Computer-Assisted Research Design and Analysis

Barbara G. Tabachnick

California State University, Northridge

Linda S. Fidell

California State University, Northridge

Allyn and Bacon

Boston ■ London ■ Toronto ■ Sydney ■ Tokyo ■ Singapore

Senior Editor: *Rebecca Pascal*
Editorial Assistant: *Whitney Brown*
Marketing Manager: *Caroline Croley*
Editorial Production Service: *Chestnut Hill Enterprises, Inc.*
Manufacturing Buyer: *Megan Cochran*
Cover Administrator: *Linda Knowles*
Electronic Composition: *Omegatype Typography, Inc.*

Library of Congress Cataloging-in-Publication Data

Tabachnick, Barbara G.
    Computer-assisted research design and analysis / Barbara G. Tabachnick, Linda S. Fidell.
        p. cm.
    Includes bibliographical references and index.
    ISBN 0-205-32178-X (alk. paper)
    1. Analysis of variance—statistics.   2. Computer-aided design.   I. Fidell, Linda S.
    II. Title.
    T175.T27 2000
    001.4–dc21   99-087332

Printed in the United States of America

10 9 8 7 6 5 4 3 2 1   05 04 03 02 01 00

C O N T E N T S

5 Factorial Randomized-Groups, Fixed-Effects Designs 152

PREFACE

Computer-Assisted Research Design and Analysis is a textbook or reference book for people who have a background in basic descriptive and inferential statistics. Although we review basic descriptive statistics in Chapter 2 and the logic of basic ANOVA in Chapter 3, the reviews are slanted toward screening data and understanding the assumptions of analyses. In most universities, the book is appropriate for senior or first-year graduate study, or for those who are taking part in a year-long research design and statistics course.

One distinctive feature of the book is the inclusion of the regression approach to ANOVA alongside the traditional approach. As we included more and more of the regression approach in our courses, we developed appreciation for the clarity and flexibility of this approach to ANOVA. The approach easily clarifies issues associated with unequal *n* and interaction contrasts, among others. It also greatly facilitates understanding of fractional factorials and other screening designs, which are the topics of Chapter 10. Although screening designs are not routinely included in a social science curriculum, they should be. They offer a powerful approach to pilot studies and an organized method of research for areas where few cases are available. With knowledge of how to set up a data set for the regression approach and the availability of regression software, you will learn to appreciate the full flexibility of ANOVA conducted through regression.

Computer-Assisted Research Design and Analysis also includes details on how to perform both simple and complicated analyses by hand through traditional means, regression, and through the most recent (at the time of writing) versions of SPSS, SAS, SYSTAT, and MINITAB. Syntax and output for both basic and complicated analyses are shown, with interpretive comments of the output. Chapters 4 through 7 review basic and complicated analyses for randomized groups, repeated measures, and mixed designs.* Then we include illustrations of analyses for basic and complicated screening, Latin-square, ANCOVA, and nesting and random-effects designs.

More material is included than some instructors may want to cover in depth in one semester, so instructors should choose the analyses most appropriate for their disciplines. However, because all chapters follow a similar outline, students can continue study on their own or readily find material they need when they encounter an unusual problem later on. We have used this book in manuscript form three times prior to publication. The first 10 weeks are used to cover material through Chapter 7 (mixed randomized-groups, repeated-measures designs). Students found the review of factorial designs at the end of Chapter 7 especially helpful. The remaining 5 weeks are used to cover the basics of ANCOVA, Latin-square, screening, and random-effects designs, and make students familiar with some of their complications. The first eight chapters comprise a fast-paced, one-quarter course.

Chapters 4 through 11 follow the same format. The introduction is followed by the research questions that can be answered by the analysis and then by the major assumptions of analysis, with recommendations if there is a violation of an assumption. The next section has an unrealistically small and often silly data set that is analyzed by traditional methods, through regression, and through the four software packages. These examples reflect our hobbies (skiing, belly dancing, and reading—primarily mystery and science fiction) and are meant to be immediately accessible to people from a

---

*We decided to use the terms that are used more widely in statistics rather than the between-subjects and within-subjects terms used in the social sciences, which are confusing in some settings.

variety of backgrounds. Except for being perhaps slightly amusing, they are intended to "get out of the way" so you can concentrate on the design and the statistical analysis. Or, if preferred, your own variable names and labels can be substituted.

The next section of each chapter discusses varieties of the basic design, if there are any, and is followed by a section that covers issues particular to the analysis. The following section illustrates a complete analysis of a real-life data set; these complete examples come from a variety of research areas. Although we are social scientists, we have consulted in many research areas and have learned the necessity of "getting up to speed" quickly in a new area. The complete examples are eclectic and are described more fully in Appendix B. Data sets for the complete examples are on our Website (http://www.abacon.com/tabachnick). Those who find some of the examples less than compelling are urged to substitute a data set from their own research area and follow the steps of analysis with it. The last section of each chapter compares the programs available for the analysis and will be most useful when buying software or trying to do something unusual. Problems are included at the end of each chapter; answers to most of them are in Appendix C.

Once students have completed this course, they should be prepared to take a course in multivariate statistics, with our other book, *Using Multivariate Statistics* (Allyn & Bacon, 4th ed., © 2001; ISBN: 0-321-05677-9), as text. Both books use the same outline for all technique chapters, making the transition from univariate to multivariate statistics easier. Further information and the data sets for both books are available at http://www.abacon.com/tabachnick

We are aware of the controversy surrounding use of tests of statistical significance instead of focusing on practical significance (effect size). We have chosen to continue the practice of using statistical significance levels to focus interpretation but have also included measures of effect size for most analyses. We also sometimes use terms such as *statistically reliable* or *reliable mean differences* instead of *statistically significant* or *significant mean differences* to serve as reminders that the word *significant* has excess connotations. The real implication of a *significant* difference is that one is likely to replicate the conclusions if one repeats the study, a concept closer to *reliable* than to *important*.

The students from two classes survived manuscript versions of this book. They made numerous helpful comments and asked to be remembered by name: Andrew Ainsworth, Marcos Arroyo, Myra Bamaca, Brent Berger, Heewon Bong, Carla Bressler, Alison Brown, Mark Cady, Julie Campbell, Desiree Despues, John Dueppen, Shirley Elan, Andrew Espinoza, Tim Goldsmith, Michael Gregory, Brian Keel, Charles Kimzey, Nicholas Krier, Kevin Laack, Ravit Lichtenberg, Kristie MacDonald, Karla Martinez, Kelly Martinez, Ellen Mastoras, Eileen McNeill, Ludwin Molina, Jason Piccone, Alva Possada, Kim Radmacher, AnnaMarie Rimicci, Alicia Robinson, Randy Sauser, Mary Schooley, Julie Smurda, and Karen Spoor. Much that is right about this book is due to their careful reading of it.

We'd like to thank all of those reviewers who helped us sort through our thoughts so that we could make this book as clear as possible. John Jamieson of Lakehead University in Canada provided helpful information about ANOVA for this book (and our other one); Dave DeYoung of the California Department of Motor Vehicles was, as always, generous with helpful suggestions. The reviews by Dennis Doverspike of the University of Akron and Barry McLaughlin of the University of California, Santa Cruz, were especially helpful. We particularly thank Carrie Green, our technical editor, who tried her best to keep us out of trouble. Much that is right about the book is due to her very careful accuracy checking. Remaining errors, of course, are ours. And the active encouragement of spouses is forever appreciated.

1   Introduction

All behavior varies. This is true of the behavior of people, assembly lines, stock markets, fabrics, equipment, bacteria, and so on. Cases that are treated one way behave differently from those treated another. Cases that are ostensibly treated the same also behave differently from each other, and over time. Sometimes differences in behavior are associated with known differences in treatment, and other times, the reason for the variability is unknown. Identification of the various factors that contribute to the variability in behavior is the goal of the set of statistical procedures described in this book.

For instance, you might be interested in factors that contribute to success in a statistics course. Factors that might be associated with success include the textbook used in the course, the teaching style of the professor, the cognitive style of the student, the number of assignments, the timing of assignments, the clarity of assignments, the number of prior statistics courses, the grades earned in those courses, the size of the class, the color of the classroom walls, the method of study, the timing of study, the age of the student, and so on. Among the many factors that might be effective, some have important effects and others have no effect or minimal effect. The statistical methods described here help you decide which factors have important effects and which are largely irrelevant.

Many different types of analysis of variance (ANOVA) techniques are covered here: one-way and factorial randomized-groups ANOVA, repeated-measures ANOVA, incomplete and partial factorial ANOVA, ANOVA with a covariate, and ANOVA with randomly chosen levels of treatment. Each analysis is appropriate in a different situation, depending on the design of the study. Guidelines for choosing the analysis to match your design are presented at the end of this chapter.

We assume that you have had one or two courses in descriptive and inferential statistics in which you covered central tendency and variance (standard deviation), the logic of the statistical hypothesis test, some fundamental terms in research design, and, perhaps, the *t*-test, simple correlation and regression, and chi square. Although we revisit these topics briefly in Chapter 2, we recommend a review of your own earlier text if our review is not sufficient. We also assume some exposure to research design in your own field of study.

1.1   The Nature of Research

1.1.1   IVs and DVs

The elements of a research design are often identified as *independent variables* (IVs) and *dependent variables* (DVs). The IVs are the factors that may or may not be effective in changing scores (values) on the DV. The IVs are manipulated by the researcher in an experimental design and are chosen for study by the researcher in a nonexperimental design. The DV is the score produced by the case. From the example, potential IVs are the textbook used in the course, the teaching style of the professor, the cognitive style of the student, the number of assignments, the number of prior statistics courses, the size of the class, the age of the student, and so on. The DV is success in the course, measured perhaps by points cumulated over examinations. The terminology comes from the nature of experiments where the outcome—the DV—is thought to be dependent on the IV.

IVs have levels. Each IV has at least two levels, but may have many more than two levels. For instance, textbook has two levels (this book or another) and size of class has three levels (15, 30, and 45 students). Timing of study has two levels (distributed or cramming). Classroom wall color has five levels (yellow, institutional green, blue, lavender, and pink). The researcher studies differences in success produced by different levels of various IVs.

1.1.2 What Is an Experiment?

Although the statistical procedures are indifferent to the sources of the data, the strength of the conclusions that can be drawn from a study differ depending on whether the study is experimental or nonexperimental. Experimental studies have at least three special characteristics: random assignment of cases to levels of IVs, manipulation of those levels, and control of extraneous variables. Levels of the IV are manipulated by deciding what the levels are, how they are implemented, and how and when cases are assigned and exposed to them.

To accomplish random assignment of cases to levels of treatment, the researcher uses a random process to determine which cases experience which level of an IV. Random assignment is used for at least two reasons. The first is to remove researcher bias from the study—to keep the researcher from assigning (however unconsciously) bigger, stronger, smarter cases to the level of treatment he or she hopes is more effective. The second reason is to let random processes *average out* differences among cases. The researcher's fondest hope is that all differences among cases are spread evenly among the levels of treatment *before* treatment is delivered.

For example, it is assumed that students come into statistics courses with preexisting differences in motivation, study habits, competing demands on time, preferences for instructors, and so on. If a flip of a coin (or some other random process) is used to assign students to classes with different textbooks, the differences in motivation, study habits, and so on should be randomly and approximately evenly spread through the classes. The classes, in short, should be roughly equivalent at the start of the study.

Flipping a coin is usually not the major method used for random assignment, because it is unlikely to result in equal sample sizes in each group. Instead, a variety of alternative random assignment strategies have been devised that differ depending on the experimental design chosen. Examples include use of a random-number table, generation of random numbers through software, poker chips whose colors represent groups, and so on. Randomization for the various designs in this book is discussed in Chapters 4 through 11 in sections labeled "Allocation of Cases." Randomization often is discussed in research design and introductory statistics texts, such as Keppel, Saufley, and Takunaga (1992).

Manipulation of the levels of treatment is undertaken so that the researcher controls both the precise nature of each level of treatment and the timing of its delivery. The researcher hopes to demonstrate that different treatments are accompanied by different average responses and that the differences in average response are produced by manipulating which group gets what type of treatment. In the example, the researcher first randomly assigns students to classrooms and then randomly assigns textbook to classroom. Because the students in the classrooms should be relatively equal to begin with, differences in success are attributed to textbook, provided that all other relevant variables have been controlled. In a nonexperimental study, the researcher merely looks at scores for classes that use different textbooks, but without any assurance of the equivalence of classes or any control over how the text is used and other features of the course.

Control of extraneous variables is undertaken to assure that the only thing that changes during the study is level of treatment. There are several ways to control extraneous variables. One way is to hold them constant for the duration of the study. For example, the same instructor teaches both classes in the same room, at the same time of day, with the same assignments, and so on (i.e., the same class in which students have different textbooks). A second way to deal with extraneous variables is to spread them randomly through the levels of treatment (much like differences among cases are controlled) in the hopes that their effects will average out. If, for example, several classes are assigned to different classrooms at different times of day and the two textbooks are randomly assigned to them, the effects of room and time should be neutralized in the study. A third way to deal with extraneous variables is to take control of them and counterbalance their effects. For example, if there are four classes, two are scheduled for morning and two for afternoon, with each textbook used for one morning and one afternoon class. Finally, one can turn an extraneous variable into another IV. For example, time of day is turned into a second IV and studied in conjunction with textbook. These possibilities are discussed at length as they arise in the context of various research designs.

One class of extraneous variables can occur when researchers and/or cases are aware of the nature of the experiment and their part in it. Researchers may be biased toward or against one or more of the IV levels, as may cases. Control of these extraneous variables sometimes is possible by making the cases "blind" to the level of treatment to which they are exposed (e.g., by making placebos and experimental drugs look the same), or by "double-blinding" both cases and those who administer the treatments.

When cases have been randomly assigned so differences among them are not associated with treatment, when the researcher has delivered levels of treatment under precisely controlled conditions at known times, and when all extraneous variables have been controlled, differences in scores are attributed to differences in the level of treatment because there is no other explanation for systematic changes in the DV.

If there are several IVs in a study, only one of them needs to be manipulated for the study to be considered an experiment. However, studies without any manipulated IVs are considered *observational*, or *correlational*, or *nonexperimental*. Studies in which some, but not all, of the requirements for an experiment are met are called *quasi-experiments*. For example, the researcher might have two classes available for study, in which one textbook is randomly assigned to one class, the other textbook to the other class, and all other features of instruction are equivalent. However, this is still a quasi-experiment rather than an experiment if it was not possible to randomly assign cases to the two classes.

Even if a study is properly experimental in all respects, inference of a causal relationship between DV and IV is hazardous until the study is successfully replicated one or more times. Researchers only begin to believe that there is a causal relationship between two variables when a study is repeated and similar results found. Even then, the argument for a causal relationship is strengthened by asking the research question using a variety of research strategies and achieving similar results each time.

1.1.3 What If It Isn't an Experiment?

When there is neither random assignment of cases, manipulation of the levels of at least one IV, nor control of extraneous variables, the study is not an experiment and the researcher cannot attribute changes in DV scores to differences in the level of an IV. The researcher is only able to say that differences in the DV are *related to* or *associated with* differences in levels of the IV.

The inference is limited in part because of the third-variable problem. When extraneous third variables have not been properly controlled (including potential differences among groups of cases), there is always the chance that some of them have contributed to apparent treatment effects. And, worse, if some changes in extraneous variables happen to coincide with changes in the level of treatment (i.e., if values of the extraneous variable are confounded with the levels of the IV), it is not possible to determine which is responsible for the change in the DV. The variability in the DV may appear to be coming from different levels of treatment when it is actually coming from changes in an extraneous variable. For example, if two different instructors are used along with two different textbooks, differences in success of students could be due to either textbook or instructor, and it is impossible to determine which has been effective.

Inference is also limited by the problem of direction of causality that occurs when the researcher does not manipulate the timing of delivery of the levels of the IV. In this case, it isn't always clear which came first, whether the IV produces changes in the DV or the DV produces changes in the IV. The researcher knows that IV and DV are changing together, but not which occurred first. For example, if the researcher does not first assign the textbook and then observe differences in success, it is not clear if differences in textbook lead to differences in success, or if differences in success lead to more effective use of textbook, whichever textbook is used.

The statistical methods, however, are blissfully unaware of all these subtleties. The numbers are crunched and the estimates of probability are produced regardless of the source of the numbers. It is up to the researcher to be aware of the limitations of the design and to reach conclusions that are justified by it.

1.1.4 Relationship Between Design and Analysis

There is almost a one-to-one correspondence between the design of the study and the statistical methods used to analyze it. In fact, one step in planning a study is to plan the statistical methods because you want to be sure that the planned study can be analyzed. One of us encountered a data set for a Ph.D. dissertation recently, data already collected by the graduate student over several years, without thought as to how the data were to be analyzed, for which there was no analysis.

There are several considerations in the choice of statistical methods. One of them is the scale on which the DV is measured. Some analyses are appropriate when the DV is continuous (interval or ratio), other analyses when it is discrete (nominal), and yet others when it is ordinal. Another consideration is whether cases provide a score to just one level of treatment or provide scores to several levels of treatment. A third consideration is relevant when there is more than one IV; you have to determine whether all possible *combinations* of all levels of all IVs are presented to cases. A fourth consideration is the potential presence of other variables, called covariates, whose effects need to be neutralized in the analysis. A fifth consideration is whether the researcher deliberately chose the specific levels of treatment or whether levels of treatment were randomly selected. These and yet other considerations are part of the decision about the appropriate analysis, as discussed throughout the book.

1.1.5   Monitoring Processes to Aid in Experimental Design

How do you decide what is important to study? Which IVs should be included and at what levels? What is the appropriate DV? In basic research, theory guides the selection of IVs and their levels, as well as the selection of the DV. In applied research, you often know the DV you are interested in, but are less certain about which IVs influence that DV.

For example, in industry, you know that you want to improve the quality of a product, and you may have some ideas about factors to improve quality. One way to pinpoint potential IVs is to monitor the production process, recording quality over a period of time while also keeping track of things that change over time such as temperature of the production facility, maintenance schedule of the machines that fabricate the product, characteristics of the operators who produce each product, changes in materials used for the product, and so on. The same principle pertains in other applied research settings. For example, what is happening when a class of students is more successful than usual? What is happening when symptoms of a disease change over time? What is happening as pilots respond to in-flight interruptions? Some of the quality control charts introduced in Chapter 2 are useful for monitoring many types of processes in an effort to uncover the IVs that are important to include in a more formal study.

It also is sometimes useful to monitor processes continuously during the course of a study, to help refine the design and start over, or to call an end to the experiment, as in the case of an obviously successful drug trial.

1.2   Types of Research Designs

One of the basic considerations in choosing a design and its associated analysis is how cases are allocated to treatments. Does a case participate in just one level of treatment (or one combination of levels of treatments) or does the case participate in several levels of treatment (and/or their combinations)? Stated differently, does each case provide a single DV score or several DV scores, each in response to a different level of treatment? You may also want to consider possible features of the cases themselves (e.g., age) that are almost certainly going to affect outcome, and treat such features as nonexperimental IVs in the design and analysis of research.

1.2.1   Randomized-Groups Designs

Randomized-groups designs, also called completely randomized designs (Chapters 4 and 5), have different cases in every level (or combinations of levels) of the IV(s) and each case provides a single observation on the DV.[1] The terminology comes from experimental methodology, in which cases are randomly assigned to levels of treatment so the group of cases in each level is different, hence randomized groups. This is called a *between-subjects design* in the social sciences because differences due to the level of treatment are tested between different groups of subjects. In other contexts, cases are screws, trainees, fabrics, college undergraduates, or whatever, but each of them is measured only once. Table 1.1 shows the allocation of cases to three levels of treatment (designated as a_1, a_2, and a_3) in a randomized-groups design. Note that the nine different cases in this example are designated

---

[1]There is a single DV unless the design is multivariate in which several different DVs are measured at one time for each case. This complicates the analysis, however, as described in Chapter 9 of Tabachnick and Fidell (2001).

TABLE 1.1   Assignment of Cases in a One-Way Randomized-Groups Design

Treatment		
a_1	a_2	a_3
s_1	s_4	s_7
s_2	s_5	s_8
s_3	s_6	s_9

with a lowercase subscripted *s*. (The subscripted *s* indices do *not* imply sequential assignment; they are merely identifiers.)

In the example, the cases are students randomly assigned to classes that use three different textbooks (or classes of three different sizes, or whatever). The researcher is looking for differences in success associated with differences in level of treatment.

This design is necessary when, for instance, cases are used up in the process of measurement. It is also necessary when either treatment or the measurement process produces relatively permanent changes in the cases. With this design, each case is naive with respect to treatment because it only participates in one level of treatment; thus, this design is also desirable when lack of naivete produces its own changes in behavior. For example, having cases read more than one résumé in an experiment designed to study stereotyping may reveal too much about the purposes of the study. However, the design requires the availability (willingness?) of more numerous cases than some of the other designs.

1.2.2   Repeated-Measures Designs

Each case participates in two or more levels of treatment and is measured once at each level in repeated-measures designs (Chapter 6). Thus, there will be as many DV scores for each case as there are levels (or combinations of levels) of the IV(s). This is called a *within-subjects design* in the social sciences, because differences due to treatments are measured within the same set of subjects. Table 1.2 shows the allocation of cases to three levels of treatment (designated as a_1, a_2, and a_3) in a repeated-measures design. Note that the three different cases in this design are represented by subscripts. In the example, students take three tests during the semester, providing one score for each test. The DV, success, is measured three times on the same measurement scale.

This design is appropriate when the desire is to monitor changes in the DV that occur over time, or with repeated exposure to treatment, or with repeated measurement. It is also appropriate when the naivete of the cases is not important or is controlled through use of a Latin square (Chapter 9) or some other procedure. The design has additional advantages when there are individual differences in the cases and the researcher wants to take those differences into account. The design is efficient in its use of cases; it uses far fewer cases than the randomized-groups design (three in this example instead of nine), and once you are set up to measure them, the measurement often goes more quickly than when many different cases have to be set up. However, the design has a restrictive assumption that makes its use problematic in many situations. Chapter 6 also describes a variation of

TABLE 1.2　Assignment of Cases in a One-Way Repeated-Measures Design

Treatment		
a_1	a_2	a_3
s_1	s_1	s_1
s_2	s_2	s_2
s_3	s_3	s_3

the design in which different cases are matched and then treated as if they were the same case during analysis.

1.2.3　One-Way and Factorial Designs

Many research studies have a single IV with two or more levels. In this book, a single IV is identified by a capital letter, A. The number of levels of the IV is designated with a lowercase letter, a, and each separate level is designated with a subscripted lowercase letter, say, a_1, a_2, and a_3. Designs with only one IV are called one-way designs. Tables 1.1 and 1.2 show allocation of cases in a one-way randomized-groups design and in a one-way repeated-measures design, respectively.

The design is two-way when a second IV is added, three-way with a third IV, and so on (cf. Chapters 5 and 6). Each additional IV is designated with an additional capital letter, B, then C, and so on, with their respective number of levels designated b and c, and each level of each IV designated as, for instance, b_1 and b_2, and c_1, c_2, and c_3, if $b = 2$ and $c = 3$. Second and third IVs often are in factorial arrangement with A. In a factorial arrangement, all *combinations* of all levels of all IVs are included. For instance, if there are two IVs with $a = 3$ and $b = 2$, cases are tested under the following combinations of levels: a_1b_1, a_1b_2, a_2b_1, a_2b_2, a_3b_1, and a_3b_2. Sometimes it is undesirable or inconvenient to present all possible combinations of levels of all IVs, and the design is not factorial, but rather incomplete, unbalanced, or partially factorial, as discussed in Chapters 9 and 10.

1.2.4　Blocking Designs

Often a second or third IV is a blocking variable introduced as a form of control for an extraneous variable. A blocking variable is often a characteristic of the cases that the researcher turns into a non-experimental IV. The analysis then provides information about differences associated with the manipulated IV, differences produced by the blocking IV, and differences produced by the combination of the two IVs. For example, the researcher might block on age of student and then study the effects of size of class on success in a statistics class. When the cases are people, they are often blocked on variables such as gender, age, income, educational level, or skill.

A blocking variable also can be a feature of the testing situation, perhaps not of major interest itself, but with potential impact on the DV. For example, the classroom in which the statistics course is taught is not of substantive interest, but is, nonetheless, a potential factor in the design that could be turned into a blocking variable.

1.2.5 Crossing and Nesting

In order to understand the factors and their error terms in research design and analysis, you have to come to grips with the concepts of crossing and nesting. Crossing occurs when all levels of one variable completely cross (occur in combination with) all levels of another variable. When the IVs are completely crossed, the design is described as *factorial*. Consider the two-way design of Table 1.3(a) in which there are two IVs, A and B, in factorial arrangement, labeled an $A \times B$ design. Each IV has two levels, and the levels of A completely cross the levels of B (and vice versa); that is, all combinations of effects occur in the design, a_1b_1, a_1b_2, a_2b_1, and a_2b_2. For example, suppose A is textbook

TABLE 1.3   Crossing and Nesting in Arrangements of IVs

(a) Two-way factorial design

	Treatment A	
Treatment B	a_1	a_2
b_1	a_1b_1	a_2b_1
b_2	a_1b_2	a_2b_2

(b) Three-way factorial design

		Treatment A	
Treatment C	**Treatment B**	a_1	a_2
c_1	b_1	$a_1b_1c_1$	$a_2b_1c_1$
	b_2	$a_1b_2c_1$	$a_2b_2c_1$
c_2	b_1	$a_1b_1c_2$	$a_2b_1c_2$
	b_2	$a_1b_2c_2$	$a_2b_2c_2$

(c) Treatment C nested in AB combinations

	Treatment A	
Treatment B	a_1	a_2
b_1	$c_1 - a_1b_1c_1$	$c_5 - a_2b_1c_5$
	$c_2 - a_1b_1c_2$	$c_6 - a_2b_1c_6$
b_2	$c_3 - a_1b_2c_3$	$c_7 - a_2b_2c_7$
	$c_4 - a_1b_2c_4$	$c_8 - a_2b_2c_8$

(this one and another) and B is size of class (large and small). In a factorial design, each textbook occurs in combination with—is used in—both large classes and small ones.

A third IV, C, is fully crossed with A and B in Table 1.3(b) forming an $A \times B \times C$ design. In this design, C crosses levels of A, levels of B, and combinations of levels of A and B. Essentially, the $A \times B$ design of Table 1.3(a) is repeated at each level of C. If C is classroom, then all combinations of textbook, class size, and classroom appear in the design, this textbook with the large class in the classroom with pink walls, the other textbook with the large class in the classroom with green walls, and so on until all combinations of the three variables are present.

The third IV, C, is added to the factorial arrangement of A and B in a different way in Table 1.3(c). In this design, there are *different* levels of C at each *combination* of levels of A and B. For instance, c_1 and c_2 are in the a_1b_1 combination, c_5 and c_6 are in the a_2b_1 combination, and so forth. The eight levels of C are said to *nest* in each AB combination. The frontslash notation is used to designate nesting; in this example, the notation is C/AB (C nested in AB combinations). For example, suppose C is still classrooms and there are eight classrooms in which statistics classes are taught. Classrooms c_1 and c_2 are randomly assigned to receive this textbook and a large class; c_3 and c_4 receive this textbook and a small class; c_5 and c_6 receive the other textbook and a large class; and c_7 and c_8 receive the other textbook and a small class.

In Tables 1.3(b) and 1.3(c), levels of the third IV C either cross AB combinations or nest within them. Most commonly, it is cases that cross the levels of the other IV (Table 1.2) or nest within the levels of the other IV (Table 1.1). In the repeated-measures design, cases cross levels of $A - A \times S$, while in the randomized-groups design, cases nest in levels of $A - S/A$.

Becoming familiar with this terminology is important because you need to understand the pattern of crossing and nesting in your design in order to pick the right analysis. Ask yourself whether each IV crosses over all levels of all other IVs. In more complicated designs (cf. Chapters 9 and 10), some IVs cross completely and others do not. That is, not all combinations of levels may appear in the design; you may, for instance, have the $a_1b_1c_1$ combination, but not the $a_1b_1c_2$ combination. Then ask yourself if *cases* cross all levels of all IVs (as in the repeated-measures design of Table 1.2) or whether cases are nested in levels of IVs (as in the randomized-groups design of Table 1.1). Later, you will discover that cases may nest in levels of some IVs while they cross levels of other IVs in designs that are said to be mixed.[2]

1.3   Types of Treatments

The levels of an IV sometimes differ from each other in type and sometimes differ from each other in amount. Some choices about the appropriate analysis depend on whether the levels differ in type (a qualitative IV) or in amount (a quantitative IV).

1.3.1   Qualitative IVs

Qualitative IVs have levels that differ in type. For instance, textbook is a qualitative IV whose levels differ in type (this text versus another text). Or the IV is type of personnel training procedure,

---

[2]This is one use of the term *mixed*. You will discover that *mixed* is also used to designate designs with fixed and random effects, described in Chapter 11. Most confusing!

manual-based or video-based. Frequently used blocking IVs are sex (male or female) or gender (men or women) whose levels also (happily) differ in type.

1.3.2   Quantitative IVs

Quantitative IVs have levels that differ in amount. For example, number of assignments (5, 10, or 15) is a quantitative IV. Or the IV is amount of personnel training, 4 or 8 hours. Frequently used quantitative blocking IVs are age (20–29, 30–39, or 40–49) or years of education (8, 12, or 16) or income. Note that in these examples, the levels are spaced the same distance apart. This is not a requirement, but it does simplify some of the computations.

When an IV is quantitative, a special analysis, called a *trend analysis*, is available that looks for a linear (straight-line) relationship between the DV and the levels of the IV, or a quadratic (having a single curve) relationship between the DV and the levels of the IV, or both.[3] This fascinating topic is discussed in detail in Chapters 4, 5, and 6.

A study is likely to have some IVs that are qualitative and some that are quantitative. And some that are hard to fathom. For instance, what do you call an IV that has two levels, one with none of something and one with lots of something? Do the levels differ in quality or quantity? Well. . . . Since there are only two levels, you really do not have to decide because the analysis is the same, and addition of a third level would clarify the situation, in any event. In this case, most researchers would call the *none-of-something* level the control condition, and the *lots-of-something* level the treatment, and let it go at that.

1.4   Outcome Measures

There are also various types of DVs: continuous, ordinal, and discrete. Determining which type of DV you have is not a trivial matter because it is one of the fundamental considerations when choosing the appropriate analysis.

1.4.1   Types of Outcome Measures

Outcome measures also may be quantitative or qualitative, differing in amount or type. Qualitative outcome measures are always discrete, and discrete outcomes with only two categories are called *dichotomous*. Quantitative outcomes may be continuous, ordinal, or discrete.[4] Thus, discrete outcomes may be quantitative or qualitative.

Continuous outcomes assess the *amount* of the DV; there is a continuum of possible values and the size of the observed value of the DV depends on the sensitivity of the measuring device. As the measuring device becomes more sensitive, so does the precision with which the DV is assessed. Examples of continuous DVs are time to complete a task, amount of fabric used in various manufacturing processes, or score on an essay exam.

Ordinal DVs reveal the rank order of the outcomes vis-à-vis each other, but do not indicate the extent to which one outcome exceeds another. For instance, if the quality of several different paint

---

[3]There are also much more complicated relationships, depending on the number of levels of the IV.

[4]The term *categorical* often is used to refer to either ordinal or nominal DVs.

jobs is rank-ordered, the researcher knows which is the best, but not by how much. The best paint job might be a lot better than the next best one, or it might be just a little bit better; there is no way to know. There are fewer statistical methods available for analysis of ordinal variables.

Discrete DV responses are classified into categories. There are usually only a few possible values of discrete DVs, and the values are chosen so that every response can be classified into one and only one of the categories. For instance, employees are classified as properly trained or not; eggs are divided into small, medium, large, extra large, and jumbo; respondents answer either "yes" or "no"; manufactured parts either pass or do not pass quality control; or dessert choice is sorbet, tiramisu, chocolate mousse, or apple tart.

Notice that in the eggs example, the DV is continuous if the eggs are weighed, but the DV is discrete (and a little ordinal) if the eggs are classified into categories. This brings up the point that a continuous DV can be changed to an ordinal or discrete one (with some loss of information), but the reverse is not true. There is not enough information to change a discrete DV to a continuous one.

Often, the issue of type of DV is simply decided by the researcher. The decision is basically a matter of how much faith the researcher has in the measuring process and whether a difference makes a meaningful difference. For instance, although eggs could be weighed to small fractions of a kilogram, does it make any sense to do so? What is the meaningful level of measurement for this particular DV? There is lively debate as to the extent to which noncontinuous DVs are appropriately analyzed by statistical procedures designed for continuous outcomes, such as ANOVA. Researchers with all but the simplest research designs find themselves attempting to justify the appropriateness of treating DVs as if they are continuous in order to exploit the flexibility of ANOVA.

In practice, we usually treat DV values as if they are continuous when the underlying scale is thought to be continuous but the measured scale actually is ordinal, the number of categories is large—say seven or more—and the data meet other assumptions of the analysis. For instance, the number of correct items on an objective test is technically not continuous because fractional values are not possible, but is thought to measure some underlying continuous variable such as course mastery. Another example of a DV with ambiguous measurement is one measured on a Likert-type scale in which consumers rate their attitudes toward a product as "strongly like," "moderately like," "mildly like," "neither like nor dislike," "mildly dislike," "moderately dislike," or "strongly dislike." Occasionally, even dichotomous DVs are treated as if continuous when the two categories of the DV occur fairly equally in each level of the IV.

For the most part, the designs and analyses in this book are limited to outcomes that either are measured on a continuous scale or can be treated as such. Thus, we use the term "continuous" throughout the remainder of this book whether the measured scale itself is continuous or the DV is to be treated as if continuous. We use the term "discrete" for outcomes with a few categories, whether the categories differ in type or quantity.

1.4.2   Number of Outcome Measures

A single DV is measured in the designs discussed in this book. The same DV can be measured once or more than once, but just one DV is assessed. For instance, the instructor might measure success in the statistics course with a single test at the end or measure success as the average of scores achieved on several tests. In either situation, success is inferred from only one DV. Or success might be measured by several equivalent tests given during the semester. In either situation, though, success is measured by a single type of DV, test score. Designs with a single DV are often referred to as univariate.

There are many designs, however, in which several different DVs are measured, either all at once or all several times. For instance, the researcher could be interested in both test scores and attitude toward statistics. Scores and attitude are both DVs and both could be measured only once for each case at the end of the course or several times for each case during the course. Designs with several different DVs are called *multivariate*; they are described by Tabachnick and Fidell (2001).

1.5   Overview of Research Designs

1.5.1   Continuous Outcomes

In the preceding example, the scores on tests form a continuous DV. The most common analysis for a continuous DV is ANOVA.[5] ANOVA summarizes the responses at each level of a treatment (or combination of treatments) by averaging the responses and then determines whether there is a reliable difference among them. Do the treatments at some levels raise means whereas others lower means? Details of the analysis used to answer these questions are presented in Chapter 3, along with an explanation for why an analysis of *variance* makes inferences about *means*.

There are about half a dozen different kinds of ANOVA and a near infinite number of ways to combine them. The flexibility of the analytic procedure is astonishing. For this reason, it is used in almost all branches of science. Once you understand the great variety of research designs that can be analyzed through ANOVA, you can tailor your design to meet precisely your research needs.

1.5.1.1   *Randomized-Groups ANOVA*

The one-way randomized-groups design is very popular. This design has one IV, *A*, with two or more levels, and there are different cases in every level of *A*. A one-way randomized-groups design with three levels of *A* is illustrated in Table 1.1. If *A* represents different class sizes (say 15, 30, or 45 students), the researcher asks if the average DV score is different for classes with different numbers of students. One-way randomized-groups ANOVA is discussed in Chapter 4.

If there are two or more IVs each with two or more levels deliberately chosen by the researcher, if all combinations of levels are present, and if each combination of levels has different cases, the design is a factorial randomized-groups design, as illustrated in Table 1.3(a). If the preceding researcher is interested in the possible impact of textbook in addition to class size, all combinations of the two variables are used and each student generates a single DV score, as illustrated in Table 1.3(b). The researcher asks if success is different in classes of different size, if success is different with different textbooks, and whether some combinations of textbook and class size work particularly well (say, this textbook with a small class, but another textbook with a large class). Factorial randomized-groups ANOVA is the topic of Chapter 5.

1.5.1.2   *Repeated-Measures ANOVA*

Another general class of ANOVA is used with repeated-measures designs. These designs are characterized by having the same outcome measured more than one time for each case, as illustrated in Table 1.2. If several tests are given during the course and each score is used, a one-way repeated-measures ANOVA is appropriate. The researcher asks if there are reliable mean differences in test

---

[5]ANOVA was also the stage name used by one of us in our somewhat less than reputable belly dancing days.

scores as the semester progresses. One-way and factorial repeated-measures ANOVAs are discussed in Chapter 6.

The mixed design combines features of the randomized-groups design with features of the repeated-measures design. There are different cases in levels of the randomized groups IV, but cases are measured repeatedly at the levels of the repeated-measures IV, as seen in Table 1.4. For example, suppose one class is assigned this textbook and another is assigned the other textbook, but three tests are given in the semester and each test score is used separately. The design is randomized groups with respect to textbook, but repeated measures with respect to test scores. ANOVA for mixed designs is discussed in Chapter 7.

When a very large number of DV scores are measured on an ongoing basis (say, 50 or more), time-series analysis, rather than repeated-measures ANOVA, is appropriate. The researcher studies changes that occur over time before and after introduction of a treatment. For instance, water consumption for a municipality is measured monthly for several years, before and after a campaign is mounted to conserve water. Or records of number of accidents per week are kept for a year or more and compared with the number in the weeks after the start of a safety campaign. Time-series analysis, as discussed in Tabachnick and Fidell (2001), is appropriate for these kinds of data.

1.5.1.3 Analysis of Covariance, ANCOVA

Another variety of ANOVA is analysis of covariance, known as ANCOVA. The term *covariance* comes from use of a *covariate* (CV) in the analysis. A CV is a continuous variable that is related to the DV but, at least in experimental work, independent of the IV(s). In experimental work, the CV often is the same as the DV, but measured *before* levels of treatment are applied. The goal of the analysis is to examine mean differences on the DV associated with levels of the IV after DV scores are adjusted for pretreatment differences on the CV. For example, a pretest of knowledge of statistics is measured for all students *before* the levels of treatment are applied and the pretest scores serve as the CV. These pretest scores reflect differences in motivation, past instruction, number of previous courses, time since previous course, and so on, that students bring into the experiment. Scores on the DV are adjusted for differences on the CV and then adjusted mean differences associated with levels of treatment are analyzed. The researcher asks if there are mean differences due to treatment after cases are equalized for preexisting differences on the CV. ANCOVA is the topic of Chapter 8.

TABLE 1.4   Mixed Design Where *A* Is a Randomized-Groups IV and *B* Is a Repeated-Measures IV

	Treatment *B*		
Treatment *A*	b_1: Test 1	b_2: Test 2	b_3: Test 3
a_1: This Text	s_1	s_1	s_1
	s_2	s_2	s_2
a_2: Another Text	s_3	s_3	s_3
	s_4	s_4	s_4

1.5.1.4   Latin-Square ANOVA

Sometimes the researcher wants to control for nuisance variables in the randomized-groups design or for the order in which levels of the repeated measure are presented to cases in the repeated-measures design. A Latin square design is used if a fully crossed (full factorial) design is not desirable or feasible. The Latin square is only part of the full factorial arrangement of levels of IVs. Latin-square analyses provide tests of mean differences among the levels of each IV, but not their interactions. Latin-square analyses are described in Chapter 9.

1.5.1.5   ANOVA for Screening and Other Incomplete Designs

Another fairly common situation occurs in the early stages of a research program when the researcher is not yet sure which IVs are important or when all combinations of treatments are not feasible. Screening and other incomplete designs are appropriate in these situations because numerous IVs are included, but they are not fully crossed. That is, there is no attempt to implement the IVs in a full factorial design, with all their combinations. The effects of the levels of each IV are assessed, but not interactions among IVs, or at least not all of them. For instance, in the early stages of research, the researcher may want to examine potential effects of teaching style of instructor, number of assignments, timing of assignments, color of walls in classroom, and so on, in addition to textbook and size of class. A fully factorial arrangement of all these IVs with at least two levels each is nearly overwhelming. However, use of a screening or other incomplete design, as described in Chapter 10, makes the project manageable.

1.5.1.6   Random-Effects ANOVA

A final variety of ANOVA has to do with the way levels of the IV are selected. In most research designs, the researcher selects the specific levels of the IV because they are the ones of research interest. This is a fixed-effects IV. Results generalize to the levels actually included in the study. However, another option is to randomly select the levels of the IV. The researcher lists the population of all possible levels (or all possible levels within a range of interest) and then randomly selects a few of them. This is a random-effects IV. For instance, the researcher lists all possible statistics instructors at a university and then randomly selects two of them to teach the courses. Results generalize to the population of all possible levels (or all levels within the range of interest). Random-effects ANOVA, including the nested design of Table 1.3(c), are described in Chapter 11.

1.5.2   Rank-Order Outcomes

There are far fewer analytical techniques for ordinal DVs. There are nonparametric counterparts to one-way randomized-groups and repeated-measures ANOVA but they are not covered in this book. For instance, the rank sums test (when $a = 2$) and the Kruskall-Wallis test (when $a > 2$) are available for one-way randomized-groups designs, and the sign test (when $a = 2$) and the Friedman test (when $a > 2$) are available for one-way repeated-measures designs. These analyses are described in Siegel and Castellan (1988) and are available through most statistical packages. ANOVA is sometimes applied to ordinal outcomes, as discussed in Section 1.4.1, when the research design is one for which no nonparametric technique is available and the distribution of outcomes is (or can be transformed to be) relatively normal.

1.5.3   Discrete Outcomes

Analysis of a discrete DV is accomplished through simple chi-square analysis, if there is only one discrete IV, or through log-linear models or logistic regression if there are several IVs. Chi-square analysis is described in Chapter 2 and in most elementary statistics textbooks. For example, suppose the researcher categorizes the students' scores into either "pass" or "fail." Chi square is used to determine if there is a relationship between success and textbook.

1.5.3.1   *Log-Linear Models*

When there is one discrete DV and several discrete IVs, log-linear models (sometimes referred to as *multiway frequency analysis*) are used. These models are extensions of chi-square analysis that yield information about frequencies on the DV associated with each IV separately, and then with combinations of IVs. For instance, suppose the researcher includes textbook, classroom wall color, and teaching style of instructor as IVs, and then classifies the test score for each case as either pass or fail. The researcher asks if success is associated with each IV separately and all combinations of them. Log-linear models are described in Chapter 7 of Tabachnick and Fidell (2001).

1.5.3.2   *Logistic Regression*

Logistic regression is used when there is one discrete DV and one or more IVs, which may be discrete, continuous, or a combination of discrete and continuous. For instance, if the DV is classified as pass or fail, and IVs are textbook and teaching style of instructor (both discrete), along with age of student (continuous), logistic regression is used for the analysis. Logistic regression is described in Chapter 12 of Tabachnick and Fidell (2001).

1.5.4   Time as an Outcome

The DV in some applications is elapsed time until something happens. For instance, the DV might be the length of time that students study statistics when they are given two different types of classes for the first course, or length of time patients survive following two types of chemotherapy, or length of time parts made of different alloys survive in a testing chamber. When the DV is length of time until something happens, survival (or failure[6]) analysis is appropriate, as described in Chapter 15 of Tabachnick and Fidell (2001).

1.6   Overview of Issues Encountered in Most Designs

1.6.1   Statistical Inference

This section is intended as a brief review of a complicated topic rather than a complete exposition of it. If you mastered the intricacies of statistical inference in a previous course or if you believe that statistical inference is misguided (see Section 1.6.5), this section can be skipped.

---

[6]Is the cup half full or half empty?

Statistical inference is used to make rational decisions under conditions of uncertainty. Inferences (decisions) are made about populations based on data from samples that contain incomplete information. Different samples taken from the same population probably differ from one another and from the population. Therefore, inferences regarding the population are always a little risky.

The traditional solution to this problem is the application of statistical inference. Two hypothetical states of reality are set up, each representing a probability distribution of means that come from alternative hypotheses about the true nature of the population. One distribution represents the hypothesis that treatment makes no difference, and is affectionately known as the null hypothesis, H_0. The other distribution represents the hypothesis that treatment makes a difference and is known as the alternative hypothesis, H_a. Given sample results, a best guess is made as to which distribution the sample was taken from, a tricky proposition because, as you recall from your introductory statistics course, the distributions overlap (Figure 1.1). Formalized statistical rules are used to define "best." Section 3.2.3.3 discusses the application of statistical inference to ANOVA.

H_0 and H_a represent alternative realities, only one of which is true. When the researcher is forced to decide whether to retain or reject H_0, four things can happen. If the null hypothesis is true, a correct decision is made if the researcher retains H_0 and an error (Type I error) is made if the researcher rejects it. If the probability of making the wrong decision is α, the probability of making the right decision is $1 - \alpha$. If, on the other hand, H_a is true, the probability of making the right decision by rejecting H_0 is $1 - \beta$ and the probability of making the wrong decision is β (a Type II error).

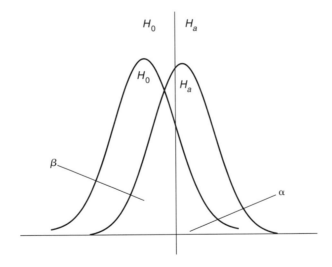

FIGURE 1.1   Overlapping Distributions Representing the Null (H_0) and Alternative (H_a) Hypotheses. A Type I error (with probability of a) occurs if the result comes from the H_0 distribution, but the decision is made to reject H_0. A Type II error (with probability of β) occurs if the result comes from the H_a distribution but the decision is made to retain H_0.

This information is summarized in a *confusion matrix* (aptly named, according to beginning statistics students) showing the probabilities of each of these four outcomes:

		Reality	
		H_0	H_a
Statistical	Retain "H_0"	$1 - \alpha$	β (Type II error)
Decision	Reject "H_0"	α (Type I error)	$1 - \beta$
		1.00	1.00

1.6.2   Power

The lower right-hand cell of the confusion matrix represents the most desirable outcome and the power of the research. Usually, the researcher believes that H_a is true and hopes that the sample data lead to rejection of H_0. Power is the probability of rejecting H_0 when H_a is true. Many of the choices in designing research are made with an eye toward increasing power because research with low power is not often worth the effort.

One way to increase power is to increase the probability of making a Type I error. However, it cannot be changed much or Type I error rates reach an unacceptable level. Given the choice between .05 and .01 for α error, though, use of .05 increases power. A second strategy is to apply a stronger treatment. This has the effect of moving the distributions farther apart so that they do not overlap so much. For example, distributions will be farther apart if differences are sought between supercomputer and PC performance than if differences are sought between PC and Macintosh performance. Other strategies to decrease overlap of the distributions involve reducing the variability among scores in each treatment by exerting greater experimental control and increasing the sample sizes.

There is also the danger of *too much power*. The null hypothesis is probably never exactly true and any treatment is likely to have some effect, however small. As sample size increases, rejection of H_0 becomes more and more likely. For that reason, a "minimal meaningful difference" should guide the selection of sample size. The sample size should be large enough to reveal a meaningful difference but not so large as to reveal any difference whatsoever.

1.6.3   Effect Size

Statistical significance tests assess the *reliability* of the association between the IV(s) and DV. Is the null hypothesis likely to be rejected again if the study is repeated? Measures of effect size assess *how much* association there is by assessing the degree of relationship between the IV(s) and DV. It is important to assess the degree of relationship to avoid publicizing trivial results as though they had practical utility or spending money to change to a new procedure that actually makes very little difference.

Most measures of effect size assess the proportion of variance in the DV that is associated with levels of an IV. That is, they assess the amount of total variance in the DV that is predictable from knowledge of the levels of the IV. If the total variances of the DV and the IV are represented by circles, as in a Venn diagram, measures of effect size assess the degree of overlap of the circles, as seen in Figure 1.2. In this example, the first IV, A, is rather strongly related to the DV, Y; the second IV, B, is unrelated to Y, and the interaction of $A \times B$ is modestly related to Y.

1.6.4 Parameter Estimates

What are the likely population means for cases exposed to the various levels of the IV(s)? If the entire population is measured instead of only a sample of cases, what mean is expected? If several populations are measured, what means are expected? The population means are the unknown parameters; the observed DV scores provide estimates of them. That is, sample means are used as parameter estimates. In fact, descriptions of entire populations are *parameters*, not statistics. Because we never know the parameters exactly without measuring the entire population, we use the sample statistics to create a range of values within which the population values are likely to fall. These are called *confidence intervals*.

The ability to estimate parameters for a population from a sample depends on how representative the sample is of the population. If you take a random sample from the population (and then, perhaps, randomly assign cases to levels of treatment), sample statistics provide estimates of the population values. If the sample is one of "convenience," however, it is hazardous to estimate population values from it.

1.6.5 To Test or Not to Test

There is a recurring controversy about the value of using statistical inference (Harlow, Mulaik, and Steiger, 1997). This has grown out of a history of overemphasis on simply deciding whether a null hypothesis can be rejected, and an underemphasis on considerations of power, effect size, and parameter estimates. Historically, a research project was considered for publication only if the statistical test was significant—the null hypothesis was rejected—without regard for the degree of association between the IV and DV. The result was many journal articles about trivial treatment effects and file

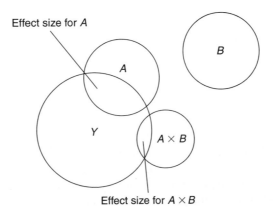

**FIGURE 1.2 Venn Diagram of Effects Sizes
for A, B, and $A \times B$**

drawers full of unpublished studies rejected for publication because of Type II errors. To ameliorate this result, some have recommended abandoning the inferential test altogether.

Our position is that significance testing is still useful for a number of purposes, but needs to be accompanied by consideration of effect size, parameter estimates, and power. In large and complex studies, inference provides a convenient guide for determining which results deserve further attention. However, complex designs provide numerous significance tests, some likely to be spurious if all are tested at liberal α levels such as .05. By considering effect size and power along with the significance test, one minimizes the likelihood of interpreting very small and perhaps unreliable treatment differences as important. By reporting effect sizes and either significance tests or confidence intervals (or including information that allows the reader to compute confidence intervals), one minimizes publication of reliable, but trivial, results.

A new development that may one day assist decision making is estimation of a confidence interval around an effect size. This interval contains information about both effect size and the significance test because an effect-size interval that includes zero is also a nonsignificant result. However, these confidence intervals have not yet been worked out for most of the ANOVA designs in this book, and are not yet implemented in major statistical packages (Steiger and Fouladi, 1997). These issues and other approaches to dealing with these problems are discussed at length by Harlow and colleagues (1997).

1.7   Generalizing Results

The trick with statistics is using the values from a sample of cases to make decisions about a population of cases; the sample of cases itself is often of no or very limited interest. The sample is merely a convenient mechanism for estimating values for the population. There is usually no need for inferential statistics if you measure the whole population or if you have no desire to generalize beyond your sample.

Ideally, the researcher carefully defines the population of interest and then randomly samples from it.[7] The sample is said to be representative if it has the same distributions of relevant characteristics as are found in the population. A great deal of work and interest have gone into strategies for gathering random samples in nonexperimental, observational, or correlational research. Indeed, the usefulness and quality of the work are often determined by the representativeness of the sample. Less attention has been paid to this issue in experimental studies, although it probably deserves more focus.

The concept of sampling has somewhat different connotations in nonexperimental and experimental research. In nonexperimental research, you investigate relationships among variables in a predefined population (e.g., college students or agricultural plots in California) from which you have randomly drawn cases. In experimental research, you often use convenient cases (e.g., students taking introductory psychology at a particular school or available agricultural plots in a particular field) and then attempt to *create* different populations by treating subgroups of cases differently (exposing students to different teaching styles or giving plots different fertilizer). The goal in experiments is to assure that all cases (students or plots) come from the same population before you treat them differently. Instead of random sampling from all students or plots in California, there is random assignment of cases to treatment groups (levels of the IV) to ensure that, before treatment, the subsamples

---

[7]Strategies for random sampling are discussed in detail in such texts as Rea and Parker (1997).

are homogeneous. Statistical tests provide evidence as to whether, after treatment, the samples are still homogeneous.

In experiments, *strict* statistical generalization about treatment effectiveness is limited to the population from which you randomly assigned cases to treatments (e.g., the students who signed up for your study). In practice, *logical* generalization usually goes beyond that to the type of cases who participated in the study. For example, if a particular group of freshmen and sophomores in introductory psychology courses at your university signed up for your study, you often generalize to freshmen and sophomores in universities like yours, after appropriate justification of their representativeness.

It is also possible to randomly select the levels of the IV, as described in the random-effects designs of Chapter 11. Generalization about the effectiveness of treatment is to the population of levels when the levels of the IV are randomly selected from a population of levels.

1.8   Computer Assistance

Nobody does statistics by hand any more, except in initial learning stages when application of pencil to paper and finger to calculator has a salutatory effect on understanding (and on developing appreciation for the computer). Instead, the work of statistical analysis and, increasingly, experimental design is done with one or more software packages. Throughout this book, we demonstrate syntax and output from the four most popular statistical packages and from several packages for designing experiments, calculating sample size, and the like.

1.8.1   Programs for Statistical Analysis

Syntax and output are presented throughout this book from SPSS 10.0 (SPSS Inc., 1999a, 1999b, 1999c, 1999d), SAS 7.0 (SAS Institute Inc., 1990, 1998), SYSTAT 9.0 (SPSS Inc., 1999e), and MINITAB 12.21 (Minitab, Inc., 1997). These are the most recent releases at the time of writing. However, newer releases of some of them may be available in a year or two, and your facility may still be running an older version of one or more of them. Pay some attention to which release you are running because the syntax and output may look different, because errors in older releases are often corrected in newer ones, and because new descriptive and inferential statistical methods may have become available.

You are fortunate if you have access to all four packages. Programs within the packages do not completely overlap, and some problems are better handled through one package than another. For example, doing several versions of the same basic analysis on the same set of data is particularly easy with SPSS. SYSTAT and MINITAB are good for fast, interactive work. SYSTAT also has excellent graphics. SAS has extensive front-end data-handling capabilities. We illustrate all four packages because different facilities have different ones. You may start out using SPSS, for instance, and then move to a facility that has SAS. It can take several days to familiarize yourself with a new package and it helps to have some examples of it side by side with examples from the package you already know.

Most routine analyses are available through menu systems in all these packages. Online help and manuals are also available and there is additional documentation in various newsletters, pocket guides, technical reports, and other materials that are printed as the programs are continuously corrected, revised, and upgraded. At this point, hard copy documentation for all four packages fills a rather sizeable bookcase. The documentation accompanying the packages is usually adequate; however, without considerable experience, it is sometimes still very difficult to produce the analysis you need. When the menu system is incomplete, you have to use the syntax to get the analysis. You let the menu system take you as far as it will, and then modify it through syntax if you need to. For this reason, we present the syntax that produced each output, although for many examples, we used the menu system to write the syntax.

One of the problems with these big, flexible statistical packages is that they usually produce something, but not necessarily the analysis you want. Because the output is visually appealing, it is tempting to believe that it is also the desired analysis. That may be a rash assumption. Start by running a small data set with the same design as your problem, where the result is known, to compare the results. When the results are identical, you know you have the right syntax, and you know how to read the results in the program you are running. You are now ready to run your larger problem.

Another problem is that the packages present results in different order, and often with different jargon, so you have to learn how to read the output. Such learning is facilitated by annotated output in the manuals and online help that provides a verbal description of various statistics. We attempt to foster this learning by presenting and describing output from all four programs. Although you may only want to consider output from one of the packages right now, the others are available when you need them.

Chapters 4 through 11 of this book offer explanations and illustrations from a variety of analyses within each package and compare the features of the programs. Our hope is that once the techniques are understood, you will be able to generalize to other programs within the packages and to packages not reviewed here. However, be prepared to detest and find vastly inferior the second and all subsequent packages encountered. In our experience, people form unwarranted loyalties to the first package encountered, whichever it is.

1.8.2   Programs for Designing Experiments

Computer programs are available to assign cases to treatments in randomized-groups designs as well as other, more complicated designs that involve different orders of treatments for different cases and treatments that are not fully crossed. SYSTAT, SAS, and MINITAB have built-in programs for experimental design, whereas SPSS has a separate product, Trial Run, to design experiments (with, mercifully, a single manual; SPSS Inc., 1997b). NCSS 2000 (Number Crunching Statistical System, 1997) also has extensive capabilities for designing experiments and is illustrated along with the other programs in Chapters 9 and 10 for complicated designs.

Another set of programs helps the data analyst estimate sample sizes needed to run studies with desired power. These programs include PASS and PC-SIZE, which are described in Section 4.5.2. That section also gives a URL (internet address) for a World Wide Web site devoted to power programs.

A final type of program useful to the researcher (and the teacher) is one that generates mock data for a research design. Complicated designs are often best understood by doing the associated statistical analyses. However, it is sometimes too late to figure out how to analyze data after they are collected. A good strategy when in doubt about the mechanics of an analysis is to generate a small sample of simulated data and run the proposed analyses on them. The small, hypothetical, sample data sets of Chapters 4 through 11 were generated, for the most part, through DATASIM (Bradley, 1988), a program that generates data sets for a variety of ANOVA designs.

1.9 Organization of the Book

Chapter 2 gives an overview of data entry and basic descriptive statistics for screening data, including several newer graphical methods. It also briefly summarizes bivariate correlation and regression as well as chi-square analysis. Chapter 3 provides a review of the rationale behind one-way randomized-groups ANOVA, including the basic assumptions of analysis, and a demonstration of the analysis through regression. For those with an adequate statistical background, Chapters 2 and 3 can be skimmed or skipped altogether. However, even if you understand the statistics, it may be helpful to glance through these chapters to familiarize yourself with the notational system we use and our way of discussing statistics.

Chapters 4 through 11 cover specific research designs and associated statistical techniques. The chapters follow a common format and, although they proceed from simple to more complex analyses, are intended to be taken up in any order, or omitted, at the discretion of the reader. Once you are familiar with the format, it should be relatively easy to find the answer to your question about an analysis in a particular chapter.

The chapters each begin with an overview of the design and analysis and the major research questions that can be asked using them. Then conceptual and practical limitations and assumptions of analysis are summarized, including recommendations for proceeding after violation of an assumption. Next, a tiny, inadequate, and usually silly, data set is analyzed by hand to illustrate the computations and by software to illustrate the corresponding syntax and output for each of the major packages. These examples are intended to be readily grasped by people from diverse backgrounds, and perhaps entertaining, if not compelling from a research perspective. A section then follows describing variations of the technique, if any. The next section discusses special issues and complexities that arise with the particular analysis. Then there is a guided tour through one or two real-world data sets for which the analysis is appropriate. These data sets come from a variety of research areas that those who become proficient in statistical analyses may encounter if they serve as consultants. This section concludes with an example of a Results section in American Psychological Association format[8] describing the outcome of the statistical analysis appropriate for submission to a professional journal. The tour concludes with both a tabular and verbal comparison of the features of the programs available through the statistical packages. Problem sets are, of course, available at the end of each chapter for the edification of the student.

1.10 Choosing a Design: Some Guidelines

Table 1.5 is a flow chart to assist you in choosing the appropriate type of analysis for your data set. In order to use the chart, you have to first identify the type of DV you have: Is it continuous, discrete, or ordinal?[9] The next step is to identify the number of IVs, the number of levels of each IV, the arrangement of IVs (factorial or incomplete), the type of each IV (randomized groups, repeated measures, a little of both—mixed—or random effects), and then, if you have a continuous DV, whether you have a covariate in your design. For the inexperienced researcher, these decisions are not always easy to make. After a while, however, this will become old hat, so that a quick glance at Table 1.5 will verify your plan of analysis.

---

[8]You may need to adjust the write-up of the results to the practices of your own journal.

[9]This book deals only with analyses for continuous DVs or those that can be treated as if continuous.

TABLE 1.5   Guidelines for Selection of Statistical Analysis

Type of DV	No. of IVs (No. of Levels)	Arrangement of IVs	Type of IV	Covariate	Analysis
Continuous	1 (2)		RG	No	RG ANOVA or *t*-Test
			RG	Yes	ANCOVA
			RM		RM ANOVA or *t*-Test
	1 (3+)		RG	No	RG ANOVA, Planned Comparisons
			RG	Yes	RG ANCOVA, Planned Comparisons
			RM		RM ANOVA, Planned Comparisons
	2+ (2+)	Factorial	RG	No	RG ANOVA
			RG	Yes	RG ANCOVA
			RM		RM ANOVA
			Mixed	No	ANOVA
			Mixed	Yes	ANCOVA
			Random Effects		Random-Effects ANOVA
		Incomplete	RG		Latin Square, Screening
			RM		RM Latin Square, Screening

RG = Randomized-groups

RM = Repeated-measures

(continued)

TABLE 1.5   Continued

Type of DV	#No. of IVs (No. of Levels)	Arrangement of IVs	Type of IV	Covariate	Analysis
Ordinal	1 (2)	RG			Mann-Whitney U Test
		RM			Wilcoxon T Test
	1 (3+)	RG			Kruskall-Wallis H Test, Ryans
		RM			Friedman Test, Nemenyi

Type of DV	No. of IVs (No. of Levels)	Arrangement of IVs	Type of IV	Covariate	Analysis
Discrete	1 (2+)		Discrete (RG)		Chi Square
			Discrete (RM)		McNemar's Change Test
	2+ (2+)		Discrete		Log-Linear Models
			Discrete + Continuous		Logistic Regression

1.11   Problem Sets

1.1   An experiment is designed to determine how loudness is affected by speaker size. The researcher measures loudness of 30 speakers randomly chosen from the factory floor, 10 each that are 8, 10, and 12 inches in diameter.

   a. Identify the IV and its levels.
   b. Are cases arranged to form a randomized-groups or repeated-measures IV?
   c. Is the IV quantitative or qualitative?
   d. Identify the DV. What type of outcome is it?
   e. What kind of design is this?
   f. What type of statistical error would you be making if speaker size really affected loudness but your experiment failed to uncover that difference?
   g. How would you change speaker sizes to make this experiment more powerful?

1.2 Dr. Optimist believes he has discovered a "smarts" pill that will increase IQ by 15 points. He first measures the IQ of 90 college juniors and then randomly assigns them to one of two groups: 45 of them take the smarts pill and 45 take a placebo pill. He then measures the IQ of all of them at three intervals: 1 month after starting, 6 months after starting, and 1 year after starting.

    a. Identify all IVs and their levels.
    b. For each IV, are cases arranged to form a randomized-groups or repeated-measures IV?
    c. Identify whether each IV is quantitative or qualitative.
    d. Identify the DV. What type of outcome is it?
    e. What kind of design is this?
    f. What type of statistical error would Dr. Optimist have made if he reported that his pill worked when it really was no better than a placebo?

1.3 A manufacturer wonders whether adding polyester to a pants suit makes it last longer. She randomly assigns half of her female and half of her male employees to a group that wears uniforms with polyester added and the remaining employees to a group that wears uniforms without polyester. She then observes the uniforms to see how long it takes for them to wear out.

    a. Identify all IVs and their levels.
    b. For each IV are cases arranged to form a randomized-groups or repeated-measures IV?
    c. Identify whether each IV is quantitative or qualitative.
    d. Identify whether each IV is manipulated or not.
    e. Identify the DV. What type of outcome is it?
    f. What kind of design is this?

1.4 Create a potential experiment with three IVs, each having three levels, and a continuous DV to be analyzed as a factorial randomized-groups ANOVA.

    a. Identify all IVs and their levels.
    b. Identify whether each IV is quantitative or qualitative.
    c. Identify whether each IV is manipulated or not.

1.5 Suppose a researcher at a hospital wants to identify the combination of disinfectant and temperature most effective against a new strain of bacteria. Each disinfectant is used at all temperatures. Several different wards in the hospital are identified, and two different wards are randomly assigned to use each combination of disinfectant and temperature. The cases are various pieces of equipment in use in various wards. Identify the pattern of crossing and nesting in this design.

Extending the Concepts

1.6 Expand on Table 1.3 to show a four-way factorial design and then a design in which Treatment *D* is nested within *ABC* combinations.

1.7 Give yourself a pat on the back for surviving your first assignment.

2

Organizing, Describing, and Screening Data

2.1 Organizing Data for a Computer

All of the statistical packages reviewed here use data organized in a similar fashion; a data set organized for SPSS is also appropriate for SAS or SYSTAT, MINITAB, or NCSS. The data set can be entered into a file through a spreadsheet, a word processor (and saved in ASCII format), or a database, and then read by the statistical package, or it can be entered directly into the specialized data-entry program of the statistical package. The packages also have conversion facilities that allow them, with varying levels of difficulty, to import data created by some of the other packages.[1]

The statistical packages have a great deal of flexibility for manipulating variables once they are entered into a file. You can convert continuous variables to discrete variables, change numeric values attached to levels of discrete variables, rescale values of continuous variables using logarithmic or other transformations, add, average, or otherwise manipulate values from two or more variables, and so on. In other words, the numbers entered into the data set are potentially only the starting point for the values that are analyzed.

The packages also have some built-in flexibility for handling missing values. Missing values occur when, for one reason or another, some data for a case are unavailable. The default option for the programs is to delete a case with data missing on one or more of the variables currently in use. In randomized-groups designs, deletion of the case is appropriate. Deletion of a case, however, often results in unequal numbers of cases in various levels of the IV(s); problems associated with unequal n (unbalanced designs) are discussed in Chapter 5. In repeated-measures designs, one or more of the DV measures may be missing for a case when other DVs are available. Then, missing values may be imputed (guessed at) by various means instead of dropping the case. This problem and the various remedies for it are discussed in Chapter 6.

2.1.1 Discrete, Continuous, and Ordinal Data

Data for each case are entered in a different row in a data file. The data in the row can be any mix of discrete, continuous, and ordinal variables, and entered in any sequence, but all cases have to use the

---

[1]SPSS, SYSTAT, MINITAB, and NCSS require that data be converted to their own formats although some can import data from other formats. SAS command mode is capable of using ASCII files directly.

same order for the variables. The order itself does not matter because variables are named and then manipulated by their names. However, for purposes of proofreading, it is usually easier to enter the data in the order in which they are collected.[2]

Each row of data typically is for a different case[3] and each column of data is for a different variable. The values that are entered into a column depend on the type of variable. If the variable is a discrete/categorical/nominal/enumerated/group membership variable, the researcher assigns an arbitrary number to each category and inserts the appropriate number for the case in the column. Most programs permit you to assign names rather than arbitrary numbers for these kinds of variables, but you may later find that assignment of names has reduced your flexibility. For example, if a discrete variable represents group membership (experimental versus control), or the outcome of quality assessment (pass or fail), the researcher arbitrarily assigns, say, 1 to experimental group/pass, and 2 to control group/fail; the column for the variable contains 1's and 2's, each appropriate for a particular case. If the variable is to be treated as continuous, the entries in the column are the actual values (scores) each case receives on the continuous variable. If the variable is ordinal/rank order, the entry is the rank order assigned to each case or by each case.

By the way, we strongly recommend that you avail yourself of the built-in capacity of the programs for attaching labels to the values of discrete variables. For instance, if you are assessing whether a case passes or fails quality control, you could either use 1 to represent "pass" or 1 to represent "fail." At the time that you create the data set, you are sure you will never forget your choice. However, 3 months and a couple of data sets later, you are likely to be less sure of your decision. Interpretive labels attached to the values during creation of the data set and printed automatically on the output go a long way toward removing this source of confusion. Or create a code book for the data set and be meticulous with its location.

If a datum is missing for a case, also remember to leave the appropriate column empty or insert a missing-values code. A missing-values code is a default code used by the program or a code chosen by the researcher to indicate missing values. Most current programs use a period (.) as a default missing-values code. If you do not acknowledge the missing value somehow, the numbers after the missing value may be shifted left into the wrong columns.

2.1.2   Randomized-Groups Designs

The minimum randomized-groups design has one discrete variable and one continuous variable. The discrete variable represents levels of the IV and the continuous variable the DV. The data set has a minimum of two columns. The column for the IV has numbers in it that represent the level of the IV experienced by each case. The column for the DV contains the scores for the cases. It is common practice to use a third column to represent case number. The data organization for a one-way randomized-group design with six cases and three levels of A appears in Table 2.1(a).

---

[2]Large data sets cannot really be proofread. Instead, you have to rely on the "reasonableness" of the descriptive statistics for the distributions of each variable to reveal errors in data entry.

[3]Sometimes there is so much data for each case that you may want to wrap the data for each case around into more than one row so that you can view or print out all the values. In any event, each case must begin with a new row.

TABLE 2.1   Organization of Data for Randomized-Groups Designs

(a) One-way randomized-groups design with three levels of *A*

Case	*A*	DV
1	1	14.23
2	1	17.70
3	2	16.94
4	2	17.05
5	3	21.55
6	3	19.46

(b) Two-way factorial randomized-groups design with two levels of *A* **and two levels of** *B*

Case	*A*	*B*	DV
1	1	1	6
2	1	1	10
3	1	2	22
4	1	2	17
5	2	1	4
6	2	1	11
7	2	2	19
8	2	2	15

A randomized-groups design with two IVs, *A* and *B*, requires a minimum of three columns: one to code level of *A*, one to code level of *B*, and one for the scores on the DV. The data organization for a two-way factorial design with eight cases, two levels of *A*, and two levels of *B* appears in Table 2.1(b). An additional column is required to code the levels for each additional IV, whether or not it is in factorial arrangement with the other IVs. If a CV (covariate, Chapter 8) also is measured, an additional column is required for its values. The data organization for a two-way factorial randomized-groups design with a DV and a CV is in Table 2.1(c)

Much of the time, data sets contain more variables than are currently being analyzed. It is common in the social sciences, for instance, to have demographic information for each case in addition to its status on IVs and the DV. Each additional variable requires an additional column. This information may never be analyzed or may be useful only with certain outcomes of the major analysis. We have generally found it easier to enter all information when the data set is created rather than to

TABLE 2.1   Continued

(c) Two-way factorial randomized-groups design with two levels of *A*, two levels of *B*, a DV, and a CV

Case	A	B	DV	CV
1	1	1	6	122
2	1	1	10	146
3	1	2	22	108
4	1	2	17	112
5	2	1	4	107
6	2	1	11	134
7	2	2	19	93
8	2	2	15	72

go back and add it later. In other words, it is usually better to put in all the information you have and never use some of it than to go back and (painfully) add it later. You can always save a subset of the variables needed for a particular analysis into another file, with a unique name.

2.1.3   Repeated-Measures Designs

Each case provides a score at each level of an IV or each combination of levels of IVs in a repeated-measures design. Table 2.2(a) shows the layout of data for a one-way repeated-measures design with five cases and three levels of *A*. Table 2.2(b) shows the layout of data for a two-way repeated-measures design with five cases, three levels of *A*, and two levels of *B*. Table 2.2(c) shows layout of data for a mixed design where *A* is a randomized-group IV and *B* is a repeated-measures IV. The layout of data for a mixed design is a combination of the layout for randomized groups and for repeated measures. As designs become larger, more columns are needed, but the organizational principles remain the same.

The scores for each case at each level of a repeated-measures IV are entered in the data set, not the codes for levels of the IV.[4] The name of the repeated measures IV, its number of levels, and the labels for the levels are defined through facilities provided by the software "on the fly," so to speak. If there is more than one repeated-measures IV, it is very helpful to use some naming convention like the one suggested in Table 2.2(b) in which the DV corresponding to particular combinations of levels of *A* and *B* are very clearly indicated.

---

[4]Sometimes it is useful to enter repeated-measures data with IV codes (and case codes) in randomized-groups format (cf. Chapters 6 and 9).

TABLE 2.2   Organization of Data for Repeated-Measures and Mixed Designs

(a) One-way repeated-measures design with three levels of A

Case	DV at a_1	DV at a_2	DV at a_3
1	0.0047	0.0042	0.0032
2	0.0083	0.0081	0.0078
3	0.0063	0.0059	0.0055
4	0.0075	0.0075	0.0070
5	0.0051	0.0047	0.0043

(b) Two-way factorial repeated-measures design with three levels of A and two levels of B

Case	DV at a_1b_1	DV at a_1b_2	DV at a_2b_1	DV at a_2b_2	DV at a_3b_1	DV at a_3b_2
1	138	140	155	139	157	155
2	126	126	131	128	130	133
3	140	139	144	138	141	140
4	120	118	119	122	123	130
5	149	144	145	139	148	145

(c) Two-way factorial mixed design with two levels of A (randomized group) and two levels of B (repeated measures)

Case	A	DV at b_1	DV at b_2
1	1	0.11	0.17
2	1	0.14	0.20
3	2	0.23	0.24
4	2	0.22	0.20

2.2   Describing Data from One Variable

This section and the one that follows are intended as reminders of material already mastered in a first course in descriptive and inferential statistics. If you are encountering this material for the first time, you may wish to study it in greater detail in a more elementary book such as Spatz (1997).

There are two ways to summarize the data from a single variable: statistical and graphical. Statistical methods involve presenting certain summary values that represent an entire distribution of numbers with just a few statistics. A measure of central tendency usually is presented, along with a measure of dispersion. The measure of central tendency is the single number that best represents the entire distribution. It is a single point on a scale (score line) and the value that one would guess if asked to make a prediction about the score of a new case. The measure of dispersion indicates the variability in the numbers and the extent to which the scores in the distribution differ from central tendency. The dispersion measure is a distance along a scale (score line). If the measure of dispersion is small, the value of central tendency is a good prediction because all cases have scores that are close to each other. If the measure of dispersion is large, the prediction is not as good because cases have scores that are very different and are widely spread along the scale.

The second method, and the one gaining popularity, is graphic. The researcher seeks to present information about a distribution in a visually compelling, immediately comprehensible display. Different graphical methods are useful for displaying different kinds of data, and new methods are constantly being developed. Truly stunning graphical methods are sometimes available with modern computers to convey the information about a single variable or the relationships among two or more variables, sometimes in motion. Some of these new methods are summarized by Cleveland (1994), who also provides numerous helpful hints for improving the usefulness of all graphical displays. Tukey (1977) shows many of these methods that are useful in exploratory data analysis. Hoaglin, Mosteller, and Tukey (1991) demonstrate graphical displays especially useful for exploratory ANOVA. Tufte (1983) is also helpful.

The following discussion briefly summarizes statistical and graphical methods useful for different types of variables. Output from SPSS, SAS, MINITAB, or SYSTAT is used to illustrate some of these methods. However, the choice of package for type of data is more or less random because they all provide similar information. The data set (DESCRPT.* on the data disk that accompanies this text[5]) is randomly generated with 50 cases and five variables (unimaginatively labeled Var_A, Var_B, Var_C, Var_D, and Var_E), the first four continuous and the last discrete. The distributions for the continuous variables have been generated to illustrate certain properties of data such as normality, skewness, and outliers.

2.2.1 Discrete Variables

Recall that discrete variables have only a few levels or values (categories). IVs in ANOVA are always discrete (categorical) variables. (DVs also may be discrete, but usually are not in ANOVA.) For example, a discrete IV might be type of drug with three levels: placebo, stimulant, and tranquilizer. (A discrete DV might be improvement with two values: not improved and improved.)

2.2.1.1 *Central Tendency and Dispersion for Discrete Variables*

Because numbers often are arbitrarily assigned to name categories of discrete variables, there are very few statistics that are useful to summarize their distributions. The mode is used as the measure of central tendency, where the mode is the category with the greatest number of cases. Sometimes there are two such categories and the distribution is said to be bimodal. Often, it is useful to report the percentage (and sometimes number) of cases in each category, as well, to give your reader an idea of the dispersion of cases into categories.

---

[5]The README.TXT file on the disk describes the naming conventions for the data sets.

2.2.1.2   *Graphical Methods for Discrete Variables*

Frequency histograms, bar charts, and pie charts often are used to display data from a discrete variable. The length of the bar or the size of the slice that represents each category gives a clear, rapid, visual summary of the popularity of the various categories and the dominance of the modal category, as shown in Figure 2.1 in charts produced by SYSTAT GRAPH. The LABEL instruction requests that slices of the pie chart be labeled with the percentage for each value of Var_*E*.

It is apparent from either the bar chart or the pie chart that the middle category (2) is the most popular with 21 of the cases (42% of 50 cases); this is the category that one would predict for a new case. Category 3 has 19 cases (38%) and category 1 has 10 cases (20%). Category 2, then, is not a great deal more popular than category 3, but both are more popular than category 1.

2.2.2   Ordinal Variables

Rank-order/ordinal data are obtained when the researcher assesses the relative positions of cases in a distribution of cases (e.g., most talented, least efficient), when the researcher has others rank order several items (most important to me, etc.), or when the researcher has assessed numerical scores for cases, but does not trust them. In the last situation, the researcher believes that the case with the highest score has the most (or least) of something, but is not comfortable analyzing the numerical scores themselves, so the data are treated as ordinal. Numbers reveal which case is in what position, but there is no assurance that the distance between the first and second cases is the same as, for instance, the distance between the second and third cases, or any other adjacent pair.

```
PIE VAR_E/ LABEL
BAR VAR_E
```

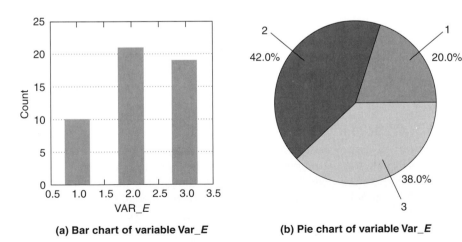

(a) **Bar chart of variable Var_*E***   (b) **Pie chart of variable Var_*E***

**FIGURE 2.1   Syntax, Bar Chart, and Pie Chart from
SYSTAT GRAPH for Discrete Var_*E***

2.2.2.1 *Central Tendency and Dispersion for Ordinal Variables*

The median (the value of the middle case) is used as the measure of central tendency because the size of adjacent differences is not stable. The median is the value associated with the middle case when there is an odd number of them. When there is an even number of cases, the median is the average of the values for the two middle cases. The median is the value at the 50th percentile; 50% of the cases have values above the median and 50% below.

Dispersion is assessed in two ways: by range and by quartiles. The range is the highest score minus the lowest score. The quartiles are the values that cut off the upper and lower 25% of the cases. In other words, the lower quartile is the 25th percentile, the median is the 50th percentile, and the upper quartile is the 75th percentile.

The data set, DESCRPT.*, contains four continuous variables and one discrete variable. Suppose that the researcher has doubts about the measurement of Var_A and feels more justified considering it ordinal than continuous. That is, the researcher is willing to take advantage of the order property of the numbers but is uncomfortable about treating them as continuous. Appropriate summary statistics are median for central tendency, with range and interquartile range (75th percentile minus the 25th percentile)[6] for dispersion, shown using SPSS FREQUENCIES in Table 2.3. The

TABLE 2.3 SPSS Syntax and Descriptive Statistics for Var_A Treated as Ordinal

```
FREQUENCIES
  VARIABLES=var_a
  /NTILES=4
  /STATISTICS=RANGE MINIMUM MAXIMUM MEDIAN
  /BARCHART FREQ
  /ORDER ANALYSIS.
```

Statistics

VAR_A

N	Valid	50
	Missing	0
Median		50.0000
Range		40.00
Minimum		32.00
Maximum		72.00
Percentiles	25	43.7500
	50	50.0000
	75	58.0000

[6]The semi-interquartile range that sometimes is reported is one-half the interquartile range.

NTILES = 4 instruction requests quartiles. Also requested are relevant statistics and a bar chart based on frequencies (i.e., a frequency histogram). The ORDER ANALYSIS instruction is produced by default using the SPSS menu system.

The range is equal to the maximum score minus the minimum score ($72 - 32 = 40$). The interquartile range is the value associated with the 75th percentile minus the value associated with the 25th percentile ($58 - 43.75 = 14.25$), and the semi-interquartile range is half the interquartile range, $14.25/2 = 7.125$.

2.2.2.2 *Frequency Histogram for Ordinal Variables*

A frequency histogram is appropriate if a graphical display of an ordinal variable created from an originally continuous variable is desired. Figure 2.2 is a frequency histogram produced by SPSS FREQUENCIES. From this display, one can judge the overall shape of the distribution, and with the information in Table 2.3 visualize the position of the median and the width of the interquartile range.

2.2.3 Continuous Variables

Numerous statistics are available for continuous variables. The mean measures central tendency; standard deviation and variance measure dispersion. Skewness and kurtosis describe the shape of the distribution so that normality may be assessed. Measures of central tendency and dispersion for discrete and ordinal data also are interesting for continuous variables. Histograms, bar charts, stem-and-leaf charts, box plots, and normal probability plots are just a few of the types of graphs available for visual inspection of continuous distributions.

The data set contains four continuous variables built to illustrate different features of distributions. All the variables center around 50 and could potentially range between 0 and 100. Var_A is

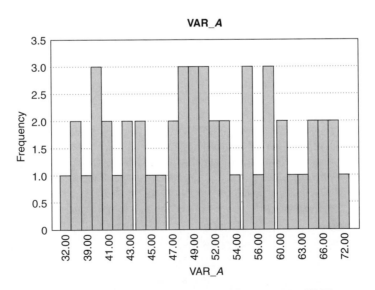

**FIGURE 2.2   Bar Chart of Var_A as Produced by SPSS
FREQUENCIES (Syntax is in Table 2.3)**

fairly normally distributed with a somewhat wide dispersion. Var_B is similar, but with narrow dispersion. Var_C is positively skewed and Var_D contains an outlier (a case with an outrageous value). These properties of the variables emerge as the distributions are investigated.

2.2.3.1 *Central Tendency and Dispersion for Continuous Variables*

The mean is the appropriate measure of central tendency for a continuous variable with a distribution that is symmetrical above and below its center. The mean is the sum of the scores divided by the number of scores. The mean also is something like a central value of gravity for a distribution because it is the value around which the sum of the deviations is zero. That is, if you subtract the mean from each score, and sum the resulting deviations, the sum is always zero. (These relationships are seen later for one numerical example in Table 2.4.)

This property of the mean creates havoc with otherwise commonsense measures that might be developed to assess dispersion. A first thought about an appropriate measure of dispersion might be something like the sum of the deviations of the scores from the mean. However, because the sum of the deviations is always zero, this is unhelpful. For this reason, the deviations are *squared* before being summed to compute standard deviation. A problem then arises with the sum of squared deviations as a potential measure of dispersion; variables from large data sets are likely to have larger dispersion than variables from smaller data sets simply because more squared deviations are added together. For this reason, the squared deviations are *averaged* in computation of standard deviation. Finally, squaring the deviations changes the scale from the one in which the variable was originally measured. For this reason, the *square root* of the average squared deviation is taken in computation of standard deviation, as shown in Equation 2.1.

$$S_N = \sqrt{\frac{\sum (Y - \overline{Y})^2}{N}} \tag{2.1}$$

The standard deviation of a sample of raw scores is the *square root* of the *average of the squared deviations* of the scores about their mean, where N is the number of scores.

Equation 2.1 for standard deviation is appropriate when the researcher wants a summary of the dispersion of a particular sample of numbers. Frequently, however, the researcher is more interested in estimating the dispersion in a population from the dispersion in a sample, and Equation 2.1 yields a value that is, on average, slightly too small. That is, on average, the sample standard deviation underestimates the standard deviation in a population because the values in the sample are a bit too close to their own mean. Equation 2.1, then, provides a *biased estimate* of standard deviation when applied to a population. The correction for this underestimation is simple; N is decreased by 1 in the denominator. Equation 2.2 provides an *unbiased estimate* and is used to estimate the dispersion in a population, σ (sigma), from scores in a sample:

$$s_{N-1} = \sqrt{\frac{\sum (Y - \overline{Y})^2}{N - 1}} \tag{2.2}$$

The standard deviation used to estimate a population dispersion value from a sample uses $N - 1$ in the denominator, instead of N.

If the square root is not taken of the average squared deviation, the result is the variance, as shown in Equation 2.3.

$$s^2_{N-1} = \frac{\sum (Y - \overline{Y})^2}{N - 1} \tag{2.3}$$

The variance is a numerical assessment of dispersion in squared units of the scale in which the variable is measured. This makes variance harder to understand, although you do develop a feel for it after awhile. However, a conceptual relationship between variance and Venn diagrams is a helpful and powerful way to understand relationships among variables (Figure 2.3) as introduced in Chapter 1 and used in later chapters.

The total variance of a variable is illustrated as a circle in a Venn diagram. The extent of a relationship between two variables is represented by the degree of overlap between their two circles. If the relationship is strong, the overlap is high; if the relationship is low or nonexistent, there is small or no overlap. In Figure 2.3, the circle labeled X represents the total variance of X, the circle labeled Y represents the total variance in Y (which, as illustrated, has more variance than X—it is a bigger circle), and the overlapping area represents a moderate degree of relationship between X and Y.

There are two equations for standard deviation and variance; one is easier to understand and the other is easier to compute and less subject to rounding error. The standard deviation equation that is easier to understand is Equation 2.2.[7] Should you find yourself on a desert island with your calculator but no computer, the raw score version that is easier to calculate is Equation 2.4:

$$s_{N-1} = \sqrt{\frac{\sum Y^2 - \frac{(\sum Y)^2}{N}}{N - 1}} \tag{2.4}$$

2.2.3.2   Parameter Estimates, Confidence Intervals, and Sampling Distributions

The desire to estimate central tendency in a population from the mean of a sample leads to parameter estimation and the computation of confidence intervals. The mean in the population is the para-

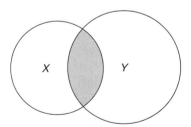

FIGURE 2.3   Variance and Degree of Relationship between Variables Using Venn Diagrams

---

[7]Believe it or not.

meter to be estimated in ANOVA.[8] Confidence limits are boundaries placed around the sample mean to create an interval of values that indicate which populations are likely to have means (μ: mu) which could have produced the sample mean.[9] A common size (and the default for many programs) is the 95% confidence interval. The interval based on the sample mean contains the true population mean in 95% of all samples (Mulaik, Raju, and Harshman, 1997). If 99% confidence limits are used instead, the confidence interval is wider and the interval based on the sample mean contains the true population mean in 99% of all samples. Confidence intervals with other limits also are possible, depending on the particular application. Confidence intervals are computed using Equation 2.5.

$$\overline{Y} \pm t s_{\overline{y}} \tag{2.5}$$

A confidence interval for a population mean, μ, is the sample mean plus or minus the t value[10] at the required probability level times the standard deviation of the sampling distribution of means, $s_{\overline{y}}$.

The standard error is a special kind of standard deviation which comes from a sampling distribution in which statistics are distributed, not raw scores. The standard error of the mean comes from distribution of sample means. A sampling distribution is more theoretical than actual because it is a distribution of all of the values of the *statistics* (means, in this case[11]) computed for all samples of a given size drawn from a population. For instance, you draw a first sample of, say, 37 cases, from a population of 4000 cases, and compute the mean. That mean becomes one entry in the sampling distribution. You put these 37 cases back into the population, draw a different sample of 37 cases, compute their mean, and keep going until you have drawn and computed the mean for some huge number of different samples of size 37 from this population of 4000 cases. The standard error of the mean is the standard deviation of the distribution of means. Fortunately, you do not have to draw these samples; the simple equation for using a sample standard deviation to estimate a standard error for a sampling distribution of means is

$$s_{\overline{Y}} = \frac{s_{N-1}}{\sqrt{N}} \tag{2.6}$$

The standard error for the sampling distribution of the sample means (the standard error of the mean) is the standard deviation used to estimate dispersion in a population divided by the square root of sample size.[12]

---

[8]The observed values of statistics estimated for populations are called *parameter estimates*; the population values themselves are called *parameters* and usually are depicted by Greek letters. Population parameters are hypothesized, estimated, or known; they are not calculated unless one happens to have all the data from the population.

[9]Confidence intervals also may be estimated for the difference between two means. These are the bounds within which the population difference is expected to fall. If the interval includes zero, the null hypothesis of no difference between means cannot be rejected.

[10]Tables of probabilities associated with t values are in all introductory statistics texts, such as Spatz (1997). Confidence intervals are based on z rather than t when the population standard deviation (σ) is known (e.g., from a standardized test) and replaces s_{N-1} in equation 2.6.

[11]There are many other sampling distributions: distributions of differences between two means, distributions of ratios of two variances, and so on.

[12]The sample size, N, is used in the equation even when the known population standard deviation (σ) replaces its estimated value (s_{N-1}). The standard error of the mean is then labeled $\sigma_{\overline{y}}$.

One pleasant feature of sampling distributions is that their shapes are often known. For instance, the Central Limit Theorem tells us that a sampling distribution of means has an approximately normal distribution if samples of about size 30 or larger are drawn from the population of raw scores. The distribution of raw scores does not have to be normal or anywhere near normal for the sampling distribution of means to be normal. Therefore, as long as one is dealing with the sampling distribution, and not the raw scores, known properties of a normal curve (or whichever curve is appropriate) can be used. This advantage of sampling distributions allows one to go back and forth between statistical values and probabilities in statistical inference.

The sample of numbers in Table 2.4 is used to illustrate computations of standard deviation, variance, and a 95% confidence interval.

The mean is

$$\overline{Y} = \frac{\sum Y}{N} = \frac{43}{10} = 4.3$$

Following Equation 2.1, the standard deviation for the sample is

$$S_N = \sqrt{\frac{70.1}{10}} = 2.65$$

TABLE 2.4   Data Set for Illustration of Mean, Standard Deviation, Variance, and Standard Error

Y	$(Y - \overline{Y})$	$(Y - \overline{Y})^2$
4	$4 - 4.3 = -.3$	.09
1	$1 - 4.3 = -3.3$	10.89
7	$7 - 4.3 = 2.7$	7.29
3	$3 - 4.3 = -1.3$	1.69
2	$2 - 4.3 = -2.3$	5.29
9	$9 - 4.3 = 4.7$	22.09
7	$7 - 4.3 = 2.7$	7.29
3	$3 - 4.3 = -1.3$	1.69
6	$6 - 4.3 = 1.7$	2.89
1	$1 - 4.3 = -3.3$	10.89
$\sum Y = 43$	$\sum (Y - \overline{Y}) = 0$	$\sum (Y - \overline{Y})^2 = 70.1$

The estimated standard deviation of the population (Equation 2.2) is

$$S_{N-1} = \sqrt{\frac{70.1}{9}} = 2.79$$

The estimated population variance (Equation 2.3) is

$$S_{N-1}^2 = (2.79)^2 = 7.78$$

The standard error of the mean (standard deviation for the sampling distribution of means—Equation 2.6) is

$$S_{\overline{Y}} = \frac{2.79}{\sqrt{10}} = 0.88$$

And, therefore, the 95% confidence interval (with $t = 2.26$ when there are 9 degrees of freedom[13]) for the population mean (Equation 2.5) is

$$4.3 \pm 2.26 \ (0.88)$$

so that we are 95% confident that the population mean (μ) is in the interval between 2.31 and 6.29.

Fun though all of this is, most people rely on computers to provide simple descriptive statistics. Table 2.5 contains appropriate descriptive statistics for the continuous variables through the SAS Interactive Data Analysis menu system. Menu selections are listed because, unlike other SAS procedures, Interactive Data Analysis does not produce syntax in the SAS log. Note that SAS does not accept variable names with underbars.

It takes a bit of experience to learn to read output but it is well worth the effort. Numerous descriptive statistics for four variables, each with 50 cases, are summarized here, accurately, in a fraction of a second. The same information could be produced by hand, but it would take about half a day and be of dubious accuracy. Summarized for each variable is N, the sum of the weights (Sum Wgts), the Mean, the sum of the values of the variable, the standard deviation (Std Dev), Variance, Skewness, Kurtosis, the uncorrected sum of squares (USS), the corrected sum of squares (CSS), the coefficient of variation (CV), the standard error of the mean (Std Mean), and the 95% Confidence Intervals for the mean, standard deviation, and variance.

Notice in Table 2.5 that standard deviation (Std Dev) and the confidence interval for the mean are quite a bit smaller for Var_B than Var_A, indicating that the values in Var_B are more like each other, although all variables center at about 50. The CV value reported for each variable is the coefficient of variation, the standard deviation divided by the mean. If the mean is very large and the dispersion very small, the coefficient of variation is quite small, signaling a potential problem with the accuracy with which older computers render the numbers. Std Mean is the standard error of the mean (standard deviation of the sampling distribution of $\overline{Y}$). USS and CSS are sums of squared

---

[13]Degrees of freedom (df) are discussed more thoroughly in Chapter 3 and elsewhere.

TABLE 2.5 Menu Selections and Output from SAS Interactive for Var_A, Var_B, Var_C, and Var_D

1. Open SAS Interactive Data Analysis with appropriate data set (here SASUSER.DESCRPT).
2. Choose Analyze and then Distribution(Y).
3. Select Y variables: VARA, VARB, VARC, and VARD.
4. In Output dialog box, select Moments and Basic Confidence Intervals.

▶ | VARA

Moments

N	50.0000	Sum Wgts	50.0000
Mean	51.1600	Sum	2558.0000
Std Dev	9.4747	Variance	89.7698
Skewness	0.2202	Kurtosis	−0.6498
USS	135266.000	CSS	4398.7200
CV	18.5197	Std Mean	1.3399

95% Confidence Intervals

Parameter	Estimate	LCL	UCL
Mean	51.1600	48.4673	53.8527
Std Dev	9.4747	7.9145	11.8067
Variance	89.7698	62.6398	139.3989

▶ | VARB

Moments

N	50.0000	Sum Wgts	50.0000
Mean	49.7200	Sum	2486.0000
Std Dev	1.9171	Variance	3.6751
Skewness	0.0373	Kurtosis	−0.6842
USS	123784.000	CSS	180.0800
CV	3.8557	Std Mean	0.2711

95% Confidence Intervals

Parameter	Estimate	LCL	UCL
Mean	49.7200	49.1752	50.2648
Std Dev	1.9171	1.6014	2.3889
Variance	3.6751	2.5644	5.7069

TABLE 2.5   Continued

▶ VARC

Moments			
N	50.0000	Sum Wgts	50.0000
Mean	49.8000	Sum	2490.0000
Std Dev	11.6759	Variance	136.3265
Skewness	1.3582	Kurtosis	1.8361
USS	130682.000	CSS	6680.0000
CV	23.4456	Std Mean	1.6512

95% Confidence Intervals			
Parameter	Estimate	LCL	UCL
Mean	49.8000	46.4817	53.1183
Std Dev	11.6759	9.7533	14.5497
Variance	136.3265	95.1263	211.6944

▶ VARD

Moments			
N	50.0000	Sum Wgts	50.0000
Mean	51.1200	Sum	2556.0000
Std Dev	8.1407	Variance	66.2710
Skewness	-0.2307	Kurtosis	-0.0263
USS	133910.000	CSS	3247.2800
CV	15.9247	Std Mean	1.1513

95% Confidence Intervals			
Parameter	Estimate	LCL	UCL
Mean	51.1200	48.8064	53.4336
Std Dev	8.1407	6.8002	10.1444
Variance	66.2710	46.2428	102.9088

deviations around the mean, uncorrected for the mean and corrected, respectively. These values are helpful in hand calculation of ANOVA, as described in Chapter 3. Notice that all variables have Sum Wgts = 50, indicating that each case has been allocated equal weight (by default). Skewness and kurtosis values are described in what follows.

2.2.3.3   *Normality*

Normal distributions are symmetrical about the mean with a defined shape and height. Mean, median, and mode are the same, and the percentages of cases between the mean and various standard deviation units from the mean are known. For this reason, you can rescale a normally distributed continuous variable to a z score scale (with mean 0 and standard deviation 1) and look up the probability that corresponds to a particular range of raw scores. The legitimacy of using the z score scale and its associated probabilities depends on the normality of the distribution of the continuous variable. Equation 2.7 is used for conversion of a raw score to a z score.[14]

$$ z = \frac{Y - \overline{Y}}{s_{N-1}} \tag{2.7} $$

There are both statistical and graphical methods of assessing the normality of the distribution of a continuous variable. Skewness and kurtosis are descriptive statistics; skewness assesses the symmetry of the distribution and kurtosis its peakedness. Distributions are not normal if they are not symmetrical or if they are too peaked or too flat. A positively skewed distribution has a pileup of cases at small values and a few cases with large values that lengthen the tail of the distribution at high values. A negatively skewed distribution has a pileup of cases at large values and a few cases with small values that lengthen the tail of the distribution at small values. A *leptokurtic* distribution (one with positive kurtosis) is too peaked; a *platykurtic* distribution (one with negative kurtosis) is too flat (think "flatty"). Both have a different percentage of cases between standard deviation units than does the normal distribution, so z score conversions, inferential tests, and the like, with nonnormal distributions are often misleading (Wilcox, 1998). A normal distribution is called *mesokurtic*. Figure 2.4 shows a normal curve and several that depart from normality.

In a normal distribution, skewness and kurtosis are zero. The standard error of skewness is

$$ s_{\text{skewness}} = \sqrt{\frac{6}{N}} \tag{2.8} $$

For the fictitious data set of DESCRPT.* with $N = 50$, the standard error of skewness for all variables is

$$ s_{\text{skewness}} = \sqrt{\frac{6}{50}} = 0.346 $$

The standard error of kurtosis is

$$ s_{\text{kurtosis}} = \sqrt{\frac{24}{N}} \tag{2.9} $$

---

[14]The sample standard deviation, S_N, is appropriate for some uses of z scores if there is to be no generalization of them beyond the sample tested. For example, classroom grades are sometimes based on sums (or averages) of z scores of exams over the course of a semester.

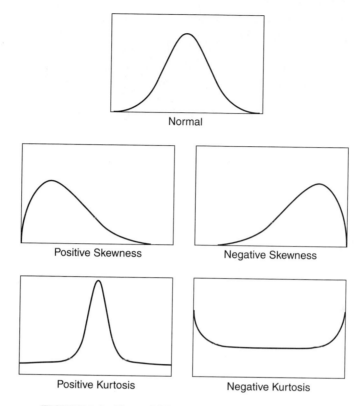

FIGURE 2.4 **Normal Distribution, Distributions with Skewness, and Distributions with Kurtoses**

For the fictitious data of DESCRPT.*:

$$s_{kurtosis} = \sqrt{\frac{24}{50}} = 0.693$$

Either of these standard errors can be used to see if a distribution departs from normality by dividing the skewness or kurtosis value for the distribution by its respective standard error and looking up the result as a z score from a standard normal table of values. For skewness:

$$z_{skewness} = \frac{skewness - 0}{s_{skewness}} \qquad (2.10)$$

and for kurtosis:

$$z_{kurtosis} = \frac{kurtosis - 0}{s_{kurtosis}} \qquad (2.11)$$

Table 2.5 shows skewness and kurtosis values for the continuous variables in the data set. After calculating the standard errors using Equations 2.8 and 2.9, the z score for Var_A for skewness is $0.220/0.346 = 0.64$ and the z score for kurtosis is -0.94. For Var_C, which was generated to have skewness, the z score for skewness is 3.92 and the z score for kurtosis is 2.65.[15] Conventional but conservative (.01 or .001) two-tailed alpha levels (along with inspection of the shape of the distribution) are used to evaluate the significance of skewness and kurtosis with small to moderate samples.[16] By these criteria, Var_A is normal but Var_C has statistically significant positive skewness. But if the sample is large, it is better to inspect the shape of the distribution instead of using formal inference because the equations for standard error of both skewness and kurtosis contain N, and normality is likely to be rejected with large samples even when the deviation is slight.

Some advanced analyses require evaluation of normality by testing skewness and kurtosis. Requirements for normality are often satisfied by transforming the DV (discussed in Section 3.5.7) if the z scores for skewness and/or kurtosis are too discrepant. The problem with transformation is that results are interpreted in terms of the transformed DV, not the original scale of the DV, an often awkward state of affairs.

2.2.3.4   Outliers

Outliers are deviant cases that may have undue impact on the results of analysis. They can raise means or lower means and, by doing so, create artificial significance (increase Type I error rate: Section 1.6.1) or cover up real significance (increase Type II error rate). They almost always increase measures of dispersion, making finding significance less likely. Their inclusion in a data set, in short, makes the outcome of analysis unpredictable and not generalizable unless to a population that happens to include the same sort of outlier.

An outlier is a score that is unusually far from the mean and apparently disconnected from the rest of the scores. The z score distribution is used to assess the distance of a raw score from its mean. Equation 2.7 is used to convert a raw score to a z score. If the sample is fairly large, say, 100 or more, a case with an absolute z value of 3.3 or greater is probably an outlier because the probability of sampling a score of this size in random sampling from the population of interest is .001 or less (two-tailed). If the sample is smaller, an absolute value of $z = 2.58$ ($p < .01$, two-tailed) is appropriate. But visual inspection of the distribution is needed before firmly concluding that a case is an outlier, as seen in what follows.

If you discover a case that might be an outlier, the first step is to check the score for the case to make sure that it is accurately entered into the data file. If the datum is accurately entered, you next check that missing values have been correctly specified. If not, the computer may be reading the missing values code as a raw score. If the datum is accurately entered and missing values specified, you next decide whether the case is properly part of the population from which you intended to sample. If the case is not part of the population, it is deleted with no loss of generalizability of results to your intended population.[17] The description of outliers is a description of the kinds of cases to which

---

[15]Var_D also has a z score indicative of skewness, but it is due to the presence of an outlier, as becomes clear in the next section.

[16]There also are formal statistical tests for the significance of the departure of a distribution from normality, such as Shapiro, Wilks' W statistic, and the Anderson-Darling test (available in MINITAB), but they are very sensitive and often signal departures from normality that do not really matter.

[17]Deletion of cases in ANOVA produces unequal sample sizes in cells representing levels of the IV(s). This, in turn, raises other issues (see, e.g., Sections 4.5.4 and 6.5.6).

the results do not apply. Besides, investigation of the conditions associated with production of the outlying score can reveal the effects of unintended changes in your research program (i.e., shifts in delivery of treatment).

If you decide that the outlier is properly sampled from your population of interest, it remains in the analysis, but steps are taken to reduce its impact—the distribution is transformed or outlying scores are changed. The first option for reducing impact is transformation of *all* the scores to change the shape of the entire distribution to more nearly normal (cf. Chapter 3). In this case, the outlier is considered to have come from a nonnormal distribution with tails that are too heavy so that too many cases fall at extreme values. The same transformations used to produce normality (Section 3.5.7) thus are appropriate to reduce the impact of an outlier: square root, logarithmic, or inverse. A case that is an outlier in the untransformed distribution is still on the tail of the transformed distribution, but its impact is reduced.

The second option is to change the score for just the outlying case so that it is deviant, but not as deviant as it was. For instance, the outlying case can be assigned a raw score that is one unit larger (or smaller) than the next most extreme score in the distribution. This is an attractive alternative to reduce the impact of an outlier if measurement is rather arbitrary anyway.

Researchers often are reluctant to deal with outliers. They feel that the sample should be analyzed "as is." However, not dealing with outliers is also dealing with them, just in another way. They remain in the analysis but change the population to which one can generalize to a population that contains a similar outlier. Not dealing with outliers is a bit like burying one's head in the sand and hoping that the problem will simply disappear.

Any deletions, changes of scores, or transformations are reported together with the rationale. And be skeptical as you read a paper that makes no mention of outliers. The authors either dealt with them but failed to mention it or did not consider the problem, which raises questions about the findings.

In the example data set, Var_D was created with an outlying score. Features of SPSS EXPLORE appropriate for identifying outliers are shown in Table 2.6. The PLOT instruction requests a BOXPLOT; the STATISTICS instruction requests EXTREME values (to identify outliers) as well as DESCRIPTIVES. The remaining instructions are default values generated by the SPSS menu system.[18]

The output segment labeled Descriptives contains most of the important descriptive statistics for a continuous variable, and that labeled Extreme Values shows information relevant for identifying outliers. The cases with the highest and lowest five values are listed along with the values. For Var_A, the highest and lowest values do not differ much from the values near them, but for Var_D, the lowest value of 13 differs considerably from the next higher value of 32, which, in turn, does not differ much from the next higher value of 34. The z score associated with the value of 13 is extreme: at $(13 - 50.52)/9.71 = -3.86$ according to Equation 2.7.

Further evidence that the score is an outlier comes from the boxplot for Var_D, where case 12 is identified as below the interval containing the rest of the values. In the boxplot for Var_A, there is no case with a value outside the interval. The interval in the boxplot is based on the interquartile range—the range between the 75th and 25th percentile and that contains 50% of the cases. These borders are called *hinges*. The median is the line through the box. If the median is off center, there is some skewness to the data. The lines outside the box are 1.5 times the interquartile range from their own hinges. That is, the top line is 1.5 (75th percentile − 25th percentile) above the 75th percentile, and the lower line is 1.5 (75th percentile − 25th percentile) below the 25th percentile. These two

---

[18]If you want boxplots from two or more groups side by side, use the box and whisker plots available through quality control menus.

TABLE 2.6 Identification of Outliers through SPSS Explore: Syntax and Output

```
EXAMINE
  VARIABLES=var_a var_d
  /PLOT BOXPLOT
  /COMPARE GROUP
  /STATISTICS DESCRIPTIVES EXTREME
  /CINTERVAL 95
  /MISSING LISTWISE
  /NOTOTAL.
```

Explore

Descriptives

			Statistic	Std. Error
VAR_A	Mean		51.1600	1.3399
	95% Confidence	Lower Bound	48.4673	
	Interval for Mean	Upper Bound	53.8527	
	5% Trimmed Mean		51.1000	
	Median		50.0000	
	Variance		89.770	
	Std. Deviation		9.4747	
	Minimum		32.00	
	Maximum		72.00	
	Range		40.00	
	Interquartile Range		14.2500	
	Skewness		.220	.337
	Kurtosis		−.650	.662
VAR_D	Mean		50.5200	1.3727
	95% Confidence	Lower Bound	47.7615	
	Interval for Mean	Upper Bound	53.2785	
	5% Trimmed Mean		51.1111	
	Median		50.0000	
	Variance		94.214	
	Std. Deviation		9.7064	
	Minimum		13.00	
	Maximum		69.00	
	Range		56.00	
	Interquartile Range		10.5000	
	Skewness		−1.218	.337
	Kurtosis		3.498	.662

TABLE 2.6   Continued

Extreme Values

			Case Number	Value
VAR_A	Highest	1	20	72.00
		2	16	67.00
		3	2	67.00
		4	39	66.00
		5	36	66.00
	Lowest	1	45	32.00
		2	8	36.00
		3	22	36.00
		4	1	39.00
		5	30	.[a]
VAR_D	Highest	1	48	69.00
		2	40	64.00
		3	5	63.00
		4	41	62.00
		5	38	.[b]
	Lowest	1	12	13.00
		2	34	32.00
		3	2	33.00
		4	46	35.00
		5	32	38.00

a. Only a partial list of cases with the value 40 are shown in the table of lower extremes.
b. Only a partial list of cases with the value 62 are shown in the table of upper extremes.

VAR_A

VAR_D

lines are called the upper and lower inner fences, respectively.[19] Any score, such as that for case 12, that is above or below the inner fences is likely to be an outlier.

If this were a real data set, with the scale of measurement of Var_D somewhat arbitrary, the researcher might decide (after checking the accuracy of data entry and missing values codes) to convert the 13 to a value around 30.

2.2.3.5 Graphical Methods for Continuous Variables

Along with examining the statistics, you also want to look at graphical representations of the distributions of continuous variables. Graphical methods include, among others, frequency histograms, stem-and-leaf charts, and normal probability plots. SPSS FREQUENCIES produced the frequency histograms in Figure 2.5 for Var_A, which is normally distributed, and Var_C, which is not. The nor-

FIGURE 2.5 Syntax and Frequency Histogram with Normal Curve Overlay from SPSS FREQUENCIES for Var_A and Var_C

---

[19]There can be outer fences as well (which are three times the interquartile range from their respective hinges) but only if there are very extreme data points.

mal curve overlay is selected along with the frequency histogram to assist in judgment of normality. The positive skewness of Var_C is readily apparent from the graph.

Stem-and-leaf plots also are available for assessing the overall shape of distributions but they take a little getting used to. They actually display every number in the distribution by using the largest digit (thousands, hundreds, tens, or whatever) to identify the rows and then the smaller digit(s) as the entries in the rows. Figure 2.6 shows a stem-and-leaf plot for Var_A generated by SPSS EXPLORE.

The rows (stems) in Figure 2.6 are in tens (as identified near the end of the table) and the elements in the rows (leaves) are in single units. The first column gives the frequency count for values in that range. Thus, there is one number in the first row (a 32) and three numbers in the next row (36, 36, and 39).

Normal probability plots also require some explanation. In these plots, the scores are first sorted and ranked. Then an expected normal value is computed and plotted against the actual normal value for each case. The expected normal value is the z score that a case with that rank holds in a normal distribution; the actual normal value is the z score it has in the actual distribution. If the actual distribution is normal, the two z scores are similar and the points fall along the diagonal running from lower left to upper right, with some minor deviations due to random processes. Deviations from normality shift the points away from the diagonal. Figure 2.7 contains normal probability plots (requested as **NPPLOT**) for Var_A and Var_C produced by SPSS EXPLORE.

```
EXAMINE
 VARIABLES=var_a
 /PLOT STEMLEAF
 /COMPARE GROUP
 /STATISTICS NONE
 /CINTERVAL 95
 /MISSING LISTWISE
 /NOTOTAL.


VAR_A Stem-and-Leaf Plot

Frequency     Stem & Leaf
     1.00       3.  2
     3.00       3.  669
    10.00       4.  0001123344
    10.00       4.  5677888999
     8.00       5.  00022334
     7.00       5.  5556888
     4.00       6.  0013
     6.00       6.  556677
     1.00       7.  2

 Stem width:    10.00
 Each leaf:      1 case(s)
```

**FIGURE 2.6   Syntax and Stem-and-Leaf Plot
Produced by SPSS EXPLORE for Var_A**

```
EXAMINE
 VARIABLES=var_a var_c
 /PLOT NPPLOT
 /COMPARE GROUP
 /STATISTICS NONE
 /CINTERVAL 95
 /MISSING LISTWISE
 /NOTOTAL.
```

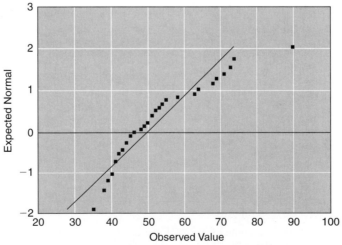

**FIGURE 2.7 Syntax and Normal Probability Plots of Var_*A*
and Var_*C* Produced by SPSS EXPLORE**

As shown in Figure 2.7, the data points fall very close to the diagonal in the plot for Var_A but some distance from it for Var_C. The low values and the high values of Var_C have z scores that are a bit too low, whereas the z scores for the middle values are a bit too high. The data point far from the others in the upper right-hand part of the plot for Var_C looks suspiciously like an outlier and, if the data set were real, deserves further investigation.

Usually, it is preferable to examine graphical distributions of variables before or along with an examination of the statistics. Often, you find that you have to use both methods, anyway, to fully understand the variables you are analyzing.

2.3 Describing Relationships Between Two Variables

Often the researcher is interested in the relationship between two variables as well as the distributions of both of them. Both statistical methods and graphical methods of examining relationship depend on the types of both variables. If both variables are discrete, chi-square analysis and bar charts are used. If both are continuous, correlation and regression along with scattergrams are used. If one is discrete and the other continuous, ANOVA and line graphs are used.

All of these two-variable analyses contain both descriptive and inferential components. Inferential tests for chi square and correlation are in this chapter along with descriptive components. Remaining inferential analyses are in subsequent chapters.

2.3.1 Both Variables Discrete

Chi-square (χ^2) analysis is used to examine the relationship between two discrete variables. For instance, χ^2 is the appropriate analysis if one wants to examine a potential relationship between three different machines for producing a part and the number of parts that pass (and fail) quality control.

The null hypothesis (cf. Section 1.6.1) in χ^2 analysis generates expected frequencies against which observed frequencies are tested. If the observed frequencies are similar to the expected frequencies, the value of χ^2 is small and the null hypothesis is retained; if they are sufficiently different, the value of χ^2 is large and the null hypothesis is rejected. The relationship between the size of χ^2 and the difference in observed and expected frequencies can be seen readily from the computational equation for χ^2:

$$\sum_{ij} (f_o - F_e)^2/F_e \tag{2.12}$$

where f_o represents observed frequencies, and F_e represents the expected frequencies in each cell. Summation is over all the cells in a two-way table. Expected frequencies are estimated during the analysis.

Usually, the expected frequencies for a cell are generated from its row sum and its column sum.

$$\text{Cell } F_e = (\text{row sum})(\text{column sum})/N \tag{2.13}$$

When this procedure is used to generate the expected frequencies, the null hypothesis tested is that the variable on the row (say, pass/fail quality control) is independent of the variable on the column (type of machinery). If the fit of expected to observed frequencies is good (so that χ^2 is small), then one concludes that the two variables are probably independent; a poor fit leads to a large χ^2, rejection of the null hypothesis, and the conclusion that the two variables are probably related.

The degrees of freedom (df) for the analysis are

$$(R - 1)(C - 1) \tag{2.14}$$

the number of rows minus one times the number of columns minus one. You probably remember the concept of df from your previous course when it was discussed as the number of numeric elements that are free to take on any value before the last ones can be found by subtraction. Or you may have encountered the loss of df as the number of parameters that are estimated.

Table 2.7 contains a fictitious data set appropriate for χ^2 analysis that relates three pieces of machinery to the number of items that either pass or fail inspection. Table 2.7(a) *describes* the relationship between machines and outcomes—whether they pass or fail. Columns include the three

TABLE 2.7   Data Set for Illustration of Chi-Square Analysis

(a) Observed outcomes for each type of machine

Outcome	Type of Machine			
	a_1	a_2	a_3	
Pass (b_1)	73	62	28	163
Fail (b_2)	27	18	22	67
	100	80	50	230

(b) χ^2 analysis of outcomes for each type of machine

Cell	f_o	F_e	$(f_o - F_e)^2/F_e$
$a_1 b_1$	73	$163(100)/230 = 70.9$	$(73 - 70.9)^2/70.9 = 0.06$
$a_1 b_2$	27	$67(100)/230 = 29.1$	$(27 - 29.1)^2/29.1 = 0.15$
$a_2 b_1$	62	$163(80)/230 = 56.7$	$(62 - 56.7)^2/56.7 = 0.50$
$a_2 b_2$	18	$67(80)/230 = 23.3$	$(18 - 23.3)^2/23.3 = 1.21$
$a_3 b_1$	28	$163(50)/230 = 35.4$	$(28 - 35.4)^2/35.4 = 1.55$
$a_3 b_2$	22	$67(50)/230 = 14.6$	$(22 - 14.6)^2/14.6 = 3.75$
			$\chi^2 = 7.22$

machines for producing parts and rows include the information for each machine. Table 2.7(b) contains information for the *inferential* component of the relationship. Columns include observed and expected frequencies for each cell (each combination of type of machine and outcome). The final column contains the χ^2 component for each cell and ends with the sum over the six cells. That calculated χ^2 value (sum of individual cell values) in Table 2.7(b) is 7.22. In this case, there are 2 df $[(2-1)(3-1)]$, so that the critical χ^2 value for rejecting the null hypothesis is 5.99 at $\alpha = .05$ (cf. Table A.2 in Appendix A). Because 7.22 exceeds 5.99, the null hypothesis of no relationship between the variables is rejected in favor of the conclusion that the different machines produce different quality control pass rates.

Bar charts often are used to graphically display the relationship between two discrete variables. Figure 2.8 contains the display for the data in Table 2.7(a), produced by SYSTAT GRAPH using the data in CHISQ. SYD. One concludes from this display and rejection of the null hypothesis that the third machine produces a less favorable pass/fail ratio than the other two machines.

The statistics and charts of Section 2.2.1, derived separately for each of the discrete variables, also might be interesting.

2.3.2   Both Variables Continuous

Correlation and regression are used when both variables are continuous. Correlation is used to measure the size and direction of the relationship between the two variables; regression is used to predict one variable from the other. Correlation and regression are first cousins both logically (if there is no

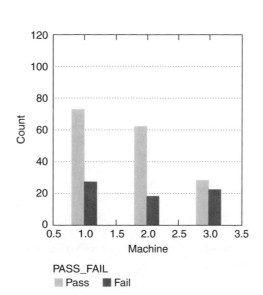

**FIGURE 2.8   Syntax and SYSTAT GRAPH
Bar Chart for Two Discrete Variables**

relationship, prediction is also not possible) and computationally, as indicated in what follows. Correlation and regression are preceded by separate descriptive statistics and/or graphs for each of the continuous variables (Section 2.2.3).

2.3.2.1 Correlation

The Pearson product-moment correlation coefficient, r, is a frequently used measure of association between two continuous variables, X and Y. The most easily understood equation for Pearson r is

$$r = \frac{\sum z_X z_Y}{N - 1} \tag{2.15}$$

where Pearson r is the "average" cross product of standardized X and Y variable scores.

$$z_Y = \frac{Y - \overline{Y}}{s_{Y_{N-1}}} \quad \text{and} \quad z_X = \frac{X - \overline{X}}{s_{X_{N-1}}}$$

and s_{N-1} is as defined in Equation 2.2.

Pearson r is independent of scale of measurement (because both X and Y scores are converted to standard scores) and independent of sample size (because of division by $N - 1$). The value of r ranges between $+1.00$ and -1.00, where .00 represents no relationship or predictability between the X and Y variables. An r value of $+1.00$ or -1.00 indicates perfect predictability of one score when the other is known. When correlation is perfect, scores for all subjects in the X distribution have the same relative positions as corresponding scores in the Y distribution.[20]

The direction of the relationship is indicated by the sign of r. When r is positive, Y values increase as X values increase. When r is negative, Y values decrease as X values increase. The absolute value of r indicates the size of the relationship, whether positive or negative. Thus, an r value of .65 indicates a relationship of the same size as an r value of $-.65$. However, the direction of the relationship is opposite in the two cases.

There also is a raw score form of Equation 2.15, helpful on that desert island:

$$r = \frac{\sum XY - [(\sum X)(\sum Y)]/N}{\sqrt{[\sum X^2 - (\sum X)^2/N][\sum Y^2 - (\sum Y)^2/N]}} \tag{2.16}$$

Compare the numerator of Equation 2.16 with the numerator of Equation 2.4. Notice that they are the same except that a Y has been inserted into the numerator in place of one of the Xs (or an X for one of the Ys). With this replacement, the numerator becomes (the sum of squares for) covariance instead of (the sum of squares for) variance. Correlation, then, really is asking about the substitutability of one variable for the other. When correlation is perfect, you can replace X with Y (or the reverse) with no loss of information.

Table 2.8 demonstrates calculation of values used in correlation and regression with fictitious continuous variables labeled X and Y.

---

[20]When correlation is perfect, $z_X = z_Y$ for each pair and the numerator of Equation 2.15 is, in effect, $\sum z_X z_X$. Because $\sum z_X^2 = N - 1$, Equation 2.15 reduces to $(N - 1)/(N - 1)$, or 1.00.

TABLE 2.8   Data Set for Illustration of Correlation and Regression

Case	X	X^2	Y	Y^2	XY
1	3	9	8	64	24
2	7	49	3	9	21
3	9	81	2	4	18
4	2	4	7	49	14
5	4	16	8	64	32
6	6	36	5	25	30
7	1	1	8	64	8
8	8	64	4	16	32
9	7	49	4	16	28
10	2	4	9	81	18
	$\sum X = 49$	$\sum X^2 = 313$	$\sum Y = 58$	$\sum Y^2 = 392$	$\sum XY = 225$

By using Equation 2.16, Pearson r for the data set in Table 2.8 is

$$r = \frac{225 - \frac{(49)(58)}{10}}{\sqrt{\left(313 - \frac{49^2}{10}\right)\left(392 - \frac{58^2}{10}\right)}} = -.93$$

The null hypothesis in correlation is that there is no relationship between the two variables in the population: $\rho = 0$ where ρ (rho) is the population correlation. This hypothesis most easily is tested by referring to tables of values of r that differ reliably from zero with probability levels .05 and .01, given the degrees of freedom for the test (the number of pairs of scores minus 2). The null hypothesis is rejected if the computed value of r exceeds the tabled value. These tables are available in introductory statistics texts. For example, the critical value at $\alpha = .05$ for the 8 df of Table 2.8 (10 pairs of scores $-$ 2) is .63 (absolute). We can reject the null hypothesis of no relationship between X and Y because this is exceeded by the calculated value of .93 (absolute).

Squared correlation (r^2—also called effect size or coefficient of determination) is used to interpret the degree of relationship if it is found to be reliable. In a Venn diagram (Figure 2.3 earlier), the variance of each variable is represented as a circle and the relationship between the two variables is represented by the overlapping area between them. If r is zero, the circles do not overlap. If $r = .32$, $r^2 = .10$ and about 10% of the area in the circles overlaps. Absolute values of correlations less than about .30, then, are usually considered minimal, even if they are found to be reliable, because less than 10% of the variance in $\overline{Y}$ can be attributed to its linear association with $\overline{X}$ and vice versa. When $|r| = .71$, $r^2 = .50$ and about half the area in the circles is overlapping. Depending on the research area, such a correlation might be considered small, moderate, or very strong.

The data in Table 2.8 show a strong, negative relationship. If $r = -.93$, then $r^2 = .86$ for an 86% overlap between the variance of X and the variance of Y. The direction of the correlation is negative, meaning that scores on Y decrease as scores on X increase.

2.3.2.2 Regression

Whereas correlation assesses the size and direction of the linear relationship between two variables, regression is used to predict a score on one variable from a score on the other. In bivariate (two-variable) simple linear regression, a straight-line relationship between the two variables is found. The best-fitting straight line goes through the means of X and Y and minimizes the sum of the squared vertical distances between the data points and the line.

To find the best-fitting straight line for predicting $\overline{Y}$ from $\overline{X}$, Equation 2.17 is solved:

$$Y' = bX + a \tag{2.17}$$

where Y' = predicted score

b = slope of the line (change in Y divided by change in X)

X = value for which Y is to be predicted

a = value of Y when X is 0.00

The differences between the predicted and the obtained values of Y for each case represent errors of prediction, called *residuals*. The best-fitting straight line is the line that minimizes the squared errors of prediction/residuals. For this reason, this type of regression is called *least squares regression*.

To solve Equation 2.17, both b and a are found.

$$b = \frac{\sum XY - [(\sum X)(\sum Y)]/N}{\sum X^2 - (\sum X)^2/N} \tag{2.18}$$

The bivariate regression coefficient, b, is the ratio of the covariance of the variables to the variance of the one from which predictions are made.

Note the differences and similarities between Equation 2.16 (for correlation) and Equation 2.18 (for the regression coefficient). Both have covariance as the numerator but differ in the denominator. In correlation, the variances of both are used in the denominator. In regression, the variance of the predictor variable serves as the denominator: If Y is predicted from X, variance of X is the denominator, but if X is predicted from Y, variance of Y is the denominator.

The value of the intercept, a, also is calculated to complete the solution.

$$a = \overline{Y} - b\overline{X} \tag{2.19}$$

The intercept is the mean of the observed values of the predicted variable minus the product of the regression coefficient times the mean of the predictor variable.

The slope for regression for predicting Y from X in the data of Table 2.8 using Equation 2.18 is

$$b = \frac{225 - \dfrac{(49)(58)}{10}}{313 - \dfrac{49^2}{10}} = -.81$$

And the intercept, from Equation 2.19, is

$$a = 5.8 - (-.81)4.9 = 9.8$$

Equation 2.17 is used to predict Y from X as follows:

$$Y' = (-.81)X + 9.8$$

If a new case has an X score of 3, the predicted Y score for the case is

$$Y' = (-.81)3 + 9.8 = 7.4$$

This result is consistent with the negative signs of r and b, which mean that scores on Y go down as scores on X go up.

The null hypothesis in regression is that the regression coefficient in the population (β) is equal to zero—that Y cannot be predicted from X. One way to test the null hypothesis is to calculate r from the same data. The test for r also is the test for b. In the example, then, we can reject the hypothesis of no prediction because we rejected the hypothesis of no relationship.

The relationship between the two variables usually is visualized using a scattergram, as shown in Figure 2.9 produced by SYSTAT SPLOM. This particular display has the added advantage of showing frequency histograms for the two variables on the margins. The slope is displayed by the request for **SMOOTH=LINEAR**. Data are in REGRESS.SYD.

It is clear from the graph in the lower left box that Y scores go down as X scores go up, consistent with the negative correlation and the negative regression coefficient. The line representing the slope ends at the lower right corner if $b = -1.00$ and $a = 0$.

Although regression typically is used with two continuous variables, it also can be used when one of the variables is dichotomous. In this case, one is said to be taking the regression approach to ANOVA. This application is demonstrated in Chapter 3. This approach sometimes offers greater conceptual clarity than the normal ANOVA approach and is a strategy that is used when helpful throughout this book.

2.3.3 One Discrete and One Continuous Variable

The relationship between a discrete and a continuous variable is usually studied through ANOVA when the discrete variable is the IV and the continuous variable is the DV. The many varieties and complexities of ANOVA are the subject of the rest of this book. This section concentrates on graphical displays. The files on disk named DESGROUP.* contain 48 cases: three levels of an IV with 16 cases in each level and a single DV.

SPLOM X Y / HALF SMOOTH=LINEAR

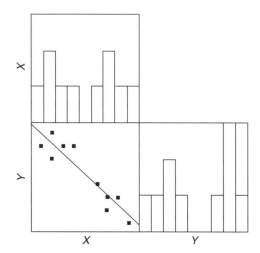

**FIGURE 2.9   Scattergram and Frequency
Histograms for Two Continuous Variables:
SYSTAT SPLOM Syntax and Output**

One of the nicer programs for visualizing the relationship between a discrete variable and a continuous variable is MINITAB. Histograms with a normal curve overlay are available for each level of the IV (the discrete variable). A potential outlier appears as a data point far from its own mean and disconnected from the rest of the data in its own level. Syntax and output for two runs of this program with hypothetical data in DESGROUP.MTW are in Tables 2.9(a) and 2.9(b). The DV is the variable to be `Described`. The IV is identified as the grouping variable in the `By` instruction. The output produced by `%Describe` is specified in the menu by requesting a graphical summary in the Graphs window.

There are no outliers in any of the three levels of the IV in Table 2.9(a), but there is a probable outlier in the first level of the IV reproduced in Table 2.9(b), created by changing a value of 21 in the data set of Table 2.9(a) to a 1 (in what might be a common typographical data-entry error). This data point has a z score of $(1 - 16.500)/5.633 = -2.75$ and is apparently disconnected from the rest of the data in its group. The outlier pulls down the mean for the first group.

A line graph of the group means is useful when a significant difference between means is found in ANOVA, as shown in Figure 2.10, produced by SPSS UNIANOVA for the data used in Table 2.9(a). The graph is requested in the PLOT=PROFILE instruction, with the label of the IV in parentheses. The remaining syntax is produced by the SPSS menu system once the IV and DV are identified, and is explained in subsequent chapters.

There is a single line on this graph because there is only one IV. If there is a second IV, separate lines (say, dotted and dashed) are used to show the mean values of one IV at each level of the second IV. It is clear from Figure 2.10 that the highest mean DV score from the sample is at the first level of the IV, the lowest mean at the second level, and an intermediate mean at the third level.

TABLE 2.9   Relationship Between a Discrete IV and Continuous DV. Minitab %Describe Syntax and Output

```
MTB> %Describe 'DV';
SUBC> By 'IV'.
```

(a) No outliers

Descriptive Statistics

95% Confidence Interval for Mu

95% Confidence Interval for Median

Variable: DV
Group: 1

Anderson-Darling Normality Test
A-Squared: 0.235
P-Value: 0.750

Mean   17.7500
StDev   3.9243
Variance   15.4
Skewness   −2.3E-01
Kurtosis   0.685919
N   16

Minimum   9.0000
Ist Ouartile   15.2500
Median   17.5000
3rd Quartile   20.5000
Maximum   25.0000

95% Confidence Interval for Mu
15.6589   19.8411
95% Confidence Interval for Sigma
2.8989   6.0736
95% Confidence Interval for Median
15.7627   19.4746

Descriptive Statistics

95% Confidence Interval for Mu

95% Confidence Interval for Median

Variable: DV
Group: 2

Anderson-Darling Normality Test
A-Squared: 0.795
P-Value: 0.031

Mean   13.3125
StDev   4.6722
Variance   21.8292
Skewness   1.10080
Kurtosis   0.430983
N   16

Minimum   8.0000
Ist Quartile   10.0000
Median   12.0000
3rd Quartile   16.5000
Maximum   24.0000

95% Confidence Interval for Mu
10.8229   15.8021
95% Confidence Interval for Sigma
3.4514   7.2311
95% Confidence Interval for Median
10.0000   15.4746

(continued)

TABLE 2.9   Continued

Descriptive Statistics

Variable: DV
Group: 3

Anderson-Darling Normality Test
A-Squared: 0.228
P-Value: 0.775

Mean   15.8125
StDev   4.3084
Variance   18.5625
Skewness   0.226477
Kurtosis   −1.5E-01
N   16

Minimum   8.0000
Ist Quartile   12.0000
Median   16.0000
3rd Quartile   18.7500
Maximum   24.0000

95% Confidence Interval for Mu

95% Confidence Interval for Mu
13.5167   18.1083
95% Confidence Interval for Sigma
3.1827   6.6681
95% Confidence Interval for Median
12.0000   18.2373

95% Confidence Interval for Median

(b) Probable outlier in Group: 1 of the IV

Descriptive Statistics

Variable: DV
Group: 1

Anderson-Darling Normality Test
A-Squared: 0.671
P-Value: 0.064

Mean   16.5000
StDev   5.6332
Variance   31.7333
Skewness   −1.32211
Kurtosis   3.12336
N   16

Minimum   1.0000
1st Quartile   15.0000
Median   17.0000
3rd Ouartile   19.0000
Maximum   25.0000

95% Confidence Interval for Mu

95% Confidence Interval for Mu
13.4983   19.5017
95% Confidence Interval for Sigma
4.1613   8.7185
95% Confidence Interval for Median
15.0000   19.0000

95% Confidence Interval for Median

```
UNIANOVA
  dv BY iv
  /METHOD=SSTYPE(3)
  /INTERCEPT=INCLUDE
  /PLOT=PROFILE(iv)
  /CRITERIA=ALPHA(.05)
  /DESIGN=iv.
```

Profile Plots

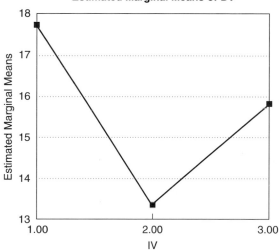

FIGURE 2.10   Line Graph of Mean DV Scores at Each Level of the IV; Syntax and Output from SPSS GLM

Although the means are not the same, the graph does not reveal if they are reliably different. For that, a formal statistical analysis is required. Also note that the scale of Figure 2.10 may exaggerate differences among levels because the lowest value of the Y axis is not zero.

The graphical procedures just discussed for the relationship between a discrete IV and a continuous variable DV are appropriate for experimental data but probably less so for observational data. When observations are underway, either as an end in themselves or in preparation for conducting an experiment, some graphical procedures developed for quality control may be more helpful. One of these, the stratified control chart, is appropriate when the DV is continuous, and another, the attribute control chart, when the DV is discrete and you have counted the number of such discrete outcomes in a period of time. Both of these charts plot DV scores against other observed variables.

Stratification of control charts help pinpoint factors associated with observations that are extreme by showing mean values as well as upper (UCL) and lower (LCL) confidence limits. In a typical example, diameters of manufactured parts are measured every day for 20 days. There are three different machines (A386, A455, and C334) on which the parts are manufactured and four different operators (DRJ, CMB, RMM, and MKS) using the machines. Data are in DIAMETER.SD7, provided by SAS as part of the SASUSER directory.

Figure 2.11 shows the syntax and stratified control chart for SAS SHEWART. Stratification by machines is indicated by putting it in parentheses after the IV: DAY (MACHINE). Operators are identified by different symbols on the chart. The syntax after the forward slash is produced by default through the SAS QC menu system.

Machines are indicated at the top of the chart and operators by the use of different symbols for points in the chart itself. The chart shows that the diameter is too large when RMM is operating the A455 machine. There also is some indication that RMM produces more variable diameters, particularly on machine A386. However, there was no random assignment of operators to machines and no observations of CMB on machine A455, so the data are strictly correlational.

In the social or biological sciences, a researcher might be interested in fluctuating anxiety scores or temperature, or the like. Such scores are monitored over a period of time while also tracking the occurrence of other variables (e.g., operators) that are potentially related, but not manipu-

```
symbol1 w=1 v=PLUS c=RED;
symbol 2 v=STAR c=GREEN;
symbol 3 v=CIRCLE c=BLUE;
symbol 4 v=SQUARE c=CYAN;
proc skewhart data= SASUSER.DIAMETER ;
  XRCHART DIAMETER * DAY ( MACHINE ) = OPERATOR /
     llimits=2 blockpos=1 blocklabtype=TRUNCATED cconnect=BLACK
     coutfill=RED tableall (noprint exceptions) ;
run;
```

FIGURE 2.11   Stratified Statistical Control Chart Produced by SAS SHEWART: Syntax and Output

lated. The stratified control chart is used to assist in discovering the variables that are most closely associated with changes in the DV.

Attribute control charts are helpful when the outcome is not measured as continuous scores, but instead as a head count of discrete values that occur in a period of time. Suppose, for a typical example, that you have operators with two levels of training, expert and novice, and are sampling 200 parts each hour, which are inspected for defects (the DV) under two environmental conditions (air conditioning on and off). The data are in TRAINING.SD7, provided by SAS as part of the SASUSER directory.

Figure 2.12 shows syntax and an attribute chart through SAS SHEWART. HOUR is the subgrouping variable (the major IV). HOUR(TRAINING AC) indicates that TRAINING and AC are consecutive stratification variables (stratification is optional for attribute control analysis). The instructions show that there are 200 items produced each hour. The remaining syntax is produced by default through the SAS QC menus.

Figure 2.12 shows that the process goes out of control under a novice operator, beginning while the air conditioning is on. The process seems to be coming back into control as the air conditioning is turned off. Attribute control charts also are produced by NCSS and MINITAB.

```
proc skewhart data= SASUSER.TRAINING ;
  PCHART DEFECTS * HOUR ( TRAINING AC ) = subgroupn=200
    llimits=2 blockpos=1 blocklabtype=TRUNCATED cconnect=BLACK
    coutfill=RED tableall (noprint exceptions) ;
run;
```

FIGURE 2.12   Attribute Control Chart; SAS SHEWART Syntax and Output

In the social sciences, one might count the number of temper tantrums of a child each day and also record the values of several other variables potentially related to those tantrums. Use of the attribute control chart could help reveal which of the other variables are potentially related to the occurrence of more numerous tantrums.

2.4   Problem Sets

2.1 Compute the sample standard deviation, the estimated population standard deviation, and the standard error for the continuous variable shown. Compute the 95% confidence interval for the population mean for the same data. Use a statistical computer program to produce the same statistics.

45	45	23	23
42	43	10	40
33	16	25	42
27	31	43	32
35	44	42	37
28	18	29	19
14	38	38	50
32	29	25	26

2.2 Use appropriate graphical means to inspect the data in Problem 2.1. Use both statistical and graphical methods to determine if the distribution is relatively normal.

2.3 Use statistical and graphical methods to inspect the distribution of the continuous variable shown for the presence of outliers. (Note that this distribution is not quite the same as that in Problem 2.1.)

45	45	23	23
42	43	10	40
33	16	25	42
27	31	43	32
35	44	42	37
28	18	29	19
14	78	38	50
32	29	25	26

2.4 Compute chi square for the relationship between the two discrete variables shown. Is there a relationship? Evaluate the relationship using Table A.2 of Appendix A.

	Response to Question		
	Yes	No	
Treatment Group	34	19	53
Control Group	26	27	53
	60	46	106

2.5 Compute correlation and regression for the two continuous variables shown. Generate a scatterplot to inspect the relationship. Generate a Venn diagram to represent the size of the relationship.

Plant	Height of Plant	Number of Seeds
1	10	50
2	11	44
3	13	43
4	11	39
5	12	38
6	14	60
7	14	43
8	14	45
9	12	60
10	14	44
11	11	39
12	12	39
13	11	43
14	11	51
15	13	49
16	12	42
17	9	38

3

Basic ANOVA: Logic of Analysis and Tests of Assumptions

3.1   Introduction

Analysis of variance tests the reliability (significance)[1] of mean differences—central tendency—among different groups of scores. The different groups of scores may correspond to different levels of a single IV or to different combinations of levels of two or more IVs. The groups of scores may come from different cases or from the same cases measured repeatedly. If a difference between means is statistically reliable (significant), the difference is expected (with a certain probability) to reappear if the study is replicated. A nonsignificant difference implies that you cannot rule out the possibility that the mean differences that do exist in the sample data occurred by chance.

The simplest design for which ANOVA is appropriate has one IV with two levels and a single DV measured on a continuous scale. The IV consists of one control group of cases and one treatment group of cases, and the researcher asks if means on the DVs for each group are reliably different. If another treatment group is added to the design, the researcher inquires about the reliability of the differences among the three means, and so on.[2]

For example, in a drug testing program in which a control group is given a placebo and a treatment group is given a new analgesic, the researcher asks if the average report of pain (the DV) is reliably different in the two groups. However, even if the new analgesic is completely worthless in relieving pain, the control group and the treatment group are likely to have slightly different means in reported pain. Indeed, it would be surprising if the means were identical, given variability in pain assessments. A yardstick is needed to test the *reliability* of the difference between the two means. That yardstick is developed in ANOVA in which the difference between the means is compared to an estimate of naturally occurring variability in pain to see if the difference is big enough to be reliable (where "big enough," as you recall, is statistically defined).

---

[1]We use the terms *significance* and *reliability* interchangeably throughout the text to remind the reader that rejecting the null hypothesis does not mean that the finding is important (significant), but rather that the mean difference is large enough that a difference is likely to reappear in a replication of the study (reliable).

[2]Levels of the IV (groups) to be investigated are chosen explicitly by the researcher in this *fixed-effects* design. *Random-effects* designs (Chapter 11) are those in which levels of the IV to be investigated are chosen randomly by the researcher from a larger set of levels.

3.2 Analysis of Variance

One of us had endless difficulty as a student understanding why an analysis that tested for differences in central tendency was called an analysis of variance. The following is an effort to spare you similar trouble.

3.2.1 The General Linear Model

ANOVA is part of the general linear model (GLM). Some software packages acknowledge that by using GLM as a general designation for their ANOVA programs. However, the general linear model is a good deal more general than ANOVA, and a thorough discussion of it is beyond the scope of this book.[3]

A simple form of the GLM appropriate for ANOVA is

$$Y = \mu + \alpha + e \qquad (3.1)$$

This equation asserts that a score, Y, can be decomposed into three elements, the population mean, μ, the effects of an independent variable, α, and error, e. That is, each score can be conceptualized as the grand mean modified by the potential effects of an IV, A, and error. ANOVA tests whether the effects of A are reliable. The idea is that different levels of A systematically change scores from the value of the grand mean; the treatments associated with some levels of A tend to raise scores, the treatments associated with other levels of A tend to lower them, and other levels may leave the mean unaffected.

All of this is, of course, tempered by error. Error is composed of uncontrolled influences on scores. The nature of error differs from discipline to discipline, and from study to study. In some settings, it is variation in the operation of equipment; in others, variation in the cases; in yet others, variation in the testing situation or the researcher; or all of these. The error term is the composite of all the effects you have not measured or controlled and do not know about (although you may well have suspicions). Like levels of an IV, the effect of some kinds of error is to raise scores, whereas the effect of other kinds of error is to lower scores. It should be clear from Equation 3.1 that a very large error term can "swamp" the effects of the IV, burying it in the noise, so to speak. For this reason, a great deal of effort is directed toward minimizing the error term.

But the error term also is useful as a metric to judge whether the effects of the IV are reliable. Even if the IV is a complete bust, one would not expect the means of different groups of scores to be exactly equal. They should be a bit different due simply to the vagaries of repeatedly taking different samples of scores from the same population for each level of A. For this reason, the yardstick is needed against which to test the mean differences. That yardstick should be measured on the same scale as the means and reflect naturally occurring variability in scores, without the influence of an IV. The error term, e, is used for this important function in ANOVA. The idea, then, is to test mean differences against naturally occurring variability in scores as represented by e.

---

[3]Chapter 17 of Tabachnick and Fidell (2001) treats you to a brief overview of the GLM, including the MGLM (multivariate general linear model). You might want to wait until you are well into this book before you tackle it.

3.2.2 Generation of a Data Set

The easiest way to understand ANOVA is by generating a tiny data set using the GLM and then see-ing how ANOVA processes it. As a first step, let us set the grand mean, μ, to 5 for a data set with 10 cases, as shown in Table 3.1.[4] In this table, at this point, all 10 cases have a score of 5.

The next step is to add the effects of the IV. Suppose that the effect of the treatment at a_1 is to raise scores by 2 units, and the effect of the treatment at a_2 is to lower scores by 2 units. At this point, as shown in Table 3.2, all the scores and the mean at a_1 are 7 and all the scores and the mean at a_2 are 3.

TABLE 3.1   Generation of a Data Set for ANOVA, $Y = \mu$

\multicolumn{2}{c}{a_1}		\multicolumn{2}{c}{a_2}	
Case	Score	Case	Score
s_1	5	s_6	5
s_2	5	s_7	5
s_3	5	s_8	5
s_4	5	s_9	5
s_5	5	s_{10}	5

TABLE 3.2   Generation of a Data Set for ANOVA, $Y = \mu + a$

\multicolumn{2}{c}{a_1}		\multicolumn{2}{c}{a_2}	
Case	Score	Case	Score
s_1	$5 + 2 = 7$	s_6	$5 - 2 = 3$
s_2	$5 + 2 = 7$	s_7	$5 - 2 = 3$
s_3	$5 + 2 = 7$	s_8	$5 - 2 = 3$
s_4	$5 + 2 = 7$	s_9	$5 - 2 = 3$
s_5	$5 + 2 = 7$	s_{10}	$5 - 2 = 3$
$\sum Y_{a_1} =$	35	$\sum Y_{a_2} =$	15
$\sum Y_{a_1}^2 =$	245	$\sum Y_{a_2}^2 =$	45
$\overline{Y}_{a_1} =$	7	$\overline{Y}_{a_2} =$	3

[4]This data set is too small for many research applications that use ANOVA. Small data sets often are analyzed using the Wilcoxon-Mann-Whitney Test, with adjustment for small sample size, or another appropriate nonparametric test. We use a very small data set here for didactic purposes.

The changes produced by treatment are the deviations of the scores from μ. Over all of these cases, the sum of the squared deviations is

$$5(2^2) + 5(-2)^2 = 40$$

This is the sum of the (squared) effects of treatment if all cases are influenced identically by the various levels of A and there is no error.

The third step is to complete the GLM with addition of error. Table 3.3 contains the complete GLM for the tiny data set with numbers representing error added to each score.

By using the variance form of Equation 2.4, the variance for the a_1 group is

$$a_1: \quad s^2_{N-1} = \frac{\sum Y^2 - \frac{(\sum Y)^2}{N}}{N-1} = \frac{251 - \frac{35^2}{5}}{4} = 1.5$$

and the variance for the a_2 group is

$$a_2: \quad s^2_{N-1} = \frac{51 - \frac{15^2}{5}}{4} = 1.5$$

The average of these two numbers also is 1.5. Keep in mind that these numbers represent error variance, that is, they represent random variability in scores within each group where all cases are ostensibly treated the same and, therefore, are uncontaminated by effects of the IV.

TABLE 3.3   Generation of a Data Set for ANOVA, $Y = \mu + a + e$

	a_1		a_2		
Case	*Score*	*Case*	*Score*		**Sum**
s_1	$5 + 2 + 2 = 9$	s_6	$5 - 2 + 0 = 3$		
s_2	$5 + 2 + 0 = 7$	s_7	$5 - 2 - 2 = 1$		
s_3	$5 + 2 - 1 = 6$	s_8	$5 - 2 + 0 = 3$		
s_4	$5 + 2 + 0 = 7$	s_9	$5 - 2 + 1 = 4$		
s_5	$5 + 2 - 1 = 6$	s_{10}	$5 - 2 + 1 = 4$		
$\sum Y_{a_1} =$	35	$\sum Y_{a_2} =$	15		$\sum Y = 50$
$\sum Y^2_{a_1} =$	251	$\sum Y^2_{a_2} =$	51		$\sum Y^2 = 302$
$\overline{Y}_{a_1} =$	7	$\overline{Y}_{a_2} =$	3		$\overline{Y} = 5$

The variance for this group of 10 numbers, *ignoring group membership,* is

$$s_{N-1}^2 = \frac{302 - \dfrac{50^2}{10}}{9} = 5.78$$

3.2.3 The Basic Analysis

The simplest design for ANOVA has one IV with two levels and different cases at each level. For the traditional approach, DV scores are gathered and arranged in a table similar to Table 3.3, with *a* columns representing levels of the IV and *n* scores within each level.[5] Table 3.4 contains the same scores as Table 3.3, in standard ANOVA format, without listing individual cases or GLM breakdown.[6] New notation in the table is described in subsequent sections.

3.2.3.1 Basic ANOVA: The Deviation Approach

For development of equations, each score is designated Y_{ij}, where $i = 1, 2, ..., n$, observations at each level of *A*, and *j* represents group/level. GM represents the grand mean of all scores over all groups. The difference between each score and the grand mean $(Y_{ij} - \text{GM})$ is broken into two components: (1) the difference between the score and its own group mean and (2) the difference between that group mean and the grand mean.

$$(Y_{ij} - \text{GM}) = (Y_{ij} - \overline{Y}_j) + (\overline{Y}_j - \text{GM}) \tag{3.2}$$

TABLE 3.4   Standard Setup for ANOVA Data Set

A		Sum
a_1	a_2	
9	3	
7	1	
6	3	
7	4	
6	4	
$\sum Y_{a_1} = A_1 = 35$	$\sum Y_{a_2} = A_2 = 15$	$\sum Y = T = 50$
$\sum Y_{a_1}^2 = 251$	$\sum Y_{a_2}^2 = 51$	$\sum Y^2 = 302$
$\overline{Y}_{a_1} = 7$	$\overline{Y}_{a_2} = 3$	$\overline{Y} = \text{GM} = 5$

[5]Throughout the book, *n* is used for number of scores within a single level and *N* is used for total number of scores.

[6]It would be most helpful if cases *did* report the breakdown for their scores in terms of the GLM but that would put a lot of statisticians out of work. We have to rely on ANOVA to discover the breakdown instead.

This result is achieved by first subtracting and then adding information about group membership—the group means—to the equation. The first difference $(Y_{ij} - \overline{Y}_j)$—between a score and its own group mean—represents error (all the cases in each level have, after all, been treated identically, so deviations from the group mean are unexplained). The second difference $(\overline{Y}_j - GM)$—between a group mean and the grand mean—represents the effects of the IV (plus error—more later). For the first case, then

$$(9 - 5) = (9 - 7) + (7 - 5)$$

The score for the first case can be conceptualized as either a difference between the score and the grand mean $(9 - 5)$, or as the difference between the score and its own group mean $(9 - 7)$ plus the difference between its own group mean and the grand mean $(7 - 5)$.

Each parenthetical term in Equation 3.2 is then squared and summed separately to produce the sum of squares for error and the sum of squares for treatment, respectively. The basic partition holds because, conveniently, the cross-product terms produced by squaring and summing cancel each other out. Across all scores, the partition is

$$\sum_i \sum_j (Y_{ij} - GM)^2 = \sum_i \sum_j (Y_{ij} - \overline{Y}_j)^2 + n \sum_j (\overline{Y}_j - GM)^2 \qquad (3.3)$$

This is the deviation form of basic ANOVA where each of the quantities is represented as a difference (a deviation) between two elements. Representing variance as a deviation is the easiest way to *understand* the partition, although equations presented in Section 3.2.3.2, which follows, are easier to use for computation.

Each of these terms is a *sum of squares* (SS)—a sum of squared differences between two individual elements. That is, each term is a special case of the numerator of a variance equation, such as Equation 2.4. The term to the left of the equal sign is the total sum of squared differences between scores and the grand mean, SS_{total} or SS_T. This, when "averaged," is the total variance in the set of scores, ignoring group membership. The first term to the right of the equal sign is the sum of squared deviations between each score and its group mean, summed over all groups. This component is variously called SS within groups (SS_{wg}), or SS error (SS_{error}), or $SS_{S/A}$. The second term to the right of the equal sign is the sum of squared deviations between each group mean and its grand mean, variously called SS between groups (SS_{bg}) or SS_A. The partition of total variance of Equation 3.3 is also frequently symbolized (with reversed terms on the right hand side) as[7]

$$SS_{total} = SS_{bg} + SS_{wg} \qquad (3.4)$$

It is important to realize that the total variance in the set of scores is partitioned into two sources, one representing the effects of the IV and the other representing all other effects, error. In this sense, it is truly an analysis of variance. Because the effects of the IV are assessed by changes in the central tendencies of the groups, the inferences that come from ANOVA are about differences in central tendency.

---

[7]The order of terms on the right has been reversed from that in Equation 3.3.

But sums of squares are not yet variances. To become variances, they are "averaged." The denominators for averaging SS in ANOVA are called degrees of freedom. The degrees of freedom (df) partition the same way as the sums of squares:

$$df_{total} = df_{bg} + df_{wg} \tag{3.5}$$

Total degrees of freedom is the total number of scores, N, minus 1, lost when the grand mean is estimated. N can also be represented as a, the number of groups, times n, the number of scores in each group (if the number of scores in each group is equal). Therefore,

$$df_{total} = N - 1 = an - 1 \tag{3.6}$$

Within-groups (error) degrees of freedom is the number of scores, N, minus the number of groups, a. One df is lost when the mean for each of the a groups is estimated. Therefore,

$$df_{wg} = N - a = an - a = a(n - 1) \tag{3.7}$$

Between-groups (treatment) degrees of freedom is the a group means minus one, lost when the grand mean is estimated, so that

$$df_{bg} = a - 1 \tag{3.8}$$

Verifying the equality proposed in Equation 3.5, we have

$$N - 1 = N - a + a - 1$$

As in the partition of sums of squares, information about group membership is subtracted out of the equation and then added back in.

Degrees of freedom are best understood as the number of numbers that are free to vary before the last number gets "fixed." Imagine you are told that the mean of a group of numbers is 5, that there are four numbers, and that the first three are 2, 8, and 7. What is the fourth number? It has to be 3 because $5 = (2 + 8 + 7 + X)/4$. Or, if you know that the first three numbers are 111, -24, and 2, the fourth number has to be. . . . [8] The point is that this problem has 3 df because the first three numbers can be anything, but the fourth number is fixed because of the mean. In ANOVA, df_{total} is $N - 1$ because the numbers have to work out to the GM. The a means for each group also have to work out to the GM, so there are $a - 1$ df. Finally, there are two ways to think about df for the error term. First, each group has $n - 1$ df (because each group of numbers has to work out to the mean for its own group of size n) and there are a such groups, so there are $a(n - 1)$ df. Or there are N scores and a df are lost as the mean of each group is estimated, leaving $N - a$ df. Figure 3.1 is a graphic representation of the partition.

For the simplest ANOVA design, the partition of Equation 3.4 is

$$SS_T = SS_A + SS_{S/A} \tag{3.9}$$

---

[8] −69.

(a) Sums of squares   (b) Degrees of freedom

FIGURE 3.1   Partitions of (a) Total Sum of Squares into Sum of Squares Due to Differences between the Groups and Due to Differences among Cases within the Groups and (b) Total Degrees of Freedom into Degrees of Freedom Associated with the Groups and Associated with Cases within the Groups

In this notation, the total sum of squares (SS_T) is partitioned into a sum of squares for treatment A, SS_A, and a sum of squares error, $SS_{S/A}$ (scores nested within A).[9]

Variance is an "averaged" sum of squares. The division of a sum of squares by df produces variance, called *mean square,* MS, in ANOVA. ANOVA produces three variances: one associated with total variability among scores (MS_T); one with variability between groups (MS_{bg} or MS_A); and one associated with variability within groups (MS_{wg} or $MS_{S/A}$). The equations for mean squares are

$$MS_A = \frac{SS_A}{df_A} \tag{3.10}$$

and

$$MS_{S/A} = \frac{SS_{S/A}}{df_{S/A}} \tag{3.11}$$

MS_T is total variance in scores across all groups, s_{N-1}^2, and is generally not a useful quantity for ANOVA.

The F distribution is a sampling distribution of the ratio of two variances. In ANOVA, MS_A and $MS_{S/A}$ provide the variances for the F ratio to test the null hypothesis that $\mu_1 = \mu_2 = \cdots = \mu$.

$$F = \frac{MS_A}{MS_{S/A}} \qquad df = (a-1), (N-a) \tag{3.12}$$

If the null hypothesis is true and there are no treatment effects to make the numerator larger, the F ratio boils down to a ratio between two estimates of the same error. In this case, the likely value for F is a number around one (more later).

Once F is obtained (computed), it is tested against critical F looked up in a table (such as Table A.1 in Appendix A)[10] with numerator $df = a - 1$ and denominator $df = N - a$ at desired alpha level.

---

[9]The order of terms on the right has been reversed from that in Equation 3.3.

[10]Actually, when the analysis is done by computer, the exact probability associated with the obtained F is given, so it is no longer necessary to look up the critical value in a table.

If obtained F is equal to or larger than critical F, the null hypothesis that the means are equal is rejected in favor of the hypothesis that there is a difference among the means in the a groups.

Anything that increases obtained F increases power, the probability of rejecting a false null hypothesis. Equation 3.12 tells us that power is increased by increasing differences among means in the numerator (MS_A) or by decreasing the error variability in the denominator ($MS_{S/A}$).

3.2.3.2   Standard Computational Form

The deviation equations in the preceding section are useful for understanding the partition of sums of squares in ANOVA, but inconvenient for calculating sums of squares from a data set.[11] The more convenient equation for calculating a sum of squares is

$$SS_Y = \sum Y^2 - \frac{(\sum Y)^2}{N} \tag{3.13}$$

Actually, $\sum Y^2$ is divided by 1, the number of "scores" in each Y, thus can be expressed as $\frac{\sum Y^2}{1}$.

All of the SS equations in Section 3.2.3.1 have a more convenient form, but first we need to develop a notational scheme and apply it to the data in Table 3.4.

Y is used to designate a single score (9, 7, …, 4 in the example).

A (uppercase italicized A without a subscript) is used to designate the IV.

a (lowercase italicized a without a subscript) is used to designate the number of levels of A (2 in this example).

a_1 and a_2 (lowercase italicized a with subscript) are used to designate specific levels of treatment A.

A_1 and A_2 (uppercase italicized A with subscript) are used to designate totals at each level of treatment (35 and 15, respectively).

T is used to designate the grand total $\left(\sum Y = 35 + 15 = 9 + 7 + \cdots + 4 = 50 \right)$.

$\sum Y^2$ = total of all the squared scores ($9^2 + 7^2 + \cdots + 4^2 = 302$).

n is used to designate the number of scores in each group (5 in this example).[12]

N or an designates the total number of scores (10 in this example).

In this notational scheme, the equation for SS_A, sums of squares treatment, is

$$SS_A = \frac{\sum A^2}{n} - \frac{T^2}{an} \tag{3.14}$$

Unlike $\sum Y^2$ of Equation 3.13, $\sum A^2$ has n rather than 1 scores in each value of A.

---

[11]For one thing, calculating means and then deviations from them is fraught with rounding error.

[12]n would be used with a subscript (n_j) if there were unequal numbers of scores in each group.

The equation for $SS_{S/A}$, sum of squares error, is

$$SS_{S/A} = \sum Y^2 - \frac{\sum A^2}{n} \tag{3.15}$$

And the equation for SS_T is

$$SS_T = \sum Y^2 - \frac{T^2}{an} \tag{3.16}$$

Each equation has two elements, the second subtracted from the first. Notice that these elements repeat over the three equations; although two appear in each equation, there are only three of them altogether. Notice also that in each element, the denominator is the number of scores in the values summed in the numerator before squaring. For instance, $\sum Y^2$ is divided by one (because each Y that is squared is a single score), $\sum A^2$ is divided by n (because each A that is squared is the sum of n scores), and T^2 is divided by an (because the T that is squared is the sum of an scores). Table 3.5 shows sums of squares for the example:

Take a moment to compare SS_A with the value of 40 for sum of squared deviations calculated in Section 3.2.2 from Table 3.2. SS_A can be interpreted as the SS due to treatment effects alone if all cases respond identically to treatment. It can also be interpreted as an answer to the question, "What is the SS if all cases are at the mean for their own group?"

Table 3.6 shows degrees of freedom for the example. Mercifully, the partitions of SS and the partitions of df both sum to their respective totals. If they do not sum to SS_T and df_T, there has been a computational error.

Variance (mean square) for each source is obtained by dividing SS by df. Table 3.7 shows calculation of mean squares for treatment and error sources of variance.

Finally, Table 3.8 is a source table that summarizes the results of Tables 3.5 through 3.7, and adds the F ratio of Equation 3.12. Take a moment to compare these values with those in Section 3.2.2 calculated from the data in Table 3.3. The variances within each group are 1.5, as is their average. $MS_{S/A}$ is, then, the average within-group variance. This fact becomes important later when we consider the homogeneity of variance assumption of ANOVA in Section 3.4.3. Also compute MS_T from Table 3.8 $(52/9 = 5.78)$ and compare it with the total variance computed for all the scores from the data in Table 3.3; MS_T *is* the total variance for the scores, ignoring group membership.

TABLE 3.5 Calculation of Sums of Squares for Basic One-Way ANOVA

$$SS_A = \frac{35^2 + 15^2}{5} - \frac{50^2}{10} = 40.0$$

$$SS_{S/A} = 302 - \frac{35^2 + 15^2}{5} = 12.0$$

$$SS_T = 302 - \frac{50^2}{10} = 52.0$$

TABLE 3.6 Calculation of Degrees of Freedom for Basic ANOVA

$$df_A = a - 1 = 2 - 1 = 1$$

$$df_{S/A} = N - a = 10 - 2 = 8$$

$$df_T = an - 1 = 10 - 1 = 9$$

TABLE 3.7   Calculation of Mean Squares for Basic ANOVA

$$MS_A = \frac{SS_A}{df_A} = \frac{40}{1} = 40$$

$$MS_{S/A} = \frac{SS_{S/A}}{df_{S/A}} = \frac{12}{8} = 1.5$$

TABLE 3.8   Source Table for Basic ANOVA

Source	SS	df	MS	F
A	40.0	1	40.0	26.67
S/A	12.0	8	1.5	
T	52.0	9		

3.2.3.3   Statistical Inference in ANOVA

Section 1.6 described the rationale for deciding whether the differences among sample means are likely to have occurred by chance. Recall that the denominator of the F ratio is an estimate of how much the means are likely to differ on the basis of random variation/error alone. The numerator of the F ratio is an estimate of the difference among means due to treatment plus error (Section 3.2.3.4), whereas the denominator is differences in scores due to error. If there are no treatment effects (i.e., if the null hypothesis is true and $\mu_{a_1} = \mu_{a_2} = \cdots = \mu_{a_j}$), then differences among means equal differences among scores and both the numerator and denominator represent error, so the F ratio is likely to be around 1.0.[13] It might be less than 1.0, or it might be a bit greater than 1.0, or it might be much greater than 1.0, although that would be improbable. Figure 3.2 shows the shape of the F ratio when the null hypothesis is true. The vertical line on the left represents the mean of this distribution, at $F = 1$.

Therefore, the notion that differences among means are due to random variation is unlikely to be true if the F ratio is large enough. How large is large enough? That depends on degrees of freedom for both the numerator (df_A) and the denominator ($df_{S/A}$). Table A.1 in Appendix A shows the critical F ratio for combinations of numerator and denominator df, and for various levels of Type I error (willingness to risk erroneously deciding that the mean differences are due to treatment rather than random variation). If the calculated (obtained) F ratio of Equation 3.12 is equal to or greater than the critical F ratio from Table A.1, the null hypothesis that means differ only by random variation is rejected, and we rejoice in our research success.

Say, for the example, that our willingness to risk a Type I error is 5%. (For the remainder of this book, we will assume $\alpha = .05$, two-tailed test, unless otherwise stated.) With numerator df = 1 and denominator df = 8, the critical value of F in Table A.1 is 5.32. The calculated (obtained) F of 26.67 is larger than 5.32; therefore, the null hypothesis is rejected. The right vertical line in Figure 3.2 shows the distribution at the point that $F = 5.32$. Five percent of the distribution falls to the right of that point, so that 5% of the time an F ratio this large or larger could occur even when the null hypothesis is true. On the other hand, it is much more likely that an F ratio this large is the result of a *different* distribution—one in which the null hypothesis is *not* true and $F > 1.00$. Therefore, we conclude that $\mu_{a_1} \neq \mu_{a_2}$, that the mean for the first group, 7, is reliably different from (larger than) the mean of the second group, 3.

---

[13]However, it is unlikely to be exactly 1.0 because error is estimated differently in the numerator and denominator (more later).

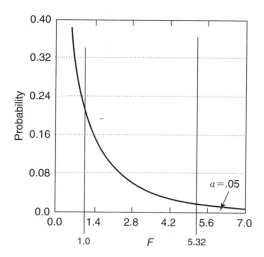

**FIGURE 3.2   Distribution of the F Ratio
When the Null Hypothesis Is True. Generated
Through SYSTAT GRAPH**

3.2.3.4   More Later

It is time for a confession regarding the data generated from GLM in Table 3.3. Notice that, within both a_1 and a_2, the sum of the numbers for error is zero. When the sum of the errors inside each group is zero, the means for each group are the same as the population values. However, nature is rarely so accommodating. Ordinarily, the error terms are spread around through the whole data set, summing to zero, but over the whole data set, not within each group. When that is the case, the means for each group are shifted a bit, too, depending on exactly how the errors are distributed, as shown in Table 3.9.

The numbers for deviations due to error are the same deviations as those in Table 3.3, but now error is spread around randomly. The sum of the error effects at a_1 is -1, and the mean has changed from 7 to 6.8; similarly, the sum of the error effects at a_2 is $+1$, and the mean has changed from 3 to 3.2. This is alarming, but recall that researchers almost always have to use sampled values to estimate population values and the estimation is rarely exact. When estimating the population values (i.e., parameters) for the mean of each group, confidence intervals are created around the sample means that contain the population means with a specified confidence (e.g., 95%).

This slippage of the means also explains why the F ratio is sometimes written as

$$F = \frac{\text{treatment} + \text{error}}{\text{error}} \tag{3.17}$$

When the group means are shifted by the distribution of errors, the numerator reflects both the effects of treatment and the effects of error. If there are no treatment effects, the F ratio should be about 1, but probably not exactly 1 due to the differences in the way error is estimated in the numerator and denominator. If there are treatment effects, the F ratio should exceed 1, perhaps by enough to exceed the critical value so we can have faith in the mean difference.

TABLE 3.9   A More Typical Data Set for ANOVA, $Y = GM + A + e$

a_1		a_2	
Case	Score	Case	Score
s_1	$5 + 2 + 2 = 9$	s_6	$5 - 2 + 0 = 3$
s_2	$5 + 2 - 2 = 5$	s_7	$5 - 2 + 0 = 3$
s_3	$5 + 2 + 0 = 7$	s_8	$5 - 2 + 2 = 5$
s_4	$5 + 2 + 0 = 7$	s_9	$5 - 2 + 0 = 3$
s_5	$5 + 2 - 1 = 6$	s_{10}	$5 - 2 - 1 = 2$
$\sum Y_{a_1} = A_1 =$	34	$\sum Y_{a_2} = A_2 =$	16
$\sum Y_{a_1}^2 =$	240	$\sum Y_{a_2}^2 =$	56
$\overline{Y}_{a_1} =$	6.8	$\overline{Y}_{a_2} =$	3.2

3.3   The Regression Approach to ANOVA

Analysis of variance is a special case of regression and both of them are special cases of the GLM. All ANOVA problems can be solved through regression, but the reverse is not true: Not all regression problems can be solved using traditional ANOVA. This is because continuous variables can be "backed down" to ordinal or discrete variables, but discrete variables cannot be made continuous. Regression is most often used to study the relationship between two continuous variables, but it can also be used if one of the variables is discrete and represents group membership—exactly the setting for ANOVA.

Bivariate—two-variable—regression for two continuous variables is summarized in Chapter 2, Section 2.3.2. Bivariate regression is sufficient to analyze the simple ANOVA problem of Section 3.2. As the ANOVA problem grows, however, multiple (many-variable) regression is needed for the solution, as shown in Chapter 4 and elsewhere.

Because both the traditional approach and the regression approach produce identical results, many of our students seem to think that we include the regression approach to ANOVA out of some sadistic impulse. However, about halfway through the course, they often realize that the regression approach is often conceptually "cleaner" than the traditional ANOVA approach. The design of the study is completely replicated in the columns necessary for the regression approach and separate elements of the design are readily identified and available for analysis. As the design becomes more complicated, the clarity and specificity of the regression approach remain. In fact, screening designs and problems created by unequal n are easily understood through the regression approach but very difficult to fathom without it. Finally, as the design becomes more and more complicated, perhaps with numerous IVs, unequal n, and covariates, and perhaps even with continuous IVs, you retain complete control over the analysis by using the regression approach.

In the chapters that follow, we illustrate this flexibility and use whichever approach is easier. And even if you never choose to use this approach yourself, you will benefit by increased flexibility and depth in your understanding of ANOVA.[14]

3.3.1 Bivariate Regression and Basic ANOVA

In a typical data set for bivariate regression, such as that in Table 2.8, the cases each have scores for two continuous variables, X and Y. In the regression approach to ANOVA, the Y column (vector) is usually written first and the X column is filled with coding that represents group membership. There are several different types of coding (cf. Section 3.5.5), each with its own advantages and disadvantages. We use contrast coding here because of its many advantages in the regression approach to ANOVA. By using this coding for the example, every case in a_1 receives an X "score" (a code) of 1, and every case in a_2 receives a score of -1.

The data set of Table 3.4 is organized in regression format in Table 3.10. The first column indicates the level of A (and is included for your convenience); the second column, the case; the third

TABLE 3.10 Columns for Regression Approach to ANOVA with Two Treatment Levels

Level of A	Case	Y	X	YX
	s_1	9	1	9
	s_2	7	1	7
a_1	s_3	6	1	6
	s_4	7	1	7
	s_5	6	1	6
	s_6	3	-1	-3
	s_7	1	-1	-1
a_2	s_8	3	-1	-3
	s_9	4	-1	-4
	s_{10}	4	-1	-4
Sum		50	0	20
Squares summed		302	10	
N		10		
Mean		5		

[14]There is yet another approach to ANOVA, the cell means model, which requires matrix algebra for a solution. The decision was made to omit demonstration of the cell means model in this book, although it sometimes is used internally by software programs. Interested readers are referred to Kirk (1995); Woodward, Bonett, and Brecht (1990); and the SYSTAT manual (SPSS Inc., 1999e).

column, Y; the fourth column, X (contrast coding for group membership); and the fifth column, the product of columns Y and X. The number of X columns needed to separate the groups is equal to $df_A = a - 1$. Since $a = 2$, in this example, a single X column is required to separate a_1 from a_2. The sum of each column, the sum of the squared values in the column, the number of scores, and relevant means are given at the bottom of the table.

The next step is to calculate the prliminary sum of squares (SS) and the sum of products (SP) for the problem. Computational equations and values for the example in Table 3.10 appear in Table 3.11. Notice the happy event that occurs in the equations for SS(X) and SP(YX): The second terms reduce to zero. This is because the codes used in the X column sum to zero. This feature simplifies the computations, and is one of the advantages of contrast coding when there are equal sample sizes in each group.

Equation 3.1 describes the general linear model in terms suitable for the deviation (traditional) approach to basic ANOVA. The corresponding equation suitable for the regression approach to two-group ANOVA is

$$Y = a + bX + e \tag{3.18}$$

This equation asserts that a score, Y, can be decomposed into three elements. The intercept, a, corresponds to the mean, μ of Equation 3.1 with the contrast coding described earlier. Note that this intercept, a, has nothing to do with number of levels of the IV (also designated a, just to maximize confusion). The slope, b, when multiplied by the code (1 or -1) representing the level of the IV (X), corresponds to the main effect of the independent variable: α of Equation 3.1. And the error term, e, is the same in both equations.

This equation may seem familiar; it is the bivariate regression Equation 2.16 with the addition of the error term and the change of predicted Y' to the actual value of the DV, Y. Indeed, error is defined as the difference between an observed score and the predicted score:

$$e = Y - Y' \tag{3.19}$$

Thus, Equations 2.16 to 2.18 are used to find slope, intercept, and predicted score for two-level randomized-group ANOVA, as shown in Table 3.12.

TABLE 3.11 Preliminary Sums of Squares and Sum of Products for Regression Approach to Basic ANOVA

$$SS(Y) = \sum Y^2 - \frac{(\sum Y)^2}{N} = 302 - \frac{50^2}{10} = 52$$

$$SS(X) = \sum X^2 - \frac{(\sum X)^2}{N} = 10 - \frac{0^2}{10} = 10$$

$$SP(YX) = \sum YX - \frac{(\sum Y)(\sum X)}{N} = 20 - \frac{(50)(0)}{10} = 20$$

With contrast coding of the X column $(1, -1)$ and equal sample sizes, the intercept, a, is equal to the grand mean. When the contrast code for a case is inserted in the prediction equation (as shown in the lower right-hand portion of the table), the predicted score for each case is the mean of that case's own treatment group. Thus, for cases in level a_1, with a contrast code of 1, Y' is 7, and for cases in level a_2, with a contrast code of -1, Y' is 3.

The preliminary SS and SP values in Table 3.11 are also used to compute a final sum of squares for regression, SS(reg.), used to test the null hypothesis that the slope, b, is zero, and, simultaneously, that the correlation, r, is zero. The equation for final SS(reg.) is a first cousin to the equation for slope:

$$SS(\text{reg.}) = \frac{[SP(YX)]^2}{SS(X)} \tag{3.20}$$

Once SS(reg.) is known, and SS(Y) is computed, an error term, called sum of squares residual, SS(resid.), is computed as the difference between them, as shown in Table 3.13.

SS(reg.) has as many df as there are X columns (columns to code levels of the IV). The df(resid.) are found as the difference between df(total) and df(reg.). Degrees of freedom for the example are in Table 3.14.

Table 3.15 summarizes the information in Tables 3.13 and 3.14 in a source table, rearranged to mimic that of Table 3.8.

TABLE 3.12   Slope and Intercept Estimates for Regression Approach to Basic ANOVA

$$b = \frac{\sum XY - [(\sum X)(\sum Y)]/N}{\sum X^2 - (\sum X)^2/N} = \frac{SP(YX)}{SS(X)} = \frac{20}{10} \quad = 2$$

$$a = \overline{Y} - b\overline{X} \qquad\qquad = 5 - 2(0) \quad = 5$$

$$Y' = a + bX$$

For $a_1, X = 1$:

$$= 5 + (2)(1) \quad = 7$$

For $a_2, X = -1$:

$$= 5 + (2)(-1) - 3$$

TABLE 3.13   Final Sums of Squares for Basic ANOVA through Regression

$$SS(\text{reg.}) = \frac{[SP(YX)]^2}{SS(X)} = \frac{20^2}{10} = 40$$

$$SS(\text{total}) = SS(Y) = 52$$

$$SS(\text{resid.}) = SS(\text{total}) - SS(\text{reg.}) = 52 - 40 = 12$$

TABLE 3.14   Calculation of Degrees of Freedom for Basic ANOVA through Regression

df(reg.)   = number of predictors
            (X vectors, columns)   = 1

df(total) = number of cases (N) − 1 = 10 − 1 = 9

df(resid.) = df(total) − df(reg.)   = 9 − 1   = 8

TABLE 3.15   Source Table for Basic ANOVA through Regression

Source	SS	df	MS	F
Regression	40	1	40.0	26.67
Residual	12	8	1.5	
Total	52	9		

The values in Table 3.15 are identical to those in Table 3.8; only the names have been changed to protect the innocent. The regression source is the treatment effect, A, and the residual source is the estimate of error, S/A. The F ratio is the same as in Table 3.8:

$$F = \frac{MS(reg.)}{MS(resid.)} = \frac{40}{1.5} = 26.67$$

Table A.1 is used to find the critical value of F for testing null hypotheses, as in the traditional approach to ANOVA. Three null hypotheses are tested at one time through the regression approach: (1) the population correlation between X and Y is equal to zero, (2) the population regression coefficient (slope or b), is equal to zero, and (3) $\mu_1 = \mu_2$. The third hypothesis, of course, is the null hypothesis in the form typically stated for the traditional approach to ANOVA.

3.3.2   Why Bother?

With simple designs, the traditional approach to ANOVA is clearly more efficient. However, as designs become more complicated, the traditional approach often loses its advantage. The traditional computational scheme becomes convoluted for some types of problems and requires something of a leap of faith as to its accuracy. The regression approach, however, with the design of the study clearly laid out in the X columns, remains straightforward. The logic of the process is easy to follow, although the computations require an extra step; i.e., preliminary calculations of sums of squares or sums of products for each of the columns, followed by final calculation of SS(reg.) from the preliminary calculations. With use of a spreadsheet such as Excel or Quattro Pro, the computations are also easy enough to make the approach attractive. Or you could use a multiple-regression program available in one of the statistics software packages instead of an ANOVA program. These multiple-regression programs have facilities for controlling the entry of variables sequentially, giving you complete control over the analysis.

3.4   Assumptions of Analysis

Certain assumptions are made about the nature of the data when inferential tests are devised. It is simply not possible, most of the time, to develop an inferential test for all possible types of data sets. It may be that the inferential test works well for many types of data sets, including some that violate some of the assumptions; an inferential test is said to be *robust* if it gives the correct answer despite violation of some assumption(s). However, the applicability of an analytic strategy to data sets with various properties has to be investigated. When an inferential test is used for a data set that violates important assumptions, the probabilities that are estimated are not necessarily accurate. The researcher may intend to use an α level of, say, .05, but actually have an α level of, say, .23. For this reason, it is important to consider the fit between the assumptions of analysis and your data set before using the analysis. Some ANOVA designs have specialized assumptions that are not discussed here, but instead are addressed in the third sections of the chapters devoted to those designs.

3.4.1   Normality of Sampling Distribution of Means

An assumption of ANOVA is that the sampling distribution of means for each level (or combination of levels) of the IV(s) is normal. The assumption is for the sampling distribution, not the raw scores. If the raw scores are normally distributed, the sampling distribution of their means is also normally distributed. However, even if the raw scores are not normally distributed, the Central Limit Theorem assures us that the sampling distribution of means is normally distributed for large enough samples.

Normality of sampling distributions is usually assured by having sufficiently large and relatively equal sample sizes among levels (or combinations of levels) of the IV. *With relatively equal sample sizes and two-tailed tests (and no outliers), robustness is expected with 20 degrees of freedom for error.* For basic ANOVA, degrees of freedom for error are calculated using Equation 3.7. Single-sided (one-tailed) tests require larger samples.

Rather often, experiments have small sample sizes and fail to provide sufficient df. If error df are low, tests for skewness and kurtosis are applied to the raw scores within each group (Section 2.2.3.3). If these tests also indicate problems, the researcher has to compensate. If sample sizes are unequal or too small and there is excessive skewness or kurtosis, or if outliers are present, data transformation may be necessary to achieve normality of distributions of raw scores within each group. Transformations are discussed in Section 3.5.7. Recall from Chapter 2 that the transformation is applied to *all* DV scores, not just the scores in one group. Nonparametric methods also are available for small, nonnormally distributed data sets. Siegel and Castellan (1988) and Conover (1980) are rich sources for nonparametric tests. Most statistical computer packages also provide nonparametric analyses.

3.4.2   Independence of Errors

The last term in the GLM is *e*, the error term. Another assumption of analysis is that the errors are independent of one another, that the size of the error for one case is unrelated to the size of the error for cases near in time, near in space, or whatever. This assumption is easily violated if, for instance, equipment drifts during the course of the study and cases measured near each other in time have more similar errors of measurement than cases measured farther apart in time. In each research setting, care is needed to control the numerous factors that could cause violation of the assumption of independence of errors because violation of the assumption can lead to both larger error terms (due to inclusion of additional factors that are not accounted for in the analysis) and potentially misleading results if nuisance variables are confounded with levels of treatment.

If cases are entered into the data set in sequential order, and the problem is analyzed through regression, there is a formal test of contingencies among errors in time, called the Durbin-Watson statistic. This statistic assesses autocorrelation (self-correlation) among residuals. If the errors (residuals) are independent, autocorrelation is zero. If you suspect violation of this assumption due to contingencies in the sequence of the cases, use of this analysis is appropriate. If violation is found, addition of another IV representing time (say, early, middle, and late in the course of the study) might account for this source of variability in the data set.

The assumption of independence of errors also is violated if an experiment is not properly controlled. For experimental IVs, errors within groups are related (not independent) if all cases within a level are tested together (unless all cases from all levels are tested simultaneously) because cases tested together are subject to the same nuisance variables. For example, a participant may laugh out loud inappropriately in the presence of other members of a group assigned to watch a sad movie. Thus, a mean difference found between groups could be due to the nuisance variables unique to the group rather than the treatment unique to the group.[15] The seriousness of confounding nuisance variables with levels of treatment by testing groups separately depends on the expected sizes of the effects of the nuisance variables on the DV. If there are potentially important nuisance variables, *test cases individually or simultaneously for all levels, not in groups defined by levels.*

This assumption rarely is applicable for nonexperimental IVs. In the absence of random assignment to levels, there is no justification for causal inference to the treatments, so that the assumption of independence loses relevance.

3.4.3   Homogeneity of Variance

The ANOVA model *tests* whether population *means* from different levels of the IV are equal. However, the model *assumes* that population *variances* in different levels of the IV are equal. That is, it is assumed in ANOVA that the variance of DV scores within each level of the design is a separate estimate of the same population variance. Recall from Sections 3.2.2 and 3.2.3.2 that the error term, $MS_{S/A}$, is an average of the variances within each level. If those variances are separate estimates of the same population variance, averaging them is sensible. If the variances are quite different, and are not separate estimates of the same population variance, averaging them to produce a single error term is not sensible.

---

[15]Nested designs, in which groups are necessarily tested together, are discussed in Chapter 11.

ANOVA is known to be robust to violation of this assumption as long as there are no outliers, sample sizes are large and fairly equal, the sample variances within levels (or combinations of levels) are relatively equal, and a two-tailed hypothesis is tested. The ratio of largest to smallest sample size should be no greater than 4:1. The ratio of largest to smallest variance should be no greater than approximately 10:1 when an F_{max} ratio is calculated in which

$$F_{max} = \frac{s^2_{largest}}{s^2_{smallest}} \tag{3.21}$$

Homogeneity of variance requires that F_{max} be no greater than 10. *If these conditions are met, there is adequate homogeneity of variance.*

If sample sizes are too discrepant, a formal test of homogeneity of variance is useful; some of them are described in detail by Winer, Brown, and Michels (1991), Keppel (1991), and others. However, these tests tend to be too sensitive, leading to overly conservative rejection of the use of ANOVA. Many of these tests also are sensitive to nonnormality of the DV. One of the tests, Levene's (1960) test of homogeneity of variance, is typically not sensitive to departures from normality, although like the others is usually too sensitive to heterogeneity of variance. Levene's test performs ANOVA on the absolute values of the residuals (differences between each score and its group mean) derived from a standard ANOVA and is available in SPSS ONEWAY and GLM. Significance indicates possible violation of homogeneity of variance.

Violations of homogeneity often can be corrected by transformation of the DV scores (Section 3.5.7), however, interpretation is limited to the transformed scores. Another option is to use a more stringent α level (e.g., for nominal $\alpha = .05$, use .025 with moderate violation and .01 with severe violation of homogeneity) with untransformed DV scores.

Heterogeneity of variance always should be reported and, in any event, is usually of interest in itself. *Why* is spread of scores in groups related to level of treatment? Do some levels of treatment affect all the cases about the same, whereas other levels of treatment affect only some cases or affect some cases much more strongly? This finding may turn out to be one of the most interesting in the study and should be dealt with as an issue in itself, not just as an annoyance in applying ANOVA.

3.4.4 Absence of Outliers

Outliers are discussed in some detail in Chapter 2, Section 2.2.3.4. Outliers are a pervasive problem in data sets and are the subject of a great deal of gossip among statisticians at cocktail parties ("Remember the time that an outlier was found—a 2000-year-old man . . . ?"). The effects of outliers are unpredictable; they can hide real significance or create apparent significance in ANOVA. They severely limit the generalizability of the results. For this reason, it is important to screen data sets for outliers prior to analysis. Remember that they are sought separately in each level (or combination of levels) of a design.

There may be outlying scores on the DV in one or more levels of the IV. An outlier is a score that is unusually far from the mean of its own group and apparently disconnected from the rest of the scores in the group. The z score distribution is used to assess the distance of raw scores from their

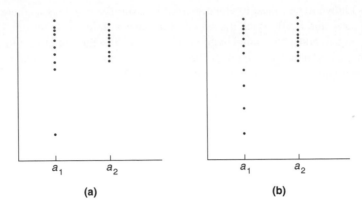

(a)   **(b)**

**FIGURE 3.3   Assessing Outliers through Disconnectedness
Where the Low Score at a_1 in (a) Is More Likely to Be a True
Outlier than the Same Low Score in (b)**

own group mean. A z score (Equation 2.7) is calculated as the difference between the score for a deviant case and its group mean divided by the standard deviation for its group. If there are 20 or more df for error, a case with a z (absolute) value of 3.3 or greater is probably an outlier because the probability of sampling a score of this size if it is truly from the population of interest is .001 or less. If there are fewer than 20 df for error, an absolute value of $z = 2.58$ is appropriate (corresponding to a probability of .01 or less).

Disconnectedness is assessed by visual inspection of the distribution of DV scores in each group. As shown in Figure 3.3, if there is a large distance between the potential outlier and the other scores in the group, and the score has a z value of 3.3 or higher, that case is most probably an outlier. If, on the other hand, the score seems to be connected with the rest of the cases because intervening cases "fill the gap," then the case may not be an outlier. Rather, you may be dealing with a nonnormal distribution.

If one or more outliers are found, they are dealt with by transforming *all* the DV scores (Section 3.5.7), or by deleting the cases producing outlying scores, or by changing just the scores for the outlying cases to make them less deviant, as discussed in Section 2.2.3.4. These options have different consequences, however. If all scores are transformed, interpretation of the results of ANOVA is limited to the transformed means. If cases are deleted, the sample is changed and so is the scope of generalizability. If scores are changed, you need to reassure your readers that the decision was made prior to and without consideration of its effects on ANOVA. In any case, treatment of outliers is included in the report of the analysis.

3.5   Other Recurring Issues

There are several recurring issues in ANOVA, discussed in all the chapters that follow. They are also discussed briefly here to give you a preview of coming attractions.

3.5.1   Effect Size

In some disciplines, there is currently lively debate about the use of the term *significance* to describe mean differences that are judged reliable. The problem is partially semantic and involves the excess baggage attached to the word significant. In ordinary parlance, the term also connotes important, a meaning that is inappropriate when applied in a statistical setting. Mean differences in well-controlled experiments are often reliable, but quite small and unimportant from any practical standpoint. There is growing awareness, then, of a need to examine effect size, which does indicate importance, as well as reliability. This issue is discussed in Chapter 2 in the context of squared correlation and Venn diagrams. Discussion of this issue is expanded, and measures of effect size provided, in the chapters that follow.

3.5.2   Power

Power is the probability of correctly rejecting a false null hypothesis. In somewhat plainer English, power is the probability of supporting your research hypothesis if it really is true. If the probability is low, there is very little reason to do the research because you are unlikely to find evidence in favor of the conclusion you seek, even if it is true. In most settings, a power level of about .80 or so is needed to justify the time and expense of conducting the research.

Power and sample size are interrelated. Larger samples have greater power, all other things being equal. One of the more common things a statistician is asked to do is to estimate the sample size needed for the requisite power. The researcher wants to have a big enough sample for adequate power without going overboard and using too many cases. There are numerous programs available for assisting in the assessment of power. These and related concepts are also discussed in the chapters that follow.

3.5.3   Comparisons

When there are only two levels of an IV, the results of ANOVA are unambiguous. If the difference is reliable (significant), the larger population mean probably (with error $= \alpha$) is greater than the smaller one. The two means are estimates of central tendency from two different populations. If the difference is not reliable (nonsignificant), the two population means probably (with error $= \beta$) are the same; that is, they are separate estimates of central tendency in a single population.

However, when there are more than two levels of an IV, the results of routine (omnibus) ANOVA are ambiguous. The result tells you that there probably is a difference somewhere among the population means, but not which means are different. If there are three means, for instance, you could have $\mu_{a_1} \neq \mu_{a_2} \neq \mu_{a_3}$ (all three means different), or $\mu_{a_1} = \mu_{a_2} \neq \mu_{a_3}$ (the first two means equal, but unequal to the third), or $\mu_{a_1} = \mu_{a_3} \neq \mu_{a_2}$ (first and third means equivalent, but unequal to the second), or . . . well, you get the point.

In order to resolve the ambiguity, comparisons (also called contrasts) are performed. Comparisons are either done in lieu of ANOVA, in a process called planned comparisons, or after ANOVA, in a process called post hoc comparisons. If you have enough information to plan your comparisons, there is a clear advantage in terms of Type I error rates and power. Post hoc analyses are used if you do not know what to expect, but power is lower.

There are many varieties of comparisons each with a different trade-off between power and flexibility. This issue also arises repeatedly in the chapters that follow.

3.5.4   Orthogonality

Orthogonality is perfect *non*relationship between two or more variables. When two variables are orthogonal, their correlation is zero. The issue of orthogonality arises in several places, one in the context of comparisons. The regression approach to ANOVA, for instance, involves setting up a bunch of comparisons and it "works" easily because orthogonal codes are used in the X columns (Table 3.10); similarly, comparisons in a traditional analysis are enhanced by choosing orthogonal coding coefficients (Chapter 4).

The issue of orthogonality also arises when designs include more than one IV, as discussed in Chapters 5 (for randomized-groups designs) and 6 (for repeated-measures designs) and Chapter 7 (for mixed designs). Additional IVs are in factorial arrangement in the designs discussed in these chapters because all combinations of all levels of all IVs are included in the design. As long as the designs are factorial and have equal numbers of scores in every cell, the IVs are orthogonal and each source of variability in the design is assessed independently (except for use of a common error term); that is, the F tests for all of the IVs are independent.

However, there are two situations when designs become nonorthogonal. The first is when sample sizes are not equal in all cells in the design, and the second is when IVs are added, but are not in factorial arrangement with other IVs in the design. Chapter 5, Section 5.6.5, has a lengthy discussion of the problem of nonorthogonality associated with unequal n. Chapters 9 (Latin-square designs), 10 (screening designs), and 11 (nested designs) discuss analyses for designs when IVs are not in factorial arrangement. The covariates introduced in Chapter 8 are also not orthogonal to the rest of the design.

3.5.5   Coding

Coding is used to perform the specialized work of comparisons, the basis for the regression approach to ANOVA. Codes (also called weighting coefficients) are numerical values used to leave out some levels of an IV, or compare the means from two groups with each other, or pool groups together for the purposes of testing the pooled mean from two or more groups against the mean for other groups (pooled or not). Consider, for example, the four levels of treatment in Table 3.16, with two control groups (waiting list and placebo) and two treatment groups (Treatment I and Treatment II). The basic idea is to weight scores in groups by numbers to perform some work, as described in the last column of the table.

Often, the work done by numerical codes is simply to separate levels of an IV from each other, for example, to separate a_1 from a_2 and a_3. There are several schemes for doing that, as illustrated in Table 3.17, dummy variable coding, effects coding, and contrasts coding. As many codes are needed as there are degrees of freedom for the groups. For instance, there are three groups in the example, a_1, a_2, and a_3, so there are two degrees of freedom and two columns of codes (X_1 and X_2) necessary to separate the groups from each other, no matter which coding scheme is used.

In all these schemes, the cases at a_1 have a different set of codes from the cases at a_2 and a_3. By looking at the rows, members of group a_1 have codes of 1, 0 for X_1 and X_2 with dummy variable coding and effects coding, but 2, 0 for contrasts coding. Members of a_2 have 0, 1 codes with dummy variable coding and effects coding, but -1, 1 for contrasts coding, whereas members of a_3 have 0, 0

TABLE 3.16   Coding Coefficients to Delete Groups, to Compare Means of Groups, and to Pool Means of Groups

Waiting List	Placebo	Treatment I	Treatment II	Work of Codes (Weighting Coefficients)
0	0	1	−1	Leave out waiting list and placebo groups and compare mean of Treatment I against mean of Treatment II.
1	1	−1	−1	Pool waiting list and placebo groups and pool Treatment I and Treatment II and compare pooled mean of control groups against pooled mean of treated groups.
0	2	−1	−1	Leave out waiting list and compare the means of the placebo group against the pooled means from the two treatment groups.

TABLE 3.17   Three Types of Coding, Dummy Variable, Effects, and Contrasts, to Separate Groups from Each Other

Groups	Dummy Variable Coding		Effects Coding		Contrasts Coding	
	X_1	X_2	X_1	X_2	X_1	X_2
a_1	1	0	1	0	2	0
a_2	0	1	0	1	−1	1
a_3	0	0	−1	−1	−1	−1

codes for dummy variable coding, but −1, −1 for effects and contrasts coding. By looking down the columns, and thinking about the information in Table 3.16, the X_1 column separates a_1 from a_2 and a_3 in dummy variable coding, compares a_1 against a_3 in effects coding, and compares a_1 against a_2 and a_3 in contrasts coding. Ask yourself what the X_2 column is doing in the three types of coding.

Because contrasts coding is orthogonal, and for other reasons that are too complicated to go into here, we use contrasts coding in the regression examples for most of the book. This is also the type of coding that corresponds to the coding used for comparisons in the traditional approach to ANOVA. Be warned, however, that you will encounter effects coding in Chapter 10 (screening designs) and dummy variable coding from time to time in your study of advanced statistics and in the literature.

3.5.6   Missing Values

In randomized-groups designs, each case provides a single DV score. When that score is missing, the case is deleted from the analysis and the problem of missing values becomes a problem of unequal *n*. In repeated-measures designs and mixed designs, on the other hand, there are other scores for a case that can be used to estimate the size of the missing value. As the number of DV scores taken for each case increases, it becomes more probable that there will be missing values, but also better estimates of them.

There are several ways to estimate—impute—missing values. Some of them involve honest best guesses about the likely size of a missing value. Others use regression equations to predict the missing score from one or several other scores that are available for a case, as shown in Section 2.3.2.2. Others impute missing values from average DV score for the case, and average for the level of treatment in which the missing DV occurs. Others match the case with a missing value to another case with complete values and use the value from the complete case as the estimate. Yet others draw a random sample from among the scores of the complete cases. When there are specialized methods of estimating a missing value for a particular analysis, they are discussed in the relevant chapter.

3.5.7   Transformations

Data transformations are often undertaken when a data set violates assumptions such as normality and homogeneity of variance or when there are outliers. If you decide to transform, it is important to check that the distribution is improved by transformation. If a variable is only moderately positively skewed, for instance, a square root transformation may make the variable moderately negatively skewed, and there is no advantage to transformation. Often, you need to try first one transformation and then another until you find the transformation that produces the skewness and kurtosis values nearest zero, homogeneity of variance, and/or the fewest outliers.

Variables differ in the extent to which they diverge from normal. Figure 3.4 presents distributions with several degrees of nonnormality, together with the transformations that are likely to render them normal. If the distribution differs moderately from normal, a square root transformation is tried first. If the distribution differs substantially, a log transformation is tried. If the distribution differs severely, the inverse is tried. According to Bradley (1982), the inverse is the best of several alternatives for J-shaped distributions, but even it may not render the distribution acceptably normal. Finally, if the departure from normality is severe and no transformation seems to help, you may want to try dichotomizing the variable.

The direction of the deviation is also considered. When distributions have positive skewness, as discussed previously, the long tail is to the right. When they have negative skewness, the long tail is to the left. If there is negative skewness, the best strategy is to "reflect" the variable and then apply the appropriate transformation for positive skewness. To reflect a variable, find the largest score in the distribution and add 1 to it to form a constant that is larger than any score in the distribution.[16]

---

[16]If the distribution contains negative numbers, add a large enough constant so that the smallest number in the entire distribution is 1 before performing the transformation.

TRANSFORMATION

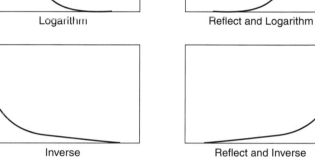

**FIGURE 3.4   Distributions with Varying Degrees of Nonnormality
and Their Potential Transformations**

Then create a new variable by subtracting each score from the constant. In this way, a variable with negative skewness is converted to one with positive skewness prior to transformation. When you interpret a reflected variable, be sure to reverse the direction of the interpretation as well. For instance, if big numbers meant good things prior to reflecting the variable, big numbers mean bad things afterwards.

Instructions for transforming variables in four software packages are given in Table 3.18. Notice that a constant is also added if the distribution contains a value less than 1. A constant (to bring the smallest value to at least 1) is added to each score to avoid taking the log, square root, or inverse of zero.

It should be clearly understood that this section merely scratches the surface of the topic of transformations, about which a great deal more is known. The interested reader is referred to Emerson (1991) or the classic Box and Cox (1964) for a more flexible and challenging approach to the problem of transformation.

TABLE 3.18 Original Distributions and Common Transformations to Produce Normality

	MINITAB	SPSS	SAS	SYSTAT
	LET[a]	COMPUTE	DATA	DATA TRANSFORM
Moderate positive skewness	LET NEWX=SQRT(X).	NEWX=SQRT(X)	NEWX=SQRT(X);	LET NEWX=SQR(X)
Substantial positive skewness with zero	LET NEWX=LOGTEN(X).	NEWX=LG10(X)	NEWX=LOG10(X);	LET NEWX=L10(X)
Severe positive skewness, L-shaped with zero	LET NEWX=LOGTEN(X + C).	NEWX=LG10(X + C)	NEWX=LOG10(X + C);	LET NEWX=L10(X + C)
	LET NEWX=1/X.	NEWX=1/X	NEWX=1/X;	LET NEWX=1/X
Moderate negative skewness	LET NEWX=1/(X + C).	NEWX=1/(X + C)	NEWX=1/(X + C);	LET NEWX=1/(X + C)
Substantial negative skewness	LET NEWX=SQRT(K - X).	NEWX=SQRT(K-X)	NEWX=SQRT(K - X);	LET NEWX=SQR(K - X)
Severe negative skewness, J-shaped	LET NEWX=LOG(K - X).	NEWX=LG10(K-X)	NEWX=LOG10(K - X);	LET NEWX=L10(K - X)
	LET NEWX=1/(K - X).	NEWX=1/(K-X)	NEWX=1/(K - X);	LET NEWX=1/(K - X)

[a]Calc provides transforms in the MINITAB Windows menu system.

C: a constant added to each score so that the smallest score is 1.

K: a constant from which each score is subtracted so that the smallest score is 1; usually equal to the largest score $+1$.

92

3.6   Overview of Remaining Chapters

Chapters 4 through 11 describe analyses appropriate to various research designs. Chapter 4 describes basic one-way, randomized-group, fixed-effects ANOVA. This is the simplest analysis, and the place to begin your study of ANOVA. Chapter 5 provides a generalization of the one-way analysis to a design with two or more IVs. The concept of interaction arises at this point and is the next level of complexity in ANOVA. Chapter 6 describes repeated measures and Chapter 7 mixed-design ANOVAs where cases are measured more than one time. Some important assumptions affect these analyses, increasing their complexity over the material in Chapters 4 and 5. Chapter 7 ends with a summary of the designs of Chapters 5 through 7. We recommend, then, that you take on these chapters in order (unless you are already familiar with the material in one or more of them). After that, the order in which you approach Chapters 8 through 11 is best driven by your needs.

In working with the analysis chapters, it is recommended that you select a set of variables appropriate to your own discipline and insert those variable names, as appropriate, into the examples we give. It is also suggested that you apply the various analyses to some interesting data set from your own discipline. Many data banks are readily accessible through computer installations. One online source of such data sets is http://lib.stat.cmu.edu/DASL/DataArchive.html.

3.7   Problem Sets

3.1 Pain is measured on a scale of 0 to 30 for two groups of pain sufferers, control group and a group given drug treatment in the following data set. Check the assumptions for the analysis of this data set.

a_1: Control	a_2: Treatment
14	15
13	12
15	11
14	12
12	12
30	14
16	14
11	10
13	14
14	13
25	10
14	12

3.2 Resolve any problems you found in Problem 3.1 and use the standard computational approach for ANOVA for this problem.

3.3 Redo Problem 3.1 using the regression approach and contrasts coding 1, −1.

Extending the Concepts

3.4 Redo Problem 3.1 using the regression approach with other numbers (say, 3, − 3). Remember that every case in the same group has the same code and that the codes for the two groups are different. (*Hint:* Make your life easy and pick small numbers.)

4 One-Way Randomized-Groups Analysis of Variance, Fixed-Effects Designs

4.1 General Purpose and Description

This simple one-way ANOVA asks if different groups of cases have reliable mean differences on a DV. The different groups form different levels of a single IV; the DV is a continuous variable that potentially has different means in the different groups. For example, do two different types of therapy produce mean differences in self-esteem? The levels of the single IV are the two types of therapy; the DV is self-esteem. The research question is whether the therapies differ in their ability to enhance self-esteem. The null hypothesis is that the two therapies produce about the same average self-esteem. Or, if the IV is type of on-the-job personnel training program with three levels (a no-training control group, a text-based training program, and a video-based training program) and the DV is the supervisor's overall rating of job performance, ANOVA determines if there are reliable mean differences in supervisor ratings associated with type of training program. The research hypothesis might be that the video-based training program is superior to the text-based program, which in turn is better than no training at all. The null hypothesis is that there are no mean differences in ratings among the three training programs.

ANOVA *compares* means, so the minimum number of levels of the IV is 2: one of the levels may be a control and one a treatment, or they may be two different treatments. Although there must be at least two levels of treatment, there may be many levels of treatment. However, designs with very large numbers of levels often become unwieldy.

The levels of treatment differ in either type or amount. Examples of levels that differ in type are the two different types of therapy or the three different types of on-the-job training. Examples of levels that differ in amount are the same therapy for two different lengths of time (say, 1 month or 2 months), or the same type of on-the-job training conducted for, say, one session, two sessions, or three sessions. A special type of technique, called a trend analysis, is available when there are three or more levels of treatment that differ in amount.

This chapter discusses completely randomized, fixed-effects, one-way ANOVA, also known as one-way between-subjects ANOVA. The analysis is appropriate when there is a single DV and (1) there is only one IV (one-way), (2) there are different cases in each level of the IV (completely randomized), and (3) all of the levels of the IV are specifically chosen by the researcher (fixed effects) because they are the levels of research interest. Designs with more than one IV are discussed in Chapter 5. Designs in which the same cases are measured repeatedly, or in which cases are matched in some way before random assignment, are discussed in Chapters 6 and 7. Designs in which levels of IVs are not fixed, but are randomly selected by the researcher, are discussed in Chapter 11. Designs with more than one DV (say, self-esteem and level of anxiety) are discussed in Chapters 9 and 10 of Tabachnick and Fidell (2001).

This type of ANOVA is often used to analyze the results of experimental research. If the study is an experiment, there is random assignment of cases to levels of the IV, manipulation of the levels of the IV by the researcher, and control of extraneous variables. The analysis also is frequently and appropriately used for non- and quasi-experimental research where it is impossible to randomly assign cases to levels of treatment or to manipulate the levels of the IV, but interpretation of results is limited in the absence of full experimental control.

4.2   Kinds of Research Questions

The primary question in one-way ANOVA is whether there are reliable mean differences on the DV among the different treatment groups. If reliable mean differences are found, population means (and often standard deviations and/or standard errors) are estimated and reported for each group along with estimates of the strength of the treatment effect. If there are more than two levels of the IV, comparisons are usually desired to pinpoint the location of reliable mean differences among groups. Comparisons are conducted in addition to or instead of ANOVA.

4.2.1   Effect of the IV

Are there reliable mean differences on the DV associated with the different levels of the IV? That is, holding all else constant,[1] are the mean differences among the different groups of cases larger than would be expected if mean differences are due solely to random fluctuations in scores? For example, is there a reliable mean difference in self-esteem depending on therapy type? Is there a mean difference in rating of job performance depending on the training group to which an employee has been assigned?

These questions are answered by applying F tests to the data, as demonstrated in Sections 3.2.3.3 and 4.4. This F test is called an omnibus test because it assesses the overall reliability of differences among treatment means but does not reveal the source of the difference(s) if there are more than two treatments.

4.2.2   Specific Comparisons

If there are more than two groups and a mean difference is found, what is the source of the difference? For the job-training example with three levels, is the text-based training program different from no training at all? Is the video-based program different from the text-based program? Is the average performance of trained employees different from that of employees without on-the-job training? Or, if the IV is quantitative, as in length of training, is there a linear relationship between length of training and supervisor ratings? Does supervisor rating increase and then level off with increased training? These questions are answered by applying comparison procedures as discussed in Section 4.5.5.

---

[1]Devices discussed in Section 1.1 are used to "hold all else constant" in an experimental design.

Comparisons to pinpoint the source of mean differences can be conducted in lieu of the omnibus F test (planned) or following the omnibus F test (post hoc). The advantages and disadvantages of planned and post hoc tests are also discussed in Section 4.5.5.

4.2.3   Parameter Estimates

If a treatment could be applied to an entire population, what mean would be expected? What mean job performance rating would we expect for a population of employees who participated in a video-based training program? Population values estimated from samples are called parameter estimates. Parameter estimates reported following ANOVA are group means, standard deviations, standard errors, and/or confidence intervals for the mean (which incorporate both means and standard errors). Means as well as standard deviations or standard errors are reported in narrative form, shown in a table, or presented in a graph. Estimation of parameters is illustrated in Section 4.6.2.

4.2.4   Effect Sizes

The size of group mean differences may provide sufficient information to assess the magnitude of treatment effect when the DV is a familiar one such as size, weight, or a physical measure such as number of bacteria. If, however, inspection of means is insufficient, a measure of effect size is useful. It also is useful to report effect sizes so that future researchers may include your study in meta-analyses, which combine the results of many published studies. There are two types of effect-size measures. One type is based on proportion of variance in a DV that can be attributed to differences among treatments, and another type expresses differences among group means in standard deviation units. Both types are discussed in Section 4.5.1.

4.2.5   Power

How high is the probability of showing that there are mean differences among groups if, indeed, treatment has an effect? For example, if the video-based training program is indeed superior to the text-based program or to no program at all, what is the probability of demonstrating that superiority? Estimates of power made prior to running a study are used to help determine sample size. Estimates of power as part of the analysis of a completed study are primarily used to determine why the research hypothesis did not find support. Power is discussed in Section 4.5.2.

4.3   Assumptions and Limitations

4.3.1   Theoretical Issues

The statistical test does not insure that changes in the DV are caused by the IV. Causal inference depends on the design of the study, not on the statistical test used. Considerations discussed in Sections 1.1 and 1.2 determine the legitimacy of causal inference. As a statistical test, ANOVA is also appropriate for nonexperimental IVs as long as results are interpreted cautiously.

Strict generalizability is limited to populations from which random samples are taken, as discussed in Section 1.7. Results in an experiment generalize to the population of cases available for random assignment to levels of the IV. In nonexperimental studies, it usually is impossible to determine the available population unless there is careful random sampling from the population of interest. Therefore, generalization becomes a logical argument.

4.3.2 Practical Issues

The ANOVA model assumes normality of sampling distributions, homogeneity of variance, independence of errors, and absence of outliers, as described in Section 3.4. Unequal sample sizes, which create nonorthogonality, also pose problems for some assumptions and some comparisons in ANOVA, as discussed in Section 4.5.5.

4.4 Fundamental Equations

One-way randomized-groups designs have one IV with at least two levels. The analysis for two levels is demonstrated in Section 3.2.3. This section shows allocation of cases to three levels, partition of variance, and calculation of the one-way randomized-groups ANOVA by both the traditional and the regression approach. Analyses with more than three levels are calculated in the same manner as those with three levels.

4.4.1 Allocation of Cases

The cases in an experiment are randomly assigned to one of two or more levels of the IV through any of the methods discussed in Section 1.1.2. Table 4.1 shows how cases are assigned to groups within this design. Notice that every level of A has a different group of cases assigned to it. A is a fixed effect because the three levels are specifically chosen by the researcher because they are the ones of interest, not randomly selected from some larger set of levels. Cases, however, are a random effect because they are randomly assigned to the levels of A from the full set of cases available. This is still considered a fixed-effects design because cases are experimental units, not effects to be tested.

For the traditional approach, once DV scores are gathered, they are arranged in such a table, with a columns representing groups (levels of the IV) and n scores within each group.[2]

TABLE 4.1 Assignment of Cases in a One-Way Randomized-Groups Design

Treatment		
a_1	a_2	a_3
s_1	s_4	s_7
s_2	s_5	s_8
s_3	s_6	s_9

[2]Recall that n is used for sample size within a single group or level and N is used for total sample size.

Cases in a nonexperimental study are also assigned to the levels of the IV, but not on the basis of random assignment. For example, cases could be classified on the basis of their age group (21–35, 36–50, 51–65) or their religious affiliation. That is, levels of the IV to which cases are assigned are determined by the case themselves or their characteristics, not by the researcher.

4.4.2   Partition of Sources of Variance

The partition of variance in basic ANOVA is described in Section 3.2.3.1. This partition applies to the one-way randomized-groups design with equal sample sizes in each group no matter how many levels of A.

4.4.3   Traditional ANOVA Approach (Three Levels)

Section 3.2.3 shows the traditional ANOVA approach with two levels of an IV. This example is a generalization of that approach to three (or more) levels. Table 4.2 shows a silly, hypothetical, and very small data set in which rating of a ski vacation (the DV) is evaluated as a function of view from the hotel room (the IV). Skiers are randomly assigned on arrival at a mythical ski resort to a hotel room with a view of the parking lot, a view of the ocean (we said it was mythical), or a view of the ski slopes. We assume proper controls have been instituted to avoid communication among skiers in the experiment. Sample size is inadequate for answering real research questions but allows relatively painless hand calculation of the ANOVA.

Equations 3.13 through 3.16 are used to calculate the sums of squares for this example in Table 4.3. Table 4.4 shows degrees of freedom for the example. Note that the partitions of SS and the partitions of df both sum to their respective totals.

Recall that variance (mean square) associated with each source is obtained by dividing SS by df, because SS is the numerator and df is the denominator of variance. Table 4.5 shows calculation of mean squares associated with treatment and error sources of variance.

Finally, Table 4.6 is a source table that summarizes the results of Tables 4.3 through 4.5, and adds the F ratio of Equation 3.12. Note that SS_A and $SS_{S/A}$ add up to SS_T. However, MS_A and $MS_{S/A}$ *do not* add up to MS_T.

TABLE 4.2   Hypothetical Data Set for a One-Way Design with Three Levels

A: Type of View		
a_1: Parking Lot View	a_2: Ocean View	a_3: Ski Slope View
1	3	6
1	4	8
3	3	6
5	5	7
2	4	5
$A_1 = 12$	$A_2 = 19$	$A_3 = 32$

TABLE 4.3 Calculation of Sums of Squares for Traditional One-Way ANOVA with Three Levels

$$SS_A = \frac{12^2 + 19^2 + 32^2}{5} - \frac{63^2}{15} = 41.2$$

$$SS_{S/A} = 325 - \frac{12^2 + 19^2 + 32^2}{5} = 19.2$$

$$SS_T = 325 - \frac{63^2}{15} = 60.4$$

TABLE 4.4 Calculation of Degrees of Freedom for Traditional One-Way ANOVA with Three Levels

$$df_A = a - 1 = 3 - 1 = 2$$

$$df_{S/A} = an - a = 15 - 3 = 12$$

$$df_T = an - 1 = 15 - 1 = 14$$

TABLE 4.5 Calculation of Mean Squares for Traditional One-Way ANOVA with Three Levels

$$MS_A = \frac{SS_A}{df_A} = \frac{41.2}{2} = 20.6$$

$$MS_{S/A} = \frac{SS_{S/A}}{df_{S/A}} = \frac{19.2}{12} = 1.6$$

TABLE 4.6 Source Table for Traditional One-Way ANOVA with Three Levels

Source	SS	df	MS	F
A	41.2	2	20.6	12.88
S/A	19.2	12	1.6	
T	60.4	14		

Section 3.2.3.3 describes the process for deciding whether the differences among sample means are likely to have occurred by chance. Suppose, for example, our willingness to risk a Type I error is 5%. With numerator $df = 2$ and denominator $df = 12$, the critical value of F in Table A.1 of Appendix A is 3.88. The calculated (obtained) F of 12.88 is larger than 3.88; therefore, the null hypothesis is rejected. We conclude that rating of a ski vacation does, indeed, depend on the view from the hotel room.

4.4.4 Regression Approach (Three Levels)

As discussed in Sections 3.3.1 and 3.5.5, the regression approach to ANOVA uses columns of numbers to code group membership. Because there are only two groups in the example of Section 3.3.1, a single column is sufficient to separate the cases into two groups (1 if a case belonged to one group, -1 if a case belonged to the other group). However, with more than two groups, more than one column is required to separate the a groups from each other. For an example, with three groups, the first column could separate group 3 from groups 1 and 2, and the second column separates groups 1 and 2. So, instead of the single X column of Section 3.3.1, several X columns are necessary, and multiple rather than bivariate regression is required.

The number of X columns needed to separate the groups is equal to $df_A = a - 1$. If, in addition, the numbers in the columns are chosen so that they sum to zero in each column and the columns are orthogonal (cf. Sections 3.5.4 and 4.5.5.2), the sum of the sums of squares for the $a - 1$ X columns ($a - 1$ of them) equals the sum of squares for the treatment effect, A.

Table 4.7 shows the scores on the DV, Y,[3] with one of the many possible sets of orthogonal contrast codes in the two X columns. The numbers in the X column are chosen to correspond to research questions relevant to this example. The X_1 column separates a_3 from a_1 and a_2 (the ski slope view from the parking lot and ocean views), and the X_2 column separates a_1 from a_2 (the parking lot view from the ocean view). Of the many sets of codes that could be devised, these are probably the most interesting for purposes of comparisons, as we will see in Section 4.5.5.1. The remaining columns are found by multiplication.

Table 4.8 shows the sums of squares calculated from Table 4.7. Notice that the second terms in the equations for $SS(X_1)$ and $SS(X_2)$ reduce to zero. This is because the codes we have chosen for columns X_1 and X_2 sum to zero for their columns. This feature is worth the simplification in calculation alone, but also is part of the requirement for the columns to be orthogonal.

TABLE 4.7   Columns for Regression Approach to Analysis of Variance with Three Treatment Levels

Level of A	Case	Y	X_1	X_2	YX_1	YX_2	X_1X_2
	s_1	1	1	-1	1	-1	-1
	s_2	1	1	-1	1	-1	-1
a_1	s_3	3	1	-1	3	-3	-1
	s_4	5	1	-1	5	-5	-1
	s_5	2	1	-1	2	-2	-1
	s_6	3	1	1	3	3	1
	s_7	4	1	1	4	4	1
a_2	s_8	3	1	1	3	3	1
	s_9	5	1	1	5	5	1
	s_{10}	4	1	1	4	4	1
	s_{11}	6	-2	0	-12	0	0
	s_{12}	8	-2	0	-16	0	0
a_3	s_{13}	6	-2	0	-12	0	0
	s_{14}	7	-2	0	-14	0	0
	s_{15}	5	-2	0	-10	0	0
Sum		63	0	0	-33	7	0
Squares summed		325	30	10			
N		15					
Mean		4.2	0	0			

---

[3]The column labeling a_i is only for your convenience in identifying group membership; it does not enter into calculations.

**TABLE 4.8 Preliminary Sums of Squares for
Regression Approach to ANOVA with Three Levels**

$$\text{SS}(Y) = \sum Y^2 - \frac{(\sum Y)^2}{N} = 325 - \frac{63^2}{15} = 60.4$$

$$\text{SS}(X_1) = \sum X_1^2 - \frac{(\sum X_1)^2}{N} = 30 - \frac{0^2}{15} = 30.0$$

$$\text{SS}(X_2) = \sum X_2^2 - \frac{(\sum X_2)^2}{N} = 10 - \frac{0^2}{15} = 10.0$$

**TABLE 4.9 Sums of Cross Products for Regression Approach to
ANOVA with Three Levels**

$$\text{SP}(YX_1) = \sum YX_1 - \frac{(\sum Y)(\sum X_1)}{N} = -33 - \frac{(63)(0)}{15} = -33$$

$$\text{SP}(YX_2) = \sum YX_2 - \frac{(\sum Y)(\sum X_2)}{(N)} = 7 - \frac{(63)(0)}{15} = 7$$

$$\text{SP}(X_1X_2) = \sum X_1X_2 - \frac{(\sum X_1)(\sum X_2)}{N} = 0 - \frac{(0)(0)}{15} = 0$$

Table 4.9 shows the sums of cross products that are produced by the columns in Table 4.7. The second terms in the first two sums of cross-products of Table 4.9 also reduce to zero, as does the entire sum of cross-products for X_1X_2. This holds for columns that are coded orthogonally as long as sample sizes in each group are equal.

Equation 2.16 for the GLM in regression format needs to be modified to account for additional columns. With two columns, the equation becomes

$$Y' = a + b_1X_1 + b_2X_2 \tag{4.1}$$

where each column, X_j, has its own slope, b_j, and the slope-column products (b_jX_j) are summed over the $a - 1$ columns.

In general, then, the regression equation for any number of levels of A is

$$Y' = a + \sum_{j=1}^{a-1} b_jX_j \tag{4.2}$$

Note again the two uses of a: the intercept and the number of levels of the IV.

Table 4.10 shows equations for estimating slopes and intercept for computation of ANOVA through regression. The equations for slope (b) are quite a bit more complicated than for the two-level design of Table 3.12, and are facilitated by matrix algebra once the number of X columns

TABLE 4.10 Slope and Intercept Estimates for Regression Approach to ANOVA with Three Levels

$$b_1 = \frac{[SP(YX_1)][SS(X_2)] - [SP(YX_2)][SP(X_1X_2)]}{[SS(X_1)][SS(X_2)] - SP(X_1X_2)^2} = \frac{(-33)(10) - (7)(0)}{(30)(10) - 0^2} = -1.1$$

$$b_2 = \frac{[SP(YX_2)][SS(X_1)] - [SP(YX_1)][SP(X_1X_2)]}{[SS(X_1)][SS(X_2)] - SP(X_1X_2)^2} = \frac{(7)(30) - (33)(0)}{(30)(10) - 0^2} = 0.7$$

$$a = \overline{Y} - \overline{X}_1(b_1) - \overline{X}_2(b_2) \qquad = 4.2 - 0(-1.1) - 0(0.7) = 4.2$$

$$Y' = a + b_1(X_1) + b_2(X_2)$$

For group 1, when $X_1 = 1, X_2 = -1$:
$$Y' = 4.2 + (-1.1)(1) + (0.7)(-1) = 2.4$$

For group 2, when $X_1 = 1, X_2 = 1$:
$$Y' = 4.2 + (-1.1)(1) + (0.7)(1) = 3.8$$

For group 3, when $X_1 = -2, X_2 = 0$:
$$Y' = 4.2 + (-1.1)(-2) + (0.7)(0) = 6.4$$

exceeds 2. However, it is not necessary to calculate these slope and intercept values when the purpose of the analysis is to test the reliability of differences among means, the goal of ANOVA.

The reduction of some of the terms to zero with orthogonal contrast coding of columns (and equal sample sizes) continues in the equations for regression coefficients, b_1 and b_2. With contrast coding, the intercept, a, is equal to the grand mean, $\overline{Y}$. When the codes in the X columns for the group membership for a case are inserted into the prediction equation (as shown in the lowest section of the table), the predicted score for each skier is the mean of that skier's own treatment group.[4]

Sums of squares for the regression analysis are shown in Table 4.11. Degrees of freedom for regression are shown in Table 4.12. Table 4.13 summarizes the information in Tables 4.11 and 4.12 in a source table, rearranged to mimic that of Table 4.6.

The values in Table 4.13 are identical to those in Table 4.6; only the names have been changed. The regression source is the treatment effect, A, and the residual source is the estimate of error, S/A. The F ratio is

$$F = \frac{MS(\text{reg.})}{MS(\text{resid.})} = \frac{20.6}{1.6} = 12.88$$

as in Table 4.6. Table A.1 is used to find the critical value of F for testing the null hypothesis. Three null hypotheses are tested at once through the regression approach: (1) that the population correlation between actual and predicted Y is equal to zero, (2) that each of the population regression coefficients is equal to zero, and (3) that $\mu_1 = \mu_2 = \mu_3$, the null hypothesis in the form typically stated for the traditional approach to ANOVA.

---

[4]Section 5.6.5 discusses unequal sample sizes, in which columns are no longer orthogonal. Sequential multiple regression is discussed in that section as one way of dealing with nonorthogonality of columns in factorial designs.

TABLE 4.11 Sums of Squares for ANOVA through Regression with Three Treatment Levels

$$SS(\text{reg.}) = SS(\text{reg. } X_1) + SS(\text{reg. } X_2) = \frac{SP(YX_1)^2}{SS(X_1)} + \frac{SP(YX_2)^2}{SS(X_2)} = \frac{(-33)^2}{30} + \frac{7^2}{10}$$

$$= 36.3 + 4.9 \qquad = 41.2$$

SS(total)	$= SS(Y)$	$= 60.4$
SS(resid.)	$= SS(\text{total}) - SS(\text{reg.}) \quad = 60.4 - 41.2$	$= 19.2$

TABLE 4.12 Calculation of Degrees of Freedom for ANOVA through Regression with Three Treatment Levels

df(reg.) $=$ number of predictors (X vectors) $= 2$

df(total) $=$ number of cases (N) $- 1 = 15 - 1 = 14$

df(resid.) $=$ df(total) $-$ df(reg.) $\quad = 14 - 2 = 12$

TABLE 4.13 Source Table for One-Way ANOVA through Regression with Three Levels

Source	SS	df	MS	F
Regression	41.2	2	20.6	12.88
Residual	19.2	12	1.6	
Total	60.4	14		

TABLE 4.14 Hypothetical Data Set for One-Way ANOVA in Form Suitable for Computer Analysis

VIEW	RATING
1	1
1	1
1	3
1	5
1	2
2	3
2	4
2	3
2	5
2	4
3	6
3	8
3	6
3	7
3	5

4.4.5 Computer Analyses of Small-Sample One-Way Design

Table 4.14 shows how data are entered for a one-way ANOVA. Data may be entered in a word processing program and saved in text mode, entered in a spreadsheet program and saved in text mode, or entered through facilities provided by the statistical program. Data sets entered through word processors or spreadsheets may include only numbers, without the column headings shown in Table 4.14; data sets entered through statistical programs typically include variable names at the tops of columns.

Each row is a single case. The first column uses 1, 2, or 3 to represent the level of the IV (a_i) for each case. The second column contains the DV score for the case. An additional column, case number, may be added for your convenience in editing the data file.

Tables 4.15 through 4.18 show computer analyses of the small-sample example of the one-way randomized-groups small-sample ANOVA through SPSS ONEWAY, MINITAB ONEWAY, SAS ANOVA, and SYSTAT ANOVA, respectively.

Table 4.15 shows syntax and output for SPSS ONEWAY.[5] This program, as all SPSS analysis of variance programs, specifies the name of the DV (rating) followed by the keyword BY, followed by the name of the IV (VIEW). The instruction, /MISSING ANALYSIS, is the default for handling missing values. Means, standard deviations, standard errors, 95% confidence interval for the mean, maximum, and minimum values are requested by /STATISTICS DESCRIPTIVES. One-way analysis of variance also may be done through SPSS GLM. This set of programs is demonstrated in subsequent chapters.

The output begins with a table of descriptive statistics. This is followed by a source table, entitled ANOVA (compare with Table 4.6). The column labeled Sig. provides the probability, to four

TABLE 4.15   One-Way Randomized-Groups ANOVA for Sample Example through SPSS ONEWAY

```
ONEWAY
   rating BY view
   /STATISTICS DESCRIPTIVES
   /MISSING ANALYSIS.
```

Oneway

Descriptives

RATING

	N	Mean	Std. Deviation	Std. Error	95% Confidence Interval for Mean Lower Bound	95% Confidence Interval for Mean Upper Bound	Minimum	Maximum
Parking lot	5	2.4000	1.6733	.7483	.3223	4.4777	1.00	5.00
Ocean	5	3.8000	.8367	.3742	2.7611	4.8389	3.00	5.00
Ski slope	5	6.4000	1.1402	.5099	4.9843	7.8157	5.00	8.00
Total	15	4.2000	2.0771	.5363	3.0497	5.3503	1.00	8.00

ANOVA

RATING

	Sum of Squares	df	Mean Square	F	Sig.
Between Groups	41.200	2	20.600	12.875	.001
Within Groups	19.200	12	1.600		
Total	60.400	14			

[5]If SPSS Windows menus are used, the ONEWAY program is accessed through the Statistics menu, Compare Means submenu, and then a choice of One-way ANOVA.

decimal places, that an observed F ratio this large or larger could have occurred as a result of chance variation. Thus, the probability that this result could have occurred by chance is .001.

Table 4.16 shows syntax and output from MINITAB ONEWAY. The DV label is listed first, followed by the IV label. Both are in single quotes.

The One-way Analysis of Variance table is the source table (compare with Table 4.6), in which S/A is labeled ERROR. The P column provides the probability that an outcome this extreme or more extreme could have occurred as a result of chance variation, here .001. This is followed by sample sizes, means, and standard deviations (StDev) for the three groups. The 95% confidence intervals are shown graphically for each mean.

Table 4.17 shows SAS ANOVA syntax and output for the small-sample example. SAS PROC GLM also may be used for this analysis, and is nearly identical to PROC ANOVA for this application. The IV, VIEW, is identified as the classification variable. The model instruction follows regression syntax, with the DV (RATING) identified on the left side of the equation and the IV on the right. Descriptive statistics are requested by the means statement.

Two source tables are given. The first is for the full model with all IVs combined; the second identifies IVs (and their interactions) as separate sources of variability. Since there is only one IV in this example, both source tables are the same. S/A is identified as Error in the first source table (compare with Table 4.6). The probability that the F value this large or larger could have occurred by chance variation is provided in the Pr > F column. This table includes R-Square, the proportion of variance accounted for by the whole model (cf. Section 4.5.1). Also shown are the square root of

TABLE 4.16 One-Way Randomized-Groups ANOVA for Small-Sample Example through MINITAB ONEWAY

```
MTB > Oneway 'RATING' 'VIEW'.
```

One-way Analysis of Variance

```
Analysis of Variance for RATING
Source     DF        SS        MS       F        P
VIEW        2     41.20     20.60   12.88   0.001
Error      12     19.20      1.60
Total      14     60.40

                                Individual 95% CIs For Mean
                                Based on Pooled StDev
Level    N     Mean    StDev   -----+---------+---------+---------+-
1        5    2.400    1.673   (-----*-----)
2        5    3.800    0.837         (-----*-----)
3        5    6.400    1.140                     (-----*-----)
                               -----+---------+---------+---------+-
Pooled
StDev=        1.265             2.0       4.0       6.0       8.0
```

TABLE 4.17   One-Way Randomized-Groups ANOVA through SAS ANOVA

```
proc anova data=SASUSER.RAND_GRP;
  class VIEW;
  model RATING = VIEW;
  means VIEW;
run;
```

                    Analysis of Variance Procedure
                      Class Level Information

                    Class   Levels   Values
                    VIEW   3   1 2 3

              Number of observations in data set = 15

                  Analysis of Variance Procedure

Dependent Variable: RATING

                          Sum of
Source   DF   Squares   Mean Square   F Value   Pr>F
Model   2   41.20000000   20.60000000   12.88   0.0010
Error   12   19.20000000   1.60000000
Corrected Total   14   60.40000000

        R-Square   C.V.   Root MSE   RATING Mean
        0.682119   30.11693   1.2649110   4.20000000

Source   DF   Anova SS   Mean Square   F Value   Pr>F
VIEW   2   41.20000000   20.60000000   12.88   0.0010

                  Analysis of Variance Procedure

              Level of   -----------RATING----------
              VIEW   N   Mean   SD
              1   5   2.40000000   1.67332005
              2   5   3.80000000   0.83666003
              3   5   6.40000000   1.14017543

the MS$_{S/A}$ (**Root MSE**), the grand mean of the DV (**Y Mean**), and the coefficient of variation (**C.V.**, the square root of the error mean square divided by the grand mean, multiplied by 100). Descriptive statistics for each level of the IV are provided after the second source table.

Table 4.18 shows syntax and output of the small-sample analysis through SYSTAT ANOVA. Setup for ANOVA simply requires identification of the DV, RATING, as the DEPEND variable and

TABLE 4.18   One-Way Randomized-Groups ANOVA through SYSTAT ANOVA

```
PRINT=MEDIUM
ANOVA
CATEGORY VIEW
COVAR
DEPEND RATING
ESTIMATE
```

Effects coding used for categorical variables in model.

Categorical values encountered during processing are:
VIEW (3 levels)
```
        1,        2,        3
```

Dep Var: RATING   N: 15   Multiple R: 0.826   Squared multiple R: 0.682

Analysis of Variance

Source	Sum-of-Squares	DF	Mean-Square	F-Ratio	P
VIEW	41.200	2	20.600	12.875	0.001
Error	19.200	12	1.600		

Least-squares means.

		LS Mean	SE	N
VIEW	=1	2.400	0.566	5
VIEW	=2	3.800	0.566	5
VIEW	=3	6.400	0.566	5

Least Squares Means

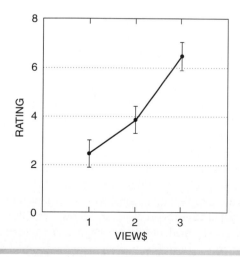

the IV, `VIEW`, as the `CATEGORY` variable. The request for `PRINT=MEDIUM` provides means and standard errors. Remaining syntax is produced by the SYSTAT Windows menu system. The analysis also may be done through SYSTAT GLM, but syntax differs, requiring MODEL language using regression syntax, similar to SAS GLM.

`Squared multiple R` is the proportion of variance accounted for by the set of all effects (cf. Section 4.5.1). The probability that an F ratio this large or larger is due to chance appears in the column labeled `P` in the source table. S/A is labeled `Error`. SYSTAT provides group means in the section labeled `Least-squares means` and plots them as well. The `SE` (standard error) column shows a single value for all levels of the IV. These values are found by dividing the square root of $MS_{S/A}$ by the square root of n and are plotted as bars surrounding the means: one SE above and one SE below (cf. Section 2.2.3.2).

4.5 Some Important Issues

Several of the issues discussed in this section apply to other kinds of designs as well. The issues are discussed here because this is the first opportunity to do so. Subsequent chapters refer back to this section when appropriate.

4.5.1 Effect Size

Finding a statistically significant effect tells you only that your IV probably made a difference—that it is unlikely that the observed mean difference among groups occurred by chance. There is nothing in the inferential test that tells how much of a difference your IV made. Although a bigger F ratio often implies a bigger effect, the size of the F ratio depends on error variability and degrees of freedom as well as on differences among means. For this reason, measures of effect size (also called strength of association, treatment magnitude, or magnitude of effect) are often used.

Effect size should always be reported if the effect is significant. There is disagreement, however, as to whether effect size should be reported if the mean differences are not reliable. Some argue that if an effect is not statistically reliable, there is no evidence of an effect, so effect size cannot be reported as different from zero. Thus, these researchers believe that effect size should not be reported when the null hypothesis is retained. Others argue that all treatments produce *some* differences, however small, and that finding a nonsignificant effect is due to lack of power (Section 4.5.2), not lack of a real effect. If that is the case, reporting effect size provides useful information to researchers who want to use the information to design a more powerful study or perform a meta-analysis (in which researchers statistically combine the results of multiple studies of the same variables). We place ourselves firmly on the fence of this controversy.

Occasionally, the DV is so well understood that a mere statement of parameter estimates (cell means) in appropriate units tells all you need to know about effect size. For example, if a particular prenatal regime produces babies weighing 500 grams (about 1.1 lb) more at birth, the magnitude of the effect of the treatment is obvious (although some would perhaps prefer a translation into ounces). Estimates of parameters do not always reveal effect size, however. Often the unit of measurement of the DV is arbitrary, derived, transformed, or otherwise not easily understood. Also, different studies often have measured DVs on different scales, making a comparison of their results from parameter estimates difficult. A variety of effect size measures are available to solve these problems.

The most common measures of effect size express treatment magnitude as the proportion of variability in the DV associated with the effect. The easiest way to conceptualize these measures is through a Venn diagram, as shown in Figure 4.1. All of the variability in the DV, from whatever source (measurement error, extraneous variables, etc.), is the circle of interest. The other circle, labeled A, represents the effect of the IV. The extent of overlap is the proportion of variability in the DV that is associated with, related to, predictable from, or accounted for by the effect. Small effects have only a tiny proportion of the variability in the DV associated with them and a correspondingly tiny overlap. Larger effects have larger and larger proportions of the variability in the DV associated with them and larger areas of overlap. If all of the variability in the DV is predictable by the effect, the circles overlap completely.

The simplest measure of effect size is η^2 (also called R^2); η^2 (eta squared) is the sum of squares for the effect divided by the total sum of squares:

$$\eta^2 = R^2 = \frac{SS_A}{SS_T} \tag{4.3}$$

For the example of Section 4.4.3 (cf. Table 4.6),

$$\eta^2 = R^2 = \frac{41.2}{60.4} = .68$$

Thus, about 2/3 of the variability in ratings of a ski vacation is due to the view from the room. You have a very good idea of how highly a vacation is rated by knowing the view from the room.

A drawback to η^2 is that the measure is simply a descriptive statistic; it describes the proportion of variability in the DV accounted for by the effect in the particular sample, but, on average, overestimates the effect size in the population from which the sample was drawn. That is, η^2 is a biased estimate of the parameter. An alternative measure, called $\hat{\omega}^2$ (omega squared), is an unbiased parameter estimate that generalizes to the population. Because it adjusts for the overestimation of effect size by

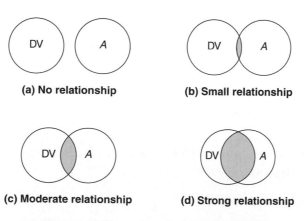

(a) No relationship   **(b) Small relationship**

(c) Moderate relationship   **(d) Strong relationship**

FIGURE 4.1   Different Strengths of Relationship between the DV and A Using Venn Diagrams

η^2, $\hat{\omega}^2$ is always smaller than η^2. Equation 4.4 for $\hat{\omega}^2$ starts with the two sums of squares used in η^2, and then something is subtracted from the numerator and added to the denominator.

$$\hat{\omega}^2 = \frac{SS_A - df_A(MS_{S/A})}{SS_T + MS_{S/A}} \tag{4.4}$$

For the small-sample example,

$$\hat{\omega}^2 = \frac{41.2 - 2(1.6)}{60.4 + 1.6} = .61$$

less than the .68 calculated for η^2.

When you merely want to describe effect size in a sample, η^2 is the measure of choice. When you want to estimate effect size for a population from a sample, $\hat{\omega}^2$ is your choice. However, computation of $\hat{\omega}^2$ becomes very complicated when the design is other than randomized groups with equal sample sizes in all levels of the IV. The descriptive measure η^2, on the other hand, easily generalizes to a variety of ANOVA designs and is often used with complicated designs despite the limits to its generalizability.

Another kind of measure of effect size expresses mean differences in standard deviation units. This is called Cohen's d (1977), or "effect-size index." In its simplest form, it is the absolute difference between the largest and smallest means, divided by the common standard deviation.

$$d = \frac{|\overline{Y}_l - \overline{Y}_s|}{\sqrt{MS_{S/A}}} \tag{4.5}$$

where l and s subscripts denote largest and smallest means, respectively.

This simplest form of the measure requires that there be an even number of means, that they be concentrated at each of the extremes, and that there be equal sample sizes within each level. Thus, the measure only works for some single-factor designs. It becomes increasingly complicated when dealing with other arrangements of means within their range or unequal sample sizes. Thus, d is a less convenient measure than $\hat{\omega}^2$ or η^2. Cohen (1977) shows the varieties of d and equations for converting d to η^2.

Effect sizes also are useful in evaluating specific comparisons. These are described in Section 4.5.5.7.

4.5.2 Power and Sample Size

Power, as discussed in Sections 1.6.2 and 3.5.2, is the sensitivity of a research design: the probability that one will be able to reject a false null hypothesis. Power considerations drive many features of research design and experimental control.

4.5.2.1 Designing Powerful Studies

Analyzing the power of a study is most usefully accomplished in the design stage, *before* the data are collected. It is too late to change the design after data have been collected and an unfavorable outcome is observed. The most that can be done then is to redesign and rerun the study, usually a frustrating and costly enterprise.

One factor influencing power is the size of the effect in the population. Small effects are harder to detect than larger ones—thus small effects generate less power, all other things being equal. One way to increase power, then, is to be sure to choose strong and very different levels of treatment. This will increase the size of the mean differences that produce MS_A and, therefore, increase the numerator of F.

Error variability also has a profound effect on power; the smaller the error variability, the greater the power. Measures to control extraneous variables and (perhaps) to randomly assign a *homogeneous* sample of cases to different levels of treatment are instituted to minimize $SS_{S/A}$. Controlling extraneous variables is accomplished by holding them constant over levels of treatment, counterbalancing (or partially counterbalancing) their effects, or letting random processes disperse their effects evenly through levels of treatment. In practical terms, this means one must have equipment that is running reliably, experimental technicians who are performing their job consistently, and so on, through the long list of variables that can increase the variability in the DV. Randomly assigning a homogeneous sample of cases to different levels of treatment has the effect of minimizing variability due to differences in cases. This will also decrease the size of $SS_{S/A}$.

Another way to minimize $MS_{S/A}$, the denominator of the F ratio, is to increase *its* denominator by increasing $df_{S/A}$. This is reflected in the notion that large sample sizes generate more power. With the same sum of squares for error, mean square for error decreases as degrees of freedom for error increase.

Finally, the level of α chosen for testing hypotheses affects power. The stricter (smaller) the level of α (e.g., using .01 instead of .05), the less the power. Recall from Section 1.6.1 that power is $1 - \beta$, so that α and β errors are negatively related. That is, there is a trade-off between Type I and Type II errors in designing research studies.

These relationships have several implications for designing research studies to maximize power:

1. *Select levels of the IV that are very different.* All other things being equal, it is more useful to choose levels of an IV that are as different from each other as possible if you hope to find a statistically significant outcome. That is, larger effect sizes are more likely to lead to favorable results than are smaller ones. A needle is harder to find in a haystack than a nail. Or, if small effects are to be detected, be prepared to make other compromises, such as testing very large samples.

2. *Use the most liberal legitimate α level for testing hypotheses.* Legitimacy depends on the use of the results. Scientific publication traditionally has required use of α levels of .05 or smaller for declaring results to be statistically significant. However, requirements for studies designed for purposes other than scientific publication may justify more liberal α levels. For example, if a choice is to be made between two materials in a manufacturing process, equal in cost and other production factors, with no prior reason for choosing one over the other, the choice could be made on the basis of an observed difference where α is as great as .49. There is, of course, a strong possibility that the "wrong" material is chosen, but that error still is less than would be associated with an arbitrary choice or a flip of a coin. Large Type I errors also may be tolerated if the consequences of Type II errors are grave (e.g., diagnosing a disease that is fatal if not treated) and power cannot be increased in other ways.

3. *Control error variability to the extent possible.* Error variability in randomized-groups designs is the variability of scores within groups given the same treatment. Thus, anything done to control for extraneous influences on the DV tends to increase power. The more homogeneous the sample of cases within treatments, the less that error variability is likely to be. Samples of wheat taken from a single field and then randomly assigned to different treatments are likely to be more similar than samples of wheat taken from a variety of fields. (The problem with this, of course, is that generalizability is limited to the field[s] supplying the samples—cf. Section 1.7.) Individual studies vary in their response to the necessary trade-off between power and generalizability.[6] Assuring that cases are tested under identical conditions (but for levels of the IV) likewise increases homogeneity. Sloppy research hurts power.

   4. *Compute the sample size necessary to achieve the desired power as part of the research design.* The goal is to avoid wasting resources looking for trivial effects, or expending resources needlessly in a search for a very large effect that you are unlikely to miss in any event.

4.5.2.2   *Estimating Sample Size*

A variety of techniques are available for estimating needed sample size, ranging from the quick and dirty to the elaborate. Many view these techniques as tedious when performed by hand. However, several computer programs also are available for estimating sample size, some at minimal cost. An example of one of these is GANOVA, included in Woodward and colleagues (1990), which solves for power as well as needed sample size. Another is PC-SIZE (Dallal, 1986), a shareware program that deals with one-way and two-way randomized-groups designs, among others. NCSS PASS (1996) is an example of a comprehensive commercial power analysis and sample size program. Other programs are regularly reviewed in methodological journals, such as *Behavior Research Methods, Instruments, and Computing.* PC-SIZE and other shareware programs may be accessed through a Web site devoted to power analysis. The URL is http://www.sustain.forestry.ubc.ca/cacb/power/. The site also includes links to power programs that may be used online.

   Some decisions must be made before estimating needed sample size, whether by hand or through computer programs. First, you need to determine your α level and whether you want a one- or two-tailed test of the null hypothesis (some computer programs assume a two-tailed test, but you can trick them into a one-tailed test by doubling the α value that you enter). Second, you need to decide on the power you want to achieve, recognizing that the greater the value you set, the larger sample size you will need. Values in the range of .75 to .90 are typically considered reasonable in scientific research.

   You also need to estimate the size of the effect you expect to achieve. These estimates can be either in the form of expected mean differences or in the form of expected effect size. Finally, you need some idea of the within-group (error) variability that is likely to occur given your ability to control extraneous influences on the DV. This last is perhaps the most difficult to estimate. What do you predict to be the distribution of scores on the DV for cases given the same treatment? If you are using a standardized measure as a DV (such as a measure of IQ), the population standard deviation of the scale is probably known (e.g., $\sigma = 15$). Or, previous research may have used the same DV and reported the within-group variability. Or, in the absence of these conveniences, a highly recommended method for estimating variability of a DV is a pilot study. Try out your DV on a small sam-

---

[6]Nonhomogeneous samples may be made more homogeneous by moving to a factorial design, however. For example, create an additional IV with different fields as levels to increase homogeneity within each cell (a combination of both treatment and field), as discussed in Chapter 5.

ple of cases, giving them no treatment or only one of the treatments, and calculate the standard deviation.[7] Or, if all else fails, divide your anticipated range in scores by 5 for a very rough estimate of error variability.

A classic quick-and-dirty method for estimating sample size is illustrated here primarily because it makes clear the relationships among design decisions.

$$n = \frac{2\sigma^2}{\delta^2}(z_{1-\alpha} + z_{1-\beta})^2 \tag{4.6}$$

where n = sample size for each group

σ^2 = estimated MS_{error} = $MS_{S/A}$ for this design

$z_{1-\alpha}$ = normal deviate corresponding to $1 - \alpha$ (see Table 4.19 for typical values)

$z_{1-\beta}$ = normal deviate corresponding to $1 - \beta$ (see Table 4.19 for typical values)

δ = desired minimal difference between means to be detected

The equation clearly shows the trade-off between α and β error, and the increase in sample size necessary for smaller effects and greater error variances. The greater the variability in the DV (σ^2), the larger the retention region for the null hypothesis ($1 - \alpha$), and the more power desired ($1 - \beta$), the larger the needed sample size; whereas the larger the expected mean difference (δ), the smaller the needed sample size.

Equation 4.6 is meant for simple one-way designs with two levels. It can be used with multi-level designs by defining δ as the smallest mean difference in the set that is to be detected. This method often results in an overestimation of sample size in multilevel designs because you are solving for the smallest difference, rather than any difference at all. However, you will have at least the power you have selected, and probably much more.

Say, for example, that before running the experiment described in Section 4.4.3, you postulate a mean difference between ski slope view and ocean view of about 2.5 rating points, and $MS_{S/A} = 2$ (from a pilot study). Suppose that the desired significance test is two-tailed with α level set at .05, so that $1 - \alpha = .95$ and $z_{1-\alpha} = 1.96$. (Note that this actually is $z_{1-\alpha/2}$ because it is a two-tailed test.)

TABLE 4.19   Selected Values of z for Sample-Size Equation

	p	z (2-tail)	z (1-tail)
$1 - \alpha$	.99	**2.58**	2.33
	.95	**1.96**	1.65
$1 - \beta$	.85	1.44	**1.04**
	.80	1.28	**0.84**
	.75	1.15	**0.67**

[7]If you decide to use more than one treatment, be sure to calculate variances separately for cases within each treatment, and then find the average standard deviation.

Suppose also that the desired power $(1 - \beta)$ is set at .85, so that $z_{1-\beta} = 1.04$. The one-tail test is used since the research hypothesis predicted an advantage in favor of the ski slope view.[8] Solving the equation, then,

$$n = \frac{2(2)}{2.5^2}(1.96 + 1.04)^2 = 5.76$$

Fractional numbers are rounded upward, so that there are at least as many cases as required for the stated power. Thus, six skiers need to be randomly assigned to each type of room to achieve a significant result ($p < .05$) with a probability of .85 for the difference between ocean and ski slope views, if such a difference truly exists.

Notice an interesting simplification with these particular choices of α and β. The z values add to 3.00, so that the last part of the expression, squared, is 9.00. As a result, an even quicker and dirtier form of the sample-size formula is

$$n = \frac{18\sigma^2}{\delta^2} \tag{4.7}$$

More precise estimates are available with the use of power tables, such as are available in Keppel (1991). Better yet, use of software such as PC-SIZE streamlines sample-size determination. Assume for the example that the means for the three room views were hypothesized to be 2.5, 4.0, and 6.5. The program requires variability in the form of a standard deviation rather than a variance, so that $(2)^{1/2} = 1.414$ is used. In addition, α is chosen as .05 and power as .85. Table 4.20 shows the setup and results for this problem through PC-SIZE. (Note that selected values appear below the instructions in printed output.)

TABLE 4.20   Sample-Size Determination Through PC-SIZE

```
                    PC-Size
        A Program for Sample Size Determinations
                  Version 2.13
                  (c) 1985, 1986

          "One of many STATOOLS(tm) . . . "
                      by

              Gerard E. Dallal
              53 Beltran Street
              Malden, MA 02148

Please acknowledge PC-SIZE in any publication that
makes use of its calcluations. A suitable reference
is Dallal, G. E. (1986), "PC-SIZE: A Program for
Sample Size Determinations," The American
Statistician,40,52.
```

[8]Null hypotheses are usually bidirectional, indicating a two-tailed test, whereas research hypotheses are usually unidirectional, indicating a one-tailed test.

TABLE 4.20   Continued

```
This program operates in seven modes:

    1  --   single factor design
    2  --   two factor design
    3  --   randomized blocks design
    4  --   paired t-test
    5  --   generic F
    6  --   correlation coefficient
    7  --   proportions

Choose a mode [1]:
    1

Enter the level of the test [ .050]:
  .50000E-01
Enter the required power [ .800]:
  .85000
Enter the number of groups [ 2]:
    3

There are three ways to specify the alternative:

    1  --   Specify individual effects.
    2  --   Specify a range throughout which group
                means are uniformly distributed.
    3  --   Specify average squared effect divided
                by the error variance.
Choose a method [2]:
    1
Enter estimate of effect for group 1 [ .00000 ]:
  2.5000
Enter estimate of effect for group 2 [ .00000 ]:
  4.0000
Enter estimate of effect for group 3 [ .00000 ]:
  6.5000
Enter estimate of within cell standard deviation
[0.00]:
1.4140

Level of the test: .0500
Non-centrality parameter: 4.0846 * sample size

    SAMPLE
     SIZE      POWER
  (per cell)

       2      .32311
       3      .66977
       4      .86682
```

Only four skiers in each group are required for power of .87, at the chosen α level with means and within-cell standard deviation as specified. This provides power to find *any* differences among the three groups. That is, there is enough power to find an omnibus effect. If the desire truly is to find a particular difference between just two of the groups, this software may be used as if only those two groups were run. This use assumes a planned comparison, in which no power is lost by adjusting for post hoc analysis, as per Section 4.5.5.

4.5.2.3 Power of a Nonsignificant Effect

The procedures of Section 4.5.2 usually are used to determine needed sample size before gathering data. However, they can be turned around to solve for power after the analysis is run if a nonsignificant result is obtained. This gives you some idea of how far off your study was from producing a significant effect. For example, PC-SIZE shows in Table 4.20 that had we run an experiment with $n = 2$ and achieved the stated means and within-cell standard deviation, the power would have been .32 (indicating a Type II error rate of .68) and a need to run more subjects in a second study if significance is to be expected.

The PASS program (NCSS, 1996) permits power solutions in the case when information about sample size, means, and error variance is used. The program requires that you provide σ_m for the effect of A either by calculation or by entering the observed means into the "sigma calculator." The three means for the sample data from Section 4.4 (2.4, 3.8, and 6.4) produce $\sigma_m = 1.657$. Then you find $\sigma = \sqrt{MS_{S/A}} = 1.26$. Table 4.21 shows output from NCSS for the data in the one-way ANOVA of Section 4.4.3.

Thus, the hypothetical data analyzed in Section 4.4.3 had a probability of .98 of detecting a true mean difference in ratings among the three ocean views. The program also produces effect size in the form of d (cf. Section 4.5.1). SPSS GLM also gives power and effect size (in the form of η^2) for each effect as part of the analysis if certain menu selections are made, as demonstrated in Section 5.4.5.

4.5.3 Unequal Sample Sizes

Unequal sample sizes in levels of the IV pose no particular difficulty for computation of one-way omnibus ANOVA, but may pose intractable problems if the inequality is caused by differential dropout from some levels of the IV in an experiment designed to have equal sample sizes. For example, if some levels of treatment cause some employees to leave an experiment, or rats to die, or fabrics to disintegrate, the original random assignment to levels of the IV is no longer random by the time the DV is measured. Therefore, it is no longer an experiment.

TABLE 4.21 Output of NCSS PASS for Results of One-way ANOVA with Three Levels

Numeric Results for One-Way Analysis of Variance

Power	n	k	Alpha	Beta	Sigma m	Sigma	Effect Size
0.98357	5.00	3	0.05000	0.01643	1.66	1.26	1.30998

Another complication of unequal sample sizes is that orthogonality is lost in both the traditional and regression approaches (and therefore in comparisons) even when the coding itself is orthogonal. For example, note in Table 4.7 that the sums of X_1, X_2, and $X_1 X_2$ are not zero if one or more cases is missing from any group.

Suppose the last case in the small sample provided unusable data, resulting in only four scores in a_3. Table 4.22 shows the resulting data set and group means. For the example, then, SS_A is found using Equation 3.14, with modification to the denominators for unequal n. With three levels of A, for example, Equation 3.14 becomes

$$SS_A = \left(\frac{A_1^2}{n_1} + \frac{A_2^2}{n_2} + \frac{A_3^2}{n_3} \right) - \frac{T^2}{N} \tag{4.8}$$

and for the data of Table 4.24,

$$SS_A = \left(\frac{12^2}{5} + \frac{19^2}{5} + \frac{27^2}{4} \right) - \frac{58^2}{14} = 42.96$$

and $MS_A = SS_A / df_A = 42.96/2 = 21.48$.

For the error term, the sum of squares is found by a modification of Equation 3.15 for unequal n as follows:

$$SS_{S/A} = \sum Y^2 - \left(\frac{A_1^2}{n_1} + \frac{A_2^2}{n_2} + \frac{A_3^2}{n_3} \right) \tag{4.9}$$

TABLE 4.22   Hypothetical Data Set with Unequal Sample Sizes for One-Way ANOVA

A: Type of View		
a_1: Parking Lot View	a_2: Ocean View	a_3: Ski Slope View
1	3	6
1	4	8
3	3	6
5	5	7
2	4	
$A_1 = 12$	$A_2 = 19$	$A_3 = 27$
$\overline{Y}_{A_1} = 2.4$	$\overline{Y}_{A_2} = 3.8$	$\overline{Y}_{A_3} = 6.75$
$Y_{A_1}^2 = 40$	$Y_{A_2}^2 = 75$	$Y_{A_3}^2 = 185$

and for the data of Table 4.22,

$$SS_{S/A} = (40 + 75 + 185) - \left(\frac{12^2}{5} + \frac{19^2}{5} + \frac{27^2}{4}\right) = 16.75$$

Degrees of freedom for error is the number of scores within each group minus 1, or $4 + 4 + 3 = 11$ so that

$$MS_{S/A} = \frac{16.75}{4 + 4 + 3} = 1.52$$

$$F = \frac{21.48}{1.52} = 14.13$$

and critical F at $\alpha = .05$ from Table A.1 with 2 and 11 df is 3.98, indicating a statistically significant difference in rating of vacation as a function of view from room.

In this situation, the traditional approach to ANOVA is clearer than the regression approach because some of the columns do not sum to zero and the computations become much more complex. A feel for the kind of adjustments that are necessary is obtained by looking at the equations for slope in Table 4.10.

4.5.4   Homogeneity of Variance

Section 3.4.3 discusses the ratio of largest to smallest variance as an indication of compliance with the assumption of homogeneity of variance. To repeat Equation 3.20,

$$F_{max} = \frac{s^2_{largest}}{s^2_{smallest}}$$

Variances (squared standard deviations) in the small-sample example of Section 4.4.3 (with equal n) are $(1.673)^2$, $(0.837)^2$, and $(1.140)^2$ for the three groups, respectively, as shown in Tables 4.15 through 4.17. Thus,

$$F_{max} = \frac{(1.673)^2}{(0.837)^2} = 4.00$$

Recall that the assumption of homogeneity of variance is robust to violation when (1) $F_{max} \leq 10$, (2) the ratio of largest to smallest sample size is less than 4:1, (3) two-tailed tests are used, and (4) an omnibus analysis is performed. All of these requirements are met for the small-sample omnibus ANOVA, so the probability associated with the critical value of F is close to the tabled value. Departure from homogeneity of variance is more serious for comparisons than for omnibus analyses, as shown in Section 4.5.5.

Recall from Section 3.4.3 that heterogeneity of variance should always be reported and is often of interest in itself. Differences in dispersion of scores in groups could come from differences in the cases in groups (indicating a failure of random assignment) or from variability in the reactions of various cases to the same treatment. Cases may respond consistently to some levels of treatment and inconsistently to other levels. What is it about the level of treatment and/or the cases that causes variability in response? Ferreting out the source of this variability often leads the research in unexpected and fruitful directions.

4.5.5 Specific Comparisons

An analysis of variance as described in preceding sections provides only limited information if there are more than two levels of the IV. The overall test of the effect, the omnibus analysis, indicates that there are differences somewhere among the means, but gives no hint as to exactly which means are different from one another. Specific *comparisons* (also called *contrasts*) are necessary to provide more focused tests of differences among means.

Specific comparisons may either *replace* omnibus ANOVA (planned comparisons) or *follow* omnibus ANOVA (post hoc comparisons). Planned comparisons are far more powerful than post hoc comparisons and are therefore preferred. An analysis "uses up" degrees of freedom, best thought of as a precious, nonrenewable resource. Those degrees of freedom can be used either conducting a one-way omnibus ANOVA or conducting planned comparisons. The one-way omnibus ANOVA uses up $a - 1$ df; those df could, instead, be spent performing planned comparisons that provide specific information regarding the location of mean differences.

If ANOVA is done first, several types of post hoc comparisons are available, all with different goals and different levels of power. The two that are discussed here in greatest detail are the Scheffé procedure for performing numerous and complex comparisons and the Tukey test for comparing all possible pairs of means. The Scheffé procedure is the most flexible, but also the most conservative of the post hoc procedures. Failure to apply appropriate adjustment for post hoc analyses results in (grossly) inflated Type I error. Section 4.5.5.5 deals with some adjustment techniques.

The only difference between planned comparisons and several types of post hoc comparisons is which critical F is used to test the F obtained for the comparison; a larger critical value of F is required when the same comparison is done post hoc. That is, F obtained for a comparison is the same whether planned or post hoc; it is the inferential test of the comparison that changes depending on when it is performed.

Gaining the power of planned comparisons imposes restrictions, in addition to the need for preplanning. First, there should only be as many comparisons as there are df_A.[9] For example, in a one-way design with four levels, three comparisons, each with a single df, are available for analysis. Second, it is desirable to use an orthogonal set of weighting coefficients (numerical codes) for the comparisons. Weighting coefficients are chosen to express hypotheses. If possible, these coefficients are chosen in such a way that the hypotheses tested are independent—that the set of coefficients completely analyzes all available variability without reanalyzing any parts of it.

Figure 4.2 uses Venn diagrams to illustrate the difference between orthogonal and nonorthogonal comparisons. In Figure 4.2(a), there are as many comparisons as there are df_A and the set of comparisons is orthogonal. In this case, the comparisons completely partition the area representing the relationship between the DV and A, with none of the area reanalyzed. Figure 4.2(b) represents a case of nonorthogonal comparisons, where not all of the relationship between the DV and A is analyzed, and some of the area is analyzed by more than one comparison.

---

[9]If greed sets in and more planned comparisons are desired than the available df, the Bonferroni correction is applied, as discussed in Section 4.5.5.4.

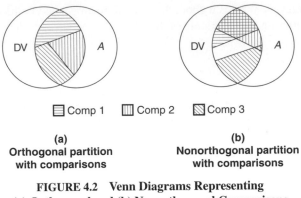

□ Comp 1   ▥ Comp 2   ▨ Comp 3

(a)
Orthogonal partition
with comparisons

(b)
Nonorthogonal partition
with comparisons

FIGURE 4.2   Venn Diagrams Representing
(a) Orthogonal and (b) Nonorthogonal Comparisons

4.5.5.1 *Weighting Coefficients for Comparisons*

Comparison of treatment means begins by assigning a weighting factor (w) to the mean of each level of the IV so the weights reflect your null hypotheses. Suppose you have a one-way design with a means and you want to make comparisons. For each comparison: (1) A weight is assigned to each mean. (2) At least two of the means have to have nonzero weights. (3) Weights of zero are assigned to means (groups) that are left out of a comparison. (4) Means that are contrasted with each other are assigned weights with opposite signs (positive or negative) with the constraint that (5) the weights sum to zero, that is,

$$\sum_{1}^{a} w_j = 0$$

For example, consider an IV with four levels, producing $\overline{Y}_{a_1}$, $\overline{Y}_{a_2}$, $\overline{Y}_{a_3}$, and $\overline{Y}_{a_4}$. If you want to test the null hypothesis that, in the population, $\mu_{a_1} - \mu_{a_3} = 0$, appropriate weighting coefficients are 1, 0, -1, 0 producing $1\overline{Y}_{a_1} + 0\overline{Y}_{a_2} + (-1)\overline{Y}_{a_3} + 0\overline{Y}_{a_4}$. $\overline{Y}_{a_2}$ and $\overline{Y}_{a_4}$ are left out while $\overline{Y}_{a_1}$ is compared with $\overline{Y}_{a_3}$. Or, if you want to test the null hypothesis that $(\mu_{a_1} + \mu_{a_2})/2 - \mu_{a_3} = 0$ (to compare the average of means from the first two groups with the mean of the third group, leaving out the fourth group), weighting coefficients are $\frac{1}{2}, \frac{1}{2}, \frac{1}{2}, -1, 0$, (or any multiple of them, such as 1, 1, -2, 0), respectively. Or, if you want to test the null hypothesis that $(\mu_{a_1} + \mu_{a_2})/2 - (\mu_{a_3} + \mu_{a_4})/2 = 0$ (to compare the average mean of the first two groups with the average mean of the last two groups), the weighting coefficients are $\frac{1}{2}, \frac{1}{2}, -\frac{1}{2}, -\frac{1}{2}$, (or 1, 1, -1, -1).

Notice that some of these comparisons involve pooling (averaging) means to contrast them with another mean (or another pooled mean). But no matter how complicated the pooling procedure becomes, a comparison always boils down to a test of the difference between two means. For this reason, the F test for a comparison has just one degree of freedom in the numerator.

The idea behind the test is that the difference between the weighted means is equal to zero when the null hypothesis is true. The more the sum diverges from zero, the greater the obtained F and the greater the confidence with which the corresponding null hypothesis is rejected.

In the small-sample example, for instance, to test whether the ocean view differs significantly from the parking lot view, the coefficients assigned to the three levels of the IV are $-1, 1, 0$ for parking lot, ocean, and ski slope views, respectively. Notice that these are also the X_2 coefficients applied to the three levels in the regression approach to ANOVA (Table 4.7). The other set of coefficients, in X_1, contrasts the combination of parking lot and ocean view with the ski slope view. At this point, you have probably recognized that the weighting coefficients for comparisons are the same as the numerical codes in the columns for the regression approach to ANOVA. Indeed, the regression approach has comparisons imbedded as an integral part of the analysis.

4.5.5.2   Orthogonality of Weighting Coefficients for Comparisons

Any pair of comparisons is orthogonal if the sum of the cross-products of the weights for the two comparisons is equal to zero. For example, in the following three comparisons:

	w_1	w_2	w_3
Comparison 1	1	1	-2
Comparison 2	-1	1	0
Comparison 3	1	0	-1

the sum of the cross-products of weights for Comparison 1 and Comparison 2 is

$$(1)(-1) + (1)(1) + (-2)(0) = 0$$

Therefore, the first two comparisons are orthogonal. This corresponds to the sum of the X_1X_2 column of Table 4.7, in which codes for each case have been cross multiplied. The use of orthogonal coding in the regression approach to ANOVA *builds in* orthogonal comparisons.

Comparison 3, however, is orthogonal to neither of the first two comparisons. For instance, checking it against Comparison 1,

$$(1)(1) + (1)(0) + (-2)(-1) = 3$$

In general, there are as many orthogonal comparisons as there are degrees of freedom for effect. Because $a = 3$ in the example, $df_A = 2$. There are, then, only two orthogonal comparisons when there are three levels of an IV, only three orthogonal comparisons when there are four levels of an IV, and so on. (However, there are always several possible sets of orthogonal comparisons.)

There are advantages to use of orthogonal comparisons if a set is available that asks the appropriate research questions. First, there are only as many of them as there are degrees of freedom for effect, so the temptation to "overspend" degrees of freedom is avoided. Second, as shown in Figure 4.2, orthogonal comparisons analyze nonoverlapping variance; if one of them is significant, it has no bearing on the significance of any of the others. Last, because they are independent, if all $a - 1$ orthogonal comparisons are performed, the sum of the sum of squares for the comparisons is the same as the sum of squares for the IV in omnibus ANOVA. That is, the sum of squares for the effect has been completely partitioned into the $a - 1$ orthogonal comparisons that comprise it. This is, of course, the tack that is taken in the regression approach to ANOVA.

It should be emphasized that answering the right research question is more important than having an orthogonal set of comparisons. Sometimes an orthogonal set answers the right questions so you can take advantage of its mathematical properties. However, answering the right research questions is always more important than maintaining orthogonality in the set of comparisons.

4.5.5.3   Obtained F for Comparisons

Once the weighting coefficients are chosen, the following equation is used to obtain F for the comparison if sample sizes are equal in each group. (Section 4.5.5.5.1 shows an equation to use for unequal n.)

$$F = \frac{n(\sum w_j \overline{Y}_j)^2 / \sum w_j^2}{\text{MS}_{S/A}} \tag{4.10}$$

where n = number of scores in each group

$(\sum w_j \overline{Y}_j)^2$ = squared sum of the weighted means

$\sum w_j^2$ = sum of the squared coefficients

$\text{MS}_{S/A}$ = mean square for error in the ANOVA

The numerator of Equation 4.10 is both sum of squares and mean square for the comparison because a comparison has only one degree of freedom.

In the small-sample example, with $n = 5$ and $\text{MS}_{S/A} = 1.6$, if the parking lot and ocean views are pooled and contrasted with the ski slope view:

$$F = \frac{5[(1)(2.4) + (1)(3.8) + (-2)(6.4)]^2 / [1^2 + 1^2 + (-2)^2]}{1.6} = 22.69$$

This is the same F ratio that is found if the regression approach is used to test X_1 of Table 4.11.

$$F = \frac{\text{SS}(\text{reg}.X_1)}{\text{MS}(\text{resid}.)} = \frac{36.3}{1.6} = 22.69$$

Once you have obtained F for a comparison, whether by hand calculation or computer, the obtained F is compared with a critical F to see if the mean difference is reliable. If obtained F exceeds critical F, the null hypothesis represented by the weighting coefficients is rejected. But which critical F is used depends on whether the comparison is planned or post hoc (and other niceties such as equal n and homogeneity of variance).

4.5.5.4   Planned Comparisons

Choice of tests for planned comparisons depend on the number of comparisons to be done, whether the planned comparisons are orthogonal, and whether the assumption of homogeneity of variance is met. Table 4.23 shows the choices.

TABLE 4.23   Choosing among Tests for Planned Comparisons

Type of Comparison	Number of Comparisons	Orthogonal?	Homogeneity of Variance?	Test
Complex	$a - 1$	yes	Yes	$F(1, df_{S/A})$: Section 4.5.5.4.1
			No	$F(1, df_{S/A})$: with Welch's df correction: Section 4.5.5.4.2
		no	Yes	Bonferroni: Section 4.5.5.4.3
			No	Bonferroni with Welch's df correction: Sections 4.5.5.4.3 and 4.5.5.4.2
	More than $a - 1$		Yes	Bonferroni: Section 4.5.5.4.3
			No	Bonferroni with Welch's df correction: Sections 4.5.5.4.3 and 4.5.5.4.2
Pairwise			Yes	Bonferroni: Section 4.5.5.4.3
			No	Bonferroni with Welch's df correction: Sections 4.5.5.4.3 and 4.5.5.4.2
Control vs. each treatment			Yes	Dunnett: Section 4.5.5.4.4
			No (and/or unequal n)	Dunnett with Welch's df correction: Section 4.5.5.4.4

4.5.5.4.1   An Orthogonal Set

If you are in the enviable position of having planned your comparisons prior to data collection, you have planned no more of them than you have degrees of freedom for the effect, the set of planned comparisons is orthogonal, and there is homogeneity of variance, the significance of F for the comparison is read directly from the output just as in routine ANOVA. Or, if obtained F is compared with critical F from a table such as Table A.1, each comparison is tested against critical F at chosen alpha with one degree of freedom in the numerator and df_{error} ($df_{S/A}$) in the denominator. If obtained F is larger than critical F, the null hypothesis represented by the weighting coefficients is rejected.

In the small-sample example, $df_{S/A} = 12$. The critical value from Table A.1 with 1 and 12 df at $\alpha = .05$ is 4.75. With obtained $F = 22.69$, the null hypothesis of no difference between the mean of the ski slope view versus pooled mean of the other two views is rejected.

Table 4.24 shows how the set of orthogonal comparisons is done through SPSS, SAS, and SYSTAT software, by adding contrast coefficients to existing syntax for one-way ANOVA.

The MINITAB GLM procedure does not have a provision for user-specified contrasts. However, they may still be done through GLM (or REGRESSION) by adding a column of X coefficients to the data file for each orthogonal comparison and running multiple regression using the new columns as IVs.

TABLE 4.24 Syntax for Orthogonal Comparisons

Program	Syntax	Section of Output	Name of Effect

SPSS ONEWAY	ONEWAY
	  rating BY view
	  /CONTRAST= 1 1 –2
	  /CONTRAST= –1 1 0
	  /MISSING ANALYSIS.
		Contrast Tests	Assume equal variances[a]

SAS GLM	proc glm data=SASUSER. RAND_GRP;
	      class VIEW;
	      model RATING = VIEW;
	      contrast 'X1' VIEW 1 1 –2;
	      contrast 'X2' VIEW –1 1 0;
	run;
		Contrast	X1, X2

SYSTAT ANOVA	ANOVA CATEGORY VIEW COVAR DEPEND RATING ESTIMATE HYPOTHESIS EFFECT=VIEW NOTE 'SLOPE VS OTHERS' CONTRAST[1 1 –2] TEST HYPOTHESIS EFFECT=VIEW NOTE 'PARKING VS OCEAN' CONTRAST[–1 1 0] TEST	Test of Hypothesis Source	Hypothesis

[a]t is given rather than F; recall that $t^2 = F$ with df = 1 in the numerator and df$_{S/A}$ in the denominator.

Table 4.25 shows the data set in which the orthogonal comparisons of Table 4.7 are used as variables. Table 4.26 shows the MINITAB GLM syntax and output for the analysis. Note that the variables of interest are designated COVARIATES[10] for purposes of this analysis. `Brief 2` is a default value produced by the MINITAB menu system and suppresses some optional output.

Notice that the `Adj SS` for `X1` and `X2` match the component values for SS(reg.X_1) and SS(reg.X_2) in Table 4.11, as does the `Error` term. The `F` for `X1` matches the hand-calculated value in Section 4.5.5.3. The `Coef` for `X1` and `X2` match the regression coefficients (b_1 and b_2) of Table 4.10 and the `Constant` is the intercept, a. Finally, notice that the `T` values for `X1` and `X2` are the

[10]Covariates are discussed in Chapter 8. For current purposes, the covariate designation simply indicates that variables are to be treated as continuous rather than discrete.

TABLE 4.25   Data Set for Analyzing Orthogonal Comparisons through Regression

VIEW	RATING	X1	X2
1	1	1	−1
1	1	1	−1
1	3	1	−1
1	5	1	−1
1	2	1	−1
2	3	1	1
2	4	1	1
2	3	1	1
2	5	1	1
2	4	1	1
3	6	−2	0
3	8	−2	0
3	6	−2	0
3	7	−2	0
3	5	−2	0

TABLE 4.26   Orthogonal Comparisons through MINITAB GLM: Syntax and Selected Output

```
MTB > GLM 'RATING' = X1 X2;
SUBC> Covariates 'X1' 'X>2';
SUBC> Brief 2.
```

General Linear Model

```
Factor     Type Levels Values
Analysis of Variance for RATING, using Adjusted SS for Tests
```

Source	DF	Seq SS	Adj SS	Adj MS	F	P
X1	1	36.300	36.300	36.300	22.69	0.000
X2	1	4.900	4.900	4.900	3.06	0.106
Error	12	19.200	19.200	1.600		
Total	14	60.400				

Term	Coef	StDev	T	P
Constant	4.2000	0.3266	12.86	0.000
X1	−1.1000	0.2309	−4.76	0.000
X2	0.7000	0.4000	1.75	0.106

square roots of Fs. The test of the Constant (that the mean RATING differs significantly from zero) is not of research interest. (Actually, orthogonal comparisons may be done in any regression or GLM program by entering X columns as data and treating them as continuous IVs.)

With planned comparisons, the results for omnibus ANOVA are not attended; the researcher moves straight to the results for the comparisons. Once the degrees of freedom are spent on the planned comparisons, however, it is perfectly acceptable to snoop the data using the less powerful post hoc procedures (Section 4.5.5.5).

4.5.5.4.2   Welch's Correction for Heterogeneity of Variance

All of the tests in Table 4.23, including the orthogonal set of comparisons in Section 4.5.5.4.1 above, assume homogeneity of variance. Therefore, the omnibus ANOVA that provides the error term should also be examined for homogeneity of variance using the procedures of Section 4.5.4.[11] If the guidelines are violated, Welch's correction is applied to $df_{S/A}$ when looking up critical F to compensate for inflated Type I error rate. The adjusted df_{error} is based on Welch (1947).

$$df_{error'} = \frac{\left(\dfrac{w_1^2 s_1^2}{n_1} + \dfrac{w_2^2 s_2^2}{n_2} + \cdots + \dfrac{w_a^2 s_a^2}{n_a} \right)^2}{\dfrac{w_1^4 s_1^4}{n_1^2(n_1 - 1)} + \dfrac{w_2^4 s_2^4}{n_2^2(n_2 - 1)} + \cdots + \dfrac{w_a^4 s_a^4}{n_a^2(n_a - 1)}} \tag{4.11}$$

Using the variances from the small-sample example, $(1.673)^2$, $(0.837)^2$, and $(1.140)^2$ for demonstration purposes, even though they are not heterogeneous, and assuming the comparison coefficients are 1, 1, −2:

$$df_{error'} = \frac{\left(\dfrac{1^2(1.673)^2}{5} + \dfrac{1^2(0.873)^2}{5} + \dfrac{(-2)^2(1.140)^2}{5} \right)^2}{\dfrac{1^4(1.673)^4}{5^2(5-1)} + \dfrac{1^4(0.873)^4}{5^2(5-1)} + \dfrac{(-2)^4(1.140)^4}{5^2(5-1)}} = \frac{(1.750)^2}{0.354} = 8.65$$

Thus, error df are cut from 12 to 9 to adjust for violation of the assumption of homogeneity of variance. Critical F at $\alpha = .05$ with df $= 1, 9$ in Table A.1 is 5.32, so the comparison is statistically reliable even after this (unnecessary in this example) adjustment to df.

Note that this equation also incorporates unequal n, if present, which may exacerbate the seriousness of heterogeneity of variance.

4.5.5.4.3   Bonferroni Correction

Sometimes the researcher plans more comparisons than degrees of freedom for the effect. For instance, you may plan to compare all pairs of means (pairwise comparisons), but this requires too many degrees of freedom. When there are too many tests, the α level across all tests—the familywise

---

[11]Variances can be obtained through any of the software modules that provide descriptive statistics, or calculated by hand.

Type I error rate—exceeds the α level for any one test even if comparisons are planned. The reason for the precipitous rise in error rate is the necessity of making many separate decisions, all of them correctly. When there is only one test, the Type I error rate is .05, so the probability of correctly retaining a true null hypothesis is .95. With two tests, each at $\alpha = .05$, the probability of retaining two true null hypotheses is $(.95)(.95) = .90$. This comes from the desire to make the correct decision on the first test *as well as* the correct decision on the second. The probability of an incorrect decision about at least one of the hypotheses is $1 - .90 = .10$. That is, although each test uses $\alpha = .05$, when the familywise error rate is computed, the error rate for both tests combined is .10. With three tests, the joint probability of retaining three true null hypotheses is $(.95)(.95)(.95) = .86$ and the familywise error rate is .14. When there are five hypothesis tests to be conducted, the familywise error rate is about .23, meaning that there is roughly one chance in four of committing a Type I error in the chain of five decisions. As a rough guide, the familywise Type I error rate is the number of tests to be conducted multiplied by the chosen α level.

When there are too many significance tests, then, some adjustment of α for the tests are needed. It is common practice to use a Bonferroni-type adjustment in which more stringent α levels are used with each test to keep the familywise α across all tests at reasonable levels. For instance, if five comparisons are planned and each one of them is tested at $\alpha = .02$, the alpha across all tests is an acceptable .10 (roughly, .02 times 5, the number of tests). Overall familywise error rates of between .05 and .15 are acceptable in many situations. Thus, the simplest form of the Bonferroni correction is applied by dividing the acceptable familywise error rate by the number of comparisons to be made.

However, this familywise error rate need not be apportioned equally among all comparisons. If you want to keep overall α at, say, .10, and you have five tests to perform, you can assign each of them $\alpha = .02$, or you can assign two of them $\alpha = .04$ with the other three evaluated at $\alpha = .01$, for an overall Type I error rate of roughly .11. Keppel (1991) suggests a modified Bonferroni procedure that takes into account the number of tests legitimately performed as planned comparisons as well as those in excess of the legitimate number. The decision about how to apportion α through the tests is part of planning the analysis and is made prior to data collection.

A problem of inflated Type I error rate also occurs when the researcher plans $a - 1$ comparisons, but they are nonorthogonal. The problem arises because the researcher is reanalyzing the same sum of squares (Figure 4.2). The suggested remedy is to apply the Bonferroni correction (with Welch's adjustment if homogeneity of variance is violated), as seen in Table 4.23. Most software programs provide a Bonferroni correction to pairwise comparisons, but not to complex comparisons.[12]

As an aside, it is important to realize that routine ANOVA designs with numerous main effects and interactions suffer from the same problem of inflated Type I error rate across all tests as planned comparisons where there are too many tests. Some adjustment of α for separate tests is needed in big ANOVA problems as well if all effects are evaluated.

4.5.5.4.4 Dunnett's Test for Control Group vs. Each Treatment

Dunnett's test is applicable to a specific design when there is a single control group and multiple treatment groups and the researcher plans to compare the mean of each treatment, in turn, with the

---

[12]An alternative, slightly more powerful, method for apportioning familywise Type I error rate is the Sidak correction, available for pairwise comparisons in GLM programs of SAS, SPSS, and MINITAB.

mean of the control. In this situation, there are $a - 1$ comparisons, but they are not orthogonal. Thus, Dunnett's test controls α_{FW} (familywise Type I error rate) for $a - 1$ nonorthogonal comparisons.

Obtained F for these comparisons uses Equation 4.10, simplified because each comparison involves only two means, coded 1 and -1. If the parking lot view is considered a control condition in the small-sample example, the two F ratios for the Dunnett comparisons are 3.06 for ocean and 25.00 for ski slope.

The critical F ratio for the Dunnett test, F_D, is

$$F_D = q_D{}^2 \tag{4.12}$$

where q_D is the value from Table A.4, entered with df_{error} ($df_{S/A}$ for the randomized-groups design), a (the number of means including the control), and your selection of .05 or .01 as α_{FW}.

For the example, with $df_{S/A} = 12$, $a = 3$, and $\alpha_{FW} = .05$ (two-tailed), the value from Table A.4 is 2.50, which when squared produces $F_D = 6.25$. By the criterion of the Dunnett test, the ski slope view differs significantly from the parking lot control, but the ocean view does not.

The procedure demonstrated here is for the two-tailed Dunnett test, to be used with a nondirectional alternative hypothesis. This form of the Dunnett test is available in the GLM programs of MINITAB, SAS, SPSS, and SYSTAT. These software implementations also permit a one-sided Dunnett test, with the control group hypothesized to have either a lower (or higher) mean than the treatment groups. MINITAB GLM also has procedures by which Sidak or Bonferroni (rather than Dunnett) adjustments are made to assess each difference between a treatment group and the control.

Dunnett's test assumes equal n and a special form of homogeneity of variance. It is assumed that the variance of the control group is equal to the pooled variance of the treatment groups. When these assumptions are not met, you can use Dunnett's test with Welch's correction for error df of the previous section.

4.5.5.5   *Adjustments for Post Hoc Comparisons*

If you are unable to plan your comparisons and choose instead to start with routine ANOVA, you almost always follow up a significant main effect (with more than two levels) with post hoc comparisons to find the treatment means that are different from one another. Because you have already spent your degrees of freedom in routine ANOVA and are likely to capitalize on chance differences among means that you notice in the data, some form of adjustment of α is necessary.

A staggering array of procedures for dealing post hoc with inflated Type I error rate is available. The tests differ in the number and type of comparisons they permit, the amount of adjustment required of α, and availability in software. The tests that permit more numerous comparisons have correspondingly more stringent adjustments to critical F. Therefore, the fewer comparisons that are possible, the less conservative (i.e., more powerful) the test. The name of the game is to choose the most liberal (powerful) test that permits you to perform the comparisons of interest.

Section 4.5.5.5.1 demonstrates the most flexible but conservative adjustment procedure, the Scheffé test. This test permits numerous and complex comparisons and controls familywise error rate over all comparisons that can be devised. Section 4.5.5.5.2 demonstrates the Tukey HSD test, which controls familywise error for all pairwise comparisons among means. Because the Scheffé test permits comparison of all pairs of means, as well as comparisons where means are pooled, the adjustment is more severe. These are the two most popular post hoc procedures, but require equal n

and homogeneity of variance in their simplest forms. Alternative procedures are available when the assumptions are violated, as seen in Table 4.27. Note that the Dunnett tests listed in Table 4.27 are for pairwise comparisons and differ from the Dunnett test described in Section 4.5.5.4.4.

Other comparison procedures available in software include the Duncan test, the Student-Newman-Keuls test, the least-significant difference and modified least-significant difference tests, an alternative Tukey procedure, and so on. Generally, these tests are known to be too liberal under certain circumstances, and are not recommended.

Different selections of these post hoc adjustment techniques are available in statistical computing packages. Section 4.7 compares one-way ANOVA programs and indicates which techniques are available in each.

4.5.5.5.1 Scheffé Post Hoc Test for Complex Comparisons

The test described here (Scheffé, 1953) is the most flexible and most conservative (least powerful) of the methods of post hoc adjustment. The Scheffé adjustment for familywise error rate is applied to critical F. Once this critical F is computed, you use it for all pairwise comparisons and for all combinations of treatment means pooled and contrasted with other treatment means, pooled or not, as desired.[13] And once you pay the "price" in conservatism for this flexibility, you might as well conduct all the comparisons that make sense given your research design.

TABLE 4.27   Choosing among Post Hoc Analyses

Type of Comparison	Equal n?	Homogeneity of Variance?	Number of Error df	Test
Complex	Yes	Yes		F_s: Section 4.5.5.5.1
	Yes	No		F_s with Welch's df correction: Sections 4.5.5.5.1 and 4.5.5.4.2
	No	Yes		Modified F_s: Section 4.5.5.5.1
	No	No		Modified F_s with Welch's df correction: Sections 4.5.5.5.1 and 4.5.5.4.2
Pairwise	Yes	Yes		Tukey HSD: Section 4.5.5.5.2
	Yes	No	75 or more	Dunnett C: Section 4.5.5.5.3
	Yes	No	Less than 75	Dunnett T3: Section 4.5.5.5.3
	No	Yes		Tukey-Kramer: Section 4.5.5.5.3
	No	No	75 or more	Dunnett C: Section 4.5.5.5.3
	No	No	Less than 75	Dunnett T3: Section 4.5.5.5.3

---

[13]Some possibilities for pooling are illustrated in Section 4.5.5.1.

The Scheffé adjustment to critical F for a comparison on marginal means is

$$F_S = (a - 1)F_c \qquad (4.13)$$

where F_S = Scheffé-adjusted critical F

$a - 1$ = degrees of freedom for the effect

F_c (critical F) = tabled F with $a - 1$ degrees of freedom in the numerator and degrees of freedom associated with the error term in the denominator

If obtained F is larger than critical F_S, the null hypothesis represented by the weighting coefficients for the comparison is rejected in favor of a two-tailed alternative hypothesis. For example, had the small-sample comparison of the ski slope view against the pooled means of the ocean and parking lot views been done as part of a post hoc analysis, critical F_S would have been $(3 - 1)(3.88) = 7.76$. The obtained $F = 22.69$ is still statistically reliable, meaning that the null hypothesis of equality between the mean of the ski slope view contrasted with the pooled means of the parking lot and ocean views is rejected.

The Scheffé test assumes homogeneity of variance; violation is dealt with by applying Welch's correction to error df (Equation 4.11). The Scheffé test also assumes equal n, violation of which requires modifying Equation 4.10 as follows:

$$F = \frac{(\sum w_j \overline{Y}_j)^2 / \sum (w_j^2 / n_j)}{\mathrm{MS}_{S/A}} \qquad (4.14)$$

Each coefficient is divided by its own group size, instead of multiplying weighted means by a single sample size. For example, using the unequal-n data of Section 4.5.3, the comparison of ski slope vs. other views with coefficients 1, 1, and -2 produces obtained F:

$$F = \frac{[(1)(2.4) + (1)(3.8) + (-2)(6.75)]^2 / [(1^2/5 + 1^2/5 + (-2)^2/4]}{1.52} = 25.04$$

4.5.5.5.2   Tukey HSD Test for Pairwise Comparisons

The Tukey HSD (honestly significant difference) test, or studentized range statistic, is designed to test all means against each other pairwise; each mean compared, in turn, with every other mean. This set of comparisons does not include comparisons with pooled or averaged means. Obtained F is calculated using Equation 4.10, the same as for any other comparison except that the equation is simplified because the pair of means of interest are given codes 1 and -1 and the remaining means are omitted because their codes are zero. In the small-sample example, the three obtained F ratios are as follows:

Parking lot view vs. ocean view:

$$F = \frac{5[(1)(2.4) + (-1)(3.8)]^2 / [1^2 + (-1^2)]}{1.6} = 3.06$$

Parking lot view vs. ski slope view:

$$F = \frac{5[(1)(2.4) + (-1)(6.4)]^2/[1^2 + (-1^2)]}{1.6} = 25.00$$

Ocean view vs. ski slope view:

$$F = \frac{5[(1)(3.8) + (-1)(6.4)]^2/[1^2 + (-1^2)]}{1.6} = 10.56$$

The critical F ratio in the Tukey test is

$$F_T = \frac{q_T{}^2}{2} \qquad\qquad (4.15)$$

where q_T is the value from Table A.3. To enter Table A.3, you use df_{error} ($df_{S/A}$), a (the number of levels of the IV), and one of two choices for familywise α_{FW} (.05 or .01). The adjustment to critical F for controlling α_{FW} is built into the two-tailed tabled q_T value.

For the small-sample example, $df_{S/A} = 12$, $a = 3$, and α_{FW} is chosen to be .05. Table A.3 shows that $q_T = 3.77$. Therefore, $F_T = (3.77)^2/2 = 7.11$. Thus, the means for parking lot and ocean views do not differ reliably, but the remaining two pairs of means are significantly different. The critical value for the Tukey test (7.11) is smaller than the corresponding critical value for the Scheffé test (7.76), making the null hypothesis easier to reject because the Tukey procedure permits fewer comparisons.

A useful computational procedure for the Tukey test when there is a large number of means involves solving for the critical mean difference rather than critical F_T. All pairwise differences between means that are greater than this critical mean difference are statistically significant. The critical mean difference, $\bar{d}_T$ is defined as

$$\bar{d}_T = q_T\sqrt{\frac{MS_{S/A}}{n}} \qquad\qquad (4.16)$$

In this example, the critical mean difference is

$$\bar{d}_T = 3.77\sqrt{\frac{1.6}{5}} = 2.13$$

Thus, the difference between means for parking lot view and ocean view ($3.8 - 2.4 = 1.4$) is not statistically significant, but the other two mean differences exceed 2.13.

Tukey tests are available in MINITAB, SPSS ONEWAY and GLM, SAS ANOVA and GLM, and SYSTAT ANOVA and GLM. SPSS ONEWAY and GLM also have an alternative Tukey procedure (TUKEY-b) which has different critical values for means that are different rank distances apart.[14]

---

[14]Tukey-b is one of several "multiple range tests" available in software, as shown in Table 4.32.

SPSS and SAS GLM have numerous additional tests for pairwise comparisons, but some of these, like Scheffé, are far too conservative when applied to pairwise comparisons, and others, such as Student-Newman-Keuls, are often too liberal.

4.5.5.5.3 Pairwise Comparisons When Assumptions Are Violated

Tukey tests assume equal n and homogeneity of variance. There are two additional Dunnett tests (not to be confused with the Dunnett planned comparison test for comparing a control with each treatment) that modify the Tukey test to accommodate unequal n and heterogeneity of variance, as seen in Table 4.27. The first, Dunnett C, is more powerful when there are 75 or more error df. The other, Dunnett T3, is more powerful when sample sizes are smaller (Dunnett, 1980). Both of these are appropriate with either equal or unequal sample sizes. Both are available in SPSS GLM, but not in any of the other software packages reviewed. Both are discussed by Kirk (1995), who has a comprehensive coverage of multiple comparison tests.

When the assumption of homogeneity of variance is met, but there is unequal n, the Tukey-Kramer modification to the error MS of Equation 4.16, $\sqrt{MS_{S/A}/n}$, is applied separately for each comparison:

$$\sqrt{\left[MS_{S/A}\left(\frac{1}{n_i}+\frac{1}{n_j}\right)\right]\Big/2} \tag{4.17}$$

where n_i and n_j = sample sizes for the applicable pair of means.

All of the GLM programs (SPSS, SAS SYSTAT, and MINITAB) as well as SPSS ONEWAY apply the Tukey-Kramer modification for unequal sample sizes.

4.5.5.5.4 Summary of Some Critical Values for Comparisons

Table 4.28 summarizes the critical values for our example when $\alpha = .05$ (with $a = 3$ and $n = 5$) for the omnibus ANOVA, for orthogonal planned comparisons, for comparisons of a control with each treatment, and with two types of adjustments for post hoc analysis.

TABLE 4.28   Critical Values for Omnibus ANOVA and Comparisons with $a = 3$ and $n = 5$

Type of Test	Relevant Statistical Table	Maximum Number of Tests	Critical Value for Rejecting H_0 at $\alpha = .05$
Omnibus ANOVA	A.1	1	3.88
Planned comparisons	A.1	2	4.75
Dunnett test	A.4	2	6.25
Tukey test	A.3	3	7.11
Scheffé test	A.1	6	7.76

Table 4.28 shows the loss of power as more tests, and less restrictive ones, are permitted. Although the same number of tests is permitted for planned and Dunnett comparisons, the planned comparisons are more restrictive because they are orthogonal. Note that the difference in critical values between Tukey and Scheffé adjustments is small when $a = 3$, but grows as the number of levels of a increases. For example, with $a = 6$ and $n = 5$, the critical value for a Tukey test is $(4.37)^2/2 = 9.55$, but the critical value for a Scheffé test is $(5)(2.62) = 13.10$.

4.5.5.6 *Trend Analysis*

The functional relationship between the IV and the DV typically is of interest when the levels of the IV differ in amount rather than in type. That is, when differences in levels of the IV are *quantitative* rather than *qualitative,* one often wants to know how the DV changes as a function of the level of the IV. For instance, a qualitative IV is different types of view from a window, whereas a quantitative IV is the same view at different window sizes. If the IV is quantitative, one might ask, "Does rating of quality of the vacation increase with window size?" Or, is there an optimal size above which ratings decline? Or do ratings increase up to a point and then level off as window sizes become ever larger?

These questions are answered by a trend analysis (polynomial decomposition) using Table A.5. These weighting coefficients are used in Equation 4.10 just as are any other weighting coefficients. These weighting coefficients are orthogonal, and, if $a - 1$ of them are used, they completely analyze the variance in the DV associated with treatment. Further, their use may be planned or post hoc (for which a post hoc Scheffé adjustment to critical F is required). In other words, a trend analysis is just like planned orthogonal comparisons or post hoc comparisons with a Scheffé adjustment to critical F except that you look the coefficients up instead of making them up.

A trend analysis checks the *shape* of the relationship between the DV and the levels of the IV. The simplest shape is a linear trend where the means of the DV at various levels of the IV fall along a straight line. The line may have positive slope (where the means increase with increasing levels of the IV) or negative slope (where the means decrease with increasing levels of the IV). The closer the means come to falling along a line with nonzero slope, the higher the F value and the greater the chance of rejecting the null hypothesis of equality among the means.[15]

With more than two levels of the IV, higher-order trends become possible. In general, there are $a - 1$ possible trends, although not all of them may be of much interest. If there are four levels of the IV, there are three possible trends: linear, quadratic, and cubic. The shape that is investigated by each trend is seen by plotting the trend coefficients against successive means. Figure 4.3 plots the trend coefficients for the three possible trends when there are four levels of the IV. As can be seen, the shapes become increasingly esoteric as the number of levels of the IV increases. In many applications, only the linear and quadratic trends are interpretable.

Combinations of trends are possible because the coefficients are orthogonal, and each trend is independent of all others. It is rather common to find a combination of linear and quadratic trend, for instance, in the shape of the relationship of means of the DV at various levels of the IV. Figure 4.4 represents several different shapes that would all produce both significant linear and significant quadratic trend (if the error term is small enough).

---

[15]If there are only two levels of the IV, the only trend possible is linear ("two points determine a line") and omnibus ANOVA is also the test of linear trend.

(a) Linear trend
$(-3, -1, 1, 3)$

(b) Quadratic trend
$(1, -1, -1, 1)$

(c) Cubic trend
$(-1, 3, -3, 1)$

FIGURE 4.3   Shapes Represented by Linear, Quadratic, and Cubic Trend When $a = 4$

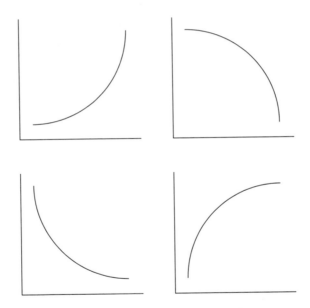

FIGURE 4.4   Shapes Represented by a Combination of Linear and Quadratic Trends

The interpretation of these various trends is different. If the only significant trend is linear, it means that over the range of sizes of the levels of the IV tested, the DV goes steadily up (or down). Quadratic trend usually implies that there is some optimal level of the IV where the DV scores are at their highest (or lowest). Combinations of linear and quadratic trend usually imply that the process grows (or declines) rapidly and then levels off, or that the process is level for a while before it rapidly grows (or declines). Interpretation of yet higher-order trends and combinations of them is left to the vivid imagination of the reader.

If the levels of the IV in the ski slope example are *size* of window of ski slope view (say, 250, 500, and 750 cm²) rather than type of view (parking lot, ocean, or ski slope), a trend analysis is

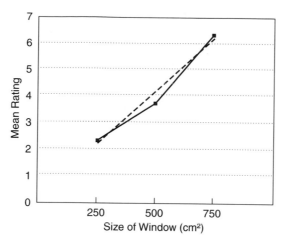

**FIGURE 4.5   Mean Rating of Ski Vacation as a
Function of Window Size**

appropriate. A plot of the means for the example appears in Figure 4.5. The means seem basically to fall in a straight line (represented by the dashed line), but not exactly along it. The coefficients for linear trend of the three means are $-1, 0, 1$ and $\sum w_i^2 = 2$.[16] Applying Equation 4.10 to the small-sample data with $MS_{S/A} = 1.6$ and $n = 5$:

$$F = \frac{5[(-1)(2.4) + (0)(3.8) + (1)(6.4)]^2/2}{1.6} = 25.00$$

At this point, we know that the rating of the vacation increases with the increasing view of the ski slope.

The quadratic trend tests whether two best-fit lines drawn through the means have significantly different slopes. Figure 4.5 shows that the slope from a_1 to a_2 is not identical to the slope from a_2 to a_3, but we do not know whether the difference is statistically reliable. Table A.5 provides the coefficients for quadratic trend, $1, -2, 1$, and $\sum w_i^2 = 6$. Applying Equation 4.10,

$$F = \frac{5[(1)(2.4) + (-2)(3.8) + (1)(6.4)]^2/6}{1.6} = 0.75$$

The linear trend is statistically significant by either a planned or post hoc criterion. The quadratic trend is reliable by neither criterion. Therefore, we conclude that rating of the vacation increases linearly with increasing size of ski slope view.

SPSS ONEWAY (as demonstrated in Section 4.7.2) and SYSTAT ANOVA/GLM have special syntax to produce a trend analysis, but SYSTAT requires a separate run for each trend (demonstrated in Section 4.7.2). SAS GLM requires specification of the coefficients of Table A.5.

---

[16]Yes, these are the same coefficients used to test the mean of the first vs. the mean of the last level of the IV. If means for these levels are significantly different, the best-fit line drawn through the three means is not horizontal, so its slope is not zero. The value of the middle mean does not matter.

MINITAB GLM (or any other GLM or regression program) can do linear and quadratic trend analysis by adding the coefficients for each trend of interest to the data set and then doing multiple regression, as per Tables 4.25 and 4.26.

The coefficients in Table A.5 assume that the levels of the IV increase or decrease in equal increments, say, from 250 to 500 to 750 cm^2, and that sample sizes are equal in all levels of the IV. Otherwise, coefficients must be devised to reflect the inequality of spacing among levels of the IV and/or inequality in sample sizes. Derivation of coefficients for unequally spaced IVs is difficult by hand,[17] but some canned programs provide for them by allowing you to enter an integer for each level of the IV (say, 200, 250, and 325 cm^2) when levels are unequally spaced, and by dealing with unequal sample sizes (see Section 4.6). Programs that allow unequal spacing for randomized-groups designs are SPSS GLM and SYSTAT ANOVA. SAS GLM provides for unequal spacing only for repeated-measures IVs. Section 4.7.2 shows a planned trend analysis (with unequal sample sizes and equal spacing) through SPSS ONEWAY. Trend analysis with unequal spacing is demonstrated in Section 11.6.3.

4.5.5.7   Effect Sizes for Comparisons

Section 4.5.1 describes estimation of effect sizes for the omnibus test of the IV. What is the proportion of variability in the DV associated with differences in levels of A? Effect sizes for comparisons may be regarded in two ways. What proportion of the variability in the DV is associated with the comparison? Or what is the proportion of variability in the main effect of A that is associated with the comparison? The numerator in both types of comparisons is the same—the variability associated with the comparison. The denominator reflects the base against which you are evaluating the comparison—either the entire variability of the DV or the variability associated with the omnibus main effect.

Consider the comparison of ski slope view with the average of parking lot and ocean views of Section 4.5.5.3. The SS for the comparison is 36.3. Tables 4.6 and 4.13 show that $SS_T = 60.4$, $SS_A = 41.2$, and $SS_{S/A} = 19.2$.

A variant of Equation 4.3 is used to evaluate the comparison relative to total variability:

$$\eta^2 = \frac{SS_{A\,comp}}{SS_T} = \frac{36.3}{60.4} = .60 \tag{4.18}$$

This indicates that 60% of the variance in ratings of a ski vacation is associated with the difference between a ski slope view and the other views.

A different denominator is used to evaluate the variability in the comparison relative to the variability in the main effect of A,

$$\eta^2 = \frac{SS_{A\,comp}}{SS_A} = \frac{36.3}{41.2} = .88 \tag{4.19}$$

This indicates that 88% of the difference due to views (levels of A) is in the ski slope view versus the other two views.

---

[17]See Myers (1979) for an approach to deriving coefficients with unequal spacing between levels of the IV.

4.6   Complete Example of One-Way ANOVA

The experiment analyzed here studied the number of facets in the eyes of each fly hatched in one of nine incubators that varied in temperature. This grand old classic study (Hersh, 1924) is described more fully in Appendix B. Data files are FLY.*.

The nine incubator temperatures varied from 15 to 31°C in increments of 2°C. The number of facets was reported in units on a logarithmic scale. The strategy here is a planned trend analysis to evaluate the number of facets as a function of increasing temperature.

4.6.1   Evaluation of Assumptions

4.6.1.1   Accuracy of Input, Independence of Errors, Sample Sizes, and Distributions.

Table 4.29 shows syntax and output for a SYSTAT GRAPHS run on the DV, `facets`, followed by a SYSTAT STATS run. The output is requested to be shown separately for each level of the IV in the `BY temp` instruction. Histograms with a normal curve superimposed are requested in the graphs run by specifying two `DENSITY` functions overlaid, the first a histogram and the second a `NORMAL` curve with blank `AXES` and labels. Statistics requested include `N` (the sample size), the `Mean`, `Minimum`, `Maximum`, `SD` (standard deviation), `Variance`, `Kurtosis`, `SEK` (standard error of kurtosis), `Skewness`, and `SES` (standard error of skewness).

Output reproduced in Table 4.29 is merged over the STATS and DENSITY runs for ease of interpretation. Sample sizes are unequal, ranging from 54 (for both 17 and 31°C) to 137 (for 27°C). The raw score distributions vary over the nine groups as well, but normality of sampling distributions is assured by the very large number of df available with 9 groups and 823 observations: $df_{S/A} = N - a = 823 - 9 = 814$. Only 6 of the 9 groups are shown in Table 4.29.

Negative values for the DV in some of the groups look suspicious until one realizes that the measurement of number of facets has been subjected to a logarithmic transformation. A constant added to each value before transformation would have avoided this anomaly.

Independence of errors is questionable because flies within a single incubator were not hatched individually. Evidence is needed that there were no systematic differences among incubators other than temperature, and that environments within incubators differed only in temperature.

4.6.1.2   Outliers

Table 4.29 in its full form provides means, standard deviations, minima, and maxima for each group necessary to identify outliers through standard scores (z scores) within each group. Standard scores for the minimum and maximum values are calculated within each group, and if the absolute value of one of them exceeds $|z| > 3.3$, the case with the maximum (or minimum score) is an outlier. Attention then turns to the case with the next highest (or lowest) score.

The first group has no outliers. Standard scores for the minimum and maximum values are $z = (1.07 - 4.548)/1.56 = -2.23$ and $z = (8.07 - 4.548)/1.56 = 2.26$, respectively. The first possible outlier encountered is in the 21°C group, with $z = (7.07 - 0.32)/1.898 = 3.56$ for the maximum score. Note, however, that the histogram in Table 4.29 shows this score is not notably disconnected from the remaining scores given the scale of the plot (cf. Section 3.4.4). Another possible outlier is the case with the minimum score in the 25°C group, with $z = -4.48$. This score, however, indeed is

TABLE 4.29 Descriptive Statistics and Histograms Through SYSTAT STATS and Density for Fly Data: Syntax and Partial Output

```
BY TEMP
BEGIN
  DENSITY facets / FILL = 0
  DENSITY facets / NORMAL AXES=NONE SCALE=NONE XLAB=' ' YLAB= ' '
END
STATS
STATS FACETS / Kurtosis Maximum Mean Minimum SD SEK SES Skewness Variance N
```

The following results are for: TEMP = 15.000

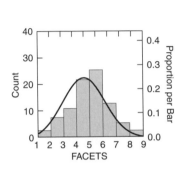

	FACETS
N of cases	90
Minimum	1.070
Maximum	8.070
Mean	4.548
Standard Dev	1.560
Variance	2.432
Skewness(G1)	−0.040
SE Skewness	0.254
Kurtosis(G2)	−0.062
SE Kurtosis	0.503

The following results are for: TEMP = 17.000

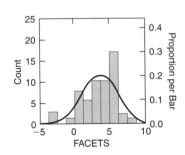

	FACETS
N of cases	54
Minimum	−2.930
Maximum	8.070
Mean	3.514
Standard Dev	2.345
Variance	5.497
Skewness(G1)	−0.735
SE Skewness	0.325
Kurtosis(G2)	0.689
SE Kurtosis	0.639

The following results are for: TEMP = 21.000

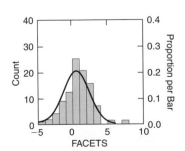

	FACETS
N of cases	100
Minimum	−4.930
Maximum	7.070
Mean	0.320
Standard Dev	1.898
Variance	3.604
Skewness(G1)	0.057
SE Skewness	0.241
Kurtosis(G2)	1.300
SE Kurtosis	0.478

TABLE 4.29   Continued

The following results are for: TEMP   =   25.000

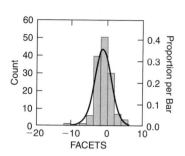

	FACETS
N of cases	122
Minimum	−11.930
Maximum	4.070
Mean	−1.627
Standard Dev	2.299
Variance	5.287
Skewness(G1)	−0.582
SE Skewness	0.219
Kurtosis(G2)	2.870
SE Kurtosis	0.435

The following results are for: TEMP   =   27.000

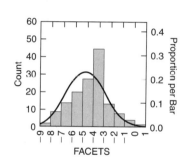

	FACETS
N of cases	137
Minimum	−8.930
Maximum	0.070
Mean	−4.623
Standard Dev	1.722
Variance	2.964
Skewness(G1)	−0.188
SE Skewness	0.207
Kurtosis(G2)	0.089
SE Kurtosis	0.411

The following results are for: TEMP   =   31.000

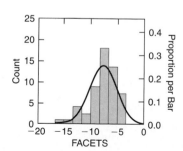

	FACETS
N of cases	54
Minimum	−15.930
Maximum	−3.930
Mean	−7.819
Standard Dev	2.575
Variance	6.629
Skewness(G1)	−1.120
SE Skewness	0.325
Kurtosis(G2)	1.031
SE Kurtosis	0.639

disconnected from the remaining scores. The next lowest score is not an outlier. Thus, the case with the minimum score in the sixth group is considered an outlier in the data set. Variability noted in temperature measurement over time and within incubators (this was 1924, after all) suggests that this extreme case may have had a different actual hatching temperature, indicating that the case may be deleted. Also, sample sizes in all groups are large enough that there is no problem in deleting this case from subsequent analyses, leaving a total $N = 822$.

TABLE 4.30   Planned Trend Analysis for One-Way Randomized-Groups Design: SYSTAT Syntax and Selected Output

```
BY
IF (TEMP=25) AND (FACETS=<-11) THEN LET FACETS=.
ANOVA
CATEGORY TEMP
COVAR
DEPEND FACETS
ESTIMATE
HYPOTHESIS
EFFECT=temp
NOTE 'LINEAR TREND'
CONTRAST/POLYNOMIAL ORDER=1
TEST
HYPOTHESIS
EFFECT=temp
NOTE 'QUADRATIC TREND'
CONTRAST /POLYNOMIAL ORDER=2
TEST
```

.
.
.

```
HYPOTHESIS
EFFECT=temp
NOTE '8th ORDER TREND'
CONTRAST /POLYNOMIAL ORDER=8
TEST
```

Effects coding used for categorical variables in model.

Categorical values encountered during processing are:
TEMP (9 levels)

15,	17,	19,	21,	23,	25,	27,
29,	31					

1 case(s) deleted due to missing data.

Dep Var: FACETS   N: 822   Multiple R: 0.877   Squared multiple R: 0.769

TABLE 4.30   Continued

Analysis of Variance

Source	Sum-of-Squares	df	Mean-Square	F-ratio	P
TEMP	12383.033	8	1547.879	339.084	0.000
Error	3711.254	813	4.565		

Least squares means.

		LS Mean	SE	N
TEMP	=15	4.548	0.225	90
TEMP	=17	3.514	0.291	54
TEMP	=19	2.492	0.235	83
TEMP	=21	0.320	0.214	100
TEMP	=23	-2.430	0.230	86
TEMP	=25	-1.542	0.194	121
TEMP	=27	-4.623	0.183	137
TEMP	=29	-6.590	0.217	97
TEMP	=31	-7.819	0.291	54

LINEAR TREND

Test for effect called: TEMP

Test of Hypothesis

Source	SS	df	MS	F	P
Hypothesis	11084.807	1	11084.807	2428.276	0.000
Error	3711.254	813	4.565		

QUADRATIC TREND

Test for effect called: TEMP

Test of Hypothesis

Source	SS	df	MS	F	P
Hypothesis	19.904	1	19.904	4.360	0.037
Error	3711.254	813	4.565		

8TH ORDER TREND

Test for effect called: TEMP

Test of Hypothesis

Source	SS	df	MS	F	P
Hypothesis	149.385	1	149.385	32.375	0.000
Error	3711.254	813	4.565		

4.6.1.3   *Homogeneity of Variance*

Variances are shown in Table 4.29. The smallest variance is in the group of flies hatched at the lowest temperature, Variance $= 2.432$, and the largest variance is in the group hatched at the highest temperature, Variance $= 6.629$. The resulting $F_{max} = 6.629/2.432 = 2.73$ (less than 10) poses no threat to homogeneity of variance, especially with a discrepancy in sample sizes no greater than about 2.5:1.

4.6.2   Planned Trend Analysis for One-Way Randomized-Groups Design

SYSTAT ANOVA is selected for the planned analysis, as shown in Table 4.30. The BY instruction turns off the processing by groups useful for Table 4.30. The IF instruction deletes the outlier from group 6. The model first is ESTIMATEd by declaring the IV (CATEGORY) to be TEMP and the DV (DEPEND) to be FACETS. Then each ORDER of the POLYNOMIAL (i.e., trend) is requested in a separate HYPOTHESIS run. The NOTEs label each of the trends to make the output more readable.

The output shows the omnibus Analysis of Variance, which we will ignore because we have planned a trend analysis instead of the omnibus ANOVA. This is followed by LS Means, standard errors (SE), and sample size for each group. SYSTAT ANOVA (as well as GLM) does specific comparisons on unweighted means when sample sizes are unequal. The unweighted analysis adjusts all trends for each other. Type I error rate for each of the five trends to be evaluated is set at .01, producing a familywise error rate of about .08 (cf. Section 4.5.5.4.3). Each source table lists Hypothesis as the label for the trend and a common Error (S/A) term for testing each effect.

The results show a strong LINEAR TREND, $F(1,813) = 2428.28$. Strength of association between the transformed number of facets and the linear trend of temperature is remarkably large for an experiment, $\eta^2 = 11084.81/16094.28 = .69$ (Equation 4.18, with SS_T found as the sum of the two sources of variance in the omnibus ANOVA table). Four of the other trends also are statistically significant at $\alpha = .01$ but account for little variance in the number of facets. The QUINTIC TREND (5th-order, not shown) is reliable, $F(1, 813) = 10.33$, $\eta^2 = .01$. The 6th ORDER TREND (not shown) also is statistically reliable, $F(1, 813) = 15.10$, $\eta^2 = .02$, as well as the 7th ORDER TREND (not shown), $F(1, 813) = 16.60$, $\eta^2 = .02$, and the 8th ORDER TREND, $F(1, 813) = 32.73$, $\eta^2 = .04$.

The significant but small deviations from linear trend in this analysis may have resulted from the nature of the manipulation. The recorded temperature for each incubator was the nominal value, with variation of as much as 1°C above or below that nominal value. Variation occurred with time and was not constant throughout a single incubator. Thus, small deviations in trend should not preclude an interpretation of an overall linear trend of decrease in number of facets with increasing temperature.

The standard error of the mean is calculated by

$$SE_M = \sqrt{\frac{MS_{Error}}{df_{Error}}} = 0.075$$

(see Equation 2.6 for the basic formula for calculating the standard error of the mean). Recall that a 95% confidence interval may be built as two standard errors above and below each mean.

Figure 4.6 plots the means and standard errors for the nine groups, illustrating the strong linear trend, as produced by SYSTAT. This is a modified version of the graph produced by the syntax of Table 4.29.

Table 4.31 is a checklist for one-way randomized-groups ANOVA. An example of a Results section, in journal format, follows for the study just described.

```
LINE FACETS*TEMP / SERROR XLABEL='Temperature (C)' YLABEL='MEAN FACETS' ,
YMIN=-16 YMAX=9 YTICK=8 DASH=1, 11, 7
```

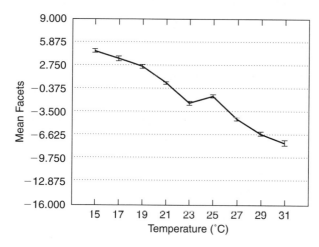

FIGURE 4.6   Mean Number of Facets (and Standard Errors) as a Function of Incubator Temperature: SYSTAT GRAPH Syntax and Output

TABLE 4.31   Checklist for One-Way Randomized-Groups ANOVA

1. Issues
   a. Independence of errors
   b. Unequal sample sizes
   c. Normality of sampling distributions
   d. Outliers
   e. Homogeneity of variance
2. Major analyses: planned comparisons or omnibus F, if significant:
   a. Effect size
   b. Parameter estimates (means and standard deviations or standard errors or confidence intervals for each group)
3. Additional analyses
   a. Post hoc comparisons
   b. Discussion of departure from homogeneity of variance, if appropriate

Results

A planned trend analysis for a one-way randomized-groups design was performed on a transformed value of the number of facets in eyes of newly hatched Drosophila melanogaster Meig heterozygotes. Flies were hatched in nine incubators varying in temperature from 15°C to 31°C in increments of 2°C. Numbers of facets were transformed into units that make the measurement scale essentially logarithmic.

Total N of 823 was reduced to 822 with the deletion of an outlier. One fly from the 23°C incubator had an unusually small number of facets (z = −4.48). The assumption of homogeneity of variance was met, with sample sizes ranging from 54 to 137.

The planned trend analysis at α = .01 for each comparison showed a strong negative linear trend of incubator temperature, F(1, 812) = 2428.28, p < .05, η^2 = .69, SE_M = 0.075. Figure 4.6 shows mean(transformed) number of facets as a function of temperature, with standard errors.

There also were significant, but small (each η^2 < .05), higher-order trends as well. The 5th-, 6th-, 7th- and 8th-order trends met a criterion of p < .02, F(1, 813) = 10.33, 15.10, 16.60, and 32.73, respectively.

Deviations from the negative linear trend may be explained at least in part by the inexact nature of the manipulation of temperature. Groups were classified by nominal incubator temperature, which varied over time and within each incubator by as much as 1°C above or below the nominal value. Thus, small deviations in trend should not preclude an interpretation of an overall decrease in the logarithm of the number of facets with increasing temperature.

4.7 Comparison of Programs

Each of the four major packages has a number of programs for ANOVA, almost all of which may be used for one-way randomized-groups ANOVA. Table 4.32 reviews one program from each package, typically the simplest one to use for this design. Subsequent chapters review the other programs.

TABLE 4.32   Comparison of SPSS, SYSTAT, MINITAB, and SAS Programs for One-Way Randomized-Groups ANOVA

Feature	SPSS ONEWAY	MINITAB ONEWAY	SAS GLM[a]	SYSTAT ANOVA and GLM[a]
Input				
Specify sample-size estimate for post hoc comparisons	Harmonic	No	No	No
Specify α level for post hoc comparisons	Yes	Yes	ALPHA	No[b]
Special specification for trend (polynomial) analysis	Polynomial	No[c]	No	Polynomial
Separate-variance tests for comparisons	Yes	No	No	Separate
Specify error terms for comparisons	No	No	Yes	Yes
Output				
ANOVA table	Yes	Yes	Yes	Yes
Means for each group	Yes	Yes	Yes	LS mean
Standard deviations for each group	Yes	Yes	Yes	No
Standard error for each group	Yes	No	Yes	No
Pooled within-group standard error	No	No	Std Err LSMEANS	Yes
Pooled within-group standard deviation	No	Yes	No	No
Minimum and maximum values, each group	Yes	No	No	No
Descriptive statistics for all groups combined	Yes	No	No	No

(Continued)

TABLE 4.32 Continued

Feature	SPSS ONEWAY	MINITAB ONEWAY	SAS GLM[a]	SYSTAT ANOVA and GLM[a]
Confidence intervals for each mean	Yes	No	CLM	No
Error coefficient of variation	No	No	Yes	No
Levene's test for homogeneity of variance	Yes	No	No	No
R^2 (η^2)	No	No	R-Square	Squared multiple R
User-specified comparisons	Yes	No	Yes	Yes
Tukey HSD test for pairwise differences	TUKEY	Yes	TUKEY	TUKEY[d]
Tukey-B multiple-range test for pairwise differences	BTUKEY	No	NO	No
Dunnett test for control vs. treatment	DUNNETT	Yes	DUNNETT	DUNNETT[c]
Scheffé test (for pairwise differences only)	SCHEFFE	No	SCHEFFE	SCHEFFE[c]
LSD/Fisher (pairwise t-tests)	LSD	No	LSD	Yes
Bonferroni tests for pairwise differences	BONFERRONI	Yes	BON	BONF[d]
Bonferroni correction for control vs. treatment	No	Yes	No	No
Duncan test for pairwise differences	DUNCAN	No	DUNCAN	No
Student-Newman-Keuls test for pairwise differences	SNK	No	SNK	No
Dunnett C and T3 tests for pairwise differences with heterogeneity of variance	C, T3	No	No	No
Gabriel test for pairwise differences	GABRIEL	No	GABRIEL	No
Ryan-Eniot-Gabriel-Welch F stepdown procedure for multiple comparisons	FREGW	No	REGWF	No

TABLE 4.32   Continued

Feature	SPSS ONEWAY	MINITAB ONEWAY	SAS GLM[a]	SYSTAT ANOVA and GLM[a]
Ryan-Eniot-Gabriel-Welch Range stepdown procedure for multiple comparisons	QREGW	No	REGWQ	No
Hochberg multiple comparison and range test	GT2	No	GT2	No
Waller-Duncan multiple comparison test	WALLER	No	WALLER	No
Tamahane pairwise comparisons for unequal n	T2	No	No	No
Games-Howell pairwise comparisons for unequal n	GH	No	No	No
Sidak tests for pairwise differences	SIDAK	Yes	SIDAK	No
Sidak correction for control vs. treatment	No	Yes	No	No
Confidence limits for pairwise differences	Yes	Yes	CLDIFF	No
Probability values for pairwise differences	Yes	No	PDIFF	Yes
Confidence limits for predicted values for each case	No	No	Yes	No
Outliers (studentized residual criterion)	No	No	P	Yes
Durbin-Watson statistic	No	No	P	Yes
Plots				
Means for each group	Yes	No	No	Yes
Standard errors shown on plot of means	No	No	No	Yes
Confidence interval for each group	No	Yes	No	No
Histogram of residuals	No	Yes	No	No
Normal probability plot of residuals	No	Yes	No	No

(Continued)

TABLE 4.32   Continued

Feature	SPSS ONEWAY	MINITAB ONEWAY	SAS GLM[a]	SYSTAT ANOVA and GLM[a]
Residuals vs. predicted (fitted) values	No	Yes	No	No
Residuals vs. sequence of data	No	Yes	No	No
Residuals vs. any variable	No	Yes	No	No
Saved to file				
Residuals	No	Yes	Yes	Yes
Predicted (fitted, adjusted) values, i.e., mean for each case	No	Yes	Yes	Yes
Additional statistics, including those for outliers	No	No	Yes	Yes
Means, standard deviations and frequencies	Yes	No	Yes	No

[a]Additional features reviewed in subsequent chapters.

[b]Probability values provided for comparisons.

[c]Linear and quadratic trends are done through GLM.

[d]GLM only.

4.7.1   SPSS Package

SPSS has several programs for ANOVA: ONEWAY, and a group of GLM (general linear model) programs.[18] Table 4.32 reviews ONEWAY, devoted solely to one-way randomized-groups ANOVA and the easiest of the SPSS analysis of variance programs to use. ONEWAY is accessed in Windows through the Statistics menu, Compare Means submenu, and then a choice of One-way ANOVA.

ONEWAY provides a comprehensive set of descriptive statistics, including the 95% confidence interval for the mean for each of the groups. Levene's test for homogeneity of variance is available along with separate-variance (as differentiated from pooled-variance) tests for comparisons if homogeneity of variance is violated. A wide variety of post hoc comparison procedures are available. Among programs reviewed in Table 4.32, ONEWAY is the only one with a provision for handling unequal n by specifying equal weighting[19] of sample sizes for post hoc comparisons (the harmonic mean). Trend analysis is easily specified.

---

[18]SPSS GLM replaces MANOVA. The earlier program is available in syntax.

[19]These weights are different from the coefficients used to form specific comparisons.

4.7.2   SAS System

SAS has two programs for ANOVA: GLM and ANOVA. The ANOVA program runs faster and uses less storage but is limited to equal sample sizes in each group. The one-way omnibus test is accurate in both programs, but ANOVA may produce inaccurate results for comparisons. Therefore, only GLM is reviewed in Table 4.32 and in subsequent chapters.

PROC GLM produces two source tables for omnibus ANOVA: one table (designated the model source of variance) that reports a test of all effects combined and another table that reports a test of each effect separately. These tables provide redundant information in one-way omnibus ANOVA when there is only one effect. Several descriptive statistics are available by request.

This program has a large number of post hoc comparison procedures and provides confidence intervals for differences among means for some of them on request. A measure of effect size, η^2 (labeled `R-Square`), is provided for the omnibus ANOVA.

The program provides an indication of outliers through the studentized residual criterion and also evaluates autocorrelation of cases through the Durbin-Watson statistic. Autocorrelation causes difficulty only if order of cases is related to treatments, which should not occur when treatments are randomly assigned. Although GLM and ANOVA produce no plots, any of the values saved to file may be plotted through the PROC PLOT.

4.7.3   SYSTAT System

SYSTAT ANOVA is a subset of GLM for analysis of variance with a different setup but largely the same output. The few features that are different are noted in Table 4.32.

SYSTAT ANOVA/GLM provides the mean for each group accompanied by a pooled standard error of the mean, as long as the option chosen for output length using ANOVA is PRINT= MEDIUM or PRINT=LONG. The standard error of the mean differs among groups only if sample sizes are unequal. Additional descriptive statistics are requested through the STATS program. An effect size measure, η^2 (labeled `Squared Multiple R`), is reported for the omnibus analysis. Outliers (identified by the studentized residual criterion) are highlighted and the Durbin-Watson autocorrelation statistic is given in the event that the order of cases is not random. Four of the most popular post hoc comparison procedures are available. Separate-variance tests are available for specific comparisons but not for post hoc procedures.

4.7.4   MINITAB Programs

MINITAB has a number of programs for ANOVA. One of them, AOVONEWAY—labeled One-way (Unstacked) in the Windows menu—even can do a one-way ANOVA with responses from each group in a separate column. GLM can be used for one-way ANOVA as well. Additional programs are discussed in subsequent chapters.

ONEWAY has several post hoc pairwise comparison procedures and offers alternatives to Dunnett's adjustment for testing each treatment against a control group. Although there is no provision for trend analysis or user-specified contrasts, these may be done through GLM by adding coefficient columns to the data set, as shown in Tables 4.25 and 4.26. ONEWAY provides a useful plot of confidence intervals for each mean, and is rich in various types of residuals plots. Residuals and fitted (predicted) values may be saved. Features of GLM are demonstrated in subsequent chapters.

4.8   Problem Sets

4.1   Do an analysis of variance on the following data set. Assume the IV is minutes of presoaking a dirty garment and the DV is rating of cleanliness.

	Presoak Time		
a_1 5 min	a_2 10 min	a_3 15 min	a_4 20 min
2	3	8	6
6	9	11	7
6	9	9	9
6	5	9	6
5	7	6	9
3	5	12	9

a. Test for homogeneity of variance.
b. Provide a source table.
c. Check results by running the data set through at least one canned computer program.
d. Calculate effect size.
e. Write a results section for the analysis.
f. Do a trend analysis with an appropriate post hoc adjustment.

4.2   Do an analysis of variance on the following pilot data set.

a_1	a_2	a_3	a_4	a_5
6	5	5	6	6
5	6	5	5	7
5	6	7	9	7
	7	5	7	6
	6		7	
			6	

a. Provide a source table.
b. Check results by running the data set through at least one canned computer program.
c. How many cases would need to be run to get a statistically significant main effect at $\alpha = .05$ and $\beta = .20$? Use a canned program if available; otherwise, assume that the minimum difference you are seeking is between a_1 and a_5.

4.3   Do an analysis of variance for the following, with $n = 10$. (Recall that $MS_{S/A}$ is the average of the group variances when sample sizes are equal.)

	a_1	a_2	a_3
Mean	20	22	28
Variance	42	46	43

a. Provide a source table.
b. Calculate effect size.
c. Do a Tukey test at $\alpha = .05$.
d. Do a post hoc test of a_3 vs. the other two groups.

4.4 Suppose a researcher is interested in the effects of hours of sleep on performance on a statistics exam. Students are randomly assigned to get 2, 4, 6, or 8 hours of sleep prior to the exam. The DV is exam score. Assume that a_1 is 2 hours of sleep, a_2 is 4 hours of sleep, and so on. Write the coefficients you would need to answer the following questions.

a. Is there a linear trend of exam scores for hours of sleep?
b. Do students who sleep 8 hours do better than those who sleep less?
c. Is there a difference in average performance between those who sleep 2 hours and those who sleep 4 hours?
d. Do students who sleep 2 or 4 hours do worse than those who sleep 6 or 8 hours?
e. Write an orthogonal set of coefficients that makes the most sense to you given the meaning of the levels of the IV.

4.5 Assume that a researcher runs a drug study for three analgesics against two types of control groups. There are five groups in all (a_1 to a_5, respectively): a waiting list control group, a placebo control group, a group that receives the old analgesic, and two other groups, each assigned to one of the two new analgesics. The DV is pain relief. Write the coefficients you need to answer each of the following questions.

a. Do the two types of control groups produce different levels of pain relief?
b. Are the combined control groups different from the combined analgesic groups?
c. Does the old analgesic differ from the combination of newer analgesics?
d. Do the two newer analgesics differ from each other?
e. Is the response of the first of the new analgesics (a_4) different from the placebo group?
f. Is the response of the second of the new analgesics different from the placebo group?

5 Factorial Randomized-Groups, Fixed-Effects Designs

5.1 General Purpose and Description

This design is a generalization of the one-way, randomized-groups design to a study in which there is more than one IV. For example, the first IV in a two-way design might be type of on-the-job personnel training, with three levels such as a no-training control group, a text-based training program, and a video-based training program. A second IV might be job classification, with two levels such as clerical personnel and security personnel. The DV might be supervisor's overall job performance rating. This example could also be referred to as a 3×2 factorial design because there are two IVs, one with 3 levels, and the other with 2 levels. A factorial design with three IVs, with 3, 2, and 4 levels, respectively, is called a $3 \times 2 \times 4$ design; the order in which IVs are listed is arbitrary.

The omnibus ANOVA for this design develops separate statistical tests for each of the IVs and their interaction. For type of on-the-job training, potential mean differences between the video-based training program, the text-based program, and the no-training program are examined. For job classification, the potential mean difference between those trained for clerical and for security jobs is examined. The interaction of type of training and job classification examines potential differences in the *pattern* of response of clerical and security personnel to the different types of on-the-job training. For example, security personnel might respond more favorably to the video-based program, whereas clerical personnel respond equally to both types of training. Interpretation of interactions is discussed in detail in Section 5.6.1.

The minimum number of IVs for a factorial design is 2. A design is factorial when there are two or more IVs and all levels of one IV are used in combination with all levels of the others. The example is factorial because both security and clerical trainees receive no training, text-based training, and video-based training. If, say, security personnel never receive text-based training, the design is not fully factorial. This is a randomized-groups design because different security and clerical trainees are randomly assigned to each of the three levels of training.

In general, the distinguishing characteristics of a completely randomized, fixed-effects design are that (1) different cases are randomly assigned to each *combination* of levels of the IVs, (2) each research unit is measured once, and (3) all of the levels of all of the IVs are fixed (deliberately chosen by the researcher and not randomly chosen from among a range of levels). Such designs are usually also factorial (fully crossed) because cases receive all possible combinations of levels of the IVs.

Exceptions to the latter are the dangling group design discussed in Section 5.5.2 and the incomplete designs of Chapters 9 and 10.

There may be any number of IVs with any number of levels each. However, fully crossed randomized-groups designs become unwieldy when there are many IVs and/or many levels for each IV. The number of combinations of levels of IVs is a product of the levels of each. For instance, if there are three IVs (a three-way design), the first with three, the second with four, and the third with two levels, there are $3 \times 4 \times 2 = 24$ combinations to present. Running a study of this size can become a logistical nightmare and the number of cases required can become excessive. For example, 120 cases are needed if five cases are randomly assigned to each of the combinations of levels.

A factorial randomized-groups design is an experiment if at least one of the IVs is manipulated, with random assignment to its levels. In the two-way example, type of training is an experimental IV and job classification is nonexperimental. The omnibus ANOVA is also appropriate for nonexperimental and quasi-experimental designs, but interpretation of results is limited to those appropriate for nonexperimental designs.

5.2   Kinds of Research Questions

5.2.1   Main Effects of the IVs

Averaging across all combinations of levels of all other IVs, are there reliable mean differences among the levels of this IV? That is, when the effects of all other IVs are held constant by averaging across their effects, do the means at different levels of this IV differ by more than would be expected by chance? For example, is there a mean difference in job performance rating depending on the training group to which an employee is assigned? Is there a mean difference in job performance ratings between clerical and security personnel?

These questions are answered by applying separate F tests to each IV, as demonstrated in Section 5.4. Procedures discussed in Section 1.1.2 are used to "hold constant" all other effects in an experimental design.

5.2.2   Effects of Interactions among IVs

Holding the effects of other IVs constant, does the pattern of means for one IV change at different levels of another IV? For example, does the pattern of differences in means among training programs depend on whether clerical or security personnel are being trained? This is called the training program by job classification interaction.

F tests are conducted separately for each interaction (if there is more than one) and, except for the use of a common error term, are independent of tests of main effects of individual IVs if there are equal numbers of cases at all combinations of levels and the design is fully crossed. There is an interaction for each combination of IVs, so if there are three IVs (A, B, and C), there is an $A \times B$ interaction, an $A \times C$ interaction, a $B \times C$ interaction, and an $A \times B \times C$ interaction. The greater the number of IVs, the greater the number of interactions generated. If, for example, age of trainee is added to the training program and job classification IVs, there are two additional two-way interactions (training program by age group and job classification by age group) and the three-way interaction (training program by job classification by age group). The three-way interaction asks if the difference in effectiveness of training programs for clerical versus security employees depends on their age group. Two-way and higher-order interactions are discussed more fully in Section 5.6.1.

5.2.3 Specific Comparisons

If a difference in means among more than two groups is found, what is the source of the difference? For example, is the text-based training program more effective than no training at all? Is the video-based program better than the text-based program? Is the average performance of trained employees better than that of employees without on-the-job training? Is there a difference between text- and video-based programs for clerical employees? These questions may be answered by applying one of a wide variety of post hoc comparison procedures, some of which are discussed in Section 5.6.4.

Alternatively, some of these specific questions may be answered by conducting a planned set of comparisons instead of testing omnibus main effects and interactions. The advantage of doing so is greater power for these tests when planned than when hypotheses are posed after omnibus differences are observed. Planned comparisons also are discussed in Section 5.6.4.

5.2.4 Parameter Estimates

What population means are expected given a particular treatment or combination of treatments? What job performance rating would we expect for a clerical worker who participated in a video-based training program? Parameter estimates reported in factorial designs (as well as one-way designs) are means, standard deviations, standard errors, and/or confidence intervals for the mean.

Parameter estimates for main effects are marginal means,[1] the mean of each level of the IV averaged over all the levels of the other IV(s). When sample sizes are not the same for all cells, there are different ways to average over the other IVs. Section 5.6.5 discusses this and other complications of studies with unequal sample sizes. Marginal means most often appear in narrative format in a results section, but may be presented in tabular or graphic format, particularly if the IV has many levels and/or those levels represent some underlying quantitative dimension such as amount of treatment.

Parameter estimates for interactions are cell means, also either reported in narrative format, shown in a table, or plotted in a graph. Graphs typically are used with a statistically reliable interaction. Frequently these are line graphs,[2] as shown in the examples in Section 5.6.1.

5.2.5 Effect Sizes

As for one-way ANOVA, effect sizes typically are reported in terms of proportion of variance in the DV that is associated with a main effect or interaction. Effect sizes are usually reported for all statistically reliable effects. Section 5.6.2 demonstrates calculation of effect sizes.

---

[1] And sometimes also standard deviations or standard errors.

[2] Bar graphs are technically more correct when the levels of the IV are qualitatively different, but sometimes are more difficult to interpret.

5.2.6 Power

How high is the probability of showing main effects and interactions if, indeed, IV(s) have effects? For example, what is the probability of finding a difference in performance rating among groups given different training types if the difference actually exists? What is the probability of finding a difference between clerical and security workers? What is the probability of finding that the pattern of performance ratings among training types is different for clerical and security workers?

Estimates of power made prior to running a study are used to help determine sample size, as for a one-way design. Estimates of power made after completing a study help determine why research hypotheses were not supported. Power is discussed in Section 5.6.3.

5.3 Assumptions and Limitations

5.3.1 Theoretical Issues

Theoretical issues in a factorial design are identical to those in a one-way design. Thus, issues of causal inference and generalizability are of the same concern in factorial designs.

5.3.2 Practical Issues

Whether one-way or factorial, the ANOVA model assumes normality of sampling distributions, homogeneity of variance, independence of errors, and absence of outliers. Unequal sample sizes pose additional problems for factorial ANOVA and are discussed in Section 5.6.5.

5.3.2.1 Normality of Sampling Distributions

Issues of normality of sampling distributions apply to data in the *cells* (combinations of levels of IVs) of a factorial design, where n is the sample size of each cell. However, the criteria are the same as for a one-way design (Section 3.4.1). Similarly, solutions for questionable normality are the same as for a one-way design, except that fewer nonparametric tests are available. If a test of differences between medians is desired, a generalization of the χ^2 test of independence is available where each IV is a factor and the DV from ANOVA becomes an additional factor when it is transformed into a categorical variable (using a median or some other split). Thus, a two-way ANOVA becomes a three-way χ^2 (with the DV as the additional factor), and so on. Tabachnick and Fidell (2001, Chapter 7) discuss multiway frequency analysis.

5.3.2.2 Homogeneity of Variance

Homogeneity of variance usually is tested in the cells of a factorial design. The guidelines for assessing compliance with the assumption and solutions for violation are the same as for a one-way design except that cells formed by the combination of IVs are tested instead of levels of a single IV. That is, homogeneity of variance is tested in the six cells of a factorial design (formed by combining, say, one IV with two levels with a second IV with three levels) the same way as in a one-way design when the IV has six levels (cf. Sections 3.4.3 and 4.5.5). Procedures are also available to test homogeneity of variance separately for each main effect and interaction of a factorial design should these be desired.

5.3.2.3   *Independence of Errors*

The ANOVA model assumes that errors (deviations of individual scores around their respective means) are independent of one another, both within each cell and between cells of a design. The assumption is identical to that for a one-way design, but applied to cells rather than levels of a single IV. This assumption is evaluated in the same way as for one-way designs (cf. Section 3.4.2).

5.3.2.4   *Absence of Outliers*

Univariate outliers can occur in the DV in one or more cells of the design. Issues surrounding testing and dealing with outliers are the same as for a one-way design (Section 3.4.4), with outliers defined by their cells rather than levels of a single IV.

5.4   Fundamental Equations

Factorial designs consist of two or more IVs, each of which has at least two levels. The design is factorial if all levels of one IV occur in combination with all levels of the other IVs. Equation 3.22 shows the GLM in traditional deviation format for two-way randomized-groups ANOVA:

$$Y = \mu + \alpha + \beta + \alpha\beta + e$$

where α = deviation of a score, Y, from the grand mean, μ, due to the main effect of
                the first IV, A
        β = deviation of a score due to the main effect of the second IV, B
        $\alpha\beta$ = deviation of a score due to the interaction—the effect of the combination
                of A and B on Y above and beyond their individual main effects on Y

Thus, a factorial design with two IVs provides three tests for the "price" of one: two that you would get from two separate one-way studies, one on each IV, and a freebie. Say, the first IV is the same as in the one-way design of Section 4.4: The IV is view from the room (parking lot, ocean, and ski slope) and the DV is rating of the vacation. The test of the main effect of type of view is the same test as in the one-way ANOVA. If the second IV is profession of rater (say, administrators, belly dancers, and politicians), you also get a test of possible mean differences in rating of vacation associated with type of profession. The third test—of interaction—is not available if you simply run two studies, one for each IV. The test of interaction asks if the effect of one IV depends on the level of the other IV. For example, does the effect of view on rating of vacation differ for the different professions?

5.4.1   Allocation of Cases

Cases are randomly assigned to each level of an experimentally manipulated IV. Table 5.1 shows assignment of cases to two treatments, A and B, with two levels each. Twelve different cases are randomly assigned to the four cells representing combinations of levels of A and B, leaving $n = 3$ for each cell. Recall that indices for s do not imply sequential assignment but are only for convenience.

TABLE 5.1   Assignment of Cases in Two-Way Randomized-Groups ANOVA with Both IVs Manipulated

Treatment A	Treatment B	
	b_1	b_2
a_1	s_1 s_2 s_3	s_7 s_8 s_9
a_2	s_4 s_5 s_6	s_{10} s_{11} s_{12}

TABLE 5.2   Assignment of Cases in Two-Way Randomized-Groups ANOVA with One Nonmanipulated IV

Case Type A	Treatment B	
	b_1	b_2
a_1	$s_{a_1,b_1,1}$ $s_{a_1,b_1,2}$ $s_{a_1,b_1,3}$	$s_{a_1,b_2,1}$ $s_{a_1,b_2,2}$ $s_{a_1,b_2,3}$
a_2	$s_{a_2,b_1,1}$ $s_{a_2,b_1,2}$ $s_{a_2,b_1,3}$	$s_{a_2,b_2,1}$ $s_{a_2,b_2,2}$ $s_{a_2,b_2,3}$

If the design has one manipulated and one nonmanipulated IV, cases are randomly assigned to levels of the manipulated IV within each level of the nonmanipulated IV. This sometimes is called a treatment by blocks design, or a blocking design. Table 5.2 shows a design with a manipulated IV, Treatment B, and a nonmanipulated IV, Case Type A. Cases are classified into either a_1 or a_2. Blocking variables test the generalizability of the effects of the manipulated IV through the test of interaction. Does the effect of the manipulated IV depend on the level of the blocking variable? In our current example, type of profession is a blocking variable—the design is said to be blocked on profession; cases are randomly assigned to view but classified as to profession. Common types of blocking variables are environmental, situational, or correlational variables associated with cases.

The six cases classified as a_1 are randomly assigned to the two levels of B, as are the six cases classified as a_2. If there is one nonmanipulated and two manipulated IVs, cases are randomly assigned to every combination of levels of the manipulated IVs within each level of the nonmanipulated IV, and so on.

In a completely nonexperimental design, levels of both A and B are observed, neither is manipulated. Cases are classified into all levels on the basis of their characteristics with respect to A and B. For example, cases are classified into A on the basis of profession and into B on the basis of, say, age. The statistical analysis is identical for the fully randomized design, the treatment by blocks design, and the fully nonexperimental design; only the interpretation with respect to causality differs for the variants of the design.

5.4.2   Partition of Sources of Variance

SS_{bg} of Equation 3.4, expressed as $n \sum_j (\overline{Y} - GM)^2$ in Equation 3.3, is further partitioned into SS associated with the first IV, A; SS associated with the second IV, B; and SS associated with the interaction, AB (discussed in Section 5.6.1). That is,

$$SS_{bg} = SS_A + SS_B + SS_{AB} \tag{5.1}$$

or

$$n_{jk} \sum_j \sum_k (\overline{Y}_{AB} - \text{GM})^2 = n_j \sum_j (\overline{Y}_A - \text{GM})^2 + n_k \sum_k (\overline{Y}_B - \text{GM})^2$$

$$+ \left[n_{jk} \sum_j \sum_k (\overline{Y}_{AB} - \text{GM})^2 - n_j \sum_j (\overline{Y}_A - \text{GM}^2 - n_k \sum_k (\overline{Y}_B - \text{GM})^2 \right]$$

The sum of squared differences between cell means $(\overline{Y}_{AB})$ and the grand mean is partitioned into (1) sum of squared differences between means associated with different levels of A $(\overline{Y}_A)$ and the grand mean; (2) sum of squared differences between means associated with different levels of B $(\overline{Y}_B)$ and the grand mean; and (3) sum of squared differences associated with combinations of A and B $(\overline{Y}_{AB})$ and the grand mean, from which differences associated with A and with B are subtracted. Each n is the number of scores composing the relevant marginal or cell mean; n_{jk} is the number of scores in a cell, n_j is the number of scores in each level of A, and n_k is the number of scores in each level of B.

Note that the interaction is what is left over after influences associated with each of the IVs are subtracted. That is, any differences among cell means remaining after marginal mean differences are eliminated are associated with the interaction.

The full partition for the factorial randomized groups design is

$$\sum_i \sum_j \sum_k (Y_{ijk} - \text{GM})^2 = n_j \sum_j (\overline{Y}_A - \text{GM})^2 + n_k \sum_k (\overline{Y}_B - \text{GM})^2$$

$$+ \left[n_{jk} \sum_j \sum_k (\overline{Y}_{AB} - \text{GM})^2 - n_j \sum_j (\overline{Y}_A - \text{GM})^2 - n_k \sum_k (\overline{Y}_B - \text{GM})^2 \right] \quad (5.2)$$

$$+ \sum_i \sum_j \sum_k (Y_{ijk} - \overline{Y}_{AB})^2$$

or

$$\text{SS}_T = \text{SS}_A + \text{SS}_B + \text{SS}_{AB} + \text{SS}_{S/AB}$$

The notation for the error term is S/AB, which indicates subjects (cases) within the groups formed by combinations of A and B—subjects *nested* within the various AB combinations.

Total degrees of freedom remains the number of scores (expressed as N or abn) minus 1, lost when the grand mean is estimated (cf. Equation 3.6). Degrees of freedom for A are the number of levels of A minus 1, lost because the $\overline{Y}_{a_j}$ average to the grand mean, so $a - 1$ of the means can take on any values whatever, but the last mean is fixed.

$$\text{df}_A = a - 1 \quad (5.3)$$

Similarly, degrees of freedom for B are the number of levels of B minus 1, lost because the $\overline{Y}_{b_k}$ also average to the grand mean, so the first $b - 1$ of them can take on any value, but the last one is fixed.

$$df_B = b - 1 \tag{5.4}$$

Degrees of freedom for the AB interaction are the degrees of freedom for A times the degrees of freedom for B.

$$df_{AB} = (a - 1)(b - 1) \tag{5.5}$$

Finally, degrees of freedom for error are the total degrees of freedom minus a times b, the number of cell means estimated.

$$df_{S/AB} = N - ab \tag{5.6}$$

Verifying the equality of degrees of freedom,

$$N - 1 = a - 1 + b - 1 + (a - 1)(b - 1) + N - ab$$

Rearranging terms and multiplying terms within parentheses,

$$N - 1 = N - ab + a - 1 + b - 1 + ab - a - b + 1$$

Figure 5.1 diagrams the partition of sums of squares and degrees of freedom.

Mean squares are formed by dividing sums of squares by degrees of freedom, as for one-way designs, but now there are more of them:

$$MS_A = \frac{SS_A}{df_A} \qquad MS_B = \frac{SS_B}{df_B}$$
$$MS_{AB} = \frac{SS_{AB}}{df_{AB}} \qquad MS_{S/AB} = \frac{SS_{S/AB}}{df_{S/AB}} \tag{5.7}$$

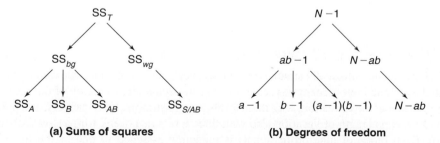

(a) Sums of squares   (b) Degrees of freedom

**FIGURE 5.1   Partition of (a) Sums of Squares and (b) Degrees of Freedom
for Two-Way Factorial Randomized-Groups ANOVA**

F ratios are formed for each of the three sources of variance to be evaluated: *A*, *B*, and *AB*. Each *F* ratio is formed by dividing the appropriate MS by the estimate of random-error variation, $MS_{S/AB}$.

F_A evaluates differences among marginal means for levels of *A*, called the main effect of *A*. The null hypothesis for this test is the same as for a one-way ANOVA, now expressed as $\mu_{a_1} = \mu_{a_2} = \cdots = \mu_{a_j}$. The obtained F_A is

$$F_A = \frac{MS_A}{MS_{S/AB}} \qquad df = (a-1), (abn - ab) \qquad (5.8)$$

Obtained F_A is tested against critical *F* from Table A.1 in Appendix A with numerator df $= a - 1$ and denominator df $= N - ab$. The null hypothesis is rejected if the obtained F_A is equal to or exceeds critical *F*.

F_B evaluates differences among marginal means for levels of *B*, called the main effect of *B*. The null hypothesis for this test is that $\mu_{b_1} = \mu_{b_2} = \cdots = \mu_{b_k}$.

$$F_B = \frac{MS_B}{MS_{S/AB}} \qquad df = (b-1), (abn - ab) \qquad (5.9)$$

Obtained F_B is tested against critical *F* from Table A.1 with numerator df $= b - 1$ and denominator df $= N - ab$. The null hypothesis is rejected if the obtained F_B is equal to or exceeds critical *F*.

F_{AB} evaluates differences that remain among cell means after differences among marginal means are subtracted: the *AB* interaction. The null hypothesis is that *remaining* cell means are all equal: For example, that $\mu_{a_1b_1} = \mu_{a_1b_2} = \mu_{a_2b_1} = \mu_{a_2b_2}$ after effects of *A* and *B* are removed or, alternatively, that the mean differences between the levels of *B* are the same at the different levels of *A*, for example, that $(\mu_{a_1b_1} - \mu_{a_1b_2}) = (\mu_{a_2b_1} - \mu_{a_2b_2})$. A deeper understanding of the meaning of interaction is available through the regression approach, as discussed in Section 5.4.4.

$$F_{AB} = \frac{MS_{AB}}{MS_{S/AB}} \qquad df = (a-1)(b-1), (abn - ab) \qquad (5.10)$$

Obtained F_{AB} is tested against critical *F* from Table A.1 with numerator df $= (a-1)(b-1)$ and denominator df $= N - ab$. The null hypothesis is rejected if the obtained F_{AB} is equal to or exceeds critical *F*.

5.4.3   Traditional ANOVA Approach (3 × 3)

Table 5.3 shows an unrealistically small, silly, hypothetical data set in which the rating of a vacation is evaluated as a function of length of vacation and professional identification of the rater. The first IV, *A*, is professional identification, with three levels (administrators, belly dancers, and politicians). The second IV, *B*, is length of vacation also with three levels (a 1-week trip, a 2-week trip, or a 3-week trip). Each block of nine professionals is randomly assigned to one of the three vacation lengths, resulting in *n* = 3 for each combination of levels of *A* and *B*. Thus, vacation length is an experimental IV and profession is not.

TABLE 5.3   Hypothetical Data Set for 3 × 3 ANOVA

A: Profession	B: Vacation Length		
	b_1: 1 week	b_2: 2 weeks	b_3: 3 weeks
a_1: Administrators	0 1 0	4 7 6	5 8 6
a_2: Belly Dancers	5 7 6	5 6 7	9 8 8
a_3: Politicians	5 6 8	9 9 9	3 3 2

$$\sum Y^2 = 0^2 + 1^2 + \cdots + 2^2 = 1046$$
$$a = 3, b = 3, n = 3$$

TABLE 5.4   Cell Totals and Marginal Sums for Hypothetical Data Set for 3 × 3 ANOVA

A: Profession	B: Vacation Length			Marginal Sums for A
	b_1: 1 week	b_2: 2 weeks	b_3: 3 weeks	
a_1: Administrators	1	17	19	$A_1 = 37$
a_2: Belly Dancers	18	18	25	$A_2 = 61$
a_3: Politicians	19	27	8	$A_3 = 54$
Marginal sums for B	$B_1 = 38$	$B_2 = 62$	$B_3 = 52$	$T = 152$

A matrix of sums, such as that in Table 5.4, is very helpful to work with in order to calculate sums of squares. The table contains sums for the cells (AB) as well as sums for the margins of both A and B.

Table 5.5 shows computational equations for sums of squares for A, B, AB, and S/AB. Note that for each quantity, the divisor is the number of cases added together to produce the sums that are to be squared in the numerator. In the first equation, for example, scores are summed in each level of

TABLE 5.5 Computational Equations for Sums of Squares for Two-Way ANOVA

$$SS_A = \frac{\sum A^2}{bn} - \frac{T^2}{abn} = \frac{37^2 + 61^2 + 54^2}{9} - \frac{152^2}{27}$$

$$SS_B = \frac{\sum B^2}{an} - \frac{T^2}{abn} = \frac{38^2 + 62^2 + 52^2}{9} - \frac{152^2}{27}$$

$$SS_{AB} = \frac{\sum (AB)^2}{n} - \frac{\sum A^2}{bn} - \frac{\sum B^2}{an} + \frac{T^2}{abn} = \frac{1^2 + 17^2 + 19^2 + 18^2 + 18^2 + 25^2 + 19^2 + 27^2 + 8^2}{3}$$

$$- \frac{37^2 + 61^2 - 54^2}{9} - \frac{38^2 + 62^2 + 52^2}{9} + \frac{152^2}{27}$$

$$SS_{S/AB} = \sum Y^2 - \frac{\sum (AB)^2}{n} = 0^2 + 1^2 + 0^2 + 4^2 + \cdots + 3^2 + 2^2$$

$$- \frac{1^2 + 17^2 + 19^2 + 18^2 + 18^2 + 25^2 + 19^2 + 27^2 + 8^2}{3}$$

$$SS_T = \sum Y^2 - \frac{T^2}{abn} = 0^2 + 1^2 + 0^2 + 4^2 + \cdots + 3^2 + 2^2 - \frac{152^2}{27}$$

$A(A_1 + A_2 + A_3)$ before squaring, and there are bn cases in each level of A. Table 5.6 shows the final calculations for sums of squares for the example.

Table 5.7 summarizes the calculation results and shows the mean squares and F values based on Equations 5.2 through 5.10. Each of the F ratios is evaluated separately. With $\alpha = .05$, the critical values for the main effects of A and B are the same because each has 2 df in the numerator and 18 df in the denominator. The critical F from Table A.1 is 3.55. Because both of the calculated F ratios for main effects are larger than 3.55, the null hypotheses of equality of means on both margins are rejected. We conclude that there is a difference in ratings due to length of ski trip and also that ratings differ by profession.

The interaction of length of trip and profession is evaluated with numerator df = 4 and denominator df = 18. With a critical F value of 2.93 (from Table A.1), we also conclude that the ratings of cases with different lengths of vacation depend on profession (or, conversely, that the effect of pro-

TABLE 5.6 Sums of Squares for Traditional 3 × 3 ANOVA with Three Levels of Each IV

SS_A	$= 889.55 - 855.7$	$= 33.85$
SS_B	$= 888 - 855.7$	$= 32.30$
SS_{AB}	$= 1026 - 889.55 - 888 + 855.7$	$= 104.15$
$SS_{S/AB}$	$= 1046 - 1026$	$= 20.00$
SS_T	$= 1046 - 855.7$	$= 190.30$

TABLE 5.7 Source Table for Traditional Two-Way ANOVA

Source	SS	df	MS	F
A	33.85	2	16.93	15.25
B	32.30	2	16.15	14.55
AB	104.15	4	26.04	23.46
S/AB	20.00	18	1.11	
T	190.30	26		

fession depends on length of vacation). That is, administrators, belly dancers, and politicians have different patterns in their preferences for length of vacation. A glance at the totals in Table 5.4 suggests that administrators are mild in their preferences for either 2- or 3-week vacations, belly dancers like vacations of any length but seem to prefer 3-week vacations, and politicians seem to prefer 2-week vacations, but these patterns need to be confirmed by further analyses. Put another way, the significant interaction implies that one must know both the length of the vacation and the profession of the case in order to predict the rating of the vacation. Interpretation of interactions is discussed in Section 5.6.1, where plots of means (parameter estimates) are also constructed.

5.4.4   Regression Approach (3×3)

As discussed in Section 4.4.4, the regression approach "works" by using orthogonal weighting coefficients—contrast coefficients—in the columns that code each IV. One column is required for each df associated with main effects and interactions. Two columns are required for the $a - 1$ ($3 - 1 = 2$) df for the main effect of A and two for the $b - 1$ ($3 - 1 = 2$) df for the main effect of B; four columns are required for the $(a - 1)(b - 1)$ df for the AB interaction. Altogether eight columns are thus required for the 3×3 factorial design.[3] SS(reg.) for separate columns are then combined when necessary to form main effects and interactions, just as they are combined to form a main effect in a one-way design with more than two levels.

To separate the three groups of professions from each other, two columns are needed. The weighting coefficients in one column are arbitrarily chosen to separate administrators from both belly dancers and politicians, and the coefficients in the second column to separate belly dancers from politicians. Two columns are also needed to separate the three levels of vacation length from each other, but here the weighting coefficients for trend analysis seem most appropriate. The first column provides a test of the linear trend and the second column of the quadratic trend.

Table 5.8 shows the scores on the DV, Y, in the first column, and then weighting coefficients for the eight columns representing main effects and interaction, and then cross-products calculated from the first nine columns. The coding for the X_1 column compares rating of administrators with pooled ratings from belly dancers and politicians. The X_2 column compares ratings of belly dancers with those of politicians. These two columns are orthogonal. Weighting coefficients for trend analysis are found in Table A.5. The X_3 column has the weighting coefficients for the linear trend of vacation length, and the X_4 column has weighting coefficients for the quadratic trend of vacation length. These two columns are orthogonal to each other and also orthogonal to the first two X columns. These two sets of orthogonal weighting coefficients are chosen based on the meaning of the levels of A and B in this example. However, any set of orthogonal weighting coefficients will also be orthogonal to another orthogonal set as long as sample sizes are equal in the cells.

The X columns for interaction are found by cross-multiplication of each of the X columns for A with each of those for B. Consider first a simple case in which there are only two levels of A and two levels of B. As shown in Table 5.9 (where DV scores, Y, are not included), the X_1 column distinguishes a_1 from a_2 and the X_2 column distinguishes b_1 from b_2. Interaction is coded in the X_3 column, which is a cross-product of the weighting coefficients in X_1 and the weighting coefficients in X_2. Note that all three columns are orthogonal. Note also that in the interaction column, groups labeled a_1b_1 and

---

[3]This is the same number that would be required for a one-way design with nine levels. Thus, analysis of a factorial design may be seen as simply a set of comparisons developed for a one-way design, with each column representing a single comparison.

TABLE 5.8   Columns for Regression Approach to Analysis of Variance with Three Treatment Levels in Both A and B

		A		B		AB				SP							
						X_1*X_3	X_1*X_4	X_2*X_3	X_2*X_4	$Y*X_1$	$Y*X_2$	$Y*X_3$	$Y*X_4$	$Y*X_5$	$Y*X_6$	$Y*X_7$	$Y*X_8$
	Y	X_1	X_2	X_3	X_4	X_5	X_6	X_7	X_8	X_9	X_{10}	X_{11}	X_{12}	X_{13}	X_{14}	X_{15}	X_{16}
a_1b_1	0	2	0	−1	1	−2	2	0	0	0	0	0	0	0	0	0	0
	1	2	0	−1	1	−2	2	0	0	2	0	−1	1	−2	2	0	0
	0	2	0	−1	1	−2	2	0	0	0	0	0	0	0	0	0	0
a_1b_2	4	2	0	0	−2	0	−4	0	0	8	0	0	−8	0	−16	0	0
	7	2	0	0	−2	0	−4	0	0	14	0	0	−14	0	−28	0	0
	6	2	0	0	−2	0	−4	0	0	12	0	0	−12	0	−24	0	0
a_1b_3	5	2	0	1	1	2	2	0	0	10	0	5	5	10	10	0	0
	8	2	0	1	1	2	2	0	0	16	0	8	8	16	16	0	0
	6	2	0	1	1	2	2	0	0	12	0	6	6	12	12	0	0
a_2b_1	5	−1	1	−1	1	1	−1	−1	1	−5	5	−5	5	5	−5	−5	5
	7	−1	1	−1	1	1	−1	−1	1	−7	7	−7	7	7	−7	−7	7
	6	−1	1	−1	1	1	−1	−1	1	−6	6	−6	6	6	−6	−6	6
a_2b_2	5	−1	1	0	−2	0	2	0	−2	−5	5	0	−10	0	10	0	−10
	6	−1	1	0	−2	0	2	0	−2	−6	6	0	−12	0	12	0	−12
	7	−1	1	0	−2	0	2	0	−2	−7	7	0	−14	0	14	0	−14
a_2b_3	9	−1	1	1	1	−1	−1	1	1	−9	9	9	9	−9	−9	9	9
	8	−1	1	1	1	−1	−1	1	1	−8	8	8	8	−8	−8	8	8
	8	−1	1	1	1	−1	−1	1	1	−8	8	8	8	−8	−8	8	8
a_3b_1	5	−1	−1	−1	1	1	−1	1	−1	−5	−5	−5	5	5	−5	5	−5
	6	−1	−1	−1	1	1	−1	1	−1	−6	−6	−6	6	6	−6	6	−6
	8	−1	−1	−1	1	1	−1	1	−1	−8	−8	−8	8	8	−8	8	−8
a_3b_2	9	−1	−1	0	−2	0	2	0	2	−9	−9	0	−18	0	18	0	18
	9	−1	−1	0	−2	0	2	0	2	−9	−9	0	−18	0	18	0	18
	9	−1	−1	0	−2	0	2	0	2	−9	−9	0	−18	0	18	0	18
a_3b_3	3	−1	−1	1	1	−1	−1	−1	−1	−3	−3	3	3	−3	−3	−3	−3
	3	−1	−1	1	1	−1	−1	−1	−1	−3	−3	3	3	−3	−3	−3	−3
	2	−1	−1	1	1	−1	−1	−1	−1	−2	−2	2	2	−2	−2	−2	−2
Sum	152	0	0	0	0	0	0	0	0	−41	7	14	−34	40	−8	18	34
Sum of sq	1046	54	18	18	54	36	108	12	36								
N	27																

164

TABLE 5.9   Regression Approach to a 2 × 2 Factorial Design

Group	A X_1	B X_2	AB $X_1 * X_2 = X_3$
a_1b_1	1	1	1
a_1b_2	1	−1	−1
a_2b_1	−1	1	−1
a_2b_2	−1	−1	1

a_2b_2 are coded 1 and those for a_1b_2 and a_2b_1 are coded −1. Thus, the null hypothesis tested by the interaction is that the pooled mean for a_1b_1 and a_2b_2 is the same as the pooled mean for a_1b_2 and a_2b_1. This is the simplest interpretation of interaction as a comparison between pooled means from the two sides of a cross that links the four groups of a 2 × 2 factorial design. The interaction can also be interpreted as a difference between mean differences, that is, between $\mu_{a_1b_1} - \mu_{a_1b_2}$ and $\mu_{a_2b_1} - \mu_{a_2b_2}$.

In the larger 3 × 3 example, weighting coefficients in the X_5 column are a product of weighting coefficients in X_1 and weighting coefficients in X_3. Weighting coefficients in the X_6 column are a product of weighting coefficients in the X_1 and X_4 columns. Weighting coefficients in the X_7 column are a product of X_2 and X_3, and finally, weighting coefficients in X_8 are a product of weighting coefficients in X_2 and X_4. For the first case in the a_1b_1 group (an administrator's rating a 1-week ski trip), then, the weighting coefficients in the X_5 to X_8 columns, respectively, are

$$X_5 = X_1X_3 = 2(-1) = -2$$
$$X_6 = X_1X_4 = 2(1) = 2$$
$$X_7 = X_2X_3 = 0(-1) = 0$$
$$X_8 = X_2X_4 = 0(1) = 0$$

Remaining cases are coded in like fashion, multiplying a weighting coefficient from a column representing A by a weighting coefficient from a column representing B.

The GLM in regression format of Equation 4.2 thus applies to this factorial design with $j = 8$. However, the equations for the bs are most conveniently expressed in matrix format, with matrix algebra used for solution. Mercifully, computation of the solution of the bs (slopes) and a (intercept) is not necessary for testing ANOVA hypotheses.

Table 5.10 shows the general forms of equations for sums of squares and sums of products for the regression approach. Table 5.11 shows the equations for finding the sums of squares for the main effect of A, type of profession. Note that this matches the SS_A of Table 5.6.

Table 5.12 shows the equations for finding the sums of squares for the main effect of B, length of vacation.

TABLE 5.10   Preliminary Sums of Squares and Cross-Products Terms for Regression Equations and Final SS for Regression

$$SS_Y \quad = \sum Y^2 - \frac{(\sum Y)^2}{N}$$

$$SS(X_i) \quad = \sum X_i^2 - \frac{(\sum X_i)^2}{N}$$

$$SP(YX_i) \quad = \sum YX_i - \frac{(\sum Y)(\sum X_i)}{N}$$

$$SS(\text{reg.}X_i) = \frac{[SP(YX_i)]^2}{SS(X_i)}$$

TABLE 5.11   Equations for the Sum of Squares for the Main Effect of A

$$SS(\text{reg.}X_1) = \frac{[SP(YX_1)]^2}{SS(X_1)} \qquad = \frac{(-41)^2}{54} \qquad = 31.13$$

$$SS(\text{reg.}X_2) = \frac{[SP(YX_2)]^2}{SS(X_2)} \qquad = \frac{7^2}{18} \qquad = \ 2.72$$

$$SS_A \qquad = SS(\text{reg.}X_1) + SS(\text{reg.}X_2) \ = 31.13 + 2.72 = 33.85$$

TABLE 5.12   Equations for the Sum of Squares for the Main Effect of B

$$SS(\text{reg.}X_3) = \frac{[SP(YX_3)]^2}{SS(X_3)} \qquad = \frac{14^2}{18} \qquad = \ 10.89$$

$$SS(\text{reg.}X_4) = \frac{[SP(YX_4)]^2}{SS(X_4)} \qquad = \frac{(-34)^2}{54} \qquad = \ 21.41$$

$$SS_B \qquad = SS(\text{reg.}X_3) + SS(\text{reg.}X_4) \ = 10.89 + 21.41 \ = \ 32.30$$

Finally, the sum of squares for the interaction of type of profession with vacation length is calculated as per Table 5.13 (with a bit of rounding error in SS_{AB}). Sum of squares for error is found by subtracting all of the sums of squares for effects from the total sum of squares.

$$SS_Y = 1046 - \frac{152^2}{27} = 190.30$$

TABLE 5.13   Equations for the Sum of Squares for the *AB* Interaction

$$SS(\text{reg.}X_5) = \frac{[SP(YX_5)]^2}{SS(X_5)} \qquad = \frac{40^2}{36} \qquad = 44.44$$

$$SS(\text{reg.}X_6) = \frac{[SP(YX_6)]^2}{SS(X_6)} \qquad = \frac{(-8)^2}{108} \qquad = 0.59$$

$$SS(\text{reg.}X_7) = \frac{[SP(YX_7)]^2}{SS(X_7)} \qquad = \frac{18^2}{12} \qquad = 27.00$$

$$SS(\text{reg.}X_8) = \frac{[SP(YX_8)]^2}{SS(X_8)} \qquad = \frac{34^2}{36} \qquad = 32.11$$

$$SS_{AB} \quad = SS(\text{reg.}X_5) + SS(\text{reg.}X_6) \quad = 44.44 + 0.59$$
$$+ SS(\text{reg.}X_7) + SS(\text{reg.}X_8) \quad + 27.00 + 32.11 = 104.15$$

SS_Y is the same as SS_T in Table 5.6, and

$$SS_{S/AB} = SS_Y - SS_A - SS_B - SS_{AB}$$
$$= 190.30 - 33.85 - 32.30 - 104.15 = 20.00$$

Each X column represents a single df comparison. Thus, the df for effects in Table 5.7 are the same as the numbers of columns for each effect. Total degrees of freedom (df_Y) are $N - 1 = 27 - 1 = 26$ (as in Table 5.7). Degrees of freedom for the error term are found by subtraction or by calculating $N - v - 1$, where v is the number of X columns. Thus, $\text{df}_{S/AB} = 27 - 8 - 1 = 18$.

MS values and F ratios then are calculated as in Table 5.7. Interpretation is identical to that of ANOVA calculated by traditional means.

5.4.5   Computer Analyses of Small-Sample Factorial Design

Table 5.14 shows how data are entered for this type of two-way ANOVA. Data may be entered in text format (e.g., through a word processor or a spreadsheet and then saved in text format), or entered through facilities provided by the statistical program. Data entered as text format include only numbers, without the column headings shown in Table 5.14; data entered through statistical programs typically include variable names at the tops of columns. Each row is a single case, one column is needed to code the levels of each IV (a column for LENGTH and a column for PROFESS, in this case), and a column is needed for the DV (RATING). An additional column, case number, may be added for convenience in viewing and editing the data file.

Tables 5.15 through 5.18 show computer analyses of the small-sample example of Section 5.4.3 through SPSS GLM (UNIVANOVA[4]), SYSTAT ANOVA, MINITAB GLM, and SAS GLM, respectively.

---

[4]Accessed through SPSS for Windows as Statistics, General linear model, General Factorial. UNIANOVA is the syntax generated by the menu selection.

**TABLE 5.14   Hypothetical Data Set for
3 × 3 ANOVA in a Form Suitable for
Computer Analysis**

PROFESS	LENGTH	RATING
1	1	1
1	1	0
1	1	1
1	2	4
1	2	7
1	2	6
1	3	5
1	3	8
1	3	6
2	1	5
2	1	7
2	1	6
2	2	5
2	2	6
2	2	7
2	3	9
2	3	8
2	3	8
3	1	5
3	1	6
3	1	8
3	2	9
3	2	9
3	2	9
3	3	3
3	3	3
3	3	2

The SPSS GLM (UNIANOVA) syntax lists the DV (rating), followed by the keyword BY, followed by a list of the IVs (length and profess). EMMEANS instructions request marginal and cell means; DESCRIPTIVE in the /PRINT instruction requests descriptive statistics for cells. ETASQ and OPOWER request effect size and observed power statistics. DESIGN requests the full factorial two-way ANOVA, and is the default. Remaining syntax (METHOD, INTERCEPT, and CRITERIA) shows the default values produced by SPSS menus.

Cell means and standard deviations are printed as a result of the PRINT = DESCRIPTIVE instruction. Below the segment of output labeled Tests of Between-Subjects Effects is a traditional ANOVA source table with S/AB (Table 5.7) labeled Error. The column labeled Sig shows the probability (to three decimal places) that an F ratio this large or larger would be achieved if the null hypothesis were true. The Corrected Model source of variation is a composite of the LENGTH and PROFESS main effects and the LENGTH*PROFESS interaction. The probability that each of these results occurred by chance if the null hypothesis is true is less than .0005. The Total source of variance includes the sum of squares for intercept (grand mean in the coding scheme used by SPSS).

TABLE 5.15 Two-Way Randomized-Groups ANOVA for Small-Sample Example through SPSS GLM (UNIANOVA)

```
UNIANOVA
  rating BY length profess
  /METHOD = SSTYPE(3)
  /INTERCEPT = INCLUDE
  /EMMEANS = TABLES(length)
  /EMMEANS = TABLES(profess)
  /EMMEANS = TABLES(length*profess)
  /PRINT = DESCRIPTIVE ETASQ OPOWER
  /CRITERIA = ALPHA(.05)
  /DESIGN = length profess length*profess.
```

Univariate Analysis of Variance

Between-Subjects Factors

		Value Label	N
VACATION LENGTH	1.00	1 WK	9
	2.00	2 WK	9
	3.00	3 WK	9
PROFESSION	1.00	ADMIN	9
	2.00	BELLY	9
	3.00	POLITIC	9

Descriptive Statistics

Dependent Variable: RATING

VACATION LENGTH	PROFESSION	Mean	Std. Deviation	N
1 WK	ADMIN	.3333	.5774	3
	BELLY	6.0000	1.0000	3
	POLITIC	6.3333	1.5275	3
	Total	4.2222	3.0732	9
2 WK	ADMIN	5.6667	1.5275	3
	BELLY	6.0000	1.0000	3
	POLITIC	9.0000	.0000	3
	Total	6.8889	1.8333	9
3 WK	ADMIN	6.3333	1.5275	3
	BELLY	8.3333	.5774	3
	POLITIC	2.6667	.5774	3
	Total	5.7778	2.6352	9
Total	ADMIN	4.1111	3.0596	9
	BELLY	6.7778	1.3944	9
	POLITIC	6.0000	2.8723	9
	Total	5.6296	2.7054	27

(continued)

TABLE 5.15   Continued

Tests of Between-Subjects Effects

Dependent Variable: RATING

Source	Type III Sum of Squares	df	Mean Square	F	Sig.	Eta Squared	Noncent. Parameter	Observed Power[a]
Corrected Model	170.296[b]	8	21.287	19.158	.000	.895	153.267	1.000
Intercept	855.704	1	855.704	770.133	.000	.977	770.133	1.000
LENGTH	32.296	2	16.148	14.533	.000	.618	29.067	.996
PROFESS	33.852	2	16.926	15.233	.000	.629	30.467	.997
LENGTH * PROFESS	104.148	4	26.037	23.433	.000	.839	93.733	1.000
Error	20.000	18	1.111					
Total	1046.000	27						
Corrected Total	190.296	26						

a. Computed using alpha = .05

b. R Squared = .895 (Adjusted R Squared = .848)

Estimated Marginal Means

1. VACATION LENGTH

Dependent Variable: RATING

VACATION LENGTH	Mean	Std. Error	95% Confidence Interval Lower Bound	95% Confidence Interval Upper Bound
1 WK	4.222	.351	3.484	4.960
2 WK	6.889	.351	6.151	7.627
3 WK	5.778	.351	5.040	6.516

The **Corrected Total** excludes the sum of squares for intercept and is the more useful sum for effect size calculations (cf. Section 5.6.2). The column labeled **Eta Squared** contains partial η^2 as a measure of effect size (Section 5.6.2). **R squared** in footnote **b** is the proportion of total variance that is predictable from the sum of all effects. **Adjusted R Squared** adjusts that value for bias due to small-sample sizes (cf. Tabachnick & Fidell, 2001, Section 5.6.3). **Observed Power** is described in Section 5.6.3 of this chapter, and the **Noncent. Parameter** (noncentrality) is relevant to calculation of power.

TABLE 5.15   Continued

2. PROFESSION

Dependent Variable: RATING

| | | | 95% Confidence Interval | |
PROFESSION	Mean	Std. Error	Lower Bound	Upper Bound
ADMIN	4.111	.351	3.373	4.849
BELLY	6.778	.351	6.040	7.516
POLITIC	6.000	.351	5.262	6.738

3. VACATION LENGTH * PROFESSION

Dependent Variable: RATING

| VACATION LENGTH | PROFESSION | Mean | Std. Error | 95% Confidence Interval | |
				Lower Bound	Upper Bound
1 WK	ADMIN	.333	.609	−.945	1.612
	BELLY	6.000	.609	4.721	7.279
	POLITIC	6.333	.609	5.055	7.612
2 WK	ADMIN	5.667	.609	4.388	6.945
	BELLY	6.000	.609	4.721	7.279
	POLITIC	9.000	.609	7.721	10.279
3 WK	ADMIN	6.333	.609	5.055	7.612
	BELLY	8.333	.609	7.055	9.612
	POLITIC	2.667	.609	1.388	3.945

Marginal and cell means appear at the end of the output together with a common standard error for each level of each factor and the 95% confidence interval for the mean. The common standard error is found by dividing the square root of $MS_{S/A}$ (labeled Error in the output) by the square root of the number of cases in each marginal or cell mean.

Table 5.16 shows syntax and partial output for SYSTAT ANOVA. The DV is named in the DEPEND instruction; IVs are named in the CATEGORY instructions. PRINT=MEDIUM produces cell and marginal means and standard errors.

Squared multiple R is the proportion of variance predicted by all effects combined, as in SPSS. The probability that an outcome is due to chance appears in the column labeled P in the source table (cf. Table 5.7). S/AB is labeled Error. SYSTAT provides marginal as well as cell means in the section labeled Least squares means. The SE column shows a single estimate of standard error for all marginal means and for all cell means. These values are found by dividing the square root of

TABLE 5.16 Two-Way Randomized-Groups ANOVA of Small-Sample Example through SYSTAT ANOVA: Syntax and Selected Output

```
PRINT=MEDIUM
ANOVA
CATEGORY LENGTH PROFESS
COVAR
DEPEND RATING
ESTIMATE
```

Effects coding used for categorical variables in model.

Categorical values encountered during processing are:
LENGTH (3 levels)
        1,   2,   3
PROFESS (3 levels)
        1,   2,   3

Dep Var: RATING   N: 27   Multiple R: 0.946   Squared multiple R: 0.895

Analysis of Variance

Source	Sum-of-Squares	df	Mean-Square	F-ratio	P
LENGTH	32.296	2	16.148	14.533	0.000
PROFESS	33.852	2	16.926	15.233	0.000
LENGTH*PROFESS	104.148	4	26.037	23.433	0.000
Error	20.000	18	1.111		

Least squares means.

		LS Mean	SE	N
LENGTH	=1	4.222	0.351	9
LENGTH	=2	6.889	0.351	9
LENGTH	=3	5.778	0.351	9

Least Squares Means

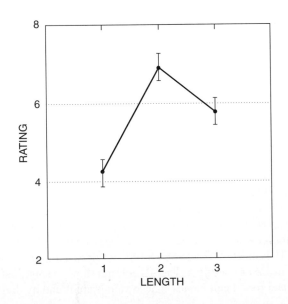

172

TABLE 5.16 **Continued**

PROFESS	=1	4.111	0.351	9
PROFESS	=2	6.778	0.351	9
PROFESS	=3	6.000	0.351	9

Least Squares Means

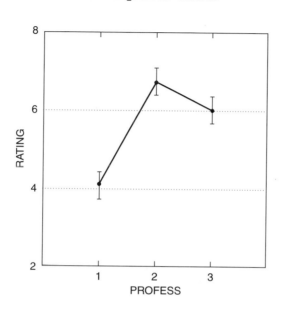

LENGTH	=1			
PROFESS	=1	0.333	0.609	3
LENGTH	=1			
PROFESS	=2	6.000	0.609	3
LENGTH	=1			
PROFESS	=3	6.333	0.609	3
LENGTH	=2			
PROFESS	=1	5.667	0.609	3
LENGTH	=2			
PROFESS	=2	6.000	0.609	3
LENGTH	=2			
PROFESS	=3	9.000	0.609	3
LENGTH	=3			
PROFESS	=1	6.333	0.609	3
LENGTH	=3			
PROFESS	=2	8.333	0.609	3
LENGTH	=3			
PROFESS	=3	2.667	0.609	3

$MS_{S/A}$ by the square root of either the marginal or cell sample size. SYSTAT provides graphs for marginal and cell means; however, the cell means (not shown here) are in an inconvenient format (separate graphs for each level of one IV).

Table 5.17 shows syntax and output for the analysis through MINITAB GLM. The DV is on the left side of the GLM equation. IVs and the interaction are specified on the right side of the GLM equation. Marginal and cell means are requested in the MEANS instruction.

TABLE 5.17   Two-Way Randomized-Groups ANOVA for Small-Sample Example through MINITAB GLM

```
MTB > GLM 'RATING' = LENGTH PROFESS LENGTH*PROFESS;
SUBC>    Brief 2;
SUBC>    Means LENGTH PROFESS LENGTH*PROFESS.
```

General Linear Model

```
Factor        Type Levels Values
LENGTH        fixed      3 1 2 3
PROFESS       fixed      3 1 2 3
```

Analysis of Variance for RATING, using Adjusted SS for Tests

Source	DF	Seq SS	Adj SS	Adj MS	F	P
LENGTH	2	32.296	32.296	16.148	14.53	0.000
PROFESS	2	33.852	33.852	16.926	15.23	0.000
LENGTH*PROFESS	4	104.148	104.148	26.037	23.43	0.000
Error	18	20.000	20.000	1.111		
Total	26	190.296				

Least Squares Means for RATING

LENGTH		Mean	StDev
1		4.2222	0.3514
2		6.8889	0.3514
3		5.7778	0.3514
PROFESS			
1		4.1111	0.3514
2		6.7778	0.3514
3		6.0000	0.3514
LENGTH*PROFESS			
1	1	0.3333	0.6086
1	2	6.0000	0.6086
1	3	6.3333	0.6086
2	1	5.6667	0.6086
2	2	6.0000	0.6086
2	3	9.0000	0.6086
3	1	6.3333	0.6086
3	2	8.3333	0.6086
3	3	2.6667	0.6086

After the output indicating numbers of levels in each IV, MINITAB GLM (or BALANCED) provides the source table (corresponding to Table 5.7): Analysis of Variance for RAT-ING.... The column labeled P shows, to three decimal places, the probability that an outcome this large or larger could have occurred by chance if the null hypothesis were true. S/AB is called Error by MINITAB. Marginal Means along with numbers of cases and standard deviations (StDev) are given for each of the main effects, followed by cell means, with cell sizes and standard deviations. These are the values labeled Std. Error by SPSS and SE by SYSTAT, that is, the square root of $MS_{S/A}$ divided by the square root of either the marginal or cell sample size.

SAS GLM syntax and output appear in Table 5.18. Discrete IVs are identified in the class instruction; the model instruction shows (in regression format) that the DV is a function of the IVs

TABLE 5.18 Two-Way Randomized-Groups ANOVA for Small-Sample Example through SAS GLM: Syntax and Selected Output

```
proc    glm data = SASUSER.FAC_RAND;
        class LENGTH PROFESS;
        model RATING = LENGTH PROFESS LENGTH*PROFESS;
        means LENGTH PROFESS LENGTH*PROFESS;
run;
```

```
                General Linear-Models Procedure
                  Class Level Information

              Class     Levels     Values

              LENGTH       3       1 2 3

              PROFESS      3       1 2 3

        Number of observations in data set = 27

              General Linear-Models Procedure
```

Dependent Variable: RATING

Source	DF	Sum of Squares	Mean Square	F Value	Pr > F
Model	8	170.29629630	21.28703704	19.16	0.0001
Error	18	20.00000000	1.11111111		
Corrected Total	26	190.29629630			

R-Square	C.V.	Root MSE	RATING Mean
0.894901	18.72401	1.0540925	5.62962963

Source	DF	Type III SS	Mean Square	F Value	Pr > F
LENGTH	2	32.29629630	16.14814815	14.53	0.0002
PROFESS	2	33.85185185	16.92592593	15.23	0.0001
LENGTH* PROFESS	4	104.14814815	26.03703704	23.43	0.0001

(continued)

TABLE 5.18   Continued

General Linear-Models Procedure

Level of LENGTH	N	--------RATING---------	
		Mean	SD
1	9	4.22222222	3.07318149
2	9	6.88888889	1.83333333
3	9	5.77777778	2.63523138

Level of PROFESS	N	--------RATING---------	
		Mean	SD
1	9	4.11111111	3.05959329
2	9	6.77777778	1.39443338
3	9	6.00000000	2.87228132

Level of LENGTH	Level of PROFESS	N	--------RATING---------	
			Mean	SD
1	1	3	0.33333333	0.57735027
1	2	3	6.00000000	1.00000000
1	3	3	6.33333333	1.52752523
2	1	3	5.66666667	1.52752523
2	2	3	6.00000000	1.00000000
2	3	3	9.00000000	0.00000000
3	1	3	6.33333333	1.52752523
3	2	3	8.33333333	0.57735027
3	3	3	2.66666667	0.57735027

and their interaction. Marginal (LENGTH and PROFESS) and cell (LENGTH*PROFESS) means are requested in the means instruction.

Three source tables are given. The first is for evaluating the entire Model (sum of all the effects), with the Error (S/AB) as well as the Total (identified as Corrected). This table includes R-Square, the proportion of variance predictable from all effects combined. Also shown are the square root of $MS_{S/A}$ (Root MSE), the grand mean (RATING Mean), and the coefficient of variation (C.V.—the square root of the error mean square divided by the grand mean, multiplied by 100).

The second and third source tables show the three effects, with the last column (Pr > F) indicating the probability of obtained F this large or larger under the null hypothesis. Type I SS (not shown) and Type III SS results differ only if there are unequal sample sizes (cf. Section 5.6.5). Marginal and cell means and standard deviations follow.

5.5   Other Types of Randomized-Groups Designs

Factorial designs may be expanded to any number of IVs, producing higher-order factorials. A variant on this design is one in which an additional group, typically a control group, is added to an otherwise factorial design.

5.5.1 Higher-Order Factorial Designs

Higher-order randomized-groups factorial designs have more than two IVs, each with two or more levels. In an experiment, at least one of the IVs is experimentally manipulated with the remaining IVs also experimentally manipulated, or not. Quasi-experimental or nonexperimental designs have no experimentally manipulated IVs. Table 5.19 shows allocation of cases in the simplest higher-order factorial design, a $2 \times 2 \times 2$ design.

This design can be considered a replication of an A by B factorial design at both c_1 and c_2. Seven effects are tested, each of the three main effects (A, B, and C), the 3 two-way interactions (AB, AC, and BC), and the three-way interaction (ABC). Thus, the between-groups sum of squares is partitioned as follows:

$$SS_{bg} = SS_A + SS_B + SS_C + SS_{AB} + SS_{AC} + SS_{BC} + SS_{ABC} \tag{5.11}$$

TABLE 5.19 Assignment of Cases in a Three-Way Randomized-Groups Design with All IVs Experimentally Manipulated

Treatment C

c_1

Treatment A	Treatment B	
	b_1	b_2
a_1	s_1 s_2 s_3	s_7 s_8 s_9
a_2	s_4 s_5 s_6	s_{10} s_{11} s_{12}

c_2

Treatment A	Treatment B	
	b_1	b_2
a_1	s_{13} s_{14} s_{15}	s_{19} s_{20} s_{21}
a_2	s_{16} s_{17} s_{18}	s_{22} s_{23} s_{24}

The error sum of squares remains the within-cell variability, now designated $SS_{S/ABC}$, so that the partition of the total sum of squares is

$$SS_T = SS_A + SS_B + SS_C + SS_{AB} + SS_{AC} + SS_{BC} + SS_{ABC} + SS_{S/ABC} \qquad (5.12)$$

Table 5.20 shows degrees of freedom and expanded (multiplied out) degrees of freedom for each of the effects and the corresponding computational equations for SS. Spend some time comparing the expanded degrees-of-freedom equations and the computational equations: The value that is squared in the numerator of the computational equations is the corresponding value from the expanded degrees-of-freedom equation. The only exceptions are that 1s in the degrees-of-freedom statements are each replaced by T^2 in the computational equations, and that Ns are replaced by $\sum Y^2$. Notice also that each segment of the computational equations contains all the factors in the study (A, B, C, in this case) and n, and that the elements that are not in the numerator of a segment are in the

TABLE 5.20   Degrees of Freedom and SS Equations for Three-Way ANOVA

Source	Degrees of Freedom and Expanded df	Sum of Squares Equations
A	$a - 1$	$\dfrac{\sum A^2}{bcn} - \dfrac{T^2}{abcn}$
B	$b - 1$	$\dfrac{\sum B^2}{acn} - \dfrac{T^2}{abcn}$
C	$c - 1$	$\dfrac{\sum C^2}{abn} - \dfrac{T^2}{abcn}$
AB	$(a-1)(b-1)$ $= ab - a - b + 1$	$\dfrac{\sum AB^2}{cn} - \dfrac{\sum A^2}{bcn} - \dfrac{\sum B^2}{acn} + \dfrac{T^2}{abcn}$
AC	$(a-1)(c-1)$ $= ac - a - c + 1$	$\dfrac{\sum AC^2}{bn} - \dfrac{\sum A^2}{bcn} - \dfrac{\sum C^2}{abn} + \dfrac{T^2}{abcn}$
BC	$(b-1)(c-1)$ $= bc - b - c + 1$	$\dfrac{\sum BC^2}{an} - \dfrac{\sum B^2}{acn} - \dfrac{\sum C^2}{abn} + \dfrac{T^2}{abcn}$
ABC	$(a-1)(b-1)(c-1)$ $= abc - ab - ac - bc$ $+ a + b + c - 1$	$\dfrac{\sum ABC^2}{n} - \dfrac{\sum AB^2}{cn} - \dfrac{\sum AC^2}{bn} - \dfrac{\sum BC^2}{an}$ $+ \dfrac{\sum A^2}{bcn} + \dfrac{\sum B^2}{acn} + \dfrac{\sum C^2}{abn} - \dfrac{T^2}{abcn}$
S/ABC	$N - abc$	$\sum Y^2 - \dfrac{\sum ABC^2}{n}$
T	$N - 1$	$\sum Y^2 - \dfrac{T^2}{abcn}$

denominator. Lastly, notice the pattern in the sequences of addition and subtraction: The factor with the most elements (*ABC*, in this case) is added, and then all two-way combinations of those elements are subtracted, and then all one-way elements are added, and then the *T* element is subtracted.[5] The segments of the computational equation, in short, follow the same pattern of addition and subtraction as the expanded degrees-of-freedom statement. Once this pattern is apparent to you, you can generate the computational equations for any factorial design from the expanded degrees of freedom.

Figure 5.2 diagrams the partition of sums of squares and degrees of freedom for the three-way factorial randomized-groups ANOVA.

Suppose we are investigating the eagerness (the DV) of a bull in the presence of a cow. Factor *A* is deprivation time for the bull (short vs. long), *B* is familiarity of cow (familiar vs. unfamiliar), and *C* is decoration of the pen (unpainted wood vs. floral wallpaper). Table 5.21 shows a hypothetical data set for this experiment. Table 5.22 shows the syntax and output for a SYSTAT ANOVA run on these data.

The source table, with S/ABC labeled `Error`, shows that all three main effects are statistically significant. Means for each of the levels of the main effects appear in the table labeled `Least square means`. For example, the mean eagerness of bulls after short deprivation is 2.6 and the mean eagerness after long deprivation is 6.0. Among the interactions, only the two-way interaction

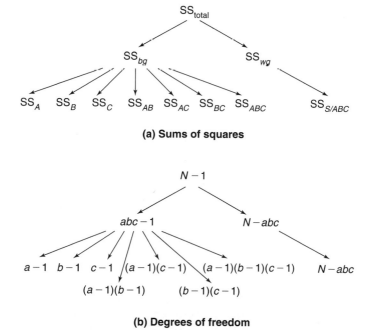

(a) Sums of squares

(b) Degrees of freedom

**FIGURE 5.2   Partition of (a) Sums of Squares and
(b) Degrees of Freedom for Three-Way Factorial
Randomized-Groups Design**

[5]In a four-way study, after the four-way interaction (*ABCD*) is included, the three-way interactions are subtracted, and then the two-way combinations are added, and then the one-way elements are subtracted, and, finally, the *T* element is added.

TABLE 5.21   Hypothetical Data Set for Three-Way Randomized-Groups ANOVA

Deprivation	Familiarity	Decor	Eagerness
1	1	1	4
1	1	1	3
1	1	1	2
1	1	1	3
1	1	1	0
1	1	2	3
1	1	2	0
1	1	2	2
1	1	2	1
1	1	2	4
1	2	1	0
1	2	1	2
1	2	1	2
1	2	1	0
1	2	1	2
1	2	2	6
1	2	2	5
1	2	2	5
1	2	2	5
1	2	2	3
2	1	1	0
2	1	1	5
2	1	1	4
2	1	1	1
2	1	1	3
2	1	2	6
2	1	2	7
2	1	2	6
2	1	2	6
2	1	2	6
2	2	1	9
2	2	1	6
2	2	1	6
2	2	1	6
2	2	1	7
2	2	2	6
2	2	2	10
2	2	2	9
2	2	2	9
2	2	2	8

**TABLE 5.22   Three-Way Randomized-Groups ANOVA through SYSTAT ANOVA:
Syntax and Selected Output**

```
PRINT=MEDIUM
ANOVA
CATEGORY DEPRIVATION FAMILIARITY DECOR
COVAR
DEPEND EAGERNESS
ESTIMATE
```

Effects coding used for categorical variables in model.

Categorical values encountered during processing are:
DEPRIVATION (2 levels)
         1,   2
FAMILIARITY (2 levels)
         1,   2
DECOR (2 levels)
         1,   2

Dep Var: EAGERNESS   N: 40   Multiple R: 0.891   Squared multiple R: 0.794

Analysis of Variance

Source	Sum-of-Squares	DF	Mean-Square	F-Ratio	P
DEPRIVATION	115.600	1	115.600	58.904	0.000
FAMILIARITY	40.000	1	40.000	20.382	0.000
DECOR	44.100	1	44.100	22.471	0.000
DEPRIVATION *FAMILIARITY	14.400	1	14.400	7.338	0.011
DEPRIVATION*DECOR	2.500	1	2.500	1.274	0.267
FAMILIARITY*DECOR	2.500	1	2.500	1.274	0.267
DEPRIVATION *FAMILIARITY*DECOR	22.500	1	22.500	11.465	0.002
Error	62.800	32	1.963		

Least squares means.

	LS Mean	SE	N
DEPRIVATION =1	2.600	0.313	20
DEPRIVATION =2	6.000	0.313	20

| FAMILIARITY =1 | 3.300 | 0.313 | 20 |
| FAMILIARITY =2 | 5.300 | 0.313 | 20 |

| DECOR   =1 | 3.250 | 0.313 | 20 |
| DECOR   =2 | 5.350 | 0.313 | 20 |

(continued)

TABLE 5.22   Continued

	LS Mean	SE	N
DEPRIVATION =1			
FAMILIARITY =1	2.200	0.443	10
DEPRIVATION =1			
FAMILIARITY =2	3.000	0.443	10
DEPRIVATION =2			
FAMILIARITY =1	4.400	0.443	10
DEPRIVATION =2			
FAMILIARITY =2	7.600	0.443	10
DEPRIVATION =1			
DECOR =1	1.800	0.443	10
DEPRIVATION =1			
DECOR =2	3.400	0.443	10
DEPRIVATION =2			
DECOR =1	4.700	0.443	10
DEPRIVATION =2			
DECOR =2	7.300	0.443	10
FAMILIARITY =1			
DECOR =1	2.500	0.443	10
FAMILIARITY =1			
DECOR =2	4.100	0.443	10
FAMILIARITY =2			
DECOR =1	4.000	0.443	10
FAMILIARITY =2			
DECOR =2	6.600	0.443	10
DEPRIVATION =1			
FAMILIARITY =1			
DECOR =1	2.400	0.626	5
DEPRIVATION =1			
FAMILIARITY =1			
DECOR =2	2.000	0.626	5
DEPRIVATION =1			
FAMILIARITY =2			
DECOR =1	1.200	0.626	5
DEPRIVATION =1			
FAMILIARITY =2			
DECOR =2	4.800	0.626	5
DEPRIVATION =2			
FAMILIARITY =1			
DECOR =1	2.600	0.626	5
DEPRIVATION =2			
FAMILIARITY =1			
DECOR =2	6.200	0.626	5
DEPRIVATION =2			
FAMILIARITY =2			
DECOR =1	6.800	0.626	5
DEPRIVATION =2			
FAMILIARITY =2			
DECOR =2	8.400	0.626	5

of deprivation by familiarity ($P = 0.011$) and the three-way interaction of deprivation by familiarity by decoration ($P = 0.002$) are statistically reliable. Plots of marginal and cell means are omitted here. Interpretation of interactions for three-way designs is discussed in Section 5.6.1.2.

Generating computational equations for factorial designs with more than three IVs follows a simple pattern.

1. List all IVs. There is a main effect for each IV, with degrees of freedom equal to the number of levels of that IV minus 1.
2. Form all combinations of two-way interactions among IVs. Degrees of freedom for each interaction are the product of the degrees of freedom for each of the IVs forming the interaction.
3. Form all combinations of three-way interactions among IVs. Again, degrees of freedom are the products of the degrees of freedom for component IVs.
4. Continue forming combinations of interactions until the highest-order interaction is listed (e.g., *ABCDE*).
5. The error term is the within-cell variability: *S* before the slash, the highest-order interaction after the slash, for example, *S/ABCDE*.
6. Expand degrees-of-freedom equations to develop the segments needed and their patterns of addition and subtraction (cf. Table 5.20).
7. Form the computational equations with all elements in either the numerator or denominator of each segment and follow the rules of substitution for 1s and *N*s.

Computer analysis of higher-order factorials requires a column in the data file for each IV and a column for the DV. Then the IVs are listed in the appropriate syntax instruction for factors used by the statistical program. Interactions are formed and tested automatically by SPSS and SYSTAT ANOVA. SYSTAT GLM, MINITAB GLM, and SAS require that they be specified in the model instruction (cf. Table 5.18).

5.5.2 Factorial Design with a Single Control

Sometimes factorial designs have two or more IVs representing levels of experimental treatments but only a single control group. Consider a study with two types of drugs and two levels of dosage, say, 5 and 10 mg. If the researcher also wants a control group with no drug treatment (no *A* or *B*), there is only one such group since 0 mg of the first drug is just the same as 0 mg of the second drug. Or consider an experiment in which the researcher is interested in the effects of type (classical and heavy metal) and loudness (40 and 80 dB) of background music during study on examination scores. If the researcher also wants a 0-dB control group, there is only one because 0 dB of classical music sounds just like 0 dB of heavy metal.

This is sometimes called a *dangling group design*. Table 5.23 shows a layout for the simplest form of such a design. The factorial portion of this design can have any number of IVs with two or more levels of each IV; the distinguishing feature is the single control group.

The first step in the analysis is to turn the design into a one-way design with, in this example, five levels. The error term is $SS_{S/A}$, found as in Sections 3.2.3.2 and 4.4.3. Degrees of freedom for the error term are found by multiplying the total number of groups ($a = 5$ in this example) by $n - 1$. This error term is easily found by computer by using a column of numbers that identifies group membership; this is the appropriate error term for all the tests.

The second step is to use comparisons, preferably planned beforehand (see Section 5.6.4), to test relevant hypotheses. One likely test is of the control condition mean against the pooled means

TABLE 5.23   Factorial Design with Two Levels Each of Two Drug Treatments and a Single Control

		B: Dosage	
		b_1: 5 mg	b_2: 10 mg
	a_1: First drug	a_1b_1: Group 1	a_1b_2: Group 2
A: Type of Drug	a_2: Second drug	a_2b_1: Group 3	a_2b_2: Group 4
			Control: 0 mg Group 5

for four drug conditions (with weighting coefficients of 1, 1, 1, 1, −4). An example of this step of the analysis is in Section 5.6.4.1.2. The other three comparisons might well be an omnibus analysis of the 2 × 2 factorial part of the design into *A*, *B*, and *AB*. The weighting coefficients for these comparisons are in Table 5.9 to be used with the procedures of Section 5.6.4.1.2. These four comparisons are a complete orthogonal partition of the sum of squares for the design. Analysis of these designs is also discussed by Himmelfarb (1975), Keppel (1982), and Winer and colleagues (1991).

5.6   Some Important Issues

Several of the issues discussed in this section also apply to designs other than randomized groups. For example, the interpretation of interactions is the same for any factorial design. They are discussed here only because this is the first opportunity to do so. Subsequent chapters refer back to this section when appropriate.

5.6.1   Interpreting Interactions

Presence of an interaction indicates that the effect of one IV on the DV depends on the level of another IV. Absence of an interaction indicates that the effect of one IV on the DV is similar for all levels of another IV. The null hypothesis is that there is no interaction. Rejection of the null hypothesis indicates that there probably is, in reality, an interaction.

5.6.1.1   Two-Way Designs

Interactions in a two-way design may be expressed in either direction or from a prediction perspective. For example, the interaction between length of stay and profession in the 3 × 3 example of Section 5.4.3 may be stated either as "The effect of different lengths of stay on ratings of a vacation depends on type of profession" or as "The effect of different professions on ratings of a vacation depends on length of stay." Or, from a prediction perspective, one could say that "Prediction of the rating of the vacation requires knowledge of both the type of profession and the length of stay."

Tests of interactions are also tests of differences among mean *differences*. For example, the interaction in the two-way design also may be stated as "The differences between mean ratings of vacations of various lengths are different for the different professions" or 'The differences between mean ratings for different professions are different for the three lengths of stay." The means for the small-sample example of Section 5.4.3 are in Table 5.24.

Interactions are best illustrated in graphs of means in which levels of one IV define the abscissa, the DV is on the ordinate, and the second IV is represented by separate lines. For example, a plot of the cell means of Table 5.24 is in Figure 5.3.

TABLE 5.24 Cell and Marginal Means for Hypothetical Data Set for 3 × 3 ANOVA of Table 5.3

A: Profession	B: Vacation Length			Marginal Means for A
	b_1: 1 week	b_2: 2 weeks	b_3: 3 weeks	
a_1: Administrators	0.33	5.67	6.33	4.11
a_2: Belly Dancers	6.00	6.00	8.33	6.78
a_3: Politicians	6.33	9.00	2.67	6.00
Marginal means for B	4.22	6.89	5.78	5.63

FIGURE 5.3 Mean Rating of Vacation as a Function of Length of Stay and Profession

This plot shows differences among professions in vacation ratings as a function of length of stay. Politicians prefer 2-week vacations and do not much like 3-week vacations. Belly dancers like vacations of any length but prefer 3-week vacations. Administrators really dislike 1-week vacations and may prefer 3-week vacations to 2-week vacations. This is just an eyeball description of the patterns. Specific comparisons (Section 5.6.4) are necessary to make definite statements about preferences.

The interaction could also be plotted in the other direction, with profession defining the abscissa and length of stay represented by separate lines, as shown in Figure 5.4.[6] This figure is a bit more difficult to interpret verbally because it suggests an interpretation in terms of weeks rather than profession. Three-week vacations are disliked by politicians but most preferred by belly dancers; 2-week vacations are preferred by politicians but produce moderate ratings by the other two groups; 1-week vacations receive moderate ratings by politicians and belly dancers but are heartily disliked by administrators.

Both orientations are equally legitimate. The choice is yours as a researcher, but ease of interpretation is the final criterion. The following guidelines may be useful:

1. If one IV is quantitative (e.g., weeks) and the other is qualitative (e.g., profession), interpretation is usually easier if the quantitative IV defines the abscissa.
2. If one IV is a blocking variable (e.g., profession), interpretation is often easier if the blocking IV is plotted as separate lines.
3. If one IV has more levels than the other, interpretation is often easier if the IV with more levels defines the abscissa.

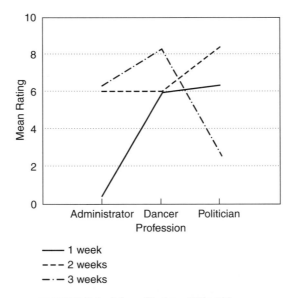

FIGURE 5.4   Mean Rating of Vacation as a Function of Length of Stay and Profession

---

[6]By convention, interaction is plotted as a line graph to emphasize parallelism of lines. The use of a line graph with profession defining the abscissa does not imply that profession is a quantitative variable. Strictly speaking, bar graphs are more appropriate when IVs are qualitative, but line graphs often are more easily interpreted.

In practice, the researcher frequently produces both plots and chooses the one that is more easily "verbalized."

When there is interaction, the lines are not parallel. The null hypothesis for an interaction can also be expressed as parallelism of the lines, with rejection of the null hypothesis when there is significant departure from parallelism. Suppose that belly dancers consistently rate their vacations higher than politicians and that politicians rate their vacations higher than administrators. Suppose also that everybody prefers a 2-week vacation to a 1-week vacation, and a 3-week vacation to a 2-week vacation, and by about the same amounts. In this case, there is no interaction and the lines are parallel, as shown in Figure 5.5.[7]

This figure shows that differences in ratings between professions are the same for all levels of length of vacation or that differences in ratings between different lengths of vacation are the same for all professions. There are no differences among mean differences.

Notice that Figure 5.5 makes it easy to interpret main effects, assuming that they are statistically reliable. The line for the belly dancers is consistently higher than the line for politicians, which, in turn, is consistently higher than the line for administrators. On average, 3-week vacations get higher ratings than 2-week vacations, and so on. Differences in means for main effects are often visible even when lines are not parallel. For example, Figure 5.3 also shows higher ratings by belly dancers than administrators, and, on average, higher ratings for 2-week vacations than 1-week vacations.

Caution is needed when interpreting significant main effects in the presence of a significant interaction. One way of looking at the presence of interaction is that the effects of one IV on the DV

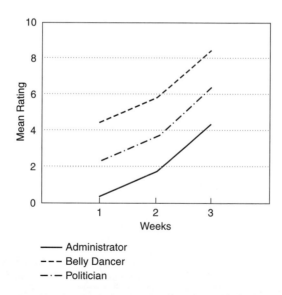

**FIGURE 5.5   Mean Rating of Vacation as a Function
of Length of Vacation and Profession, Assuming No Interaction**

[7]Lines do not have to be precisely parallel to conclude that there is no significant interaction. Failing to reject the null hypothesis for interaction means that lines do not deviate reliably from parallelism.

do not generalize over the levels of the other IV. Once you know that the effects of one IV are tempered by or contingent on the levels of another IV, interpretation of either IV alone is problematic. Some (e.g., Keppel, 1991) recommend only interpreting significant main effects when there is no interaction or if the interaction is significant but effect size is small relative to main effects and there is an ordinal pattern to the means. If the means are ordinal (as in Figure 5.5), they line up in the same order at all levels of the other IV, so the lines do not cross each other even if they are not parallel. The means in Figures 5.3 and 5.4 are disordinal because the lines cross. In any event, main effects should be interpreted cautiously or not at all when the interaction is both reliable and strong.

Consider, for example, the tests of main effects in an experiment involving ADHD (hyperactive) kids and non-ADHD kids who are given either stimulants or tranquilizers. ADHD kids have a paradoxical response to these two drugs and become *more* active when given tranquilizers and *less* active when given stimulants. Non-ADHD kids respond the other way to the two drugs. Table 5.25 shows the typical pattern of behavior.

Results of ANOVA on data like these are probably a significant interaction but a nonsignificant main effect for type of drug and for type of kid. This is because the means on the margins are very similar when averaged over both high and low scores. Taken at face value, the tests of main effects imply that ADHD kids and non-ADHD kids have the same behavior, as do kids given stimulants and tranquilizers, clearly misleading conclusions, but indicative of the potential problem of interpreting main effects in the presence of interaction.

5.6.1.2   Higher-Order Factorials

Numerous interactions are tested in higher-order factorials. For example, a three-way design with *A*, *B*, and *C* provides tests of all two-way interactions (*AB*, *AC*, and *BC*) plus the three-way interaction (*ABC*). Any of these or all of these may be statistically significant. If the three-way interaction is not significant, but one or more of the two-way interactions are significant, they are plotted and interpreted as if a two-way design had been analyzed.

For example, in the three-way design of Section 5.5.1, the two-way interaction between deprivation and familiarity is statistically reliable (cf. Table 5.22). Figure 5.6 plots the means involved in that interaction. The plot shows that the effect of deprivation time on eagerness is greater in the presence of unfamiliar rather than familiar cows.

But when the three-way interaction is significant as well, interpretation of lower-order interactions and main effects is also problematic. From a prediction perspective, a three-way interaction

TABLE 5.25   Problematic Nature of Main Effects When Interaction Is Significant

		Type of Drug		Main Effect of Kid
		Stimulant	*Tranquilizer*	
Type of Kid	*ADHD*	Low	High	Medium
	Non-ADHD	High	Low	Medium
Main Effect of Drug		Medium	Medium	

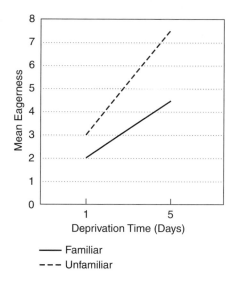

**FIGURE 5.6   Mean Eagerness of Bull as a Function
of Deprivation Time and Familiarity of Cow**

means that the researcher must know the status on all three IVs in order to accurately predict a score for a case on the DV. That is, the generalizability of two-way interactions and main effects is contingent on the level of the third variable so that

1. the *AB* interaction varies with the level of *C*, or
2. the *AC* interaction varies with the level of *B*, or
3. the *BC* interaction varies with the level of *A*

Figure 5.7 plots all of the cell means for the three-way interaction found in Section 5.5.1.

The interaction between deprivation and familiarity shown in Figure 5.7 is different for wood- and wallpaper-decorated pens. There is little interaction in the presence of floral wallpaper. At c_2 (floral wallpaper), deprivation and familiarity are said to be additive (i.e., there is no interaction) because eagerness is a simple sum of the effects of longer deprivation and unfamiliar cow. There is an interaction in the presence of wood, however, in which the effect of deprivation on eagerness occurs only in the presence of unfamiliar cows (note the nearly horizontal line for familiar cows). Notice that this figure also suggests main effects of all three IVs. Plotted points are higher on average for wallpaper than for wood decoration, are higher on average for 5 days than 1 day of deprivation, and are higher on average for unfamiliar than familiar cows.

If there were no three-way interaction, the relationship between deprivation and familiarity would be the same in both types of pens. For example, both plots of Figure 5.7 might have the same interaction as found in the presence of wood. Or both plots might have the same lack of interaction found in the presence of wallpaper.

Full interpretation of a three-way interaction requires further analysis through specific comparisons, just as does full interpretation of a two-way interaction, or main effects with more than two levels.

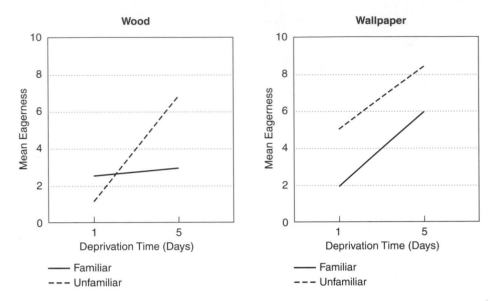

FIGURE 5.7   Mean Eagerness of Bull as a Function of Familiarity of Cow, Days of Deprivation, and Decoration of Pen

5.6.2   Effect Size

Recall that effect size is the proportion of variability in the DV that is associated with or accounted for by an IV (cf. Section 4.5.1). In a Venn diagram (e.g., Figure 4.3), where the circle for the DV represents all of the variability in the DV, effect size is the overlapping area between the DV and an IV (a main effect or an interaction). Effect sizes in a factorial design are reported for all statistically significant effects. Sometimes researchers also choose to report effect size for nonsignificant effects.

The generalization of η^2 for factorial designs is

$$\eta^2_{\text{effect}} = R^2_{\text{effect}} = \frac{\text{SS}_{\text{effect}}}{\text{SS}_T} \tag{5.13}$$

where $\text{SS}_{\text{effect}}$ is the sum of squares for A or B or AB, or whatever.

The three significant effects for the two-way small-sample example of Table 5.7 thus produce, for profession:

$$\eta^2_A = R^2_A = \frac{33.85}{190.30} = .18$$

and for length of stay:

$$\eta^2_B = R^2_B = \frac{32.30}{190.30} = .17$$

and for interaction of length of stay with profession:

$$\eta^2_{AB} = R^2_{AB} = \frac{104.15}{190.30} = .55$$

The two main effects, length of stay and profession of rater, account for approximately the same proportion of variance in the rating of a vacation. The interaction, however, accounts for a much greater proportion of variance. In a factorial design with equal n, these effects are orthogonal and additive, so that .90 (.17 + .18 + .55) of the variability in rating of vacation is predictable from the combination of IVs.

With factorial designs and several significant sources of variability, this measure of effect size can be quite small because the denominator contains systematic effects other than the one of current interest. The denominator (SS_T) is thus larger than it would be if a one-way ANOVA had been run on one of the factors, say, A, making the ratio smaller. A solution is to compute partial η^2 in which the denominator consists only of the effect of interest and the error; this produces a better guess of the effect size that might be found in a one-way design with just factor A:

$$\text{Partial } \eta^2 = \frac{SS_{\text{effect}}}{SS_{\text{effect}} + SS_{\text{error}}} \tag{5.14}$$

where SS_{error} is the error sum of squares ($SS_{S/AB}$, $SS_{S/ABC}$, or whatever).

For the main effect of A, profession, in the two-way example, for instance,

$$\text{Partial } \eta^2_A = \frac{33.85}{33.85 + 20.00} = .63$$

a much larger estimate than that produced by standard η^2. This is the **Eta Squared** that is produced by SPSS GLM (cf. Table 5.15). However, when partial η^2 is used, effect sizes from various sources are *not* additive.

Effect sizes for comparisons may be calculated with respect to the total SS or with respect to the effect they are decomposing. These are demonstrated in context of the various types of comparisons in Section 5.6.4.

As in the one-way analysis, η^2 (or partial η^2) is a descriptive statistic, not a parameter estimate. The corresponding parameter estimate, $\hat{\omega}^2$, may also be applied to factorial designs. As in one-way designs, $\hat{\omega}^2$ adjusts for overestimation by η^2 and is always smaller than η^2. For factorial designs in which only one effect is significant:

$$\hat{\omega} = \frac{SS_{\text{effect}} - df_{\text{effect}}(MS_{\text{error}})}{SS_T + MS_{\text{error}}} \tag{5.15}$$

where MS_{error} is $MS_{S/AB}$, $MS_{S/ABC}$, or whatever is appropriate for the design.

Although there is more than one significant effect in the design so that application of Equation 5.15 is problematic, $\hat{\omega}^2$ for the main effect of A in the two-way example is

$$\hat{\omega}^2_A = \frac{33.85 - 2(1.11)}{190.30 + 1.11} = .17$$

smaller than the .18 produced by η^2.

The partial form of $\hat{\omega}^2$ is available when there is more than one significant effect (Keren and Lewis, 1979):

$$\text{Partial } \hat{\omega}^2 = \frac{\text{df}_{\text{effect}}(\text{MS}_{\text{effect}} - \text{MS}_{\text{error}})/N}{\left[\text{df}_{\text{effect}}(\text{MS}_{\text{effect}} - \text{MS}_{\text{error}})/N\right] + \text{MS}_{\text{error}}} \tag{5.16}$$

Applied to the main effect of A,

$$\text{Partial } \hat{\omega}^2_A = \frac{2(16.93 - 1.11)/27}{[2(16.93 - 1.11)]/27 + 1.11} = .53$$

This estimate is smaller than partial η^2, but much larger than unadjusted $\hat{\omega}^2$.

A drawback of $\hat{\omega}^2$ (whether adjusted or not) is that it becomes much more complicated when the layout is other than a randomized-groups design with equal sample sizes in all cells. The descriptive measures η^2 or partial η^2, on the other hand, easily generalize to a variety of ANOVA designs.

Cohen's d (1977), described in Section 4.5.1, works well for main effects if means are evenly spaced throughout their range. However, it also becomes complicated for other arrangements of means within their range and when applied to interactions in factorial designs (see Cohen, 1977, Chapter 8). Thus, d is a less convenient measure than $\hat{\omega}^2$ or η^2, especially for factorial designs.

5.6.3   Power and Sample Size

Considerations for designing a powerful factorial research study are the same as those for designing a powerful one-way study, as discussed in Section 4.5.2.

5.6.3.1   Estimating Sample Size

Some techniques discussed in Section 4.5.2 are available for estimating sample size in factorial designs. However, the "quick-and-dirty" methods of Equations 4.6 and 4.7 are problematic with factorial designs because of the many possible mean differences to be evaluated.

One approach is to solve Equation 4.6 or 4.7 separately for each main effect and each interaction in a factorial design and then use the largest resulting sample size. For the interaction, the difference between means, δ, is defined as the smallest difference between mean differences to be detected.[8]

---

[8]Interpretation of interactions as differences among mean differences is discussed in Section 5.4.

Say, for example, that a pilot study for a 2×2 experiment produces $MS_{S/AB} = 1$ and the cell and marginal means of Table 5.26.

Sample-size estimation for either of the main effects follows procedures of Section 4.5.2.2, using $MS_{S/AB}$ as the estimate of error variance, and realizing that the resulting sample size is divided among levels of the other IV. For example, the main effect of B has $\delta = 6.65 - 6.1 = 0.55$ in the pilot study, which may be used as an estimate of the smallest difference to be detected. Entering into Equation 4.7 (which assumes $\alpha = .05$ and $\beta = .15$):

$$n = \frac{18\sigma^2}{\delta^2} = \frac{18(1)}{0.55^2} = 59.5$$

This value is divided by the number of levels of A to produce cell-size estimates, so that $n = 59.5/2 = 29.75$, or 30 per cell.

For the interaction, the difference among mean differences is $\delta = (7.5 - 6.6) - (5.8 - 5.6) = 0.7$. When entered in Equation 4.7:

$$n = \frac{18(1)}{0.7^2} = 36.73$$

This value must be multiplied by 2 because each difference is based on two cells, so that $n = 2(36.73) = 73.46$. Rounding up, $n = 74$ per cell.

PC-SIZE (Dallal, 1986) and NCSS PASS work well for estimating sample size for main effects in a factorial design, but interaction estimates are complicated. GANOVA (Woodward et al., 1990), however, handles all effects in factorial designs quite well. Table 5.27 shows the output from GANOVA for the 2×2 example, assuming $\alpha = .05$ and $\beta = .15$. To use GANOVA, you have to specify the design, your choice of α error level and power $(1 - \beta)$, and the effects you want to test. The sample size for the main effect of A is requested by the numeral 1, the main effect of B by the numeral 2, and the AB interaction by 12.

The output provides separate sample-size estimates for each effect; choose the largest sample size if you want all effects to be statistically reliable. Both cell and total sample sizes are provided for planned tests as well as Scheffé-adjusted post hoc tests (see Section 5.6.4.3). Thus, a sample of 74 cases per cell (the same as estimated from the quick-and-dirty method) is needed for the proposed study, 296 altogether.

TABLE 5.26   Hypothetical Means from a Pilot Study for a 2×2 Design

	b_1	b_2	Mean A
a_1	5.6	5.8	5.7
a_2	6.6	7.5	7.05
Mean B	6.1	6.65	

TABLE 5.27   **Sample-Size Determination through GANOVA**

```
                         GANOVA 4
          (Preliminary Professional Version-1/30/92)
       ANALYSIS OF LINEAR MODELS FOR EXPERIMENTAL DESIGN
                     POWER/SAMPLE SIZE


                      Copyright 1990
          M. L. Brecht, J. A. Woodward, D. G. Bonett



SUMMARY OF THE DESIGN
-----------------------------------------------------
2 -WAY ANOVA WITH FIXED EFFECTS


   2 BETWEEN-GROUP FACTORS        LEVELS
     ( 1 )FACTOR 1                   2
     ( 2 )FACTOR 2                   2
   -------------------------------------------------


   -------------------------------------------------
   -------------------------------------------------
HYPOTHESIS ON BETWEEN-GROUP FACTORS:
  MAIN EFFECT OF FACTOR 1
  ----------------------------

     ALPHA=.0500  POWER=.850

  NUMBER         TOTAL
 PER CELL     SAMPLE SIZE    POWER
 ----------------------------------------------------
ONE PLANNED TEST
      30           120        0.848
      31           124        0.859
 ----------------------------------------------------
SCHEFFE POST HOC TEST
      49           196        0.847
      50           200        0.856
 ----------------------------------------------------
```

5.6.3.2   *Power of a Nonsignificant Effect*

The GANOVA program (Woodward et al., 1990) also facilitates power estimates for a completed factorial design when information about the design, sample size, means, and error variance are entered. Power estimates are often used at this point to investigate the reason for a nonsignificant finding. Output includes power estimates both for planned and post hoc analyses. Table 5.28 shows output from GANOVA for the data in the 3×3 ANOVA of Section 5.4.3. All of the effects in the small-sample example had power in excess of 99%. Note that these are the same values available from SPSS GLM in Table 5.15.

TABLE 5.27 Continued

```
---------------------------------------------------
---------------------------------------------------
HYPOTHESIS ON BETWEEN-GROUP FACTORS:
  MAIN EFFECT OF FACTOR 2
-------------------------------

    ALPHA=.0500  POWER=.850

 NUMBER        TOTAL
PER CELL    SAMPLE SIZE   POWER
---------------------------------------------------
ONE PLANNED TEST
     5           20        0.809
     6           24        0.882
---------------------------------------------------
SCHEFFE POST HOC TEST
     8           32        0.791
     9           36        0.854
---------------------------------------------------
---------------------------------------------------

---------------------------------------------------
HYPOTHESIS ON BETWEEN-GROUP FACTORS:
  INTERACTION OF 1
            AND 2
-------------------------------

    ALPHA=.0500  POWER=.850

 NUMBER        TOTAL
PER CELL    SAMPLE SIZE   POWER
---------------------------------------------------
ONE PLANNED TEST
    73          292        0.846
    74          296        0.851
---------------------------------------------------
SCHEFFE POST HOC TEST
   120          480        0.847
   121          484        0.851
---------------------------------------------------
```

5.6.4 Specific Comparisons

A significant main effect in an omnibus analysis is ambiguous when the main effect has more than two levels. Just as in a one-way design with three or more levels, ANOVA tells you that the means are not equal, but gives no clue as to which means are different from each other. And a significant interaction, even in the 2×2 design in which both IVs have two levels, almost always warrants closer inspection. Various comparison procedures provide more focused tests of differences among means.

TABLE 5.28   Output of GANOVA for Results of 3 × 3 Factorial ANOVA

```
                        GANOVA 4
          (Preliminary Professional Version—1/30/92)
       ANALYSIS OF LINEAR MODELS FOR EXPERIMENTAL DESIGN
                     POWER/SAMPLE SIZE

                     Copyright 1990
            M. L. Brecht, J. A. Woodward, D. G. Bonett

SUMMARY OF THE DESIGN
-------------------------------------------------------------------


2 -WAY ANOVA WITH FIXED EFFECTS

   2 BETWEEN-GROUP FACTORS        LEVELS
       ( 1 )FACTOR 1                3
       ( 2 )FACTOR 2                3


-------------------------------------------------------------------
-------------------------------------------------------------------
-------------------------------------------------------------------
HYPOTHESIS ON BETWEEN-GROUP FACTORS:
   MAIN EFFECT OF FACTOR 1
                                             POWER
   NUMBER     ALPHA    NON-CENTRALITY     ONE          SCHEFFE
   PER CELL            PARAMETER      PLANNED TEST  POST-HOC TEST
-------------------------------------------------------------------
      3     .0500       29.167         0.996          0.303
-------------------------------------------------------------------


-------------------------------------------------------------------
-------------------------------------------------------------------
HYPOTHESIS ON BETWEEN-GROUP FACTORS:
   MAIN EFFECT OF FACTOR 2
                                             POWER
   NUMBER     ALPHA    NON-CENTRALITY     ONE          SCHEFFE
   PER CELL            PARAMETER      PLANNED TEST  POST-HOC TEST
-------------------------------------------------------------------
      3     .0500       30.504         0.997          0.333
-------------------------------------------------------------------


-------------------------------------------------------------------
-------------------------------------------------------------------
HYPOTHESIS ON BETWEEN-GROUP FACTORS:
   INTERACTION OF 1
             AND 2
                                             POWER
   NUMBER     ALPHA    NON-CENTRALITY     ONE          SCHEFFE
   PER CELL            PARAMETER      PLANNED TEST  POST-HOC TEST
-------------------------------------------------------------------
      3     .0500       93.718         1.000          0.715
-------------------------------------------------------------------
```

As for a one-way design, comparisons may be either planned or post hoc (Section 4.5.5). Comparisons done post hoc are more conservative (less powerful), so it is better to plan them if you can. Or, as advocated by Keppel (1991), you can mix the two by following a sequential plan in which the choice of post hoc comparisons depends on the outcome of omnibus tests.

5.6.4.1 Types of Comparisons

Comparisons test differences among means or combinations of means by applying weighting coefficients to them and forming F ratios that are tested using critical values of F based on either planned or post hoc rules of assessment. Three kinds of comparisons are available for factorial designs: comparisons of marginal means for main effects, comparisons applied to cell means for investigating special designs (such as the dangling control group), and comparisons intended to dissect an interaction (as discussed in Section 5.6.4.4).

5.6.4.1.1 Comparisons on Marginal Means

When a main effect with more than two levels is significant, or when there is a plan to investigate a main effect, comparisons on marginal means are often desirable. Remember, however, that comparisons on marginal effects are problematic when there is significant interaction, as discussed in Section 5.6.1. Significant interaction implies that the effect of one IV differs depending on the level of another IV. If you already know that a main effect has limited generalizability, its interpretation on the margin is often misleading.

To conduct a comparison on the margin (e.g., $SS_{A\,comp}$ or $SS_{B\,comp}$), coefficients are generated and applied to marginal means as they are in a one-way design. The means for each of the levels, averaged across all the levels of other IVs, are weighted by coefficients with the constraint that the coefficients sum to 0 for each comparison. Two comparisons are orthogonal if, in addition, the sum of the cross-products of weighting coefficients is 0.

There are two approaches to ANOVA, the traditional approach and the regression approach, as discussed in Section 5.4. The regression approach as illustrated in Section 5.4.4 builds marginal comparisons into the X columns themselves. The first column of Table 5.8, X_1, applies the coefficients $2 -1 -1$ to the three levels of A. The sum of squares for regression for this column *is* the sum of squares for that comparison on the marginal means for A ($SS_{A\,comp1}$). The second column, X_2, applies the coefficients $0\ 1 -1$ to the levels of A. The sum of squares for regression for this column is the sum of squares for that comparison on the marginal means ($SS_{A\,comp2}$).

The traditional ANOVA approach to the same comparisons is available through Equation 5.17. Because comparisons each have 1 df, the sum of squares is the same as the mean square, so the F ratio for marginal comparisons is obtained in one step.

$$F = \frac{n_{\overline{Y}}(\sum w_j \overline{Y}_j)^2 / \sum w_j^2}{MS_{error}}$$

(5.17)

where $n_{\overline{Y}}$ = number of scores in each of the means to be compared

$(\sum w_j \overline{Y}_j)^2$ = squared sum of the weighted means

$\sum w_j^2$ = sum of the squared coefficients

MS_{error} = mean square for error in the ANOVA

By using Equation 5.17 for the traditional ANOVA approach to data of the small-sample example, the coefficients for the comparison of administrators against belly dancers and politicians combined $(2 -1 -1$, just as for the regression approach) are applied to the marginal means of A (4.11, 6.78, 6.00), representing type of profession:

$$F = \frac{9[(2)(4.11) + (-1)(6.78) + (-1)(6.00)]^2/2^2 + (-1)^2 + (-1)^2}{1.11} = \frac{31.19}{1.11} = 28.10$$

The $n_{\overline{Y}}$ for this analysis is 9, the number of scores in each of the marginal means for A. Note that the numerator (which is both $SS_{A\,comp1}$ and $MS_{A\,comp1}$) is equivalent (when computations are carried to four decimal places) to $SS(reg.X_1)$ of Table 5.11. The same procedure is available for the second comparison on A, and, when the coefficients defining that comparison are used in Equation 5.17, yields $SS(reg.X_2)$ in the numerator (which is also both $SS_{A\,comp2}$ and $MS_{A\,comp2}$). If the trend coefficients for X_3 and X_4 in Table 5.8 are applied to marginal means of B (4.22, 6.89, 5.78—for length of stay), the numerators of Equation 5.17 become $SS(reg.X_3)$—$SS_{B\,comp1}$—and $SS(reg.X_4)$—or $SS_{B\,comp2}$—respectively. Comparisons of marginal means are interpreted as if in a one-way design.

Effect size for this comparison may be calculated in two ways. First, η^2 may be calculated for the comparison as a proportion of the total sum of squares for the factorial design:

$$\eta^2 = \frac{SS_{A\,comp}}{SS_T} = \frac{31.19}{190.30} = .16 \tag{5.18}$$

Alternatively, η^2 may be calculated for the comparison as a proportion of the main effect of which it is a component:

$$\eta^2 = \frac{SS_{A\,comp}}{SS_A} = \frac{31.19}{33.85} = .92 \tag{5.19}$$

The interpretation of these two versions of η^2 is quite different, so specify which you used when you report your results.

5.6.4.1.2   Comparisons on Cell Means

Usually, when weighting coefficients are applied to cell means, the researcher is attempting to understand an interaction; procedures appropriate to dissecting an interaction in a factorial design are discussed in Section 5.6.4.4. Sometimes, however, there is an unusual design, and coefficients are applied to cell means to analyze features of the design.

One example of an unusual design when comparisons might be applied to cell means is the dangling group design of Section 5.5.2. In this design, the researcher is very likely to want to know if the mean for the control group differs from the combined mean of the four treated groups. To accomplish this comparison, each of the four groups is assigned a coefficient of 1 and the control group a coefficient of -4. Table 5.29 shows the arrangement with the assigned coefficients. Suppose the means for the five groups are as shown in Table 5.30.

TABLE 5.29   Assignment of Weighting Coefficients in a Factorial Design with Two Levels Each of Two Drug Treatments and a Single Control

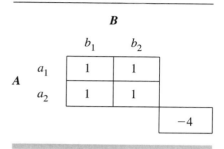

TABLE 5.30   Hypothetical Means for a Factorial Design with Two Levels Each of Two Drug Treatments and a Single Control

		B	
		b_1	b_2
A	a_1	5.6	5.8
	a_2	6.6	7.5
			4.0

The $n_{\overline{Y}}$ of Equation 5.17 is the cell sample size; if we assume that $n = 5$ and that $MS_{S/A} = 2.3$ in this example,

$$F = \frac{5[(1)(5.6) + (1)(5.8) + (1)(6.6) + (1)(7.5) + (-4)(4)]^2/1^2 + 1^2 + 1^2 + 1^2 + (-4)^2}{2.3} = 9.81$$

Obtained F is evaluated as either planned or post hoc, depending on when the decision to do the comparison was made. Effect size is calculated as the proportion of total variance associated with the effect:

$$\eta^2 = \frac{SS_{comp}}{SS_T} \tag{5.20}$$

A solution requires calculation of SS_T, which, in turn, requires the raw scores not given in this example.

5.6.4.2   *Critical* **F** *for Planned Comparisons*

If you have planned your comparisons prior to data collection and if you have planned no more of them than you have degrees of freedom for the effect to be tested, critical F is obtained from the tables just as in routine ANOVA. Each comparison is tested against critical F at routine α with one degree of freedom in the numerator and degrees of freedom associated with MS_{error} in the denominator. If obtained F is larger than critical F, the null hypothesis represented by the weighting coefficients is rejected.

In the 3×3 small-sample example, error df $= 18$ (see Table 5.7), and the critical value in Table A.1 is 4.41 at $\alpha = .05$. The obtained $F = 28.10$ for the first marginal comparison, A_{comp1}, clearly exceeds the critical value, leading to the conclusion that there is a significant mean difference in ratings of vacations by administrators versus belly dancers and politicians.

In the dangling control group example, denominator df $= a(n-1) = 5(5-1) = 20$. The critical value from Table A.1 with 1 and 20 df and $\alpha = .05$ is 4.35. With obtained $F = 9.81$, the null hypothesis of no mean difference between the control group and the pooled treated groups is rejected.

As for the one-way design, the Bonferroni correction is applied if more comparisons are planned than are justified by the available df (Section 4.5.5.4.3).

5.6.4.3 Adjustments for Post Hoc Comparisons

Criteria for post hoc tests in the factorial design are the same as for the one-way design. The researcher chooses the most powerful post hoc method that allows the comparisons of interest. Both Scheffé and Tukey adjustments are available for marginal tests in factorial designs or for unusual designs. The Dunnett test is typically not applied in factorial designs. An exception is the design with a single control, which is treated as a one-way design for purposes of the Dunnett test (Section 4.5.3.5.3). Additional post hoc tests available in software are summarized in Table 4.28.

5.6.4.3.1 Scheffé
The Scheffé method for computing critical F for a comparison on marginal means is

$$F_S = (k-1)F_c \tag{5.21}$$

where $\quad F_S = $ adjusted critical F

$\quad (k-1) = $ degrees of freedom for the effect with k levels (a or b)

$\qquad F_c = $ tabled F with effect degrees of freedom in the numerator and degrees of freedom associated with the error term in the denominator

If obtained F is larger than F_S, the null hypothesis represented by the weighting coefficients for the comparison is rejected.

For example, for comparisons on the marginal means of A, critical $F_S = 2(3.55) = 7.10$. Obtained $F_{A\text{comp1}} = 28.10$ for comparing the means for administrators against the pooled mean for belly dancers and politicians exceeds even this strong adjustment. The same critical value is used for post hoc tests on marginal means of B because in this example the number of levels of B is also 3.

The adjustment for tests of cell means instead of marginal means for unusual designs is more drastic because there are usually numerous levels and, therefore, many possible comparisons. To find the total number of levels, you transform the factorial segment of the design into a one-way design with $a \times b$ levels and then add the remaining cells. Thus, the 2×2 part of the dangling control groups example yields 4 levels, plus the level for the control group, for a total of 5. If the dangling control groups comparison is done as part of a post hoc analysis, the critical value F_s is based on F_c with 4 and 20 df, so that $F_S = (5-1)(2.87) = 11.48$. The obtained $F = 9.81$, in this case, is not statistically reliable.

5.6.4.3.2 Tukey
There are two ways to use the Tukey test on main effects in a factorial design. The first, and probably most sensible, option is to do Tukey tests separately for each significant main effect. If done by hand, obtained F is calculated by assigning coefficients to marginal means (as in Section 5.6.4.1.1), whereas critical F_T is based on the number of marginal means. In Section 5.6.4.1.1, obtained F for the

difference in mean ratings between administrators and the other two groups is 28.10. Critical $F_T = (3.61)^2/2 = 6.52$ (Equation 4.15) for the three marginal means of A. Therefore, the mean difference for the comparison is significant by the Tukey criterion. This approach to the Tukey test is available in the GLM programs of SPSS,[9] MINITAB, SAS, and SYSTAT (but not SYSTAT ANOVA).

The second approach is simply to ignore the factorial arrangement and treat the means on the margins as if from a one-way design. That is, the cells are recoded into a one-way design as illustrated later in Table 5.31 and elsewhere. The Tukey test then is identical to that described in Section 4.5.5.5.2. This approach may also be taken with software for other pairwise comparisons that are available for one-way ANOVA, such as Bonferroni or Sidak.

If this approach is taken, the 3×3 example of Section 5.4.3 is treated as a one-way design with 9 groups and 36 possible pairwise comparisons. Obtained F's are calculated by assigning coefficients of 1 and -1 separately to each pair of means and critical F_T is based on 9 means, so that, in the example, $F_T = (4.96)^2/2 = 12.3$ at $\alpha = .05$. With so many possible comparisons, it is usually best to put the mean differences in order and test the smallest mean difference first, followed by the next smallest, and so on until the first significant difference is found. The larger differences also are significant. (Alternatively, you can test the largest difference first, and work down until a nonsignificant difference is found.) Or, the minimum significant mean difference, $\overline{d}_T$, may be found, as per Equation 4.16.

5.6.4.4   *Analyzing Interactions*

There are two approaches to pinpointing the location of the mean differences when the interaction is significant in omnibus ANOVA: a simple-effects analysis or an interaction contrast analysis. There is a helpful notational scheme that clearly labels these various types of comparison.

Simple-effects analysis includes both simple main effects and simple comparisons. Both back a factorial design down into a series of one-way designs by examining one IV separately at each level of another IV. A *simple main effect* holds one IV constant at a chosen level and examines mean differences among all levels of the other IV. For instance, one could compute $SS_{A \text{ at } b_1}$ (to test the cell means for A at the first level of B) or $SS_{B \text{ at } a_1}$ (to test the cell means for B at the first level of A). Then, if either A or B has more than two levels, *simple comparisons* are possible. For instance, one could compute $SS_{A\text{comp1 at } b_1}$ (to compare the two means formed by applying weighting coefficients to the cell means of A at the first level of B) or $SS_{B\text{comp1 at } a_1}$ (to compare the two means formed by applying weighting coefficients to the cell means of B at the first level of A). For the example, $SS_{A \text{ at } b_1}$ represents the sum of squares for the mean difference in ratings among administrators, belly dancers, and politicians for a 1-week vacation. $SS_{A\text{comp1 at } b_1}$ represents the sum of squares for the difference between administrators and the other two groups for a 1-week vacation.

An interaction contrasts analysis examines interaction by forming smaller interactions with weighting coefficients applied to either A or B or both. When weighting coefficients are applied to A while all levels of B are used, one assesses $F_{A\text{comp}\times B}$. When weighting coefficients are applied to B while all levels of A are used, one assesses $F_{A\times B\text{comp}}$. These are sometimes called partial factorials. If weighting coefficients are applied to both A and B, one assesses $F_{A\text{comp}\times B\text{comp}}$. For our example, $F_{A\text{comp1}\times B}$ is a test of the interaction of administrators versus the other two groups with vacations of all three lengths: Do administrators show the same pattern of responses to vacations of the same length as the other two groups? $F_{A\times B\text{comp1}}$ is a test for the interaction of the linear trend of vacation

---

[9]SPSS GLM also has a Dunnett C test, which does not require homogeneity of variance, but uses the same test distribution as the Tukey test.

length for all three professions: Do all three professions have the same linear trend? Finally, $F_{A\,comp1 \times B\,comp1}$ is a test of the similarity of the linear trend of vacation length for administrators versus the other two groups: Do administrators have the same linear trend as the other two groups?

Either simple effects or interaction contrasts can be part of a comprehensive sequential plan such as that recommended by Keppel (1991, Chapters 11, 12, and 20), where the decision about which post hoc analyses to use depends on the outcome of the omnibus ANOVA. The general strategy for a sequential analysis considers the significance of all interaction(s) and main effects. If the interaction is significant, and at least one main effect is *not* significant, use simple-effects analysis. If the interaction is significant, but so are all of the main effects, use interaction contrasts. If the interaction is significant, and none of the main effects is significant, use either simple effects or interaction contrasts, whichever is the easier to explain.

The sequential plan usually follows the results of omnibus ANOVA, so post hoc adjustments are required. However, either simple-effects or interaction contrasts also could be planned. If you plan no more than three or four comparisons, and eschew omnibus ANOVA, adjustment is unnecessary. If, however, you plan more comparisons than that, a Bonferroni correction (cf. 4.5.5.4.2) is prudent.

Simple-effects and interaction contrasts analyses are demonstrated through software in the following sections, with analysis by hand also discussed to some extent. Briefly, simple-effects analyses are done by hand by performing a one-way ANOVA with follow-up comparisons, as described in Chapter 4, on the appropriate row or column of data. (Equations and hand-worked examples for the traditional ANOVA approach are also demonstrated in Keppel, 1991.) Interaction contrasts are most easily done by hand by using the regression strategy in conjunction with a spreadsheet program or by creating the needed coefficients as illustrated later in Table 5.36 and using them in syntax for one of the software packages.

5.6.4.4.1   *Simple Effects*

In simple-effects analysis, one IV is held constant at a selected level, and mean differences are examined on the levels of the other IV, as shown in Figure 5.8. For instance, the level of A is held constant at administrator, and mean differences are examined in ratings of 1-, 2-, and 3-week vacations (Figure 5.8[a]). The researcher asks if administrators have mean differences in their ratings of 1-, 2-, and 3-week vacations by assessing $F_{B\,at\,a_1}$. Or length of vacation is held constant at 1 week, and mean differences are explored among professions (Figure 5.8[c]). The researcher asks whether the three types of professions have different mean ratings of 1-week vacations by assessing $F_{A\,at\,b_1}$. Each test of these simple main effects has 2 df in the numerator because, in this example, A and B both have three levels. A simple main-effects analysis could then be followed by simple comparisons (Figures 5.8[b] and 5.8[d]), where the numerator again has 1 df. These simple comparisons may be among single cells, as in Figure 5.8(d), or among combined cells, as in Figure 5.8(b).

Simple-effects analysis partitions one of the main effects from the omnibus ANOVA in addition to the interaction. When A is held constant at a single level to analyze B, both the sum of squares for interaction and the sum of squares for B are reapportioned into SS for simple effects of B. When levels of B are held constant and A is analyzed, both the sum of squares for interaction and the sum of squares for A are reapportioned into SS for simple effects of A. Because, in simple-effects analyses, the interaction sum of squares is confounded (intermingled) with one or the other of the main effects, it seems best to confound them with a nonsignificant main effect where possible.

In the small-sample 3×3 example of Section 5.4.3, both main effects and the interaction are significant. Because all effects are significant, the guidelines suggest that interaction contrasts are

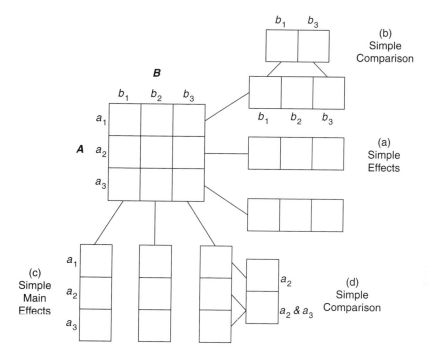

FIGURE 5.8 Simple-Effects Analysis Exploring (a) Differences among *B*
for Each Level of *A*, **Followed by (b) Simple Comparison between Levels of** *B*
for One Level of *A***; and (c) Differences among** *A* **for Each Level of** *B*, **Followed by**
(d) Simple Comparison between Levels of *A* **for One Level of** *B*

appropriate rather than simple effects. For didactic purposes, however, the simple effects of *A* (pro-fession) will be analyzed at each level of *B* (vacation length).

Hand calculations for simple effects are straightforward: You do a one-way ANOVA on each "slice" of the design. For example, to do simple effects on *A* at each level of *B*, you do 3 one-way ANOVAs: *A* at b_1, *A* at b_2, and *A* at b_3, by applying the equations of Section 4.4.3. This provides you with $MS_{A \text{ at } b_j}$ and $MS_{S/A \text{ at } b_j}$.[10]

To form the *F* ratio, $MS_{A \text{ at } b_j}$ is divided by either $MS_{S/A \text{ at } b_j}$ or $MS_{S/AB}$, the error term for the factorial design. $MS_{S/AB}$ is normally used because it is considered more stable since it is based on more numerous estimates of the same within-cell error variability (all the cells instead of just some of them). However, if there are rather larger differences in the variability in the cells (failure or near fail-ure of homogeneity of variance at some levels of *B*), it makes more sense to use the error term devel-oped specifically for the simple effect. Whichever error term you choose, calculating the ANOVAs by hand may prove more efficient for small data sets than using software.

Table 5.31 shows syntax and location of output for simple-effects analysis through SPSS GLM, SAS GLM, and SYSTAT GLM with $MS_{S/AB}$ as the error term. Recall that MINITAB has no

---

[10]These one-way ANOVAs can also be performed through software by selecting data for just one level of *B* at a time and doing the analysis, with comparisons if desired, that way.

TABLE 5.31 Syntax for Simple Main-Effects Analysis

Program	Syntax	Section of Output	Name of Effect

SPSS GLM	```UNIANOVA```
	``` rating BY profess length```
	``` /METHOD = SSTYPE(3)```
	``` /INTERCEPT = INCLUDE```
	``` /CRITERIA = ALPHA(.05)```
	``` /LMATRIX = "profess at one week"```
	``` profess 2 -1 -1 profess*length 2 0 0 -1 0 0 -1 0 0;```
	``` profess 0 1 -1 profess*length 0 0 1 0 0 -1 0 0```
	``` /LMATRIX = "profess at two weeks"```
	``` profess 2 -1 -1 profess*length 0 2 0 0 -1 0 0 -1 0;```
	``` profess 0 1 -1 profess*length 0 0 0 1 0 0 -1 0```
	``` /LMATRIX = "profess at three weeks"```
	``` profess 2 -1 -1 profess*length 0 0 2 0 0 -1 0 0 -1;```
	``` profess 0 1 -1 profess*length 0 0 0 0 0 1 0 0 -1```
	``` /DESIGN profess, length, profess*length.```
		Custom Hypothesis Test #1, etc.	Test Results

SAS GLM	```data BTFILES.FAC_RANG;```
	``` set BTFILES. FAC_RAND;```
	``` IF PROFESS=1 AND LENGTH=1 THEN GROUP=1;```
	``` IF PROFESS=1 AND LENGTH=2 THEN GROUP=2;```
	``` IF PROFESS=1 AND LENGTH=3 THEN GROUP=3;```
	``` IF PROFESS=2 AND LENGTH=1 THEN GROUP=4;```
	``` IF PROFESS=2 AND LENGTH=2 THEN GROUP=5;```
	``` IF PROFESS=2 AND LENGTH=3 THEN GROUP=6;```
	``` IF PROFESS=3 AND LENGTH=1 THEN GROUP=7;```
	``` IF PROFESS=3 AND LENGTH=2 THEN GROUP=8;```
	``` IF PROFESS=3 AND LENGTH=3 THEN GROUP=9;```
	```PROC GLM;```
	``` CLASS GROUP;```
	``` MODEL RATING = GROUP;```
	``` CONTRAST 'PROFESS AT 1 WK' GROUP 2 0 0 -1 0 0 -1 0 0,```
	``` GROUP 0 0 0 2 0 0 -1 0 0 -1;```
	``` CONTRAST 'PROFESS AT 2 WK' GROUP 0 2 0 0 -1 0 0 -1 0,```
	``` GROUP 0 0 0 2 0 0 -1 0 0 -1;```
	``` CONTRAST 'PROFESS AT 3 WK' GROUP 0 0 2 0 0 -1 0 0 -1;```
	```RUN;```
		Contrast	PROFESS AT 1 WK. etc.

TABLE 5.31 Continued

Program	Syntax	Section of Output	Name of Effect
SYSTAT GLM	IF (PROCESS=1) AND (LENGTH=1) THEN LET GROUP=1	Test of Hypothesis	Hypothesis
	IF (PROCESS=1) AND (LENGTH=2) THEN LET GROUP=2		
	IF (PROCESS=1) AND (LENGTH=3) THEN LET GROUP=3		
	IF (PROCESS=2) AND (LENGTH=1) THEN LET GROUP=4		
	IF (PROCESS=2) AND (LENGTH=2) THEN LET GROUP=5		
	IF (PROCESS=2) AND (LENGTH=3) THEN LET GROUP=6		
	IF (PROCESS=3) AND (LENGTH=1) THEN LET GROUP=7		
	IF (PROCESS=3) AND (LENGTH=2) THEN LET GROUP=8		
	IF (PROCESS=3) AND (LENGTH=3) THEN LET GROUP=9		
	GLM		
	CATEGORY GROUP		
	COVAR		
	DEPEND RATING		
	ESTIMATE		
	HYPOTHESIS		
	EFFECT=group		
	NOTE 'PROFESS AT WEEK1'		
	CONTRAST [2 0 0 -1 0 0 -1 0 0 0 0 0 1 0 0 -1 0 0]		
	TEST		
	HYPOTHESIS		
	EFFECT=group		
	NOTE 'PROFESS AT WEEK2'		
	CONTRAST [0 2 0 0 -1 0 0 -1 0 0 0 0 0 1 0 0 -1 0]		
	TEST		
	HYPOTHESIS		
	EFFECT=group		
	NOTE 'PROFESS AT WEEK3'		
	CONTRAST [0 0 2 0 0 -1 0 0 -1 0 0 0 0 0 1 0 0 -1]		
	TEST		

provision for user-specified comparisons, other than adding columns that represent the comparison to the data set.

Simple main effects in SPSS GLM are done through LMATRIX syntax, where weighting coefficients are provided by the researcher for the effect to be analyzed (profess) and for the interaction. For example, the first LMATRIX is identified (within quotes) as testing the simple main effect of profess at one week. The LMATRIX instruction has two parts, one for each degree of freedom in the profess main effect, separated by a semicolon. Within each part, coefficients are provided for the first degree of freedom for the main effect of profess (2 −1 −1) and for the profess*length interaction at 1 week (2 0 0 −1 0 0 −1 0 0) and then for the second degree of freedom for the main effect of profess (0 1 −1) and its profess*length interaction at 1 week (0 0 0 1 0 0 −1 0 0). LMATRIX instructions then follow for the 2 df for a 2-week vacation and for the 2 df for a 3-week vacation. The results of both simple comparisons are combined in the output because both are within a single LMATRIX instruction. The output for the first LMATRIX instruction is labeled Custom Hypothesis #1, and so on.

Table 5.32 helps clarify the specification for the interaction, where A is type of profession and B is length of vacation. Because profess is named before length, the nine cells of the design are laid out in the order specified in the table. The coefficients are assigned to select the appropriate level of B for each comparison. Note, for instance, that when the comparison is "at b_1," coefficients are only present in the b_1 columns.

Table 5.31 shows syntax for the simple effects analysis through SAS GLM that produces the same results as the other programs. The **DATA** step recodes the design into a nine-level one-way layout, with the IV labeled **GROUP**. SAS GLM requires separate **CONTRAST** instructions for simple effects of profession at each level of length (B). A set of coefficients is derived for each df of the simple-effects analysis. Two sets of coefficients, separated by a comma, are necessary because there are three levels of profession. Here the set includes (2 −1 −1) and (0 1 −1) applied to the appropriate cells of the design representing the level of length selected, with zeros applied to all other cells. These are the same coefficients used for SPSS GLM.

SYSTAT GLM also requires recoding of the design into a nine-level one-way layout. The model first is estimated to produce the single error term, and then separate hypothesis tests are specified for each level of one of the variables. The NOTEs in the syntax help label the output because otherwise all hypothesis source tables look alike.

TABLE 5.32   Order of Cells for Specification of Weighting Coefficients for Simple-Effects Analyses

	a_1b_1	a_1b_2	a_1b_3	a_2b_1	a_2b_2	a_2b_3	a_3b_1	a_3b_2	a_3b_3
A comp1 at b_1	2	0	0	−1	0	0	−1	0	0
A comp2 at b_1	0	0	0	1	0	0	−1	0	0
A comp1 at b_2	0	2	0	0	−1	0	0	−1	0
A comp2 at b_2	0	0	0	0	1	0	0	−1	0
A comp1 at b_3	0	0	2	0	0	−1	0	0	−1
A comp2 at b_3	0	0	0	0	0	1	0	0	−1

All programs test the three simple main effects as if they are planned. If these analyses are done post hoc, however, the printed significance levels are inappropriate and a Scheffé adjustment is needed to control for inflated familywise Type I error. For these tests, the Scheffé adjustment is

$$F_s = (a - 1)F_{(a-1),\,(df_{error})} \tag{5.22}$$

where a = number of levels in the main effect being analyzed

df_{error} = df for omnibus error term

For the example, using $\alpha = .05$,

$$F_s = (3 - 1)F_{2,18} = 7.10$$

All three simple main effects survive the Scheffé adjustment, with F values of 30.70, 9.10, and 22.30, respectively, indicating that there are differences among professions for all three levels of length of vacation. However, these simple effects each have 2 df (because there are three levels of A). Therefore, a further decomposition of the interaction (and main effect of A) into separate degrees-of-freedom comparisons is in order.

As seen in Figure 5.8(d), simple comparisons are possible on A at each level of B because A has three levels. A set of orthogonal comparisons tests (1) the mean difference between the administrators and the other two professions, and then (2) the mean difference between belly dancers and politicians. The weighting coefficients for the first comparison are 2 −1 −1, and the coefficients for the second comparison are 0 1 −1. These comparisons are done by hand by applying Equation 5.17 to cell means, where n_Y is the number of scores per cell, and weights are applied to cell rather than marginal means. F ratios are formed with $MS_{S/A\,at\,b_j}$ or $MS_{S/AB}$ as the error term in the denominator. Here again you may find it more efficient to do hand calculations for small data sets than to set up the rather complex syntax required by software programs.

Table 5.33 shows syntax and location of output for simple comparisons through SPSS GLM, SAS GLM, and SYSTAT ANOVA with $MS_{S/AB}$ as the error term.

Note that syntax for the SPSS and SAS is very similar to that used for simple main effects, except that here there is a separate set of contrast coefficients for each comparison. SAS and SYSTAT require recoding of the two IVs into a single IV in a one-way layout.

It may have occurred to you that the nine coefficients in the syntax look suspiciously like coefficients in the columns of the regression approach, as indeed they are. Simple main effects and simple comparisons are done through regression by the simple expedient of applying zeros to the levels of the variable currently omitted from analysis. The columns necessary to compute $SS_{A\,comp1\,at\,b_1}$ and $SS_{A\,comp2\,at\,b_1}$ are shown in Table 5.34. The sum of SS(reg.) for these two columns is $SS_{A\,at\,b_1}$.

Table 5.35 shows how simple-effects analysis partitions a main effect and the interaction, and is further decomposed into simple comparisons. Degrees of freedom and sums of squares in parentheses are those that are replaced by finer-grained analyses. A_{comp1} and A_{comp2} refer to the first and second comparisons on A, respectively. In the table, the 6 df from the combination of the main effect of A and the AB interaction are partitioned, first into simple main effects with 2 df each and then into the 6 single df comparisons. Table 5.35 also shows the results of the tests of simple comparisons produced by the syntax in Table 5.33.

TABLE 5.33   Syntax for Simple Comparisons in a Two-Way Factorial Design

Program	Syntax	Section of Output	Name of Effect

SPSS GLM	UNIANOVA
	  rating BY profess length
	  /METHOD = SSTYPE(3)
	  /INTERCEPT=INCLUDE
	  /CRITERIA = ALPHA(.05)
	  /LMATRIX = "admin vs others at one week"
	     profess 2 −1 −1 profess*length 2 0 0 −1 0 0 −1 0 0
	  /LMATRIX = "belly vs politic at one week"
	     profess 0 1 −1 profess*length 0 0 0 1 0 0 −1 0 0
	  /LMATRIX = "admin vs others at two weeks"
	     profess 2 −1 −1 profess*length 0 2 0 0 −1 0 0 −1 0
	  /LMATRIX = "belly vs politic at two weeks"
	     profess 0 1 −1 profess*length 0 0 0 0 1 0 0 −1 0
	  /LMATRIX = "admin vs others at three weeks"
	     profess 2 −1 −1 profess*length 0 0 2 0 0 −1 0 0 −1
	  /LMATRIX = "belly vs politic at three weeks"
	     profess 0 1 −1 profess*length 0 0 0 0 0 1 0 0 −1
	  /DESIGN profess, length, profess*length.
		Custom Hypothesis Tests #1, etc.	Test Results

SAS GLM	`proc glm`[a]
	  `class GROUP;`
	  `model RATING = GROUP;`
	  `contrast 'admin vs others at one week'`
	    `GROUP 2 0 0 -1 0 0 -1 0 0;`
	  `contrast 'belly vs politic at one week'`
	    `GROUP 0 0 0 1 0 0 -1 0 0;`
	  `contrast 'admin vs others at two weeks'`
	    `GROUP 0 2 0 0 -1 0 0 -1 0;`
	  `contrast 'belly vs politic at two weeks'`
	    `GROUP 0 0 0 0 1 0 0 -1 0;`
	  `contrast 'admin vs others at three weeks'`
	    `GROUP 0 0 2 0 0 1 0 0 -1;`
	  `contrast 'belly vs politic at three weeks'`
	    `GROUP 0 0 0 0 0 1 0 0 -1;`
	`run;`
		`Contrast`	`admin vs others at one week, etc.`

SYSTAT ANOVA	`IF (PROCESS=1) AND (LENGTH=1) THEN LET GROUP=1`
	`IF (PROFESS=1) AND (LENGTH=2) THEN LET GROUP=2`
	`IF (PROFESS=1) AND (LENGTH=3) THEN LET GROUP=3`
	`IF (PROFESS=2) AND (LENGTH=1) THEN LET GROUP=4`
	`IF (PROFESS=2) AND (LENGTH=2) THEN LET GROUP=5`
	`IF (PROFESS=2) AND (LENGTH=3) THEN LET GROUP=6`
	`IF (PROFESS=3) AND (LENGTH=1) THEN LET GROUP=7`
	`IF (PROFESS=3) AND (LENGTH=2) THEN LET GROUP=8`
	`IF (PROFESS=3) AND (LENGTH=3) THEN LET GROUP=9`
		`Test of Hypothesis Source`	Hypothesis

TABLE 5.33   Continued

Program	Syntax	Section of Output	Name of Effect
SYSTAT ANOVA (cont.)	ANOVA		
	CATEGORY GROUP		
	COVAR		
	DEPEND RATING		
	ESTIMATE		
	HYPOTHESIS		
	NOTE 'admin vs others at one week'		
	EFFECT=GROUP		
	CONTRAST [2 0 0 -1 0 0 -1 0 0]		
	TEST		
	HYPOTHESIS		
	NOTE 'belly vs politic at one week'		
	EFFECT=GROUP		
	CONTRAST [0 0 0 1 0 0 -1 0 0]		
	TEST		
	HYPOTHESIS		
	NOTE 'admin vs others at two weeks'		
	EFFECT=GROUP		
	CONTRAST [0 2 0 0 -1 0 0 -1 0]		
	TEST		
	HYPOTHESIS		
	NOTE 'belly vs politic at two weeks'		
	EFFECT=GROUP		
	CONTRAST [0 0 0 0 1 0 0 -1 0]		
	TEST		
	HYPOTHESIS		
	NOTE 'admin vs others at three weeks'		
	EFFECT=GROUP		
	CONTRAST [0 0 2 0 0 -1 0 0 -1]		
	TEST		
	HYPOTHESIS		
	NOTE 'belly vs politic at three weeks'		
	EFFECT=GROUP		
	CONTRAST [0 0 0 0 0 1 0 0 -1]		
	TEST		

[a] Preceded by coding into one-way design as per Table 5.31.

If planned with a Bonferroni adjustment of α to .02 for all comparisons, ratings of administrators differ from the others for 1-week and 2-week, but not 3-week, vacations, whereas belly dancers differ from politicians for 2-week and 3-week vacations. If tested post hoc, $F_s = 2\,(F_{2,18}) = 7.10$ and ratings of administrators differ from the others for 1-week, but not 2- or 3-week, vacations, whereas belly dancers still differ from politicians for both 2- and 3-week vacations.

TABLE 5.34   Columns for Regression Approach to Simple-Effects Analysis

	Y	A at b_1	
		A comp1 at b_1 X_1	A comp2 at b_1 X_2
a_1b_1	0 1 0	2 2 2	0 0 0
a_1b_2	4 7 6	0 0 0	0 0 0
a_1b_3	5 8 6	0 0 0	0 0 0
a_2b_1	5 7 6	−1 −1 −1	1 1 1
a_2b_2	5 6 7	0 0 0	0 0 0
a_2b_3	9 8 8	0 0 0	0 0 0
a_3b_1	5 6 8	−1 −1 −1	−1 −1 −1
a_3b_2	9 9 9	0 0 0	0 0 0
a_3b_3	3 3 2	0 0 0	0 0 0

Effect sizes may be calculated with respect to total SS or the combination of the interaction and the effect being decomposed, in this case the combination of AB and A. For the simple effect of A at b_1 (assuming that a further decomposition into simple comparisons is not done),

$$\eta^2 = \frac{SS_{A\ at\ b_1}}{SS_T} = \frac{68.22}{190.30} = .36 \tag{5.23}$$

TABLE 5.35   Source Table for Simple Main-Effects Analysis Followed by Simple Comparisons

Source	SS	df	MS	F
B: Length of Vacation	32.30	2	16.15	14.55
A: Profession	[(33.85)]	[(2)]		
AB	[(104.15)]	[(4)]		
A at b_1	(68.22)	(2)		
A_{comp1} at b_1	68.06	1	68.06	61.25
A_{comp2} at b_1	0.17	1	0.17	0.16
A at b_2	(20.22)	(2)		
A_{comp1} at b_2	6.72	1	6.72	6.05
A_{comp2} at b_2	13.50	1	13.50	12.15
A at b_3	(49.56)	(2)		
A_{comp1} at b_3	1.39	1	1.39	1.25
A_{comp2} at b_3	48.17	1	48.17	43.35
S/AB	20.00	18	1.11	
T	190.30	26		

or

$$\eta^2 = \frac{SS_{A \text{ at } b_1}}{SS_A + SS_{AB}} = \frac{68.22}{33.85 + 104.15} = .49 \qquad (5.24)$$

For the simple comparison, A_{comp1} at b_1,

$$\eta^2 = \frac{SS_{A \text{ comp at } b_1}}{SS_T} = \frac{68.06}{190.30} = .36 \qquad (5.25)$$

or

$$\eta^2 = \frac{SS_{A \text{ comp at } b_1}}{SS_A + SS_{AB}} = \frac{68.06}{33.85 + 104.15} = .49 \qquad (5.26)$$

As usual, it is important to report which form of η^2 you are using.

Suppose you are planning an analysis in which you expect a main effect of B and an AB interaction, but no main effect of A. This might be an expectation if A is a control variable that you hypothesize to interact with B (your primary IV), but to have no effect on its own. Further, suppose your interest in B is on mean differences between the first level and the other two (especially appropriate if the first level of B is a control condition), and then mean differences between the last two levels. The simple comparisons of this section are appropriate as an analytic strategy: Do one simple comparison in which b_1 is compared to the combination of b_2 and b_3 at each level of A, and then b_2 is compared with b_3 at each level of A. This analysis "spends" 6 df and produces a familywise error rate of approximately .12 if each simple comparison is evaluated at the .02 alpha level.

It should be noted that simple interactions are also possible when there are more than two IVs. If there are three IVs, for instance, one could ask if AB interactions are present at each level of C (or if AC interactions are present at each level of B or if BC interactions are present at each level of A). When significant interactions are found, simple main effects might follow to investigate, for example, the simple main effect of A at each BC combination and then, perhaps, the simple comparison of A at each BC combination.

5.6.4.4.2   Interaction Contrasts

Interaction contrasts are more appropriate than simple-effects analysis when both main effects are significant or you expect them to be. Interaction contrasts are not confounded with main effects because their sum of squares comes from the omnibus interaction. Thus, interaction contrasts are always appropriate. However, most researchers (and their readers) find simple effects easier to understand, so we recommend using interaction contrasts only when the main effects also are significant.

In interaction contrast analysis, the interaction between two IVs is examined through one or more smaller interactions, as depicted in Figure 5.9. Smaller interactions are obtained by deleting levels of one or more of the IVs, or by combining levels with use of appropriate weighting coefficients, or both. For instance, the significant interaction in a 3×3 design might be reduced to examination of a possible interaction between just two levels of A and two levels of B, as in Figure 5.9(a). Or you could combine, say, two of the levels of A and two of the levels of B to test the interaction of the four cells that are produced, as in Figure 5.9(b). Or you could select just two levels of one IV while using all levels of the other, as in Figure 5.9(c).

Interaction contrasts are formed by applying weighting coefficients to either A or B or both, to evaluate $F_{A \text{comp} \times B}$ (where coefficients are applied only to A), or $F_{A \times B \text{comp}}$ as in Figure 5.9(c) (where coefficients are applied only to B), or $F_{A \text{comp} \times B \text{comp}}$ as in Figures 5.9(a) and 5.9(b) (where coefficients are applied to both A and B). When the weighting coefficients are applied to just one IV, the analysis is sometimes called a partial factorial. Interactions can be formed from single cells as in Figures 5.9(a) and 5.9(c) or by combining cells of one or both IVs, as in Figure 5.9(b).

Weighting coefficients for interactions contrasts are found by cross-multiplying the weighting coefficients for each of the two IVs. First, appropriate weighting coefficients are chosen for each comparison (say, $2 -1 -1$ for A and $-1\ 0\ 1$, for B), and then they are cross-multiplied to find the coefficients to apply to the means of the cells, given in parentheses below the coefficients in Table 5.36. For the current example, this analysis asks if administrators have the same linear trend of vacation length as belly dancers and politicians.

It is at this point that the traditional approach to ANOVA becomes tricky, whereas the regression approach remains straightforward. Simple interaction contrasts that involve weighting coefficients of 0, 1, and -1 are fairly straightforward when done by hand, but contrasts that involve

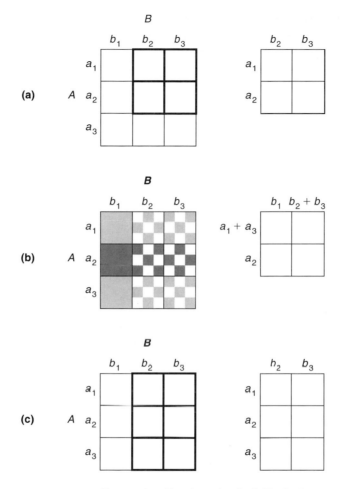

**FIGURE 5.9   Interaction Contrasts Analysis Exploring
Small Interaction Formed by Partitioning a Large (3 × 3)
Interaction: (a) 2 × 2 with Selected Single Levels
of Both A and B, (b) 2 × 2 with Combined Levels of A
(Lighter Gray Levels Are Combined) and B
(Patterned Levels Are Combined), and (c) 2 × 3 with
All Levels of A and Selected Levels of B (Partial Factorial)**

fractional weighting coefficients or weighting coefficients larger than 1 become complex. Keppel (1991, pp. 258–266) does as clear a presentation as is possible, but the logic of the procedure is still difficult to understand. The regression approach on the other hand remains clear.

Consider the numbers in the X_5 column of Table 5.8, for instance. They are identical to the weighting coefficients derived for the interaction contrast in Table 5.36. This is because the numbers in the X_5 column are a product of the coefficients in the X_1 and X_3 columns, which are the same as the coefficients for A and B, respectively. The regression approach, then, has interaction contrasts built in.

TABLE 5.36   Weighting Coefficients and Their Cross-Products for the First Interaction Contrast on the Small-Sample Example: (Cell Means in Parentheses)

	$b_1 = -1$	$b_2 = 0$	$b_3 = 1$
$a_1 = 2$	-2	0	2
	(0.33)	(5.67)	(6.33)
$a_2 = -1$	1	0	-1
	(6.00)	(6.00)	(8.33)
$a_3 = -1$	1	0	-1
	(6.33)	(9.00)	(2.67)

Table 5.37 shows syntax and location of output for interaction contrasts through SPSS GLM, SAS GLM, and SYSTAT ANOVA. The weighting coefficients for the first interaction contrast are derived in Table 5.36; the weighting coefficients for the other three interaction contrasts are found through the same procedures, as in columns X_6, X_7, and X_8 in Table 5.8. Because the sets of coefficients for A and B on the margins are orthogonal, the set of interaction contrasts is orthogonal, as well. However, a nonorthogonal set could be chosen if it were more meaningful. Note that SYSTAT ANOVA requires first recoding the two IVs into a one-way layout.

Results of the interaction contrast analyses produced by syntax of Table 5.37 are in Table 5.38. Table 5.38 shows how interaction contrast analysis partitions the interaction when orthogonal weighting coefficients are used on the two main effects and there is equal n in each cell. Degrees of freedom and sums of squares for the large interaction (in parentheses) are replaced by finer-grained analysis.

Note that the sums of squares for the contrasts match the sums of squares for the interaction columns, X_5 to X_8, of Table 5.13, where factorial ANOVA is done through multiple regression. If each of the sums of squares for the interaction columns is tested individually, rather than combined for the omnibus test of interaction, results are identical to these interaction contrasts. Thus, this multiple-regression approach to factorial ANOVA builds interaction contrasts into the fabric of the analysis.

Effect sizes for interaction contrasts are calculated with respect to either total SS or SS_{AB} (the effect being decomposed). For A_{comp1} by B_{linear},

$$\eta^2 = \frac{SS_{A\,\text{comp1} \times B\,\text{linear}}}{SS_T} = \frac{44.44}{190.30} = .23 \tag{5.27}$$

or

$$\eta^2 = \frac{SS_{A\,\text{comp1} \times B\,\text{linear}}}{SS_{AB}} = \frac{44.44}{104.15} = .43 \tag{5.28}$$

TABLE 5.37 Syntax for Interaction Contrasts in a Two-Way Factorial Design

Program	Syntax	Section of Output	Name of Effect

SPSS GLM	UNIANOVA
	  rating BY profess length
	  /METHOD = SSTYPE(3)
	  /INTERCEPT = INCLUDE
	  /CRITERIA = ALPHA(.05)
	  /LMATRIX = "admin vs. others by linear"
	    profess*length -2 0 2 1 0 -1 1 0 -1
	  /LMATRIX = "admin vs. others by quadratic"
	    profess*length -2 4 -2 1 -2 1 1 -2 1
	  /LMATRIX = "belly vs. polit by linear"
	    profess*length 0 0 0 1 0 -1 -1 0 1
	  /LMATRIX = "belly vs. polit by quadratic"
	    profess*length 0 0 0 -1 2 -1 1 -2 1
	  /DESIGN profess, length, profess*length .
		Custom Hypothesis Tests #1, etc.	Test Result

SAS GLM	proc glm data=SASUSER.FAC_RAND;
	    class PROFESS LENGTH;
	    model RATING = PROFESS LENGTH PROFESS*LENGTH;
	contrast 'admin vs. others by linear'
	  PROFESS*LENGTH -2 0 2 1 0 -1 1 0 -1;
	contrast 'admin vs. others by quadratic'
	  PROFESS*LENGTH -2 4 -2 1 -2 1 1 -2 1;
	contrast 'belly vs. polit by linear'
	  PROFESS*LENGTH 0 0 0 1 0 -1 -1 0 1;
	contrast 'belly vs. polit by quadratic'
	  PROFESS*LENGTH 0 0 0 -1 2 -1 1 -2 1;
	run;
		Contrast	admin vs others by linear, etc.

(continued)

TABLE 5.37 Continued

Program	Syntax	Section of Output	Name of Effect
SYSTAT		Test of	Hypothesis
ANOVA		Hypothesis	
		Source	
	IF (PROFESS=1) AND (LENGTH=1) THEN LET GROUP=1		
	IF (PROFESS=1) AND (LENGTH=2) THEN LET GROUP=2		
	IF (PROFESS=1) AND (LENGTH=3) THEN LET GROUP=3		
	IF (PROFESS=2) AND (LENGTH=1) THEN LET GROUP=4		
	IF (PROFESS=2) AND (LENGTH=2) THEN LET GROUP=5		
	IF (PROFESS=2) AND (LENGTH=3) THEN LET GROUP=6		
	IF (PROFESS=3) AND (LENGTH=1) THEN LET GROUP=7		
	IF (PROFESS=3) AND (LENGTH=2) THEN LET GROUP=8		
	IF (PROFESS=3) AND (LENGTH=3) THEN LET GROUP=9		
	ANOVA		
	CATEGORY GROUP		
	COVAR		
	DEPEND RATING		
	ESTIMATE		
	HYPOTHESIS		
	NOTE `admin vs others by linear'		
	EFFECT=GROUP		
	CONTRAST [-2 0 2 1 0 -1 1 0 -1]		
	TEST		
	HYPOTHESIS		
	NOTE `admin vs. others by quadratic'		
	EFFECT=GROUP		
	CONTRAST [-2 4 -2 1 -2 1 1 -2 1]		
	TEST		
	HYPOTHESIS		
	NOTE `belly vs. polit by linear'		
	EFFECT=GROUP		
	CONTRAST [0 0 0 1 0 -1 -1 0 1]		
	TEST		
	HYPOTHESIS		
	NOTE `belly vs. polit by quadratic'		
	EFFECT=GROUP		
	CONTRAST [0 0 0 -1 2 -1 1 -2 1]		
	TEST		

TABLE 5.38   Source Table for Interaction Contrast Analysis

Source	SS	df	MS	F
A	33.85	2	16.93	15.25
B	32.30	2	16.15	14.55
AB	(104.15)	(4)		
$A_{comp1} \times B_{linear}$	44.44	1	44.44	40.00
$A_{comp1} \times B_{quad}$	0.59	1	0.59	0.53
$A_{comp2} \times B_{linear}$	27.00	1	27.00	24.30
$A_{comp2} \times B_{quad}$	32.11	1	32.11	28.90
S/A	20.00	18	1.11	
	190.30	26		

Interaction contrasts may be done as part of a planned analysis (replacing the omnibus test of the interaction) or a post hoc analysis to dissect a significant interaction. The Scheffé adjustment for post hoc analysis for inflated Type I error rate is

$$F_S = (a-1)(b-1)F_{(a-1)(b-1), (df_{error})} \qquad (5.29)$$

In this case, with $\alpha = .05$:

$$F_S = (3-1)(3-1)(2.93) = 11.72$$

Whether these interaction contrasts are done as planned or post hoc analyses, there is a difference in linear trend between administrators and others ($F = 40.00$), and a difference in linear trend between belly dancers and politicians ($F = 24.30$), and a difference in quadratic trend between belly dancers and politicians ($F = 28.90$).

Interpretation of a significant interaction contrast involves plotting the means compared in the interaction. The means for the significant linear trend of administrators versus others are shown in Table 5.39. The first interaction contrast is plotted in Figure 5.10.

The plot of means suggests that administrators are far less satisfied with 1-week vacations than the others, as a group. If further clarification is desired, a significant interaction contrast is followed up with one or more simple comparisons. For example, a simple comparison is run between administrators and others at the 1-week level of vacation. Or a simple comparison is run for administrators between 1 and 3 weeks of vacation. Procedures for simple comparisons like these are in Table 5.35, previously illustrated as a follow-up to simple main-effects analysis. These simple comparisons need a Scheffé adjustment for post hoc testing.

5.6.4.5   Extending Comparisons through the Regression Approach

Table 5.40 presents a verbal layout of the eight columns of the regression approach to our current problem. At this point, the marginal comparisons for both A and B are available, as well as the four orthogonal interaction contrasts.

TABLE 5.39   Means Compared in Interaction Contrast of Linear Trend of Administrators versus Others

	One-Week Vacation	Three-Week Vacation
Administrators	0.33	6.33
Others	$(6.00 + 6.33)/2 = 6.16$	$(8.33 + 2.67)/2 = 5.50$

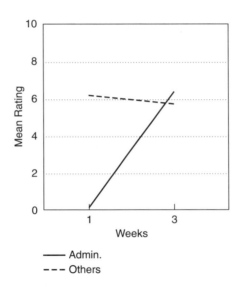

FIGURE 5.10   Interaction Contrast of Linear Trend between Administrators versus Others

However, additional information can be gleaned from the table by adding together various columns, as shown in Table 5.41. $A_{comp1} \times B$ asks if there is an interaction between administrators and others at the three levels of B. $A_{comp2} \times B$ asks if there is an interaction between belly dancers and politicians at the three levels of B. $A \times B_{linear}$ asks if the linear trends are the same for the three professions, and $A \times B_{quad}$ asks if the quadratic trends are the same for the three professions.

It should be noted that if you have the error term, you do not need to work out the complete regression problem in order to compute the sum of squares for a particular element of the design. For example, if you want the sum of squares for the interaction contrast of $A_{comp1} \times B_{linear}$, you need only compute the preliminary sum of squares for X_5 and the sum of products for $Y \times X_5$. The sum of squares regression for the interaction contrast is obtained by applying Equation 3.20.

As with all comparisons, effect size is calculated with respect to total sum of squares or the sum of squares for the effect being decomposed; in this case SS_A is the denominator of η^2 for A_{comp1} and A_{comp2}, and SS_{AB} in the denominator of η^2 for, say, $A \times B_{linear}$ or $A_{comp1} \times B_{linear}$.

TABLE 5.40   Columns for Randomized-Groups ANOVA through Regression

X_1	X_2	X_3	X_4	X_5	X_6	X_7	X_8
				$X_1 \times X_3$	$X_1 \times X_4$	$X_2 \times X_3$	$X_2 \times X_4$
A_{comp1}	A_{comp2}	B_{linear}	B_{quad}	$A_{comp1} \times B_{linear}$	$A_{comp1} \times B_{quad}$	$A_{comp2} \times B_{linear}$	$A_{comp2} \times B_{quad}$
A		B		$A \times B$			

TABLE 5.41   Partial Factorials through Regression

$A_{comp1} \times B$	$X_5 + X_6$	$A_{comp1} \times B_{linear} + A_{comp1} \times B_{quad}$
$A_{comp2} \times B$	$X_7 + X_8$	$A_{comp2} \times B_{linear} + A_{comp2} \times B_{quad}$
$A \times B_{linear}$	$X_5 + X_7$	$A_{comp1} \times B_{linear} + A_{comp2} \times B_{linear}$
$A \times B_{quad}$	$X_6 + X_8$	$A_{comp1} \times B_{quad} + A_{comp2} \times B_{quad}$

5.6.4.6   Comparisons in Higher-Order Designs

The highest-order interaction sets the stage for comparisons in higher-order designs. If the highest-order interaction is not statistically reliable, the analysis is treated as a next lower-level design. For example, if the highest-order interaction is nonsignificant in a three-way design, the 3 two-way interactions are examined and treated as if from 3 separate two-way designs. Thus, any two-way interaction that is statistically reliable is dealt with as in Sections 5.6.4.4 through 5.6.4.5. So, for example, a significant $A \times C$ interaction (with values in the ac cells summed over levels of B) is followed by either simple main effects or interaction contrasts that in turn are followed by simple comparisons. Any significant main effects that are not involved in a significant interaction (as B might be in this example) are followed by simple comparisons on marginal means.

   If the higher-order interaction is statistically reliable, either the simple-effects or interaction comparisons strategy again is adopted. Now, however, the first stage in a simple-effects analysis is simple interactions. For example, a significant three-way interaction is followed by tests of the two-way interactions at each level of the third IV, for example, $A \times B$ at c_1, $A \times B$ at c_2, and so on. The strategy that involves least confounding (intermingling of SS) is to test a nonsignificant (or the least substantial) interaction or, if comparisons are planned beforehand, one that is expected to be nonsignificant. For example, the choice of $A \times B$ at c_i assumes that the $A \times B$ interaction is not significant or has the smallest effect size of the three. (An interaction contrast approach is preferable if all three interactions are or are expected to be significant and substantial.)

   Any significant two-way interaction (at one level of the third IV) is then treated as in a two-way design. That is, two-way interactions are followed up with simple main effects or interaction comparisons, which in turn are followed up by simple comparisons. In the example of Table 5.22, the appropriate simple-effects strategy is based on one of the two nonsignificant two-way interactions: DEPRIVATION by DECOR at each level of FAMILIARITY, or FAMILIARITY by DECOR at each level of DEPRIVATION. A simple-effects interaction analysis is demonstrated in Section 7.7.2.2 for a three-way mixed randomized-groups repeated-measures design.

If all lower-order interactions as well as the highest-order interaction are statistically reliable, interaction contrasts are appropriate, as per Section 5.6.4.4.2. These are formed by applying contrasts coefficients to each of the IVs that have more than two levels. For example, you might base interaction contrasts on a mix of comparisons and trends in a $3 \times 3 \times 3$ design. You would have eight tests of the form $A_{comp} \times B_{comp} \times C_{comp}$. For example, two of the comparisons might be $A_{comp1} \times B_{linear} \times C_{comp1}$ and $A_{comp2} \times B_{quad} \times C_{comp1}$, and so on.

5.6.5 Unequal Sample Sizes

All of the problems of unequal n discussed in Section 4.5.3 for one-way designs carry over to factorial designs, and that is just the beginning. The first, and largest, problem is still the logical one. If unequal sample sizes are caused by one of the treatment levels in a design meant to have equal sample sizes, interpretation is problematic. Results, if interpreted, generalize only to cases that provide complete data. Such cases may be substantially different from cases that are unable (or unwilling) to provide complete data.

The next two problems are statistical. First, orthogonality of effects is lost for all of the main effects and all of the lower-order interactions in higher-order designs. The only effect that is unrelated to all of the others is the highest-order interaction, because the sum of squares for the interaction is found by subtracting the sums of squares for the main effects (cf. Equation 5.2 and Table 5.5) in the traditional ANOVA equations.[11] Nonorthogonality is most easily seen for the simple two-way factorial design of Table 5.9, where A and B both have only two levels. In Table 5.42, the same design is represented where there is equal $n = 3$ in Table 5.42(a) and one cell $(a_1 b_2)$ with only two cases in Table 5.42(b). Notice that in Table 5.42(a), the correlation between column X_1 and column X_2 is zero because 1 and -1 are paired equally often with each other. However, in Table 5.9(b), where there is unequal n, the correlation between column X_1 and column X_2 is no longer zero. In this case, the sum of squares for the X_1 column (SS_A) and the sum of squares for the X_2 column (SS_B) are nonorthogonal. The analysis of a design with unequal n has to take this nonorthogonality (overlapping sum of squares) into account.

Notice that with unequal n, the X_3 (interaction) column also is nonorthogonal with the other two, but again its overlap with the main effects is eliminated in the traditional analysis by subtraction of sums of squares associated with both A and B. Figure 5.11 demonstrates the overlap in Venn diagrams in the traditional analysis.

The second statistical problem with unequal sample sizes has to do with ambiguity regarding the marginal means. The data in Table 5.42 for a_1, at both b_1 and b_2, are duplicated in Table 5.43. There are two ways to compute $\overline{Y}_{a_1}$. The first way is to compute the mean of the scores in the column. The second way is to compute the mean of the two cell means. When there is equal n, these two methods of computing the marginal mean yield the same value (5.67), as shown in Table 5.43(a). When there is unequal n, these two methods of computing the marginal mean yield different values

---

[11]All effects, including the highest-order interaction, are nonorthogonal in the regression approach and require matrix calculations. Also, most adjustments require a sequential series of regression equations rather than the single one demonstrated in Section 3.2.

**TABLE 5.42   Effects of Equal and Unequal *n*
on the Orthogonality of Columns in ANOVA**

(a) Equal *n* in all four cells

	Case	Y	X_1 (A)	X_2 (B)	$X_3 = X_1 X_2$ (AB)
$a_1 b_1$	1	5	1	1	1
	2	3	1	1	1
	3	4	1	1	1
$a_1 b_2$	4	7	1	−1	−1
	5	7	1	−1	−1
	6	8	1	−1	−1
$a_2 b_1$	7	3	−1	1	−1
	8	5	−1	1	−1
	9	4	−1	1	−1
$a_2 b_2$	10	4	−1	−1	1
	11	1	−1	−1	1
	12	3	−1	−1	1

(b) Unequal *n* when case 6 is lost in the $a_1 b_2$ cell

	Case	Y	X_1 (A)	X_2 (B)	$X_3 = X_1 X_2$ (AB)
$a_1 b_1$	1	5	1	1	1
	2	3	1	1	1
	3	4	1	1	1
$a_1 b_2$	4	7	1	−1	−1
	5	7	1	−1	−1
$a_2 b_1$	7	3	−1	1	−1
	8	5	−1	1	−1
	9	4	−1	1	−1
$a_2 b_2$	10	4	−1	−1	1
	11	1	−1	−1	1
	12	3	−1	−1	1

(5.2 and 5.5), as shown in Table 5.43(b). ANOVA, which lives to test for mean differences, is in a quandary with unequal *n*. The researcher has to specify which marginal mean is to be tested. This ambiguity exists for all means in a larger factorial design except for those associated with the cells of the highest-order interaction.

Again, there are two approaches to calculating marginal means in a factorial design. One approach is to find the cell means for each level of one IV at a level of the other IV, add them up, and divide by the number of cell means. This is the procedure used in Table 5.43, when, for instance, the 4 and 7 are averaged to produce a marginal mean of 5.5. This procedure produces unweighted means, because cells are weighted equally, regardless of the number of cases each has. The other approach is to add up all of the scores in that level of the IV, ignoring the other IV(s), and divide by the number of

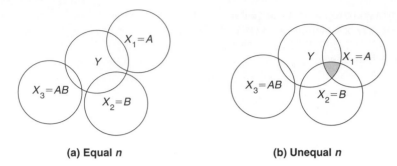

(a) Equal _n_   **(b) Unequal _n_**

FIGURE 5.11   Relationships among Effects in Orthogonal and Nonorthogonal Two-Way Designs: (a) No Overlapping Variance among Main Effects with Equal _n_; and (b) Overlap among Main Effects with Unequal _n_

TABLE 5.43   Ambiguity of Marginal Means in Unequal _n_ Designs

	(a) Equal _n_ in every cell			**(b) Unequal _n_ in one cell**		
	Case	**Y**	**Cell Means**	**Case**	**Y**	**Cell Means**
a_1b_1	1	5		1	5	
	2	3	$\overline{Y}_{a_1b_1} = 4$	2	3	$\overline{Y}_{a_1b_1} = 4$
	3	4		3	4	
a_1b_2	4	7		4	7	
	5	7	$\overline{Y}_{a_1b_2} = 7.33$	5	7	$\overline{Y}_{a_1b_2} = 7$
	6	8				
Marginal Means	$\overline{Y}_{a_1} =$	$(5 + \cdots + 8)/6$ $= 5.67$	$(4 + 7.33)/2$ $= 5.67$	$\overline{Y}_{a_2} =$	$(5 + \cdots + 7)/5$ $= 5.2$	$(4 + 7)/2$ $= 5.5$

scores. In Table 5.43, this procedure produces the marginal mean of 5.2. This procedure produces weighted[12] means, because cell means are weighted by their cell sample sizes. The marginal mean, in this case, is closer to the cell mean with the larger sample size. With two potential candidates for the mean, which marginal mean do we want to analyze? Which mean reflects population values?

In an experiment designed with equal sample cell sizes, with some random dropout here and there, the unweighted means are more appropriate: There is no justification for weighting smaller cells less heavily because their small size occurred by chance. On the other hand, in nonexperimental designs or when there are one or more nonexperimental IVs, the inequality in sample sizes may

---

[12]Note that these weights are sample sizes and are different from the coefficients that are used to weight means for specific comparisons.

be caused by population size differences. If type of job training and gender are IVs, for example, there may really be more women than men, for instance, in the particular job for which training is being offered. A design that weights cell means by their cell sample sizes makes more sense because, in the population, the marginal mean would, indeed, be closer to the mean for women.

However, with unequal sample sizes, there is the further complication of overlapping variance. Some way to subtract out the overlap is needed. In the unweighted-means approach, the overlap is subtracted from the effects. None of the effects takes credit for it. The sums of squares for effects plus error do not add up to the total SS because total SS includes the area of overlap. In the weighted-means approach, the researcher *decides* which effect deserves the credit (gets the overlapping variance) and gives it higher priority. The sums of squares for effects plus error then add up to total SS.

There are some guidelines for assigning priority to IVs. The decision is based on the roles the various IVs are playing in the design. If there are two or more IVs, give the one of greater interest the higher priority because, in that position, it will also most probably have higher power. On the other hand, if one or more of the IVs is a blocking variable, you may want to adjust the treatment IV (e.g., vacation length) for differences due to the blocking variable (e.g., profession) before testing mean differences on the treatment IV. The blocking IV—gender—becomes a covariate, as discussed in Chapter 8. For example, in the type of job training by gender example, you might want to adjust for gender differences before looking for mean differences due to type of job training. Or if your IVs occur in a time sequence, assign the ones that happen earlier the higher priority so that later events are adjusted for earlier ones. All of these considerations also apply to lower-order interactions in higher-order factorials. Intermediate interactions overlap among themselves and with main effects. In any design, however, the highest-order interaction is independent of all other effects, whether sample sizes are equal or unequal, because the sum of squares for the highest-order interaction is formed by subtracting sums of squares for all lower-order effects in traditional ANOVA calculations.

Researchers usually use the unweighted-means approach in experiments, where overlapping sums of squares are simply unanalyzed unless there is compelling reason to assign priority. If one of the experimental IVs is of overriding interest, the only strategy that is likely to make a meaningful difference in its power is assigning it highest priority. All other strategies are likely to yield the same, possibly sad, results.

Some software programs are limited to the unweighted-means approach or to algorithms that are consistent with that strategy. SYSTAT ANOVA and GLM offer only the unweighted-means analysis and SAS ANOVA cannot handle unequal n. However, a weighted-means analysis can be produced by any of these software packages if the regression programs are used in conjunction with the setups for the regression strategy. Much more detail about this approach is available in Chapter 5 of Tabachnick and Fidell (2001).

Table 5.44 shows SPSS REGRESSION syntax and selected output for a sequential (sometimes called hierarchical) regression analysis (in which all effects are adjusted for higher priority effects) of the data in Tables 5.42 and 5.43(b).[13] The **METHOD** instructions specify that X_1 (i.e., A) is entered first (given highest priority and all overlapping sums of squares); then X_2 (i.e., B) is entered to test the nonoverlapping sums of squares for B. Finally, X_3 (i.e., $A \times B$) is entered in the final step of the sequence. If on the other hand B is to be given priority over A, it is entered first into the equation. The **CHANGE** statistic is selected to produce the sequential tests of effects; remaining options are produced by default through the SPSS Windows menus.

---

[13]Note that the X_3 column may be entered in the data set or created through transformation.

TABLE 5.44   Weighted-Means ANOVA through Sequential Regression: SPSS REGRESSION Syntax and Selected Output

```
REGRESSION
 /MISSING LISTWISE
 /STATISTICS COEFF OUTS R ANOVA CHANGE
 /CRITERIA=PIN(.05) POUT(.10)
 /NOORIGIN
 /DEPENDENT y
 /METHOD=ENTER x1 /METHOD=ENTER x2 /METHOD=ENTER x3 .
```

Model Summary

Model	R	R Square	Adjusted R Square	Std. Error of the Estimate	Change Statistics R Square Change	F Change	df1	df2	Sig. F Change
1	.548[a]	.300	.223	1.57	.300	3.864	1	9	.081
2	.575[b]	.330	.163	1.63	.030	.358	1	8	.566
3	.852[c]	.726	.609	1.11	.396	10.111	1	7	.015

a. Predictors: (Constant), X1
b. Predictors: (Constant), X1, X2
c. Predictors: (Constant), X1, X2, X3

The tests of effects are in the **F Change** column. Thus, $F_A(1, 9) = 3.86$ with $p = .081$ indicates no reliable main effect of A. Similarly, there is no main effect of B with $F_B(1, 8) = 0.36$, $p = .566$. However, there is a significant interaction with $F_{AB}(1, 7) = 10.11, p = .015$.

ANOVA programs that offer several options for dealing with unequal n are SPSS GLM, MINITAB GLM, and SAS GLM. These programs use similar notation and procedures. Table 5.45, adapted from Tabachnick and Fidell (2001), summarizes the various options in the programs.

Overall and Spiegel's (1969) Method 1 is the unweighted-means analysis. The remaining methods are various ways of applying weighted-means analyses, as discussed at great length in Tabachnick and Fidell (2001, Section 8.5.2.2). Method 1, the unweighted-means analysis in which all effects are adjusted for each other, is usually appropriate for experimental work. Method 3 is most commonly used for nonexperimental work in which differences in cell sizes represent population differences and all effects are adjusted for higher priority effects. This is the weighted-means method that requires a priority order of effects.

5.7   Complete Example of Two-Way Randomized-Groups ANOVA

This example of factorial randomized-groups ANOVA is from a study of the bonding strength of periodontal dressings, tested in vitro at one of two times. The five dressings were all commercially available and were tested at 3 or 24 hours after application. Researchers were interested in differ-

TABLE 5.45 Terminology for Strategies for Adjustment of Unequal Sample Sizes

Research Type	Overall and Spiegel (1969)	SPSS GLM	MINITAB GLM	SYSTAT	SAS
1. Experiments designed to be equal *n* with random dropout. All cells equally important.	Method 1	METHOD= SSTYPE(3): (default) METHOD= SSTYPE(4)[a]	SUBC> Ssquares 3 (default)	Default	TYPE III and TYPE IV[a]
2. Nonexperimental research in which sample sizes reflect importance of cells. Main effects have equal priority.[b]	Method 2	METHOD= SSTYPE(2)	N.A.	N.A.[c]	TYPE II
3. Like number 2, except all effects have unequal priority.	Method 3	METHOD= SSTYPE(1)	SUBC> Ssquares 1	N.A.[c]	TYPE I
4. Research in which cells are given unequal weight on basis of prior knowledge.	N.A.	N.A.	SUBC> WEIGHTS in {variable}	N.A.[c]	N. A.

[a] Type III and IV differ only if there are missing cells.

[b] The programs take different approaches to adjustment for interaction effects.

[c] Instructions are given in the SYSTAT manual to produce adjustments other than Method 1.

ences among the dressings in bonding strength, between the 3- and 24-hour bonding strength, and in any interaction between time and dressing. The dependent variable was tensile bond strength, measured in units of KN/m^2. There were 10 observations in each of the 10 combinations of dressing and setting time, resulting in $N = 100$. The study is described in more detail in Appendix B. Data files are DENTAL.*.

5.7.1 Evaluation of Assumptions

5.7.1.1 *Sample Sizes, Normality, and Independence of Errors*

There are 10 cases in all cells of the design, so that $df_{error} = N - ab = 90$, well over the 20 required to support normality of sampling distributions. Independence of errors is assumed because trials were run individually. Table 5.46 shows an SPSS FREQUENCIES run of the data for diagnostic purposes. The file is first sorted and split so that descriptive statistics are produced separately for each group. Histograms are requested with a normal curve superimposed. All statistics are requested. SESKEW and SEKURT are standard errors for skewness and kurtosis, respectively. The /FORMAT=NOTABLE instruction suppresses the table of frequencies and percentages for each DV value. Only a few of the groups are shown.

TABLE 5.46   Diagnostic Run for Two-Way ANOVA through SPSS Frequencies: Syntax and Selected Output

```
SORT CASES BY dressing hours.
SPLIT FILE
  SEPARATE BY dressing hours.
FREQUENCIES
  VARIABLES=strength
  /FORMAT=NOTABLE
  /STATISTICS=STDDEV VARIANCE MINIMUM MAXIMUM MEAN SKEWNESS SESKEW
    KURTOSIS SEKURT
  /HISTOGRAM NORMAL
  /ORDER ANALYSIS.
```

Frequencies

Type of dressing = care, Time after application = 3

Statistics[a]

Bond strength KN/sq m

N	Valid	10
	Missing	0
Mean		354.90
Std. Deviation		147.93
Variance		21884.32
Skewness		.368
Std. Error of Skewness		.687
Kurtosis		−.276
Std. Error of Kurtosis		1.334
Minimum		140
Maximum		596

a. Type of dressing = care, Time after application = 3

Type of dressing = peripac, Time after application = 24

Statistics[a]

Bond strength KN/sq m

N	Valid	10
	Missing	0
Mean		130.00
Std. Deviation		37.64
Variance		1416.89
Skewness		.878
Std. Error of Skewness		.687
Kurtosis		1.534
Std. Error of Kurtosis		1.334
Minimum		83
Maximum		211

a. Type of dressing = peripac, Time after application = 24

TABLE 5.46   Continued

Type of dressing = putty, Time after application = 24
Statisticsª
Bond strength KN/sq m

N	Valid	10
	Missing	0
Mean		852.20
Std. Deviation		227.17
Variance		51606.40
Skewness		.395
Std. Error of Skewness		.687
Kurtosis		−1.029
Std. Error of Kurtosis		1.334
Minimum		553
Maximum		1225

a. Type of dressing = putty, Time after application = 24

5.7.1.2   *Homogeneity of Variance*

Output of Table 5.46 contains indications that variances are heterogeneous rather than homogeneous (cf. Section 3.4.3). The standard deviations range from 37.642 to 227.17 and the ratio of largest to smallest variance far exceeds 10: $F_{max} = 51606.40/1416.89 = 36.41$. This suggests that a square root or log transform of the DV should be considered.

Table 5.47 shows syntax and results of these transformations. The **COMPUTE** instructions provide square root and log transforms of the DV, **strength**, to produce **sstren** and **lstren**, respectively. Only variances, minima, and maxima are requested in this **FREQUENCIES** run.

With the square root transformation of the DV, $F_{max} = 16.1436/1.6609 = 9.72$, a bit less than 10. With the log transformed DV, $F_{max} = .04493/.00223 = 20.13$.

5.7.1.3   *Outliers*

Runs producing Tables 5.46 and 5.47 provide maximum and minimum values for each treatment to check for outliers. All scores are well within 3.3 standard deviations of their means and apparently connected to other scores in their groups, so that outliers pose no problem in this data set.

5.7.2   Randomized-Groups Analysis of Variance

There is a choice for the omnibus ANOVA at this point: the ANOVA on the square root transform of strength or the ANOVA on the original, untransformed data with α set at a somewhat more stringent level (e.g., .01 rather than .05) given the strong heterogeneity. Because all analyses produce essentially the same results at $\alpha = .01$, the preference is for the simplest (untransformed) analysis. However, the report of results will include a statement of the finding of heterogeneity of variance and an attempt to interpret it, if warranted.

TABLE 5.47   SPSS Frequencies to Request Variances with Square Root and Log Transforms: Syntax and Selected Output

```
COMPUTE sstren=SQRT(strength)
COMPUTE lstren=LG10(strength)
FREQUENCIES
VARIABLES=sstren lstren /FORMAT=NOTABLE
/STATISTICS=VARIANCE MINIMUM MAXIMUM
/ORDER ANALYSIS .
```

Type of dressing = care, Time after application = 3

Statistics[a]

		SSTREN	LSTREN
N	Valid	10	10
	Missing	0	0
Variance		16.1436	3.97E-02
Minimum		11.83	2.15
Maximum		24.41	2.78

a. Type of dressing = care, Time after application = 3

Type of dressing = peripac, Time after application = 3

Statistics[a]

		SSTREN	LSTREN
N	Valid	10	10
	Missing	0	0
Variance		4.9930	4.49E-02
Minimum		5.83	1.53
Maximum		12.96	2.23

a. Type of dressing = peripac, Time after application = 3

Type of dressing = peripac, Time after application = 24

Statistics[a]

		SSTREN	LSTREN
N	Valid	10	10
	Missing	0	0
Variance		2.6119	1.52E-02
Minimum		9.11	1.92
Maximum		14.53	2.32

a. Type of dressing = peripac, Time after application = 24

TABLE 5.47   Continued

Type of dressing = putty, Time after application = 24

Statistics[a]

		SSTREN	LSTREN
N	Valid	10	10
	Missing	0	0
Variance		14.9817	1.35E-02
Minimum		23.52	2.74
Maximum		35.00	3.09

a. Type of dressing = putty, Time after application = 24

5.7.2.1   Omnibus Tests

Table 5.48 shows the SPSS GLM ANOVA for the original untransformed scores. Both of the main effects and the interaction are highly significant, $p < .001$. Tables of Estimated Marginal Means show standard errors of means for each effect, to be reported in the Results section. Treatment magnitude varies widely among the three effects, however. Applying Equation 5.16 (preferable to the Eta Squared of Table 5.48) for the effects:

$$\text{Partial } \hat{\omega}_D^2 = \frac{4(2098498.5 - 19696.8)/100}{4(2098498.5 - 19696.8)/100 + 19696.8} = .81$$

$$\text{Partial } \hat{\omega}_H^2 = \frac{1(1131244.96 - 19696.8)/100}{1(1131244.96 - 19696.8)/100 + 19696.8} = .36$$

$$\text{Partial } \hat{\omega}_{DH}^2 = \frac{4(212895.09 - 19696.8)/100}{4(212895.09 - 19696.8)/100 + 19696.8} = .28$$

A great deal of systematic variance is accounted for in these partial analyses.

SYSTAT is used to produce Figure 5.12, where plots of means and standard errors aid in interpretation of the interaction. (Recall that the 95% confidence interval is bounded by two standard errors on either side of the mean.) SYSTAT syntax appears at the top of the figure.

All of the dressings show greater strength at 24 hours than 3 hours, but the difference is small for Putty and Peripac. The Zone dressing tested at 24 hours appears superior to all of the others. The most straightforward way to interpret these differences (and lack of them) is pairwise comparison of all 10 treatments.

5.7.2.2   Comparisons among Cell Means

Omnibus analysis of variance is followed by post hoc pairwise comparisons of means and by post hoc pairwise comparisons of variance. SPSS GLM offers pairwise tests that do not assume homogeneity of variance. The Dunnett C[14] test [requested as POSTHOC=GROUP(C)] is convenient because it is

[14]Note from Table 4.28 that this is simply an alternative test for all pairwise comparisons, and differs from the Dunnett test in which various treatments are compared with a control.

TABLE 5.48 Two-Way Analysis of Variance of Strength through SPSS GLM (UNIANOVA): Syntax and Selected Output

```
UNIANOVA
    strength BY dressing hours
    /METHOD = SSTYPE(3)
    /INTERCEPT = INCLUDE
    /CRITERIA = ALPHA(.05)
    /DESIGN = dressing hours dressing*hours .
```

Univariate Analysis of Variance

Tests of Between-Subjects Effects

Dependent Variable: Bond strength KN/sq m

Source	Type III Sum of Squares	df	Mean Square	F	Sig.	Eta Squared	Noncent. Parameter	Observed Power[a]
Corrected Model	10376820[b]	9	1152980.0	58.536	.000	.854	526.827	1.000
Intercept	38668499	1	38668499	1963.183	.000	.956	1963.183	1.000
DRESSING	8393994.9	4	2098498.7	106.540	.000	.826	426.160	1.000
HOURS	1131245.0	1	1131245.0	57.433	.000	.390	57.433	1.000
DRESSING * HOURS	851580.34	4	212895.09	10.809	.000	.324	43.234	1.000
Error	1772715.2	90	19696.836					
Total	50818034	100						
Corrected Total	12149535	99						

a. Computed using alpha = .05

b. R Squared = .854 (Adjusted R Squared = .840)

Estimated Marginal Means

1. Type of dressing

Dependent Variable: Bond strength KN/sq m

Type of dressing	Mean	Std. Error	95% Confidence Interval	
			Lower Bound	Upper Bound
care	519.100	31.382	456.754	581.446
coe	677.600	31.382	615.254	739.946
peripac	121.000	31.382	58.654	183.346
putty	845.050	31.382	782.704	907.396
zone	946.450	31.382	884.104	1008.796

TABLE 5.48 Continued

2. Time after application

Dependent Variable: Bond strength KN/sq m

Time after Application	Mean	Std. Error	95% Confidence Interval	
			Lower Bound	Upper Bound
3	515.480	19.848	476.049	554.911
24	728.200	19.848	688.769	767.631

3. Type of dressing * Time after application

Dependent Variable: Bond strength KN/sq m

Type of Dressing	Time after Application	Mean	Std. Error	95% Confidence Interval	
				Lower Bound	Upper Bound
care	3	354.900	44.381	266.729	443.071
	24	683.300	44.381	595.129	771.471
coe	3	573.600	44.381	485.429	661.771
	24	781.600	44.381	693.429	869.771
peripac	3	112.000	44.381	23.829	200.171
	24	130.000	44.381	41.829	218.171
putty	3	837.900	44.381	749.729	926.071
	24	852.200	44.381	764.029	940.371
zone	3	699.000	44.381	610.829	787.171
	24	1193.900	44.381	1105.729	1282.071

231

```
BAR STRENGTH*DRESSING / OVERLAY GROUP=HOURS SERROR
XLABEL='Periodontal Dressing' , YLABEL='Mean bond strength '
```

FIGURE 5.12   Mean Bond Strength (and Standard Errors)
as a Function of Periodontal Dressing and Setting Time:
SYSTAT GRAPH Syntax and Output

based on the studentized range, as per the Tukey test. Table 5.49 shows SPSS GLM (UNIANOVA) syntax and selected output showing the pairwise Dunnett C comparisons. Critical $\alpha = .01$ is used instead of .05 because of the large number of comparisons. A new variable, group, is added manually to the data set, formed out of the 10 combinations of dressing and hours.

Significant differences at $\alpha = .01$ are marked with an asterisk (*) in this output. The dressing with the highest mean, Zone after 24 hours, is stronger than any other dressings except Putty after either 3 or 24 hours. Therefore, a decision in favor of any of the three combinations is statistically supported—Putty if quicker setting time is important. There are no reliable mean differences between 3 and 24 hours for Putty or for Peripac, but time differences are statistically reliable for the three other dressings.

5.7.2.3   Interpreting Heterogeneity of Variance

Some variances in strength are far larger than others, although this finding did not compromise the major analyses. Pairwise F tests of variances are conducted post hoc with α set to .001 because there are 45 pairs where

$$F = \frac{s^2_{\text{larger}}}{s^2_{\text{smaller}}}$$

TABLE 5.49   SPSS GLM (UNIANOVA) Syntax and Partial Output for Pairwise Comparisons among Means with Dunnett C Adjustment

```
UNIANOVA
  strength BY group
  /METHOD = SSTYPE(3)
  /INTERCEPT = INCLUDE
  /POSTHOC = group (C)
  /CRITERIA = ALPHA(.01)
  /DESIGN = group .
```

Multiple Comparisons

Dependent Variable: Bond strength KN/sq m
Dunnett C

(I) GROUP	(J) GROUP	Mean Difference (I – J)	Std. Error	99% Confidence Interval Lower Bound	Upper Bound
care3	care24	−320.40(*)	62.764	−643.72	−13.08
	coe3	−218.70	62.764	−487.07	49.67
	coe24	−426.70(*)	62.764	−730.54	−32.86
	peri3	242.90	62.764	−15.46	501.26
	peri24	224.90	62.764	−30.92	480.72
	putty3	−483.00(*)	62.764	−886.39	−79.61
	putty24	−497.30(*)	62.764	−951.62	−42.98
	zone3	−344.10(*)	62.764	−672.51	−15.69
	zone24	−839.00(*)	62.764	−1253.71	−424.29
care24	care3	328.40(*)	62.764	13.08	643.72
	coe3	109.70	62.764	−110.57	329.97
	coe24	−98.30	62.764	−360.63	164.03
	peri3	571.30(*)	62.764	363.35	779.25
	peri24	553.30(*)	62.764	348.50	758.10
	putty3	−154.60	62.764	−527.72	218.52
	putty24	−168.90	62.764	−596.57	258.77
	zone3	−15.70	62.764	−306.14	274.74
	zone24	−510.60(*)	62.764	−895.93	−125.27
coe3	care3	218.70	62.764	−49.67	487.07
	care24	−109.70	62.764	−329.97	110.57
	coe24	−208.00(*)	62.764	−411.50	−4.50
	peri3	461.60(*)	62.764	335.74	587.46
	peri24	443.60(*)	62.764	323.03	564.17
	putty3	−264.30	62.764	−598.69	70.09
	putty24	−278.60	62.764	−672.94	115.74
	zone3	−125.40	62.764	−364.04	113.24
	zone24	−620.30(*)	62.764	−968.26	−272.34
coe24	care3	426.70(*)	62.764	122.86	730.54
	care24	98.30	62.764	−164.03	360.63
	coe3	208.00(*)	62.764	4.50	411.50
	peri3	669.60(*)	62.764	479.50	859.70
	peri24	651.60(*)	62.764	464.96	838.24
	putty3	−56.30	62.764	−419.77	307.17
	putty24	−70.60	62.764	−489.88	348.68
	zone3	82.60	62.764	−195.33	360.53
	zone24	−412.30(*)	62.764	−788.30	−36.30
peri3	care3	−242.90	62.764	−501.26	15.46
	care24	−571.30(*)	62.764	−779.25	−363.35
	coe3	−461.60(*)	62.764	−587.46	−335.74
	coe24	−669.60(*)	62.764	−859.70	−479.50

(continued)

TABLE 5.49   Continued

(I) GROUP	(J) GROUP	Mean Difference (I – J)	Std. Error	99% Confidence Interval	
				Lower Bound	Upper Bound
	peri24	−18.00	62.764	−114.24	78.24
	putty3	−725.90(*)	62.764	−1052.31	−399.49
	putty24	−740.20(*)	62.764	−1127.79	−352.61
	zone3	−587.00(*)	62.764	−814.32	−359.68
	zone24	−1081.90(*)	62.764	−1422.20	−741.60
peri24	care3	−224.90	62.764	−480.72	30.92
	care24	−553.30(*)	62.764	−758.10	−348.50
	coe3	−443.60(*)	62.764	−564.17	−323.03
	coe24	−651.60(*)	62.764	−838.24	−464.96
	peri3	18.00	62.764	−78.24	114.24
	putty3	−707.90(*)	62.764	−1032.30	−383.50
	putty24	−722.20(*)	62.764	−1108.11	−336.29
	zone3	−569.00(*)	62.764	−793.43	−344.57
	zone24	−1063.90(*)	62.764	−1402.28	−725.52
putty3	care3	483.00(*)	62.764	79.61	886.39
	care24	154.60	62.764	−218.52	527.72
	coe3	264.30	62.764	−70.09	598.69
	coe24	56.30	62.764	−307.17	419.77
	peri3	725.90(*)	62.764	399.49	1052.31
	peri24	707.90(*)	62.764	383.50	1032.30
	putty24	−14.30	62.764	−510.49	481.89
	zone3	138.90	62.764	−245.35	523.15
	zone24	−356.00	62.764	−816.19	104.19
putty24	care3	497.30(*)	62.764	42.98	951.62
	care24	168.90	62.764	−258.77	596.57
	coe3	278.60	62.764	−115.74	672.94
	coe24	70.60	62.764	−348.68	489.88
	peri3	740.20(*)	62.764	352.61	1127.79
	peri24	722.20(*)	62.764	336.29	1108.11
	putty3	14.30	62.764	−481.89	510.49
	zone3	153.20	62.764	−284.22	590.62
	zone24	−341.70	62.764	−847.13	163.73
zone3	care3	344.10(*)	62.764	15.69	672.51
	care24	15.70	62.764	−274.74	306.14
	coe3	125.40	62.764	−113.24	364.04
	coe24	−82.60	62.764	−360.53	195.33
	peri3	587.00(*)	62.764	359.68	814.32
	peri24	569.00(*)	62.764	344.57	793.43
	putty3	−138.90	62.764	−523.15	245.35
	putty24	−153.20	62.764	−590.62	284.22
	zone24	−494.90(*)	62.764	−891.02	−98.78
zone24	care3	839.00(*)	62.764	424.29	1253.71
	care24	510.60(*)	62.764	125.27	895.93
	coe3	620.30(*)	62.764	272.34	968.26
	coe24	412.30(*)	62.764	36.30	788.30
	peri3	1081.90(*)	62.764	741.60	1422.20
	peri24	1063.90(*)	62.764	725.52	1402.28
	putty3	356.00	62.764	−104.19	816.19
	putty24	341.70	62.764	−163.73	847.13
	zone3	494.90(*)	62.764	98.78	891.02

Based on observed means.

* The mean difference is significant at the .01 level.

and df $= 9$ and $9(n - 1)$ for each of the F tests. This test is similar to the F_{max} test, except that a tabled critical value is used and all pairs of variances are tested, not just the largest and smallest pair. The critical value from Appendix A.6 for these variance tests is 10.37.

Table 5.50 shows (with an asterisk) which of the variances differed reliably. In general, this analysis shows that Peripac, the dressing with least strength, is also less variable than the stronger dressings, Zone after 24 hours and Putty after 3 and 24 hours. Peripac also is less variable in strength than some of the intermediate dressings. The weakest dressing produced the most consistent results.

Table 5.51 is a checklist for factorial randomized-groups ANOVA. An example of a Results section, in journal format, follows for the study described.

TABLE 5.50   Significant (*) Differences among Variances in Strength of Dressings after 3 and 24 Hours

	Zone 3 hr	Zone 24 hr	Putty 3 hr	Putty 24 hr	Coe 3 hr	Care 24 hr
Peripac 3 hr		*	*	*	*	*
Peripac 24 hr	*	*	*	*		*

TABLE 5.51   Checklist for Factorial Randomized-Groups ANOVA

1. Issues
   a. Independence of errors
   b. Unequal sample sizes
   c. Normality of sampling distributions
   d. Outliers
   e. Homogeneity of variance
2. Major analyses
   a. Main effects or planned comparisons. If significant:
      (1) Effect size(s)
      (2) Parameter estimates (marginal means and standard deviations or standard errors or confidence intervals)
   b. Interactions or planned comparisons. If significant:
      (1) Effect size(s)
      (2) Parameter estimates (cell means and standard deviations or standard errors or confidence intervals in table or plot)
3. Additional analyses
   a. Post hoc comparisons
   b. Interpretation of departure from homogeneity of variance

Results

A 5 × 2 randomized-groups ANOVA was performed on bond strength of periodontal dressings tested in vitro. Dressings, commercially available, were Zone, Perio Putty, Coe Pak, PerioCare+, and Peripac. Half the 20 samples of each dressing were tested for tensile bond strength after 3 hours and half tested after 24 hours. Severe heterogeneity of variance was noted, however, no substantive distortion of the results was evident. Obtained probability levels were far enough beyond the preset α = .05 to compensate for any inflation in Type I error due to heterogeneity. Therefore, no additional adjustment for heterogeneity was made. Figure 5.12 plots means and standard errors for all combinations of dressing and time.

Strong, statistically significant differences among dressing were evident, averaged over the two time periods, $F(4, 90)$ = 106.54, p < .001, SE_M = 31.38, partial $\hat{\omega}^2$ = .81. Tensile strength varied from a mean high of 946.56 KN/m^2 for Zone dressing to a mean low of 121.00 KN/m^2 for Peripac.

A smaller, but still significant, effect of time also was evident, averaged over dressings, $F(1, 90)$ = 57.43, p < .001, SE_M = 19.85, partial $\hat{\omega}^2$ = .36. Average strength was less after 3 hours (M = 515.48 KN/m^2) than after 24 hours (M = 728.2 KN/m^2). These main effects were modified by a small but statistically significant interaction between dressing and time, $F(1, 90)$ = 10.81, p < .001, SE_M = 44.38, partial $\hat{\omega}^2$ = .10.

All pairwise comparisons among means were tested using a Dunnett C correction at α = .01. These comparisons showed that the dressing with the strongest mean, Zone after 24 hours, was superior to all other dressings except Perio Putty after either 3 or 24 hours. These findings suggest a choice in favor of Perio Putty if setting time is important.

However, pairwise comparisons among variances in strength among the 10 sets of samples showed greatest variance for the strongest dressings; strength measurements for Zone after 24 hours and Putty after 3 and 24 hours were less consistent than were strength measurements for the weakest dressings: Peripac after 3 and after 24 hours. Peripac after 3 hours was also significantly less variable in strength than PerioCare+ after 3 hours and Coe Pak after 3 hours. Peripac after 24 hours was significantly less variable in strength than Zone after 3 hours and PerioCare+ after 3 hours. All of the samples using Zone after 24 hours and using Putty, however, were stronger than any of the samples using Peripac.

5.8   Comparison of Programs

Table 5.52 reviews programs from SPSS, SAS, MINITAB, and SYSTAT that are appropriate for factorial randomized-groups ANOVA. Only the features applicable to these designs are reviewed here; other features are reviewed elsewhere.

5.8.1   SPSS Package

GLM (UNIANOVA) is the SPSS program available for factorial analysis of variance.[14] GLM offers the standard features such as source tables and the major descriptive statistics and has options for unequal sample sizes. SPSS GLM is the only program reviewed that provides achieved power and effect sizes. GLM has a vast array of post hoc tests—20 in all, including several choices of pairwise comparisons that do not require homogeneity of variance. GLM also provides tests for homogeneity of variance, predicted values and residuals, plots of residuals, plots of means versus variances (Box-Cox plots—handy for diagnosis of homogeneity of variance), and plots of means to aid interpretation.

5.8.2   SAS System

SAS GLM has all of the general features of ANOVA programs along with several unique features. However, GLM's capacity to do a wide variety of multivariate general linear modeling makes it more difficult to use than some of the more specialized ANOVA programs. For instance, modeling syntax is necessary to specify IVs and the DV. SAS ANOVA is less computer-intensive, but is no easier to use than GLM and is limited to data sets with equal sample sizes in all cells.

---

[14]In SPSS for Windows, on the General Linear Models submenu, UNIANOVA program is identified as GLM-General Factorial. An earlier program, MANOVA, is available in syntax.

TABLE 5.52   Comparison of SPSS, SYSTAT, and SAS Programs for Factorial Randomized-Groups ANOVA

Feature	MINITAB GLM[a]	SPSS GLM	SAS GLM[a]	SYSTAT ANOVA and GLM[a]
Input				
Maximum number of IVs	9	No limit	No limit	No limit
Options for unequal n	Yes	Yes	Yes	Yes[b]
Specify α level for post hoc comparisons	Yes	No	ALPHA	No[d]
Special specification for trend (polynomial) analysis	No	Yes	No	Polynomial
Unequal spacing of levels for trend analysis	N.A.	Yes	No	Yes
Streamlined specification for simple effects	No	No	SLICE	No
Specify error terms for effects and/or contrasts	No	Yes	Yes	Yes
Specify number of Bonferroni comparisons	No	No	No	No
Custom hypothesis matrices	No	Yes	Yes	Yes
Case weighting	No	Yes	Yes	No
Specify tolerance	Yes	EPS	SINGULAR	Yes
Output				
ANOVA table	Yes	Yes	Yes	Yes
Cell means	Yes	Yes	Yes	No
Confidence interval for cell means	No	No	No	No
Unadjusted marginal means	No	No	Yes	No
Cell standard deviations	No	Yes	Yes	No
Confidence interval for adjusted cell means	No	No	Yes	No
Standard errors for adjusted cell means	Yes	No	Data file	Yes

TABLE 5.52   Continued

Feature	MINITAB GLM[a]	SPSS GLM	SAS GLM[a]	SYSTAT ANOVA and GLM[a]
Adjusted marginal means	Yes	EMMEANS	LS MEANS	Yes
Standard errors for adjusted marginal means	Yes	EMMEANS	STDERR	Yes
Descriptive statistics for all groups combined	No	Yes	No	No
Power analysis and effect sizes	No	Yes	No	No
Tests for pairwise contrasts that do not require homogeneity of variance	No	Yes	No	No
t test for all pairs of cell means	No	No	Yes	Yes
Tukey comparisons for main effects	Yes	Yes	Yes	No
Bonferroni pairwise comparisons for main effects	Yes	Yes	Yes	No
Scheffé pairwise comparisons for main effects	No	Yes	Yes	No
LSD pairwise comparisons for main effects	No	Yes	Yes	No
Sidak pairwise comparisons for main effects	Yes	Yes	Yes	No
Additional post hoc tests with adjustments[f]	Yes	Yes	Yes	Yes
User-specific contrasts	No	Yes	Yes	Yes
Multiple R and/or R^2	No	Yes	Yes	Yes
Levene's test for homogeneity of variance	No	Yes	No	No
Predicted values and residuals	No	Yes	Yes	Data file
Confidence limits for predicted values	No	No	Yes	No
Outliers (studentized residual criterion)	No	Yes	P	Yes
Durbin-Watson statistic	No	No	P	Yes

TABLE 5.52   Continued

Feature	MINITAB GLM[a]	SPSS GLM	SAS GLM[a]	SYSTAT ANOVA and GLM[a]
Plots				
Means	No	Yes	No	Yes
Box-Cox plots for homogeneity of variance (group means vs. group standard deviations)	No	Yes	No	No
Plots of residuals	Yes	Yes	No	No
Histogram of residuals	Yes	No	No	No
Normal probability plot of residuals	Yes	No	No	No
Residuals vs. predicted (fitted) values	Yes	No	No	No
Residuals vs. order of data	Yes	No	No	No
Residuals vs. any variable	Yes	No	No	No
Saved to file				
Residuals	Yes	Yes	Yes	Yes
Predicted (fitted, adjusted) values, i.e., mean for each case	Yes	Yes	Yes	Yes
Additional statistics, including those for outliers	Yes	Yes	Yes	Yes
Means, standard deviations and frequencies	No	No	Yes	Yes

[a] Additional features reviewed in other chapters.

[b] Requires multiple runs for any but Method 1.

[c] Scheffé and Bonferroni confidence intervals for parameter estimates.

[d] Probability values provided for comparisons.

[e] Not available for unique sums of squares (see Table 5.45).

[f] See Table 4.31 for additional details about post hoc tests.

[g] May be done through WEIGHT procedure.

GLM has an especially rich array of options for planned and post hoc comparisons, and all sorts of matrices may be hypothesized and printed out for the more sophisticated analyst. The program produces predicted values and residuals for each case, as well as confidence limits for those values, on request. Information about outliers is available, along with the Durbin-Watson statistic if case order is meaningful.

5.8.3   SYSTAT System

SYSTAT ANOVA is a subset of the GLM program; both produce the same output and have the same features, but ANOVA uses a simpler syntax for identification of IVs and the DV. GLM uses modeling syntax, similar to SAS.

The program has several of the more popular post hoc comparison procedures, along with user-specified weighting coefficients. However, the program is somewhat short on descriptive statistics, among them standard deviations within cells. (Instead, a standard error is printed that is the square root of the pooled within-cell variance divided by the square root of the cell size.) This means that other modules within the system are necessary to evaluate homogeneity of variance.

Studentized residual outliers are automatically printed as is the Durbin-Watson statistic. Plots of means are provided, however, they are not in the usual "factorial" format. SYSTAT ANOVA and GLM produce an unweighted means analysis by default if sample sizes are unequal. Any other option for dealing with unequal n requires multiple runs.

5.8.4   MINITAB Programs

MINITAB has several programs to analyze factorial designs: TWO-WAY (available by menu); BALANCED, requiring equal n; and GLM. Output is virtually identical for the three programs, but GLM has the most flexibility and options, and so is the only one described in Table 5.52.

GLM uses model language and requires explicit listing of interactions as well as main effects in a regressionlike equation. Three options for unequal n are available, as well as four types of post hoc pairwise comparisons. A major failing is the lack of user-specified contrasts. Thus, codes for contrasts must be explicitly listed as variables in the data set and declared to be "covariates" (cf. Tables 4.23 and 4.24). As for SYSTAT, descriptive statistics (with actual cell standard deviations and variances) are unavailable in GLM. However, the program has a good selection of residuals plots and saves plenty of statistics to file.

5.9   Problem Sets

5.1 Do an analysis of variance on the following data set. Assume that A is type of fabric, B is minutes of presoaking a garment, and the DV is rating of cleanliness.

	Presoak Time			
	b_1 5 min	b_2 10 min	b_3 15 min	b_4 20 min
a_1: Cotton	2	3	8	6
	6	9	11	7
	6	9	9	9
a_2: Polyester	6	5	9	6
	5	7	6	9
	3	5	12	9

a. Test for homogeneity of variance.
b. Provide a source table.
c. Check results by running the data set through at least one canned computer program.
d. Calculate effect size(s).
e. Write a Results section for the analysis.
f. Use one of the canned computer programs to do a trend analysis and apply an appropriate post hoc adjustment.

5.2 Table 5.38 shows several significant interaction contrasts for the small sample data of Table 5.3. One of these is plotted in Figure 5.10. Plot one of the remaining significant contrasts.

5.3 Do an analysis of variance (through a canned computer program) on the following pilot data set, assuming these are pilot data for an experiment in which cell sample sizes will be equal.

	b_1	b_2	b_3	b_4	b_5
a_1	6	5	5	6	6
	5	6	5	5	7
			6		
	5	6	7	9	7
a_2	8	7	5	7	6
		6		7	
				6	

a. Provide a source table.
b. Show appropriate marginal means.
c. How many cases would need to be run to get a statistically significant main effect of B at $\alpha = .05$ and $\beta = .20$?

5.4 Suppose a researcher is interested in the effects of hours of sleep and type of beverage consumed on test performance in a statistics course. Students in the course are randomly assigned to get either 4, 6, or 8 hours of sleep, and to get either coffee, fruit juice, or beer in the 24 hours prior to the exam. Consider type of beverage factor A and hours of sleep factor B. For each question, indicate the type of analysis required (marginal comparison, simple main effect, simple comparison, or interaction contrast) and use A and B symbols to specify the analysis (e.g., Acomp at b_3).
a. Do students who get 8 hours of sleep perform better than those who get 4 or 6 hours?
b. Do those who drink coffee perform better than those who drink fruit juice?
c. For those sleeping 6 hours, do the different beverages produce different exam scores?
d. For those drinking fruit juice, is there a linear trend of hours of sleep?
e. For coffee drinkers, is there a difference in exam scores between those who sleep 4 hours and those who sleep 8 hours?
f. For those drinking beer, is there a difference in scores depending on hours of sleep?
g. For those sleeping 4 hours, is there a difference between fruit juice and coffee drinkers?
h. Do coffee drinkers and fruit juice drinkers have a different linear trend of hours of sleep?

Extending the Concepts

5.5 Do a three-way ANOVA using the data set of Table 5.21.
a. Test for homogeneity of variance.
b. Provide a source table.
c. Check results by running the data set through at least one canned computer program.
d. Calculate effect size(s).
e. Write a Results section for the analysis.
f. Use one of the canned computer programs to test the simple effect of deprivation at each level of familiarity. Assume this was part of the sequential analysis plan. (*Hint:* If using SPSS, recode into 8 groups and analyze as per SYSTAT or use coefficients in ONEWAY contrasts as per Chapter 4.)

5.6 Develop the IV coding columns for a $2 \times 3 \times 3$ ANOVA using the regression approach.

6 Repeated-Measures Designs

6.1 General Purpose and Description

Each case is measured more than once on the same DV in repeated-measures designs. In randomized-groups designs, each case is measured a single time.[1] Repeated-measures designs are often used to track changes in a DV over time. For instance, a marketing firm might be interested in changes in sales of a new product in the 6 months after introduction into a city. Sales figures are collected in each of several sales districts (the cases) for each month and analyzed using repeated-measures ANOVA. Are sales higher at the end? Is there a difference between the first and second month of sales? When did sales really "pick up"? Are sales still going up or have they leveled off?

Although the IV often is a variable such as time or distance whose levels are in a fixed order, repeated-measures designs are also used with IVs whose levels are measured in any order. For instance, a hospital might be interested in the efficacy of several different disinfectants for cleaning pieces of equipment. The levels of the IV are the different disinfectants. The cases are the same pieces of equipment, cleaned repeatedly, each time using a different disinfectant. The order in which the disinfectants are used is completely arbitrary. In this application of repeated measures, special controls for the potential effects of order are necessary, as described in Section 6.5.1 and Chapter 7.

Two or more repeated-measures IVs are often used in factorial combination in the same study. For instance, different disinfectants are used in combination with different temperatures of washing solution (high and low) to find, if possible, the particular combination of disinfectant and temperature that is the most efficacious. A repeated-measures IV can also be used in combination with one or more randomized-groups IVs in a mixed design, the topic of Chapter 7.

Repeated-measures designs are favored in many settings because they often are more efficient and powerful than randomized-groups designs. They are more efficient for at least two reasons. The first is that they use far fewer cases than a corresponding randomized-groups design. For instance, a randomized-groups design with three levels probably requires about 10 cases per level, for a total of 30 cases. In a repeated-measures design, the same 10 cases are measured three times. This feature of repeated measures is especially valuable if cases are rare or expensive. Second, it often takes con-

---

[1]There are designs in which cases are measured once, but on several DVs, and analyzed using MANOVA (multivariate analysis of variance); or in which cases are measured several times, each time on several DVs, and analyzed using repeated-measures MANOVA. See Tabachnick and Fidell, 2001.

siderable time and effort to access and prepare a case. Once a case is ready, it is often more efficient to measure it several times unless there is some reason not to.

Repeated-measures analysis often is more powerful than randomized-groups analysis because differences associated with the cases themselves are assessed and subtracted from the error term. In ANOVA, anything measured more than one time is eligible for analysis as a source of variability. In repeated measures, cases are measured more than one time. Differences between cases, then, are eligible for analysis. For instance, in the marketing example, differences in sales districts are assessed and subtracted from the error term; in the hospital example, differences in the pieces of equipment are assessed and removed from the error term. The error term in a repeated-measures design, then, frequently is smaller than the error term in a corresponding randomized-groups design, making the overall ANOVA more powerful. Repeated-measures designs often are chosen to capitalize on this feature of the analysis.

However, there are no free lunches, so increases in efficiency and power with this design are sometimes offset by a restrictive assumption that makes analysis by traditional ANOVA problematic. The assumption, sphericity, is discussed in Sections 6.3.2.3, and 6.6.2. When the assumption is violated, routine analysis is untenable. There are several alternatives, some of them involving more complicated statistical analyses and some involving reconceptualization of the design.

6.2   Kinds of Research Questions

The research questions asked in repeated-measures designs are basically the same as those of randomized-groups designs. Are there reliable mean differences associated with the levels of an IV? Do combinations of levels of IVs interact to produce changes of their own in the means? If so, parameters and effect size are estimated. If an IV has more than two levels, comparisons are appropriate in lieu of or after ANOVA.

6.2.1   Effect of the IVs

The main effect of each IV in the design is available for analysis. Are there reliable mean differences associated with different levels of each IV? Are there mean differences in the sales figures for the 6 months? Do different disinfectants produce different levels of cleanliness? There is, however, another main effect available for analysis in a one-way design should it prove interesting, and that is for cases. Do cases have different average scores on the DV? Do the sales districts differ? Are pieces of equipment different in cleanliness? In some settings, differences due to cases are extremely interesting, and in others, they are merely a nuisance. These questions are answered as in randomized-groups ANOVA, by applying F tests to the data, as demonstrated in Section 6.4.1.

6.2.2   Effect of Interactions among IVs

Does the effect of one IV depend on the level of another IV? Are there particular combinations of levels of IVs that are better (or worse) than other combinations? Is the effectiveness of type of disinfectant different at various levels of temperature of the washing solution? Section 6.4.2 demonstrates application of the F test to answer questions about interaction.

6.2.3 Parameter Estimates

What mean DV score is predicted for each level of the IV in the population? For each combination of levels of IVs? What average cleanliness score is predicted for each type of disinfectant? Parameter estimates reported for reliable IVs are sample means and either standard deviations, standard errors, or confidence intervals around the means. Reliable mean differences are often shown graphically, as in Figure 2.10.

6.2.4 Effect Sizes

How much of the variability in the DV is associated with differences in levels of the IV? Or with differences in combinations of levels of IVs? How much of the total variability in sales is associated with month? How much of the total variability in cleanliness is associated with the type of disinfectant? Computation of effect size for repeated-measures IVs is discussed in Section 6.6.4.

6.2.5 Power

What is the probability of finding a mean difference on the IV if the DV really does change with different levels of the IV? More formally, if the alternative hypothesis is true (the null hypothesis is false), what are the chances of concluding in its favor? If there really are differences in disinfectants, what is the probability of finding a mean difference in cleanliness? Are enough cases (pieces of equipment) being tested so that the outcome is likely to be statistically significant? Computation of power in repeated measures is discussed in Section 6.6.3.

6.2.6 Specific Comparisons

If there are more than two levels of an IV, which means are reliably different from which other means? Do some levels of the IV produce similar means while other levels produce different mean DV scores? Are all of the disinfectants different from each other? Are some of them the same whereas others are different? Is the best one significantly better than the next best one? As in randomized-groups designs, comparisons are either planned and performed in lieu of ANOVA or, with lower power, performed post hoc. Comparisons are a nasty topic in repeated-measures designs, as discussed in Section 6.6.6.

6.3 Assumptions and Limitations

6.3.1 Theoretical Issues

If the repeated-measures IV is passage of time (whose levels are chosen, but cannot be manipulated), the study is not an experiment, and causal inference is inappropriate. When the levels are manipulated (e.g., type of music), issues of causal inference are resolved by attention to the details of the design of the study, as in randomized-groups designs.

Control of extraneous variables may be especially difficult because of the passage of time during repeated measurement. Have extraneous variables been adequately controlled? What conditions, if any, change during the course of the study? Is equipment stable? Do testing conditions remain the same? Do the researchers behave consistently over time? If cases are people, are they just as perky and involved at the last measurement as at the first? Is their attention stable or does it waver over time? Do people become more skilled at performing the DV over time regardless of the IV? If the levels of the IV can be presented in any order, and if there is reason to expect change over repeated measurement, you are wise to implement a Latin-square design as an additional control over these changes, as discussed in Chapter 9.

There is also the issue of generalizability of findings: How are cases obtained and what population do they represent? Because repeated-measures designs use fewer cases than randomized-groups designs, generalization is more problematic, making the representativeness of the sample more critical than for randomized-groups design. Also, the pattern of effects of the IV can only be generalized to cases that have been exposed to all levels of the IV. Thus, generalization usually is more restricted in a repeated-measures design than in a randomized-groups design. These and other questions are resolved by attention to the details of the research design and not to the statistics.

6.3.2 Practical Issues

Practical issues of normality of sampling distributions, homogeneity of variance, and absence of outliers are similar in repeated-measures and randomized-groups designs. However, the assumption of independence has greater relevance in this design and additivity (absence of interaction between cases and levels of the IV) is an additional assumption. Although logically different, they play out as the assumption of sphericity, special to repeated measurement. This assumption is critical to the analysis and often violated with both real and made up data sets.

All of the analyses in this chapter also assume equal spacing between adjacent levels of IVs (e.g., 10, 20, 30 seconds), not unequal spacing (e.g., 5, 20, 30 seconds). Analysis of unequally spaced levels of IVs is discussed in Section 11.6.3.

6.3.2.1 Normality of Sampling Distributions

In randomized-groups designs, normality of sampling distributions of means is expected if there are relatively equal numbers of cases in every cell and 20 df for error. In repeated measures, there is only one value in every combination of case and IV level (i.e., one case in each cell as shown in Table 6.1(a)) and the number of cases at each level of the IV is equal because the same cases participate at all levels. If there is only one IV, *normality of the sampling distribution of means is anticipated if there are 20 df for the error term.*

However, a complexity arises with small N studies and factorial repeated measures. In factorial repeated measures, several error terms are developed, a different one for each IV and combination of IVs in the design. Some error terms may have sufficient df to assure normality but others may not. If df are sparse for the error terms associated with some effects, look at the skewness and kurtosis values associated with the DV for those effects, as described in Section 2.2.3.3. If the values are satisfactory, normality of sampling distributions is anticipated. To look at skewness and kurtosis, you have to generate the DV scores for each IV or combination of IVs because the scores that are actually tested are not the raw scores, but rather the sums of raw scores, as shown in Tables 6.1(b) and 6.1(c). It is the distributions of summed scores (10, 4, 14) for a_1, and summed scores (10, 6, 14) for a_2 that need to be fairly normally distributed to test the main effect of A, and similarly to test the main effect of B, b_1 (7, 3, 11) versus b_2 (13, 7, 17).

TABLE 6.1   Conversion of Raw Scores to Scores Tested by each IV in a Factorial Repeated-Measures Design

(a) Raw scores

	a_1		a_2	
	b_1	b_2	b_1	b_2
s_1	3	7	4	6
s_2	1	3	2	4
s_3	5	9	6	8

(b) Scores tested in main effect of A

	a_1	a_2
	$b_1 + b_2$	$b_1 + b_2$
s_1	$3 + 7 = 10$	$4 + 6 = 10$
s_2	$1 + 3 = 4$	$2 + 4 = 6$
s_3	$5 + 9 = 14$	$6 + 8 = 14$

(c) Scores tested in main effect of B

	b_1	b_2
	$a_1 + a_2$	$a_1 + a_2$
s_1	$3 + 4 = 7$	$7 + 6 = 13$
s_2	$1 + 2 = 3$	$3 + 4 = 7$
s_3	$5 + 6 = 11$	$9 + 8 = 17$

The principle involved with generating these scores is the same no matter how complex the design becomes: You sum together the numbers over the IV that is currently "left out" for each level of the IV you are interested in. For instance, if you are creating a data set for the main effect of A, you sum together the scores for B at a_1 and repeat the process at a_2, and so on, as illustrated in Table 6.1(b). If the design has three IVs, when you are interested in the main effect of A, you sum over both B and C. When you are interested in the $A \times B$ interaction, you sum over scores for levels of C. All of the programs have convenient facilities for combining scores in this manner.

If nonnormality threatens the analysis, a data transformation of the DV scores may be desirable; if so, *all* of the scores at all levels of the repeated-measures IV are transformed. Various transformations are discussed in Section 2.2.3.3. Nonparametric methods are available for small, nonnormally distributed data sets if there is only one IV. The Wilcoxon Signed Ranks Test is available when $a = 2$; the Friedman test is available for $a > 2$. Most statistical computer packages provide these nonparametric analyses.

6.3.2.2   Homogeneity of Variance

There is only one DV score in each cell of a design in which all cases participate in all levels of all IVs, so the assumption of homogeneity of variance within each cell is not relevant. However, homogeneity of variance for all the scores contributing to a level of an IV or a combination of levels of IVs is required. Variances are computed for scores at each level of an IV or each combination of levels of

IVs and examined for homogeneity of variance. Because DV scores for each level or each combination of levels of IVs are in a separate column of the data set in a repeated-measures design (as shown in Table 6.13 later), compute the variance for each column separately and compare the variances. The guidelines and procedures in Section 4.5.4 or 5.3.2.2 are also appropriate for a repeated-measures design.

6.3.2.3   *Independence of Errors, Additivity, Homogeneity of Covariance, and Sphericity*

Although assumptions of independence of errors, homogeneity of covariance, and additivity are conceptually different, they are practically combined into an assumption of sphericity in the repeated-measures design. The reason is that the error term for the design confounds random error (the independence of error assumption) and the $A \times S$ (IV by cases) interaction (related to the additivity assumption). One's fondest hope in repeated measures is that there is no genuine (population) $A \times S$ interaction, so the error term is only random error. This is a forlorn hope with many real data sets because of contingencies in the responses of the same cases as they are repeatedly measured over time.

Violation of independence of errors occurs because of reassessment of the same cases, because of effects over time, and because of differences in the similarities of levels of treatment. The error components for each case are almost certainly associated with each other over levels of A because they are the same cases. Also, cases are likely to have idiosyncratic responses to different levels of treatment. Some may respond strongly to some levels, whereas others respond strongly or not at all to other levels. This produces $A \times S$ interaction, which violates additivity.[2]

A second source of violation is potential nonindependence of errors due to passage of time. Not only cases, but also equipment and the testing situation are likely to drift over time. Measurements made close to each other in time are probably more similar than measurements made farther apart in time. The third source of violation is patterns of similarity in the different levels of A. If some levels of A are similar to each other, but different from other levels, there are likely to be higher correlations in the error components among those that are more similar. These sources contribute to violation of homogeneity of covariance.

Section 6.6.2 discusses these assumptions and the tests of them more technically. It also discusses the alternative analytic strategies available when a data set violates the assumptions.

6.3.2.4   *Absence of Outliers*

Outliers have the same devastating effect on repeated-measures designs as on randomized-groups designs. Outliers are sought among the same sets of DV scores as those used to assess homogeneity of variance: separately in each level or combination of levels of repeated-measures IVs. Therefore, potential outliers are sought for each DV column in the data set (shown in Table 6.13 later). The guidelines of Section 3.4.5 or 4.3.2.4 are appropriate for this design as well. If an outlier is found, deletion of the case, transformation of all the DV scores, or adjustment of the single score is appropriate.

---

[2]If you can identify some characteristic of the cases (such as age, gender, or socioeconomic status) that is associated with differences in response to different levels of A, you can block cases on it. This creates a mixed design (Chapter 7) and makes the formerly pesky interaction directly available for analysis and interpretation.

6.3.2.5   *Missing Data*

If data are missing in randomized-groups designs, there is very little that can be done because there is no other information from which to estimate the size of the missing value. In repeated measures, however, there are other DV scores for the case from which to estimate (impute) the missing value. If only one or two DV scores are missing, it is often better to estimate them rather than lose all the other information for those cases. Various estimation procedures are described in Section 6.6.5.

6.4   Fundamental Equations

There are several varieties of repeated-measures designs. The simplest is a design with a single IV. The next most complicated design has two IVs in factorial combination. These are covered in the sections that follow. Designs, of course, sometimes have three or more IVs, but the analytical principles remain the same and are easily generalized from the two-IV situation. Designs that have at least one randomized-group IV in addition to at least one repeated-measures IV are discussed in the following chapter.

6.4.1   One-Way Repeated-Measures ANOVA

6.4.1.1   *Allocation of Cases*

All cases participate at all levels of *A* in a one-way repeated-measures design. Table 6.2 shows how cases are used in a one-way design with three levels. Notice that every level of *A* has the same cases and each case participates at every level of *A*. Once DV scores are gathered, they are arranged in a table, with *a* columns representing levels of the IV, one row for each case, and *s* scores within each level.

6.4.1.2   *Partition of Sources of Variance*

Anything that is measured more than one time is potentially a source of variance in ANOVA. In repeated-measures designs, cases are measured more than one time and are therefore analyzed as a

TABLE 6.2   Assignment of Cases in a One-Way Repeated-Measures Design

Treatment		
a_1	a_2	a_3
s_1	s_1	s_1
s_2	s_2	s_2
s_3	s_3	s_3
s_4	s_4	s_4

potential source of variability in the DV. The other identifiable source of variability is factor A. Once these two sources of variability are computed, the remaining variability serves as the error term. Total variability (SS_T), then, is partitioned into that due to treatment, to cases, and to error.

$$SS_T = SS_A + SS_S + SS_{AS} \tag{6.1}$$

Notice that this partition of total variability is identical to that of the main effects and interaction in a two-way randomized-groups design, A and B and $A \times B$. That is, there is a main effect of A, a main effect of S, and the interaction of A with S. Levels of S (cases) cross levels of A; all combinations of A and S appear in the design. In a two-way randomized-groups design, however, there is an additional source of variability, S/AB—cases nested within AB combinations—that serves as the error term. In the repeated-measures design, as shown in Table 6.2, there is only one score at each AS combination.[3] Therefore, there is no variability in scores within each cell. In the absence of the traditional error term, $A \times S$ is used as the error term. This term is both the interaction of cases with treatment (the idiosyncratic responses of cases to levels of treatment) and random variability (error). More about that later.

Degrees of freedom in ANOVA partition the same way as sums of squares:

$$df_T = df_A + df_S + df_{AS} \tag{6.2}$$

Total degrees of freedom is the total number of scores, as, minus 1, lost when the grand mean is estimated. Therefore,

$$df_T = as - 1 \tag{6.3}$$

Note that s is the notation used for number of cases so that $as = N$, the total number of scores.

Degrees of freedom for treatment are identical to those in a corresponding randomized-group design:

$$df_A = a - 1 \tag{6.4}$$

Degrees of freedom for cases are

$$df_S = s - 1 \tag{6.5}$$

And degrees of freedom for the error term are

$$df_{AS} = (a - 1)(s - 1) \tag{6.6}$$

This is a complete partition of the degrees of freedom (and, by extension, sum of squares):

$$as - 1 = a - 1 + s - 1 + as - a - s + 1$$

---

[3]This is the reason that repeated-measures designs sometimes are labeled one-score-per-cell.

Figure 6.1 is a graphic representation of the partition. The figure shows the partition of SS_T in a randomized-groups design and then in a repeated-measures design. Notice that SS_A is the same in the two designs. Notice also that SS_S and SS_{AS} come out of the error term, $SS_{S/A}$, in the randomized-groups design. This explains why the error term for repeated measures is often smaller than the error term for randomized groups: differences due to cases are assessed and removed as a source of variability. Notice, however, that df for the repeated-measures error term also are reduced.

Variances (mean squares) are produced by dividing SS by df. Thus, equations for mean squares are

$$MS_A = \frac{SS_A}{df_A} \tag{6.7}$$

and

$$MS_S = \frac{SS_S}{df_S} \tag{6.8}$$

and

$$MS_{AS} = \frac{SS_{AS}}{df_{AS}} \tag{6.9}$$

In many research applications, MS_S, the variability in cases, is not a useful quantity.

The F distribution is a ratio of two variances. In repeated-measures ANOVA, MS_A and MS_{AS} provide the variances for the F ratio to test the null hypothesis that $\mu_{a_1} = \mu_{a_2} = \cdots = \mu_{a_j}$.

$$F = \frac{MS_A}{MS_{AS}} \qquad df = (a-1), (a-1)(s-1) \tag{6.10}$$

If the null hypothesis is true and there are no treatment effects and no $A \times S$ interaction, the F ratio boils down to a ratio of two estimates of the same error and is likely to be around one.

(a) Sums of squares   **(b) Degrees of freedom**

**FIGURE 6.1   Partition of (a) Sums of Squares and (b) Degrees of Freedom
in a Randomized-Groups Design and Then in a Repeated-Measures Design**

Once F is obtained, it is tested against critical F (Table A.1 in Appendix A) with numerator df $= a - 1$ and denominator df $= (a - 1)(s - 1)$ at desired alpha level. If obtained F equals or exceeds critical F, the null hypothesis is rejected in favor of the hypothesis that there is a difference among the means in the a levels.

6.4.1.3   Traditional One-Way Repeated-Measures ANOVA

Table 6.3 shows a data set in which number of science fiction books read per month serves as the DV. There are five readers in this small, inadequate, and hypothetical data set. (Note that this is not an experiment because time cannot be manipulated.) The last column contains the sum of the DV scores for each case over the 3 months. It is these values that are used to assess differences among the cases because they reflect overall differences in preferences for reading, or skill levels, or whatever.

By using the notational scheme developed for randomized groups, the equation for SS_A, sum of squares attributable to treatment, is

$$SS_A = \frac{\sum A^2}{s} - \frac{T^2}{as} \tag{6.11}$$

The equation for SS_S, sum of squares attributable to cases, is

$$SS_S = \frac{\sum S^2}{a} - \frac{T^2}{as} \tag{6.12}$$

The equation for SS_{AS}, sum of squares attributable to error, calculated as the $A \times S$ interaction, is

$$SS_{AS} = \sum Y^2 - \frac{\sum A^2}{s} - \frac{\sum S^2}{a} + \frac{T^2}{as} \tag{6.13}$$

TABLE 6.3   Hypothetical Data Set for a One-Way Repeated- Measures Design with Three Levels

	A: Month			Case Totals
	a_1: Month 1	a_2: Month 2	a_3: Month 3	
s_1	1	3	6	$S_1 = 10$
s_2	1	4	8	$S_2 = 13$
s_3	3	3	6	$S_3 = 12$
s_4	5	5	7	$S_4 = 17$
s_5	2	4	5	$S_5 = 11$
Treatment Totals	$A_1 = 12$	$A_2 = 19$	$A_3 = 32$	$T = 63$

And the equation for SS_T is

$$SS_T = \sum Y^2 - \frac{T^2}{as} \qquad (6.14)$$

Notice that the elements in these equations are Y, A, S, and T, each divided by the number of scores added together to produce the total that is squared. Notice also that the symbols in the denominator are the symbols *not* in the numerator. Verify that these elements are a complete partition of SS_T.

Table 6.4 shows sums of squares for the example. Take a moment to compare these results with those from the randomized-groups example of Chapter 4. Notice first that the data in Table 4.2 are the same as the data in Table 6.3. The same data set was used partly out of sloth and partly to illustrate a very important point: Computation of the main effect of A and computation of SS_T is identical for the two designs. When computing main effects (and interactions), the way cases are allocated is irrelevant. Then notice that the sum of SS_S (9.7) and SS_{AS} (9.5) is equal to $SS_{S/A}$ (19.2) from the randomized-groups design (Table 4.3). Variability due to cases (along with their df) is subtracted from the error term in a corresponding randomized-groups design, making, it is hoped, the error term in the repeated-measures design, MS_{AS}, smaller.

SS are converted to MS by dividing by df. Table 6.5 shows degrees of freedom for the example. It is reassuring that the partitions of SS and the partitions of df both sum to their respective totals. If they do not sum to SS_T and df_T, there has been a computational error.

Table 6.6 shows calculation of mean squares for treatment and error sources of variance. Compare these values with those in Table 4.5. MS_A has not changed because neither the SS nor the df have changed from the randomized-groups design. The error term for the repeated-measures design, MS_{AS}, on the other hand, is smaller than the error term for the randomized-groups design, $MS_{S/A}$ ($1.2 < 1.6$). This is because there are some differences due to cases when the data are analyzed as repeated measures. If there are no differences due to cases, the repeated-measures design is usually equal to or lower in power than the randomized-groups design (because of the loss of df for error), although it may still be more efficient to run the cases through several levels of A once they are set up to be measured (e.g., volunteers are already in the research cubicle).

Finally, Table 6.7 is a source table that summarizes the results of Tables 6.4 to 6.6 and includes the F ratio. The F ratio is tested with 2 and 8 df. If our willingness to risk a Type I error is 5%, the

TABLE 6.4   Calculation of Sums of Squares for Traditional One-Way Repeated-Measures ANOVA with Three Levels

$$SS_A = \frac{12^2 + 19^2 + 32^2}{5} - \frac{63^2}{3(5)} \qquad\qquad = 41.2$$

$$SS_S = \frac{10^2 + 13^2 + 12^2 + 17^2 + 11^2}{3} - \frac{63^2}{3(5)} \qquad = 9.7$$

$$SS_{AS} = 325 - \frac{12^2 + 19^2 + 32^2}{5} - \frac{10^2 + 13^2 + 12^2 + 17^2 + 11^2}{3} + \frac{63^2}{3(5)} = 9.5$$

$$SS_T = 325 - \frac{63^2}{3(5)} \qquad\qquad\qquad = 60.4$$

TABLE 6.5   Calculation of Degrees of Freedom for Traditional One-Way Repeated-Measures ANOVA with Three Levels

$$df_A \ = a - 1 \qquad\quad = 3 - 1 \qquad\qquad = \ 2$$

$$df_S \ = s - 1 \qquad\quad = 5 - 1 \qquad\qquad = \ 4$$

$$df_{AS} = (a-1)(s-1) = (3-1)(5-1) = \ 8$$

$$df_T \ = as - 1 \qquad\ = 15 - 1 \qquad\quad = 14$$

TABLE 6.6   Calculation of Mean Squares for Traditional One-Way Repeated-Measures ANOVA with Three Levels

$$MS_A \ = \frac{SS_A}{df_A} \ = \frac{41.2}{2} = 20.6$$

$$MS_S \ = \frac{SS_S}{df_S} \ = \frac{9.7}{4} \ = \ 2.4$$

$$MS_{AS} = \frac{SS_{AS}}{df_{AS}} = \frac{9.5}{8} \ = \ 1.2$$

TABLE 6.7   Source Table for One-Way Repeated-Measures ANOVA

Source	SS	df	MS	F
A	41.2	2	20.6	17.17
S	9.7	4	2.4	
A × S	9.5	8	1.2	
T	60.4	14		

critical value of F in Table A.1 is 4.46. Because the F ratio of 17.17 is larger than 4.46, the null hypothesis is rejected in favor of the hypothesis that there is a reliable difference in mean numbers of science fiction books read over the 3 months of the study. Note that the effect of S (cases) is not tested as part of the analysis. If they were to be tested, they would be a random effect (cf. Chapter 11). That is, cases in this study are assumed to be randomly selected (at least in an experiment) from some larger population of cases.

6.4.1.4   The Regression Approach to One-Way Repeated Measures

The regression approach uses columns to code IV levels as in the randomized-groups analysis. In general, df_A such columns are required to compute SS_A. In this example, $df_A = 2$, so two columns are required to code levels of A. Because levels of A represent passage of time, it makes sense to use the codes for trend analysis for this example, which are $-1, 0, 1$ for linear trend, and $1, -2, 1$ for quadratic trend. Table 6.8 shows the scores on the DV, Y, with trend coefficients in the two X columns. Column X_1 contains the linear-trend coefficients, and column X_2 the quadratic. Sums for cases are in column X_3, repeated three times, once at each level of A. This shortcut using case totals only works in the one-way repeated-measures design. Remaining columns are found by multiplication.

Table 6.9 shows the preliminary sums of squares calculated from Table 6.8. Table 6.10 shows the sums of cross-products that are produced by the columns in Table 6.8. And finally, sums of squares for the regression analysis are shown in Table 6.11.

TABLE 6.8   Regression Approach to One-Way Repeated-Measures Analysis of Variance with Three Treatment Levels

	Y	X_1	X_2	X_3	YX_1	YX_2	YX_3
		A		**S^a**			
a_1	1	−1	1	10	−1	1	10
	1	−1	1	13	−1	1	13
	3	−1	1	12	−3	3	36
	5	−1	1	17	−5	5	85
	2	−1	1	11	−2	2	22
a_2	3	0	−2	10	0	−6	30
	4	0	−2	13	0	−8	52
	3	0	−2	12	0	−6	36
	5	0	2	17	0	10	85
	4	0	−2	11	0	−8	44
a_3	6	1	1	10	6	6	60
	8	1	1	13	8	8	104
	6	1	1	12	6	6	72
	7	1	1	17	7	7	119
	5	1	1	11	5	5	55
Sum	63	0	0	189	20	6	823
Sum sq	325	10	30	2469			
N	15						

[a] Alternatively, cases can be divided into $s − 1 = 4$ orthogonal columns as in the two-way design of Table 6.26.

TABLE 6.9   Preliminary Sums of Squares for Regression Approach to Repeated-Measures ANOVA

$$SS_Y = \sum Y^2 - \frac{(\sum Y)^2}{N} = 325 - \frac{63^2}{15} = 60.4$$

$$SS(X_1) = \sum X_1^2 - \frac{(\sum X_1)^2}{N} = 10 - \frac{0^2}{15} = 10$$

$$SS(X_2) = \sum X_2^2 - \frac{(\sum X_2)^2}{N} = 30 - \frac{0^2}{15} = 30$$

$$SS(X_3) = \sum X_3^2 - \frac{(\sum X_3)^2}{N} = 2469 - \frac{189^2}{15} = 87.6$$

TABLE 6.10   Sums of Cross-Products for Regression Approach to Repeated-Measures ANOVA

$$SP(YX_1) = \sum YX_1 - \frac{(\sum Y)(\sum X_1)}{N} = 20 - \frac{(63)(0)}{15} = 20$$

$$SP(YX_2) = \sum YX_2 - \frac{(\sum Y)(\sum X_2)}{N} = 6 - \frac{(63)(0)}{15} = 6$$

$$SP(YX_3) = \sum YX_3 - \frac{(\sum Y)(\sum X_3)}{N} = 823 - \frac{(63)(189)}{15} = 29.2$$

TABLE 6.11   Sums of Squares for Repeated-Measures ANOVA through Regression

$$SS_A = SS(\text{reg. } X_1) + SS(\text{reg. } X_2) = \frac{[SP(YX_1)]^2}{SS(X_1)} + \frac{[SP(YX_2)]^2}{SS(X_2)} = \frac{(20)^2}{10} + \frac{(6)^2}{30} = 41.2$$

$$SS_S = SS(\text{reg. } X_3) = \frac{[SP(YX_3)]^2}{SS(X_3)} = \frac{(29.2)^2}{87.6} = 9.7$$

$$SS_T = SS_Y = 60.4$$

$$SS(\text{resid.}) = SS_T - SS_A - SS_S = 60.4 - 41.2 - 9.7 = 9.5$$

Degrees of freedom for regression are in Table 6.12. If this information is rearranged into the format of Table 6.7, the results are identical.

6.4.1.5   Computer Analyses of Small-Sample One-Way Repeated-Measures Design

Data are entered in the format of Table 6.3 for the GLM programs of SPSS, SAS, and SYSTAT, as well as SYSTAT ANOVA (but not for MINITAB GLM). That is, each line of data represents a case and contains sequential DV values for each level of the repeated-measures IV. Each line also may include a case identification number, as shown in Table 6.13.

Tables 6.14 through 6.16 show computer analyses of the small-sample example of the one-way repeated-measures ANOVA through SPSS GLM, SAS GLM, and SYSTAT ANOVA, respectively.

Table 6.14 shows syntax and output for SPSS GLM, Repeated Measures. The repeated measure is defined as month with three levels. Once the three levels are defined as month_1, month_2, and month_3, the /MEASURE identifies books as the DV. Options selected for printing are means (EMMEANS), descriptive statistics, estimates of effect size (ETASQ), and obtained power (OPOWER). The rest of the syntax in Table 6.14 is produced by default by the SPSS Windows menu program.

Confirmation of the DV used at each level of month is shown first, followed by means, standard deviations, and number of scores for each level. Multivariate tests of the mean difference for month is next; this is one of the options when sphericity is violated (Section 6.6.2), and is default output. By using Wilks' Lambda (a multivariate test criterion described by Tabachnick and Fidell,

TABLE 6.12 Calculation of Degrees of Freedom for ANOVA through Regression with Three Treatment Levels

df_A	= number of predictors (X vectors): $(a-1) = 3-1$			= 2
df_S	= number of cases -1: $(s-1)$		$= 5-1$	= 4
df_T	= number of scores -1: $(as-1)$		$= 15-1$	= 14
df(resid.) = $df_T - df_A - df_S$			$= 14-2-4 =$	8

TABLE 6.13 Hypothetical Data for One-Way ANOVA in a Form Suitable for SPSS, SAS, and SYSTAT Analysis

CASE	MONTH 1	MONTH 2	MONTH 3
1	1	3	6
2	1	4	8
3	3	3	6
4	5	5	7
5	2	4	5

2001), the difference in means is significant at $p = .047$. **Observed Power** for the multivariate test follows (.631). Next is **Mauchly's Test of Sphericity**; because the test is not significant (**Sig.** = .363), sphericity (see Section 6.6.2) is acceptable. The next table contains results of the Huynh-Feldt adjustment, as described in Section 6.6.2, and the test of **MONTH, Sphericity Assumed**. This latter test is the univariate ANOVA, with **Type III Sums of Squares = 41.200, df = 2, Mean Square = 20.600, F = 17.408**, and **Sig. = .001**. If **Mauchly's Test of Sphericity** is significant, a second option is to use instead the results of the **Huynh-Feldt test** (sig. = .002). The table also includes effect size (**MONTH, Sphericity Assumed – Eta Squared = .813**) and **Observed Power (.993)**, which is greater than the power of the multivariate test here (.631). That is followed by a table of default output (useful as the third option when sphericity fails), tests of linear and quadratic trend, in a table labeled **Tests of Within-Subjects Contrasts**. In this example, the **Linear** trend is significant (.011) but the **Quadratic** trend is not (.145). The table labeled **Tests of Between-Subjects Contrasts** contains **Sums of Squares, df**, and **Mean Square** for cases, labeled **Error**. Finally, means and the 95% confidence bounds are given for parameter estimation. This voluminous output, most of it produced by default, contains the result of routine repeated-measures ANOVA, as well as tests of the three options available when sphericity is violated. In this example, all four options indicate a reliable difference in means over the 3 months.

Table 6.15 shows SAS GLM syntax and output for the one-way repeated-measures example.[4] The **model** statement reflects the absence of a randomized group IV to the right of the equal sign. The repeated-measures IV (**MONTH**) is defined in the **repeated** statement. Means also are requested.

---

[4]SAS PROC ANOVA uses the same syntax for this analysis and produces the same output.

TABLE 6.14 One-Way Repeated-Measures ANOVA for Small-Sample Example through SPSS GLM: Syntax and Output

```
GLM
month_1 month_2 month_3
/WSFACTOR = month 3 Polynomial
/MEASURE = books
/METHOD = SSTYPE(3)
/EMMEANS = TABLES(month)
/PRINT = DESCRIPTIVE ETASQ OPOWER
/CRITERIA = ALPHA(.05)
/WSDESIGN = month.
```

General Linear Model

Within-Subjects Factors

Measure: BOOKS

MONTH	Dependent Variable
1	MONTH_1
2	MONTH_2
3	MONTH_3

Descriptive Statistics

	Mean	Std. Deviation	N
MONTH_1	2.4000	1.6733	5
MONTH_2	3.8000	.8367	5
MONTH_3	6.4000	1.1402	5

Multivariate Tests[c]

Effect		Value	F	Hypothesis df	Error df	Sig.	Eta Squared	Noncent. Parameter	Observed Power[a]
MONTH	Pillai's Trace	.870	10.035[b]	2.000	3.000	.047	.870	20.070	.631
	Wilks' Lambda	.130	10.035[b]	2.000	3.000	.047	.870	20.070	.631
	Hotelling's Trace	6.690	10.035[b]	2.000	3.000	.047	.870	20.070	.631
	Roy's Largest Root	6.690	10.035[b]	2.000	3.000	.047	.870	20.070	.631

a. Computed using alpha = .05
b. Exact statistic
c. Design: Intercept
   Within Subjects Design: MONTH

TABLE 6.14 Continued

Measure: BOOKS

Mauchly's Test of Sphericity[b]

Within Subjects Effect	Mauchly's W	Approx. Chi-Square	df	Sig.	Epsilon[a]		
					Greenhouse-Geisser	Huynh-Feldt	Lower-bound
MONTH	.509	2.027	2	.363	.671	.885	.500

Tests the null hypothesis that the error covariance matrix of the orthonormalized transformed dependent variables is proportional to an identity matrix.

a. May be used to adjust the degrees of freedom for the averaged tests of significance. Corrected tests are displayed in the layers (by default) of the Tests of Within Subjects Effects table.

b.

Design: Intercept
Within Subjects Design: MONTH

Tests of Within-Subjects Effects

Measure: BOOKS

Source		Type III Sum of Squares	df	Mean Square	F	Sig.	Eta Squared	Noncent. Parameter	Observed Power[a]
MONTH	Sphericity Assumed	41.200	2	20.600	17.408	.001	.813	34.817	.993
	Greenhouse-Geisser	41.200	1.341	30.718	17.408	.006	.813	23.349	.949
	Huynh-Feldt	41.200	1.770	23.276	17.408	.002	.813	30.814	.986
	Lower-bound	41.200	1.000	41.200	17.408	.014	.813	17.408	.870
Error(MONTH)	Sphericity Assumed	9.467	8	1.183					
	Greenhouse-Geisser	9.467	5.365	1.765					
	Huynh-Feldt	9.467	7.080	1.337					
	Lower-bound	9.467	4.000	2.367					

a. Computed using alpha = .05

(continued)

TABLE 6.14 Continued

Tests of Within-Subjects Contrasts

Measure: BOOKS

Source		MONTH	Type III Sum of Squares	df	Mean Square	F	Sig.	Eta Squared	Noncent. Parameter	Observed Power[a]
MONTH		Linear	40.000	1	40.000	20.000	.011	.833	20.000	.909
		Quadratic	1.200	1	1.200	3.273	.145	.450	3.273	.286
Error(MONTH)		Linear	8.000	4	2.000					
		Quadratic	1.467	4	.367					

a. Computed using alpha = .05

Tests of Between-Subjects Effects

Measure: BOOKS
Transformed Variable: Average

Source	Type III Sum of Squares	df	Mean Square	F	Sig.	Eta Squared	Noncent. Parameter	Observed Power[a]
Intercept	264.600	1	264.600	108.740	.000	.965	108.740	1.000
Error	9.733	4	2.433					

a. Computed using alpha = .05

Estimated Marginal Means

MONTH

Measure: BOOKS

MONTH	Mean	Std. Error	95% Confidence Interval	
			Lower Bound	Upper Bound
1	2.400	.748	.322	4.478
2	3.800	.374	2.761	4.839
3	6.400	.510	4.984	7.816

TABLE 6.15　One-Way Repeated-Measures ANOVA through SAS GLM: Syntax and Selected Output

```
proc glm data=SASUSER.SS_RPTD;
    model MONTH1 MONTH2 MONTH3 =;
    repeated MONTH / mean;
run;
```

The GLM Procedure
Repeated Measures Analysis of Variance

Repeated Measures Level Information

Dependent Variable	MONTH1	MONTH2	MONTH3
Level of MONTH	1	2	3

Manova Test Criteria and Exact F Statistics for the Hypothesis
of no MONTH Effect
H = Type III SSCP Matrix for MONTH
E = Error SSCP Matrix

S=1　　M=0　　N=0.5

Statistic	Value	F Value	Num DF	Den DF	Pr > F
Wilks' Lambda	0.13003802	10.04	2	3	0.0469
Pillai's Trace	0.86996198	10.04	2	3	0.0469
Hotelling-Lawley Trace	6.69005848	10.04	2	3	0.0469
Roy's Greatest Root	6.69005848	10.04	2	3	0.0469

Univariate Tests of Hypotheses for Within Subject Effects

Source	DF	Type III SS	Mean Square	F Value	Pr > F	Adj Pr > F G-G	H-F
MONTH	2	41.20000000	20.60000000	17.41	0.0012	0.0060	0.0021
Error (MONTH)	8	9.46666667	1.18333333				

Greenhouse-Geisser Epsilon	0.6706
Huynh-Feldt Epsilon	0.8850

Means of Within-Subjects Effects

Level of MONTH	N	Mean	Std Dev
1	5	2.40000000	1.67332005
2	5	3.80000000	0.83666003
3	5	6.40000000	1.14017543

This default output for SAS GLM begins with separate ANOVAs on each DV (not shown) and follows with the multivariate test, which matches that of SPSS GLM. The `Univariate Test of Hypotheses for Within Subject Effects` shows the univariate test of `MONTH` and its error term, together with probability following the `G-G` (Greenhouse-Geisser) and `H-F` (Huynh-Feldt) adjustments to *F*. Sum of squares for cases is not given, nor is total sum of squares. The program also produces Mauchly's test of sphericity and polynomial trend analysis if requested. Means and standard deviations produced by the `mean` instruction follow.

Table 6.16 shows syntax and output of the small-sample analysis through SYSTAT ANOVA with options set to `PRINT=SHORT`. `CATEGORY` and `COVAR` lines are produced by the Windows menu system, but may be omitted for this purely repeated-measures design without covariates. The analysis may be run through GLM with slightly different syntax but identical output.

SYSTAT ANOVA shows the means at each level of `MONTH` and produces the probability associated with *F* for routine univariate repeated measures and with the `H-F` (Huynh-Feldt) correction. `Wilks' Lambda` is provided for the multivariate alternative to repeated measures. Plots of residuals against predicted values also are produced but not reprinted here.

TABLE 6.16   One-Way Repeated-Measures ANOVA through SYSTAT ANOVA: Syntax and Selected Output

```
ANOVA
CATEGORY
COVAR
DEPEND MONTH_1 MONTH_2 MONTH_3/ REPEAT =3,NAMES='MONTH'
ESTIMATE

Number of cases processed: 5
Dependent variable means

                  MONTH_1    MONTH_2    MONTH_3
                   2.400      3.800      6.400
-----------------------------------------------------------------
Univariate and Multivariate Repeated Measures Analysis

Within Subjects
----------------

Source       SS     df      MS        F       P      G-G     H-F
MONTH      41.200    2    20.600    17.408   0.001   0.006   0.002
Error       9.467    8     1.183

Greenhouse-Geisser Epsilon: 0.6706
Huynh-Feldt Epsilon:        0.8850
-----------------------------------------------------------------
Multivariate Repeated Measures Analysis

Test of: MONTH          Hypoth. df    Error df     F        P
Wilks' Lambda =  0.130       2           3      10.035    0.047
Pillai Trace  =  0.870       2           3      10.035    0.047
H-L Trace     =  6.690       2           3      10.035    0.047
```

MINITAB has no built-in provision for specifying repeated-measures designs. Therefore, an alternative arrangement of the data is required, in which each case has as many lines as there are levels of the repeated-measures IV, and each line contains a column identifying the case, another identifying the level of the IV, and another the DV value for that level. That is, case is treated as any other IV. Table 6.17 shows the small-sample data set up for MINITAB. (Note that the other programs also do repeated-measures ANOVA using this format; however, it is less convenient and informative to do so except when analyzing some of the incomplete designs of Chapters 8, 9, and 10.)

Table 6.18 shows MINITAB GLM syntax and output for the one-way repeated-measures design. Both the repeated-measures IV, months, and cases are identified as IVs for this run. Means are requested only for the IV of substantive interest, not for cases.

The `Analysis of Variance` table shows `CASE` as a source of variance (which, of course, may be ignored), but the `MONTHS` and `Error` sources match those of the other programs, as do the means. The error term here is simply the residual after variances associated with months and cases are accounted for: The months × case interaction. There is no multivariate output, nor are there tests for sphericity; the program does not "know" that this is a repeated-measures design.

6.4.2   Factorial Repeated-Measures Designs

Factorial repeated-measure designs have two or more repeated-measures IVs in factorial combination. Cases provide a DV at each combination of levels of the IVs. Beyond exhaustion of cases (and researchers), there is no limit to the number of IVs and their levels, and, therefore, combinations of levels that can be used.

The complexity that arises with this analysis is the development of a separate error term for each effect in the design. Each error term is an interaction of cases with the effect being tested. When testing the main effect of B, for instance, the error term is the $B \times S$ interaction. When testing the $A \times B$ interaction, the error term is the $A \times B \times S$ interaction, and so on.

TABLE 6.17   Data Format for One-Way Repeated-Measures ANOVA through MINITAB with One DV Value per Line

Months	Case	Books
1	1	1
1	2	1
1	3	3
1	4	5
1	5	2
2	1	3
2	2	4
2	3	3
2	4	5
2	5	4
3	1	6
3	2	8
3	3	6
3	4	7
3	5	5

TABLE 6.18 One-Way Repeated-Measures ANOVA through MINITAB GLM

```
MTB > GLM 'books' = months case;
SUBC> Brief 2;
SUBC> Means months.
```

General Linear Model

```
Factor    Type    Levels    Values
MONTHS    fixed        3    1   2   3
CASE      fixed        5    1   2   3   4   5
```

Analysis of Variance for BOOKS, using Adjusted SS for Tests

```
Source    DF    Seq SS    Adj SS    Adj MS       F       P
MONTHS     2    41.200    41.200    20.600    17.41   0.001
CASE       4     9.733     9.733     2.433     2.06   0.179
Error      8     9.467     9.467     1.183
Total     14    60.400
```

Least Squares Means for BOOKS

```
MONTHS    Mean      StDev
1         2.400     0.4865
2         3.800     0.4865
3         6.400     0.4865
```

6.4.2.1 Allocation of Cases

Allocation of cases for the simplest 2×2 design is found in Table 6.19.

6.4.2.2 Partition of Sources of Variance

The partition of SS for a two-way repeated-measures factorial design is

$$SS_T = SS_A + SS_B + SS_{AB} + SS_S + SS_{AS} + SS_{BS} + SS_{ABS} \tag{6.15}$$

In this analysis, SS_A, SS_B, and SS_{AB} represent the main effect of A, the main effect of B, and their interaction, respectively. These effects are both logically and computationally equivalent to the same effects in a two-way factorial randomized-groups design. In the last four terms of the equation, SS_S represents differences among cases, and the remaining interactions are the various error terms.

As usual, each SS has a corresponding df. The df for each effect is formed in the usual way. For a main effect, 1 is subtracted from the number of levels, for example, $df_S = s - 1$. For an interaction, it is the df for one effect times the df for the other(s), for example, $df_{AS} = (a - 1)(s - 1)$ and $df_{ABS} = (a - 1)(b - 1)(s - 1)$.

TABLE 6.19 Allocation of Cases in a Two-Way Factorial Repeated-Measures Design

	b_1		b_2	
	a_1	a_2	a_1	a_2
s_1	s_1	s_1	s_1	s_1
s_2	s_2	s_2	s_2	s_2
s_3	s_3	s_3	s_3	s_3

A graphic representation of the partition appears in Figure 6.2. As usual, each MS is formed by dividing each SS by its corresponding df, for example, $MS_{ABS} = SS_{ABS}/df_{ABS}$.

The error term for each effect is the interaction of that effect with cases. The sources A, B, and $A \times B$ then have $A \times S$, $B \times S$, and $A \times B \times S$ as error terms, respectively.[5]

$$F_A = \frac{MS_A}{MS_{AS}} \tag{6.16}$$

(a) Sums of squares

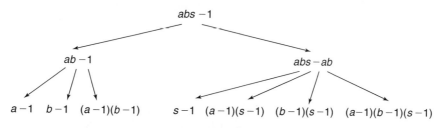

(b) Degrees of freedom

FIGURE 6.2 Partition of (a) Sums of Squares and (b) Degrees of Freedom in a Two-Way Factorial Repeated-Measures Design

[5]There is another difference between this analysis and the one-way repeated-measures analysis and that is the absence of a clear choice for the error term for S should a test of S be desired.

$$F_B = \frac{MS_B}{MS_{BS}} \qquad (6.17)$$

and

$$F_{A \times B} = \frac{MS_{AB}}{MS_{ABS}} \qquad (6.18)$$

The use of separate error terms makes sense because each error term is, computationally and logically, an interaction of cases with an effect. These interactions represent the *special* way cases reacted to the effect above and beyond the direct effects of treatment. That is, each error term is an average of the idiosyncratic reactions of the various cases to the effect in question. Why should idiosyncratic reactions to levels of B or $A \times B$ combinations be involved in a test of the reliability of A? Or idiosyncratic reactions to A be involved in a test of B, and so on?

6.4.2.3 Traditional ANOVA for Two-Way Repeated Measures

A small data set for a two-way repeated-measures design is in Table 6.20. The same five cases (and their data) as in the one-way design are used, but in this example, they are assigned to read science fiction novels and also mystery novels, each type for 3 months.[6] Month is A, with three levels, and type of novel is B, with two levels. There are, then, six combinations of month and type of novel. Number of novels read each month again serves as the DV.

The equations for the main effects of interest are the same as those in randomized-groups analysis (Chapter 5) and appear later in Table 6.22. The computational equations for interactions are

TABLE 6.20 Hypothetical Data Set for a Two-Way Factorial Repeated-Measures Design

	b_1: Science Fiction			b_2: Mystery			Case Totals
	Month 1 a_1	Month 2 a_2	Month 3 a_3	Month 1 a_1	Month 2 a_2	Month 3 a_3	
s_1	1	3	6	5	4	1	$S_1 = 20$
s_2	1	4	8	8	8	4	$S_2 = 33$
s_3	3	3	6	4	5	3	$S_3 = 24$
s_4	5	5	7	3	2	0	$S_4 = 22$
s_5	2	4	5	5	6	3	$S_5 = 25$
Treatment Totals	$A_1B_1 = 12$	$A_2B_1 = 19$	$A_3B_1 = 32$	$A_1B_2 = 25$	$A_2B_2 = 25$	$A_3B_2 = 11$	$T = 124$

[6]In this example, where type of novel is an IV whose levels can be reordered (either science fiction first or mystery first) the researcher would be well advised to use counterbalancing and Latin-square analysis, as described in Chapter 9.

the same, too, but in order to use them, you have to develop the necessary values. You have to sum together the values over cases for the $A \times B$ interaction. You sum together the values over levels of A for the $B \times S$ interaction, and you sum together the values over levels of B for the $A \times S$ interaction. This is shown in Table 6.21 for the data set of Table 6.20. Computational equations for sums of

TABLE 6.21   Computations Necessary for Computing Interaction Terms in a Two-Way Factorial Repeated-Measures Design

(a) Sums required to compute the $A \times B$ interaction

B: **Type of Novel**	a_1: Month 1	a_2: Month 2	a_3: Month 3	**Novel Totals**
	A: Month			
b_1: Science Fiction	12	19	32	$B_1 = 63$
b_2: Mystery	25	25	11	$B_2 = 61$
Month Totals	$A_1 = 37$	$A_2 = 44$	$A_3 = 43$	$T = 124$

(b) Sums required to compute the $A \times S$ interaction

	a_1: Month 1	a_2: Month 2	a_3: Month 3	**Case Totals**
	A: Month			
s_1	$1 + 5 = 6$	$3 + 4 = 7$	$6 + 1 = 7$	$S_1 = 20$
s_2	$1 + 8 = 9$	$4 + 8 = 12$	$8 + 4 = 12$	$S_2 = 33$
s_3	$3 + 4 = 7$	$3 + 5 = 8$	$6 + 3 = 9$	$S_3 = 24$
s_4	$5 + 3 = 8$	$5 + 2 = 7$	$7 + 0 = 7$	$S_4 = 22$
s_5	$2 + 5 = 7$	$4 + 6 = 10$	$5 + 3 = 8$	$S_5 = 25$
Month Totals	$A_1 = 37$	$A_2 = 44$	$A_3 = 43$	$T = 124$

(c) Sums required to compute the $B \times S$ interaction

	b_1: Science Fiction	b_2: Mystery	**Case Totals**
	B: Type of Novel		
s_1	$1 + 3 + 6 = 10$	$5 + 4 + 1 = 10$	$S_1 = 20$
s_2	$1 + 4 + 8 = 13$	$8 + 8 + 4 = 20$	$S_2 = 33$
s_3	$3 + 3 + 6 = 12$	$4 + 5 + 3 = 12$	$S_3 = 24$
s_4	$5 + 5 + 7 = 17$	$3 + 2 + 0 = 5$	$S_4 = 22$
s_5	$2 + 4 + 5 = 11$	$5 + 6 + 3 = 14$	$S_5 = 25$
Novel Totals	$B_1 = 63$	$B_2 = 61$	$T = 124$

squares for this ANOVA appear in Table 6.22. And the sums of squares in Table 6.23 with a bit of adjustment for rounding error.

Table 6.24 has the equations and computations for degrees of freedom for this example.

Finally, Table 6.25 summarizes the results of the calculations and shows the mean squares and F values for each effect. Take a moment or two to closely examine the F ratios. Notice the pattern of effects and error terms in the table.

Each effect in the table is tested against critical F with its own df. Critical F for the test of A (months) at $\alpha = .05$ with 2 and 8 df is 4.46; because 2.77 is less than 4.46, the null hypothesis of no

TABLE 6.22 Computational Equations for Sums of Squares for Two-Way Repeated-Measures ANOVA

$$SS_A = \frac{\sum A^2}{bs} - \frac{T^2}{abs} = \frac{37^2 + 44^2 + 43^2}{2(5)} - \frac{124^2}{3(2)(5)}$$

$$SS_B = \frac{\sum B^2}{as} - \frac{T^2}{abs} = \frac{63^2 + 61^2}{3(5)} - \frac{124^2}{3(2)(5)}$$

$$SS_{AB} = \frac{\sum (AB)^2}{s} - \frac{\sum A^2}{bs} - \frac{\sum B^2}{as} + \frac{T^2}{abs} = \frac{12^2 + 25^2 + 19^2 + 25^2 + 32^2 + 11^2}{5}$$
$$- \frac{37^2 + 44^2 + 43^2}{2(5)} - \frac{63^2 + 61^2}{3(5)} + \frac{124^2}{3(2)(5)}$$

$$SS_S = \frac{\sum S^2}{ab} - \frac{T^2}{abs} = \frac{20^2 + 33^2 + 24^2 + 22^2 + 25^2}{3(2)} - \frac{124^2}{3(2)(5)}$$

$$SS_{AS} = \frac{\sum (AS)^2}{b} - \frac{\sum A^2}{bs} - \frac{\sum S^2}{ab} + \frac{T^2}{abs} = \frac{6^2 + 9^2 + 7^2 + 8^2 + \cdots + 8^2}{2}$$
$$- \frac{37^2 + 44^2 + 43^2}{2(5)} - \frac{20^2 + 33^2 + \cdots + 25^2}{3(2)} + \frac{124^2}{3(2)(5)}$$

$$SS_{BS} = \frac{\sum (BS)^2}{a} - \frac{\sum B^2}{as} - \frac{\sum S^2}{ab} + \frac{T^2}{abs} = \frac{10^2 + 13^2 + 12^2 + 17^2 + \cdots + 14^2}{3}$$
$$- \frac{63^2 + 61^2}{3(5)} - \frac{20^2 + 33^2 + \cdots + 25^2}{3(2)} + \frac{124^2}{3(2)(5)}$$

$$SS_{ABS} = \sum Y^2 = 1^2 + 1^2 + 3^2 + \cdots + 0^2 + 3^2$$
$$- \frac{\sum (AB)^2}{s} - \frac{\sum (AS)^2}{b} - \frac{\sum (BS)^2}{a} \qquad - \frac{12^2 + \cdots + 11^2}{5} - \frac{6^2 + \cdots + 8^2}{2} - \frac{10^2 + \cdots + 14^2}{3}$$
$$+ \frac{\sum A^2}{bs} + \frac{\sum B^2}{as} + \frac{\sum S^2}{ab} \qquad + \frac{37^2 + 44^2 + 43^2}{2(5)} + \frac{63^2 + 61^2}{3(5)} + \frac{20^2 + \cdots + 25^2}{3(2)}$$
$$- \frac{T^2}{abs} \qquad - \frac{124^2}{3(2)(5)}$$

$$SS_T = \sum Y^2 - \frac{T^2}{abs} = 1^2 + 1^2 + 3^2 + 5^2 + \cdots + 0^2 + 3^2 - \frac{124^2}{3(2)(5)}$$

TABLE 6.23   Sums of Squares for Traditional Factorial Repeated-Measures ANOVA

SS_A	$= 515.40 - 512.53$	$= 2.87$
SS_B	$= 512.67 - 512.53$	$= 0.13$
SS_{AB}	$= 580.00 - 515.40 - 512.67 + 512.53$	$= 64.47$
SS_S	$= 529.00 - 512.53$	$= 16.47$
SS_{AS}	$= 536 - 515.40 - 529.00 + 512.53$	$= 4.13$
SS_{BS}	$= 562.67 - 512.67 - 529.00 + 512.53$	$= 33.53$
SS_{ABS}	$= 644.00 - 580.00 - 536.00 - 562.67$ $\quad + 515.40 + 512.67 + 529.00 - 512.53$	$= 9.87$
SS_T	$= 644.00 - 512.53$	$= 131.47$

TABLE 6.24   Degrees of Freedom for Traditional Factorial Repeated-Measures ANOVA

df_A	$= a - 1$	$3 - 1$	$= 2$
df_B	$= b - 1$	$2 - 1$	$= 1$
df_{AB}	$= (a-1)(b-1)$	$(3-1)(2-1)$	$= 2$
df_S	$= s - 1$	$5 - 1$	$= 4$
df_{AS}	$= (a-1)(s-1)$	$(3-1)(5-1)$	$= 8$
df_{BS}	$= (b-1)(s-1)$	$(2-1)(5-1)$	$= 4$
df_{ABS}	$= (a-1)(b-1)(s-1)$	$(3-1)(2-1)(5-1)$	$= 8$
df_T	$= abs - 1$	$3(2)(5) - 1$	$= 29$

mean difference in number of books read per month is retained. Critical F for the test of B (type of novel) at $\alpha = .05$ with 1 and 4 df is 7.71; because 0.02 is less than 7.71, the null hypothesis of no mean difference in number of science fiction and mystery novels read is retained. Finally, critical F for the test of interaction, months by type of novel at $\alpha = .05$ with 2 and 8 df is 4.46; because 26.20 is greater than 4.46, the null hypothesis of no mean difference in number of books read per month by type of book is rejected. A glance at the numbers in Table 6.20 suggests that, for science fiction books, the number of books read increases over the 3 months, whereas for mystery novels, the number decreases over the 3 months. This informal observation needs to be verified by the procedures of Section 6.6.6.

**TABLE 6.25   Source Table for Two-Way
Repeated-Measures ANOVA**

Source	SS	df	MS	F
A	2.87	2	1.44	$\dfrac{1.44}{0.52} = 2.77$
B	0.13	1	0.13	$\dfrac{0.13}{8.38} = 0.02$
AB	64.47	2	32.23	$\dfrac{32.23}{1.23} = 26.20$
S	16.47	4	4.12	
AS	4.13	8	0.52	
BS	33.53	4	8.38	
ABS	9.87	8	1.23	
T	131.47	29		

6.4.2.4 Regression Approach to Factorial Repeated Measures

The data set of Table 6.20 is rearranged into the format appropriate for regression in Table 6.26. The levels of A appear as the first column and the levels of B the second. Case designations are in the third column. These three columns are for your convenience in understanding the rearrangement of the data set and the use of coding in columns that follow. The fourth column contains DV (Y) values. The total df for this problem is 29, so it takes 29 columns to code the design (excluding the four columns already mentioned) and another 29 columns for the cross-multiplication of the DV scores with each of the design columns. The X_1 column contains the linear-trend coefficients for A and the X_2 column the quadratic trend coefficients. Column X_3 contains contrast coefficients for B, and columns X_4 and X_5 are $A_{linear} \times B$ and $A_{quad} \times B$, respectively. The next four columns, X_6 to X_9, contain contrast coding for cases; the choice of coefficients for cases is arbitrary provided that the sum of each column is zero and the products of all pairs of columns sum to zero. In this case, the coefficients used are $[4, -1, -1, -1, -1]$ for $Sc1$ (Subject contrast 1), $[0, 1, 1, -1, -1]$ for $Sc2$, $[0, 1, -1, 0, 0]$ for $Sc3$, and $[0, 0, 0, 1, -1]$ for $Sc4$.

The remaining columns are found by multiplication. Columns X_{10} to X_{29} contain all possible cross-products of columns X_1 to X_9. The X_{10} column contains codes for $A_{linear} \times Sc1$ (cross of the linear-trend coefficients for A by the code for the first df for cases). Column X_{29} contains codes for $A_{quad} \times B \times Sc4$ (cross of the quadratic coefficients for A by B by the code for the last contrast for cases). Columns X_{30} to X_{58} are Y crossed with each of the preceding columns, necessary for computation of sums of products.

In order to develop the several error terms for the factorial design, it is necessary to separate the cases from each other, unlike the one-way repeated-measures design in which cases can be combined into the $S(X_3)$ column of Table 6.8. This is accomplished in columns X_6 to X_9 of Table 6.26, separately for each of the 4 df for cases and labeled $Sc1$, $Sc2$, $Sc3$, and $Sc4$. If a different set of

TABLE 6.26 Regression Format for Factorial Repeated-Measures Design

			Y	Al X_1	Aq X_2	B X_3	Al*B X_4	Aq*B X_5	Sc1 X_6	Sc2 X_7	Sc3 X_8	Sc4 X_9	Al*Sc1 X_{10}	Al*Sc2 X_{11}	Al*Sc3 X_{12}	Al*Sc4 X_{13}
a_1	b_1	s_1	1	-1	1	1	-1	1	4	0	0	0	-4	0	0	0
		s_2	1	-1	1	1	-1	1	-1	1	1	0	1	-1	-1	0
		s_3	3	-1	1	1	-1	1	-1	1	-1	0	1	-1	1	0
		s_4	5	-1	1	1	-1	1	-1	-1	0	1	1	1	0	-1
		s_5	2	-1	1	1	-1	1	-1	-1	0	-1	1	1	0	1
	b_2	s_1	5	-1	1	-1	1	-1	4	0	0	0	-4	0	0	0
		s_2	8	-1	1	-1	1	-1	-1	1	1	0	1	-1	-1	0
		s_3	4	-1	1	-1	1	-1	-1	1	-1	0	1	-1	1	0
		s_4	3	-1	1	-1	1	-1	-1	-1	0	1	1	1	0	-1
		s_5	5	-1	1	-1	1	-1	-1	-1	0	-1	1	1	0	1
a_2	b_1	s_1	3	0	-2	1	0	-2	4	0	0	0	0	0	0	0
		s_2	4	0	-2	1	0	-2	-1	1	1	0	0	0	0	0
		s_3	3	0	-2	1	0	-2	-1	1	-1	0	0	0	0	0
		s_4	5	0	-2	1	0	-2	-1	-1	0	1	0	0	0	0
		s_5	4	0	-2	1	0	-2	-1	-1	0	-1	0	0	0	0
	b_2	s_1	4	0	-2	-1	0	2	4	0	0	0	0	0	0	0
		s_2	8	0	-2	-1	0	2	-1	1	1	0	0	0	0	0
		s_3	5	0	-2	-1	0	2	-1	1	-1	0	0	0	0	0
		s_4	2	0	-2	-1	0	2	-1	-1	0	1	0	0	0	0
		s_5	6	0	-2	-1	0	2	-1	-1	0	-1	0	0	0	0
a_3	b_1	s_1	6	1	1	1	1	1	4	0	0	0	4	0	0	0
		s_2	8	1	1	1	1	1	-1	1	1	0	-1	1	1	0
		s_3	6	1	1	1	1	1	-1	1	-1	0	-1	1	-1	0
		s_4	7	1	1	1	1	1	-1	-1	0	1	-1	-1	0	1
		s_5	5	1	1	1	1	1	-1	-1	0	-1	-1	-1	0	-1
	b_2	s_1	1	1	1	-1	-1	-1	4	0	0	0	4	0	0	0
		s_2	4	1	1	-1	-1	-1	-1	1	1	0	-1	1	1	0
		s_3	3	1	1	-1	-1	-1	-1	1	-1	0	-1	1	-1	0
		s_4	0	1	1	-1	-1	-1	-1	-1	0	1	-1	-1	0	1
		s_5	3	1	1	-1	-1	-1	-1	-1	0	-1	-1	-1	0	-1
		sum	124	0	0	0	0	0	0	0	0	0	0	0	0	0
		sqd	644	20	60	30	20	60	120	24	12	12	80	16	8	8
		ss	131.47	20	60	30	20	60	120	24	12	12	80	16	8	8
		sp		6	-8	2	34	20	-24	10	9	-3	-1	5	1	-2
		reg		1.8	1.07	0.13	57.8	6.67	4.8	4.17	6.75	0.75	0.01	1.56	0.12	0.5

(continued)

TABLE 6.26 Continued

			Aq*Sc1 X_{14}	Aq*Sc2 X_{15}	Aq*Sc3 X_{16}	Aq*Sc4 X_{17}	B*Sc1 X_{18}	B*Sc2 X_{19}	B*Sc3 X_{20}	B*Sc4 X_{21}	Al*B*Sc1 X_{22}	Al*B*Sc2 X_{23}	Al*B*Sc3 X_{24}	Al*B*Sc4 X_{25}	Aq*B*Sc1 X_{26}
a_1	b_1	s_1	4	0	0	0	4	0	0	0	−4	0	0	0	4
		s_2	−1	1	1	0	−1	1	1	0	1	−1	−1	0	−1
		s_3	−1	1	−1	0	−1	1	−1	0	1	−1	1	0	−1
		s_4	−1	−1	0	1	−1	−1	0	1	1	1	0	−1	−1
		s_5	−1	−1	0	−1	−1	−1	0	−1	1	1	0	1	−1
	b_2	s_1	4	0	0	0	−4	0	0	0	4	0	0	0	−4
		s_2	−1	1	1	0	1	−1	−1	0	−1	1	1	0	1
		s_3	−1	1	−1	0	1	−1	1	0	−1	1	−1	0	1
		s_4	−1	−1	0	1	1	1	0	−1	−1	−1	0	1	1
		s_5	−1	−1	0	−1	1	1	0	1	−1	−1	0	−1	1
a_2	b_1	s_1	−8	0	0	0	4	0	0	0	0	0	0	0	−8
		s_2	2	−2	−2	0	−1	1	1	0	0	0	0	0	2
		s_3	2	−2	2	0	−1	1	−1	0	0	0	0	0	2
		s_4	2	2	0	−2	−1	−1	0	1	0	0	0	0	2
		s_5	2	2	0	2	−1	−1	0	−1	0	0	0	0	2
	b_2	s_1	−8	0	0	0	−4	0	0	0	0	0	0	0	8
		s_2	2	−2	−2	0	1	−1	−1	0	0	0	0	0	−2
		s_3	2	−2	2	0	1	−1	1	0	0	0	0	0	−2
		s_4	2	2	0	−2	1	1	0	−1	0	0	0	0	−2
		s_5	2	2	0	2	1	1	0	1	0	0	0	0	−2
a_3	b_1	s_1	4	0	0	0	4	0	0	0	4	0	0	0	4
		s_2	−1	1	1	0	−1	1	1	0	−1	1	1	0	−1
		s_3	−1	1	−1	0	−1	1	−1	0	−1	1	−1	0	−1
		s_4	−1	−1	0	1	−1	−1	0	1	−1	−1	0	1	−1
		s_5	−1	−1	0	−1	−1	−1	0	−1	−1	−1	0	−1	−1
	b_2	s_1	4	0	0	0	−4	0	0	0	−4	0	0	0	−4
		s_2	−1	1	1	0	1	−1	−1	0	1	−1	−1	0	1
		s_3	−1	1	−1	0	1	−1	1	0	1	−1	1	0	1
		s_4	−1	−1	0	1	1	1	0	−1	1	1	0	−1	1
		s_5	−1	−1	0	−1	1	1	0	1	1	1	0	1	1
		sum	0	0	0	0	0	0	0	0	0	0	0	0	0
		sqd	240	48	24	24	120	24	12	12	80	16	8	8	240
		ss	240	48	24	24	120	24	12	12	80	16	8	8	240
		sp	3	1	−3	6	−2	−16	−7	15	11	5	7	0	−5
		reg	0.04	0.02	0.38	1.5	0.03	10.67	4.08	18.75	1.51	1.56	6.12	0.10	0.10

272

TABLE 6.26 Continued

			Aq*B*Sc2 X_{27}	Aq*B*Sc3 X_{28}	Aq*B*Sc4 X_{29}	Y*Al X_{30}	Y*Aq X_{31}	Y*B X_{32}	Y*Al*B X_{33}	Y*Aq*B X_{34}	Y*Sc1 X_{35}	Y*Sc2 X_{36}	Y*Sc3 X_{37}	Y*Sc4 X_{38}	Y*Al*Sc1 X_{39}
a_1	b_1	s_1	0	0	0	−1	1	1	−1	1	4	0	0	0	−4
		s_2	1	1	0	−1	1	1	−1	1	−1	1	1	0	1
		s_3	1	−1	0	−3	3	3	−3	3	−3	3	−3	0	3
		s_4	−1	0	1	−5	5	5	−5	5	−5	−5	0	5	5
		s_5	−1	0	−1	−2	2	2	−2	2	−2	−2	0	−2	2
	b_2	s_1	0	0	0	−5	5	−5	5	−5	20	0	0	0	−20
		s_2	−1	−1	0	−8	8	−8	8	−8	−8	8	8	0	8
		s_3	−1	1	0	−4	4	−4	4	−4	−4	4	−4	0	4
		s_4	1	0	−1	−3	3	−3	3	−3	−3	−3	0	3	3
		s_5	1	0	1	−5	5	−5	5	−5	−5	−5	0	−5	5
a_2	b_1	s_1	0	0	0	0	−6	3	0	−6	12	0	0	0	0
		s_2	−2	−2	0	0	−8	4	0	−8	−4	4	4	0	0
		s_3	−2	2	0	0	−6	3	0	−6	−3	3	−3	0	0
		s_4	2	0	−2	0	−10	5	0	−10	−5	−5	0	5	0
		s_5	2	0	2	0	−8	4	0	−8	−4	−4	0	−4	0
	b_2	s_1	0	0	0	0	−8	−4	0	8	16	0	0	0	0
		s_2	2	2	0	0	−16	−8	0	16	−8	8	8	0	0
		s_3	2	−2	0	0	−10	−5	0	10	−5	5	−5	0	0
		s_4	−2	0	2	0	−4	−2	0	4	−2	−2	0	2	0
		s_5	−2	0	−2	0	−12	−6	0	12	−6	−6	0	−6	0
a_3	b_1	s_1	0	0	0	6	8	6	6	6	24	0	0	0	24
		s_2	1	1	0	8	8	8	8	8	−8	8	8	0	−8
		s_3	1	−1	0	6	6	6	6	6	−6	6	−6	0	−6
		s_4	−1	0	1	7	7	7	7	7	−7	−7	0	7	−7
		s_5	−1	0	−1	5	5	5	5	5	−5	−5	0	−5	−5
	b_2	s_1	0	−1	0	1	1	−1	−1	−1	4	0	0	0	4
		s_2	−1	1	0	4	4	−4	−4	−4	−4	4	4	0	−4
		s_3	−1	1	0	3	3	−3	−3	−3	−3	3	−3	0	−3
		s_4	1	0	−1	0	3	0	0	0	0	0	0	0	0
		s_5	1	0	1	3	3	−3	−3	−3	−3	−3	0	−3	−3
		sum	0	0	0	6	−8	2	34	20	−24	10	9	−3	−1
		sqd	48	24	24										
		ss	48	24	24										
		sp	5	−1	0										
		reg	0.52	0.04	0										

(continued)

273

TABLE 6.26 Continued

			X_{40} Y*Al*Sc2	X_{41} Y*Al*Sc3	X_{42} Y*Al*Sc4	X_{43} Y*Aq*Sc1	X_{44} Y*Aq*Sc2	X_{45} Y*Aq*Sc3	X_{46} Y*Aq*Sc4	X_{47} Y*B*Sc1	X_{48} Y*B*Sc2	X_{49} Y*B*Sc3	X_{50} Y*B*Sc4
a_1	b_1	s_1	0	0	0	4	0	0	0	4	0	0	0
		s_2	−1	−1	0	−1	1	1	0	−1	1	−1	0
		s_3	−3	3	−5	−3	3	−3	5	−3	3	−3	−5
		s_4	5	0	2	−5	−5	0	−2	−5	−5	0	−2
		s_5	2	0	0	−2	−2	0	0	−2	−2	0	0
	b_2	s_1	0	−8	0	20	0	8	0	−20	0	−8	0
		s_2	−8	4	0	−4	8	−4	0	4	−8	4	0
		s_3	−4	0	−3	−3	4	0	3	3	−4	0	−3
		s_4	3	0	5	−5	−3	0	−5	3	3	0	5
		s_5	5	0	0	−24	−5	0	0	5	5	0	0
a_2	b_1	s_1	0	0	0	8	0	−8	0	12	0	4	0
		s_2	0	0	0	6	−8	6	0	−4	4	−3	0
		s_3	0	0	0	10	−6	0	−10	−3	3	0	5
		s_4	0	0	0	8	10	0	8	−5	−5	0	−4
		s_5	0	0	0	−32	8	−16	0	−4	−4	−8	0
	b_2	s_1	0	0	0	16	0	10	0	−16	0	5	0
		s_2	0	0	0	10	−16	0	0	8	−8	0	0
		s_3	0	0	0	4	−10	0	−4	5	−5	0	−2
		s_4	0	0	0	12	4	0	12	2	2	0	6
		s_5	0	0	0	24	12	8	0	6	6	8	0
a_3	b_1	s_1	8	8	0	−8	0	−6	0	24	0	−6	0
		s_2	6	−6	7	−6	8	0	0	−8	8	0	0
		s_3	−7	0	−5	−7	6	0	7	−6	6	0	7
		s_4	−5	0	0	−5	−7	0	−5	−7	−7	0	−5
		s_5	0	0	0	4	−5	4	0	−5	−5	−4	0
	b_2	s_1	4	0	0	−4	0	−3	0	−4	0	3	0
		s_2	3	4	0	−3	4	0	0	4	−4	0	0
		s_3	0	−3	0	0	3	0	0	3	−3	0	0
		s_4	0	0	0	0	0	0	0	0	0	0	0
		s_5	−3	0	−3	−3	−3	0	−3	3	0	3	3
		sum	5	1	−2	3	1	−3	6	−2	−16	−7	15

274

TABLE 6.26 Continued

			$Y*Al*B*Sc1$ X_{51}	$Y*Al*B*Sc2$ X_{52}	$Y*Al*B*Sc3$ X_{53}	$Y*Al*B*Sc4$ X_{54}	$Y*Aq*B*Sc1$ X_{55}	$Y*Aq*B*Sc2$ X_{56}	$Y*Aq*B*Sc3$ X_{57}	$Y*Aq*B*Sc4$ X_{58}
a_1	b_1	s_1	-4	0	0	0	4	0	0	0
		s_2	1	-1	-1	0	-1	1	1	0
		s_3	3	-3	3	0	-3	3	-3	0
		s_4	5	5	0	-5	-5	-5	0	5
		s_5	2	2	0	2	-2	-2	0	-2
	b_2	s_1	20	0	0	0	-20	0	0	0
		s_2	-8	8	8	0	8	-8	-8	0
		s_3	-4	4	-4	0	4	-4	4	0
		s_4	-3	-3	0	3	3	3	0	-3
		s_5	-5	-5	0	-5	5	5	0	5
a_2	b_1	s_1	0	0	0	0	-24	0	0	0
		s_2	0	0	0	0	8	-8	-8	0
		s_3	0	0	0	0	6	-6	6	0
		s_4	0	0	0	0	10	10	0	-10
		s_5	0	0	0	0	8	8	0	8
	b_2	s_1	0	0	0	0	32	0	0	0
		s_2	0	0	0	0	-16	16	16	0
		s_3	0	0	0	0	-10	10	-10	0
		s_4	0	0	0	0	-4	-4	0	-4
		s_5	0	0	0	0	-12	-12	0	-12
a_3	b_1	s_1	24	0	0	0	24	0	0	0
		s_2	-8	8	8	0	-8	8	8	0
		s_3	-6	6	-6	0	-6	6	-6	0
		s_4	-7	-7	0	7	-7	-7	0	7
		s_5	-5	-5	0	-5	-5	-5	0	-5
	b_2	s_1	-4	-4	-4	0	-4	-4	-4	0
		s_2	4	-3	3	0	4	-3	3	0
		s_3	3	0	0	0	3	0	0	0
		s_4	0	0	0	3	0	0	0	3
		s_5	3	3	3	3	3	3	3	3
sum			11	5	7	0	-5	5	-1	0

orthogonal coefficients is used, SS and SP for each column are different, but the total for the effect is the same, just as in any other orthogonal partition of a main effect. The df for cases in the one-way design can also be separated into different columns for the omnibus design[7] and must be separated into different columns for comparisons (cf. Section 6.6.6).

Preliminary sums of squares for the regression approach are in Table 6.27. And the sums of cross-products appear in Table 6.28. And, finally, sums of squares for the regression analysis are shown in Table 6.29.

TABLE 6.27   Preliminary Sums of Squares for Regression Approach to Factorial Repeated-Measures ANOVA

$$SS_Y = \sum Y^2 - \frac{(\sum Y)^2}{N} = 644 - \frac{124^2}{30} = 131.47$$

$$SS(X_1) = \sum X_1^2 - \frac{(\sum X_1)^2}{N} = 20 - \frac{0^2}{30} = 20$$

$$SS(X_2) = \sum X_2^2 - \frac{(\sum X_2)^2}{N} = 60 - \frac{0^2}{30} = 60$$

$$SS(X_3) = \sum X_3^2 - \frac{(\sum X_3)^2}{N} = 30 - \frac{0^2}{30} = 30$$

$$SS(X_4) = \sum X_4^2 - \frac{(\sum X_4)^2}{N} = 20 - \frac{0^2}{30} = 20$$

$$SS(X_5) = \sum X_5^2 - \frac{(\sum X_5)^2}{N} = 60 - \frac{0^2}{30} = 60$$

$$SS(X_6) = \sum X_6^2 - \frac{(\sum X_6)^2}{N} = 120 - \frac{0^2}{30} = 120$$

$$SS(X_7) = \sum X_7^2 - \frac{(\sum X_7)^2}{N} = 24 - \frac{0^2}{30} = 24$$

$$SS(X_8) = \sum X_8^2 - \frac{(\sum X_8)^2}{N} = 12 - \frac{0^2}{30} = 12$$

$$SS(X_9) = \sum X_9^2 - \frac{(\sum X_9)^2}{N} = 12 - \frac{0^2}{30} = 12$$

$$SS(X_{10}) = \sum X_{10}^2 - \frac{(\sum X_{10})^2}{N} = 80 - \frac{0^2}{30} = 80$$

$$\vdots \qquad \vdots \qquad \vdots \qquad \vdots$$

$$SS(X_{29}) = \sum X_{29}^2 - \frac{(\sum X_{29})^2}{N} = 24 - \frac{0^2}{30} = 24$$

[7]If you are masochistic.

TABLE 6.28   Sums of Cross-Products for Regression Approach to Factorial Repeated-Measures ANOVA

$$SP(YX_1) = \sum YX_1 - \frac{(\sum Y)(\sum X_1)}{N} = 6 - \frac{(124)(0)}{30} = 6$$

$$SP(YX_2) = \sum YX_2 - \frac{(\sum Y)(\sum X_2)}{N} = -8 - \frac{(124)(0)}{30} = -8$$

$$SP(YX_3) = \sum YX_3 - \frac{(\sum Y)(\sum X_3)}{N} = 2 - \frac{(124)(0)}{30} = 2$$

$$SP(YX_4) = \sum YX_4 - \frac{(\sum Y)(\sum X_4)}{N} = 34 - \frac{(124)(0)}{30} = 34$$

$$SP(YX_5) = \sum YX_5 - \frac{(\sum Y)(\sum X_5)}{N} = 20 - \frac{(124)(0)}{30} = 20$$

$$SP(YX_6) = \sum YX_6 - \frac{(\sum Y)(\sum X_6)}{N} = -24 - \frac{(124)(0)}{30} = -24$$

$$SP(YX_7) = \sum YX_7 - \frac{(\sum Y)(\sum X_7)}{N} = 10 - \frac{(124)(0)}{30} = 10$$

$$SP(YX_8) = \sum YX_8 - \frac{(\sum Y)(\sum X_8)}{N} = 9 - \frac{(124)(0)}{30} = 9$$

$$SP(YX_9) = \sum YX_9 - \frac{(\sum Y)(\sum X_9)}{N} = -3 - \frac{(124)(0)}{30} = -3$$

$$SP(YX_{10}) = \sum YX_{10} - \frac{(\sum Y)(\sum X_{10})}{N} = -1 - \frac{(124)(0)}{30} = -1$$

$$\vdots \qquad \vdots \qquad\qquad \vdots \qquad\qquad \vdots$$

$$SP(YX_{29}) = \sum YX_{29} - \frac{(\sum Y)(\sum X_{29})}{N} = 0 - \frac{(124)(0)}{30} = 0$$

Degrees of freedom for each effect in the regression approach is the number of columns—number of SS(reg. X_i)s—for the effect in the design. When SS and df are combined into a source table, the results are identical (except for minor rounding error) to the values shown for the traditional ANOVA approach, as shown in Table 6.30.

6.4.2.5   Computer Analyses of Small-Sample Factorial Repeated-Measures Design

Table 6.31 shows the data format for the two-way repeated-measures ANOVA through SPSS, SAS, and SYSTAT. Repeated-measures IVs are created out of the numerous DV values for each case by naming them and their levels. Your choice of names for the DVs and the order in which IVs and their

TABLE 6.29 Sums of Squares for Factorial Repeated-Measures ANOVA through Regression

SS_A	$SS(\text{reg. } X_1) + SS(\text{reg. } X_2)$	$\dfrac{6^2}{20} + \dfrac{(-8)^2}{60}$	$1.80 + 1.07$	2.87
SS_B	$SS(\text{reg. } X_3)$	$\dfrac{2^2}{30}$	0.13	0.13
SS_{AB}	$SS(\text{reg. } X_4) + SS(\text{reg. } X_5)$	$\dfrac{34^2}{20} + \dfrac{20^2}{60}$	$57.80 + 6.67$	64.47
SS_S	$SS(\text{reg. } X_6) + SS(\text{reg. } X_7)$ $+ SS(\text{reg. } X_8) + SS(\text{reg. } X_9)$	$\dfrac{(-24)^2}{120} + \dfrac{10^2}{24} + \dfrac{9^2}{12} + \dfrac{(-3)^2}{12}$	$4.80 + 4.17$ $+ 6.75 + 0.75$	16.47
SS_{AS}	$SS(\text{reg. } X_{10}) + SS(\text{reg. } X_{11})$ $+ SS(\text{reg. } X_{12}) + SS(\text{reg. } X_{13})$ $+ SS(\text{reg. } X_{14}) + SS(\text{reg. } X_{15})$ $+ SS(\text{reg. } X_{16}) + SS(\text{reg. } X_{17})$	$\dfrac{(-1)^2}{80} + \dfrac{5^2}{16} + \dfrac{1^2}{8} + \dfrac{(-2)^2}{8}$ $+ \dfrac{3^2}{240} + \dfrac{1^2}{48} + \dfrac{(-3)^2}{24} + \dfrac{6^2}{24}$	$0.01 + 1.56$ $+ 0.12 + 0.50$ $+ 0.04 + 0.02$ $+ 0.38 + 1.50$	4.13
SS_{BS}	$SS(\text{reg. } X_{18}) + SS(\text{reg. } X_{19})$ $+ SS(\text{reg. } X_{20}) + SS(\text{reg. } X_{21})$	$\dfrac{(-2)^2}{120} + \dfrac{(-16)^2}{24} + \dfrac{(-7)^2}{12} + \dfrac{15^2}{12}$	$0.03 + 10.67$ $+ 4.08 + 18.75$	33.53
SS_{ABS}	$SS(\text{reg. } X_{22}) + SS(\text{reg. } X_{23})$ $+ SS(\text{reg. } X_{24}) + SS(\text{reg. } X_{25})$ $+ SS(\text{reg. } X_{26}) + SS(\text{reg. } X_{27})$ $+ SS(\text{reg. } X_{28}) + SS(\text{reg. } X_{29})$	$\dfrac{11^2}{80} + \dfrac{5^2}{16} + \dfrac{7^2}{8} + \dfrac{0^2}{0}$ $+ \dfrac{(-5)^2}{240} + \dfrac{5^2}{48} + \dfrac{(-1)^2}{24} + \dfrac{0^2}{24}$	$1.51 + 1.56$ $+ 6.12 + 0$ $+ 0.10 + 0.52$ $+ 0.04 + 0$	9.87
SS_T	SS_Y	$644 - \dfrac{124^2}{30}$	$644 - 512.53$	131.47

levels are named are critical because they have to correspond. Consider the two-way factorial data set of Table 6.20. There are six DV values from 3 months and two types of novels. If the data set is organized as in Table 6.20, the 3 months are collected below each type of novel. The index for months is said to change more rapidly than the index for type of novel because, while novel is held constant (first at science fiction and then at mystery), DV values for all 3 months are presented. The data could also be rearranged so that the index for type of novel changes more rapidly than the index for month: month1 (science fiction, mystery), month2 (science fiction, mystery), and month3 (science fiction, mystery). Both of these represent the same six DVs, but in different orders.

Tables 6.32 to 6.34 present syntax and highly edited output from SPSS GLM, SAS GLM, and SYSTAT ANOVA, respectively. Except for being more lengthy due to increases in number of effects and errors, the output is the same as for the one-way design. It is the syntax that is tricky for factorial repeated-measures analysis.

SPSS GLM is shown in Table 6.32. The syntax lists all six conditions as DVs, then the /WSFACTOR instruction defines those six DVs as two repeated-measures IVs: the first with two levels and the second with three levels. Then /MEASURE names books the DV. The correspon-

TABLE 6.30   Source Table for the Regression Approach to Factorial Repeated-Measures ANOVA

Source	SS	df	MS	F
A	2.87	2	1.44	$\frac{1.44}{0.52} = 2.77$
B	0.13	1	0.13	$\frac{0.13}{8.38} = 0.02$
AB	64.47	2	32.23	$\frac{32.23}{1.23} = 26.20$
S	16.47	4	4.12	
AS	4.13	8	0.52	
BS	33.53	4	8.38	
ABS	9.87	8	1.23	
T	131.47	29		

TABLE 6.31   Hypothetical Data Set for Two-Way Repeated-Measures Design for Analysis through SPSS, SAS, and SYSTAT

CASE	SCIFI_M1	SCIFI_M2	SCIFI_M3	MSTRY_M1	MSTRY_M2	MSTRY_M3
1	1	3	6	5	4	1
2	1	4	8	8	8	4
3	3	3	6	4	5	3
4	5	5	7	3	2	0
5	2	4	5	5	6	3

dence between levels of the IVs and DVs becomes clear when you use the SPSS Windows menu system to click over the DVs that corresponds to each combination of levels. Remaining syntax in Table 6.32 is produced by the SPSS Windows menu system.

The first table in the output shows the correspondence between the levels of novel and month and the six DVs. The next table shown is for Mauchly's Test of Sphericity; both MONTH and the NOVEL *MONTH interaction have sphericity.[8] Finally, the three effects are tested against their corresponding error terms. There is no main effect of NOVEL (Sig. = .906) or of MONTH (Sig. = .122), but there is a NOVEL *MONTH interaction (Sig. = .000). Multivariate output and trend analysis are omitted here.

---

[8]The effect of novel has no test for sphericity and no adjustments because it only has two levels.

TABLE 6.32 Factorial Repeated Measures through SPSS GLM: Syntax and Selected Output

```
GLM
   scifi_m1 scifi_m2 scifi_m3 mstry_m1 mstry_m2 mstry_m3
   /WSFACTOR = novel 2 Polynomial month 3 Polynomial
   /MEASURE = books
   /METHOD = SSTYPE(3)
   /CRITERIA = ALPHA(.05)
   /WSDESIGN = novel month novel*month.
```

General Linear Model

Within-Subjects Factors

Measure: BOOKS

NOVEL	MONTH	Dependent Variable
1	1	SCIFI_M1
	2	SCIFI_M2
	3	SCIFI_M3
2	1	MSTRY_M 1
	2	MSTRY_M 2
	3	MSTRY_M 3

Mauchly's Test of Sphericity[b]

Measure: BOOKS

Within Subjects Effect	Mauchly's W	Approx. Chi-Square	df	Sig.	Epsilon[a]		
					Greenhouse-Geisser	Huynh-Feldt	Lower-bound
NOVEL	1.000	.000	0		1.000	1.000	1.000
MONTH	.796	.684	2	.710	.831	1.000	.500
NOVEL*MONTH	.252	4.135	2	.127	.572	.651	.500

Tests the null hypothesis that the error covariance matrix of the orthonormalized transformed dependent variables is proportional to an identity matrix.

a. May be used to adjust the degrees of freedom for the averaged tests of significance. Corrected tests are displayed in the layers (by default) of the Tests of Within Subjects Effects table.

b.
   Design: Intercept
   Within Subjects Design: NOVEL+MONTH+NOVEL*MONTH

TABLE 6.32   Continued

Tests of Within-Subjects Effects

Measure: BOOKS

Source		Type III Sum of Squares	df	Mean Square	F	Sig.
NOVEL	Sphericity Assumed	.133	1	.133	.016	.906
	Greenhouse-Geisser	.133	1.000	.133	.016	.906
	Huynh-Feldt	.133	1.000	.133	.016	.906
	Lower-bound	.133	1.000	.133	.016	.906
Error(NOVEL)	Sphericity Assumed	33.533	4	8.383		
	Greenhouse-Geisser	33.533	4.000	8.383		
	Huynh-Feldt	33.533	4.000	8.383		
	Lower-bound	33.533	4.000	8.383		
MONTH	Sphericity Assumed	2.867	2	1.433	2.774	.122
	Greenhouse-Geisser	2.867	1.661	1.726	2.774	.136
	Huynh-Feldt	2.867	2.000	1.433	2.774	.122
	Lower-bound	2.867	1.000	2.867	2.774	.171
Error(MONTH)	Sphericity Assumed	4.133	8	.517		
	Greenhouse-Geisser	4.133	6.645	.622		
	Huynh-Feldt	4.133	8.000	.517		
	Lower-bound	4.133	4.000	1.033		
NOVEL * MONTH	Sphericity Assumed	64.467	2	32.233	26.135	.000
	Greenhouse-Geisser	64.467	1.144	56.344	26.135	.004
	Huynh-Feldt	64.467	1.303	49.479	26.135	.003
	Lower-bound	64.467	1.000	64.467	26.135	.007
Error(NOVEL *MONTH)	Sphericity Assumed	9.867	8	1.233		
	Greenhouse-Geisser	9.867	4.577	2.156		
	Huynh-Feldt	9.867	5.212	1.893		
	Lower-bound	9.867	4.000	2.467		

Syntax and highly selected output from SAS GLM are shown in Table 6.33. SAS GLM sets up in similar fashion to the one-way repeated SAS GLM example of Table 6.15. Both the repeated factors and their number of levels are listed in the `repeated` instruction; order is important and so is the comma between the two factors. Notice that `novel` (with two levels) is named before month (with three levels) in the syntax, corresponding to the order of DVs in the data set. Means are requested.

SAS GLM prints out an inordinate amount of meaningless output (separate ANOVAs on each DV) before coming to the interesting analysis at the end. Separate source tables, with appropriate error terms, are shown for each effect tested, as well as epsilon values for evaluating homogeneity of variance/sphericity (cf. Section 6.6.2). Multivariate output is not shown. Means and standard deviations are at the end of Table 6.33.

```
proc glm data=SASUSER.SS_RPTD2;
    model SCIFIM1 SCIFIM2 SCIFIM3 MSTRYM1 MSTRYM2 MSTRYM3 = ;
    repeated NOVEL 2, MONTH 3 / mean;
run;
```

```
                    The GLM Procedure
             Repeated Measures Analysis of Variance
        Univariate Tests of Hypotheses for Within Subject Effects
```

Source	DF	Type III SS	Mean Square	F Value	Pr > F
NOVEL	1	0.13333333	0.13333333	0.02	0.9057
Error(NOVEL)	4	33.53333333	8.38333333		

Source	DF	Type III SS	Mean Square	F Value	Pr > F	Adj Pr > F G-G	H-F
MONTH	2	2.86666667	1.43333333	2.77	0.1216	0.1365	0.1216
Error(MONTH)	8	4.13333333	0.51666667				

```
             Greenhouse-Geisser Epsilon      0.8306
             Huynh-Feldt Epsilon             1.3481
```

Source	DF	Type III SS	Mean Square	F Value	Pr > F	Adj Pr > F G-G	H-F
MONTH*MONTH	2	64.46666667	32.23333333	26.14	0.0003	0.0044	0.0027
Error(NOVEL*MONTH)	8	9.86666667	1.23333333				

```
             Greenhouse-Geisser Epsilon      0.5721
             Huynh-Feldt Epsilon             0.6514

             Means of Within Subjects Effects
```

Level of NOVEL	N	Mean	Std Dev
1	15	4.20000000	2.07708587
2	15	4.06666667	2.25092574

Level of MONTH	N	Mean	Std Dev
1	10	3.70000000	2.16281709
2	10	4.40000000	1.71269768
3	10	4.30000000	2.58413966

Level of NOVEL	Level of MONTH	N	Mean	Std Dev
1	1	5	2.40000000	1.67332005
1	2	5	3.80000000	0.83666003
1	3	5	6.40000000	1.14017543
2	1	5	5.00000000	1.87082869
2	2	5	5.00000000	2.23606798
2	3	5	2.20000000	1.64316767

And, finally, Table 6.34 contains syntax and selected output for SYSTAT ANOVA with `PRINT=SHORT` output. The segment labeled `Repeated-measures factors and levels` provides reassurance that there is proper correspondence between the DVs and the combination of levels of the IVs. The rest of the output is clearly labeled, with epsilon values following the test of each effect. Epsilon values are blank for the effect of novel, because they are irrelevant for repeated-measures factors with only two levels. Multivariate output is not shown here.

MINITAB GLM, again, has no provision for repeated-measures ANOVA. This has two implications for the analysis. First, the data set must be rearranged so that each IV is coded in a column, with a single DV value per line (Table 6.35) as for the one-way repeated-measures design.

TABLE 6.34   Factorial Repeated-Measures ANOVA through SYSTAT ANOVA: Syntax and Selected Output

```
ANOVA
CATEGORY
COVAR
DEPEND SCIFI_M1 SCIFI_M2 SCIFI_M3 MSTRY_M1 MSTRY_M2 MSTRY_M3/
       REPEAT =2,3,NAMES='NOVEL','MONTH'
ESTIMATE

Repeated measures factors and levels
                  Dependent Variables
Within factor
  NOVEL           1.000  1.000  1.000  2.000  2.000  2.000
  MONTH           1.000  2.000  3.000  1.000  2.000  3.000
-------------------------------------------------------------

Univariate and Multivariate Repeated Measures Analysis

Within Subjects
---------------

Source          SS    df      MS       F      P     G-G     H-F

NOVEL         0.133    1    0.133   0.016  0.906    .       .
Error        33.533    4    8.383

Greenhouse-Geisser Epsilon:      .
Huynh-Feldt Epsilon       :      .

MONTH         2.867    2    1.433   2.774  0.122  0.136   0.122
Error         4.133    8    0.517

Greenhouse-Geisser Epsilon:    0.8306
Huynh-Feldt Epsilon       :    1.0000

NOVEL*MONTH  64.467    2   32.233  26.135  0.000  0.004   0.003
Error         9.867    8    1.233

Greenhouse-Geisser Epsilon:    0.5721
Huynh-Feldt Epsilon       :    0.6514
-------------------------------------------------------------
```

**TABLE 6.35   Data Format for Two-Way
Repeated-Measures ANOVA through
MINITAB with One DV Value per Line**

Case	Novel	Month	Books
1	1	1	1
2	1	1	1
3	1	1	3
4	1	1	5
5	1	1	2
1	1	2	3
2	1	2	4
3	1	2	3
4	1	2	5
5	1	2	4
1	1	3	6
2	1	3	8
3	1	3	6
4	1	3	7
5	1	3	5
1	2	1	5
2	2	1	8
3	2	1	4
4	2	1	3
5	2	1	5
1	2	2	4
2	2	2	8
3	2	2	5
4	2	2	2
5	2	2	6
1	2	3	1
2	2	3	4
3	2	3	3
4	2	3	0
5	2	3	3

Second, the F ratios for all effects except the highest-order interaction ($A \times B$ in this case) must be calculated by hand, because MINITAB does not permit specification of special error terms for the other effects.

Table 6.36 shows MINITAB GLM syntax and output using the data of Table 6.35. All of the sources of variance, including the interactions that serve as error terms, appear on the right side of the GLM equation. However, means (and standard deviations) are only requested for the substantive IVs and interaction.

All of the sums of squares (Adj. SS) and mean squares (Adj. MS) match those of Table 6.30 and output from the other programs. However, the only correct F ratio (and P value) are for the

TABLE 6.36   Two-Way Repeated-Measures ANOVA through MINITAB GLM

```
MTB > GLM 'books' = novel month novel*month case novel*case month*case;
SUBC> Brief 2;
SUBC> Means novel month novel*month.
```

General Linear Model

```
Factor   Type    Levels   Values
NOVEL    fixed       2    1  2
MONTH    fixed       3    1  2  3
CASE     fixed       5    1  2  3  4  5
```

Analysis of Variance for BOOKS, using Adjusted SS for Tests

Source	DF	Seq SS	Adj SS	Adj MS	F	P
NOVEL	1	0.133	0.133	0.133	0.11	0.751
MONTH	2	2.867	2.867	1.433	1.16	0.361
NOVEL*MONTH	2	64.467	64.467	32.233	26.14	0.000
CASE	4	16.467	16.467	4.117	3.34	0.069
NOVEL*CASE	4	33.533	33.533	8.383	6.80	0.011
MONTH*CASE	8	4.133	4.133	0.517	0.42	0.880
Error	8	9.867	9.867	1.233		
Total	29	131.467				

Least Squares Means for BOOKS

```
NOVEL   Mean    StDev
1       4.200   0.2867
2       4.067   0.2867
MONTH
1       3.700   0.3512
2       4.400   0.3512
3       4.300   0.3512
NOVEL*MONTH
1  1    2.400   0.4967
1  2    3.800   0.4967
1  3    6.400   0.4967
2  1    5.000   0.4967
2  2    5.000   0.4967
2  3    2.200   0.4967
```

NOVEL*MONTH interaction. This is because MINITAB uses the residual `Error` (the $A \times B \times S$ interaction) to test all effects, including those associated with cases. Main effect F ratios are found for NOVEL and for MONTH using procedures described in Section 6.4.2.2:

$$F_{novel} = \frac{MS_{novel}}{MS_{novel \times case}} = \frac{0.133}{8.383} = 0.02$$

and

$$F_{\text{month}} = \frac{\text{MS}_{\text{month}}}{\text{MS}_{\text{month} \times \text{case}}} = \frac{1.433}{0.517} = 2.77$$

6.5   Types of Repeated-Measures Designs

6.5.1   Time as a Variable

The repeating variable is time or trials in many repeated-measures designs. Cases are measured at two or more sequential times during the course of the study. The design is useful for assessing the time course of change, the growth or decline of a process over a time period. It is often useful to use planned comparisons with trend coefficients to model the change when tracking change is the goal. Is the change linear? If so, what is the slope? Is there a quadratic component to the change? Does the process first increase and then decline (or the reverse)? How long does the change last? Is there any permanent change? Is the DV the same at the end of the time period as at the beginning?

Passage of time is a variable with inherent order. The first trial is always before the second, and so on. Because trials cannot be given in different orders, control features such as randomization, counterbalancing, and Latin square (Chapter 9) are not available to control extraneous variables. Extraordinary care is needed, therefore, to eliminate or control extraneous variables over time to guarantee that there are no other influences on the process than the IVs.

The design also virtually guarantees violation of homogeneity of covariance/sphericity (Section 6.6.2). Events that are closer in time are likely to be more highly correlated than events farther apart in time. This gives even greater advantage to a planned trend analysis over an omnibus test of the effect of the IV because homogeneity of covariance/sphericity is not an issue with trend analysis.

Mere passage of time is not a manipulated variable. The researcher can choose when and how often to measure, but the levels of the repeated measure are not manipulated, so, strictly speaking, the study is not an experiment. However, if a second, manipulated IV is added to the design (e.g., type of novel), it becomes a true experiment. Often the second IV is a randomized-groups IV in which one group gets a treatment of some sort and the other serves as control. Or different amounts or types of treatment (e.g., science fiction or mystery novels) are given to cases in different groups and the consequences for the DV are studied over time. This is the popular mixed design in which changes associated with two or more treatments are studied over a period of time. Does one treatment produce a larger and/or more permanent change than another? The mixed design is topic of Chapter 7.

6.5.2   Simultaneous Repeated Measures

Sometimes the levels of the repeated-measures IV are administered simultaneously or intermixed within an experimental or other research session. For example, the levels of the IV might be verbs versus nouns, which appear haphazardly within a passage to be memorized. This is one of the few situations in which a repeated-measures IV may be used in an experiment without concern for counterbalancing or violation of sphericity.

6.5.3 Matched Randomized Blocks

Another variant on the repeated-measures design actually uses different cases in the different cells of the design, but analyzes the results as if produced by the same cases. That is, the design is really randomized groups (with one case per cell), but the analysis is repeated measures. This is the matched randomized-blocks design.[9] When applied in experiments, the design allows random assignment of cases to levels, yet has the advantage of greater power than the randomized-groups design.

The first step is to measure all the cases on some variable. In some studies, the variable on which cases are equated is the DV administered before treatment (a pretest). Sometimes several variables are measured during the first step and cases are equated on several variables simultaneously. The second step is to create equivalent blocks (sets) of cases based on their scores on the measured variable(s), with as many cases in each block as there are levels of the repeated-measures IV. If there are three levels of the repeated-measures IV, three "equivalent" cases are put into each block of cases, and so on. The third step is to randomly assign one case in each block to each level of the repeated-measures IV, as shown in Table 6.37. During the analytic phase, the cases in each block are treated as one in a routine repeated-measures analysis. The researcher argues that for these research purposes, these cases are equivalent.

This design is useful when cases need to be naive during each measurement or when cases or samples are used up by a single measurement. Because cases are actually different, they do not have previous experience with another level of the IV before their own trial. However, the researcher is putting a lot of faith into the matching process, and, if cases are matched on several variables, it is common to have them come "unglued" on some variables while trying to match them on others. It is also common to have such a reduced set of cases by the time they are matched that the generalizability of the findings is in doubt. An obvious practical requirement for the design is that all cases are measured ahead of time so the researcher can determine which are equivalent before randomly assigning them to levels of the repeated-measures IV.

TABLE 6.37   Matched Randomized-Blocks Design with $a = 4$

	A			
Block	a_1	a_2	a_3	a_4
block 1 $(s_1 = s_9 = s_{11} = s_{12})$	s_9	s_1	s_{12}	s_{11}
block 2 $(s_2 = s_3 = s_4 = s_8)$	s_4	s_8	s_3	s_2
block 3 $(s_5 = s_6 = s_7 = s_{10})$	s_5	s_7	s_6	s_{10}

[9]Some sources label the design *matched randomized*; others label it *randomized blocks*.

This design has the advantages of the greater power usually associated with the repeated-measures design (assuming the matching is effective) without the expectation that sphericity will be violated.

6.6   Some Important Issues

6.6.1   Carryover Effects: Control of Extraneous Variables

In planning a repeated-measures study, it is extremely important to consider the impact of repeated experience with levels of the IV(s) and the DV on the performance of the cases. If cases are people, is it a problem if they gain some knowledge of the purpose and nature of the study by experiencing several levels of the IV? Are cases changed by the measurement process? For instance, does measurement "use up" a case, or strengthen or weaken it somehow? If cases have memory, do they become more or less skilled in performing the DV over time, independent of the level of the IV? Does their attention or motivation change over time? Do some levels of the IV make permanent or semipermanent changes in the case, whereas others do not?

The researcher contemplating a repeated-measures study considers all these questions. Changes in cases over time regardless of the level of the IV (becoming more or less skilled in the performance of the DV, or shifting attention or motivation, or becoming stronger or weaker) are called *carryover effects*. When the IV is passage of time (trials), carryover effects *are* the focus of study; the researcher specifically wants to investigate changes over time. The area of learning in psychology, for instance, *is* the study of carryover effects. In many situations, however, the researcher has another research question, and carryover effects are potentially a dangerous nuisance. Consider, for instance, the factorial repeated-measures design of Section 6.4.2 in which people are assigned to read both science fiction and mystery novels, each for 3 months. It is entirely possible that people's reading habits change over a 3-month interval, regardless of type of novel. In Table 6.20, the sums of novels read increase over 3 months and then decrease, a pattern that might be expected of those participating in a research study as the novelty wears off.[10] If control is not exercised over the order in which types of novels are read, these carryover effects could be misinterpreted as an effect of type of novel.

There are several ways to exercise control over carryover effects. Two of the most popular are complete counterbalancing and partial counterbalancing (using Latin square designs). Complete counterbalancing involves presenting the levels of the IV in all possible orders to different groups of cases. In the example, in which there are two levels of B, some cases read b_1 (science fiction novels) first whereas others read b_2 (mystery novels) first. This "decouples" carryover effects from the effects of type of novel. Partial counterbalancing is used when there are several levels of the IV, and complete counterbalancing is impractical. In partial counterbalancing, some but not all of the potential orders are used with different cases. Partial counterbalancing through a Latin-square design is the worthy topic of Chapter 9. Counterbalancing has the added advantage of identifying order as a systematic source of variance and removing it from the error term.

A third way to decouple carryover effects from effects of the IV is to present the levels of the IV in a different random order for each case. This strategy is often used when there are many levels

---

[10]Sorry.

of the IV. With numerous levels of the IV presented over many trials, random processes should more or less equalize the different levels at each of the trials, thereby evenly distributing the carryover effects. Any order effects, however, remain in the error term(s).

A fourth way to minimize carryover effects is to wait until performance of the DV stabilizes to run the study. As cases learn to perform a DV, there is often a rapid change in performance over the first few trials followed by a period of time when scores are more or less stable. Cases are given several practice trials before the actual study begins. Sometimes researchers give a constant number of practice trials to all cases and sometimes they establish a criterion for stability of performance to be met before the trials of the study begins.

When the IV is time, the presence of carryover effects is assessed as the test of trials. When the repeated measure is something other than passage of time and controls such as complete or partial counterbalancing are used so that treatment effects and effects of trials/position/order are unconfounded, the test of trials/position/order is the test of the presence of carryover effects. This analysis is described in Chapter 9.

The most dangerous type of carryover is differential carryover, a type that results from the (relatively) long-lasting effects of some levels of the IV. For instance, in drug studies, a substantial washout period is usually required between delivery of different types (or dosages) of drugs to ensure that the first drug is thoroughly metabolized before the second is introduced. But if one of the drugs produces a permanent physiological change, no amount of delay will help, and the apparent effects of all the levels of the IV that follow are contaminated. When some levels of an IV produce long-lasting changes and others do not, there is differential carryover. Designs to assess differential carryover are described in Chapter 9, Section 9.5.8.3.

6.6.2   Assumptions of Analysis: Independence of Errors, Sphericity, Additivity, and Compound Symmetry

Independence of errors is an untenable assumption in repeated-measures ANOVA. Errors are necessarily correlated because measures are made on the same cases—any consistency in individual differences among cases produces correlated errors. In a logical sense, these correlations among errors are removed by calculating variance due to individual differences, SS_S, separately from what would have been the error term in a randomized-groups design (see Figure 6.1).

In practice, the assumption of independence of errors is replaced by the assumption of sphericity defined in Table 6.38, when there are more than two levels of the repeated-measures IV. The F test for the effect of treatment is too liberal if the assumption of sphericity is violated, thus the probability of Type I error is greater than the nominal value. Generally, sphericity is violated when the correlations among pairs of levels of A are unequal. This is most likely to occur when the IV is time; correlations tend to decrease over time and variances of difference scores between pairs of levels increase over time.

There is a somewhat complicated relationship among sphericity, additivity, and compound symmetry (the combination of homogeneity of variance and homogeneity of covariance). Each of these is described in Table 6.38, in which it is assumed that $a = 3$.

Additivity is the absence of an $A \times S$ interaction. Recall that it is this interaction that serves as the error term in a repeated-measures ANOVA, as discussed in Section 6.4.1. If there truly is an interaction between treatments and cases, this is a distorted error term because it includes a systematic

TABLE 6.38 Definitions of Sphericity, Compound Symmetry, and Additivity

Assumption	Verbal Definition	Algebraic Definition
Sphericity	Variances of difference scores between pairs of levels of A are equal.	$\sigma^2_{Y_{a_1}-Y_{a_2}} \cong \sigma^2_{Y_{a_1}-Y_{a_3}} \cong \sigma^2_{Y_{a_2}-Y_{a_3}}$
Compound symmetry		
Homogeneity of variance	Variances in different levels of A are equal.	$\sigma^2_{a_1} \cong \sigma^2_{a_2} \cong \sigma^2_{a_3}$
Homogeneity of covariance	Covariances (and correlations) between pairs of levels of A are equal; variances of difference scores are equal.	$\sigma_{a_1,a_2} \cong \sigma_{a_1,a_3} \cong \sigma_{a_2,a_3}$
Additivity	There is no $A \times S$ interaction; difference scores are equivalent for all cases. Variances of difference scores are zero.	$(Y_{1,a_1} - Y_{1,a_2}) \cong (Y_{2,a_1} - Y_{2,a_2})$ $\cong \cdots \cong (Y_{s,a_1} - Y_{s,a_2})$ $(Y_{1,a_1} - Y_{1,a_3}) \cong (Y_{2,a_1} - Y_{2,a_3})$ $\cong \cdots \cong (Y_{s,a_1} - Y_{s,a_3})$ $(Y_{1,a_2} - Y_{1,a_3}) \cong (Y_{2,a_2} - Y_{2,a_3})$ $\cong \cdots \cong (Y_{s,a_2} - Y_{s,a_3})$

source of variance (the interaction) as well as random error.[11] Because the interaction means that different cases have different patterns of response to treatment, a better, more powerful, and generalizable design would take the interaction into account by blocking on cases that have similar patterns of response to the levels of IV. For example, if men show one consistent pattern of response over the levels of the repeated-measures IV and women show a different consistent pattern of response, gender should be made an additional randomized-groups IV. This provides an explicit test of the former nonadditivity (treatment by gender interaction) and removes it from the error term.

The assumption of sphericity is that the variances of *difference* scores between *pairs* of levels of A are equal. This explains why the assumption is not relevant when there are only two levels of A; there is only one variance of difference scores and nothing for it to equal. Note that with complete additivity, there is zero variance in difference scores (Table 6.38). Since all zeros are equal, there is also sphericity. Thus, additivity is the most restrictive assumption.

After sphericity, the next most restrictive assumption is compound symmetry, that both the variances in levels of A and correlations between pairs of levels of A are equal. In this situation, the variances in differences scores are not zero (as they are with additivity), but they are equal. With

---

[11]Use of this design when there is $A \times S$ interaction is also suspect because the interaction shows up in the numerator of F_A as well (cf. Chapter 11).

either additivity or compound symmetry, then, the assumption of sphericity is met. However, it is possible to have sphericity without having either additivity or compound symmetry, as demonstrated by Myers and Well (1991).

If your data meet requirements for either additivity or compound symmetry, you can be confident about sphericity. However, if requirements for additivity or compound symmetry are not met, you may still have sphericity and meet statistical requirements for an honest (noninflated) F test of treatment. In practice, researchers rely on the results of a combination of tests for homogeneity of variance and the Mauchly (1940) test for sphericity.

SPSS GLM offers the Mauchly test of sphericity by default; SAS GLM and ANOVA produce it by request. In addition, all programs in the three packages that do repeated-measures ANOVA display epsilon factors that are used to adjust degrees of freedom should the assumption of sphericity be violated. MINITAB does not recognize repeated-measures designs, so offers no information about sphericity or correction for its violation.

If the Mauchly test is nonsignificant, and/or the adjustment based on epsilon (described in what follows) does not alter the nominal probability of rejecting the null hypothesis (e.g., .05 or .01), and conditions for homogeneity of variance are met, the F test for routine repeated-measures ANOVA is appropriate.

The Mauchly test, however, is sensitive to nonnormality of the DV as well as to heterogeneity of covariance. Therefore, it is sometimes significant when there is nonnormality rather than failure of sphericity. If the Mauchly test is significant, then closer examination of the distribution of the DV is in order. If it is markedly skewed, repeat the sphericity test after a normalizing transformation of the DV (cf. Chapter 2). If the test is now nonsignificant, the problem with the data set is probably nonnormality rather than failure of sphericity. If the test is still significant, there is probably nonsphericity. The Mauchly test also has low power for small samples and is overly sensitive with very large samples. Thus, with large samples, it is sometimes significant when departure from sphericity is slight. It is always worthwhile, then, to consider the magnitude of the epsilon factor, even when the test of sphericity is explicitly provided.

There are four options when the assumption of sphericity is not tenable: (1) Use specific comparisons on the IV in question (usually trend analysis) instead of the omnibus test, (2) use an adjusted F test, (3) use a multivariate test of the repeated-measures effect(s), or (4) use a maximum likelihood procedure that lets you specify that the structure of the variance-covariance matrix is other than compound symmetry. The variance-covariance matrix shows the variances for each level of a repeated-measures IV in the diagonal positions, and the covariances (cf. Section 2.3.2.1) for each pair of levels in the off-diagonal positions.

$$
\begin{array}{cccc}
 & Y_1 & Y_2 & Y_3 \\
Y_1 & \sigma^2_{a1} & \sigma_{a1,a2} & \sigma_{a1,a3} \\
Y_2 & \sigma_{a2,a1} & \sigma^2_{a2} & \sigma_{a2,a3} \\
Y_3 & \sigma_{a3,a1} & \sigma_{a3,a2} & \sigma^2_{a3}
\end{array}
$$

Compound symmetry, as seen in Table 6.38, assumes that all of the variances are the same and that all of the covariances are the same.

The first option—comparisons—takes advantage of the fact that sphericity is not required when $a = 2$. This option is often a good one because questions about trends in the DV over time are often the ones researchers want answered anyway, and the assumption of homogeneity of covariance is most likely to be violated when the IV is time-related. Does the DV increase (or decrease) steadily over time? Does the DV first increase and then decrease (or the reverse)? Are both patterns present superimposed on each other? Are there other, more complicated patterns in the data?

The second option involves using a more stringent F test of the effects of the IV in question. Two standard adjustments are routinely offered by all three computer programs that recognize repeated-measures designs: Greenhouse-Geisser (1959) and Huynh-Feldt (1976). Both compute an adjustment factor, epsilon (ε), based on the degree of failure of sphericity in the data.[12] Once ε is estimated, it is used to reduce df associated with both numerator and denominator of the F test. That is, the adjustment factor is less than or equal to 1 and is used to multiply both the df for treatment and the df for error to produce new (fractional) df for treatment and error. Reducing df makes the F test more conservative. Both Greenhouse-Geisser and Huynh-Feldt compute an ε value, but Greenhouse-Geisser usually produces a stronger adjustment (larger ε value) than Huynh-Feldt. The more liberal Huynh-Feldt adjustment is preferred because it seems to produce results closer to nominal α levels.

The third option is to use a multivariate test that does not require sphericity, instead of using routine ANOVA. This option is more often associated with analysis of nonexperimental studies. Description of multivariate tests is beyond the scope of this book, but is described in Chapters 9 and 10 of Tabachnick and Fidell (2001), and elsewhere.

A fourth option is to use a maximum likelihood strategy instead of ANOVA, in which the variance-covariance matrix is user-specified or is left unspecified. SAS MIXED produces this type of analysis. The appropriate variance-covariance matrix structure for a time-related repeated-measures IV, for example, is first-order autoregressive, in which correlations among pairs of levels decrease the farther apart they are in time. This is requested as **AR(1)** in SAS MIXED.

Before the sophisticated software was available, trend analysis (or other comparisons) was preferred on strictly computational grounds. A trend analysis is still preferred if the researcher has questions about the shape of the patterns in the DV over time. However, a disadvantage of trend analysis (or any set of comparisons) in a repeated-measures design is that each comparison has its own error term (cf. Section 6.6.6). This reduces the number of error degrees of freedom—and consequently the power—available for the test of the comparison.

ANOVA programs in all three packages that recognize repeated-measures designs give trend analyses, multivariate tests, and the Huynh-Feldt adjustment, so the researcher can easily choose any of those three options. Indeed, many combinations of these options are produced by default alongside the univariate F test, as shown in Tables 6.14 to 6.16. The fourth option, maximum likelihood analysis, is not included in standard ANOVA programs (see Section 6.7).

6.6.3   Power, Sample Size, and Relative Efficiency

A basic strategy for increasing power is decreasing the size of the error term in the F ratio. In repeated-measures analysis, sums of squares for differences among cases are assessed and subtracted from the error term. A repeated-measures design, then, is often more powerful than a corresponding randomized-groups design. More precisely, if the ratio of sum of squares to df for S is

---

[12]The adjustment is based on compound symmetry and is computed from the variance-covariance matrix of the data. The adjustment increases as the individual variances and covariances deviate from their own mean. Computation of ε is illustrated in Myers and Well (1991), among others.

larger than the ratio of sum of squares to df for the error term in a randomized-groups design, repeated measures is more powerful. If the ratio of sum of squares to df for S is the *same* as the ratio of sum of squares to df for the error term in a randomized-groups design, the two designs have equal power. But if the ratio of sum of squares to df for S is *smaller* than the ratio of sum of squares to df for the error term in a randomized-groups design, the repeated-measures design is less powerful because you are losing df without removing a corresponding proportion of sum of squares. If power is the main issue, then the repeated-measures design offers an advantage only when systematic differences among cases are anticipated.

Relative efficiency is a useful measure of the gain in power by using a one-way repeated-measures design over a one-way randomized-groups design. Note from Figure 6.1 that the error term in a repeated-measures ANOVA, SS_{AS}, is the error term from the randomized-groups ANOVA, $SS_{S/A}$, with individual differences, SS_S, subtracted out:

$$SS_{AS} = SS_{S/A} - SS_S \tag{6.19}$$

By taking into account the differences in df for the error terms in the two designs, relative efficiency (Fisher, 1935) is

$$\text{Relative efficiency} = \frac{MS_{S/A}}{MS_{AS}}\left(\frac{df_{AS} + 1}{df_{AS} + 3}\right)\left(\frac{df_{S/A} + 3}{df_{S/A} + 1}\right) \tag{6.20}$$

$MS_{S/A}$ is found either by running the analysis as a one-way randomized-groups design or by applying the following equation to the results of the repeated-measures ANOVA:

$$MS_{S/A} = \frac{(s-1)MS_S + (a-1)(s-1)MS_{AS}}{as - 1} \tag{6.21}$$

For the small-sample example, using $MS_{S/A}$ from Table 4.6,

$$\text{Relative efficiency} = \frac{1.6}{1.2}\left(\frac{8+1}{8+3}\right)\left(\frac{12+3}{12+1}\right) = 1.26$$

Thus, the error term (corrected for differences in df) for the randomized-groups design is about 1.26 times as large as that for the error term of the repeated-measures design—a 26% gain in efficiency for the repeated-measures analysis.

Relative efficiency also can be used to show how many cases would be necessary in each level of a randomized-groups design to match the efficiency of a repeated-measures design:

$$n = s(\text{relative efficiency}) = 5(1.26) = 6.3 \tag{6.22}$$

Rounding up, this shows that 7 cases per level of A are necessary in a randomized-groups design to get the same power as 5 cases for the repeated-measures design (or for the matched randomized-blocks design).

The basic procedures described in Sections 4.5.2 and 5.6.3 for calculating power and determining the number of cases apply. The one-way repeated-measures design is a two-way (treatment and case) layout, but sample-size estimations are typically of interest only for treatment effects. In factorial repeated measures, sample-size requirements are calculated for all effects (e.g., A, B, $A \times B$), and the result used that calls for the largest sample size.

Section 4.5.2 describes the ins and outs of estimating power for a study, including use of Dallal's PC-SIZE program. Notice in Table 4.20 that one of the options for estimating power is the paired t-test, your choice for a repeated-measures design. SPSS GLM provides observed power (OPOWER) for all significance tests on request, as demonstrated in Table 6.14.

6.6.4   Effect Size

Two problems arise with estimating effect size in repeated-measures designs. The first involves inclusion of sum of squares for cases in sum of squares total. Some argue that variability due to individual differences among cases should not be included in estimates of total variance. The second problem involves the error term in a one-way repeated-measures designs that includes both random variability and unwanted $A \times S$ interaction. An estimate of random variability is needed for effect-size computations, but it is impossible to separate random variability from the $A \times S$ interaction term in the repeated-measures design. If the test of sphericity indicates that there is no violation of the assumption, MS_{AS} is taken as an assessment of random variability. On the other hand, if there is evidence of $A \times S$ interaction or violation of sphericity, some accommodation is needed when estimating effect size.

Because of doubt regarding the wisdom of including sum of squares for cases in sum of squares total, and when there is little evidence of $A \times S$ interaction, we recommend using the form of partial $\hat{\omega}^2$ offered by Keppel (1991):

$$\text{Partial } \hat{\omega}_A^2 = \frac{\text{df}_A(\text{MS}_A - \text{MS}_{AS})}{\text{df}_A(\text{MS}_A - \text{MS}_{AS}) + as(\text{MS}_{AS})} \tag{6.23}$$

This equation is for the effect of A. When estimating effect size for other main effects and interactions in a factorial arrangement, the error terms, df, and levels for those effects are substituted into the equation.

A more conservative approach, and the one recommended by Myers and Well (1991) when $A \times S$ interaction is present, is to compute a lower and upper bound for the value of $\hat{\omega}^2$. The lower bound is

$$\hat{\omega}_L^2 = \frac{\text{df}_A(\text{MS}_A - \text{MS}_{AS})}{\text{df}_A(\text{MS}_A - \text{MS}_{AS}) + as(\text{MS}_{AS}) + s(\text{MS}_S)} \tag{6.24}$$

and the upper bound is the same as partial $\hat{\omega}^2$ (Equation 6.23). Equations 6.23 and 6.24 differ only in inclusion of the effect of cases in the denominator.

Partial $\hat{\omega}^2$ and its lower bound are computed for A (month) for the one-way repeated-measures example of Table 6.7.

$$\text{Partial } \hat{\omega}_A^2 = \frac{2(20.600 - 1.183)}{2(20.600 - 1.183) + 3(5)(1.183)} = .69$$

$$\hat{\omega}_L^2 = \frac{2(20.600 - 1.183)}{2(20.600 - 1.183) + 3(5)(1.183) + 5(2.433)} = .56$$

In the example, there is apparent sphericity, so the partial $\hat{\omega}_A^2$ value of .69 is appropriate. If Mauchly's test is significant and there is other evidence of failure of sphericity, $\hat{\omega}_A^2$ instead is estimated to fall within the range of .56 and .69. That is, between 56% and 69% of the variability in number of novels read is associated with month.

The same considerations apply to the simpler estimate of effect size, η^2. That is, partial η^2 is appropriate if there is sphericity, whereas η_L^2 is used as a lower bound if there is doubt about sphericity.

As usual,

$$\text{Partial } \eta^2 = \frac{SS_A}{SS_A + SS_{\text{error}}} = \frac{SS_A}{SS_A + SS_{AS}} \tag{6.25}$$

which, for the data in the one-way repeated small-sample example, is

$$\text{Partial } \eta_A^2 = \frac{41.2}{41.2 + 9.5} = .81$$

This is the value reported by SPSS GLM when **ETASQ** is requested.

For a lower-bound value,

$$\eta_L^2 = \frac{SS_A}{SS_T} = \frac{SS_A}{SS_A + SS_S + SS_{AS}} \tag{6.26}$$

For the small-sample one-way data,

$$\eta_L^2 = \frac{41.2}{41.2 + 9.7 + 9.5} = .68$$

The lower-bound value of η^2, then, is the same as the η^2 for a corresponding one-way randomized-groups design (Section 4.5.1). As usual, the values for η^2 and partial η^2 are larger than the corresponding $\hat{\omega}^2$ and partial $\hat{\omega}^2$ because η^2 is a descriptive statistic, not a parameter estimate (cf. Section 4.5.1).

Recall from previous chapters that effect-size estimates are also appropriate for comparisons and are done with respect to the effect(s) of which they are a part. Lower-bound values are not needed when calculating effect sizes for comparisons, because sphericity is not an issue with single degree-of-freedom tests. Partial $\hat{\omega}^2$ for components of a trend analysis is demonstrated in Section 6.8.2. An example of η^2 for an interaction contrast, as a component of the full interaction, is in Section 6.6.6.3.

6.6.5 Missing Data

Each case in repeated-measures designs participates at all levels (or all combinations of levels) of the effect(s). If a case is missing, then it is a problem of overall reduced n and lower power, rather than a problem of unequal sample size. However, a common problem in repeated-measures designs, particularly in factorial designs with numerous combinations of levels of treatment, is to have a missing DV score. If a case is missing one DV measure, one option (the default for the software) is to delete the case. Although expedient, this option is unpopular with researchers who have measured numerous other DV scores for the case. A second option is to use available information (the other DV scores) to estimate—impute—the missing value.

Several estimation procedures are available. One is to replace the missing value with a value estimated from the mean for that level of A and for that case. The following equation takes into account both the mean for the case and the mean for the level of A, as well as the grand mean.

$$Y^*_{ij} = \frac{sS'_i + aA'_j - T'}{(a-1)(s-1)} \tag{6.27}$$

where Y^*_{ij} = predicted score to replace missing score
s = number of cases
S'_i = sum of the known values for that case
a = number of levels of A
A'_j = sum of the known values of A
T' = sum of all known values

Say that the final score, s_5 in a_3, is missing from Table 6.3. The remaining scores for that case (in a_1 and a_2) sum to $4 + 2 = 6$. The remaining scores for a_3 sum to $6 + 8 + 6 + 7 = 27$. The remaining scores for the entire table sum to $63 - 5 = 58$. Plugging these values into Equation 6.27,

$$Y^*_{5,3} = \frac{5(6) + 3(27) - 58}{(2)(4)} = 6.625$$

The error term, $A \times S$, has df reduced by the number of imputed values, here $df_{AS} = (a-1)(s-1) - 1 = 7$.

Most of the other popular methods for imputing missing values, such as regression or EM available in SPSS MVA, do not take into account the commensurate nature of the measurement—the DV is measured on the same scale for all its occurrences. They also do not take into account the consistency afforded by the repeated measurement—that is, individual differences. Multiple imputation, available through SOLAS MDA (Statistical Solutions, Inc., 1997), is a procedure that is indeed applicable to longitudinal data (or any other repeated measures) but is difficult to implement. The procedure requires that you create several data sets with different imputations of missing values and derive summary statistics from analysis of all of them. Or if you happen to have BMDP5V (Dixon, 1992), the program imputes and prints out missing values for repeated-measures analysis.

Whatever estimation procedure is used, it is reported along with the other findings in your results section.

6.6.6 Specific Comparisons

Repeated-measures designs present the same issues of planned versus post hoc comparisons, degree of adjustment, and type of comparison as randomized-groups designs. That is, comparisons in repeated-measures designs can also be either planned ahead of time and performed in lieu of omnibus ANOVA or done after omnibus ANOVA, with the power advantage to planning. Also, as in randomized-groups designs, the degree of adjustment to α depends both on when the comparison is performed and on the number of comparisons that can be performed, with the Scheffé procedure the most conservative. Finally, either user-generated coefficients or trend coefficients are available for comparisons, although, when the repeated-measure IV is time, trend coefficients are likely to be more appropriate.

Repeated-measures comparisons differ from randomized-groups comparisons in development of a separate error term for each comparison. The need for this arises from the nature of the error terms as, in part, interaction. The error terms are the idiosyncratic reactions of cases to different levels of treatment, plus random error. If a comparison omits one of the levels of treatment, why should the error term for that comparison contain idiosyncratic reactions to the omitted level of treatment? When there is no $A \times S$ interaction, the error terms are all estimates of the same random variability and about the same size as MS_{AS}, so which is used has little practical consequence. When there is interaction, however, the sizes of the various error terms differ, with direct consequences for the power of various comparisons. In practice, there is no harm in developing a special error term for each comparison. If MS_{AS} includes interaction, you are safe; if not, you may have gone to some extra effort, but the analysis is still justified.

6.6.6.1   Tests of Repeated-Measures Main Effects

This section discusses procedures for conducting a comparison on an IV with more than two levels. If there is only one IV, the procedure of Section 6.6.6.1.1 is appropriate. If there are two or more IVs, the procedure of Section 6.6.6.1.2 is appropriate. Remember that interpretation of a main effect is problematic in the presence of reliable interaction, as discussed in Section 5.6.1.1.

6.6.6.1.1   Comparisons for Designs with One Repeated-Measures IV

When there are more than two levels of A, comparisons to pinpoint the source of differences in means are appropriate. The logic is the same as for a one-way randomized-groups design, Section 4.5.3. However, procedures differ because of the development of a separate error term for each comparison.

The most straightforward way to perform these comparisons by hand is to build the comparisons into a new data set and do standard analysis on the new data set. (This method also works by computer if transformations are used to convert the data or programs operate on a special data set developed for the comparison.) There are two reasons that this approach works for repeated-measures IVs but not randomized-groups IVs. The first is that because each line of data comes from a single case, there is rationale for determining which DV scores to combine over levels of the IV. The second is that the analysis develops the mean square for the new error term right along with the comparison mean square for the IV. That is, you get $MS_{A\,comp}$ and $MS_{A\,comp \times S}$ simultaneously.

Consider the data of Table 6.3. Suppose you want two comparisons, the first month versus the second, and then the first two months versus the third. The contrast coefficients are $1, -1, 0$ and $1, 1, -2$. Table 6.39 shows the new data set needed for each comparison. These data sets are then analyzed by standard procedures (Section 6.4.1.3) to test $MS_{A\,comp}$ and $MS_{A\,comp\,S}$.

The data set for the $1, -1, 0$ comparison simply deletes data for the third level of A. The data set for the $1, 1, -2$ comparison pools the DV scores for the first two levels of A and doubles the DV scores at a_3. The DV scores with positive coefficients are combined in one column and the DV scores with negative coefficients are combined into the second column. Because each comparison has 1 df, new data sets for comparisons always have only two columns.[13] This procedure readily generalizes

---

[13]This is why comparisons are considered to have $a = 2$, and sphericity is not an issue for them.

TABLE 6.39   Development of Data Sets for Comparisons in One-Way Repeated-Measures Designs

(a) Data set for the 1, –1, 0 comparison

Case	a_1: Month 1	a_2: Month 2	Case Totals
s_1	1	3	4
s_2	1	4	5
s_3	3	3	6
s_4	5	5	10
s_5	2	4	6

(b) Data set for the 1, 1, –2 comparison

Case	$a_1 + a_2$ Month 1 + Month 2	$2(a_3)$ 2(Month 3)	Case Totals
s_1	$1 + 3 = 4$	$2(6) = 12$	16
s_2	$1 + 4 = 5$	$2(8) = 16$	21
s_3	$3 + 3 = 6$	$2(6) = 12$	18
s_4	$5 + 5 = 10$	$2(7) = 14$	24
s_5	$2 + 4 = 6$	$2(5) = 10$	16

to more complicated comparisons. For instance, the linear-trend coefficients for an IV with four levels are $-3, -1, 1, 3$. To accomplish this comparison, create two columns of data. The first column contains $3(DV_{a_1}) + DV_{a_2}$ for each case and the second column contains $DV_{a_3} + 3(DV_{a_4})$ for each case. These two columns are then analyzed in routine repeated-measures ANOVA (Section 6.4.1.3).

SAS, SPSS, and SYSTAT compute the separate error terms needed for each comparison. Table 6.40 summarizes syntax and error term for trend analysis, and user-specified comparisons for the three statistical packages that recognize repeated-measures designs. Note, however, that the SAS GLM notation in Table 6.40 only can be used for pairwise comparisons.[14]

The SAS GLM CONTRAST(1) indicates that the first level of month is to be contrasted with each other level. So, for example, if you want to compare level 2 with level 3, you would need to change the number in parentheses to 2. Complex user-specified contrasts, for example, [1, 1, −2], cannot be readily specified in SAS GLM. The user-specified contrast matrix in SPSS GLM is entered in syntax; it cannot be generated through the menu system. Note that the special contrast matrix has as many rows as columns, with the first row a series of 1s.

Once you have obtained F for a comparison, whether by hand or computer, compare the obtained F with a critical F to see if the mean difference is reliable. If obtained F exceeds critical F, the null hypothesis of equality of means for the comparison is rejected. But which critical F is used

---

[14]Any of the programs, including MINITAB, can be run on a data set specifically developed for a comparison, as in Table 6.39.

TABLE 6.40   Syntax and Error Terms for Trend Analyses and User-Specified Comparisons for One-Way Repeated-Measures Designs

Type of Comparison	Program	Syntax for One-Way Example	Name of Effect/ Name of Error in Output
Trend analysis	SPSS GLM (default)	GLM month_1 month_2 month_3 /WSFACTOR month 3 POLYNOMIAL /METHOD = SSTYPE(3) /CRITERIA = ALPHA(.05) /WSDESIGN = month.	MONTH Linear/ Error(MONTH) Linear

	SAS GLM	```proc glm data=SASUSER.SS_RPTD;```
		``` model MONTH1 MONTH2 MONTH3 = ;```
		``` repeated MONTH 3```
		``` polynomial/ summary;```
		```run;```
			`MONTH_1 MEAN/ Error`

	SYSTAT GLM (default with PRINT = MEDIUM)	GLM MODEL MONTH_1 MONTH_2 MONTH_3 = CONSTANT/ REPEAT =3,NAMES='MONTH' ESTIMATE	`Polynomial Test of Order 1 (Linear)/ Error`

User-specified coefficients	SPSS GLM	GLM
		month_1 month_2 month_3
		/WSFACTOR month 3 SPECIAL (1 1 1
		                               1 −1 0
		                               1 1 −2)
		/METHOD = SSTYPE(3)
		/CRITERIA = ALPHA(.05)
		/WSDESIGN = month.
			MONTH L1/ Error(MONTH) L1

	SAS GLM	```proc glm data=SASUSER.SS_RPTD;```
		``` model MONTH1 MONTH2 MONTH3 = ;```
		``` repeated MONTH 3```
		``` contrast (1)/ summary;```
		```run;```
			`MONTH_2 MEAN/ Error`

	SYSTAT GLM	GLM MODEL MONTH_1 MONTH_2 MONTH_3 = CONSTANT/ REPEAT = 3, NAMES = 'MONTH' ESTIMATE HYPOTHESIS WITHIN="MONTH" STANDARDIZE=WITHIN CONTRAST [1 −1 0] TEST	`Hypothesis/ Error`

depends on whether the comparison is planned or performed post hoc. If planned, the probability levels reported in the output are correct and the comparison is tested against tabled F with 1 and $df_{A comp \times S}$. If post hoc, the probability levels in the output are incorrect and, instead, Equation 4.13 is used to compute F_S: $(a - 1)F_{df_A, df_{AS}}$.

Note that the regression approach of Table 6.8 has contrast coefficients built into each column. SS(reg.) for a column *is* the sum of squares (and mean square) for a comparison, whatever coefficients are used. In the example of Table 6.8, linear-trend coefficients are used in the X_1 column so SS(reg. X_1) is SS_{linear} for A. However, this approach, in which case totals are used in the X_3 column, does not automatically develop the special error term necessary to test the comparison. To do the comparison, you need to either expand the df for cases and develop the special error term by cross-multiplying the columns for cases with the column for linear trend or develop the new DV values and submit them to routine regression analysis.

6.6.6.1.2 Marginal Comparisons in Factorial Repeated-Measures Designs

Comparisons for main effects in factorial designs investigate differences in means at the margins of the data set. To perform this analysis by hand, you again have to develop the data set for the comparison, this time both by collapsing over the levels of the other IV(s) (NOVEL in this example) and by using the contrast coefficients to transform the DV scores. The new data set for the $1, -1, 0$ comparison on MONTH is in Table 6.41. Once the data set is developed, procedures of Section 6.4.1.3 are used to compute $MS_{A comp}$ and $MS_{A comp \times S}$ for the ANOVA.

To do either trend analysis or user-specified comparisons by computer, use the syntax in Table 6.42. SYSTAT, SAS, and SPSS develop the special error terms necessary for these comparisons. Trend analyses in these programs also include tests for trends of the interaction. Recall that SAS does not perform user-specified comparisons for repeated-measures effects, so that special data sets are necessary for each comparison. This is also the procedure for MINITAB, with the data entered in the one-DV-per-line format. Note in the column for "Name of Effect/Name of Error in Output" that the programs label the output for the comparisons very differently.

SYSTAT also has a peculiarity when doing user-specified comparisons. F ratios, df, and probability values are correct, but printed sums of squares are multiplied by the sum of the squared coefficients. Thus, when coefficients of $1, -1, 0$ are used, the sums of squares are twice as big as they

**TABLE 6.41   Development of Data Set for Marginal Comparison
$(1, -1, 0)$ in Two-Way Repeated-Measures Designs**

Case	a_1: Month 1 Scifi + Mystery	a_2: Month 2 Scifi + Mystery	Case Totals
s_1	$1 + 5 = 6$	$3 + 4 = 7$	13
s_2	$1 + 8 = 9$	$4 + 8 = 12$	21
s_3	$3 + 4 = 7$	$3 + 5 = 8$	15
s_4	$5 + 3 = 8$	$5 + 2 = 7$	15
s_5	$2 + 5 = 7$	$4 + 6 = 10$	17

TABLE 6.42   Syntax and Error Terms for Trend Analyses and User-Specified Comparisons for Factorial Repeated-Measures Designs

Type of Comparison	Program	Syntax for Two-Way Example	Name of Effect/ Name of Error in Output
Trend analysis	SPSS GLM (default)	GLM scifi_m1 scifi_m2 scifi_m3 mstry_m1 mstry_m2 mstry_m3 /WSFACTOR = novel 2 polynomial month 3 polynomial /MEASURE = books /METHOD = SSTYPE(3) /CRITERIA = ALPHA(.05) /WSDESIGN = novel month novel*month.	MONTH Linear/ Error(MONTH) Linear

	SAS GLM	`proc glm data=SASUSER.SS_RPTD2;`
		`  model SCIFIM1 SCIFIM2 SCIFIM3`
		`    MSTRYM1 MSTRYM2 MSTRYM3 = ;`
		`  repeated NOVEL 2, MONTH 3`
		`    polynomial /`
		`summary;`
		`run;`
			`MONIH_1`
			`MEAN/`
			`Error`

	SYSTAT GLM (default with PRINT = MEDIUM)	`GLM`
		`MODEL SCIFI_M1 SCIFI_M2 SCIFI_M3,`
		`    MSTRY_M1 MSTRY_M2 MSTRY_M3 = ,`
		`    CONSTANT/ REPEAT =2,3,`
		`  NAMES='NOVEL', 'MONTH'`
		`ESTIMATE`
			`Polynomial`
			`Test of Order`
			`1 (Linear)`
			`MONTH/Error`

User-specified coefficients	SPSS GLM	GLM
		 scifi_m1 scifi_m2 scifi_m3
		 mstry_m1 mstry_m2 mstry_m3
		/WSFACTOR = novel 2 month 3 special (1 1 1
		                                    1 −1 0
		                                    1 1 −2)
		/METHOD = SSTYPE(3)
		/CRITERIA = ALPHA(.05)
		/WSDESIGN = novel month novel*month.
			MONTH L1/
			Error(MONTH) L1

	SYSTAT GLM	`GLM`
		`MODEL SCIFI_M1 SCIFI_M2 SCIFI_M3,`
		`    MSTRY_M1 MSTRY_M2 MSTRY_M3 =`
		`CONSTANT/ REPEAT =2,3,`
		`NAMES='NOVEL', 'MONTH'`
		`ESTIMATE`
		`HYPOTHESIS`
		`WITHIN="MONTH"`
		`STANDARDIZE=WITHIN`
		`CONTRAST [ 1 −1  0 ]`
		`TEST`
			`Hypothesis/`
			`Error`

coefficients. Thus, when coefficients of $1, -1, 0$ are used, the sums of squares are twice as big as they should be. This impacts calculation of effect sizes, as shown in Section 6.6.6.3.

6.6.6.2   Tests of Repeated-Measures Interactions: Simple-Effects Analysis

In simple-effects analysis, one IV is held constant at one level, whereas mean differences are examined between the levels of the other IV (Figure 5.8). For instance, only data from a_1, the first level of month, are used and mean differences are examined in number of scifi versus mystery novels read; the researcher asks if there are differences in number of scifi and mystery novels read in the first month by assessing $F_{B\ at\ a_1}$. The same analyses can be performed for months 2 ($F_{B\ at\ a_2}$) and 3 ($F_{B\ at\ a_3}$). Or type of novel is held constant at science fiction and mean differences are explored among months using $F_{A\ at\ b_1}$; the researcher asks whether there are mean differences in the 3 months when scifi novels are read. The same analysis can be performed for mystery novels, using $F_{A\ at\ b_2}$. The test of the simple main effect of B (novels) has 1 df in the numerator of the F test because there are only two types of novels. The test of the simple main effect of A (month) has 2 df in the numerator of the F test because there are 3 months. Because month has 2 df, the simple main-effects analysis could be followed by simple comparisons (see Figures 5.7 and 5.8). However, the guidelines of Section 5.6.4.4.1 also are appropriate for factorial repeated-measures because simple-effects analyses confound main effects with interaction.

Hand calculations for simple main effects and simple comparisons are straightforward; you do a one-way repeated-measures ANOVA on each "slice" of the design. For the example, Table 6.43 contains the data sets necessary (a) to test for mean differences between novels for the first month, (b) to test for mean differences between months for scifi novels, and (c) to compare the first 2 months against the third for scifi novels.

The easiest way to do simple main-effects analyses by computer is to select just the DVs you need to create one-way repeated-measures syntax and, for simple comparisons, add appropriate syntax. Table 6.44 shows syntax from the three programs for the simple main effect of month for science fiction novels, and the simple comparison through SPSS GLM, and SYSTAT GLM of the first 2 months versus the third for science fiction novels. The syntax and output are identical to that for a one-way repeated-measures design. The only difference is in selection of only some of the available DVs. For some user-specified comparisons, SAS GLM, as before, requires a special comparison data set for the simple comparison; MINITAB requires special data sets for both simple comparisons and simple main effects.

All programs test the effects as if they are planned. If these analyses are done post hoc, the printed significance levels are inappropriate and the Scheffé adjustment is needed to control for inflated familywise Type I error.

When there are three or more IVs, simple interactions, simple main effects, and simple comparisons are all possible. Researchers back a significant three-way interaction ($A \times B \times C$) into a series of simple two-way interactions ($MS_{B\times S\ at\ a_1}$, $MS_{B\times S\ at\ a_2}$, etc.), followed by simple main-effects (followed, perhaps, by simple comparisons) analyses of those that have reliable mean differences.

6.6.6.3   Tests of Repeated-Measures Interactions: Interaction Contrasts

The second option for pinpointing the source of an interaction is interaction contrasts analysis. As you recall, interaction contrasts are often more appropriate than simple main-effects analysis in the presence of large or disordinal (crossing) effects because only the sum of squares for omnibus interaction is partitioned. In interaction contrasts analysis, the interaction between two IVs is examined through

TABLE 6.43   Simple Effects and Simple Comparisons by Hand for Factorial Repeated-Measures Designs

(a) Data set for the simple main effect of novels at the first month

Cases	Month 1		Case Totals
	Science Fiction	Mystery	
s_1	1	5	6
s_2	1	8	9
s_3	3	4	7
s_4	5	3	8
s_5	2	5	7
Novel Totals	12	25	37

(b) Data set for the simple main effect of months for science fiction novels

Case	Science Fiction			Case Totals
	Month 1	Month 2	Month 3	
s_1	1	3	6	10
s_2	1	4	8	13
s_3	3	3	6	12
s_4	5	5	7	17
s_5	2	4	5	11
Month Totals	12	19	32	63

(c) Data set for the simple comparison of the first 2 months versus the third for science fiction novels

Case	Science Fiction		Case Totals
	Month 1 + Month 2	2(Month 3)	
s_1	$1 + 3 = \ 4$	$2(6) = 12$	16
s_2	$1 + 4 = \ 5$	$2(8) = 16$	21
s_3	$3 + 3 = \ 6$	$2(6) = 12$	18
s_4	$5 + 5 = 10$	$2(7) = 14$	24
s_5	$2 + 4 = \ 6$	$2(5) = 10$	16
Month Totals	$12 + 19 = 31$	$2(32) = 64$	95

**TABLE 6.44   Syntax for Simple Main Effects and Simple Comparisons
for Factorial Repeated-Measures Designs**

Type of Comparison	Program	Syntax	Labels for Effect/ Error

Simple main effect	SPSS GLM	GLM
		  scifi_m1 scifi_m2 scifi_m3
		  /WSFACTOR = month 3 Polynomial
		  /METHOD = SSTYPE(3)
		  /CRITERIA = ALPHA(.05)
		  /WSDESIGN = month.
			MONTH/ Error(MONTH)

	SAS GLM	```proc glm data=SASUSER.SS_RPTD2;```
		``` model SCIFIM1 SCIFIM2 SCIFIM3 =;```
		``` repeated MONTH 3;```
		```run;```
			MONTH/ Error(MONTH)

	SYSTAT GLM	```GLM```
		```MODEL SCIFI_M1 SCIFI_M2 SCIFI_M3 =,```
		``` CONSTANT/,```
		``` REPEAT =3,NAMES='MONTH'```
		```ESTIMATE```
			MONTH/ Error

Simple comparison (For 1 1 -2)	SPSS GLM	GLM
		  scifi_m1 scifi_m2 scifi_m3
		  /WSFACTOR = month 3 special (1 1 1
		                       1 1 –2
		                       1 –1 0)
		
		  /METHOD = SSTYPE(3)
		  /CRITERIA = ALPHA(.05)
		  /WSDESIGN = month.
			MONTH L1/ Error(MONTH) L1

	SYSTAT GLM	```GLM```
		```MODEL SCIFI_M1 SCIFI_M2 SCIFI_M3 =```
		```CONSTANT/REPEAT=3, NAMES='MONTH'```
		```ESTIMATE```
		```HYPOTHESIS```
		```WITHIN="MONTH"```
		```STANDARDIZE=WITHIN```
		```CONTRAST [1 1 –2]```
		```TEST```
			Hypothesis/ Error

smaller interactions (cf. Figure 5.9), obtained by deleting levels of one or more of the IVs, or by combining levels using appropriate weighting coefficients.

If contrast coefficients are applied to all of the IVs (because all have more than two levels), the analysis is interaction contrasts. If contrasts are applied to some but not all of the IVs, the analysis is a partial factorial. Because novel has only two levels in this two-way example, the analysis is partial factorial. Linear trend analysis is chosen for the 3 months.

Interaction contrasts analysis is performed by hand by creating the necessary data set and redoing the ANOVA. The appropriate data set for the partial factorial of novel with the linear trend of month is in Table 6.45. For the linear trend, the second level of month is simply deleted for both scifi novels and mystery novels. Once the data are derived, a two-way repeated-measures ANOVA is performed in which the interaction term is the desired partial factorial. Alternatively, the regression approach is available, in which $SS(\text{reg.}X_4)$ provides the desired result, as seen in Table 6.26.

The syntax of Table 6.42 automatically produces the partial factorial of NOVEL $\times$ MONTH$_{\text{linear}}$ for SAS GLM and SPSS GLM. In SAS, the effect and its error are labeled `NOVEL*MONTH.1` (`MEAN` and `Error`).[15] In SPSS GLM, the effect is labeled NOVEL*MONTH Linear with Error (NOVEL*MONTH Linear). The only program that requires different syntax is SYSTAT, shown in Table 6.46, where the `CMATRIX` instruction is added.[16] The coefficients entered into the `CMATRIX` command are obtained by cross-multiplying the coefficients for novel with the linear-trend coefficients for month, as shown in Table 5.36, or, identically, by cross-multiplying the X_1 column for MONTH$_{\text{linear}}$ with the X_3 column for NOVEL, as shown in Table 6.26.

The F ratio for the interaction contrast produced by SYSTAT GLM is correct; however, the SS (and MS) are too large by a factor of the sum of the squared coefficients. Thus, the true SS for the linear contrast is $231.2/4 = 57.8$ and the true SS for error is $36.8/4 = 9.2$. An alternative strategy is to use coefficients that, when squared, sum to one $(.5\ 0\ -.5\ -.5\ 0\ .5)$.

Effect size for the linear interaction contrast, relative to the full interaction, may be done as per Equation 5.27,

$$\eta^2 = \frac{SS_{A\text{comp}1\times B}}{SS_{AB}} = \frac{57.8}{64.467} = .90$$

Thus, 90% of the AB interaction is attributable to its linear trend.

TABLE 6.45 Hypothetical Data Set for the Partial Factorial of Novel with Month$_{\text{linear}}$

Case	b_1: Science Fiction		b_2: Mystery		Case Totals
	a_1: Month 1	a_3: Month 3	a_1: Month 1	a_3: Month 3	
s_1	1	6	5	1	$S_1 = 13$
s_2	1	8	8	4	$S_2 = 21$
s_3	3	6	4	3	$S_3 = 16$
s_4	5	7	3	0	$S_4 = 15$
s_5	2	5	5	3	$S_5 = 15$
Treatment Totals	$A_1B_1 = 12$	$A_3B_1 = 32$	$A_1B_2 = 25$	$A_3B_2 = 11$	$T = 80$

[15]Recall that contrasts in SAS GLM for repeated-measures designs are restricted to built-in comparisons, which include trend analysis. There is no provision for user-specified comparisons unless separate data sets developed for the comparison are used.

[16]Interaction contrasts are not feasible for repeated-measures designs in MINITAB.

TABLE 6.46 Syntax and Selected Output for Interaction Contrasts through SYSTAT GLM

```
GLM
MODEL SCIFI_M1 SCIFI_M2 SCIFI_M3 MSTRY_M1 MSTRY_M2 MSTRY_M3 = CONSTANT/,
 REPEAT =2,3,NAMES='NOVEL','MONTH'
ESTIMATE
HYPOTHESIS
NOTE 'LINEAR'
WITHIN="MONTH"
STANDARDIZE=WITHIN
CMATRIX [ -1 0 1 1 0 -1 ]
TEST
```

```
Repeated measures factors and levels
              Dependent Variables
Within factor
  NOVEL         1.000   1.000   1.000   2.000   2.000   2.000
  MONTH         1.000   2.000   3.000   1.000   2.000   3.000
------------------------------------------------------------------
```

```
Within Subjects
---------------
```

Source	SS	df	MS	F	P	G-G	H-F
NOVEL	0.133	1	0.133	0.016	0.906	.	.
Error	33.533	4	8.383				
MONTH	2.867	2	1.433	2.774	0.122	0.136	0.122
Error	4.133	8	0.517				
NOVEL*MONTH	64.467	2	32.233	26.135	0.000	0.004	0.003
Error	9.867	8	1.233				

```
LINEAR

Hypothesis.

C Matrix
```

	1	2	3	4	5
	1.000	0.000	-1.000	-1.000	0.000

	6
	1.000

```
Test of Hypothesis
```

Source	SS	df	MS	F	P
Hypothesis	231.200	1	231.200	25.130	0.007
Error	36.800	4	9.200		

Interaction contrasts may be done as part of a planned analysis, replacing the omnibus test of the interaction, or a post hoc analysis to dissect a significant interaction that is observed. The Scheffé adjustment for post hoc analysis for inflated Type I error rate is

$$F_S = (a - 1)(b - 1)F_{(a-1)(b-1),\,(a-1)(b-1)(s-1)} \tag{6.28}$$

In this case:

$$F_S = (3 - 1)(2 - 1)(4.46) = 8.92$$

The obtained F of 25.13 exceeds critical F_c whether planned ($F_{1,8} = 5.32$) or post hoc ($F_S = 8.92$), so there is an interaction of linear trend with novel. That is, the linear trend over months is different for science fiction and mystery novels. Interpretation of the partial interaction is most easily achieved through a plot of the means, somewhat difficult to achieve for repeated-measures designs. The relevant plot is produced by SPSS GLM (edited), however, as shown in Figure 6.3. The number

```
GLM
    scifi_m1 scifi_m2 scifi_3 mstry_m1 mstry_m2 mstry_m3
    /WSFACTOR = novel 2 Polynomial month 3 Polynomial
    /METHOD = SSTYPE(3)
    /MEASURE = books
    /PLOT = PROFILE(month*novel)
    /CRITERIA = ALPHA(.05)
    /WSDESIGN = novel month novel*month
```

Profile Plots

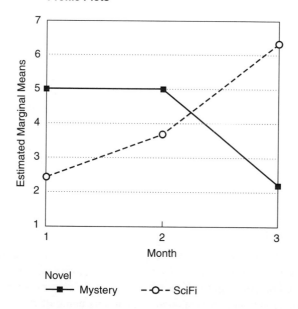

FIGURE 6.3   SPSS GLM Syntax and (Edited) Profile Plot of Means over 3 Months for Science Fiction and Mystery Novels

of science fiction novels read increases over the 3 months (positive slope), whereas the number of mystery novels read decreases over the 3 months (negative slope). The plot also suggests a quadratic trend of the interaction; that is, the curves for the two types of novels have different shapes.

6.7   Complete Example of Two-Way Repeated-Measures ANOVA

Data for this example were extracted from a study by Damos (1989) in which 20 participants were required to identify figures under various angles of rotation (0°, 60°, 120°, and 180°), each in standard and mirror-imaged orientation. The DV selected for use here is reaction time, and data selected are from the last set of 20 sessions run over a period of 2 weeks. Thus, there are two repeated-measures IVs: orientation with two levels (standard and mirror) and rotation with four levels. Previous research had shown a linear trend of increasing reaction time the greater the angle of rotation. Questions to be addressed in the current research are: (1) Are there trends other than linear? (2) Are there differences associated with mirror-imaged as opposed to standard orientation? (3) Are there differences in trend over angle of rotation for standard and mirror-imaged orientation, that is, what is the trend of the rotation by orientation interaction? Data files are REACTIME.*.

6.7.1   Evaluation of Assumptions

There are no missing data in this set. Therefore, the issues to be addressed are normality of sampling distributions, homogeneity of variance, sphericity, and absence of outliers.

6.7.1.1   Normality of Sampling Distributions

The error term for the main effect of rotation (the rotation × participant interaction) has df = $(b - 1)(s - 1) = (4 - 1)(20 - 1) = 57$, sufficient to assume normality for purposes of ANOVA. The interaction error term (orientation × rotation × participant interaction), likewise, has df = $(a - 1)(b - 1)(s - 1) = (2 - 1)(4 - 1)(20 - 1) = 57$. The error term for the main effect of orientation (standard versus mirror) has df = $(a - 1)(s - 1) = (2 - 1)(20 - 1) = 19$, close enough to the criterion of 20 to be acceptable as long as other assumptions are met.

The planned trend analysis reduces error df for each trend comparison to 19 as well, because each trend is evaluated with df = $(a - 1)(1)(s - 1) = (2 - 1)(1)(20 - 1)$, when df for *B* is reduced to 1 for each comparison. Again, this is not of concern unless other assumptions appear to be violated.

6.7.1.2   Homogeneity of Variance

Ratios of variances for this factorial design are checked for cells representing the orientation by rotation interaction. SAS MEANS is used to print out a full set of cell descriptive statistics.

Table 6.47 shows syntax and output from the SAS MEANS run. The `vardef=df` statement instructs SAS MEANS to calculate variances and standard deviations using df rather than *n* in the denominator (cf. Equations 2.1 and 2.2). Statistics requested are sample size (**N**), minimum, maxi-

TABLE 6.47   Descriptive Statistics for Two-Way Repeated-Measures ANOVA: SAS Data and Means Syntax and Output

```
proc means data=SASUSER.REACTIME vardef = df
          N MIN MAX MEAN STD VAR SKEWNESS KURTOSIS;
     var S0 S60 S120 S180 M0 M60 M120 M180;
run;
```

Variable	N	Minimum	Maximum	Mean	Std Dev
S0	20	419.0400000	550.9100000	482.9825000	41.5966443
S60	20	418.8000000	539.3600000	484.0725000	36.2295931
S120	20	432.3500000	693.6700000	506.1235000	58.8820937
S180	20	422.8400000	770.8000000	546.4735000	80.8858206
M0	20	440.5100000	592.3900000	508.9835000	53.1946684
M60	20	435.4200000	581.9700000	511.3695000	44.6091112
M120	20	430.7400000	748.6800000	523.8220000	73.6641852
M180	20	423.8000000	890.0600000	546.4510000	99.4082426

Variable	Variance	Skewness	Kurtosis
S0	1730.28	0.2594316	-1.3603214
S60	1312.58	0.0122305	-1.1656553
S120	3467.10	1.6999893	4.4887456
S180	6542.52	1.2617860	2.5805090
M0	2829.67	0.1993758	-1.6264543
M60	1989.97	-0.0246631	-1.0082450
M120	5426.41	1.4852998	3.4826521
M180	9882.00	2.2065031	7.1502194

mum, standard deviation (STD), variance, skewness, and kurtosis. Several of these are also useful for evaluating outliers.

A glance at the Variance column assures us that there is no cause for concern about heterogeneity of variance. The ratio of largest to smallest variance, $F_{max} = 9882.00/1312.58 = 7.53$, is less than 10.

6.7.1.3   Sphericity

We are interested only in trend analysis in this study, both of the main effect of rotation and of the rotation by orientation interaction. Therefore, the outcome of a test of sphericity for the omnibus effects is irrelevant. This is fortunate because the nature of the rotation IV is such that we might expect violation of sphericity (the greater the difference in angles of rotation, the lower the expected correlation).

6.7.1.4 Absence of Outliers

Table 6.47 provides information to evaluate the presence of outlying scores on the variables used for the tests. Scores are within 3.3 standard deviations of their means with one exception. The maximum score for mirror-imaged orientation with 180° rotation has $z = (890.060 - 546.451)/99.408 = 3.46$. A look at all of the variables, however, indicates generally positive skewness as well as kurtosis, and the nature of the DV, reaction time, is such that a transformation usually is applied. There is a physiological lower limit to reaction time, but very long ones can be produced by a variety of influences, many of which are unrelated to the cognitive processing strategies of interest in this research. Therefore, the decision is made to apply a square root (minimal) transform to all of the scores.

Table 6.48 shows SAS DATA syntax to perform the transformation and create a file, REACSQRT, that contains the transformed as well as original data. Table 6.48 also shows MEANS syntax and output for the transformed data.

This transformation successfully pulls in the outlier and reduces skewness and kurtosis in the entire data set.

6.7.2 Planned Trend Analysis of Two-Way Repeated-Measures Design

Table 6.49 shows SAS GLM syntax and highly selected output for the planned trend analysis. Trend analysis is requested in the polynomial instruction, along with summary to display the results of the analysis. The nom instruction suppresses multivariate output.

The output shown (much has been omitted) begins with a translation of the variables that are used to form levels of the two IVs, reassuring us that our syntax correctly identified them. All output relating to individual tests of DVs as well as the omnibus ANOVA are omitted here. Marginal and cell means and standards deviations are shown at end of the output. Table 6.49 first shows the test of type of orientation (type_1), which is solely a linear test because there are only two levels: standard and mirror. This is followed by the test of the three polynomials for angle, linear = angle_1, quadratic = angle_2, and cubic = angle_3. Finally, there are the tests of the three trends of the interaction, type_1*angle_1 = type by linear trend of angle of rotation, and so on.

The interaction is evaluated first. The section labeled type_1*angle_1 shows that the two types of trials (standard and mirror-imaged) have different slopes (linear trends) over the four angles of rotation, $F(1, 19) = 10.49$, $p = .0043$. The error term for this effect is $MS_{A \times B_{linear} \times S}$, replacing MS_{AS} in Equation 6.20:

$$\text{Partial } \hat{\omega}^2_{A \times B_{linear}} = \frac{1(4.102 - 0.391)}{1(4.102 - 0.391) + (2)(20)(0.391)} = .19$$

The two types of orientation also have different patterns (changes in slope) over rotation angle, as seen in the significant quadratic trend of the interaction (type_1*angle_2), with $F(1, 19) = 4.81$, $p = .041$. For effect size,

$$\text{Partial } \hat{\omega}^2_{A \times B_{quad}} = \frac{1(0.922 - 0.192)}{1(0.922 - 0.192) + (2)(20)(0.192)} = .09$$

There is no statistically reliable cubic trend of the interaction, $p = .7544$.

TABLE 6.48   Descriptive Statistics for Square Root Transformation of Repeated-Measures Data: SAS Data and Means Syntax and Output

```
data SASUSER.REACSQRT;
   set SASUSER.REACTIME;
   S_S0 = SQRT(S0);
   S_S60 = SQRT(S60);
   S_S120 = SQRT(S120);
   S_S180 = SQRT(S180);
   S_M0 = SQRT(M0);
   S_M60 = SQRT(M60);
   S_M120 = SQRT(M120);
   S_M180 = SQRT(M180);
run;
proc means data=SASUSER.REACSQRT vardef=df
         N MIN MAX MEAN STD VAR SKEWNESS KURTOSIS;
     var S_S0 S_S60 S_S120 S_S180 S_M0 S_M60 S_M120 S_M180;
run;
```

Variable	N	Minimum	Maximum	Mean	Std Dev
S_S0	20	20.4704665	23.4714720	21.9576297	0.9431169
S_S60	20	20.4646036	23.2241254	21.9869736	0.8242959
S_S120	20	20.7930277	26.3376157	22.4635189	1.2623367
S_S180	20	20.5630737	27.7632851	23.3195153	1.6776252
S_M0	20	20.9883301	24.3390633	22.5315384	1.1757543
S_M60	20	20.8667199	24.1240544	22.5929337	0.9888039
S_M120	20	20.7542767	27.3620175	22.8370978	1.5522365
S_M180	20	20.5864033	29.8338734	23.2957358	1.9893652

Variable	Variance	Skewness	Kurtosis
S_S0	0.8894694	0.2170095	-1.3601786
S_S60	0.6794637	-0.0377583	-1.1264405
S_S120	1.5934938	1.4753388	3.5694429
S_S180	2.8144263	0.9994462	1.9965889
S_M0	1.3823981	0.1642077	-1.6503563
S_M60	0.9777332	-0.0918186	-0.9522283
S_M120	2.4094382	1.2347343	2.5758677
S_M180	3.9575740	1.8231569	5.4112779

TABLE 6.49　Trend Analysis of Two-Way Repeated-Design:
SAS GLM Syntax and Selected Output

```
proc glm data=SASUSER.REACPLUS;
  model S_s0 S_s60 S_s120 S_s180 S_m0 S_m60 S_m120 S_m180 =;
  repeated type 2, angle 4 polynomial / mean summary nom;
run;
```

The GLM Procedure
Repeated Measures Analysis of Variance

Repeated Measures Level Information

Dependent Variable	S_S0	S_S60	S_S120	S_S180	S_M0	S_M60	S_M120	S_M180
Level of type	1	1	1	1	2	2	2	2
Level of angle	1	2	3	4	1	2	3	4

The GLM Procedure
Repeated Measures Analysis of Variance
Analysis of Variance of Contrast Variables

type_N represents the contrast between the nth level of type and
the last Contrast Variable: type_1

Source	DF	Type III SS	Mean Square	F Value	Pr > F
Mean	1	46.79768435	46.79768435	9.91	0.0053
Error	19	89.68845068	4.72044477		

angle_N represents the nth degree polynomial contrast for angle
Contrast Variable: angle_1

Source	DF	Type III SS	Mean Square	F Value	Pr > F
Mean	1	50.39520738	50.39520738	11.47	0.0031
Error	19	83.50809801	4.39516305		

Contrast Variable: angle_2

Source	DF	Type III SS	Mean Square	F Value	Pr > F
Mean	1	7.48959774	7.48959774	11.10	0.0035
Error	19	12.81538178	0.67449378		

Contrast Variable: angle_3

Source	DF	Type III SS	Mean Square	F Value	Pr > F
Mean	1	0.00129924	0.00129924	0.00	0.9585
Error	19	8.89360669	0.46808456		

TABLE 6.49   Continued

```
Contrast Variable: type_1*angle_1

     Source    DF    Type III SS    Mean Square    F Value    Pr > F

     Mean       1     4.10243072     4.10243072     10.49     0.0043
     Error     19     7.43242632     0.39118033

Contrast Variable: type_1*angle_2

     Source    DF    Type III SS    Mean Square    F Value    Pr > F

     Mean       1     0.92196416     0.92196416      4.81     0.0410
     Error     19     3.64387122     0.19178270

Contrast Variable: type_1*angle_3

     Source    DF    Type III SS    Mean Square    F Value    Pr > F

     Mean       1     0.00989138     0.00989138      0.10     0.7544
     Error     19     1.86472067     0.09814319
```

```
                  Means of Within Subjects Effects

            Level of
            type          N          Mean        Std Dev

            1            80     22.43190940     1.32069823
            2            80     22.81432640     1.47999689

            Level of
            angle         N          Mean        Std Dev

            1            40     22.24458406     1.09144922
            2            40     22.28995367     0.94947512
            3            40     22.65030832     1.40923074
            4            40     23.30762554     1.81640431

     Level of      Level of
     type          angle        N          Mean        Std Dev

     1            1            20     21.95762975     0.94311688
     1            2            20     21.98697363     0.82429586
     1            3            20     22.46351889     1.26233666
     1            4            20     23.31951533     1.67762519
     2            1            20     22.53153838     1.17575427
     2            2            20     22.59293371     0.98880394
     2            3            20     22.83709775     1.55223650
     2            4            20     23.29573576     1.98936522
```

Parameter estimates for the interaction are cell means and standard errors, produced in Table 6.50 from data in Table 6.48. In each case, the standard error of the mean is the standard deviation divided by the square root of n (i.e., $\sqrt{20} = 4.472$).

The interaction is interpreted by plotting the cell means of Table 6.50 in Figure 6.4. This is most easily done in a spreadsheet or word processing program because the absence of randomized-groups variables makes plotting difficult in all statistical software packages reviewed here except SPSS GLM.

The plot shows that the linear trend of the interaction has a shallower slope for mirror orientation trials; that is, the angle of rotation has less influence on (square root of) reaction time with mirror-imaged than standard trials. Thus, the difference between standard and mirror-imaged trials diminishes with greater angles of rotation. The quadratic trend of the interaction shows that the greater acceleration for standard trials is only for angles of rotation greater than 60°. That is, curves are parallel up to 60°; increase in reaction time between 0° and 60° is the same for standard and mirror-image trials.

There also is a significant difference in square root of reaction time due to standard versus mirror-imaged orientation, $F(1, 19) = 9.91, p = .0053$; however, interpretation of the main effect is problematic due to presence of strong interaction. If main effects are to be interpreted, marginal means are found in Table 6.48: 22.432 for standard orientation and 22.814 for mirror orientation.

Angle of rotation shows the expected significant linear trend (angle_1), with $F(1, 19) = 11.10$, $p = .0031$. There also is a significant quadratic trend (angle_2), with $F(1, 19) = 11.47, p = .0035$. No significant cubic trend is evident, $p = .9585$. Again, interpretation of trends in angle of rotation is problematic in the face of significant trends of the interaction.

Table 6.51 is a checklist for factorial repeated-measures ANOVA. An example of a Results section in journal format for the study described follows.

TABLE 6.50   Mean Square Root of Reaction Time as a Function of Type of Presentation and Angle of Rotation

	Angle of Rotation			
	0°	60°	120°	180°
Type				
Standard				
M	21.96	21.99	22.46	23.32
SE_M	0.21	0.18	0.28	0.38
Mirror				
M	22.53	22.59	22.84	23.30
SE_M	0.26	0.22	0.35	0.44

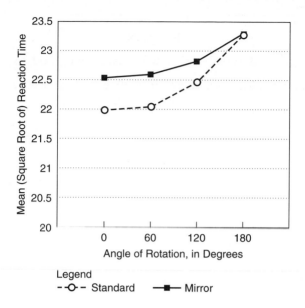

**FIGURE 6.4   Mean Square Root of Reaction Time
as a Function of Angle of Rotation
and Standard versus Mirror Orientation**

TABLE 6.51   Checklist for Factorial Repeated-Measures ANOVA

1. Issues
   a. Missing data
   b. Normality of sampling distributions
   c. Homogeneity of variance
   d. Sphericity
   e. Outliers
2. Major analyses
   a. Main effects or planned comparisons. If significant:
      (1) Effect size(s)
      (2) Parameter estimates (marginal means and standard errors or
           standard deviations or confidence intervals)
   b. Interactions or planned comparisons. If significant:
      (1) Effect size(s)
      (2) Parameter estimates (cell means in table and/or plot)
3. Additional analyses
   a. Post hoc comparisons
   b. Interpretation of departure from homogeneity of variance, if appropriate

Results

A 2 × 4 repeated-measures design was analyzed using planned trend analysis on reaction time for 20 participants. Factors were two types of orientation (standard and mirror image), and four angles of rotation (0°, 60°, 120°, and 180°). Reaction times were positively skewed, and an outlying score was noted among the mirror-imaged trials at 180°. A square root transformation of reaction times normalized the distributions adequately and the extreme score was no longer an outlier.

Cell means are shown in Table 6.50 (with standard errors) and are plotted in Figure 6.4. Statistically reliable effects included the main effect of type of orientation, linear and quadratic trends of angle of rotation, and the linear and quadratic trends of the interaction. Interpretation, therefore, is limited to interaction.

Increase in square root of reaction time as a function of increasing angle of rotation was greater for mirror-imaged than standard trials, producing a significant linear trend of the interaction, $F(1, 19) = 10.49$, $p = .0043$, partial $\hat{\omega}^2 = .19$. Thus, the greater the angle of rotation, the less the advantage of standard orientation. The quadratic trend of the interaction also was statistically reliable, $F(1, 19) = 4.81$, $p = .041$, partial $\hat{\omega}^2 = .09$, indicating that the linear trend of the interaction is limited to trials with greater angles of rotation. The difference between 0° and 60° angles is the same for standard and mirror-imaged trials.

6.8   Comparison of Programs

The programs reviewed in Table 5.52 handle repeated-measures ANOVA. MINITAB GLM requires a data set format that is different from other programs for repeated-measures ANOVA, as well as hand calculation of some F ratios. Table 6.52 summarizes features of the programs that are unique to repeated measures designs. Other features are reviewed elsewhere, particularly in Sections 4.8 and 5.8.

**TABLE 6.52   Comparison of SPSS, SYSTAT, SAS, and MINITAB Programs
for Repeated-Measures ANOVA**

Feature	SPSS GLM	SAS GLM	SAS MIXED[a]	MINITAB GLM	SYSTAT ANOVA and GLM
Input					
Special specification for trend (poly-nomial) analysis	Polynomial (default)	Yes	No	No	PRINT= MEDIUM
Simple syntax to specify unequal spacing of levels for trend analysis	Yes	Yes	No	No	Yes
Specify error terms for effects and/or contrasts	Yes	Yes	N.A.	No	Yes
Uses maximum likelihood methods rather than ANOVA	No	No	Yes	No	No
Specify structure of variance-covariance matrix	No	No	Yes	No	No
Handles missing data without deleting cases	No	No	Yes	No	No
Requires data set format with one DV value per line	No	No	No	Yes	No
Requires hand calcula-tion of some F ratios	No	No	No	Yes	No
Output					
Standard ANOVA source table	Yes	Yes	No	No[c]	Yes
Mauchly test of sphericity	Yes	PRINTE	No	No	No
Greenhouse-Geisser and Huynh-Feldt epsilons	Yes	Yes	N.A.	No	Yes

(continued)

TABLE 6.52 Continued

Feature	SPSS GLM	SAS GLM	SAS MIXED[a]	MINITAB GLM	SYSTAT ANOVA and GLM
Lower bound epsilon	Yes	No	N.A.	No	No
Epsilon-adjusted df	Yes	No	N.A.	No	No
Greenhouse-Geisser and Huynh-Feldt probabilities	Yes	Yes	N.A.	No	Yes
Multivariate tests of repeated-measures effects	Yes	Yes	No	No	Yes
Printed residuals and predicted values	Yes	Yes	PREDICTED	No	No
Residuals and predicted values saved to file	Yes	Yes	Yes	No	Yes
Plots					
Plots of residuals against predicted values[b]	Yes	No	No	No	Yes
Profile plots of means	Yes	No	No	No	No

[a]Additional features described in Section 11.8.

[b]Saved values may be plotted through other programs in package.

[c]Requires hand calculation of some F ratios.

6.8.1 SPSS Package

GLM is a program in the SPSS package for repeated-measures ANOVA. The Windows menu system is especially easy to use for these analyses. The program has all the popular features for repeated-measures designs, with Mauchly's sphericity test, trend analysis, and multivariate tests printed out by default. Also printed are details for four univariate tests for each effect: sphericity assumed, Greenhouse-Geisser adjusted, Huynh-Feldt adjusted, and with a lower-bound adjustment (usually considered far too conservative), although a simpler output format is available if requested.

Residuals may be printed and/or saved to file, and a residuals plot is available by request. Section 5.7 show additional features common to SPSS GLM analyses, such as effect size, observed power, and user-specified contrasts.

6.8.2   SAS System

SAS does repeated-measures ANOVA through PROC GLM or ANOVA. The two procedures work identically for repeated-measures designs as described in this chapter. Multivariate output is produced by default, but trend analysis requires additional syntax. Sufficient information is available to evaluate sphericity and adjust for its failure, particularly if Mauchly's test is requested. SAS does only limited user-specified comparisons for repeated-measures designs; others require a special data set developed for each comparison.

SAS MIXED is available as an alternative to repeated-measures ANOVA in the event that sphericity is violated, and the structure of the variance-covariance matrix either is known or can be assumed to be related to distance between levels of the IV (cf. Section 6.6.2).

6.8.3   SYSTAT System

SYSTAT GLM is a good, easy-to-use, repeated-measures ANOVA program, particularly if trend analysis is to be used with unequal spacing of levels. Mauchly's sphericity test is not available, but Greenhouse-Geisser and Huynh-Feldt epsilon values and adjusted probabilities are shown. If these probabilities differ from the unadjusted probabilities, steps can be taken to deal with violation of sphericity (Section 6.6.2). A request for medium-level printing of output produces trend analysis in addition to the usual univariate repeated measures ANOVA and multivariate output. Plots of residuals versus predicted values are shown by default.

6.8.4   MINITAB Programs

MINITAB has no process for identifying repeated-measures IVs. However, the analysis may be done through MINITAB GLM by explicitly declaring cases to be an IV. This ensures that individual differences are accounted for and provides a source table that includes variances for cases and interactions between cases and repeated-measures IVs. The source table shows the correct F ratio for the highest-order interaction between repeated measures IVs, and remaining F ratios may be calculated using the case by IV interactions as error terms, as shown in Tables 6.18 and 6.36. This strategy requires that data be entered in a format different from that used by other programs: Each line has a column to identify the case, a column for each repeated-measures IV to identify its level, and a single column to identify the DV value for that combination of IV levels, as shown in Tables 6.17 and 6.35.

Thus, MINITAB GLM may be used for the basic repeated-measures ANOVA, and produces marginal and cell means (and standard deviations). However, there is no test for sphericity or adjustment for violation, nor is multivariate output provided. Trend analysis and other comparisons are done by developing separate data sets for each comparison.

6.9   Problem Sets

6.1 Put together the data set of Table 6.20 for testing the normality assumption as per Table 6.1.

6.2 Do an analysis of variance, including trend analysis, through computer software of the following data set. Assume the IV is trials, and the DV is time to ski a run.

Trial			
1	2	3	4
11	7	5	4
12	8	6	6
9	8	5	5
8	5	3	2
13	8	9	6
9	6	6	4
10	5	5	3
7	3	1	0
10	5	5	0
4	3	2	1

a. Test the assumptions of normality, homogeneity of variance, and sphericity.
b. Check for outliers.
c. Calculate effect size using a form of y^2 appropriate given the results of the sphericity test.
d. Write a results section assuming the trend analysis was planned.

6.3 Reanalyze the data (either by computer or by hand) in Table 6.20 (two-way repeated-measures) as a two-way randomized-groups design and compare values.

6.4 Do a two-way repeated-measures ANOVA for the following matched randomized-blocks design. A is comprised of two kinds of altimeters, digital and analog. B is position (high, low, right, left). The DV is accuracy of altimeter reading.

	A: Altimeter Type							
	a_1: Digital				a_2: Analog			
B: Position	High	Low	Left	Right	High	Low	Left	Right
	84	45	47	90	80	49	45	73
	69	28	12	68	33	43	18	46
	99	40	35	71	36	22	56	38
	70	35	29	59	51	20	42	50
	91	18	19	85	37	44	38	39

a. Test appropriate assumptions for factorial repeated-measures ANOVA.
b. Calculate effect size(s).
c. Do any post hoc analyses you feel are appropriate.
d. Write a results section.

6.5 Complete Problem 6.4 using the regression strategy of Table 6.26.

6.6 What is the relative efficiency of the analysis of Problem 6.2 of the repeated-measures design compared with a randomized-groups design?

Extending the Concepts

6.7 Develop the variance sources, df, and error terms for a three-way repeated-measures design.

7

Mixed Randomized-Repeated Designs

7.1 General Purpose and Description

In this popular design, there are different cases at different levels of one (or more) randomized-groups IV(s), and each case is measured repeatedly on one (or more) repeated-measures IV(s). The simplest mixed design is a two-way factorial with one IV of each type. For example, a marketing firm introduces a new product with several different promotional schemes in different cities, and tracks sales over the first 6 months. The different promotional schemes, randomly assigned to cities, are the levels of the randomized-groups IV, sales districts within cities are the cases, and months are the levels of the repeated-measures IV. The DV is sales figures. Or a pharmaceutical company tests the effectiveness over several hours of a new over-the-counter analgesic for patients with three different types of pain (arthritic, headache, and lower back). Type of pain is the randomized-groups IV, trials (time) is the repeated measure, and patients are the cases. The DV is pain relief.

This design is sometimes called a split-plot design[1] due to its origins in an agricultural setting. A piece of land was split into several different plots (strips) for treatment with different fertilizers (or whatever) and repeated measures were made along the length of each strip.

This design provides an analysis of the effects of each IV separately, and their interaction(s). There is no limit (beyond the endurance of the researcher) to the number of IVs of each type that are included in the design.[2] However, if the study is an experiment, at least one of the IVs is manipulated. In the marketing example, promotional schemes are manipulated and randomly assigned. In the pharmaceutical example, the randomized-groups IV (type of pain) is a selected characteristic of the cases and the repeated measure is trials; neither is manipulated.

As in purely repeated-measures designs, the repeated-measures IVs can be of a type where the levels (or combination of levels) are in a predetermined order (trials/time, distance) or where the order in which levels are presented is arbitrary. Control of extraneous variables over the time period is essential for either type of IV. However, additional controls are possible when the order of presentation of the repeated measure is flexible. These controls are the subject of Chapter 9.

---

[1]The design also sometimes is referred to simply as "repeated measures" even though there are one or more randomized-groups IVs.

[2]One of our Ph.D. dissertations had two randomized groups and three repeated-measures IVs, this before computerized statistical software!

There are two major advantages to this type of design. The first is the test of the generalizability of the repeated-measures IV(s) over the levels of the randomized-groups IV(s) when the randomized-groups IV is a selected characteristic of cases. If a repeated-measures IV produces a different pattern of results at different levels of the randomized-groups IV, there is significant interaction and knowledge that the effects of the repeated-measures IV apply differently to different groups. For example, does the new analgesic show the same pattern of pain relief over time for those with arthritic pain, headache pain, and lower back pain (no interaction) or is there a different pattern of relief over time for different types of pain (interaction)?

The second advantage is the (usually) increased power due to the (usually) smaller error terms associated with the repeated-measures segment of the design. As in the purely repeated-measures design, differences among cases are assessed and removed from the repeated-measures error terms.[3] These error terms are used with both the repeated-measures IV(s) and the interaction(s) with repeated measures, so power for these effects is increased.

A disadvantage of the design is addition of the complexities of repeated measures to those of randomized groups. For instance, the design has all of the assumptions of randomized-groups analyses plus the assumptions of repeated-measures analyses (e.g., sphericity). It also has all of the complexity of comparisons in randomized groups plus the complexity of comparisons in repeated measures (where separate error terms are used). For example, some simple main effects are randomized groups, whereas other simple main effects are repeated measures.

7.2   Kinds of Research Questions

7.2.1   Effects of the IVs

Are the means different at different levels of the randomized-groups IV(s)? The repeated-measures IV(s)? Do the different promotional schemes produce different average sales? Are there mean differences over the 6 months of the promotion? Are there mean differences in pain relief associated with arthritic pain, headache pain, and lower back pain? Are pain assessments different over the several hours of measurement? These questions are answered in the usual ANOVA fashion by applying F tests to the data, as demonstrated in Section 7.4.

7.2.2   Effects of Interactions among IVs

Does the effect of one IV depend on the level of the other IV? For example, does one promotional scheme work well in the early months whereas another works later or not at all? Is the pattern of pain relief over hours the same for the different types of pain? For example, does the new analgesic work more rapidly for headache pain than for arthritic pain or lower back pain? F tests to answer these questions are in Section 7.4.

7.2.3   Parameter Estimates

What means are anticipated in the population for each level of the reliable effects in the design? What sales are predicted for each promotional scheme over the months? What average pain relief is pre-

---

[3]The sum of squares for differences among cases is then partitioned into the randomized-groups effects and their error term.

dicted for each type of pain over the hours of the study? These are calculated as in any factorial ANOVA, as described in Section 5.2.4.

7.2.4   Effect Sizes

How much of the variability in the DV is associated with each reliable effect in the design? How much of the variability in sales is associated with type of sales promotion? With months? With their interaction? How much of the variability in pain relief is associated with type of pain? With hours? With their interaction? Section 5.6.2 describes η^2 (Equation 5.13) and partial η^2 (Equation 5.14) for factorial designs. These equations are appropriate for mixed randomized-repeated designs with the use of the proper error term, as described in Section 7.4.

7.2.5   Power

Are there enough cases to reveal differences when the differences are real? Are enough sales districts included in each city to reveal real differences in promotional schemes? Are enough cases included for each type of pain to show that the analgesic really works better for one type of pain than another? Are consistent individual differences among cases strong enough to counteract the decrease in error df? The basic procedures described in Section 5.6.3 for calculating power and determining sample size apply.

7.2.6   Specific Comparisons

If an IV of either type has more than two levels, which levels are different from which other levels? Which sales promotion scheme is most effective? Is it more effective than the next most effective one? When are sales at their peak? Does the analgesic work better for one type of pain than another? Is there a linear or quadratic trend to pain relief over hours? Sections 7.6.1 through 7.6.5 describe procedures for specific comparisons in mixed randomized-repeated designs.

7.3   Assumptions and Limitations

7.3.1   Theoretical Issues

The same issues of causal inference and generalizability accrue to mixed designs as to randomized-groups or repeated-measures designs. If causal inference is intended, the levels of an IV are manipulated, with random assignment of cases and control of extraneous variables. Similarly, results generalize to the kinds of cases included in the design, although, as mentioned before, the generalizability of various effects is often tested directly in this design with use of selected characteristics of cases to compose (one or more of) the randomized-groups IV(s). For instance, suppose levels of A represent items/people of different age (young and old) and the levels of B represent tests at two different times (early and late). A significant interaction implies that young and old cases show a different pattern of responses over the two time periods. Or if levels of B represent two different doses of drugs, the interaction reveals that young and old cases have different reactions to the two doses. If cases are people, this result implies that prescribing should be contingent on age.

7.3.2   Practical Issues

7.3.2.1   *Normality of Sampling Distributions*

In the mixed design, normality of sampling distributions for the randomized-groups IV(s) applies to case averages (where scores have been combined over the levels of the repeated measure). For the randomized-groups IV(s), this requirement is satisfied if there are roughly equal sample sizes in each level (or combination of levels) of the randomized-groups IV(s), approximately 20 df for the randomized-groups error term, and two-tailed tests are used. If these criteria are not met, follow the procedures for randomized-groups designs as described in Chapters 4 and 5.

Criteria for the repeated-measures segments of the design are as indicated in Chapter 6. Recall that you have to generate the necessary DV scores if a test of their skewness is required. With marked skewness and inadequate df for error, data transformation often is desirable. There are no nonparametric alternatives for analysis of a mixed design.

7.3.2.2   *Homogeneity of Variance*

Homogeneity of variance in the mixed design is required at each level (or combination of levels) of the randomized-groups IV(s). Follow the procedures discussed in Chapters 4 (Sections 4.3.2.2 and 4.5.5) and 5 (Sections 5.3.2.2 and 5.8.1.2) for assessing homogeneity of variance and dealing with its violation for the randomized-groups portion of the design. Homogeneity of variance for the repeated-measures portion of the design is handled as described in Section 6.3.2.2.

7.3.2.3   *Independence of Errors, Additivity, and Sphericity*

Independence of errors is required for the randomized-groups error term, as discussed in Section 4.3.2.3. However, each repeated-measures error term confounds random variability with the cases by effects interaction, so assumptions of independence of error and additivity are intertwined. The requirement is for sphericity (as discussed in Sections 6.3.2.3 and 6.6.2) and data are tested through Mauchly's test, as in purely repeated-measures designs.[4]

SPSS GLM and SAS GLM (by request) provide Mauchly's test for each repeated-measures effect in the design. If the test fails (there is heterogeneity) for one or more effects, the usual three alternatives are available for analysis of that effect: single df comparisons, Huynh-Feldt corrections, or multivariate tests. SYSTAT provides the Huynh-Feldt correction, but not Mauchly's test. MINITAB provides no information about sphericity, because it does not recognize a repeated-measures design.

Note that the Mauchly test is for the average variance-covariance matrix over the levels of the randomized-groups IV. It is possible to have homogeneity of variance-covariance matrices for some groups but not others. Because groups are sometimes deleted during development of special error

---

[4]In the mixed design, there is a variance-covariance matrix (cf. Section 6.6.2) of the repeated-measures DVs at each level (or combination of levels) of the randomized-groups IV(s). Error terms are developed from the average variance-covariance matrix over the several groups and the reasonableness of those terms for omnibus ANOVA depends on the reasonableness of averaging. Tests of homogeneity of variance-covariance matrices are available, for example, Box's *M* test in SPSS GLM. However, these tests are overly sensitive to small departures from the assumption that may have little or no effect on nominal probabilities of Type I error rate. Although violation of homogeneity of variance-covariance matrices affects Type I error rate in the repeated-measures portion of the design, those biases are expected to be detected by Mauchly's test of sphericity.

terms for comparisons, the assumption may be met for some comparisons but not others. If you use SPSS GLM, each run for a comparison provides Mauchly's test for that comparison and you have the same options of single df comparisons, Huynh-Feldt corrections, or multivariate tests if there is violation.

7.3.2.4 Absence of Outliers

Outliers have the same unpredictable effect on analysis of the mixed design as in any other ANOVA and are identified using the same criteria of large z score and disconnectedness as in any other design. *Search for outliers separately for each cell of the design.* Thus, each repeated-measures DV is evaluated separately (as described in Section 6.3.2.4) in each level (or combination of levels) of the randomized-groups IV(s). This is demonstrated in Section 7.7. If an outlier is found, you have the same options as in any repeated-measures design.

7.3.2.5 Missing Data and Unequal Sample Sizes

Because portions of the mixed design are repeated measures, you may be able to estimate one or two data points using procedures discussed in Section 6.3.2.5. Unequal sample sizes in levels of a single randomized-groups IV pose no problem. However, unequal samples sizes create the usual problems of nonorthogonality if the randomized-groups portion of the design is itself factorial, that is, if there is more than one randomized-groups IV, as discussed in Section 5.6.5.

7.4   Fundamental Equations

In many ways, the mixed design combines material in Chapters 4, 5, and 6. Different cases appear in the different levels (or combination of levels) of the randomized-groups IV(s), but provide a DV value at each level (or combination of levels) of the repeated-measures IV(s). Therefore, the organization of data for both traditional ANOVA and the regression approach is literally a combination of the organizations for randomized groups and repeated measures. The error terms are also a literal combination of randomized-groups and repeated-measures error terms.

7.4.1   Allocation of Cases

The simplest mixed design has two IVs, one of each type, as shown in Table 7.1. The first three cases are in level a_1 and the last three cases are in level a_2. Therefore, A is a randomized-groups IV. All cases provide a DV value at both b_1 and b_2, so B is a repeated-measures IV.

Remember crossing and nesting from Section 1.2.5? In this design, cases nest in levels of A; s_1, s_2, and s_3 are nested in a_1 and s_4, s_5, and s_6 are nested in a_2. Therefore, one effect in the analysis is S/A. Meanwhile, cases cross levels of B, so another effect in the analysis is $B \times S$. Notice, however, that cases cross levels of B within each level of A. There is one $B \times S$ cross at a_1 and another $B \times S$ cross at a_2. So each $B \times S$ cross is really nested within levels of A, $B \times S/A$. Understanding this is important for understanding the error terms that are developed during the analysis. However, the main effects of A and B and the $A \times B$ interaction are logically and computationally identical to any other factorial design.

TABLE 7.1 **Allocation of Cases in a Two-Way Mixed Design**

Repeated Measures			
		b_1	b_2
Randomized Groups	a_1	s_1 s_2 s_3	s_1 s_2 s_3
	a_2	s_4 s_5 s_6	s_4 s_5 s_6

7.4.2 Partition of Sources of Variance

The partition of the sum of squares is best conceptualized as a split between the randomized-groups and the repeated-measures segments of the design:

$$SS_T = SS_{randomized} + SS_{repeated} \tag{7.1}$$

This fundamental split is differences between cases (randomized groups) and differences within cases (repeated measures). The randomized-groups segment sums to SS_S from the purely repeated-measures design. This effect is missing from the mixed design because it is further partitioned into A and S/A, the main effect of A and its error term. That is, differences in cases are due both to effects produced by levels of A and to otherwise unexplained variability in cases, just as in a randomized-groups design.

$$SS_{randomized} = SS_A + SS_{S/A} \tag{7.2}$$

The repeated-measures segment of the design is partitioned into B, $A \times B$, and $B \times S/A$ (the main effect of B, the $A \times B$ interaction, and the error term for these two sources of variability).

$$SS_{repeated} = SS_B + SS_{AB} + SS_{B \times S/A} \tag{7.3}$$

As expected, the error term for the randomized-groups segment is a nested term and the error term for the repeated-measures segment is a crossed term.

Degrees of freedom follow the partition of the sums of squares:

$$df_T = df_{randomized} + df_{repeated} = df_A + df_{S/A} + df_B + df_{AB} + df_{B \times S/A} \tag{7.4}$$

Total degrees of freedom is the total number of scores, *abs*, minus 1, lost when the grand mean is estimated; therefore:

$$df_T = abs - 1 \tag{7.5}$$

Degrees of freedom for the randomized-groups part of the design are $as - 1$, the same as the total in a one-way randomized-groups ANOVA, substituting s for n. Degrees of freedom for the randomized-groups part are further partitioned into df for the main effect of A, $a - 1$ as usual, and $a(s - 1)$, corresponding to the error term in a one-way randomized-groups design.

$$\text{df}_{\text{randomized}} = as - 1 = a - 1 + a(s - 1) \tag{7.6}$$

Degrees of freedom for the repeated portion of the design are $abs - as$, and are further partitioned into the main effect of B, $b - 1$; the $A \times B$ interaction, $(a - 1)(b - 1)$; and the interaction of B with S, which in turn is nested within A, $a(b - 1)(s - 1)$:

$$\text{df}_{\text{repeated}} = abs - as = b - 1 + (a - 1)(b - 1) + a(b - 1)(s - 1) \tag{7.7}$$

Verifying the partition for the repeated portion of the design:

$$abs - as - b - 1 + ab - a - b + 1 + abs - ab - as + a$$

Figure 7.1 diagrams the partition of sums of squares and degrees of freedom for the two-way randomized-repeated design.

There are a couple of things to notice about the analysis for a mixed design. The first is that repeated measures are kind of "sticky." The $A \times B$ interaction, for instance, contains both a randomized-group effect and a repeated-measures effect, but is analyzed in the repeated-measures part of the

(a) Sums of Squares

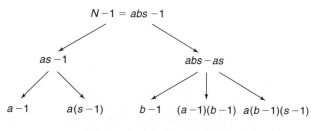

(b) Degrees of Freedom

FIGURE 7.1 Partition of (a) Sums of Squares and (b) Degrees of Freedom in a Mixed Randomized-Repeated Design

design. That is generally true: Any interaction term that contains one (or more) repeated-measures main effect(s) is analyzed as part of the repeated-measures segment of the design. The error terms for the repeated-measures effects in the design are always cases crossed with (in interaction with) effects, which in turn are nested in the randomized-groups effects in the designs. This generalizes to extensions of the design, as shown in Section 7.5.2.

7.4.3 Traditional ANOVA for the Mixed Design

An unrealistically small, hypothetical 3×3 data set for a two-way mixed design is in Table 7.2. There are three levels of each IV to illustrate comparisons. Type of novel (A) is the randomized-groups IV with three levels (science fiction, mystery, and romance). A total of 15 readers participate

TABLE 7.2   Hypothetical Data Set for a Mixed Design

		B: Month			
		b_1: Month 1	b_2: Month 2	b_3: Month 3	**Case Totals**
a_1: Science Fiction	s_1	1	3	6	$A_1S_1 = 10$
	s_2	1	4	8	$A_1S_2 = 13$
	s_3	3	3	6	$A_1S_3 = 12$
	s_4	5	5	7	$A_1S_4 = 17$
	s_5	2	4	5	$A_1S_5 = 11$
		$A_1B_1 = 12$	$A_1B_2 = 19$	$A_1B_3 = 32$	$A_1 = 63$
a_2: Mystery	s_6	3	1	0	$A_2S_6 = 4$
	s_7	4	4	2	$A_2S_7 = 10$
	s_8	5	3	2	$A_2S_8 = 10$
	s_9	4	2	0	$A_2S_9 = 6$
	s_{10}	4	5	3	$A_2S_{10} = 12$
		$A_2B_1 = 20$	$A_2B_2 = 15$	$A_2B_3 = 7$	$A_2 = 42$
a_3: Romance	s_{11}	4	2	0	$A_3S_{11} = 6$
	s_{12}	2	6	1	$A_3S_{12} = 9$
	s_{13}	3	3	3	$A_3S_{13} = 9$
	s_{14}	6	2	1	$A_3S_{14} = 9$
	s_{15}	3	3	2	$A_3S_{15} = 8$
		$A_3B_1 = 18$	$A_3B_2 = 16$	$A_3B_3 = 7$	$A_3 = 41$
		$B_1 = 50$	$B_2 = 50$	$B_3 = 46$	$T = 146$

in the study, 5 readers each randomly assigned to read only novels of one type for 3 months. Month is the repeated-measures IV, B. Number of novels read each month still serves as the DV. Both the IVs are fixed—specific levels are selected by the researcher. Readers (cases) are a random factor, but are not tested explicitly.

The equations for the main effects and interaction of interest, A, B, and $A \times B$, are identical to those in both factorial randomized-groups analysis (Chapter 5) and factorial repeated-measures analysis (Chapter 6). In general, computations for main effects and interactions are "blind" to the way cases are used in a design. The analysis is similar to repeated measures in that case totals (AS) are needed to assess overall differences among cases—a source of variability that is then partitioned into A and S/A. The last source of variability is $B \times S/A$, the error term for the repeated-measures portion of the analysis. Computational equations for sums of squares for mixed ANOVA appear in Table 7.3. As always, A and B are fixed IVs; cases (S) are random, presumably randomly selected from some larger population of cases. Sums of squares are in Table 7.4. The equations and computations for degrees of freedom for this example are in Table 7.5.

Finally, Table 7.6 summarizes the results of the calculations and shows the mean squares and F values for each effect. As you examine the F ratios, notice the pattern of effects and error terms. The error term for A is S/A and the error term for B and $A \times B$ is $B \times S/A$.

Each effect in the table is tested against critical F with its own df. Critical F for the test of A (type of novel) at $\alpha = .05$ with 2 and 12 df is 3.88; the null hypothesis of no mean differences among science fiction, mystery, and romance novels read is rejected because 4.68 is greater than 3.88. A

TABLE 7.3   Computational Equations for Sums of Squares for Mixed-Design ANOVA

$$SS_A = \frac{\sum A^2}{bs} - \frac{T^2}{abs} \qquad = \frac{63^2 + 42^2 + 41^2}{3(5)} - \frac{146^2}{3(3)(5)}$$

$$SS_{S/A} = \frac{\sum (AS)^2}{b} - \frac{\sum A^2}{bs} \qquad = \frac{10^2 + 13^2 + 12^2 + \cdots + 8^2}{3} - \frac{63^2 + 42^2 + 41^2}{3(5)}$$

$$SS_B = \frac{\sum B^2}{as} - \frac{T^2}{abs} \qquad = \frac{50^2 + 50^2 + 46^2}{3(5)} - \frac{146^2}{3(3)(5)}$$

$$SS_{AB} = \frac{\sum (AB)^2}{s} - \frac{\sum A^2}{bs} - \frac{\sum B^2}{as} + \frac{T^2}{abs} \qquad = \frac{12^2 + 19^2 + 32^2 + 20^2 + 15^2 + 7^2 + 18^2 + 16^2 + 7^2}{5}$$
$$- \frac{63^2 + 42^2 + 41^2}{3(5)} - \frac{50^2 + 50^2 + 46^2}{3(5)} + \frac{146^2}{3(3)(5)}$$

$$SS_{B \times S/A} = \sum Y^2 - \frac{\sum (AB)^2}{s} \qquad = 1^2 + 1^2 + 3^2 + 5^2 + 2^2 + 3^2 + 4^2 + 5^2 + \cdots + 1^2 + 2^2$$
$$- \frac{\sum (AS)^2}{s} + \frac{\sum A^2}{bs} \qquad - \frac{12^2 + 19^2 + 32^2 + 20^2 + 15^2 + 7^2 + 18^2 + 16^2 + 7^2}{5}$$
$$- \frac{10^2 + 13^2 + \cdots + 8^2}{3} + \frac{63^2 + 42^2 + 41^2}{3(5)}$$

$$SS_T = \sum Y^2 - \frac{T^2}{abs} \qquad = 1^2 + 1^2 + 3^2 + 5^2 + 2^2 + 3^2 + \cdots + 1^2 + 2^2 - \frac{146^2}{3(3)(5)}$$

**TABLE 7.4   Sums of Squares
for Mixed-Design ANOVA**

SS_A	$= 494.27 - 473.69$	$= 20.58$
$SS_{S/A}$	$= 520.67 - 494.27$	$= 26.40$
SS_B	$= 474.40 - 473.69$	$= 0.71$
SS_{AB}	$= 566.40 - 494.27 - 474.40 + 473.69 =$	71.42
$SS_{B \times S/A}$	$= 630 - 566.40 - 520.67 + 494.27$	$= 37.20$
SS_T	$= 630 - 473.69$	$= 156.31$

**TABLE 7.5   Degrees of Freedom
for Mixed-Design ANOVA**

df_A	$= a - 1$	$= 3 - 1$	$= 2$
$df_{S/A}$	$= a(s - 1)$	$= 3(5 - 1)$	$= 12$
df_B	$= b - 1$	$= 3 - 1$	$= 2$
df_{AB}	$= (a - 1)(b - 1)$	$= (3 - 1)(3 - 1)$	$= 4$
$df_{B \times S/A}$	$= a(b - 1)(s - 1)$	$= 3(3 - 1)(5 - 1)$	$= 24$
SS_T	$= abs - 1 = N - 1 = 3(3)(5) - 1$		$= 44$

TABLE 7.6   Source Table for Mixed-Design ANOVA

Source	SS	df	MS	F
Randomized Groups				
A	20.58	2	10.29	$\dfrac{10.29}{2.20} = 4.68$
S/A	26.40	12	2.20	
Repeated Measures				
B	0.71	2	0.36	$\dfrac{0.36}{1.55} = 0.23$
$A \times B$	71.42	4	17.86	$\dfrac{17.86}{1.55} = 11.52$
$B \times S/A$	37.20	24	1.55	
T	156.31	44		

glance at the numbers in Table 7.2 suggests that, overall, more science fiction novels are read, a conclusion tested in Section 7.6.1.1 (main effects analysis for randomized groups). Critical F for the test of B (month) at $\alpha = .05$ with 2 and 24 df is 3.40; the null hypothesis of no mean difference in number of novels read per month is retained because 0.23 is less than 3.40. Finally, critical F for the type of novel by month interaction at $\alpha = .05$ with 4 and 24 df is 2.78; the null hypothesis of no interaction of number of novels read per month by type of novel is rejected because 11.52 is greater than 2.78. The numbers in Table 7.2 suggest that the number of science fiction novels read increases over the 3 months, whereas the numbers of mystery novels and romance novels stay steady or decrease. This informal observation is tested by the procedures of Section 7.6.3 or 7.6.4 (simple-effects trend analysis or interaction contrasts).

As an aside, it should be noted that the analysis of the randomized-groups part of this design, A and S/A, is identical to a one-way randomized-groups ANOVA of the case totals.

7.4.4 Regression Approach to the Mixed Design

The mixed nature of this design carries over into the regression approach to the analysis. Columns are needed for Y and for each df in the design, 44 in this example. The 44 columns that partition the variability represent each df for main effects, for interaction, and for cases, still treated like another main effect. An additional 44 columns (not shown) are needed for the cross of each of the first 44 columns with Y. The last 44 columns produce the sums of products that are summarized under the first 44 columns as SP. The data set of Table 7.2 is rearranged for regression analysis in Table 7.7.

There are many things to notice about Table 7.7. Levels of A (3), B (3), and case designations are provided and repeated for clarification. Cases 1 to 5 repeat three times, once for each level of B at a_1; cases 6 to 10 also repeat three times, once for each level of B at a_2 and cases 11 to 15 repeat three times at a_3. The DV scores, Y, are in a single column with scores for the same cases organized by level of B. Columns X_1 and X_2 contain contrast coefficients for the two df for A; the first coefficients compare a_1 with pooled results from a_2 and a_3, the second a_2 versus a_3. These two columns are an orthogonal partition of the sum of squares for A. X_3 and X_4 contain codes for B_{linear} and B_{quad}, respectively. (Note that signs for the quadratic trend coefficients are $-1, 2, -1$ instead of $1, -2, 1$. This has no effect on the results.) These two columns are an orthogonal partition of the sum of squares for B. Columns X_5 to X_8 are columns for $A_{\text{comp1}} \times B_{\text{linear}}$, $A_{\text{comp1}} \times B_{\text{quad}}$, $A_{\text{comp2}} \times B_{\text{linear}}$, and $A_{\text{comp2}} \times B_{\text{quad}}$, respectively. These four columns are an orthogonal partition of the sum of squares for the $A \times B$ interaction.

The two error terms, one nested and one crossed, are set up in columns X_9 to X_{44}. Columns X_9 to X_{20} literally represent the nesting of the five cases at each level of A. The same arbitrary but orthogonal coefficients for cases are used and repeated at each level of A. For example, X_9 contrasts case 1 with the other cases in a_1, and X_{13} contrasts case 6 with the other cases in a_2. X_{12} contrasts cases 4 and 5 in a_1, and so on. Notice that the nesting arrangement for cases is preserved in the coding where zeros "blank out" the cases that are not in that level of A. These 12 columns (X_9 to X_{20}) are an orthogonal partition of sum of squares S/A (which has 12 df).

The last 24 columns (X_{21} to X_{44}) are the cross of B_{linear} with cases (X_{21} to X_{32}) and then B_{quad} with cases (X_{33} to X_{44}). These 24 columns are an orthogonal partition of the sum of squares for $B \times S/A$ (which has 24 df).

The remaining 44 columns are Y crossed with each of the 44 previous columns, necessary for computation of sums of products, but not shown. This problem is set up using a spreadsheet with

TABLE 7.7 Organization of Data for the Regression Approach to Mixed-Design ANOVA

			Y	A1 X_1	A2 X_2	Bl X_3	Bq X_4	A1*Bl X_5	A1*Bq X_6	A2*Bl X_7	A2*Bq X_8	A1,Sc1 X_9	A1,Sc2 X_{10}	A1,Sc3 X_{11}
		s_1	1	2	0	−1	−1	−2	−2	0	0	4	0	0
		s_2	1	2	0	−1	−1	−2	−2	0	0	−1	1	1
	b_1	s_3	3	2	0	−1	−1	−2	−2	0	0	−1	1	−1
		s_4	5	2	0	−1	−1	−2	−2	0	0	−1	−1	0
		s_5	2	2	0	−1	−1	−2	−2	0	0	−1	−1	0
		s_1	3	2	0	0	2	0	4	0	0	4	0	0
		s_2	4	2	0	0	2	0	4	0	0	−1	1	1
a_1	b_2	s_3	3	2	0	0	2	0	4	0	0	−1	1	−1
		s_4	5	2	0	0	2	0	4	0	0	−1	−1	0
		s_5	4	2	0	0	2	0	4	0	0	−1	−1	0
		s_1	6	2	0	1	−1	2	−2	0	0	4	0	0
		s_2	8	2	0	1	−1	2	−2	0	0	−1	1	1
	b_3	s_3	6	2	0	1	−1	2	−2	0	0	−1	1	−1
		s_4	7	2	0	1	−1	2	−2	0	0	−1	−1	0
		s_5	5	2	0	1	−1	2	−2	0	0	−1	−1	0
		s_6	3	−1	1	−1	−1	1	1	−1	−1	0	0	0
		s_7	4	−1	1	−1	−1	1	1	−1	−1	0	0	0
	b_1	s_8	5	−1	1	−1	−1	1	1	−1	−1	0	0	0
		s_9	4	−1	1	−1	−1	1	1	−1	−1	0	0	0
		s_{10}	4	−1	1	−1	−1	1	1	−1	−1	0	0	0
		s_6	1	−1	1	0	2	0	−2	0	2	0	0	0
		s_7	4	−1	1	0	2	0	−2	0	2	0	0	0
a_2	b_2	s_8	3	−1	1	0	2	0	−2	0	2	0	0	0
		s_9	2	−1	1	0	2	0	−2	0	2	0	0	0
		s_{10}	5	−1	1	0	2	0	−2	0	2	0	0	0
		s_6	0	−1	1	1	−1	−1	1	1	−1	0	0	0
		s_7	2	−1	1	1	−1	−1	1	1	−1	0	0	0
	b_3	s_8	2	−1	1	1	−1	−1	1	1	−1	0	0	0
		s_9	0	−1	1	1	−1	−1	1	1	−1	0	0	0
		s_{10}	3	−1	1	1	−1	−1	1	1	−1	0	0	0
		s_{11}	4	−1	−1	−1	−1	1	1	1	1	0	0	0
		s_{12}	2	−1	−1	−1	−1	1	1	1	1	0	0	0
	b_1	s_{13}	3	−1	−1	−1	−1	1	1	1	1	0	0	0
		s_{14}	6	−1	−1	−1	−1	1	1	1	1	0	0	0
		s_{15}	3	−1	−1	−1	−1	1	1	1	1	0	0	0
		s_{11}	2	−1	−1	0	2	0	−2	0	−2	0	0	0
		s_{12}	6	−1	−1	0	2	0	−2	0	−2	0	0	0
a_3	b_2	s_{13}	3	−1	−1	0	2	0	−2	0	−2	0	0	0
		s_{14}	2	−1	−1	0	2	0	−2	0	−2	0	0	0
		s_{15}	3	−1	−1	0	2	0	−2	0	−2	0	0	0
		s_{11}	0	−1	−1	1	−1	−1	1	−1	1	0	0	0
		s_{12}	1	−1	−1	1	−1	−1	1	−1	1	0	0	0
	b_3	s_{13}	3	−1	−1	1	−1	−1	1	−1	1	0	0	0
		s_{14}	1	−1	−1	1	−1	−1	1	−1	1	0	0	0
		s_{15}	2	−1	−1	1	−1	−1	1	−1	1	0	0	0
	sum		146	0	0	0	0	0	0	0	0	0	0	0
	sumsq		630	90	30	30	90	60	180	20	60	60	12	6
	ss		156.31	90	30	30	90	60	180	20	60	60	12	6
	sp			43	1	−4	4	64	−22	−2	−4	−13	−3	1
	ss(reg)			20.54	0.03	0.53	0.18	68.27	2.69	0.2	0.27	2.82	0.75	0.17

TABLE 7.7 Continued

			A1,Sc4 X_{12}	A2,Sc1 X_{13}	A2,Sc2 X_{14}	A2,Sc3 X_{15}	A2,Sc4 X_{16}	A3,Sc1 X_{17}	A3,Sc2 X_{18}	A3,Sc3 X_{19}	A3,Sc4 X_{20}	B1*Sc1 X_{21}	B1*Sc2 X_{22}
a_1	b_1	s_1	0	0	0	0	0	0	0	0	0	-4	0
		s_2	0	0	0	0	0	0	0	0	0	1	-1
		s_3	0	0	0	0	0	0	0	0	0	1	-1
		s_4	1	0	0	0	0	0	0	0	0	1	1
		s_5	-1	0	0	0	0	0	0	0	0	1	1
	b_2	s_1	0	0	0	0	0	0	0	0	0	0	0
		s_2	0	0	0	0	0	0	0	0	0	0	0
		s_3	0	0	0	0	0	0	0	0	0	0	0
		s_4	1	0	0	0	0	0	0	0	0	0	0
		s_5	-1	0	0	0	0	0	0	0	0	0	0
	b_3	s_1	0	0	0	0	0	0	0	0	0	4	0
		s_2	0	0	0	0	0	0	0	0	0	-1	1
		s_3	0	0	0	0	0	0	0	0	0	-1	1
		s_4	1	0	0	0	0	0	0	0	0	-1	-1
		s_5	-1	0	0	0	0	0	0	0	0	-1	-1
a_2	b_1	s_6	0	4	0	0	0	0	0	0	0	0	0
		s_7	0	-1	1	1	0	0	0	0	0	0	0
		s_8	0	-1	1	-1	0	0	0	0	0	0	0
		s_9	0	-1	-1	0	1	0	0	0	0	0	0
		s_{10}	0	-1	-1	0	-1	0	0	0	0	0	0
	b_2	s_6	0	4	0	0	0	0	0	0	0	0	0
		s_7	0	-1	1	1	0	0	0	0	0	0	0
		s_8	0	-1	1	-1	0	0	0	0	0	0	0
		s_9	0	-1	-1	0	1	0	0	0	0	0	0
		s_{10}	0	-1	-1	0	-1	0	0	0	0	0	0
	b_3	s_6	0	4	0	0	0	0	0	0	0	0	0
		s_7	0	-1	1	1	0	0	0	0	0	0	0
		s_8	0	-1	1	-1	0	0	0	0	0	0	0
		s_9	0	-1	-1	0	1	0	0	0	0	0	0
		s_{10}	0	-1	-1	0	-1	0	0	0	0	0	0
a_3	b_1	s_{11}	0	0	0	0	0	4	0	0	0	0	0
		s_{12}	0	0	0	0	0	-1	1	1	0	0	0
		s_{13}	0	0	0	0	0	-1	1	-1	0	0	0
		s_{14}	0	0	0	0	0	-1	-1	0	1	0	0
		s_{15}	0	0	0	0	0	-1	-1	0	-1	0	0
	b_2	s_{11}	0	0	0	0	0	4	0	0	0	0	0
		s_{12}	0	0	0	0	0	-1	1	1	0	0	0
		s_{13}	0	0	0	0	0	-1	1	-1	0	0	0
		s_{14}	0	0	0	0	0	-1	-1	0	1	0	0
		s_{15}	0	0	0	0	0	-1	-1	0	-1	0	0
	b_3	s_{11}	0	0	0	0	0	4	0	0	0	0	0
		s_{12}	0	0	0	0	0	-1	1	1	0	0	0
		s_{13}	0	0	0	0	0	-1	1	-1	0	0	0
		s_{14}	0	0	0	0	0	-1	-1	0	1	0	0
		s_{15}	0	0	0	0	0	-1	-1	0	-1	0	0
sum			0	0	0	0	0	0	0	0	0	0	0
sumsq			6	60	12	6	6	60	12	6	6	40	8
ss			6	60	12	6	6	60	12	6	6	40	8
sp			6	-22	2	0	-6	-11	1	0	1	5	5
ss(reg)			6	8.07	0.33	0	6	2.02	0.08	0	0.17	0.625	3.125

(continued)

TABLE 7.7   Continued

			Bl*Sc3 X_{23}	Bl*Sc4 X_{24}	Bl*Sc1 X_{25}	Bl*Sc2 X_{26}	Bl*Sc3 X_{27}	Bl*Sc4 X_{28}	Bl*Sc1 X_{29}	Bl*Sc2 X_{30}	Bl*Sc3 X_{31}	Bl*Sc4 X_{32}	Bq*Sc1 X_{33}
a_1	b_1	s_1	0	0	0	0	0	0	0	0	0	0	-4
		s_2	-1	0	0	0	0	0	0	0	0	0	1
		s_3	1	0	0	0	0	0	0	0	0	0	1
		s_4	0	-1	0	0	0	0	0	0	0	0	1
		s_5	0	1	0	0	0	0	0	0	0	0	1
	b_2	s_1	0	0	0	0	0	0	0	0	0	0	8
		s_2	0	0	0	0	0	0	0	0	0	0	-2
		s_3	0	0	0	0	0	0	0	0	0	0	-2
		s_4	0	0	0	0	0	0	0	0	0	0	-2
		s_5	0	0	0	0	0	0	0	0	0	0	-2
	b_3	s_1	0	0	0	0	0	0	0	0	0	0	-4
		s_2	1	0	0	0	0	0	0	0	0	0	1
		s_3	-1	0	0	0	0	0	0	0	0	0	1
		s_4	0	1	0	0	0	0	0	0	0	0	1
		s_5	0	-1	0	0	0	0	0	0	0	0	1
a_2	b_1	s_6	0	0	-4	0	0	0	0	0	0	0	0
		s_7	0	0	1	-1	-1	0	0	0	0	0	0
		s_8	0	0	1	-1	1	0	0	0	0	0	0
		s_9	0	0	1	1	0	-1	0	0	0	0	0
		s_{10}	0	0	1	1	0	1	0	0	0	0	0
	b_2	s_6	0	0	0	0	0	0	0	0	0	0	0
		s_7	0	0	0	0	0	0	0	0	0	0	0
		s_8	0	0	0	0	0	0	0	0	0	0	0
		s_9	0	0	0	0	0	0	0	0	0	0	0
		s_{10}	0	0	0	0	0	0	0	0	0	0	0
	b_3	s_6	0	0	4	0	0	0	0	0	0	0	0
		s_7	0	0	-1	1	1	0	0	0	0	0	0
		s_8	0	0	-1	1	-1	0	0	0	0	0	0
		s_9	0	0	-1	-1	0	1	0	0	0	0	0
		s_{10}	0	0	-1	-1	0	-1	0	0	0	0	0
a_3	b_1	s_{11}	0	0	0	0	0	0	-4	0	0	0	0
		s_{12}	0	0	0	0	0	0	1	-1	-1	0	0
		s_{13}	0	0	0	0	0	0	1	-1	1	0	0
		s_{14}	0	0	0	0	0	0	1	1	0	-1	0
		s_{15}	0	0	0	0	0	0	1	1	0	1	0
	b_2	s_{11}	0	0	0	0	0	0	0	0	0	0	0
		s_{12}	0	0	0	0	0	0	0	0	0	0	0
		s_{13}	0	0	0	0	0	0	0	0	0	0	0
		s_{14}	0	0	0	0	0	0	0	0	0	0	0
		s_{15}	0	0	0	0	0	0	0	0	0	0	0
	b_3	s_{11}	0	0	0	0	0	0	4	0	0	0	0
		s_{12}	0	0	0	0	0	0	-1	1	1	0	0
		s_{13}	0	0	0	0	0	0	-1	1	-1	0	0
		s_{14}	0	0	0	0	0	0	-1	-1	0	1	0
		s_{15}	0	0	0	0	0	0	-1	-1	0	-1	0
	sum		0	0	0	0	0	0	0	0	0	0	0
	sumsq		4	4	40	8	4	4	40	8	4	4	120
	ss		4	4	40	8	4	4	40	8	4	4	120
	sp		4	-1	-2	0	1	-3	-9	5	-1	-4	1
	ss(reg)		4	0.25	0.1	0	0.25	2.25	2.025	3.125	0.25	4	0.01

TABLE 7.7 Continued

			Bq*Sc2 X_{34}	Bq*Sc3 X_{35}	Bq*Sc4 X_{36}	Bq*Sc1 X_{37}	Bq*Sc2 X_{38}	Bq*Sc3 X_{39}	Bq*Sc4 X_{40}	Bq*Sc1 X_{41}	Bq*Sc2 X_{42}	Bq*Sc3 X_{43}	Bq*Sc4 X_{44}
a_1	b_1	s_1	0	0	0	0	0	0	0	0	0	0	0
		s_2	−1	−1	0	0	0	0	0	0	0	0	0
		s_3	−1	1	0	0	0	0	0	0	0	0	0
		s_4	1	0	−1	0	0	0	0	0	0	0	0
		s_5	1	0	1	0	0	0	0	0	0	0	0
	b_2	s_1	0	0	0	0	0	0	0	0	0	0	0
		s_2	2	2	0	0	0	0	0	0	0	0	0
		s_3	2	−2	0	0	0	0	0	0	0	0	0
		s_4	−2	0	2	0	0	0	0	0	0	0	0
		s_5	−2	0	−2	0	0	0	0	0	0	0	0
	b_3	s_1	0	0	0	0	0	0	0	0	0	0	0
		s_2	−1	−1	0	0	0	0	0	0	0	0	0
		s_3	−1	1	0	0	0	0	0	0	0	0	0
		s_4	1	0	−1	0	0	0	0	0	0	0	0
		s_5	1	0	1	0	0	0	0	0	0	0	0
a_2	b_1	s_6	0	0	0	−4	0	0	0	0	0	0	0
		s_7	0	0	0	1	−1	−1	0	0	0	0	0
		s_8	0	0	0	1	−1	1	0	0	0	0	0
		s_9	0	0	0	1	1	0	−1	0	0	0	0
		s_{10}	0	0	0	1	1	0	1	0	0	0	0
	b_2	s_6	0	0	0	8	0	0	0	0	0	0	0
		s_7	0	0	0	−2	2	2	0	0	0	0	0
		s_8	0	0	0	−2	2	−2	0	0	0	0	0
		s_9	0	0	0	−2	−2	0	2	0	0	0	0
		s_{10}	0	0	0	−2	−2	0	−2	0	0	0	0
	b_3	s_6	0	0	0	−4	0	0	0	0	0	0	0
		s_7	0	0	0	1	−1	−1	0	0	0	0	0
		s_8	0	0	0	1	−1	1	0	0	0	0	0
		s_9	0	0	0	1	1	0	−1	0	0	0	0
		s_{10}	0	0	0	1	1	0	1	0	0	0	0
a_3	b_1	s_{11}	0	0	0	0	0	0	0	−4	0	0	0
		s_{12}	0	0	0	0	0	0	0	1	−1	−1	0
		s_{13}	0	0	0	0	0	0	0	1	−1	1	0
		s_{14}	0	0	0	0	0	0	0	1	1	0	−1
		s_{15}	0	0	0	0	0	0	0	1	1	0	1
	b_2	s_{11}	0	0	0	0	0	0	0	8	0	0	0
		s_{12}	0	0	0	0	0	0	0	−2	2	2	0
		s_{13}	0	0	0	0	0	0	0	−2	2	−2	0
		s_{14}	0	0	0	0	0	0	0	−2	−2	0	2
		s_{15}	0	0	0	0	0	0	0	−2	−2	0	−2
	b_3	s_{11}	0	0	0	0	0	0	0	−4	0	0	0
		s_{12}	0	0	0	0	0	0	0	1	−1	−1	0
		s_{13}	0	0	0	0	0	0	0	1	−1	1	0
		s_{14}	0	0	0	0	0	0	0	1	1	0	−1
		s_{15}	0	0	0	0	0	0	0	1	1	0	1
sum			0	0	0	0	0	0	0	0	0	0	0
sumsq			24	12	12	120	24	12	12	120	24	12	12
ss			24	12	12	120	24	12	12	120	24	12	12
sp			−3	2	−3	−8	−2	3	−3	−7	11	9	−4
ss(reg)			0.38	0.33	0.75	0.53	0.17	0.75	0.75	0.41	5.04	6.75	1.33

sums, sum of squared values (sumsq), sum of squares (SS), sum of products (SP), and sum of squares for regression—SS(reg.)—computed using the spreadsheet software. Equations for computing preliminary sums of squares are in Table 6.25 and equations for computing sums of products are in Table 6.26. Table 7.8 summarizes the computations needed to produce the sum of squares for the various effects in the design.

These results are the same as those produced by the traditional ANOVA approach, within rounding error, as seen by comparing SS and df in Tables 7.6 and 7.8. The advantage is in the clarity of the layout of the design and in the separation of each df into a separate source of variability for follow-up analyses (cf. Section 7.6.5).

7.4.5   Computer Analyses of Small-Sample Mixed Design

The data set for mixed-design ANOVA is laid out as in Table 7.2. One column is needed to code the levels of each randomized-groups IV and the DV scores are given at each level of the repeated-measures IV. As in the purely repeated-measures design, the name of the repeated-measures IV and its levels are created "on the fly" through the statistical software in SPSS, SAS, and SYSTAT. If there is more than one repeated-measures IV, the DV scores are set up as in Table 6.31, with the same cautions about the necessity for consistency between the order in which DVs are presented in the data set and identified to the software.

Syntax and output from SPSS GLM for the example are in Table 7.9. Syntax is default except for the requests for /EMMEANS (marginal and cell means, standard errors, and confidence intervals).

After identification of the elements in the design, multivariate tests are given of the two effects with repeated measures, MONTH and MONTH*NOVEL, should you wish to take this approach to testing their significance. Mauchly's Test of Sphericity follows, nonsignificant in this example, indicating no violation of sphericity or homogeneity of variance-covariance matrix assumptions. Univariate tests of MONTH and MONTH*NOVEL follow, together with adjustments, including the Huynh-Feldt adjustment, if Mauchly's test is significant and you wish to take this approach to evaluating significance. This is followed by trend analysis of MONTH and MONTH*NOVEL, your third

TABLE 7.8   Sums of Squares for the Regression Approach to Mixed-Design ANOVA

Source	Columns		SS	df (Number of Columns)
A	$SS(reg.X_1) + SS(reg.X_2)$	$20.54 + 0.03$	20.57	2
S/A	$SS(reg.X_9) + SS(reg.X_{10}) + \cdots$ $+ SS(reg.X_{20})$	$2.82 + 0.75 + \cdots + 0.17$	26.40	12
B	$SS(reg.X_3) + SS(reg.X_4)$	$0.53 + 0.18$	0.71	2
$A \times B$	$SS(reg.X_5) + SS(reg.X_6)$ $+ SS(reg.X_7) + SS(reg.X_8)$	$68.27 + 2.69 + 0.20 + 0.27$	71.46	4
$B \times S/A$	$SS(reg.X_{21}) + SS(reg.X_{22}) + \cdots$ $+ SS(reg.X_{44})$	$0.62 + 3.12 + \cdots + 1.33$	37.20	24
Total	$SS(Y)$		156.31	44

TABLE 7.9   SPSS GLM Syntax and Output for Mixed-Design ANOVA

GLM
  month1 month2 month3 BY novel
  /WSFACTOR = month 3 Polynomial
  /MEASURE = books
  /METHOD = SSTYPE(3)
  /EMMEANS = TABLES(novel)
  /EMMEANS = TABLES(month)
  /EMMEANS = TABLES(novel*month)
  /CRITERIA = ALPHA(.05)
  /WSDESIGN = month
  /DESIGN=novel .

General Linear Model

Within-Subjects Factors

Measure: BOOKS

MONTH	Dependent Variable
1	MONTH1
2	MONTH2
3	MONTH3

Between-Subjects Factors

		Value Label	N
NOVEL	1.00	science fiction	5
	2.00	mystery	5
	3.00	romance	5

Multivariate Tests[c]

Effect		Value	F	Hypothesis df	Error df	Sig.
MONTH	Pillai's Trace	.062	.361[a]	2.000	11.000	.705
	Wilks' Lambda	.938	.361[a]	2.000	11.000	.705
	Hotelling's Trace	.066	.361[a]	2.000	11.000	.705
	Roy's Largest Root	.066	.361[a]	2.000	11.000	.705
MONTH * NOVEL	Pillai's Trace	.859	4.518	4.000	24.000	.007
	Wilks' Lambda	.155	8.463[a]	4.000	22.000	.000
	Hotelling's Trace	5.354	13.384	4.000	20.000	.000
	Roy's Largest Root	5.336	32.019[b]	2.000	12.000	.000

a. Exact statistic
b. The statistic is an upper bound on F that yields a lower bound on the significance level.
c.
  Design: Intercept+NOVEL
  Within-Subjects Design: MONTH

(continued)

TABLE 7.9   Continued

Mauchly's Test of Sphericity[b]

Measure: BOOKS

Within Subjects Effect	Mauchly's W	Approx. Chi-Square	df	Sig.	Epsilon[a]		
					Greenhouse-Geisser	Huynh-Feldt	Lower-bound
MONTH	.789	2.608	2	.272	.826	1.000	.500

Tests the null hypothesis that the error covariance matrix of the orthonormalized transformed dependent variables is proportional to an identity matrix.

a. May be used to adjust the degrees of freedom for the averaged tests of significance. Corrected tests are displayed in the layers (by default) of the Tests of Within-Subjects Effects table.

b.
  Design: Intercept+NOVEL
  Within-Subjects Design: MONTH

Tests of Within-Subjects Effects

Measure: BOOKS

Source		Type III Sum of Squares	df	Mean Square	F	Sig.
MONTH	Sphericity Assumed	.711	2	.356	.229	.797
	Greenhouse-Geisser	.711	1.651	.431	.229	.755
	Huynh-Feldt	.711	2.000	.356	.229	.797
	Lower-bound	.711	1.000	.711	.229	.641
MONTH * NOVEL	Sphericity Assumed	71.422	4	17.856	11.520	.000
	Greenhouse-Geisser	71.422	3.303	21.624	11.520	.000
	Huynh-Feldt	71.422	4.000	17.856	11.520	.000
	Lower-bound	71.422	2.000	35.711	11.520	.002
Error(MONTH)	Sphericity Assumed	37.200	24	1.550		
	Greenhouse-Geisser	37.200	19.818	1.877		
	Huynh-Feldt	37.200	24.000	1.550		
	Lower-bound	37.200	12.000	3.100		

alternative to evaluating significance. Then, there is output regarding the effect of the randomized-groups IV, NOVEL. Finally, marginal and cell statistics are shown in the section labeled Estimated Marginal Means. See Section 6.5 for more detailed interpretation of the repeated-measures portion of the output.

Table 7.10 contains syntax and selected output from SAS GLM for the mixed-design example. Note that means are requested separately for the repeated and randomized portions of the design.

TABLE 7.9 **Continued**

Tests of Within-Subjects Contrasts

Measure: BOOKS

Source	MONTH	Type III Sum of Squares	df	Mean Square	F	Sig.
MONTH	Linear	.533	1	.533	.320	.582
	Quadratic	.178	1	.178	.124	.731
MONTH * NOVEL	Linear	68.467	2	34.233	20.540	.000
	Quadratic	2.956	2	1.478	1.031	.386
Error(MONTH)	Linear	20.000	12	1.667		
	Quadratic	17.200	12	1.433		

Tests of Between-Subjects Effects

Measure: BOOKS
Transformed Variable: Average

Source	Type III Sum of Squares	df	Mean Square	F	Sig.
Intercept	473.689	1	473.689	215.313	.000
NOVEL	20.578	2	10.289	4.677	.031
Error	26.400	12	2.200		

Estimated Marginal Means

1. NOVEL

Measure: BOOKS

NOVEL	Mean	Std. Error	95% Confidence Interval	
			Lower Bound	Upper Bound
science fiction	4.200	.383	3.366	5.034
mystery	2.800	.383	1.966	3.634
romance	2.733	.383	1.899	3.568

(continued)

Like SPSS, SAS gives a routine univariate source table plus two of the alternatives: multivariate F tests (**Wilks' Lambda**), and probability of F after Huynh-Feldt correction (**Adj Pr > F, H - F**). Although no formal test of sphericity is given unless requested, the epsilon values near 1 for Greenhouse-Geisser and Huynh-Feldt adjustments suggest no or very little violation of the assumption. Marginal means are shown for the repeated-measures IV but not the randomized-groups IV.

TABLE 7.9   Continued

2. MONTH

Measure: BOOKS

| MONTH | Mean | Std. Error | 95% Confidence Interval | |
			Lower Bound	Upper Bound
1	3.333	.353	2.565	4.102
2	3.333	.362	2.544	4.122
3	3.067	.313	2.385	3.748

3. NOVEL * MONTH

Measure: BOOKS

| NOVEL | MONTH | Mean | Std. Error | 95% Confidence Interval | |
				Lower Bound	Upper Bound
science fiction	1	2.400	.611	1.069	3.731
	2	3.800	.627	2.434	5.166
	3	6.400	.542	5.220	7.580
mystery	1	4.000	.611	2.669	5.331
	2	3.000	.627	1.634	4.366
	3	1.400	.542	.220	2.580
romance	1	3.600	.611	2.269	4.931
	2	3.200	.627	1.834	4.566
	3	1.400	.542	.220	2.580

Marginal means for NOVEL, then, are found by averaging over MONTH1 to MONTH3 for each level of NOVEL.

Syntax and selected output from SYSTAT ANOVA for the mixed-design example are in Table 7.11. (SYSTAT GLM is also available for the analysis with different syntax but the same output; you have to define the randomized-groups IV as a categorical variable before including it in the MODEL syntax.)

By default with PRINT=SHORT, SYSTAT produces the source table for univariate repeated-measures ANOVA plus output for two of the three alternatives, the multivariate approach (Wilks' Lambda) and the Huynh-Feldt adjusted probability (H – F). PRINT=MEDIUM produces trend analysis on the repeated-measures IV and descriptive statistics in the form produced by SPSS GLM.

Recall that MINITAB does not recognize repeated-measures designs. The mixed design, however, may be analyzed by using the data setup in which each DV is on a separate line, as described in Section 6.4.1.5. The setup for the small sample data for the mixed design is in Table 7.12.

TABLE 7.10 Syntax And Selected Output from SAS GLM for Mixed ANOVA

```
proc glm data=SASUSER.SS_MIXED;
  class NOVEL;
  model MONTH1 MONTH2 MONTH3 = NOVEL;
  repeated month 3 / mean;
  lsmeans NOVEL;
run;
```

```
                      The GLM Procedure
              Repeated Measures Analysis of Variance

                Repeated Measures Level Information

       Dependent Variable    MONTH1     MONTH2     MONTH3

              Level of month      1          2          3
```

Manova Test Criteria and Exact F Statistics for the Hypothesis of
                          no month Effect
              H = Type III SSCP Matrix for month
                    E = Error SSCP Matrix

                    S=1   M=0   N=4.5

			Num	Den	
Statistic	Value	F Value	DF	DF	Pr > F
Wilks' Lambda	0.93839102	0.36	2	11	0.7049
Pillai's Trace	0.06160898	0.36	2	11	0.7049
Hotelling-Lawley Trace	0.06565385	0.36	2	11	0.7049
Roy's Greatest Root	0.06565385	0.36	2	11	0.7049

Manova Test Criteria and F Approximations for the Hypothesis of no
                        month*NOVEL Effect
            H = Type III SSCP Matrix for month*NOVEL
                    E = Error SSCP Matrix

                    S=2   M=-0.5   N=4.5

			Num	Den	
Statistic	Value	F Value	DF	DF	Pr > F
Wilks' Lambda	0.15515386	8.46	4	22	0.0003
Pillai's Trace	0.85905715	4.52	4	24	0.0073
Hotelling-Lawley Trace	5.35362220	14.40	4	12.235	0.0001
Roy's Greatest Root	5.33645857	32.02	2	12	<.0001

    NOTE: F Statistic for Roy's Greatest Root is an upper bound.
         NOTE: F Statistic for Wilks' Lambda is exact.

(continued)

TABLE 7.10   Continued

```
                    The GLM Procedure
         Repeated Measures Analysis of Variance
       Tests of Hypotheses for Between Subjects Effects
```

Source	DF	Type III SS	Mean Square	F Value	Pr > F
NOVEL	2	20.57777778	10.28888889	4.68	0.0315
Error	12	26.40000000	2.20000000		

```
              Univariate Tests of Hypotheses
                for Within Subject Effects
```

Source	DF	Type III SS	Mean Square	F Value	Pr > F	Adj Pr > F G-G	Adj Pr > F H-F
month	2	0.71111111	0.35555556	0.23	0.7967	0.7554	0.7967
month *NOVEL	4	71.42222222	17.85555556	11.52	<.0001	0.0001	<.0001
Error (month)	24	37.20000000	1.55000000				

```
              Greenhouse-Geisser Epsilon    0.8257
              Huynh-Feldt Epsilon           1.1003
```

```
           Means of Within Subjects Effects
```

Level of month	N	Mean	Std Dev
1	15	3.33333333	1.44749373
2	15	3.33333333	1.34518542
3	15	3.06666667	2.68505564

```
                The GLM Procedure
                Least Squares Means
```

NOVEL	MONTH1 LSMEAN	MONTH2 LSMEAN	MONTH3 LSMEAN
1	2.40000000	3.80000000	6.40000000
2	4.00000000	3.00000000	1.40000000
3	3.60000000	3.20000000	1.40000000

TABLE 7.11   Syntax and Selected Output for Mixed-Design ANOVA through SYSTAT ANOVA

```
ANOVA
CATEGORY NOVEL
COVAR
DEPEND MONTH1 MONTH2 MONTH3/ REPEAT =3,NAMES='MONTH'
ESTIMATE

MONTH1    MONTH2    MONTH3
 3.333     3.333     3.067
```

Univariate and Multivariate Repeated Measures Analysis

Between Subjects

Source	SS	df	MS	F	P
NOVEL	20.578	2	10.289	4.677	0.031
Error	26.400	12	2.200		

Within Subjects

Source	SS	df	MS	F	P	G-G	H-F
MONTH	0.711	2	0.356	0.229	0.797	0.755	0.797
MONTH*NOVEL	71.422	4	17.856	11.520	0.000	0.000	0.000
Error	37.200	24	1.550				

Greenhouse-Geisser Epsilon: 0.8257
Huynh-Feldt Epsilon   :   1.0000

Multivariate Repeated Measures Analysis

Test of: MONTH	Hypoth.	df	Error df	F	P
Wilks' Lambda=	0.938	2	11	0.361	0.705
Pillai Trace =	0.062	2	11	0.361	0.705
H-L Trace =	0.066	2	11	0.361	0.705

Test of: MONTH*NOVEL	Hypoth.	df	Error df	F	P
Wilks' Lambda=	0.155	4	22	8.463	0.000
Pillai Trace =	0.859	4	24	4.518	0.007
H-L Trace =	5.354	4	20	13.384	0.000
Theta = 0.842 S = 2, M = -0.5, N = 4.5 P = 0.000					

TABLE 7.12 Data Format for Mixed Randomized-Groups-Repeated-Measures ANOVA through MINITAB, with One DV Value per Line

Novel	Month	Case	Books
1	1	1	1
1	1	2	1
1	1	3	3
1	1	4	5
1	1	5	2
1	2	1	3
1	2	2	4
1	2	3	3
1	2	4	5
1	2	5	4
1	3	1	6
1	3	2	8
1	3	3	6
1	3	4	7
1	3	5	5
2	1	1	3
2	1	2	4
2	1	3	5
2	1	4	4
2	1	5	4
2	2	1	1
2	2	2	4
2	2	3	3
2	2	4	2
2	2	5	5
2	3	1	0
2	3	2	2
2	3	3	2
2	3	4	0
2	3	5	3
3	1	1	4
3	1	2	2
3	1	3	3
3	1	4	6
3	1	5	3
3	2	1	2
3	2	2	6
3	2	3	3
3	2	4	2
3	2	5	3
3	3	1	0
3	3	2	1
3	3	3	3
3	3	4	1
3	3	5	2

Table 7.13 contains syntax and selected output for the example through MINITAB GLM. The GLM equation contains the information necessary to form the correct error term, S/A, for testing the randomized-groups IV, `novel`. The S/A source of variance is formed by nesting case within `novel` using the syntax `case(novel)`.

TABLE 7.13   Syntax and Selected Output for Mixed Design through MINITAB

```
MTB > GLM 'books' = novel case(novel) month novel*month;
SUBC>   Brief 2 ;
SUBC>   Means novel month novel*month.
```

General Linear Model

Factor	Type	Levels	Values
NOVEL	fixed	3	1 2 3
CASE(NOVEL)	fixed	15	1 2 3 4 5 1 2 3 4 5 1 2 3 4 5
MONTH	fixed	3	1 2 3

Analysis of Variance for BOOKS, using Adjusted SS for Tests

Source	DF	Seq SS	Adj SS	Adj MS	F	P
NOVEL	2	20.578	20.578	10.289	6.64	0.005
CASE(NOVEL)	12	26.400	26.400	2.200	1.42	0.224
MONTH	2	0.711	0.711	0.356	0.23	0.797
NOVEL*MONTH	4	71.422	71.422	17.856	11.52	0.000
Error	24	37.200	37.200	1.550		
Total	44	156.311				

Least Squares Means for BOOKS

NOVEL		Mean	StDev
1		4.200	0.3215
2		2.800	0.3215
3		2.733	0.3215
MONTH			
1		3.333	0.3215
2		3.333	0.3215
3		3.067	0.3215
NOVEL*MONTH			
1	1	2.400	0.5568
1	2	3.800	0.5568
1	3	6.400	0.5568
2	1	4.000	0.5568
2	2	3.000	0.5568
2	3	1.400	0.5568
3	1	3.600	0.5568
3	2	3.200	0.5568
3	3	1.400	0.5568

The $B \times S/A$ term is labeled `Error`, so that F tests of `MONTH` and the `NOVEL*MONTH` interaction are correct. However, that error term also is incorrectly applied to `novel`. Instead, `CASE(NOVEL)` is the correct error term, so that

$$F_A = \frac{\text{MS}_A}{\text{MS}_{S/A}} = \frac{10.289}{2.200} = 4.68$$

as per Table 7.6.

7.5 Types of Mixed Designs

7.5.1 The Pretest–Posttest Design

One variant on the mixed design requires that the first measurement occur before any treatment is given, as shown in Table 7.14. The first trial is a pretest and all subsequent trials part of the posttest.

The mean DV scores on the first trial (pretest) are compared to see if the randomized groups are equivalent *before* treatment is given.[5] Once reassured that the groups are equivalent, interaction is examined to see if the groups have a different pattern of responses over time. A significant interaction in this design implies that the group with treatment has a different pattern of mean DV scores over trials than the control group, that is, that treatment produces some change.[6] If the control group also changes between the pretest and the posttest, one has reason to suspect the influence of uncontrolled extraneous variables.

7.5.2 Expanding Mixed Designs

As noted in Section 7.4.2, any interaction term that contains one (or more) repeated-measures main effect(s) is analyzed as part of the repeated-measures segment of the design. Also noted there, error terms for the purely randomized-groups effects in the design are always cases nested in levels (or combinations of levels) of the randomized-groups IV(s). The error terms for the repeated-measures effects in the design are always cases crossed with (in interaction with) those effects, nested in the randomized-groups effects in the designs.

TABLE 7.14   Pretest, Posttest Mixed Design

	b_1: Pretest	Treatment	b_2: Posttest
b_1: Treatment Group	Yes	Yes	Yes
b_2: Control Group	Yes	No	Yes

---

[5]If the groups are not equivalent, the pretest can be used as a covariate to adjust each case's score on the posttest by differences on the pretest, as described in Chapter 8.

[6]Analysis of difference scores between posttest and pretest produces the same result.

TABLE 7.15   Partition of Randomized-Groups and Repeated-Measures Terms in Mixed Designs with Their Error Terms

Design	Randomized-Groups IVs	Repeated-Measures IVs	Sources of Variability		
			Randomized Groups	*Repeated Measures*	*Error Terms*
Two-way mixed	A	B	A		S/A
				$B, A \times B$	$B \times S/A$
Three-way mixed	A, B	C	$A, B, A \times B$		S/AB
				$C, A \times C, B \times C, A \times B \times C$	$C \times S/AB$
	A	B, C	A		S/A
				$B, A \times B$	$B \times S/A$
				$C, A \times C$	$C \times S/A$
				$B \times C, A \times B \times C$	$B \times C \times S/A$
Four-way mixed	A, B	C, D	$A, B, A \times B$		S/AB
				$C, A \times C, B \times C, A \times B \times C$	$C \times S/AB$
				$D, A \times D, B \times D, A \times B \times D$	$D \times S/AB$
				$C \times D, A \times C \times D,$ $B \times C \times D, A \times B \times C \times D$	$C \times D \times S/AB$

These generalizations are summarized in Table 7.15, where C is the third IV. The table shows the breakdowns for a two-way mixed design, a three-way design with two randomized-groups IVs (A and B) and one repeated measure (C), a three-way design with one randomized-groups IV (A) and two repeated-measures (B and C), and, finally, a four-way design with two randomized-groups IVs (A and B) and two repeated measures (C and D).

Once you understand the pattern, you should be able to generalize to a mixed design of any complexity. If a main effect or interaction contains no repeated factors, the error term is cases within levels of randomized-groups factors. If a main effect or interaction contains one or more repeated factors, the error term is an interaction between the repeated factor(s) and cases nested within randomized-groups factors.

7.6   Some Important Issues

Issues of unequal n, power, effect size, and the like are the same for the mixed design as for the randomized-groups design (Chapters 4 and 5) and the repeated-measures design (Chapter 6). Consult these chapters for a discussion of these important issues. The difficulty with the mixed design involves comparisons. The same logic drives comparisons on the margins and tests of interaction (with either simple-effects analysis or interaction contrasts) as in the other analyses, but the process is more complicated computationally in the mixed design.

The complexity is that comparisons involving the randomized-groups IV(s) use the randomized-groups computations but different error terms for some comparisons, whereas comparisons on the repeated-measures IV(s) use repeated-measures computations and a different error term for each comparison. However, the full array of comparisons is available: comparisons on the margins, simple effects (both simple main effects and simple comparisons), and interaction contrasts.

7.6.1 Comparisons on the Margins

Comparisons on the margins are appropriate when the interaction is not significant or when it is significant but small and ordinal (not crossing). However, the marginal comparisons are conducted differently, depending on whether for a randomized-groups or repeated-measures effect, as shown in Table 7.16. In this table (like in the example of Section 7.4), A (type of novel) is a randomized-groups IV and B (month) is a repeated measure.

Contrast coefficients are chosen for A to compare the average number of science fiction books read against the pooled average of mystery and romance novels $(2, -1, -1)$. The desired error term is S/A because the contrast is concerned only with A, the randomized-groups IV. Linear-contrast coefficients $(-1, 0, 1)$ are chosen for B to see if the average number of novels read increases (or decreases) steadily over the months. The desired error term is $B_{\text{linear}} \times S/A$, a term developed specifically for this analysis.

7.6.1.1 The Randomized-Groups Margin

The effect of A and the $A \times B$ interaction are significant in the small-sample example. The $A \times B$ interaction is large, by Equation 6.25,

$$\text{Partial } \eta^2 = \frac{\text{SS}_{AB}}{\text{SS}_{AB} + \text{SS}_{B \times S/A}} = \frac{71.42}{71.42 + 37.20} = .66$$

TABLE 7.16 Comparisons on the Margins

Notes: A_{comp1} (a_1 vs. the average of a_2 and a_3) is tested against S/A and is a randomized-groups effect. B_{linear} is tested against $B_{\text{linear}} \times S/A$ and is a repeated-measures effect.

and disordinal, as shown in Figure 7.2.

Thus, 66% of the variance in number of books read is associated with the interaction between month and novel type.

Comparisons on the margins of A are inappropriate and potentially misleading under these circumstances. However, the comparison is conducted here for didactic purposes. If the comparison is calculated by hand, the sum of squares, mean square, and F for the comparison are computed using an appropriately modified version of Equation 5.16:

$$F - \frac{n_{\overline{Y}}(\sum w_j \overline{Y}_j)^2 / \sum w_j^2}{\text{MS}_{S/A}} \tag{7.8}$$

For the comparison between science fiction versus other novels,

$$F - \frac{\{3(5)[2(4.20) - 2.80 - 2.73]^2\} \big/ [2^2 + (-1)^2 + (-1)^2]}{2.20} = 9.36$$

If this comparison is planned, it is tested with 1 and 12 df and critical F at $\alpha = .05$ is 4.75. If it is tested post hoc, F_S is computed using an appropriately modified version of Equation 5.21.

$$F_S = (a - 1)F_{(a-1), a(s-1)} \tag{7.9}$$

For this example, F_S is $2(3.88) = 7.76$. Thus, the comparison is significant if planned or performed post hoc; science fiction novels are preferred to mystery and romance novels.

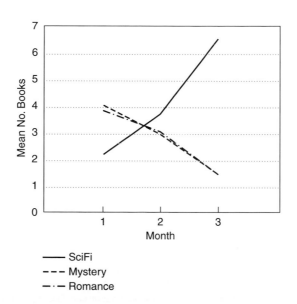

**FIGURE 7.2 Mean Number of Books Read as a
Function of Type of Novel and Month**

Syntax for performing this marginal comparison on the randomized-groups IV through SPSS GLM, SAS GLM, and SYSTAT GLM appears in Table 7.17.

The difficulty in evaluating comparisons on the randomized-groups margin in MINITAB is that the run that produces the correct MS_{Acomp} fails to produce the correct $MS_{S/A}$ error term. If the error term is available from an omnibus ANOVA (e.g., Table 7.13), the MS_{Acomp} may be found by adding a column of coefficients representing the comparison to the data set (see, e.g., Table 4.25), and then declaring that variable (e.g., X_1) to be a covariate in a model in which IVs are case and month. However, it is probably easier to do the comparison by hand.

TABLE 7.17   Syntax for Comparisons on the Margin of the Randomized-Groups IV in a Mixed Design

Program	Syntax	Section of Output	Name of Effect

SPSS GLM	GLM
	   month1 month2 month3 BY novel
	   /WSFACTOR = month 3 Polynomial
	   /METHOD = SSTYPE(3)
	   /CRITERIA = ALPHA(.05)
	   /WSDESIGN = month
	   /LMATRIX "comp1" novel 2 -1 -1
	   /DESIGN = novel .
		Custom Hypothesis Tests:
		
		Test Results
			Contrast

SAS GLM	proc glm data=SASUSER.SS_MIXED;
	   class NOVEL;
	   model MONTH1 MONTH2 MONTH3 = NOVEL;
	   contrast 'marg_com' novel −2 −1 −1;
	   repeated month 3;
	run;
		Tests of Hypotheses for Between Subjects Effects: Contrast	marg_com

SYSTAT GLM[b]	LET BOOKS = MONTH1+MONTH2+MONTH3 ANOVA CATEGORY NOVEL COVAR DEPEND BOOKS ESTIMATE HYPOTHESIS EFFECT=NOVEL CONTRAST[2 −1 −1] TEST	Test of Hypothesis	Hypothesis

[a]T-VALUE is produced instead of F; recall that $t^2 = F$ with 1 df in the numerator and df_{error} in the denominator.

[b]Note that a new DV, books, is created as the sum of the original DVs.

7.6.1.2 The Repeated-Measures Margin

Comparisons are formed on the margin of the repeated-measures IV by hand using the procedures of Section 6.6.6.1.2. Essentially, the data set is revised to build in the desired comparison and the results reanalyzed. Because the error term is developed right along with the effect, the appropriate error term is available for use.

Table 7.18 shows the data set for the $(-1\ 0\ 1)$ comparison, which simply deletes b_2 from the intact data set of Table 7.2. Routine ANOVA (Section 7.4) produces Table 7.19.[7]

Table 7.18 Hypothetical Data Set for a Mixed Design with Month 2 Eliminated for Analysis with Coefficients: (–1, 0, 1)

		B: Month		
		b_1: *Month 1*	b_3: *Month 3*	**Case Totals**
	s_1	1	6	$A_1S_1 = 7$
	s_2	1	8	$A_1S_2 = 9$
a_1: Science Fiction	s_3	3	6	$A_1S_3 = 9$
	s_4	5	7	$A_1S_4 = 12$
	s_5	2	5	$A_1S_5 = 7$
		$A_1B_1 = 12$	$A_1B_3 = 32$	$A_1 = 44$
	s_6	3	0	$A_2S_6 = 3$
	s_7	4	2	$A_2S_7 = 6$
a_2: Mystery	s_8	5	2	$A_2S_8 = 7$
	s_9	4	0	$A_2S_9 = 4$
	s_{10}	4	3	$A_2S_{10} = 7$
		$A_2B_1 = 20$	$A_2B_3 = 7$	$A_2 = 27$
	s_{11}	4	0	$A_3S_{11} = 4$
	s_{12}	2	1	$A_3S_{12} = 3$
a_3: Romance	s_{13}	3	3	$A_3S_{13} = 6$
	s_{14}	6	1	$A_3S_{14} = 7$
	s_{15}	3	2	$A_3S_{15} = 5$
		$A_3B_1 = 18$	$A_3B_3 = 7$	$A_3 = 25$
		$B_1 = 50$	$B_3 = 46$	$T = 96$

---

[7]You will have your chance at this analysis in the problem sets.

TABLE 7.19   Source Table for Mixed-Design ANOVA with Month 2 Eliminated

Source	SS	df	MS	F
Randomized Groups				
A	21.80	2	10.90	6.54
S/A	20.00	12	1.67	
Repeated Measures				
B_{comp}	0.53	1	0.53	0.32
$A \times B_{comp}$	68.47	2	34.23	20.54
$B_{comp} \times S/A$	20.00	12	1.67	
T	130.80	29		

The "main effect" of B in this analysis is the linear-trend comparison on months—B_{comp}: month 1 versus month 3—using the appropriate error term, $B_{comp} \times S/A$. Critical value for df = 1, 12 at $\alpha = .05$ for a planned comparison again is 4.75, which, of course, this F_{Bcomp} does not exceed. The Scheffé-adjusted critical value, should this comparison be done post hoc, is

$$F_S = (b - 1)F_{(b-1),a(b-1)(s-1)} \qquad (7.10)$$

which is $(2)(3.40) = 6.80$.

SAS GLM, SYSTAT GLM, and SPSS GLM (default) all have simplified syntax for trend (orthogonal polynomial) analysis on a repeated-measures factor, as shown in the first portion of Table 7.20. The second portion of the table shows syntax that generalizes to any marginal comparison on a repeated-measures factor, using the coefficients $(-1, 0, 1)$ that happen to be the ones for linear trend. Neither SAS, MINITAB, nor SYSTAT GLM does user-specified marginal comparisons on a repeated-measures factor in a mixed design. However, you can build a data set incorporating the coefficients as per Table 6.39 for all levels of the randomized-groups IV, and then analyze the comparison as if in a mixed design. That is, the newly developed data set is used for the analysis instead of the original data set. The test of the "main effect" of the repeated-measures IV then becomes the comparison of marginal means. Recall that in MINITAB GLM, you must calculate the F ratio by hand, using the S/A error term for the comparison (cf. Section 7.4.5). This procedure also is necessary for trend analysis through MINITAB.

Again, because of the difficulty in finding the correct error term in MINITAB, it is probably easier to do the comparison by hand.

7.6.2   Simple Main-Effects Analysis

One IV, either randomized or repeated, is held constant at some value while mean differences are examined on the levels of the other IV in simple main-effects analysis, as shown in Figure 5.8. The

TABLE 7.20 Syntax for Comparisons on the Margin of the Repeated-Measures IV in a Mixed Design

Type of Comparison	Program	Syntax	Section of Output	Name of Effect
Polynomial (linear trend)	SPSS GLM	GLM month1 month2 month3 BY novel /WSFACTOR = month 3 Polynomial /METHOD = SSTYPE(3) /CRITERIA = ALPHA(.05) /WSDESIGN = month /DESIGN = novel.	**Tests of Within-Subjects Contrasts**	MONTH Linear (See Table 7.9)

	SAS GLM	proc glm data=SASUSER.SS_MIXED;
		   class NOVEL;
		   model MONTH1 MONTH2 MONTH3 = NOVEL;
		   repeated MONTH 3 polynomial/summary;
		run;
			MONTH.N:
			MONTH_1
				MEAN

	SYSTAT GLM (default with PRINT=MEDIUM)	ANOVA CATEGORY NOVEL COVAR DEPEND MONTH1 MONTH2 MONTH3/, REPEAT =3, NAMES='MONTH' ESTIMATE	Single Degree of Freedom Polynomial Contrasts: Polynomial Test of Order 1 (Linear)	MONTH

User-specified	SPSS GLM	GLM
		month1 month2 month3 BY novel
		/WSFACTOR = month 3 special (1 1 1
		              -1 0 1
		              1 -2 1)
		
		/MEASURE = books
		/METHOD = SSTYPE(3)
		/CRITERIA = ALPHA(.05)
		/WSDESIGN = month
		/DESIGN = novel .
			Tests of Within-Subjects Contrasts	MONTH L1

difference between the mixed design and the completely randomized design of Chapter 5 is that simple main effects may be done on a repeated or randomized factor, and error terms differ depending on which IV is examined.

Table 7.21 shows that each simple main effect of the randomized-groups IV, A, is tested against a separate randomized-groups error term.[8] For example, the test of A at the first level of B uses S/A at b_1 as an error term. Similarly, each simple main effect of the repeated-measures IV, B, is tested against a different repeated-measures error term. For example, $B \times S$ at a_1 provides the error term for the test of B at the first level of A.

As in any simple main-effects analysis, significant effects with more than two levels may be followed up by simple comparisons among levels (see Figure 5.8). Again, each comparison among levels has its own error term.

If comparisons are done post hoc to evaluate a significant interaction, F_S for interaction is appropriate for all simple main effects, and simple comparisons, and interaction contrasts. F_S for interaction for this design is an appropriately revised version of Equation 5.28:

$$F_S = (a - 1)(b - 1)F_{(a-1)(b-1), a(b-1)(s-1)} \tag{7.11}$$

In the small-sample example of Section 7.4,

$$F_S = 2(2)F_{4, 24} = 4(2.78) = 11.12$$

7.6.2.1   Simple Main Effects for the Randomized-Groups IV

Hand calculations for simple main effects of the randomized-groups IV are done simply as one-way ANOVAs, separately on each "slice" (level of B). Equations of Sections 3.2.3.2 and 4.4.3 are used to calculate SS_A and MS_A separately at b_1, b_2, and b_3. That is, you use Equation 3.10 three times, one for each level of B. Then each numerator MS is divided by $MS_{S/A}$ at b_j calculated at that level of B. Finally, you calculate and evaluate each F, based on df_A in the numerator and $df_{S/A}$ at the level B. The result for the first level of B in the small-sample example of Section 7.4 is $F(2, 12) = 1.86, p > .05$.

TABLE 7.21   Simple Main Effects for Randomized Groups and Repeated Measures

(a) Simple main effect of A at b_1 is tested against S/A at b_1 and is a randomized-groups effect

(b) Simple main effect of B at a_1 is tested against $B \times S$ at a_1 and is a repeated-measures effect

[8]The single randomized-groups error term, provided by S/A, may be used if the df for that error term exceed 30. Tests using that error term are biased with fewer df, as noted by Winer (1971).

By computer, you also do a one-way randomized-groups ANOVA with just one of the DV measures, for example, the first month (Table 7.22).

SPSS GLM (General Factorial) may be used as an alternative to ONEWAY.

7.6.2.2 Simple Main Effects for the Repeated-Measures IV

A one-way repeated-measures ANOVA is performed on the set of DVs (levels of B) separately for each level of A. Equations 6.11 through 6.14 are used to calculate SS by hand, substituting B for A, at each level of A. The result for the first level of novel, science fiction, for the small-sample example is $F(2, 8) = 17.35, p < .01$.

Case selection is used to limit the analysis to the desired level of A for each run using SPSS, MINITAB, or SYSTAT ANOVA, as shown in Table 7.23. SAS GLM has special simple-effects language that may be used only with the repeated-measures simple effect.

7.6.3 Simple Comparisons

Simple comparisons follow significant simple main effects when there are more than two levels, to examine the specific sources of the simple main effect. As usual, they differ from simple comparisons in randomized groups or fully repeated-measures factorial designs only in the choice of error terms.

Table 7.24 shows the simple comparisons to be demonstrated for the small-sample design of Section 7.4. Comparison on the randomized-groups factor, A, is the first group (science fiction)

TABLE 7.22 Syntax for Tests of Simple Main Effects of the Randomized-Groups IV in a Mixed Design

Program	Syntax	Section of Output	Name of Effect
SPSS Compare Means	ONEWAY month1 BY novel /MISSING ANALYSIS .	**ANOVA**	Between Groups

SAS GLM	`proc glm data=SASUSER.SS_MIXED;`
	`  class NOVEL;`
	`  model MONTH1 = NOVEL ;`
	`run;`
		Dependent Variable: MONTH1 Source	NOVEL

SYSTAT ANOVA	ANOVA CATEGORY NOVEL COVAR DEPEND MONTH1 ESTIMATE	Analysis of Variance Source	NOVEL

MINITAB GLM	`MTB > SUBSET;`
	`SUBC> INCLUDE;`
	`SUBC> WHERE "MONTH=1".`
	`MTB > GLM 'books' = NOVEL.`
		Analysis of Variance for BOOKS ...	NOVEL

TABLE 7.23   Syntax for Simple Main Effects on the Repeated-Measures IV in a Mixed Design

Program	Syntax	Section of Output	Name of Effect

SPSS GLM	[DATA SELECT CASES IF (novel = 1)]
	GLM
	  month1 month2 month3
	  /WSFACTOR = month 3 Polynomial
	  /METHOD = SSTYPE(3)
	  /CRITERIA = ALPHA(.05)
	  /WSDESIGN = month .
		Tests of Within-Subjects Effects	MONTH

SAS GLM	`proc glm data=SASUSER.SS_MIXED;`
	    `by NOVEL;`
	    `class NOVEL;`
	    `model MONTH1 MONTH2 MONTH3 =;`
	    `repeated MONTH 3;`
	`run;`
		NOVEL=1
		Source:
			MONTH

SYSTAT ANOVA	SELECT (NOVEL= 1) ANOVA CATEGORY COVAR DEPEND MONTH1 MONTH2 MONTH3/ , REPEAT=3,NAMES='MONTH' ESTIMATE	Within Subjects: Source	MONTH
MINITAB GLM	MTB > SUBSET; SUBC> INCLUDE; SUBC> WHERE "NOVEL=1". MTB > GLM 'books' = month case.	Analysis of Variance for BOOKS . . .	MONTH

TABLE 7.24   Simple Comparisons in a Mixed Randomized-Repeated Design

(a) A_{comp} at b_1 is tested against S/A at b_1 and is a randomized-groups effect

(b) B_{linear} at a_1 is tested against $B_{linear} \times S/A$ at a_1 and is a repeated-measures effect versus the other two groups (mystery and romance) for the first month. Linear trend is analyzed over the repeated-measures factor, B, for science fiction novels.

7.6.3.1 Simple Comparisons for the Randomized-Groups IV

Simple comparisons for the randomized-groups IV follow naturally from the analysis of simple main effects and use the same error term. Therefore, Equation 7.8 is applied, with $MS_{S/A}$ at b_1 as the error term for any comparison following the simple main effect of A at b_1.

For the comparison of group 1 (science fiction) versus groups 2 and 3 (mystery and romance):

$$F = \frac{\{(5)[2(2.40) - 4.00 - 3.60]^2\} / [2^2 + (-1)^2 + (-1)^2]}{1.87} = 3.49$$

Critical F for a planned comparison with 1 and 12 df is 4.75, indicating that there is no reliable difference between number of science fiction books read and the number of other books read during the first month.

The analysis by computer is done by adding contrast coefficients to the one-way analysis using only the data for the first level of month as the DV (Table 7.25). Note that the special simple-effects language of SAS GLM cannot be used for this simple comparison.

TABLE 7.25 Syntax for Simple Comparisons on the Randomized-Groups IV in a Mixed Design

Program	Syntax	Section of Output	Name of Effect
SPSS GLM	ONEWAY month1 BY novel /CONTRAST= 2 -1 -1 /MISSING ANALYSIS.	**Contrast Tests**	Assume equal variances[a]

SAS GLM	`proc glm data=SASUSER.SS_MIXED;`
	   `class NOVEL;`
	   `model MONTH1 = NOVEL ;`
	   `contrast 'SCIFI_VS' NOVEL 2 -1 -1;`
	`run;`
		Dependent Variable: MONTH1 Contrast	SCIFI_VS

SYSTAT ANOVA	ANOVA CATEGORY NOVEL COVAR DEPEND MONTH1 ESTIMATE HYPOTHESIS EFFECT=NOVEL CONTRAST[2 -1 -1] TEST	Test of Hypothesis Source	Hypothesis

[a] t is given rather than F; recall that $t^2 = F$ with 1 df in the numerator and df_{error} in the denominator.

In MINITAB, once the data are subsetted to "MONTH=1," as per Table 7.22, the analysis is done by adding a column of coefficients to the data set and running a one-way randomized-groups ANOVA with the coefficient column (e.g., X_1) declared to be a covariate, as per Tables 4.25 and 4.26.

7.6.3.2   *Simple Comparisons for the Repeated-Measures IV*

Simple comparisons on the repeated-measures factor all have different error terms, as do all repeated-measures comparisons. Therefore, a data set is developed for each comparison, as in Table 6.39, based on the coefficients chosen. Indeed, the analysis is exactly the same as for the factorial repeated-measures design because only one level of novels (A) is used. That is, the design is treated as one-way repeated, with a data set generated that reflects the coefficients. For example, the data set of Table 6.39(b) is used if months 1 and 2 are to be contrasted with month 3. A data set with columns b_1 and b_3 (omitting b_2) is developed at the first level of A to test the linear trend of months for science fiction novels. The result for the small-sample example with b_2 eliminated is $F(1, 4) = 20.00$, $p < .05$.

Computer analysis simply requires selection of the level of A to be used. Contrasts, either user-specified or polynomial, are then specified (Table 7.26). SAS and MINITAB do not support user-specified comparisons on a repeated-measures IV. However, the analysis may be done through SAS or MINITAB GLM by (1) selecting the relevant level of the randomized-groups IV, (2) developing a data set for the comparison as per Table 6.39, and (3) running the analysis as described in Section 6.6.6.2.

7.6.4   Interaction Contrasts

As discussed in Section 5.6.4.4.2, interaction contrasts are appropriate when both main effects as well as the interaction are significant. The current data set has one significant main effect along with a reliable interaction. Therefore, the tests for simple main effects of A at each level of B (followed by simple comparisons) are most appropriate. However, interaction contrasts are acceptable, if not as easily interpreted.

Table 7.27 describes the interaction between the linear trend of months (B_{linear}) and science fiction versus other novels (A_{comp}). Figure 7.3 plots the combined means relevant to this test.

Month 2 is deleted from the plot because it has a coefficient of zero when coding for the linear trend. Interaction contrasts that are done by hand require development of a data set representing the cells of interest: a_1b_1, a_1b_3, $a_{2+3}b_1$, and $a_{2+3}b_3$. Again, month 2 (b_2) is omitted because it has a zero coefficient in coding for the linear trend with three levels. A standard mixed ANOVA is performed, and the interaction calculated tests $A_{comp} \times B_{linear}$. This yields $F(1, 12) = 40.96, p < .001$. Alternatively, the regression approach is used for interaction comparisons, as demonstrated in the following section.

Table 7.28 shows syntax for an interaction contrast through software. Interaction contrasts are not readily done through MINITAB GLM for mixed designs because of the difficulty in developing correct error terms.

7.6.5   Comparisons through the Regression Approach

The regression approach is preferable in many ways to the traditional ANOVA approach for comparisons in the mixed design. Each degree of freedom represents a different partition of the variability in

TABLE 7.26 Syntax for Simple Comparisons on the Repeated-Measures IV in a Mixed Design

Type of Comparison	Program	Syntax	Section of Output	Name of Effect

Polynomial (linear)	SPSS GLM	[DATA SELECT CASES IF (novel = 1)]
		GLM
		   month1 month2 month3
		   /WSFACTOR = month 3 Polynomial
		   /METHOD = SSTYPE(3)
		   /CRITERIA = ALPHA(.05)
		   /WSDESIGN = month .
			Tests of Within-Subjects Contrasts	MONTH Linear

	SAS GLM	`proc glm data=SASUSER.SS_MIXED;`
		`  where NOVEL=1;`
		`  model MONTH1 MONTH2 MONTH3 =;`
		`  repeated month 3 polynomial /`
		`  summary;`
		`run;`
			Contrast Variable: MONTH_1	MEAN

	SYSTAT ANOVA	SELECT (NOVEL= 1) ANOVA CATEGORY COVAR DEPEND MONTH1 MONTH2 MONTH3/, REPEAT=3,NAMES='MONTH' ESTIMATE HYPOTHESIS WITHIN="MONTH" CONTRAST /POLYNOMIAL TEST	Univariate 1 F Tests Effect	

User-specified (for 1, 1, -2)	SPSS GLM	[DATA SELECT CASES IF (novel = 1)]
		GLM
		   month1 month2 month3
		   /WSFACTOR = month 3 special (1 1 1
		                       1 1 -2
		                       1 -1 0)
		/MEASURE = books
		/METHOD = SSTYPE(3)
		/CRITERIA = ALPHA(.05)
		/WSDESIGN = month .
			Tests of Within-Subjects Contrasts	MONTH L1

	SYSTAT ANOVA	SELECT (NOVEL=1)
		ANOVA
		CATEGORY
		COVAR
		DEPEND MONTH1 MONTH2 MONTH3 / ,
		     REPEAT=3,
		      NAMES="MONTH"
		ESTIMATE
		HYPOTHESIS
		WITHIN="MONTH"
		CONTRAST[1 1 -2]
		TEST
			Test of Hypothesis	Hypoth-esis

TABLE 7.27   Interaction Contrasts

$A_{comp} \times B_{linear}$ is tested against $B_{linear} \times S/A$ and is a repeated-measures (interaction) effect

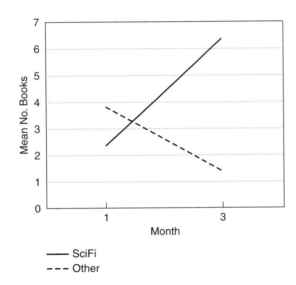

FIGURE 7.3   **Mean Number of Books Read as a Function of Science Fiction vs. Other Novels and First vs. Last Month**

the design and a different comparison or interaction contrast.[9] In Table 7.29, the information of Table 7.8 is further partitioned into its elements to illustrate the detailed analysis that is readily available.

Examination of Table 7.29 reveals that comparisons on the margins and interaction contrasts, with their corresponding error terms, are readily available from the regression breakdown. Further, partial factorial interactions are easily obtained by adding together the SS(reg.) for the columns that combine to produce an effect. For instance, if you combine SS(reg. X_5) and SS(reg. X_6), you are "going over" B_{linear} and B_{quad} for A_{comp1}. The result is $A_{comp1} \times B$. The evaluation of this sum of squares asks if the comparison on A has the same pattern over the three levels of B. Or if you combine SS(reg. X_5) and SS(reg. X_7), you are "going over" A_{comp1} and A_{comp2} for B_{linear}. The result is

[9]Simple-effects analyses (main effects and comparisons) can also be done through regression, but you have to reorganize the data set to represent the comparisons you are seeking and recompute the regression.

TABLE 7.28 Syntax for Interaction Contrasts in a Mixed Design

Type of Comparison	Program	Syntax	Location of Output / Test Results	Name of Effect

User-specified on both randomized IV (2 -1 -1) and repeated IV (-1 0 1)	SPSS GLM	GLM
		  month1 month2 month3 BY novel
		  /MMATRIX ="LINEAR" month1 -1 month2 0 month3 1
		  /MEASURE = books
		  /WSFACTOR = month 3
		  /WSDESIGN = month
		  /LMATRIX = novel 2 -1 -1
		  /DESIGN = novel.
			Test Results	Contrast

	SAS GLM	proc glm data=SASUSER.SS_MIXED;
		  class NOVEL;
		  model MONTH1 MONTH2 MONTH3 = NOVEL;
		  contrast 'Acomp1' NOVEL 2 -1 -1;
		  manova m = -1*MONTH1 + 0*MONTH2 + 1*MONTH3;
		run;
			Manova Test
			. . . .no
			Overall
			Acomp1 Effect
				Wilks'
				Lambda[a]

	SYSTAT ANOVA	ANOVA CATEGORY NOVEL COVAR DEPEND MONTH1 MONTH2 MONTH3 / REPEAT =3, NAMES='MONTH' ESTIMATE HYPOTHESIS CMATRIX [-1 0 1] EFFECT=NOVEL CONTRAST [2 -1 -1] TEST	Test of hypothesis	Hypothesis
User-specified on randomized IV (2 -1 -1); polynomial (linear) on repeated IV	SPSS GLM	Same as user-specified on both randomized and repeated, above		

	SAS GLM	proc glm data=SASUSER.SS_MIXED;
		  class NOVEL;
		  model MONTH1 MONTH2 MONTH3 = NOVEL;
		  contrast 'comp' NOVEL 2 1 -1;
		  repeated month 3 polynomial / summary;
		run;
			Contrast
			Variable:
			month_1
				comp

	SYSTAT ANOVA	Same as user-specified on both randomized and repeated, above		

[a]This is a multivariate test, but produces the same *F* ratio and df as other programs.

TABLE 7.29 Sums of Squares for the Regression Approach to Mixed-Design ANOVA

Source	Columns	SS	Name of Effect
A	SS(reg.X_1) + SS(reg.X_2)	20.54 + 0.03	
	SS(reg.X_1) = SS$_{A\text{comp1}}$	20.54	A_{comp1} on the A margin
	SS(reg.X_2) = SS$_{A\text{comp2}}$	0.03	A_{comp2} on the A margin
S/A	SS(reg.X_9) + SS(reg.X_{10}) + $\cdots$ + SS(reg.X_{20})	2.82 + 0.75 + $\cdots$ + 0.17	
B	SS(reg.X_3) + SS(reg.X_4)	0.53 + 0.18	
	SS(reg.X_3) = SS$_{B\text{linear}}$	0.53	B_{linear} on the B margin
	SS(reg.X_4) = SS$_{B\text{quad}}$	0.18	B_{quad} on the B margin
$A \times B$	SS(reg.X_5) + SS(reg.X_6) + SS(reg.X_7) + SS(reg.X_8)	68.27 + 2.69 + 0.20 + 0.27	
	SS(reg.X_5) = SS$_{A\text{comp1} \times B\text{linear}}$	68.27	Interaction contrast
	SS(reg.X_6) = SS$_{A\text{comp1} \times B\text{quad}}$	2.69	Interaction contrast
	SS(reg.X_7) = SS$_{A\text{comp2} \times B\text{linear}}$	0.20	Interaction contrast
	SS(reg.X_8) = SS$_{A\text{comp2} \times B\text{quad}}$	0.27	Interaction contrast
	SS(reg.X_5) + SS(reg.X_6) = SS$_{A\text{comp1} \times B\text{linear}}$ + SS$_{A\text{comp1} \times B\text{quad}}$ = SS$_{A\text{comp1} \times B}$	68.27 + 2.69	Partial factorial (interaction of A_{comp1} with B)
	SS(reg.X_7) + SS(reg.X_8) = SS$_{A\text{comp2} \times B\text{linear}}$ + SS$_{A\text{comp2} \times B\text{quad}}$ = SS$_{A\text{comp2} \times B}$	0.20 + 0.27	Partial factorial (interaction of A_{comp2} with B)
	SS(reg.X_5) + SS(reg.X_7) = SS$_{A\text{comp1} \times B\text{linear}}$ + SS$_{A\text{comp2} \times B\text{linear}}$ = SS$_{A \times B\text{linear}}$	68.27 + 0.20	Partial factorial (interaction of A with B_{linear})
	SS(reg.X_6) + SS(reg.X_8) = SS$_{A\text{comp1} \times B\text{quad}}$ + SS$_{A\text{comp2} \times B\text{quad}}$ = SS$_{A\text{comp1} \times B\text{quad}}$	2.69 + 0.27	Partial factorial (interaction of A with B_{quad})
$B \times S/A$	SS(reg.X_{21}) + SS(reg.X_{22}) + $\cdots$ + SS(reg.X_{44})	0.62 + 3.12 + $\cdots$ + 1.33	
	SS(reg.X_{21}) + $\cdots$ + SS(reg.X_{32})	0.62 + $\cdots$ + 4.00	Error term, $B_{\text{linear}} \times S/A$
	SS(reg.X_{33}) + $\cdots$ + SS(reg.X_{44})	0.01 + $\cdots$ + 1.33	Error term, $B_{\text{quad}} \times S/A$
Total	SS(Y)		

$A \times B_{\text{linear}}$. The evaluation of this sum of squares asks if there is a different linear trend on B among the three different levels of A. The relevant sums of squares for the specialized error terms are also obtained by adding together sums of squares for the relevant columns.

The advantage to this approach is the absolute clarity of the various elements of the design. You select the orthogonal partition for the randomized-groups IV(s), the orthogonal partition for the repeated-measures IV(s) (often a trend analysis), and the orthogonal partition for cases, and then obtain the desired results through cross-multiplying appropriate columns and evaluating their sums of squares. Addition of sums of squares regression for appropriate columns gives you the numbers needed to test various elements of the design. With modern spreadsheets, this is not even all that painful.[10]

7.7 Complete Example of Mixed Randomized-Repeated ANOVA

The data set for this example was available on the Internet (with free use authorized) and is from a statement by Texaco, Inc., to the Air and Water Pollution Subcommittee of the Senate Public Works Committee on June 26, 1973. The data were used to compare the noise produced by an Octel filter with that produced by a standard filter. Eighteen cars were tested in all, nine with each type of filter. Each type of filter was tested with cars of three sizes: small, medium, and large. Noise for each car was measured on the right and left sides. Thus, this example is a $3 \times 2 \times 2$ with two randomized-groups IVs (car size and filter type) and one repeated-measures IV (position). Data files are FILTER.*.

The goal of the original research was to show that the Octel filter was no noisier than the standard filter. More general questions about the effects of size, position, and interactions among size, position, and filter type also are addressed in the current analysis.

7.7.1 Evaluation of Assumptions

7.7.1.1 *Normality of Sampling Distributions, Missing Data, and Unequal Sample Sizes*

There are no missing data. Sample sizes are equal in each cell but small, with cells including three cases in each combination of car size, filter type, and position. Note that a corresponding completely randomized-groups design (different cases for each car position) would require 36 cases rather than the 18 in this mixed design.

Sample sizes within cells for the randomized portion of the design are too small to assure normality of sampling distributions; with only three cases per cell, $df_{S/AB} = ab(s-1) = (3)(2)(3-1) = 12$ and $df_{C \times S/AB} = ab(c-1)(s-1) = 12$. Similarly, the within-cell sample size is too small to evaluate normality either statistically or graphically. Instead, the noise scores at each level of the repeated-measures IV are examined. Table 7.30 shows overall descriptive statistics for noise at each position (left and right), as produced by SYSTAT STATS. Labels are provided to ease interpretation of output.

[10]Well. . . .

**TABLE 7.30   Descriptive Statistics of Noise at Each Position:
SYSTAT STATS Syntax and Output**

```
LABEL SIZE / 1='small' 2='medium' 3='large'
LABEL FILTER / 1='Standard' 2='Octel'
STATS LEFT RIGHT / Kurtosis Maximum Mean Minimum SD SEK SES Skewness ,
Variance N
```

	LEFT	RIGHT
N of cases	18	18
Minimum	76.000	76.500
Maximum	85.500	84.500
Mean	81.056	80.972
Standard Dev	3.412	2.434
Variance	11.644	5.926
Skewness(G1)	-0.528	-0.461
SE Skewness	0.536	0.536
Kurtosis(G2)	-1.410	-0.946
SE Kurtosis	1.038	1.038

Skewness and kurtosis are well within guidelines of Section 2.2.3.3, at least for the test of position. The critical z value for tests of skewness and kurtosis using $\alpha = .01$ is 2.58. Each skewness value is divided by its standard error, according to Equations 2.10 and 2.11. For the left side of the car,

$$z_s = \frac{-0.528}{0.536} = -0.985$$

$$z_k = \frac{1.410}{1.038} = -1.358$$

and for the right side of the car,

$$z_s = \frac{-0.461}{0.536} = -0.860$$

$$z_k = \frac{-0.946}{1.038} = -0.911$$

Therefore, there is no concern with deviation from normality as long as no outliers are found.

7.7.1.2   Homogeneity of Variance

Cells in this design are formed by the three cases in each combination of size, type, and position. The data are split into six groups, using size and type, and then the variances within the groups for both left and right noise measurements are examined. Table 7.31 shows SYSTAT STATS syntax and output for descriptive statistics for three of the six groups.

TABLE 7.31   Descriptive Statistics for Three Cells: SYSTAT STATS Syntax and Selected Output

```
BY SIZE FILTER
STATS LEFT RIGHT / Maximum Mean Minimum SD Variance N
```

The following results are for:
  SIZE = small
  FILTER = Standard

	LEFT	RIGHT
N of cases	3	3
Minimum	83.500	81.000
Maximum	83.500	82.000
Mean	83.500	81.667
Standard Dev	0.000	0.577
Variance	0.000	0.333

The following results are for:
  SIZE = large
  FILTER = Octel

	LEFT	RIGHT
N of cases	3	3
Minimum	76.000	76.500
Maximum	77.500	77.500
Mean	76.833	77.167
Standard Dev	0.764	0.577
Variance	0.583	0.333

The following results are for:
  SIZE = small
  FILTER = Octel

	LEFT	RIGHT
N of cases	3	3
Minimum	82.500	82.000
Maximum	82.500	82.000
Mean	82.500	82.000
Standard Dev	0.000	0.000
Variance	0.000	0.000

The largest variance in the data set is .583, for the large-size car, Octel filter, with noise measured on the left side. However, three of the cells have no variance at all, and it is impossible to evaluate homogeneity of variance with zero in the denominator of F_{max} (Equation 3.21). The decision is made to test all effects at $\alpha = .025$ in order to counteract any positive bias (increase in Type I error) that may be associated with heterogeneity of variance.

7.7.1.3   Outliers

Table 7.31 provides information for evaluating outliers. The first cell (small size, standard filter, right side), for example, has a **Minimum** score of 81.0, a **Mean** of 81.667, and a **Standard Dev** (standard deviation) of 0.577. Therefore, according to Equation 2.7,

$$z = \frac{81.0 - 81.667}{0.577} = -1.155$$

At $\alpha = .01$ for the small sample, critical value of $z = 2.58$, so that the score is not an outlier. Cells with no variance have no outliers, because all scores are at the mean. None of the other minimum or maximum scores are outliers within their cells.

7.7.1.4   *Independence of Errors and Sphericity*

Independence of errors for the randomized-groups portion of the design is assured by the (presumed) random assignment of cars to filter types. There is no opportunity to violate sphericity because there are only two levels of the repeated-measures IV, position.

7.7.2   Three-Way Mixed Randomized-Repeated ANOVA

7.7.2.1   *Major Analysis*

Table 7.32 shows syntax and output for SYSTAT ANOVA. BY turns off the analysis split by groups. `PRINT=MEDIUM` produces marginal and cell (not shown) means and standard errors.

Marginal means for position are labeled `Dependent variable means` and differ little at 80.972 for the right sides of the cars and 81.056 for the left sides of the cars. `Least squares means` for small cars are shown separately for right and left sides. The marginal means for car size and filter type have to be calculated; for small cars, the marginal mean is the average of the two sides: $(81.833 + 83.000)/2 = 82.416$. Remaining marginal means are found in similar fashion. Cell means are not shown because they are in the full output of Table 7.31.

The `Univariate Repeated Measures Analysis` table shows most all effects are statistically reliable at $\alpha = .025$ with the exception of the main effect of position ($F = 0.243, p = .631$) and the position by filter-type interaction ($F = 0.027, p = .872$).

The highest-order (`POSITION*SIZE*TYPE`) interaction is statistically reliable, $F(2, 12) = 9.43, p = .003$. Effect size is calculated as per Equation 5.14:

$$\text{Partial } \eta^2 = \frac{4.847}{4.847 + 3.083} = .61$$

This suggests the need for a simple-effects analysis in this three-way design in which the simple interaction between two of the IVs is plotted at each level of the third IV. As for any simple-effects analysis, the analyzed effect should be the one that is, in itself, nonsignificant because the interaction test is confounded. The only nonsignificant two-way interaction in Table 7.32 is position by filter type. This suggests that interactions between position and filter type be analyzed separately for each level of car size.

Table 7.33 shows means and standard errors for the 12 cells participating in the three-way interaction. Means and standard deviations are from Table 7.31. Standard deviations are converted to standard errors by dividing standard deviations by the square root of 3, the cell size: $\sqrt{3} = 1.732$. The three-way interaction is plotted in Figure 7.4 through a spreadsheet program (Quattro Pro). Note that three graphs are generated, one for each car size.

Figure 7.4 suggests different patterns of the interaction for each car size. The main effect of filter type is also of particular interest in this design despite the strong, slightly disordinal, interaction,

TABLE 7.32   Mixed Randomized-Repeated ANOVA: SYSTAT ANOVA Syntax and Selected Output

```
BY
PRINT=MEDIUM
ANOVA
CATEGORY SIZE FILTER
COVAR
DEPEND LEFT RIGHT/ REPEAT =2,NAMES='POSITION'
ESTIMATE

Effects coding used for categorical variables in model.

Categorical values encountered during processing are:
SIZE (3 levels)
  small, medium, large
FILTER (2 levels)
  Standard, Octel
Number of cases processed: 18
Dependent variable means

                LEFT    RIGHT
               81.056   80.972
-----------------------------------------------------------------


Least squares means.
SIZE       =small    N of Cases =      6.000

                LEFT    RIGHT
LS. Mean       83.000   81.833
SE              0.204    0.160
-----------------------------------------------------------------
SIZE       =medium   N of Cases =      6.000

                LEFT    RIGHT
LS. Mean       83.583   83.167
SE              0.204    0.160
-----------------------------------------------------------------
SIZE       =large    N of Cases =      6.000

                LEFT    RIGHT
LS. Mean       76.583   77.917
SE              0.204    0.160
-----------------------------------------------------------------
FILTER     =Standard  N of Cases =     9.000

                LEFT    RIGHT
LS. Mean       81.611   81.500
SE              0.167    0.130
-----------------------------------------------------------------
```

(continued)

TABLE 7.32   Continued

FILTER   =Octel   N of Cases =   9.000

```
               LEFT      RIGHT
LS. Mean      80.500    80.444
SE             0.167     0.130
```

Univariate Repeated Measures Analysis
Between Subjects

Source	SS	df	MS	F	P
SIZE	260.514	2	130.257	893.190	0.000
FILTER	10.563	1	10.563	72.429	0.000
SIZE*FILTER	8.042	2	4.021	27.571	0.000
Error	1.750	12	0.146		

Within Subjects

Source	SS	df	MS	F	P	G-G	H-F
POSITION	0.063	1	0.063	0.243	0.631	.	.
POSITION *SIZE	9.875	2	4.938	19.216	0.000	.	.
POSITION *FILTER	0.007	1	0.007	0.027	0.872	.	.
POSITION *SIZE*FILTER	4.847	2	2.424	9.432	0.003	.	.
Error	3.083	12	0.257				

Greenhouse-Geisser Epsilon: .
Huynh-Feldt Epsilon   :   .

because the original goal was to show that the Octel filter is no noisier than the standard filter. This is supported by the statistically reliable main effect of type, $F(1, 12) = 72.43$, $p < .001$, partial $\eta^2 = (10.563)/(10.563 + 1.75) = .86$. A look at the means of Table 7.32 shows *lower* means for the Octel filter, on average, and Figure 7.4 suggests no condition in which the Octel filter is appreciably noisier. This observation is tested as a set of simple comparisons.

7.7.2.2   Simple Interaction Comparisons

Simple interactions between position and filter type are analyzed separately for small, medium, and large cars. This is easily done in SYSTAT ANOVA by specifying that the analysis be done BY SIZE, as shown in Table 7.34. Then a simple two-way mixed analysis is requested. The printed P values

TABLE 7.33   Mean Noise as a Function of Car Size, Filter Type, and Side of Car

	FILTER TYPE			
	Standard		Octel	
	Left	*Right*	*Left*	*Right*
Car size				
Small				
$\underline{M}$	83.50	81.00	82.50	82.00
$\underline{SE}_M$	0	0.33	0	0
Medium				
$\underline{M}$	85.00	84.17	82.17	82.17
$\underline{SE}_M$	0.29	0.17	0.33	0.17
Large				
$\underline{M}$	76.33	78.67	76.83	77.17
$\underline{SE}_M$	0.33	0.17	0.44	0.33

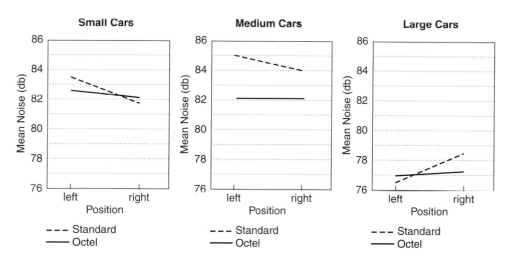

FIGURE 7.4   Mean Noise as a Function of Position, Filter Type, and Size of Car

for these simple interactions do not take into account the post hoc nature of these comparisons. Scheffé-adjusted critical F for these simple interactions requires adding the C effect (position) to Equation 7.11:

$$F_S = (a - 1)(b - 1)(c - 1)F_{(a-1)(b-1)(c-1), ab(c-1)(s-1)} \tag{7.12}$$

TABLE 7.34   Simple Interactions of Filter by Position at Each Car Size through SYSTAT ANOVA: Syntax and Selected Output

```
BY SIZE
ANOVA
CATEGORY FILTER
COVAR
DEPEND LEFT RIGHT/REPEAT =2,NAMES='POSITION'
ESTIMATE
```

The following results are for:
    SIZE   = small

Univariate Repeated Measures Analysis
Between Subjects

Source	SS	df	MS	F	P
FILTER	0.333	1	0.333	4.000	0.116
Error	0.333	4	0.083		

Within Subjects

Source	SS	df	MS	F	P	G-G	H-F
POSITION	4.083	1	4.083	49.000	0.002	.	.
POSITION *FILTER	1.333	1	1.333	16.000	0.016	.	.
Error	0.333	4	0.083				

The following results are for:
    SIZE   = medium

Univariate Repeated Measures Analysis
Between Subjects

Source	SS	df	MS	F	P
FILTER	17.521	1	17.521	76.455	0.001
Error	0.917	4	0.229		

Within Subjects

Source	SS	df	MS	F	P	G-G	H-F
POSITION	0.521	1	0.521	3.571	0.132	.	.
POSITION *FILTER	0.521	1	0.521	3.571	0.132	.	.
Error	0.583	4	0.146				

TABLE 7.34   Continued

```
The following results are for:
   SIZE    = large
```

```
Univariate Repeated Measures Analysis
Between Subjects
----------------
```

Source	SS	df	MS	F	P
FILTER	0.750	1	0.750	6.000	0.070
Error	0.500	4	0.125		

```
Within Subjects
---------------
```

Source	SS	df	MS	F	P	G-G	H-F
POSITION	5.333	1	5.333	9.846	0.035	.	.
POSITION *FILTER	3.000	1	3.000	5.538	0.078	.	.
Error	2.167	4	0.542				

For the current hypothesis at $\alpha = .025$,

$$F_S = (2)(1)(1)F_{(2)(1)(1), (3)(2)(1)(2)} = (2)F_{(2, 12)} = (2)(5.10) = 10.20$$

One of the three simple interactions is statistically reliable by this criterion, position by filter for small cars, $F(1, 4) = 16.00$. Noise is greater on the left than right side of the car using the standard filter, but no such difference is noted for the Octel filter.

The basis for calculating effect size for the simple interaction is not clear for this three-way analysis. One reasonable strategy is to look at the proportion of variance in small-car noise that is associated with the filter by position interaction. Thus,

$$\eta^2 = \frac{SS_{B \times C \text{ at } a_1}}{SS_{T \text{ at small}}} = \frac{SS_{B \times C \text{ at } a_1}}{SS_{B \text{ at } a_1} + SS_{S/B \text{ at } a_1} + SS_{C \text{ at } a_1} + SS_{B \times C \text{ at } a_1} + SS_{C \times S/B \text{ at } a_1}}$$

$$= \frac{1.333}{0.333 + 0.333 + 4.083 + 1.333 + 0.333} = .21$$

where SS_T includes all sources of variance for the small-car analysis from Table 7.34. Thus, 21% of the variance in noise among small cars is attributable to the position by filter interaction.

7.7.2.3   Simple Comparisons

Two simple comparisons are of interest in light of the simple main effect of filter (favoring the Octel filter): the higher levels of noise for the Octel filter shown in Figure 7.4 for small cars (on the right) and large cars (on the left). Table 7.35 shows SYSTAT ANOVA syntax and selected output for (a) the comparison between the filters for small cars, right side; and (b) the comparison between filters for large cars, left side. These are the only cases in which the sample Octel filters produced more noise than the sample of standard filters. Note that the BY SIZE instruction is still in effect. As expected, neither of the simple comparisons approaches statistical significance.

Table 7.36 is a checklist for mixed randomized-groups-repeated-measures ANOVA. An example of a Results section, in journal format, follows for the study described.

TABLE 7.35   Simple Comparisons between Filters

(a) Left side, small cars

```
CATEGORY FILTER
COVAR
DEPEND LEFT
ESTIMATE
```

```
The following results are for:
   SIZE   = large
```

Analysis of Variance

Source	Sum-of-Squares	df	Mean-Square	F-ratio	P
FILTER	0.375	1	0.375	0.818	0.417
Error	1.833	4	0.458		

(b) Right side, large cars

```
ANOVA
CATEGORY FILTER
COVAR
DEPEND RIGHT
ESTIMATE
```

```
The following results are for:
   SIZE   = small
```

Analysis of Variance

Source	Sum-of-Squares	df	Mean-Square	F-ratio	P
FILTER	0.167	1	0.167	1.000	0.374
Error	0.667	4	0.167		

TABLE 7.36   Checklist for Mixed Randomized-Repeated ANOVA

1. Issues
   a. Independence of errors
   b. Unequal sample sizes
   c. Normality of sampling distributions
   d. Outliers
   e. Homogeneity of variance
   f. Sphericity
2. Major analyses
   a. Main effects or planned comparisons. If significant:
      (1) Effect size(s)
      (2) Parameter estimates (marginal means and standard deviations or standard errors or confidence intervals)
   b. Interactions or planned comparisons. If significant:
      (1) Effect size(s)
      (2) Parameter estimates (cell means and standard deviations or standard errors or confidence intervals in table and/or plot)
3. Additional analyses
   a. Post hoc comparisons
   b. Interpretation of departure from homogeneity of variance

---

Results

A 2 × 3 × 2 mixed randomized-repeated ANOVA was performed on automobile noise. Half the 18 cars were tested with standard filters and half with Octel filters. Each type of filter was tested with cars of three sizes: small, medium, and large. Noise was measured on left and right sides of each car. There were three cars in each combination of size and filter type. Normality of sampling distributions and homogeneity of variance could not be evaluated in the presence of small samples and lack of variability in some cells. Therefore, α for testing all effects was set to .025 to compensate for any inflation of Type I error rate due to nonnormality or heterogeneity of variance.

There was a significant three-way interaction between car size, filter type, and side of car, $F(2, 12) = 9.43$, $p = .003$, partial η^2 = .61. Means and standard errors for the 12 cells are in Table 7.33. Means are plotted in Figure 7.4.

The interaction between position and filter type differs for the three car sizes. Therefore, interactions were compared separately for small, medium, and large cars, with a Scheffé adjustment for post hoc testing. Only for small cars was the interaction statistically reliable, $\underline{F}$(1, 4) = 16.00, $\underline{p}$ < .025. Relative to noise in small cars, η^2 = .21 for the interaction. Figure 7.4 shows a difference between left and right sides for the standard filter but not the Octel filter.

Two additional comparisons are of interest in this research, because a major goal was to demonstrate that the Octel filter is no noisier than a standard filter. The highly reliable main effect of filter type shows that, on average, the standard filter is noisier than the Octel filter, $\underline{F}$(1, 12) = 72.43, $\underline{p}$ < .001. However, Figure 7.4 suggests the Octel filter is noisier for large cars measured on the left side and small cars measured on the right side. Therefore, Scheffé-adjusted simple comparisons between the filters were made for these two conditions. Neither of the simple comparisons approached statistical significance; $\underline{F}$(1, 4) = 1.00 and 0.82 for the right side (small cars) and left side (large cars), respectively.

The main effect of size and the interaction between size and position also were statistically reliable, but not of interest in the light of the significant three-way interaction and the emphasis on filters.

7.8   Comparison of Programs

Features of the SPSS, SAS, MINITAB, and SYSTAT programs for factorial randomized-groups designs and factorial repeated-measures designs apply to mixed randomized-repeated designs and are detailed in Sections 5.7 and 6.6. The only features that are unique to mixed designs have to do with specific comparisons. These are summarized in Table 7.37.

TABLE 7.37 Comparison of SPSS, SAS, SYSTAT, and MINITAB Programs for Mixed Randomized-Repeated Measures ANOVA Specific Comparisons

Feature	SPSS GLM	SAS GLM	SYSTAT ANOVA/ GLM	MINITAB GLM
Input				
Specify comparisons on the randomized-groups margin	LMATRIX	CONTRAST	CONTRAST	No
Specify polynomial comparisons on the repeated-measures margin	Yes (default)	Yes	PRINT= MEDIUM	No
User-specified comparisons on the repeated-measures margin	SPECIAL	No	No	No
Special syntax for simple main effects on repeated-measures IV	No	BY	No	No
Specify polynomial comparisons for repeated-measures simple comparisons	Yes (default)	Yes	Yes	No
User-specified coefficients for repeated-measures simple comparisons	SPECIAL	No	CONTRAST	No
User-specified interaction contrasts for both (1) randomized and (2) repeated-measures IVs	(2) MMATRIX, (1) LMATRIX	(1) CONTRAST, (2) MANOVA	(1) CONTRAST (2) CMATRIX	No
Requires data set format with one DV value per line	No	No	No	Yes
Requires hand calculation of *F* ratio	No	No	No	Yes
Output				
Univariate results for fully user-specified interaction contrasts	Yes	No	Yes	N.A.
Multivariate results for fully user-specified interaction contrasts	No	Yes	No	N.A.

7.8.1   SPSS Package

SPSS GLM handles mixed designs with no difficulty, lacking only a special syntax for simple main-effects analysis. These are easily performed, however, by limiting the analysis to one level of the IV to be held constant. Simple-effects analysis on the randomized-groups IV also may be done through SPSS ONEWAY, as demonstrated in Table 7.20. SPSS MANOVA also is useful for interaction contrasts, because a whole set of orthogonal contrasts may be done in a single run.

7.8.2   SAS System

SAS GLM is a less satisfying program for mixed analysis, because it does not permit user-specified contrasts on the repeated-measures factor, either for marginal tests or simple comparisons. User-specified interaction contrasts are available; however, the output is in the unfamiliar form of a multivariate test. Nevertheless, the results match those of the univariate tests of the other programs. One handy feature of SAS GLM is the special syntax that permits a full set of simple main effects on the repeated-measures factor in a single run.

7.8.3   SYSTAT System

SYSTAT ANOVA (and GLM) also has some idiosyncracies in handling mixed designs. For example, user-specified coefficients may be used for repeated-measures simple comparisons, but not for comparisons on the repeated-measures margin. Marginal means are not available for the randomized-groups factor, but may be calculated easily from the cell means printed out with a request for PRINT=MEDIUM.

7.8.4   MINITAB Programs

As noted in Section 6.7.5, MINITAB does not identify repeated-measures IVs, necessitating a special data set in which each DV value is on a separate line. As is the case with any factorial design with repeated measures, some F ratios must be calculated by hand. In the case of a two-way mixed design, it is the F ratio for the randomized-groups main effect that is hand calculated. More complex designs require more hand calculation.

7.9   Putting It All Together for Factorial Designs

This section revisits material from Chapters 5 (randomized-groups), 6 (repeated-measures), and 7 (mixed randomized-groups, repeated-measures) factorial designs. The goal is to make some overall patterns apparent by comparing the three analyses. A two-way factorial design is used for the examples, each IV with three levels. Consider A qualitative (e.g., type of novel) and B quantitative (e.g., months). As more IVs are added, the analysis becomes more complex, but the basic rules generalize.

7.9.1   Allocation of Cases

Table 7.38 compares the allocation of cases (three in this example) for the randomized-groups design, the repeated-measures design, and the mixed design (where A is the randomized-groups IV and B is the repeated-measures IV).

TABLE 7.38   Allocation of Cases in 3 × 3 Randomized Groups, Repeated Measures, and Mixed Designs

(a) Randomized-groups design

	b_1	b_2	b_3
a_1	s_1	s_{10}	s_{19}
	s_2	s_{11}	s_{20}
	s_3	s_{12}	s_{21}
a_2	s_4	s_{13}	s_{22}
	s_5	s_{14}	s_{23}
	s_6	s_{15}	s_{24}
a_3	s_7	s_{16}	s_{25}
	s_8	s_{17}	s_{26}
	s_9	s_{18}	s_{27}

(a) Repeated-measures design

	a_1			a_2			a_3		
	b_1	b_2	b_3	b_1	b_2	b_3	b_1	b_2	b_3
s_1									
s_2									
s_3									

(c) Mixed randomized-groups, repeated-measures design

		b_1	b_2	b_3
a_1	s_1			
	s_2			
	s_3			
a_2	s_4			
	s_5			
	s_6			
a_3	s_7			
	s_8			
	s_9			

There are 27 cases in the randomized-groups design, each providing a single DV score. There are three cases in the repeated-measures design, each providing nine DV scores, one at each combination of levels of A and B. The mixed randomized, repeated-measures design is genuinely a blend of both designs. In this example, the design requires nine cases, each providing three scores, one at each level of B.

If cases are rare or expensive to run, the repeated-measures design has clear advantages. However, if cases need to be naive or if cases are changed by the measurement process, the randomized-groups design is preferable. If cases need to be naive with respect to one IV (A) but can provide more than one response to the other (B), the mixed design is preferable. Finally, in many settings, it is desirable to block on a variable that represents characteristics of cases (e.g., demography) to produce more homogeneous groups for development of the error term; either the randomized-groups design or the mixed design is available for this goal.

7.9.2   Assumptions of Analysis

Table 7.39 summarizes the assumptions of analysis for the three designs. Consult each chapter for alternatives if an assumption is violated.

7.9.3   Error Terms

The computations of main effects (A and B in this example), and the interactions of main effects ($A \times B$ in this example) are the same for all three designs. It is the error terms that change, depending on how cases are used in the design. Table 7.40 summarizes the error terms used for each effect, and for various types of comparisons for randomized-groups, repeated-measures, and mixed designs. For clarity, and because it is often the desirable analysis when a repeated measure is quantitative, a comparison on A is referred to as A_{comp} and a comparison on B is referred to as B_{linear}.

There are several things to notice in this table. First, in the randomized-groups design, there is a single error term throughout. Second, in the repeated-measures design, each effect is tested by that effect in interaction with cases. Third, in the mixed design, things are more complicated, but there are still some rules. Purely randomized-groups effects (in this example, only A) are tested against cases nested within those effects. Any effect with a repeated-measures component (B and $A \times B$ in this example) is tested against the repeated-measures effect(s) in interaction with cases, nested within levels of the randomized-groups design. Fourth, for both repeated measures and the repeated portion of a mixed design, when a comparison is applied to the repeated measure, it is also applied to the error term. For example, the error term for B_{linear} at a_1 is $B_{\text{linear}} \times S$ at a_1.

7.9.4   Setup for Regression

Table 7.41 contains the setup for doing a randomized-groups analysis through multiple regression. In this example, A is qualitative and has 2 df. Therefore, two columns are required to code the three levels of A. Any pair of two sets of orthogonal contrast coefficients can be used, call them A_{comp1} and A_{comp2}. B is quantitative, also with 2 df. Two columns are required to code these three levels, as well, say, B_{linear} and B_{quad}. There are 4 df for the interaction, so four columns are required to code for interaction. It is important to realize that these eight columns are also required to code the main effects and interaction for repeated-measures and mixed designs. The additional columns in these designs are required to code various elements of the error terms.

TABLE 7.39 **Assumptions of Analysis for Randomized-Groups, Repeated-Measures, and Mixed Designs**

	Randomized-Groups	Repeated-Measures	Mixed
Normality of Sampling Distributions of Means	Met with 20 df for error, roughly equal n in each cell and 2-tailed tests. In 3×3 design, requires 4 cases per cell. If df low, check normality in the cells.	Met with 20 df for each error term. In 3×3 design, requires 11 cases. If df low, check normality on the margin for each effect.	*Randomized groups:* Met with 20 df for error, roughly equal n in each group and 2-tailed tests. In 3×3 design, requires 8 cases per level of A. *Repeated measures:* Met with 20 df for each error term.
Homogeneity of Variance	Met if F_{max} across cells 10 or less with sample-size ratio $\leq$ 4:1; or Levene's test nonsignificant with sample size ratio > 4:1.	Met if F_{max} on the margin for each effect 10 or less.	*Randomized groups:* Met if F_{max} for case totals 10 or less; with sample size ratio $\leq$ 4:1; or Levene's test nonsignificant with sample-size ratio > 4:1. *Repeated measures:* Met if F_{max} on the margin for each effect 10 or less.
Independence of Errors	Depends on control of extraneous variables during testing.	Met if Mauchly's test of sphericity not significant for each effect with more than 1 df.	*Randomized groups:* Depends on control of extraneous variables. *Repeated measures:* Met if Mauchley's test of sphericity not significant for each effect with more than 1 df.
Additivity	N.A.		
Absence of Outliers	Search in each cell of the design.	Search in each separate column of the DV.	Search in each separate column of the DV at each level of the randomized-groups IV.

Cases are distinguished from each other to complete the analysis for a repeated-measures design. In this example, there are a very inadequate three cases, requiring two columns, say, Sc_1 and Sc_1. Table 7.42 contains those columns, plus the interaction of cases with each of the preceding eight columns. The interaction of cases with the main effects and interactions produces the required error terms.

After the SS(reg.) for each column is determined, various columns can be combined to produce desired error terms for comparisons. For instance, if X_{11} and X_{12} are added, the result is $A_{comp1} \times S$. If X_{17} and X_{18} are added, the result is $B_{quad} \times S$. To produce $A_{comp2} \times B \times S$, add together X_{23} through X_{26}. To produce $A_{comp1} \times B_{linear} \times S$, add together X_{19} and X_{20}.

TABLE 7.40   Error Terms Used for Various Effects in Randomized Groups, Repeated Measures, and Mixed Designs

Source	Randomized Groups (Chapter 5)	Repeated Measures (Chapter 6)	Mixed (Chapter 7)
A	S/AB	$A \times S$	S/A
B	S/AB	$B \times S$	$B \times S/A$
$A \times B$	S/AB	$A \times B \times S$	$B \times S/A$
Marginal Comparisons			
A_{comp}	S/AB	$A_{\text{comp}} \times S$	S/A
B_{linear}	S/AB	$B_{\text{linear}} \times S$	$B_{\text{linear}} \times S/A$
Simple Effects			
Simple Main Effects			
A at b_j	S/AB^{a}	$A \times S$ at b_j	S/A at b_j
B at a_i	S/AB^{b}	$B \times S$ at a_i	$B \times S$ at a_i
Simple Comparisons			
A_{comp} at b_j	S/AB^{a}	$A_{\text{comp}} \times S$ at b_j	S/A at b_j
B_{linear} at a_i	S/AB^{b}	$B_{\text{linear}} \times S$ at a_i	$B_{\text{linear}} \times S$ at a_i
Interaction Contrasts			
$A_{\text{comp}} \times B$	S/AB	$A_{\text{comp}} \times B \times S$	$B \times S/A$
$A \times B_{\text{linear}}$	S/AB	$A \times B_{\text{linear}} \times S$	$B_{\text{linear}} \times S/A$
$A_{\text{comp}} \times B_{\text{linear}}$	S/AB	$A_{\text{comp}} \times B_{\text{linear}} \times S$	$B_{\text{linear}} \times S/A$

[a]Use S/A at b_j if failure of homogeneity of variance at b_j.

[b]Use S/B at a_i if failure of homogeneity of variance at a_i.

In the repeated-measures design, cases are crossed with all effects. In the mixed design, cases cross the repeated-measures effects, but are nested in the randomized-groups effects. This pattern in the way cases participate in the design is used to develop the error terms for the mixed design, as shown for the example in Table 7.43. Assume that Sc_1 and Sc_2 represent the first three of the nine cases nested in a_1, Sc_3 and Sc_4 represent the next three cases nested in a_2, and Sc_5 and Sc_6 repre-

TABLE 7.41   Columns for Randomized-Groups ANOVA through Regression. Also First Columns for Repeated-Measures and Mixed Designs

A		B		A × B			
A_{comp1}	A_{comp2}	B_{linear}	B_{quad}	A_{comp1} $\times B_{linear}$	A_{comp1} $\times B_{quad}$	A_{comp2} $\times B_{linear}$	A_{comp2} $\times B_{quad}$
X_1	X_2	X_3	X_4	X_5	X_6	X_7	X_8
				$X_1 \times X_3$	$X_1 \times X_4$	$X_2 \times X_3$	$X_2 \times X_4$

TABLE 7.42   Additional Columns Required to Produce the Error Terms for Repeated-Measures Designs

S		A × S				B × S			
Sc_1	Sc_2	A_{comp1} $\times Sc_1$	A_{comp1} $\times Sc_2$	A_{comp2} $\times Sc_1$	A_{comp2} $\times Sc_2$	B_{linear} $\times Sc_1$	B_{linear} $\times Sc_2$	B_{quad} $\times Sc_1$	B_{quad} $\times Sc_2$
X_9	X_{10}	X_{11}	X_{12}	X_{13}	X_{14}	X_{15}	X_{16}	X_{17}	X_{18}
		$X_1 \times X_9$	$X_1 \times X_{10}$	$X_2 \times X_9$	$X_2 \times X_{10}$	$X_3 \times X_9$	$X_3 \times X_{10}$	$X_4 \times X_9$	$X_4 \times X_{10}$

A × B × S							
A_{comp1} $\times B_{linear}$ $\times Sc_1$	A_{comp1} $\times B_{linear}$ $\times Sc_2$	A_{comp1} $\times B_{quad}$ $\times Sc_1$	A_{comp1} $\times B_{quad}$ $\times Sc_2$	A_{comp2} $\times B_{linear}$ $\times Sc_1$	A_{comp2} $\times B_{linear}$ $\times Sc_2$	A_{comp2} $\times B_{quad}$ $\times Sc_1$	A_{comp2} $\times B_{quad}$ $\times Sc_2$
X_{19}	X_{20}	X_{21}	X_{22}	X_{23}	X_{24}	X_{25}	X_{26}
$X_5 \times X_9$	$X_5 \times X_{10}$	$X_6 \times X_9$	$X_6 \times X_{10}$	$X_7 \times X_9$	$X_7 \times X_{10}$	$X_8 \times X_9$	$X_8 \times X_{10}$

sent the last three cases nested in a_3. The S/A error term has $a(s - 1) = 6$ df and requires six columns. Cases then cross levels of B, while they nest in levels of A. The $B \times S/A$ error term has $a(b - 1)(s - 1) = 12$ df and requires 12 columns.

In Table 7.43, if X_{15} through X_{20} are added, the result is $B_{linear} \times S/A$, whereas if X_{21} through X_{26} are added, the result is $B_{quad} \times S/A$. Columns associated with cases are not meaningful unless there is some rationale to the comparisons applied to the cases.

It should be noted that once the columns for the regression approach are created, the analysis can be performed through one of the canned multiple-regression programs, as shown in Table 5.44. Most of the programs have the capacity for performing a sequential analysis (see Tabachnick and

TABLE 7.43   Additional Columns Required to Produce the Error Terms for Mixed Designs

S/A					
Sc_1 at a_1	Sc_2 at a_1	Sc_3 at a_2	Sc_4 at a_2	Sc_5 at a_3	Sc_6 at a_3
X_9	X_{10}	X_{11}	X_{12}	X_{13}	X_{14}

$B \times S/A$											
B_{linear} $\times Sc_1$	B_{linear} $\times Sc_2$	B_{linear} $\times Sc_3$	B_{linear} $\times Sc_4$	B_{linear} $\times Sc_5$	B_{linear} $\times Sc_6$	B_{quad} $\times Sc_1$	B_{quad} $\times Sc_2$	B_{quad} $\times Sc_3$	B_{quad} $\times Sc_4$	B_{quad} $\times Sc_5$	B_{quad} $\times Sc_6$
X_{15}	X_{16}	X_{17}	X_{18}	X_{19}	X_{20}	X_{21}	X_{22}	X_{23}	X_{24}	X_{25}	X_{26}
$X_3 \times X_9$	$X_3 \times X_{10}$	$X_3 \times X_{11}$	$X_3 \times X_{12}$	$X_3 \times X_{13}$	$X_3 \times X_{14}$	$X_4 \times X_9$	$X_4 \times X_{10}$	$X_4 \times X_{11}$	$X_4 \times X_{12}$	$X_4 \times X_{13}$	$X_4 \times X_{14}$

Fidell, 2001) in which the researcher determines the order of entry of the variables. If there is equal n in each cell, the analysis produces the same results no matter the order. However, with unequal n, the researcher can determine which effect gets overlapping variability (Figure 5.11) by entering them first into the equation. Columns for continuous variables (serving either as covariates or simply as continuous IVs) can be added, as well. In an ordinary ANCOVA (Chapter 8), covariates enter first and "take" overlapping variability. Through use of sequential regression, the priority of the covariates (or a continuous IV) can be adjusted by entering them into the equation later. Using this method, the researcher can take absolute control of the progress of the solution.

7.9.5   Developing Computational Equations from Degrees of Freedom

Once you understand the pattern of crossing and nesting in your design, you can write the degrees of freedom for each effect. The degrees of freedom can be readily expanded and "translated" into the computational equations for an effect. The expansion is shown for the two-way mixed design in Table 7.44

The elements in the design are A, B, and S. Notice that each element in the computational equations contains all three, either in the numerator or in the denominator. The letters and their combinations that are developed by expansion of the degrees of freedom refer to the numerators in the computational equations. When, in the $B \times S/A$ error term, abs is developed, it refers to a particular S at a particular AB combination. That is the same as Y, which is substituted into the computational equation. When a 1 is developed, T is substituted into the computational equation. The values in the numerator are squared and the letters that do not appear in the numerator are in the denominator. Once this pattern is apparent, you can develop the computational equations for any design from the degrees of freedom.

TABLE 7.44   Development of Computational Equations from Degrees of Freedom for the Mixed Design

Source	Degrees of Freedom	Expansion of df	Computational Equation
A	$a - 1$	$a - 1$	$\dfrac{\sum A^2}{bs} - \dfrac{T^2}{abs}$
S/A	$a(s - 1)$	$as - a$	$\dfrac{\sum (AS)^2}{b} - \dfrac{\sum A^2}{bs}$
B	$b - 1$	$b - 1$	$\dfrac{\sum B^2}{as} - \dfrac{T^2}{abs}$
$A \times B$	$(a - 1)(b - 1)$	$ab - a - b + 1$	$\dfrac{\sum (AB)^2}{s} - \dfrac{\sum A^2}{bs} - \dfrac{\sum B^2}{as} + \dfrac{T^2}{abs}$
$B \times S/A$	$a(b - 1)(s - 1)$	$\begin{aligned} a(bs - b - s + 1) \\ = abs - ab - as + a \end{aligned}$	$\sum Y^2 - \dfrac{\sum (AB)^2}{s} - \dfrac{\sum (AS)^2}{b} + \dfrac{\sum A^2}{bs}$

7.10   Problem Sets

7.1   Do a one-way randomized-groups ANOVA for the case totals in Table 7.2 and compare with results for a mixed design. That is, use A as the single IV and use the case totals (summed over B) as DV scores.

7.2   In the following two-way mixed design, the randomized-groups IV is type of music and the repeated-measures IV is time of day. The DV is rating of the music.

			Time of Day			
			9AM b_1	11AM b_2	1PM b_3	3PM b_4
Rock	a_1	s_1	8	7	5	3
		s_2	9	7	5	1
		s_3	8	5	4	1
		s_4	6	6	4	2
Classical	a_2	s_5	2	4	8	10
		s_6	6	5	9	10
		s_7	2	4	6	10
		s_8	3	5	6	9

a. Check the assumptions of normality, homogeneity of variance, and no outliers using hand calculations.

b. Do the omnibus ANOVA for this design using hand calculation.

    c. Calculate effect sizes.

    d. Use a computer program to check the preceding results and test sphericity.

    e. Write a results section.

7.3 Do the contrast in Table 7.18 using the regression approach (linear trend of month).

7.4 Do a test by hand of the simple main effect of novel at each month in the small-sample example.

Extending the Concepts

7.5 Generate error terms for the following designs:

    a. Three randomized-group IVs and one repeated-measures IV.

    b. One randomized-groups IV and three repeated-measures IVs.

7.6 Consider the following three-way design with one randomized group and two repeated factors. The randomized-groups IV is pregnancy state. Four glucose blood tests were made at hourly intervals either after fasting or after a glucose load (100 grams of glucose). The DV is glucose reading.

Hours	Fasting				Post glucose			
	1	2	3	4	1	2	3	4
	60	57	50	45	97	111	98	66
Pregnant	80	79	76	69	103	105	107	108
	74	64	70	66	109	101	103	100
	60	62	61	65	130	134	121	125
	45	83	66	71	59	85	60	73
Nonpregnant	89	90	89	77	90	144	100	121
	103	104	93	90	111	129	96	124
	77	82	82	78	86	115	93	89

    a. Use computer software to do the omnibus ANOVA and test all assumptions of the analysis.

    b. Calculate effect size(s).

    c. Do appropriate post hoc analyses suggested by the results of the omnibus ANOVA.

    d. Write a results section.

CHAPTER

8

Analysis of Covariance

8.1 General Purpose and Description

Analysis of covariance (ANCOVA) is an extension of analysis of variance in which main effects and interactions of IVs are assessed after DV scores are adjusted for differences associated with one or more covariates, variables that are measured before the DV and are correlated with it.[1] The major question for ANCOVA is the same as for ANOVA: Are mean differences among levels of the IV on the adjusted DV likely to have occurred by chance? Is there a mean difference among levels of an IV on a posttest (the DV) after posttest scores are adjusted for differences in pretest scores (the covariate)? For example, skill in assembling computers (the covariate) is assessed *before* random assignment to one of three training groups: a no-training control group, a videotaped demonstration of the assembly procedures, and hands-on training. The same test of skill then serves as the DV when administered after training. During analysis, differences in skill among cases on the pretest are removed from the error term, making the adjusted ANOVA a potentially more powerful test of the effects of treatment. Statistical analysis tests the null hypothesis that the three groups have the same mean DV score after adjustment for preexisting differences in skill.

The analysis develops a regression between the DV and the covariate(s). This regression is used to assess the "noise," where noise is the undesirable variance in the DV (individual differences among cases) estimated from scores on covariates (CVs). Although cases are randomly assigned to groups in most experiments, random assignment in no way ensures equality among groups—it only guarantees, within probability limits, that there are no preexisting *systematic* differences among groups. Random differences among cases tend to spread out scores among cases within groups (thereby increasing the error term) and may also create mean differences among groups—differences that are not associated with treatment. Either of these effects can obscure differences among groups due to levels of experimental treatment. ANCOVA removes some differences among cases from the error term (making it smaller) and adjusts the means to the levels predicted if all cases had the same score on the covariate at the beginning.

Both ANCOVA and repeated-measures ANOVA (cf. Chapter 6) are used to increase the power of a study by assessing and then removing variability associated with differences among cases from

---

[1]Much of the material for this chapter is adapted from Tabachnick and Fidell (2001).

the error term. In repeated-measures ANOVA, variance due to individual differences among cases is estimated from consistencies within cases over treatments. In ANCOVA, variance due to individual differences is estimated from the linear regression between the DV and the CV(s); the DV scores are statistically adjusted to what they would be if all cases scored identically on the CV(s), and then ANOVA is performed on the adjusted DV scores. Tests of main effects and interactions are more powerful when there are preexisting differences among cases on the DV as assessed by the CV. Otherwise, power is the same as, or lower than, in randomized-groups designs without CVs.

In the classical experimental use of ANCOVA, cases are measured on one or more CVs before the cases are randomly assigned to levels of one or more IVs. A CV is usually a continuous variable and is often measured on the same scale as the DV. However, a CV might also be some characteristic of the case (IQ, educational level, anxiety level, thickness of the fiber in an example testing fiber strength, etc.) that is measured on a different scale from the DV. In experiments, CVs are not systematically related to levels of IV(s)[2] because they are assessed prior to treatment.

ANCOVA is also used in nonexperimental studies when cases cannot be randomly assigned to treatment or levels of IVs are not manipulated. Group means are adjusted to what they would be if all cases had identical scores on the CV(s) and differences between cases on CVs are removed so that, presumably, the only mean differences that remain are related to the grouping IV(s). One problem is that differences could also be due to attributes that have not been used as CVs. A further problem is that these CVs are frequently related to the IV(s) as well as to the DV. In nonexperimental studies, then, interpretation of ANCOVA is fraught with difficulty. This application of ANCOVA is primarily for descriptive model building—the CV enhances prediction of the DV—but there is no implication of causality. If the research question involves causality, ANCOVA is no substitute for running an experiment.[3]

Although interpretations differ, the statistical operations are identical in any application of ANCOVA. In randomized-groups ANCOVA, like randomized-groups ANOVA, variance in scores is partitioned into variance due to differences between levels of the IV and variance due to differences within levels. Squared differences between scores and various means are summed and these sums of squares (when divided by appropriate degrees of freedom) provide estimates of variance attributable to main effects, interactions, and error. However, in ANCOVA, the regression of one or more CVs on the DV is estimated first, DV scores are adjusted, and ANOVA is performed on adjusted values.

Lee (1975) presents an intuitively appealing illustration of the manner in which ANCOVA reduces error variance in a one-way randomized-groups design with three levels of the IV (Figure 8.1). The vertical axis on the right-hand side of the figure illustrates scores and group means in traditional ANOVA. The error term, computed from the sum of squared deviations of DV scores around their associated group means, is substantial because there is considerable spread in scores within each group.

When the same scores are analyzed in ANCOVA, a regression line is found first that relates the DV to the CV. The error term is based on the (sum of squared) deviations of the DV scores from the

---

[2]However IV–CV relationships may occur by chance.

[3]A third application of ANCOVA is to use stepdown analysis to interpret IV differences when several DVs are used in MANOVA, as described in Chapter 9 of Tabachnick and Fidell (2001) and elsewhere.

regression line running through each group mean instead of from the means themselves. Consider the score in the lower left-hand corner of Figure 8.1. The score is near the regression line (a small deviation for error in ANCOVA) but far from the mean for its own group (a large deviation for error in ANOVA). As long as the slope of the regression lines is not zero, ANCOVA produces a smaller sum of squares for error than ANOVA. If the slope is zero, sum of squares for error is the same as in ANOVA, but mean square for error is slightly larger because each CV uses up one degree of freedom from the error term.

ANCOVA is extremely flexible. CVs can be measured on the same scale as the DV or on a different scale. CVs can be either continuous or dichotomous. CVs can be measured once or repeatedly. There may be one or more CVs, measured on the same or different scales, each measured once or repeatedly. CVs can also be used in all ANOVA designs—one-way and factorial randomized-groups designs, repeated-measures designs, mixed randomized-repeated designs, partial factorial designs, random-effects designs, and so on. Specific comparisons and trend analysis are available in ANCOVA, along with estimates of effect size. A price for this flexibility includes some additional assumptions and the necessity of testing them, along with a somewhat less straightforward interpretation of the results.

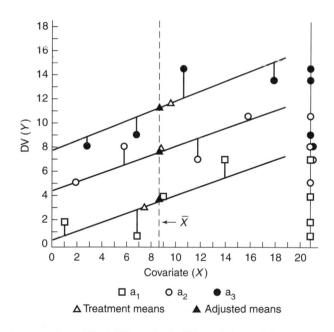

FIGURE 8.1   Plot of Hypothetical Data. The straight lines with common slope are those that best fit the data for the three treatments. The data points are also plotted along the single vertical line on the right.

(From *Experimental Design and Analysis* by Wayne Lee. Copyright © 1975 by W. H. Freeman and Company. Used with permission.)

8.2   Kinds of Research Questions

As with ANOVA, the question in ANCOVA is whether mean differences on the adjusted DV between levels (or combinations of levels) of the IV(s) are larger than expected by chance. In ANCOVA, however, there are additional questions associated with the CV(s).

8.2.1   Effect of the IV(s)

Holding all else constant, are differences in adjusted means associated with different levels of an IV larger than expected by chance? For example, is skill in assembly of computers affected by different types of training, after removing prior individual differences in assembly skill? If there is a second IV (e.g., size of computer to be assembled, with two levels, desktop and laptop), mean differences in adjusted skill in assembly are tested for this IV also. The procedures described in Section 8.4 answer this question by testing the null hypothesis that this IV also has no systematic effect on the adjusted DV.

In experimental design, "holding all else constant" is accomplished through several procedures. One of them, the topic for this chapter, is to measure the influence of extraneous variables (CVs) and hold their influence constant by adjusting for differences on them statistically. A second procedure is to institute strict experimental controls over extraneous variables to hold them constant while levels of IV(s) are manipulated. A third procedure is to turn a potentially effective extraneous variable into a blocking IV and study its effects by crossing the levels of the manipulated IV with it in factorial design. Another procedure is to randomize the levels of the extraneous variable (such as time of day) throughout the levels of the primary IV in the hopes of distributing the effects of the extraneous variable equally among treatments. A major consideration in experimental design is which (combination) of these procedures is more effective or more feasible for which extraneous variables in a given research program.

8.2.2   Effect of Interactions among IVs

Holding all else constant, does change in response over levels of one IV depend on levels of another IV? That is, do IVs interact in their effect on response?[4] For the example, when size of computer is added to type of training as a second IV, are differences in skill produced by the three levels of training the same for both desktop and laptop computers, after adjusting for preexisting differences in assembly skill? With more than two IVs, numerous interactions are generated.

Although interpreted differently from main effects, tests of interactions are statistically similar, as demonstrated in Section 8.5. Except for common error terms in some designs, each interaction is tested separately from main effects and other interactions. These tests are independent when sample sizes in all groups are equal and the design is balanced.

8.2.3   Effects of Covariates

Analysis of covariance is based on a linear regression between CV(s) and the DV, but there is no guarantee that the regression actually provides adjustment. The regression is evaluated statistically

---

[4]Chapter 5 contains an extensive discussion of interaction.

by testing the CV(s) as a source of variance in DV scores. In the computer assembly example, is pretest skill (the CV) related to posttest skill (the DV), ignoring or adjusting for effects of differential treatment? Evaluation of CV(s) is illustrated in Section 8.4.4.

8.2.4   Parameter Estimates

If a main effect or interaction is statistically significant, what adjusted population parameter (adjusted mean) is estimated for each level of the IV? What is the group mean for each level of the IV after adjustment for CVs and what are the standard errors of those means? For the example, if there is a main effect of type of training, what is the mean adjusted posttest assembly skill score in each of the three groups? If there is significant interaction, what then are the mean adjusted posttest assembly skill scores in each of the six cells formed by combining type of training with size of computer? Section 8.6.5 shows how to calculate adjusted means and Section 8.7 demonstrates their use along with standard errors in an example.

8.2.5   Effect Sizes

If a main effect or interaction is reliably associated with changes in the DV, the next logical question is: How much? How much of the variance in adjusted DV scores is associated with each main effect or interaction? For example, if the mean difference for type of training is significant, one then asks: What proportion of variance in the adjusted assembly skill scores is attributed to the IV? Estimation of adjusted effect size is described in Section 8.6.3 and demonstrated in Section 8.7.

8.2.6   Power

How high is the probability of showing that there are mean differences among groups if, indeed, treatment has an effect? For the example, if the hands-on program is superior to the video-based training program or to no program at all, what is the probability of demonstrating that superiority? Estimates of power made prior to running a study are used to help determine sample size. Estimates of power as part of the analysis of a completed study are primarily used to determine why the research hypothesis did not find support and how many cases need to be added to demonstrate significance in a replication of the study. Power is discussed in Section 8.6.4.

8.2.7   Specific Comparisons

When statistically significant effects are found for an IV with more than two levels, what is the source of the differences? Which adjusted group means differ significantly from each other? Or if the levels of the IV differ quantitatively, is there a simple trend over levels of the IV? For the example, after adjusting for individual differences in skill, (1) are the two treatment groups more effective in increasing assembly skill than the no-training control and (2) is the hands-on training more effective than video-based training?

Tests for these two questions could either be planned and performed in lieu of ANCOVA or, with some loss in sensitivity, done post hoc after finding a main effect of the IV in ANCOVA. Planned and post hoc comparisons in ANCOVA are discussed in Section 8.6.6.

8.3   Assumptions and Limitations

8.3.1   Theoretical Issues

As with ANOVA, the statistical test in no way assures that changes in the DV are caused by an IV. The inference of causality is a logical rather than a statistical problem that depends on the manner in which cases are assigned to levels of the IV(s), manipulation of levels of the IV(s) by the researcher, and controls used in the research. Statistics are available to test hypotheses from both nonexperimental and experimental research, but only in the latter case is attribution of causality justified. Nonexperimental use of CVs is both controversial and fraught with difficulty of interpretation. For example, if age is a CV, the interpretation of the results of treatment includes the caveat: "if everyone were the same age." But in a nonexperimental study, the reality may be that different treatments inherently attract cases of different ages.

Choice of CVs is a logical exercise as well. As a general rule, one wants a very small number of CVs, all correlated with the DV and none correlated with each other. The goal is maximum adjustment of the DV with minimum loss of degrees of freedom for error. Calculation of the regression of the DV on the CV(s) costs one degree of freedom for error for each CV. Thus, *the gain in power from a smaller sum of squares for error may be offset by the loss in degrees of freedom.* When there is substantial correlation between a DV and a CV, the reduction in sum of squares for error more than offsets the loss of a degree of freedom. With multiple CVs, however, a point of diminishing returns is quickly reached, especially if the CVs are correlated (see Section 8.6.1).

A frequent caution in experimental work is that the CVs must be independent of treatment. Scores on CVs are gathered before treatment is administered. Violation of this precept results in removal of that portion of the IV–DV relationship that is associated with the CV. In this situation, adjusted group means may be closer together than unadjusted means, and these adjusted means are difficult to interpret.

In nonexperimental work, sources of bias are many and subtle and can produce either under-adjustment or overadjustment of the DV. At best, the nonexperimental use of ANCOVA allows you to look at IV–DV relationships (noncausal) adjusted for the effects of CVs, as measured. Do not expect ANCOVA to permit causal inference of treatment effects with nonrandomly assigned groups. If random assignment is absolutely impossible, or if it breaks down because of nonrandom loss of cases, be sure to thoroughly ground yourself in the literature regarding use of ANCOVA in such cases, starting with Cook and Campbell (1979).

Limitations to generalizability apply to ANCOVA as they do to ANOVA or any other statistical test. One can generalize only to those populations from which a random sample is taken. ANCOVA may, in some very limited sense, adjust for a failure to randomly assign the sample to groups, but it does not affect the relationship between the sample and the population to which one can generalize.

8.3.2   Practical Issues

The ANCOVA model assumes reliability of CVs, linearity between pairs of CVs and between CVs and the DV, lack of multicollinearity among CVs, and homogeneity of regression, in addition to the usual ANOVA requirements. Experiments typically are designed with only a single CV, simplifying evaluation of linearity and outliers, and eliminating the need to consider multicollinearity. However, procedures when there are multiple CVs are described here as well.

8.3.2.1 Absence of Outliers

There are two kinds of outliers, univariate and multivariate. Univariate outliers are cases with extreme scores on a single variable (whether DV or CV), apparently disconnected from other cases in their group, as discussed in Sections 2.2.3.4 and 3.4.4. In ANCOVA, *univariate outliers are sought separately on the DV and each of the CV(s)*. They are sought separately at each level or each combination of levels of the IV(s) by looking for disconnected cases with large z scores.[5] Once potential univariate outliers are located, if there is more than one CV, the search for multivariate outliers begins.

Multivariate outliers are sought among the CVs[6] and are harder to spot because they are cases with unusual *combinations* of scores. Cases with such unusual combinations are sometimes called discrepant. The z scores on each CV separately may be reasonable, but their combination is not. For instance, a 5-foot-tall person is not unusual, nor is a person who weighs 200 pounds; however, a 5-foot-tall person who weighs 200 pounds is unusual. If height and weight are being used as CVs in a study, such a person is likely to be a multivariate outlier. The problem with outliers, generally, is that they have undue impact on the analysis. In ANCOVA, that translates as unreasonable adjustment of the DV.

Multivariate outliers may be detected by statistical or graphical methods. Between these two, statistical methods are preferred.[7] A commonly used statistical procedure is computation of Mahalanobis distance for each case. Mahalanobis distance is the distance of a case from the centroid of the remaining cases in its cell where the centroid is a point created by the means of all the CVs. For instance, if there are two CVs, height and weight, the centroid is the point that represents the intersection of the mean on height and the mean on weight. The Mahalanobis distance for a case is the distance of the point for the case's own two scores from the point representing both means. The farther the scores from the centroid, the greater the Mahalanobis distance.

The Mahalanobis distance of each case, in turn, from all other cases in its cell, is available in SYSTAT GLM and ANOVA (where the value produced is the square root of the Mahalanobis distance produced by the other programs) and in SPSS DISCRIMINANT (by requesting a display of casewise results, as demonstrated in Section 8.7.2.1.3). A very conservative probability estimate for a case being an outlier, say, $p < .001$, is appropriate with Mahalanobis distance.

Mahalanobis distances are also found through SPSS and SAS by running REGRESSION separately for each group with the CVs as predictors (IVs) and some other variable, arbitrarily chosen, as the predicted variable (the DV). Use of regression may identify a slightly different set of cases as outliers, however, because different error terms are developed in each of the separate runs, unlike the SYSTAT programs and SPSS DISCRIMINANT.

---

[5]A dichotomous CV (such as a grouping variable) is considered a univariate outlier when fewer than 10% of the cases are in one of the two groups.

[6]Multivariate outliers can also occur between the DV and the CV(s). However, in this situation, they are likely to produce heterogeneity of regression (Section 8.3.2.7), leading to rejection of ANCOVA. If CVs are serving as a convenience in most analyses, rejection of ANCOVA because there are multivariate outliers is hardly convenient.

[7]The discussion of statistical methods for detecting outliers is adapted from Tabachnick and Fidell (2001).

With SAS, there is the further complication that a value of leverage, h_{ii}, is reported instead of Mahalanobis distance. This is easily converted to Mahalanobis distance, however:

$$\text{Mahalanobis distance} = (n-1)(h_{ii} - 1/n) \qquad (8.1)$$

Or, as is sometimes more useful,

$$h_{ii} = \frac{\text{Mahalanobis distance}}{N-1} + \frac{1}{N}$$

The latter form is handy if you want to find a critical value for leverage at $\alpha = .001$ by translating the critical value for Mahalanobis distance.

Some outliers may hide behind other outliers. When one or two cases identified as outliers are deleted, the data become more consistent and then other cases become extreme. Sometimes it is a good idea to screen for outliers several times, each time dealing with cases identified as outliers on the last run, until finally no new outliers are identified. It is also a good idea to see if univariate outliers are also multivariate outliers before deciding what to do with them. Often, the same cases show up in both analyses; sometimes they do not. It is usually better to decide what to do with outliers when the total extent of the problem is known.

Recent research has pointed out unreliability of methods of outlier detection based on Mahalanobis distance or other leverage measures (e.g., Egan and Morgan, 1998; Hadi and Simonoff, 1993; Rousseeuw and van Zomeren, 1990). Unfortunately, alternative methods are computationally challenging and currently unavailable in statistical packages. Therefore, results of any method of outlier detection should be viewed cautiously.

8.3.2.2 Absence of Multicollinearity

If there are two or more CVs, they should not be highly correlated with each other. Extremely highly correlated variables are multicollinear. Perfectly correlated variables cause singularity. *One or more CVs in a set of highly correlated CVs should be eliminated* because they add very little adjustment to the DV, because they each remove a degree of freedom from the error term, and because of potential computational difficulties if they are singular or multicollinear. Software programs typically guard against multicollinearity among CVs high enough to produce computational difficulties. However, there is a net loss to the analysis by using highly correlated CVs long before that point is reached.

The size of correlation is evaluated through bivariate or multiple-regression procedures where each CV, in turn, is used as the DV with the remaining CVs treated as IVs. The squared multiple correlation is the variance in the CV currently used as DV that is associated with the other CVs. For purposes of ANCOVA, *any CV with a squared multiple correlation (SMC) in excess of .50 may be considered redundant and deleted from further analysis.* Section 8.6.1.1 shows a check for multicollinearity among CVs.

8.3.2.3 Normality of Sampling Distributions

As in all ANOVA, it is assumed that the sampling distributions of means are normal within each group. As discussed before, it is the sampling distributions of means and not the raw scores within each cell that need to be normally distributed. Section 3.4.1 provided guidelines for dealing with normality of sampling distributions. However, the alternative of using a nonparametric method when the assumption is violated is not available for ANCOVA.

8.3.2.4 Independence of Errors

The assumption that deviations of individual DV scores around their group means are independent applies equally to randomized-groups ANCOVA and ANOVA, as do the issues surrounding violation of the assumption. Independence of errors in repeated-measures IVs is dealt with through tests of sphericity, as discussed in Sections 6.3.2.3 and 6.6.2.

8.3.2.5 Homogeneity of Variance

Just as in ANOVA, it is assumed in ANCOVA that the variance of DV scores within each cell of the design is a separate estimate of the same population variance. In ANCOVA, the CV(s) are also evaluated for homogeneity of variance. If a CV fails the test, either a more stringent test of main effects and interactions is required (e.g., $\alpha = .025$ instead of .05) or the CV is dropped from the analysis. Sections 3.4.3 and 4.5.4 provide guidelines and formal tests for evaluating homogeneity of variance, and remedies for violation of the assumption.

8.3.2.6 Linearity

The ANCOVA model assesses the linear relationship between each CV and the DV and among all pairs of CVs if there is more than one. Nonlinear relationships, if present, are not captured by the analysis so that error terms are not reduced as fully as they might be, optimum matching of groups is not achieved, and group means are incompletely adjusted. In short, the power of the statistical test is reduced, producing conservative errors in statistical decision making.

If nonlinearity is suspected, *examine scatterplots of the DV with each CV and all CVs with one another* in each cell of the design. All programs including spreadsheets have modules for producing scatterplots.

If there seems to be a curvilinear relationship between the DV and a CV,[8] it may be corrected by using a transformation of the CV, or raising the CV to a higher-order power, or by simply eliminating a CV that produces nonlinearity. Nonlinear relationships between pairs of CVs can be handled by the same procedures, although it may not be worthwhile to preserve a CV that complicates interpretation.

8.3.2.7 Homogeneity of Regression

Adjustment of scores in ANCOVA is made on the basis of an average within-cell regression coefficient. The assumption is that the slope of the regression between the DV and the CV(s) within each cell is an estimate of the same population regression coefficient—that is, that the slopes are equal for all cells.

Heterogeneity of regression implies that there is a different DV–CV(s) slope in some cells of the design, or, stated another way, that there is an interaction between IV(s) and CV(s). If the IV and

---

[8]Tests for deviation from linearity are available (cf. Myers and Well, 1991), but there seems to be little agreement as to the appropriate test or the seriousness of significant deviation in the case of ANCOVA. Therefore, formal tests are not recommended.

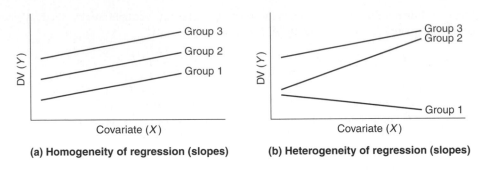

FIGURE 8.2   DV–CV Regression Lines for Three Groups Plotted
on the Same Coordinates for Conditions of (a) Homogeneity and
(b) Heterogeneity of Regression

CV(s) interact, the relationship between the CV(s) and the DV is different at different levels of the IV(s), and the CV adjustment that is needed for various cells is different. Figure 8.2 illustrates, for three groups, perfect homogeneity of regression (equality of slopes) and extreme heterogeneity of regression (inequality of slopes).

Test the assumption of homogeneity of regression using procedures described in Section 8.6.2. ANCOVA is inappropriate if the assumption is violated; alternatives to ANCOVA are discussed in Section 8.6.7.

8.3.2.8   Reliability of Covariates

It is assumed in ANCOVA that CVs are measured without error, that they are perfectly reliable. The issue is whether there is consistency in assessment of the CV score over the course of the study so that the assessment is the same at two points in time or with two types of measurement. In the case of some variables (such as diameter, or category of religious affiliation), the assumption is usually justified. With other variables (such as variables measured psychometrically or with unstable instrumentation), the assumption is not so easily made. And some CVs (such as attitude) may be reliable at the point of measurement, but fluctuate over short periods.

In experimental research, unreliable CVs lead to loss of power and a conservative statistical test through underadjustment of the error term. In nonexperimental applications, unreliable CVs can lead to either underadjustment or overadjustment of the means, as well. Thus, the issue is more serious in nonexperimental research.

8.4   Fundamental Equations

The simplest ANCOVA has one randomized-groups IV with at least two levels and one CV. This section shows allocation of cases to levels, partition of sources of variance, and computation of a one-way randomized-groups ANCOVA by the traditional method. Analyses with more than three levels are calculated in the same manner as those with three levels.

Analysis using the regression method is not as straightforward as for ANOVA because the CV is not orthogonal with the coding of the IV(s). Therefore, only the traditional approach to the analysis is demonstrated in this chapter.

8.4.1   Allocation of Cases to Conditions

Cases are assigned to groups in the same manner as they are in ANOVA, with the exception that CVs are measured before treatments are applied. Measurement of the CV(s) may be made either before or after random assignment, as long as the measurement process is precisely the same for all groups and knowledge of the CV score does not affect the randomization process. Assignment is made as in Table 4.1.

8.4.2   Partition of Sources of Variance

Equations for ANCOVA are an extension of those for ANOVA. Averaged squared deviations from means—SSs—are partitioned into SS associated with different levels of the IV (between-groups SS) and SS associated with differences in scores within groups (unaccounted for or error SS). There are three partitions, however: one for the DV, one for the CV, and one for the cross-products of CV with DV. Recall that SS for the DV in ANOVA is partitioned by summing and squaring differences between scores and various means.

$$\sum_i \sum_j (Y_{ij} - GM)^2 = n \sum_j (\overline{Y}_j - GM)^2 + \sum_i \sum_j (Y_{ij} - \overline{Y}_j)^2 \tag{8.2}$$

or

$$SS_T = SS_A + SS_{S/A}$$

The total sum of squared differences between scores on Y (the DV) and the grand mean (GM) is partitioned into two components: sum of squared differences between group means $(\overline{Y}_j)$ and the grand mean (i.e., systematic or between-groups variability); and sum of squared differences between individual scores (Y_{ij}) and their respective group means (i.e., error).

In ANCOVA, the two additional partitions involve the CV and the CV–DV relationship. First, the differences between CV scores and their GM are partitioned into between-groups and within-groups sums of squares:

$$SS_{T(x)} = SS_{A(x)} + SS_{S/A(x)} \tag{8.3}$$

The total sum of squared differences on the CV (x) is also partitioned into differences between groups and differences within groups.

Finally, the covariance (the linear relationship between the DV and the CV) is partitioned into sums of products associated with covariance between groups and sums of products associated with covariance within groups.

$$SP_T = SP_A + SP_{S/A} \tag{8.4}$$

A *sum of squares* involves taking deviations of scores from means (e.g., $X_{ij} - \overline{X}_j$ or $Y_{ij} - \overline{Y}_j$), squaring them, and then summing the squares over all cases; a *sum of products* involves taking two deviations from the same case (e.g., both $X_{ij} - \overline{X}_j$ and $Y_{ij} - \overline{Y}_j$), multiplying them together (instead of squaring), and then summing the products over all cases. As discussed in Section 3.2.3.1, the means that are used to produce the deviations are different for the different sources of variance in the research design.

The partitions for the CV (Equation 8.3) and the partitions for the association between the CV and DV (Equation 8.3) are used to adjust the sums of squares for the DV. The adjusted sum of squares for treatment is

$$SS'_A = SS_A - \left[\frac{(SP_T)^2}{SS_{T(x)}} - \frac{(SP_{S/A})^2}{SS_{S/A(x)}} \right] \tag{8.5}$$

The adjusted between-groups sum of squares (SS'_A) is found by subtracting from the unadjusted between-groups sum of squares a term based on sums of squares associated with the CV, X, and sums of products for the linear relationship between the DV and the CV.

And the adjusted sum of squares for error is

$$SS'_{S/A} = SS_{S/A} - \frac{(SP_{S/A})^2}{SS_{S/A(x)}} \tag{8.6}$$

The adjusted within-groups sum of squares $(SS'_{S/A})$ is found by subtracting from the unadjusted within-groups sum of squares a term based on within-groups sums of squares and products associated with the CV and with the linear relationship between the DV and the CV.

This can be expressed in an alternate, somewhat more intelligible, form. The adjustment for each score is the deviation of that score from the grand mean of the DV minus the deviation of the corresponding CV from the grand mean on the CV, weighted by the regression coefficient for predicting the DV from the CV. Symbolically, for an individual score:

$$(Y - Y') = (Y - GM_y) - B_{y.x}(X - GM_x) \tag{8.7}$$

The adjustment for any subject's score $(Y - Y')$ is obtained by subtracting from the unadjusted deviation score $(Y - GM_y)$ the individual's deviation on the CV $(X - GM_x)$ weighted by the regression coefficient, $B_{y.x}$.

Total degrees of freedom and df_A are the same as for ANOVA:

$$df_T = N - 1 \tag{8.8}$$

and

$$df_A = a - 1 \tag{8.9}$$

However, calculation of the regression coefficient for the DV–CV relationship (B) requires a degree of freedom so that with a single CV, $df'_T = N - 2$ and

$$df'_{S/A} = N - a - 1 = a(n - 1) - 1 = an - a - 1 \tag{8.10}$$

Figure 8.3 diagrams the partition of adjusted sums of squares and degrees of freedom for ANCOVA with a single CV.

Once adjusted sums of squares are found, mean squares are found by dividing by appropriately adjusted degrees of freedom. Thus,

$$MS'_A = \frac{SS'_A}{df'_A} \tag{8.11}$$

and

$$MS'_{S/A} = \frac{SS'_{S/A}}{df'_{S/A}} \tag{8.12}$$

MS_T is not a useful quantity for ANCOVA.

The F ratio then is

$$F = \frac{MS'_A}{MS'_{S/A}} \qquad df = (a - 1), [a(n - 1) - 1] \tag{8.13}$$

(a) Sums of squares

(b) Degrees of freedom

FIGURE 8.3   Partitions of (a) Total Adjusted Sum of Squares into Sum of Squares due to Adjusted Differences between the Groups and due to Adjusted Differences among Cases within the Groups and (b) Total Adjusted Degrees of Freedom into Degrees of Freedom Associated with Groups and Associated with Cases within the Groups

8.4.3 Traditional Approach with Three Levels and One Covariate

The unrealistically small, hypothetical data set of Table 8.1 is the same as that in Section 4.4 with the addition of a CV. Rating of a ski vacation (the DV) is evaluated as a function of view from the hotel room (the IV) adjusted for rating of past ski vacations (the CV). Skiers first provide a rating of their past ski vacations and then are randomly assigned to a hotel room with a view of the parking lot, a view of the ocean, or a view of the ski slopes (the IV). This particular vacation is assessed at the end of the trip.

Raw-score equations are more useful than deviation equations for computation of values in Equations 8.5 and 8.6. Unadjusted SS_A and $SS_{S/A}$ are as defined in Equations 3.14 and 3.15.

Treatment sum of squares for the CV is

$$SS_{A(x)} = \frac{\sum A_x^2}{n} - \frac{T_x^2}{an} \qquad (8.14)$$

Error sum of squares for the CV is

$$SS_{S/A(x)} = \sum X^2 - \frac{\sum A_x^2}{n} \qquad (8.15)$$

TABLE 8.1 Hypothetical Data Set for a One-Way Randomized-Groups ANCOVA with Three Levels and One CV

A: Type of View					
a_1: Parking Lot View		a_2: Ocean View		a_3: Ski Slope View	
X	Y	X	Y	X	Y
2	1	2	3	3	6
1	1	4	4	4	8
4	3	4	3	2	6
4	5	4	5	5	7
1	2	3	4	3	5
$A_{x_1} = 12$	$A_1 = 12$	$A_{x_2} = 17$	$A_2 = 19$	$A_{x_3} = 17$	$A_3 = 32$

$T_x = 46 \qquad \sum X^2 = 162 \qquad \sum XY = 215$

$T_y = 63 \qquad \sum Y^2 = 325$

and total sum of squares for the CV is

$$SS_{T(x)} = \sum X^2 - \frac{T_x^2}{an} \tag{8.16}$$

Sums of products between the DV and CV also are required. Error sum of products is

$$SP_{S/A} = \sum XY - \frac{\sum A_x A}{n} \tag{8.17}$$

and total sum of products is

$$SP_{total} = \sum XY - \frac{T_x T}{an} \tag{8.18}$$

When applied to the data in Table 8.1, the seven sums of squares and sums of products are as shown in Table 8.2. These values permit calculation of the adjusted sums of squares, shown in Table 8.3. Table 8.4 shows degrees of freedom for the example. Note that one degree of freedom is lost from the adjusted error term because of the single CV.

TABLE 8.2   Sums of Squares and Sums of Products for Traditional One-Way ANCOVA with Three Levels and One CV

$$SS_A = \frac{12^2 + 19^2 + 32^2}{5} - \frac{63^2}{15} = 41.2$$

$$SS_{A(x)} = \frac{12^2 + 17^2 + 17^2}{5} - \frac{46^2}{15} = 3.3$$

$$SS_{S/A} = 325 - \frac{12^2 + 19^2 + 32^2}{5} = 19.2$$

$$SS_{S/A(x)} = 162 - \frac{12^2 + 17^2 + 17^2}{5} = 17.6$$

$$SS_{T(x)} = 162 - \frac{46^2}{15} = 20.9$$

$$SP_{S/A} = 215 - \frac{(12)(12) + (17)(19) + (17)(32)}{5} = 12.8$$

$$SP_T = 215 - \frac{(46)(63)}{15} = 21.8$$

TABLE 8.3   Adjusted Sums of Squares for Traditional One-Way ANCOVA with Three Levels and One CV

$$SS'_A = 41.2 - \left[\frac{(21.8)^2}{20.9} - \frac{(12.8)^2}{17.6}\right] = 27.8$$

$$SS'_{S/A} = 19.2 - \left[\frac{(12.8)^2}{17.6}\right] = 9.9$$

TABLE 8.4   Degrees of Freedom for Traditional One-Way ANCOVA with Three Levels and One CV

$$df'_A = a - 1 = 3 - 1 = 2$$
$$df'_{S/A} = an - a - 1 = 15 - 3 - 1 = 11$$

Variance (mean square) for each source is obtained by dividing each adjusted SS by adjusted df. Table 8.5 shows calculation of adjusted mean squares for treatment and error sources of variance.

Finally, Table 8.6 is a source table that summarizes the results of Tables 8.3 through 8.5, and adds the F ratio of Equation 8.13.

The critical value for the main effect of A at $\alpha = .05$ with df = 2 and 11 is 3.98. Since 15.44 is larger than 3.98, there is a reliable mean difference in ratings of ski vacations for the three levels of treatment, after adjustment for individual differences in general rating of ski vacations. The test of the relationship between the DV and the CV is reported in Section 8.4.4; the test of the IV (treatment)–CV relationship is described in Section 8.6.2. The total SS is omitted from this source table because of ambiguity, as is discussed in subsequent sections. Note that the adjusted $SS'_T = SS'_A + SS'_{S/A} = 37.7$.

8.4.4   Computer Analyses of Small-Sample ANCOVA

Data for a one-way ANCOVA are entered as for a one-way ANOVA, with the addition of a column for each CV. With one CV, there is a column for the DV, a column coding the IV, and a column for the CV scores. Order of columns (or rows) does not matter. Tables 8.7 through 8.10 show computer analyses of the small-sample ANCOVA example of Section 8.4.3 by SAS GLM, SYSTAT GLM, SPSS GLM, and MINITAB GLM.

Table 8.7 shows syntax and output for the small-sample example through SAS GLM. Both the CV and IV are on the right side of the `model` equation, but only the IV is identified as a `class`

TABLE 8.5   Mean Squares for Traditional One-Way ANCOVA with Three Levels

$$MS'_A = \frac{SS'_A}{df'_A} = \frac{27.8}{2} = 13.9$$

$$MS'_{S/A} = \frac{SS'_{S/A}}{df'_{S/A}} = \frac{9.9}{11} = 0.9$$

TABLE 8.6   Source Table for Traditional One-Way ANCOVA with Three Levels

Source	Adjusted SS	Adjusted df	Adjusted MS	F
A	27.8	2	13.9	15.44
S/A	9.9	11	0.9	

TABLE 8.7 One-Way Analysis of Covariance for Small-Sample Example through SAS GLM

```
proc glm data=SASUSER.SSANCOVA;
    class VIEW;
    model RATING = PRE_RATE VIEW;
    lsmeans VIEW/ ;
    means VIEW ;
run;
```

Dependent Variable: RATING

Source	DF	Sum of Squares	Mean Square	F Value	Pr > F
Model	3	50.50909091	16.83636364	18.72	0.0001
Error	11	9.89090909	0.89917355		
Corrected Total	14	60.40000000			

R-Square	C.V.	Root MSE	RATING Mean
0.836243	22.57732	0.9482476	4.20000000

Source	DF	Type I SS	Mean Square	F Value	Pr > F
PRE_RATE	1	22.70254777	22.70254777	25.25	0.0004
VIEW	2	27.80654314	13.90327157	15.46	0.0006

Source	DF	Type III SS	Mean Square	F Value	Pr > F
PRE_RATE	1	9.30909091	9.30909091	10.35	0.0082
VIEW	2	27.80654314	13.90327157	15.46	0.0006

Least Squares Means

VIEW	RATING LSMEAN
1	2.88484848
2	3.55757576
3	6.15757576

Level of VIEW	N	--------RATING--------- Mean	SD	--------PRE_RATE------- Mean	SD
1	5	2.40000000	1.67332005	2.40000000	1.51657509
2	5	3.80000000	0.83666003	3.40000000	0.89442719
3	5	6.40000000	1.14017543	3.40000000	1.14017543

(categorical) variable. This signals GLM that `PRE_RATE` is a CV. Both `means` (unadjusted means) and `lsmeans` (means adjusted for the CV) are requested.

The usual two sets of SAS source tables are printed out, one showing the full model and error term, and another showing the effects of interest: the IV (`VIEW`) and the CV (`PRE_RATE`). The latter tests the reliability of the relationship between the DV and the CV. Results for `Type I` and `Type III` sums of squares differ substantially here because of nonorthogonality between the CV and the IV. The `Type I` results adjust effects in the order in which they are listed in the `model` instruction; the effect listed first is unadjusted, the second is adjusted for the first, and so on. In this example, `VIEW` is adjusted for `PRE_RATE`, but `PRE_RATE` is not adjusted for `VIEW`. The `Type I` result for the CV (`PRE_RATE`), then, is based on the correlation between `PRE_RATE` and `RATING`, without taking into account differences among groups. The `Type III` results, in which all effects are adjusted for each other, are typically of greater interest in ANCOVA (cf. Section 8.6.1).

The test of the main effect of `VIEW` matches that of Table 8.6, but for rounding error, with the `F Value` = 15.46 and `Pr > F` less than .05. Of lesser interest is the test of the CV—if we did not expect a relationship, we would not use ANCOVA—that is statistically reliable with an `F Value` of 10.35 and `Pr > F` less than .05. Mean `RATING`s for the three `VIEW` groups, adjusted for `PRE_RATE`, are in the table labeled `Least Squares Means`. Unadjusted means and standard deviations for both `RATING` and `PRE_RATE` at each level of `VIEW` are in the last table of the output.

Table 8.8 shows syntax and output for SYSTAT GLM. The CV is identified by including `PRE_RATE` in the right side of the `MODEL` list, but *not* including it in the `CATEGORY` list. Adjusted means and the regression coefficient are provided with the request for `PRINT=LONG`.

The section labeled `Estimates of effects...` shows the regression coefficient (*B* weight) for the CV, `PRE_RATE`, as used in Equation 8.8; its use is discussed in Section 8.6.5. The source table matches both Table 8.7, within rounding error, and the `Type III SS` results of Table 8.7. Adjusted means and standard errors are provided in the section labeled `Adjusted least squares means` and are plotted as well. Unadjusted means may be requested through SYSTAT STATS.

SPSS GLM UNIANOVA (General Factorial in the menu) identifies the CV after WITH in the GLM syntax, after both DV and IV are identified, as shown in Table 8.9. Adjusted means are requested by the /EMMEANS instructions and unadjusted means by the DESCRIPTIVE instruction. ETASQ and OPOWER request effect size and power statistics. PARAMETER requests *B* weights. The default method for computing sums of squares—SSTYPE(3)—is equivalent to Type III SS in SAS GLM.

The output first shows descriptive statistics, means, standard deviations, and sample sizes. Next is a source table, containing, among other things, the test of VIEW against Error (adjusted S/A) that has the same *F* ratio, within rounding error, as in Table 8.6. Of secondary interest is the test of PRE_RATE against adjusted S/A as error that shows a statistically reliable relationship between the DV and CV, after adjusting for the main effect of *A*. The Corrected Model and Corrected Total sums of squares correspond to those of SAS GLM and are based on a model in which the CV is not adjusted for the IV. Eta Squared and Observed Power are described in Sections 8.6.4 and 8.6.5, respectively.

The Parameter Estimates section shows the *B* weight for the CV, PRE_RATE, as in Equation 8.7; its use is discussed in Section 8.6.5. Note that t^2 for that parameter is equal to *F* for PRE-RATE in the source table. Estimated Marginal Means are the three group means on the DV after

TABLE 8.8   One-Way ANCOVA for the Small-Sample Example through SYSTAT GLM

```
PRINT=LONG
GLM
  CATEGORY VIEW / EFFECT
  MODEL RATING = CONSTANT + VIEW+PRE_RATE
  ESTIMATE
```

Effects coding used for categorical variables in model.

Categorical values encountered during processing are:
VIEW (3 levels)
          1,   2,   3

Dep Var: RATING   N: 15   Multiple R: 0.914   Squared multiple R: 0.836

Estimates of effects B = $(X'X)^{-1}X'Y$

                          RATING

CONSTANT		1.970
VIEW	1	-1.315
VIEW	2	-0.642
PRE_RATE		0.727

                Analysis of Variance

Source	Sum-of-Squares	df	Mean-Square	F-ratio	P
VIEW	27.807	2	13.903	15.462	0.001
PRE_RATE	9.309	1	9.309	10.353	0.008
Error	9.891	11	0.899		

Adjusted least squares means.

		Adj. LS Mean	SE	N
VIEW	=1	2.885	0.450	5
VIEW	=2	3.558	0.431	5
VIEW	=3	6.158	0.431	5

adjustment for the CV (cf. Section 8.6.5). The section also shows standard errors and confidence intervals for those means.

ANCOVA in MINITAB is done through GLM, as shown in Table 8.10. The CV is included in the GLM model equation and then identified in the Covariates instruction.

The source table provides standard information, with Total matching the corrected total of SAS and SPSS. The mean and standard deviation then are provided for the CV. The request for Means provides adjusted means and standard errors for the DV. (Note that the values in the column labeled StDev actually are standard errors.) Unadjusted means and standard deviations require the descriptive statistics module.

TABLE 8.9 One-Way Analysis of Covariance for Small-Sample Example through SPSS GLM

```
UNIANOVA
  rating BY view WITH pre_rate
  /METHOD = SSTYPE(3)
  /INTERCEPT = INCLUDE
  /EMMEANS = TABLES(view) WITH(pre_rate=MEAN)
  /PRINT = DESCRIPTIVE ETASQ OPOWER PARAMETER
  /CRITERIA = ALPHA(.05)
  /DESIGN = pre_rate view .
```

Univariate Analysis of Variance

Between-Subjects Factors

		Value Label	N
View	1.00	parking lot	5
from	2.00	ocean	5
room	3.00	ski slope	5

Descriptive Statistics

Dependent Variable: RATING

View from room	Mean	Std. Deviation	N
parking lot	2.4000	1.6733	5
ocean	3.8000	.8367	5
ski slope	6.4000	1.1402	5
Total	4.2000	2.0771	15

Tests of Between-Subjects Effects

Dependent Variable: RATING

Source	Type III Sum of Squares	df	Mean Square	F	Sig.	Eta Squared	Noncent. Parameter	Observed Power[a]
Corrected Model	50.509[b]	3	16.836	18.724	.000	.836	56.173	1.000
Intercept	6.455	1	6.455	7.179	.021	.395	7.179	.685
PRE_RATE	9.309	1	9.309	10.353	.008	.485	10.353	.833
VIEW	27.807	2	13.903	15.462	.001	.738	30.925	.993
Error	9.891	11	.899					
Total	325.000	15						
Corrected Total	60.400	14						

a. Computed using alpha = .05
b. R Squared = .836 (Adjusted R Squared = .792)

404

TABLE 8.9 Continued

Parameter Estimates

Dependent Variable: RATING

| Parameter | B | Std. Error | t | Sig. | 95% Confidence Interval | | Eta Squared | Noncent. Parameter | Observed Power[a] |
					Lower Bound	Upper Bound			
Intercept	3.927	.878	4.474	.001	1.995	5.859	.645	4.474	.982
PRE_RATE	.727	.226	3.218	.008	.230	1.225	.485	3.218	.833
[VIEW=1.00]	−3.273	.641	−5.106	.000	−4.683	−1.862	.703	5.106	.996
[VIEW=2.00]	−2.600	.600	−4.335	.001	−3.920	−1.280	.631	4.335	.976
[VIEW=3.00]	0[b]	.	.	.	.	.	.	.	.

a. Computed using alpha = .05
b. This parameter is set to zero because it is redundant.

Estimated Marginal Means

View from room

Dependent Variable: RATING

| View from room | Mean | Std. Error | 95% Confidence Interval | |
			Lower Bound	Upper Bound
parking lot	2.885[a]	.450	1.894	3.875
ocean	3.558[a]	.431	2.610	4.506
ski slope	6.158[a]	.431	5.210	7.106

a. Evaluated at covariates that appeared in the model: PRE_RATE = 3.0667.

405

TABLE 8.10   One-Way Analysis of Covariance for Small-Sample Example through MINITAB GLM

```
MTB > GLM 'RATING' = VIEW PRERATE;
SUBC>    Covariates 'PRERATE';
SUBC>    Brief 2 ;
SUBC>    Means VIEW.
```

General Linear Model

```
Factor   Type    Levels  Values
VIEW     fixed        3  1 2 3
```

Analysis of Variance for RATING, using Adjusted SS for Tests

```
Source     DF   Seq SS   Adj SS   Adj MS       F       P
VIEW        2   41.200   27.807   13.903   15.46   0.001
PRE_RATE    1    9.309    9.309    9.309   10.35   0.008
Error      11    9.891    9.891    0.899
Total      14   60.400
```

```
Term          Coef    StDev       T       P
Constant    1.9697   0.7351    2.68   0.021
PRE_RATE    0.7273   0.2260    3.22   0.008
```

Means for Covariates

```
Covariate   Mean    StDev
PRE_RATE    3.067   1.223
```

Least Squares Means for RATING

```
VIEW    Mean     StDev
1      2.885    0.4500
2      3.558    0.4307
3      6.158    0.4307
```

8.4.5   Computer Analysis Using Regression Approach to ANCOVA

Although hand computation of ANCOVA through regression requires matrix algebra because the column for the CV is not orthogonal to the column(s) for the IVs, the analysis is easily performed through a standard multiple-regression program. Table 8.11 contains the small-sample data set organized appropriately for a regression analysis. Notice that, as usual, there are as many columns for the IV (VIEW) as degrees of freedom. In this case, VIEW has three levels and 2 df, so the View_1 col-

TABLE 8.11   Data Set for Regression Approach to ANCOVA

Y Rating	X_1 Pre_rate	X_2 View_1	X_3 View_2
1	2	1	1
1	1	1	1
3	4	1	1
5	4	1	1
2	1	1	1
3	2	1	−1
4	4	1	−1
3	4	1	−1
5	4	1	−1
4	3	1	−1
6	3	−2	0
8	4	−2	0
6	2	−2	0
7	5	−2	0
5	3	−2	0

umn is the comparison of the third level of view (ski slope) against the two other views pooled, and the View_2 column is the comparison of the parking lot view with the ocean view. The CV is in the Pre_rate column and the DV is in the Rating column.

Analysis of these data through SPSS REGRESSION is illustrated in Table 8.12. The key to producing the relevant output is use of NEXT on the Linear Regression menu, to specify that pre_rate (the CV) enters before view_1 and view_2 (which enter as a block—although, if they enter separately, tests of the individual comparisons are provided), and a request for R squared change through the Statistics menu. The rest of the syntax is produced by default.

The test of the IV is found in the Model Summary table, where the F Change value of 15.462 is the omnibus test of VIEW. The test of the CV that agrees with the results of the GLM programs is in the table labeled Coefficients in the column labeled t, because $F = t^2 = (3.218)^2 = 10.36$. This is a test of the CV in the equation that also includes View_1 and View_2. The test of the relationship between the CV alone and the DV is the test of Model 1 in the Model Summary table (where the F Change value is 7.829) or in the test of Model 1 in the ANOVA table. In the ANOVA table, the test of Model 2 ($F = 18.724$) is a test of the relationship between the DV and all three variables together (Pre_rate, View_1, and View_2), a test that is also provided by SAS GLM and SPSS GLM.

At this point, you have probably realized that the regression approach offers near-complete flexibility in analysis of ANOVA-like models. For instance, the CV is just a continuous variable that could as easily be considered a continuous IV. Further, the order in which IVs and CVs are entered (and, thus, adjusted for each other) is at the discretion of the researcher. The trick is to set up the columns of data appropriate for regression and then use the facilities of one of the multiple-regression programs to enter the variables, alone or in blocks, in any order desired for the analysis.

TABLE 8.12   ANCOVA for the Small-Sample Example through SPSS REGRESSION: Syntax and Output

REGRESSION
/MISSING LISTWISE
/STATISTICS COEFF OUTS R ANOVA CHANGE
/CRITERIA=PIN(.05) POUT(.10)
/NOORIGIN
/DEPENDENT rating
/METHOD=ENTER pre_rate /METHOD=ENTER view_1 view_2 .

Regression

Variables Entered/Removed[b]

Model	Variables Entered	Variables Removed	Method
1	PRE_RATE[a]	.	Enter
2	VIEW_1, VIEW_2[a]	.	Enter

a. All requested variables entered.

Model Summary

Model	R	R Square	Adjusted R Square	Std. Error of the Estimate	Change Statistics				
					R Square Change	F Change	df1	df2	Sig. F Change
1	.613[a]	.376	.328	1.7029	.376	7.829	1	13	.015
2	.914[b]	.836	.792	.9482	.460	15.462	2	11	.001

a. Predictors: (Constant), PRE_RATE
b. Predictors: (Constant), PRE_RATE, VIEW_1, VIEW_2

TABLE 8.12 Continued

ANOVA[c]

Model		Sum of Squares	df	Mean Square	F	Sig.
1	Regression	22.703	1	22.703	7.829	.015[a]
	Residual	37.697	13	2.900		
	Total	60.400	14			
2	Regression	50.509	3	16.836	18.724	.000[b]
	Residual	9.891	11	.899		
	Total	60.400	14			

a. Predictors: (Constant), PRE_RATE
b. Predictors: (Constant), PRE_RATE, VIEW_1, VIEW_2
c. Dependent Variable: RATING

Coefficients[a]

Model		Unstandardized Coefficients		Standardized Coefficients	t	Sig.
		B	Std. Error	Beta		
1	(Constant)	1.006	1.223		.823	.425
	PRE_RATE	1.041	.372	.613	2.798	.015
2	(Constant)	1.970	.735		2.679	.021
	PRE_RATE	.727	.226	.428	3.213	.008
	VIEW_1	-.979	.177	-.690	-5.524	.000
	VIEW_2	-.336	.320	-.137	-1.050	.316

a. Dependent Variable: RATING

409

8.5   Types of Designs Using Covariates

Section 8.4 demonstrates one-way randomized-groups ANCOVA with a single CV. ANCOVA also may be used in factorial randomized-groups designs, and, under some circumstances, in repeated-measures designs.

8.5.1   Randomized-Groups Factorial

When factorial randomized-groups designs (Chapter 5) incorporate one or more CVs, the CV(s) adjusts the DV (cf. Equation 8.5) for all main effects and interactions. For example, if length of vacation (1 or 2 weeks) is added to view from window in factorial arrangement, the research questions are: (1) Does length of vacation affect rating of vacation, after adjusting for individual differences in vacation ratings? (2) Does view affect rating of vacation, after adjusting for individual differences in vacation ratings? and (3) Does the effect of view on rating depend on length of vacation, after adjusting for individual differences in vacation ratings?

Computationally, adjustment of sums of squares for effects proceeds as in Section 8.4. For a two-way design, for instance, to compute the main effect of B, substitute B for A in Equations 8.3 through 8.6, and for the interaction, substitute AB in those equations while substituting S/AB for S/A. Adjusted mean squares are formed and tested in the usual fashion, by dividing adjusted sums of squares by their adjusted degrees of freedom. Remember that one degree of freedom is subtracted from the error term for each CV to produce adjusted df. Hypotheses are tested and interpreted in the usual fashion, as described in Chapter 5.

Similarly, CVs may be applied in any of the randomized-groups Latin-square designs of Chapter 9 and the screening designs of Chapter 10. After computed sums of squares, df, and mean squares are adjusted for the CV(s), hypothesis tests proceed as in those chapters.

8.5.2   Repeated Measures

Both ANCOVA and repeated measures have the goal of reducing the error term by systematic variance associated with individual differences among cases. Although the two designs assess individual differences in separate ways, the effect on the analysis is the same. Thus, a purely repeated-measures design, in which all cases participate in all combinations of levels of all IVs, usually does not benefit from use of CVs measured only once; rather, CVs lower power by reducing the df for error by a degree of freedom each. However, in other designs with repeated measures, CVs may be helpful.

8.5.2.1   Same Covariate(s) for All Cells

There are two approaches to analysis of designs with at least one repeated-measures IV, the traditional approach and the general linear model (GLM) approach. In the traditional approach, the repeated-measures effects in the designs are not adjusted for CVs. In the GLM approach, the repeated measures are adjusted by the interaction of the CV(s) with the repeated-measures effects. SPSS MANOVA takes the traditional approach to ANCOVA. Programs labeled GLM in SAS, SYSTAT, and SPSS, as well as SYSTAT ANOVA, use the general linear model approach. Recall that MINITAB has no capability for identifying repeated-measures IVs. The work-around of Section

7.4.5 does not generalize to ANCOVA because error terms are not appropriately adjusted for the CV, resulting in erroneous df.

Table 8.13 contains a hypothetical data set for a mixed ANCOVA with a single CV measured once for each case. The randomized-groups IV is type of music: a_1 = rock; a_2 = classical. The repeated-measures IV is time of day: b_1 = 9 P.M., b_2 = 11 P.M., b_3 = 1 A.M., and b_4 = 3 A.M. (labeled T1 through T4 in the data set) at which selections are rated (the DV). The CV (EASY) is a rating of an easy listening music selection, collected before random assignment of listeners to type of music.

8.5.2.1.1 Traditional Analysis

Mixed designs (with at least one randomized-groups IV) benefit by adjustment to the randomized-groups effect(s) and error term in the analysis. All randomized-groups main effects are adjusted for CV(s), as are interactions involving only randomized-groups IVs. There is no adjustment to repeated-measures main effects, nor to any interaction involving a repeated measure, nor to error terms for these effects.

Table 8.14 shows the traditional analysis of the data set of Table 8.13 through SPSS MANOVA. Syntax is similar to SPSS GLM, except that the levels of the IV (music) must be indicated in parentheses after the label. The instruction to /PRINT=SIGNIF(AVERF, EFSIZE) CELLINFO (MEANS) requests univariate results for the repeated-measures portion of the design, printing of the effect size (partial η^2), and unadjusted cell means. Adjusted marginal means for music are requested by the /PMEANS instruction. Adjusted cell means are not available with a repeated-measures IV. Adjusted marginal means for the repeated-measures IV, trials, do not differ from unadjusted means in this analysis because repeated-measures effects are not adjusted for the covariate.

The output begins with a printout of unadjusted cell means and marginal means for TRIALS (labeled For entire sample), separately for each level of the repeated-measures factor (T1 through T4). The Tests of Between-Subjects Effects source table shows the test of the CV, labeled REGRESSION, and the test of the IV, MUSIC. The randomized-groups error term (S/A) is labeled WITHIN+RESIDUAL. Effect-size measures for the CV and randomized-groups IV follow. Then information about the CV is shown in the section labeled Regression analysis for WITHIN+RESIDUAL error term. The regression analysis provides redundant information about the significance of the adjustment by the CV; recall that $F = t^2$. Both the CV and the main

TABLE 8.13   Data Set for Traditional Analysis of Mixed Randomized-Repeated ANCOVA

MUSIC	EASY	T1	T2	T3	T4
1	6	8	7	5	3
1	6	9	7	5	1
1	4	8	5	4	1
1	3	6	6	4	2
2	6	2	4	8	10
2	7	6	5	9	10
2	3	2	4	6	10
2	5	3	5	6	9

TABLE 8.14   ANCOVA for a Mixed Design with a CV Measured Once: SPSS MANOVA Setup and Selected Output

```
MANOVA
 t1 t2 t3 t4 BY music(1,2) WITH (easy)
 /WSFACTOR = trials(4)
 /MEASURE = rating
 /PRINT = SIGNIF(AVERF, EFSIZE) CELLINFO(MEANS)
 /PMEANS = TABLES(music)
 /WSDESIGN = trials
 /DESIGN.
```

```
------------------------------------------------------------------------
Cell Means and Standard Deviations
Variable.. T1
      FACTOR        CODE        Mean     Std. Dev.     N
 MUSIC           rock         7.750         1.258      4
 MUSIC        classic         3.250         1.893      4
For entire sample            5.500         2.828      8
------------------------------------------------------------------------
Variable.. T2
      FACTOR        CODE        Mean     Std. Dev.     N
 MUSIC           rock         6.250          .957      4
 MUSIC        classic         4.500          .577      4
For entire sample            5.375         1.188      8
------------------------------------------------------------------------
Variable.. T3
      FACTOR        CODE        Mean     Std. Dev.     N
 MUSIC           rock         4.500          .577      4
 MUSIC        classic         7.250         1.500      4
For entire sample            5.875         1.808      8
------------------------------------------------------------------------
Variable.. T4
      FACTOR        CODE        Mean     Std. Dev.     N
 MUSIC           rock         1.750          .957      4
 MUSIC        classic         9.750          .500      4
For entire sample            5.750         4.334      8
------------------------------------------------------------------------
Variable.. EASY
      FACTOR        CODE        Mean     Std. Dev.     N
 MUSIC           rock         4.750         1.500      4
 MUSIC        classic         5.250         1.708      4
For entire sample            5.000         1.512      8
------------------------------------------------------------------------
Variable.. EASY
      FACTOR        CODE        Mean     Std. Dev.     N
 MUSIC           rock         4.750         1.500      4
 MUSIC        classic         5.250         1.708      4
For entire sample            5.000         1.512      8
------------------------------------------------------------------------
```

TABLE 8.14   Continued

```
Variable.. EASY
     FACTOR      CODE      Mean    Std. Dev.    N
 MUSIC          rock      4.750       1.500     4
 MUSIC          classic   5.250       1.708     4
For entire sample         5.000       1.512     8
-------------------------------------------------------------------
Variable.. EASY
     FACTOR      CODE      Mean    Std. Dev.    N
 MUSIC          rock      4.750       1.500     4
 MUSIC          classic   5.250       1.708     4
For entire sample         5.000       1.512     8
-------------------------------------------------------------------
```

```
* * * * * A n a l y s i s   o f   V a r i a n c e -- design 1 * * * * * *

Tests of Between-Subjects Effects.

   Tests of Significance for T1 using UNIQUE sums of squares
   Source of Variation        SS     DF      MS       F    Sig of F

   WITHIN+RESIDUAL           3.55     5     .71
   REGRESSION               11.33     1   11.33    15.96      .010
   MUSIC                     6.44     1    6.44     9.07      .030
   ----------------------------------------------------------------
   Effect Size Measures
                           Partial
   Source of Variation     ETA Sqd

   Regression                .761
   MUSIC                     .645
   ----------------------------------------------------------------
   Regression analysis for WITHIN+RESIDUAL error term
   --- Individual Univariate .9500 confidence intervals
   Dependent variable.. T1

   COVARIATE              B       Beta    Std. Err.   t-Value    Sig. of t

   TEASY            .42742      .68387       .107      3.995        .010

   COVARIATE    Lower -95%   CL- Upper   ETA Sq.

   TEASY             .152        .702      .761
   ----------------------------------------------------------------
   Adjusted and Estimated Means
   Variable .. T1
   CELL    Obs. Mean   Adj. Mean   Est. Mean   Raw Resid.   Std. Resid.
   1         10.125      10.339      10.125        .000         .000
   2         12.375      12.161      12.375        .000         .000
   ----------------------------------------------------------------
```

(continued)

TABLE 8.14   Continued

```
------------------------------------------------------------------
* * * * * A n a l y s i s   o f   V a r i a n c e -- design 1 * * * * * *

Tests involving 'TRIALS' Within-Subject Effect.

     Mauchly sphericity test, W =     .32890
     Chi-square approx. =            5.25111 with 5 D. F.
     Significance =                   .386

     Greenhouse-Geisser Epsilon =    .61441
     Huynh-Feldt Epsilon =          1.00000
     Lower-bound Epsilon =           .33333

AVERAGED Tests of Significance that follow multivariate tests are
equivalent to univariate or split-plot or mixed-model approach to
repeated measures. Epsilons may be used to adjust d.f. for the AVERAGED
results.
------------------------------------------------------------------
------------------------------------------------------------------


* * * * * A n a l y s i s   o f   V a r i a n c e -- design 1 * * * * * *

Tests involving 'TRIALS' Within-Subject Effect.

   AVERAGED Tests of Significance for RATING using UNIQUE sums of squares
     Source of Variation      SS     DF      MS        F    Sig of F

   WITHIN+RESIDUAL          15.63    18     .87
   TRIALS                    1.25     3     .42      .48      .700
   MUSIC BY TRIALS         179.62     3   59.87    68.98      .000
   ---------------------------------------------------------------
   Effect Size Measures
                           Partial
     Source of Variation   ETA Sqd

   TRIALS                    .074
   MUSIC BY TRIALS           .920
```

effect of **MUSIC** are statistically significant. Note that the DV is misleadingly labeled **T1** instead of rating and the CV is labeled **TEASY** instead of EASY in the ANOVA tables.

The adjusted marginal means (doubled) for the randomized-groups IV (music) then follow, along with additional redundant output that is omitted here. Note that these adjusted means require a request for **AVERF** in the **PRINT** paragraph.

The repeated-measures portion of the output begins with information about the sphericity test, along with adjustment factors should the assumption be violated (see Section 6.6.2). The **Tests** involving `'TRIALS'` `Within-Subject` `Effect` source table includes tests for `TRIALS` and `MUSIC BY TRIALS`, with the error term $(B \times S/A)$ also labeled `WITHIN+RESIDUAL`. The interaction is statistically reliable, but the main effect of `TRIALS` is not. Finally, effect-size measures are provided for the repeated-measures analysis: `TRIALS` and `MUSIC BY TRIALS`. Multivariate output is deleted here.

SPSS MANOVA does not provide adjusted marginal or cell means for repeated measures in ANCOVA. The means for the main effect of the repeated-measures factor, `TRIALS`, are the same as the unadjusted means. Adjusted marginal means for the main effect of `MUSIC` and adjusted cell means are found as per Section 8.6.5. Note that the adjusted means in Section 8.6.5 are *not* the same adjusted means that result from the GLM approach.

8.5.2.1.2   General Linear Model Analysis

In the GLM approach, all of the repeated-measures sums of squares (for main effects, interactions, and error terms) are adjusted by the interaction of the repeated-measures IV(s) with the CV. Table 8.15 shows an analysis of the data set of Table 8.13 through SYSTAT GLM.

The portions of this GLM output that refer to repeated-measures IV(s) differ from those in the traditional approach because the GLM approach adjusts repeated measures. For instance, there are adjusted means for the DV over the four trials in the section labeled `Adjusted least squares means` that differ from estimates in the traditional approach. On the other hand, the adjusted marginal means for the two levels of music (means of 5.17 and 6.08 for rock and classical music, respectively) have the same adjustment as in the traditional approach. In the source table, the test of the randomized-groups IV (`MUSIC`) and the CV (`EASY`) are also the same as in the traditional approach. However, the tests of the repeated-measures effects, `TRIALS` and the `TRIALS*MUSIC` interaction are different because of their adjustment by the `TRIALS*EASY` interaction.

The `TRIALS*EASY` interaction is reported as an additional source of variance. This is a test of differences in the relationship between the DV and CV over the four trials. Does the relationship between rating of `EASY` music and rating of either rock or classical music depend on `TRIALS`? Thus, this is a test of homogeneity of regression for the repeated-measures IV, as discussed in Section 8.6.2. There is no reliable `TRIALS*EASY` interaction in this data set—no violation of the homogeneity of regression assumption for the repeated-measures IV. Nevertheless, adjustment for the effect in this example reduces sum of squares for error enough to strengthen tests of `TRIALS` and the `TRIALS*MUSIC` interaction, even after the degrees of freedom for this interaction are deducted from the repeated-measures error term.[9]

It is not clear that the GLM strategy generally makes much sense or enhances power in ANCOVA. There is usually no a priori reason to expect a different relationship between the DV and CV for different levels of the repeated-measures IV(s). If no such relationship is present, the loss of degrees of freedom for estimating this effect could more than offset the reduction in sum of squares for error and result in a less powerful test of the repeated-measures effects. When using a GLM program, you could rerun the analysis without the CV to obtain the traditional (unadjusted) repeated-measures portion of the source table to use in a traditional type of ANCOVA, as demonstrated in Section 8.7.2.2.1.

---

[9]The multivariate output, which also includes the TRIALS by EASY interaction, is omitted.

TABLE 8.15   ANCOVA with the GLM Approach for a Mixed Design with a Constant CV: SYSTAT GLM Syntax and Selected Output

```
PRINT=MEDIUM
LABEL MUSIC / 1='ROCK' 2='CLASSIC'
GLM
CATEGORY MUSIC / EFFECT
MODEL T1 T2 T3 T4 = CONSTANT + MUSIC+EASY/ REPEAT
=4,NAMES='TRIALS'
ESTIMATE
```

Effects coding used for categorical variables in model.

Categorical values encountered during processing are:
MUSIC (2 levels)
    ROCK, CLASSIC
Number of cases processed: 8
Dependent variable means

	T1	T2	T3	T4
	5.500	5.375	5.875	5.750

Adjusted least squares means.
MUSIC   =ROCK   N of Cases =   4.000

	T1	T2	T3	T4
Adj. LS Mean	7.935	6.327	4.649	1.766
SE	0.595	0.341	0.337	0.418

MUSIC   =CLASSIC   N of Cases =   4.000

	T1	T2	T3	T4
Adj. LS Mean	3.065	4.423	7.101	9.734
SE	0.595	0.341	0.337	0.418

Univariate and Multivariate Repeated-Measures Analysis

Between Subjects

Source	SS	df	MS	F	P
MUSIC	6.436	1	6.436	9.069	0.030
EASY	11.327	1	11.327	15.960	0.010
Error	3.548	5	0.710		

Within Subjects

Source	SS	df	MS	F	P	G-G	H-F
TRIALS	4.100	3	1.367	1.802	0.190	0.215	0.190
TRIALS*MUSIC	181.199	3	60.400	79.620	0.000	0.000	0.000
TRIALS*EASY	4.246	3	1.415	1.866	0.179	0.205	0.179
Error	11.379	15	0.759				

Greenhouse-Geisser Epsilon: 0.6634
Huynh-Feldt Epsilon   :   1.0000

8.5.2.2 Varying Covariates(s) over Cells

There are two common designs in which CVs differ for cells: matched randomized-blocks designs when cases in the cells of a repeated-measures IV actually are different cases (cf. Section 6.5.3), and designs when the CV is reassessed prior to administration of each level of the repeated-measures IV(s). When the CVs differ for levels of the repeated-measures IV(s), they are potentially useful in enhancing power for all effects.

A hypothetical data set for a one-way repeated-measures ANCOVA with a varying CV appears in Table 8.16. There are two levels of the repeated-measures IV, T, and also two levels of the CV (X), measured before each level of T.

8.5.2.2.1 Traditional Analysis

Table 8.17 shows SPSS MANOVA syntax and selected output, using the traditional approach to this repeated-measures ANCOVA. The critical syntax is the listing of the two CVs, `b1_x` and `b2_x` without parenthesis after the `WITH` instruction.

Unadjusted cell means and standard deviations (not shown) begin the output and are followed by tests of the intercept (also not shown), not of interest in this analysis. The meaningful output is in the tables labeled `Tests involving 'TRIALS' Within-Subject Effect` and `Regression analysis for WITHIN+RESIDUAL error term`. The DV is misleadingly labeled `T2` in both these tables. The results show a statistically reliable effect of `TRIALS`, but no significant adjustment by the CV (labeled `T4`) with `t-value` $= -.434, p = .677$.

8.5.2.2.2 General Linear Model Analysis

GLM programs in SPSS, SAS, and SYSTAT have no special syntax for specifying a CV that changes with each level of a repeated-measures IV. Instead, the problem is set up as a randomized-groups design with one IV representing cases in which measurements for each trial are on a separate line.[10] For this example, each case has two lines, one for each trial. Trial number, CV score, and DV score are on each line. The repeated-measures design is simulated by considering both cases and trials randomized-groups IVs. Table 8.18 shows the previous data set rearranged for this analysis.

TABLE 8.16 Hypothetical Data for One-Way Repeated-Measures ANCOVA with a Varying CV

Case	T_1_X	T_1_Y	T_2_X	T_2_Y
1	4	9	3	15
2	8	10	6	16
3	13	14	10	20
4	1	6	3	9
5	8	11	9	15
6	10	10	9	9
7	5	7	8	12
8	9	12	9	20
9	11	14	10	20

[10]This setup is used in Section 6.4.1.5 and elsewhere for MINITAB, which has no provision for repeated-measures ANOVA.

TABLE 8.17   Repeated-Measures ANCOVA with a Varying CV: SPSS MANOVA Syntax and Selected Output

```
MANOVA
 b1_y b2_y WITH b1_x b2_x
 /WSFACTOR = trials(2)
 /PRINT = SIGNIF(EFSIZE), CELLIFO(MEANS)
 /WSDESIGN trials
 /DESIGN.
```

```
* * * * * A n a l y s i s   o f   V a r i a n c e -- design 1 * * * * * *

Tests involving 'TRIALS' Within-Subject Effect.

    Tests of Significance for T2 using UNIQUE sums of squares
    Source of Variation          SS     DF     MS        F    Sig of F

    WITHIN+RESIDUAL           26.08      7    3.73
    REGRESSION                  .70      1     .70      .19       .677
    TRIALS                    99.16      1   99.16    26.62       .001
    ----------------------------------------------------------------

    Effect Size Measures
                            Partial
    Source of Variation     ETA Sqd

    Regression                 .026
    TRIALS                     .792
    ----------------------------------------------------------------

    Regression analysis for WITHIN+RESIDUAL error term
    --- Individual Univariate .9500 confidence intervals
    Dependent variable.. T2

    COVARIATE             B        Beta    Std. Err.   t-Value   Sig. of t

    T4             -.21805     -.16198         .502     -.434        .677

    COVARIATE   Lower -95%   CL- Upper    ETA Sq.

    T4             -1.405        .969         .026
```

Table 8.19 shows SAS GLM syntax and output for this analysis. Because no interactions are requested, the CASE by T interaction is the error term. Type III sums of squares (**SS3**) are requested to limit output.

Used this way, the SAS GLM source table provides a test of **CASE** as an IV. Results are consistent with those of SPSS MANOVA. However, there is no test for homogeneity of covariance using this setup, relevant if there are more than two levels of the repeated-measures IV.

TABLE 8.18   Hypothetical Data for Repeated-Measures ANCOVA with Varying CV: One-Line-per-Trial Setup

CASE	T	X	Y
1	1	4	9
1	2	3	15
2	1	8	10
2	2	6	16
3	1	13	14
3	2	10	20
4	1	1	6
4	2	3	9
5	1	8	11
5	2	9	15
6	1	10	10
6	2	9	9
7	1	5	7
7	2	8	12
8	1	9	12
8	2	9	20
9	1	11	14
9	2	10	20

8.6   Some Important Issues

Analysis of covariance is complex and burdened with assumptions beyond those of ANOVA. Therefore, there are a number of issues to consider, including alternative designs to enhance power.

8.6.1   Multiple Covariates

The use of multiple CVs complicates the analysis in terms of calculation, testing of assumptions (cf. Section 8.6.2), and interpreting coefficients. CVs in ANCOVA can themselves be interpreted as predictors of the DV. From a sequential regression perspective (Section 5.6.5), each CV is simply a high-priority, continuous IV with discrete IVs (main effects and interactions) evaluated after the relationship between the CV(s) and the DV is removed.

Significance tests for CVs assess their relationship with the DV. If a CV is significant, it is related to the DV. For the small-sample example of Table 8.1, the CV, PRE_RATE, is reliably related to the DV, RATING, with $F(1, 11) = 10.35$, $p < .05$, and $B = 0.727$. This relationship is interpreted in the same way as any IV in multiple regression (Section 4.4.4).

With multiple CVs, all CVs enter the multiple-regression equation at once and, as a set, are treated as a standard multiple regression, with a regression coefficient for each CV. Within the set of CVs, the significance of each CV is assessed as if it entered the equation last; only the unique rela-

TABLE 8.19 Repeated-Measures ANCOVA: Varying CV through SAS GLM

```
proc glm data=SASUSER.SPLTPLOT;
   class CASE T;
   model Y = CASE T X / SS3;
   lsmeans T/;
   means T;
run;
```

Class Level Information

Class	Levels	Values
CASE	9	1 2 3 4 5 6 7 8 9
T	2	1 2

Number of observations in data set = 18

Dependent Variable: Y

Source	DF	Sum of Squares	Mean Square	F Value	Pr > F
Model	10	295.53592314	29.55359231	7.93	0.0059
Error	7	26.07518797	3.72502685		
Corrected Total	17	321.61111111			

R-Square	C.V.	Root MSE	Y Mean
0.918923	15.17056	1.9300328	12.72222222

Source	DF	Type III SS	Mean Square	F Value	Pr > F
CASE	8	105.19011815	13.14876477	3.53	0.0569
T	1	99.15814536	99.15814536	26.62	0.0013
X	1	0.70258981	0.70258981	0.19	0.6771

Least Squares Means

T	Y LSMEAN
1	10.3575606
2	15.0868839

Level of T	N	----------Y---------- Mean	SD	----------X---------- Mean	SD
1	9	10.3333333	2.78388218	7.66666667	3.74165739
2	9	15.1111111	4.42844342	7.44444444	2.78886676

tionship between the CV and the DV is tested for significance after overlapping variability with other CVs, in their relationship with the DV, is removed. Therefore, although a CV may be significantly correlated with the DV when considered individually, it may add no significant adjustment to the DV when considered last. When interpreting the utility of a CV, it is necessary to consider correlations among CVs, correlations between each CV and the DV, and significance levels for each CV as reported in ANCOVA source tables.

Unstandardized regression coefficients, provided by most canned computer programs, have the same meaning as regression coefficients described in Section 4.4.4. However, in ANCOVA, interpretation of the coefficients depends on type of sum of squares used. When Type III sums of squares (standard multiple regression, appropriate for experiments) are used, the significance of the regression coefficients for CVs is assessed as if the CV entered the regression equation after all other CVs and after all main effects and interactions. With other types of SS, however, CVs enter the equation differently. Type I SS in GLM programs, for example, evaluates all effects, including CVs, as entering the equation in the order they are listed in the model instructions. In any event, the coefficient is evaluated at whatever point the CV enters the equation.

Each CV "costs" one degree of freedom, so that df are reduced by the number of CVs (c), and the partition of df is as shown in Figure 8.4, a generalized version of Figure 8.3(b).

Matrix algebra is required to find the c regression coefficients (Bs) and to adjust the sums of squares for the analysis. Winer and colleagues (1991) show equations for ANCOVA with multiple CVs and a numerical example with two CVs.

Software programs differ considerably in how they present ANCOVA with multiple CVs. The GLM programs (SYSTAT, SAS, MINITAB, and SPSS) provide tests of each of the CVs individually, but no test of the combined effect of the CVs on the DV (although SAS provides information to compute the combined effect, as shown in what follows). Of the software demonstrated, only SPSS MANOVA provides both individual and combined tests of multiple CVs. Regression coefficients are available in SPSS GLM with a request for parameter estimates and in SYSTAT GLM with a request for PRINT=LONG. They are automatically provided by MINITAB GLM, but are unavailable in SAS GLM.

Table 8.20 shows SPSS MANOVA syntax and output for ANCOVA in which age group and skiing experience have been added to prerating as CVs in the small-sample example.

Note that the additional two CVs have weakened the test of the IV, VIEW (cf. Table 8.10). The REGRESSION source of variance shows that the set of CVs reliably adjusts the DV, $F(3, 9) = 4.72$,

FIGURE 8.4   Partition of Total Adjusted Degrees of Freedom into Degrees of Freedom Associated with Groups and Associated with Cases within the Groups, where c is the Number of CVs

TABLE 8.20   ANCOVA with Multiple CVs through SPSS MANOVA: Syntax and Selected Output

```
MANOVA
 rating BY view(1,3) WITH agegrp exper pre_rate
 /DESIGN.
```

* * * * * *A n a l y s i s   o f   V a r i a n c e -- design 1 * * * * * *

Tests of Significance for RATING using UNIQUE sums of squares

Source of Variation	SS	DF	MS	F	Sig of F
WITHIN CELLS	7.46	9	.83		
REGRESSION	11.74	3	3.91	4.72	.030
VIEW	23.27	2	11.64	14.03	.002
(Model)	52.94	5	10.59	12.77	.001
(Total)	60.40	14	4.31		

R-Squared =   .876
Adjusted R-Squared = .808

Correlations between Covariates and Predicted Dependent Variable
    COVARIATE

VARIABLE	AGEGRP	EXPER	PRE_RATE
RATING	.592	.520	.655

Squared Correlations between Covariates and Predicted Dependent Variable

VARIABLE	AVER. R-SQ
AGEGRP	.350
EXPER	.271
PRE_RATE	.429

Regression analysis for WITHIN CELLS error term
--- Individual Univariate .9500 confidence intervals
Dependent variable.. RATING

COVARIATE	B	Beta	Std. Err.	t-Value	Sig. of t
AGEGRP	.33797	.28494	.263	1.286	.231
EXPER	.33105	.38478	.414	.800	.444
PRE_RATE	-.38753	-.22814	.871	-.445	.667

COVARIATE	Lower -95%	CL- Upper
AGEGRP	-.256	.932
EXPER	-.605	1.267
PRE_RATE	-2.357	1.582

$p = .03$. However, none of the CVs individually adjusts the DV once the other CVs are taken into account. Even PRE_RATE, which was statistically reliable in its adjustment of RATING when alone, no longer is. This suggests that the CVs are too highly correlated (cf. Section 8.6.1.1) to be fruitfully combined in the analysis; we would have been better off with only one of them. Section 8.6.1.2 discusses how to choose among potential CVs. SPSS MANOVA also provides bivariate correlations and r^2 for each of the CVs with the DV.

Table 8.21 shows syntax for the same analysis in SAS GLM. Note that the IV, VIEW, is entered before the CVs. This permits calculation of a test for the combined CVs, as discussed in what follows.

Tests for each of the CVs are provided along with the test of the IV, VIEW, in the portion of the output associated with Type III SS, in which all effects are adjusted for one another. The results for VIEW and each of the CVs are the same as in Table 8.20.

TABLE 8.21   ANCOVA with Multiple CVs through SAS GLM

```
proc glm data=SASUSER.ANCMULT;
  class VIEW;
  model RATING = VIEW PRERATE AGEGRP EXPER;
run;
```

Dependent Variable: RATING

Source	DF	Sum of Squares	Mean Square	F Value	Pr > F
Model	5	52.93864363	10.58772873	12.77	0.0007
Error	9	7.46135637	0.82903960		
Corrected Total	14	60.40000000			

R-Square	C. V.	Root MSE	RATING Mean
0.876468	21.67896	0.9105161	4.20000000

Source	DF	Type I SS	Mean Square	F Value	Pr > F
VIEW	2	41.20000000	20.60000000	24.85	0.0002
PRERATE	1	9.30909091	9.30909091	11.23	0.0085
AGEGRP	1	1.89893201	1.89893201	2.29	0.1645
EXPER	1	0.53062070	0.53062070	0.64	0.4443

Source	DF	Type III SS	Mean Square	F Value	Pr > F
VIEW	2	23.27096810	11.63548405	14.03	0.0017
PRERATE	1	0.16418242	0.16418242	0.20	0.6668
AGEGRP	1	1.37132569	1.37132569	1.65	0.2305
EXPER	1	0.53062070	0.53062070	0.64	0.4443

The test of combined CVs is easily calculated from this output as long as **TYPE I SS** results are available and the IV is entered before the CVs in the model instruction. Sum of squares for combined CVs is

$$SS_{covariates} = SS_{model} - SS_{VIEW(Type\ I\ SS)}$$

$$= 52.9386 - 41.2 = 11.7386$$

Degrees of freedom $= c = 3$ so that

$$MS_{covariates} = \frac{SS_{covariates}}{df_{covariates}}$$

$$\frac{11.73864363}{3} = 3.9129$$

and

$$F_{covariates} = \frac{MS_{covariates}}{MS_{Error}} = \frac{3.9129}{0.8290} = 4.72$$

as in Table 8.20.

8.6.1.1   Relationships among Covariates

Interpreting significance tests of CVs is aided by knowledge of relationships among them. Sometimes tests of CVs show that they are statistically significant when considered together but not when considered individually because of strong correlations among them, as in Table 8.20. Occasionally, correlations among them are high enough to cause multicollinearity (Section 8.3.2.2). In any event, correlations among multiple CVs are reported as part of the results of an ANCOVA.

Correlations among CVs are easily obtained through software correlation programs; SMCs (squared multiple correlations) are available to evaluate multicollinearity through most factor analysis programs. SPSS FACTOR provides both bivariate correlations and SMCs. For example, Table 8.22 shows syntax and selected output for an SPSS FACTOR run of the data set with multiple CVs.

Indeed, we see that bivariate correlations are very high, ranging from .77 to .93. And SMCs (Initial Communalities), although not high enough to cause statistical problems, are strong enough to pose questions about the utility of using more than one of the CVs.

8.6.1.2   Choosing Covariates

Experiments typically use a single CV, often a pretest, administered before random assignment to treatments. Sometimes, circumstances may dictate the availability or potential desirability of multiple CVs. However, a point of diminishing returns in adjustment of the DV is quickly reached when too many CVs are used and they are correlated with each other. Power is reduced because numerous correlated CVs subtract degrees of freedom from the error term while not removing commensurate sums of squares for error. Preliminary analysis of the CVs improves chances of picking a good set.

Statistically, the goal is to identify a small set of CVs that are uncorrelated with each other but highly correlated with the DV. Conceptually, one wants to select CVs that adjust the DV for pre-

TABLE 8.22   Bivariate and Squared Multiple Correlations through SPSS FACTOR: Syntax and Selected Output

```
FACTOR
 /VARIABLES exper pre_rate agegrp
 /MISSING LISTWISE
 /ANALYSIS exper pre_rate agegrp
 /PRINT INITIAL CORRELATION EXTRACTION
 /CRITERIA MINEIGEN(1) ITERATE(25)
 /EXTRACTION PAF
 /ROTATION NOROTATE
 /METHOD=CORRELATION .
```

Factor Analysis

Correlation Matrix

		EXPER	PRE_RATE	AGEGRP
Correlation	EXPER	1.000	.929	.821
	PRE_RATE	.929	1.000	.769
	AGEGRP	.821	.769	1.000

Communalities

	Initial	Extraction
EXPER	.891	.989
PRE_RATE	.863	.872
AGEGRP	.675	.680

Extraction Method: Principal Axis Factoring.

---

dictable but unwanted sources of variability. It may be possible to pick the CVs on theoretical grounds or on the basis of knowledge of the literature regarding important sources of variability that should be controlled.

If theory is unavailable or the literature is insufficiently developed to provide a guide to important sources of variability in the DV, statistical considerations assist the selection of CVs. One strategy is to look at correlations among CVs and select one from among each of those sets of potential CVs that are substantially correlated with each other, perhaps by choosing the one with the highest correlation with the DV. Table 8.23 shows the correlations among CVs, and of each CV with the DV, RATING, produced by SYSTAT CORR.

SYSTAT CORR provides means, histograms, and scatterplots by default. We see that the pretest, PRE_RATE, has the highest correlation (but not by much) with RATING and is the CV of choice among the three. Note also the very high correlations among CVs. A more sophisticated strategy that is useful with a larger set of potential CVs is to use all subsets or stepwise regression

TABLE 8.23 Correlations of CVs with Each Other and with the DV through SYSTAT CORR

CORR
PEARSON RATING PRE_RATE AGEGRP EXPER

Pearson correlation matrix

	RATING	PRE_RATE	AGEGRP	EXPER
RATING	1.000			
PRE_RATE	0.613	1.000		
AGEGRP	0.554	0.769	1.000	
EXPER	0.487	0.929	0.821	1.000

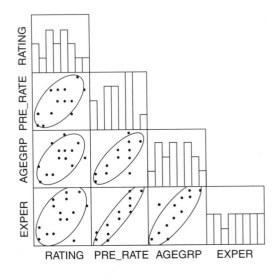

Number of observations: 15

(cf. Tabachnick and Fidell, 2001) to see which (small) set of CVs best predicts the DV, ignoring the IV. SAS REG and MINITAB BREG do all subsets regression.

Even if N is large and power is not a problem, it may still be worthwhile to select and use only a small set of CVs just for the sake of parsimony.

8.6.2 Test of Homogeneity of Regression

The assumption of homogeneity of regression is that the slopes (regression coefficients or B weights) of the regression of the DV on the CV(s) are the same for all cells of a design. Both homogeneity and heterogeneity of regression are illustrated in Figure 8.2. During analysis, slope is computed for every cell of the design and then averaged to provide the value used for adjustment. It is assumed that the slopes will differ slightly due to chance, but are really all estimates of the same population value. If the null hypothesis of equality among slopes is rejected, the analysis of covariance is inappropriate and an alternative strategy is used, as described in Section 8.6.7.

Hand calculation (with a single CV in a one-way randomizcd-groups design) requires computation of a separate sum of squares for error for the CV for each level of A, a separate sum of products between DV and CV for error for each level of A, and a separate regression coefficient for error for each level of A. These are found as follows:

$$SS_{S/A_{i(x)}} = \sum_i X_i^2 - \frac{A_{i(x)}^2}{n} \tag{8.19}$$

$$SP_{S/A_i} - \sum X_i Y_i - \frac{A_{i(x)} A_{i(y)}}{n} \tag{8.20}$$

$$B_{S/A_i} = \frac{SP_{S/A_i}}{SS_{S/A_{i(x)}}} \tag{8.21}$$

For the first level of A, parking lot view:

$$SS_{S/A_1(x)} = (2^2 + 1^2 + 4^2 + 4^2 + 1^2) - \frac{12^2}{5} = 38 - 28.8 = 9.2$$

$$SP_{S/A_1} = (2)(1) + (1)(1) + (4)(3) + (4)(5) + (1)(2) - \frac{(12)(12)}{5} = 37 - 28.8 = 8.2$$

$$B_{S/A_1} = \frac{8.2}{9.2} = 0.89$$

For the second level of A, ocean view:

$$SS_{S/A_2(x)} = (2^2 + 4^2 + 4^2 + 4^2 + 3^2) - \frac{17^2}{5} = 61 - 57.8 = 3.2$$

$$SP_{S/A_2} = (2)(3) + (4)(4) + (4)(3) + (4)(5) + (3)(4) - \frac{(17)(19)}{5} = 66 - 64.6 = 1.4$$

$$B_{S/A_2} = \frac{1.4}{3.2} = 0.44$$

And for the third level of A, ski slope view:

$$SS_{S/A_3(x)} = (3^2 + 4^2 + 2^2 + 5^2 + 3^2) - \frac{17^2}{5} = 63 - 57.8 = 5.2$$

$$SP_{S/A_3} = (3)(6) + (4)(8) + (2)(6) + (5)(7) + (3)(5) - \frac{(17)(32)}{5} = 112 - 108.8 = 3.2$$

$$B_{S/A_3} = \frac{3.2}{5.2} = 0.62$$

These values then are used to calculate a between-groups sum of squares for regression and a within-groups sum of squares for regression:

$$SS_{\text{between regression}} = \sum \left[\frac{SP^2_{S/A_i}}{SS_{S/A_{i(x)}}} \right] - \frac{(SP_{S/A})^2}{SS_{S/A_{(x)}}}, \qquad df = a - 1 \qquad (8.22)$$

and

$$SS_{\text{within regression}} = SS_{S/A} - \sum \left[\frac{(SP_{S/A_i})^2}{SS_{S/A_{i(x)}}} \right], \qquad df = N - 2 \qquad (8.23)$$

By substituting the values for the data in Table 8.1,

$$SS_{\text{between regression}} = \left[\frac{(8.2)^2}{9.2} + \frac{(1.4)^2}{3.2} + \frac{(3.2)^2}{5.2} \right] - \frac{(12.8)^2}{17.6} = 9.89 - 9.31 = 0.58$$

$$SS_{\text{within regression}} = 19.2 - \left[\frac{(8.2)^2}{9.2} + \frac{(1.4)^2}{3.2} + \frac{(3.2)^2}{5.2} \right] = 19.2 - 9.89 = 9.31$$

Mean squares and the F ratio are calculated in the usual way, as shown in Table 8.24. These two sources of variance sum to $SS'_{S/A}$, the adjusted error term for the main analysis. Thus, the homogeneity of regression analysis partitions the adjusted error into differences in slopes among groups and residual error within groups.

Homogeneity of regression is present when the obtained F ratio is *smaller* than the tabled value, in this case $F_{.05}(2, 9) = 4.26$. The assumption of homogeneity is met with this small data set.

The most straightforward programs for testing homogeneity of regression in randomized-groups designs are SYSTAT GLM or ANOVA, and SPSS MANOVA. Table 8.25 shows a test for homogeneity of regression through SPSS MANOVA. The inclusion of the IV by CV interaction (PRE_RATE by VIEW) as the last effect in the DESIGN instruction, after the CV and the IV, provides the test for homogeneity of regression. Placing this effect last and requesting METHOD=SEQUENTIAL ensures that the test for the interaction is adjusted for the CV and the IV. The ANALYSIS instruction identifies RATING as the DV. The test for PRE_RATE BY VIEW shows that there is no violation of homogeneity of regression: $p = .761$.

Programs based on the general linear model test homogeneity of regression by evaluating the CV(s) by IV(s) interaction as the last effect entering a sequential-regression model (Section 5.6.5). This procedure is demonstrated in a straightforward manner in the ANCOVA section of the SYSTAT manual (SPSS Inc., 1999e). The same procedure works for SPSS GLM and for SAS GLM through syntax, as shown in Table 8.26.

Type I SS and Type III SS provide the same test of homogeneity of regression (the interaction between PRE_RATE and VIEW) because that interaction is the last entry in the MODEL equation. The results duplicate those of Tables 8.24 and 8.25.

**TABLE 8.24   Source Table for Testing Homogeneity of
Regression in Small-Sample ANCOVA**

Source	SS	df	MS	F
Between regression	0.58	2	0.29	0.28
Within regression	9.31	9	1.03	
Adjusted S/A	9.89	11		

**TABLE 8.25   SPSS MANOVA Syntax and Selected Output
for Homogeneity of Regression**

```
MANOVA
 RATING BY VIEW(1,3) WITH PRE_RATE
 /PRINT = SIGNIF(BRIEF)
 /ANALYSIS = rating
 /METHOD = SEQUENTIAL
 /DESIGN PRE_RATE, VIEW, PRE_RATE BY VIEW.
```

```
* * * * A n a l y s i s   o f   V a r i a n c e -- design 1 * * * *

Tests of Significance for RATING using SEQUENTIAL Sums of Squares
Source of Variation      SS    DF      MS       F   Sig of F

WITHIN+RESIDUAL         9.31    9     1.03
PRE_RATE               22.70    1    22.70   21.95      .001
VIEW                   27.81    2    13.90   13.44      .002
PRE_RATE BY VIEW         .58    2      .29     .28      .761

(Model)                51.09    5    10.22    9.88      .002
(Total)                60.40   14     4.31
```

Only SPSS MANOVA permits a combined test of homogeneity of regression for multiple CVs (Table 8.27). The keyword POOL combines the three CVs in the interaction with the DV, VIEW.

The test for homogeneity of regression shows no violation, $F(6, 3) = 1.10, p = .51$. If this test shows violation of homogeneity of regression, separate tests are done on each CV to help pinpoint the source of the violation. Other programs only test CVs one at a time so that each is tested in a separate run.

GLM programs automatically test homogeneity of regression for effects of repeated-measures IVs (but not for interaction between randomized-groups and repeated-measures IVs), as shown in Table 8.17. If the assumption is not violated, you may want to eliminate this source of variance, as demonstrated in Section 8.7.2.2.1.

TABLE 8.26   SAS GLM Syntax and Selected Output Testing Homogeneity of Regression in Small-Sample ANCOVA

```
proc glm data=SASUSER.SSANCOVA;
  class VIEW;
  model RATING = VIEW PRE_RATE VIEW*PRE_RATE;
run;
```

General Linear Models Procedure

Dependent Variable: RATING

Source	DF	Sum of Squares	Mean Square	F Value	Pr > F
Model	5	51.09042642	10.21808528	9.88	0.0019
Error	9	9.30957358	1.03439706		
Corrected Total	14	60.40000000			

R-Square	C.V.	Root MSE	RATING Mean
0.845868	24.21555	1.0170531	4.20000000

Source	DF	Type I SS	Mean Square	F Value	Pr > F
VIEW	2	41.20000000	20.60000000	19.91	0.0005
PRE_RATE	1	9.30909091	9.30909091	9.00	0.0150
PRE_RATE*VIEW	2	0.58133551	0.29066776	0.28	0.7614

Source	DF	Type III SS	Mean Square	F Value	Pr > F
VIEW	2	5.27649869	2.63824935	2.55	0.1326
PRE_RATE	1	6.16112489	6.16112489	5.96	0.0373
PRE_RATE*VIEW	2	0.58133551	0.29066776	0.28	0.7614

8.6.3   Effect Size

Effect size in ANCOVA is based on adjusted sums of squares. Either η^2 or partial η^2 are reported, depending on the complexity of the design.

In a one-way design,

$$\eta^2 = \frac{SS'_A}{SS'_T} \tag{8.24}$$

For the small-sample example of Section 8.4,

$$\eta^2 = \frac{27.8}{37.7} = .74$$

TABLE 8.27   SPSS MANOVA Syntax and Selected Output for Homogeneity of Regression with Multiple CVs

```
MANOVA
 RATING BY VIEW(1,3) WITH PRE_RATE AGEGRP EXPER
 /PRINT = SIGNIF(BRIEF)
 /ANALYSIS = RATING
 /METHOD = SEQUENTIAL
 /DESIGN PRE_RATE AGEGRP EXPER VIEW,
     POOL(PRE_RATE AGEGRP EXPER) BY VIEW.
```

```
* * * * A n a l y s i s   o f   V a r i a n c e — design 1 * * * *

Tests of Significance for RATING using SEQUENTIAL Sums of Squares
```

Source of Variation	SS	DF	MS	F	Sig of F
WITHIN+RESIDUAL	2.33	3	.78		
PRE_RATE	22.70	1	22.70	29.19	.012
AGEGRP	1.00	1	1.00	1.28	.340
EXPER	5.97	1	5.97	7.67	.070
VIEW	23.27	2	11.64	14.96	.028
POOL(PRE_RATE AGEGRP EXPER) BY VIEW	5.13	6	.85	1.10	.510
(Model)	58.07	11	5.28	6.79	.071
(Total)	60.40	14	4.31		

```
R-Squared =          .961
Adjusted R-Squared = .820
```

Note that this matches the **Eta Squared** value for **VIEW** provided by SPSS GLM in Table 8.9. Be sure to include only *adjusted* sums of squares for the IV and for the error when calculating a total from output—the total provided in the output may be in error because it includes CVs.

Partial η^2 is less conservative in a factorial design:

$$\text{Partial } \eta^2 = \frac{SS'_{\text{effect}}}{SS'_{\text{effect}} + SS'_{\text{error}}} \tag{8.25}$$

where the error term is the one used to test the effect of interest.

The effect size that is reported has gained increasing importance over the last few years because of its potential use in meta analyses. ANCOVA poses something of a dilemma because effect size can be computed from either adjusted or unadjusted scores. The issue is which most closely estimates the impact of the IV on the DV in the population. Because the unadjusted estimate of effect size incorporates differences due to another variable (the CV), it is probably more appropriate to report adjusted effect size in either an experimental or nonexperimental study.

8.6.4 Power

ANCOVA (with a CV) is more powerful than a corresponding ANOVA (without the CV) if the relationship between the DV and CV(s) is large enough to overcome the loss of an error degree of freedom for each CV. An ANOVA without using PRE_RATE as a CV for the small-sample example of Section 8.4 produces Table 8.28.

Compared with results in Table 8.6, the unadjusted sums of squares are larger than the adjusted ones, but the F ratio is smaller. The loss of a degree of freedom has been offset by subtraction of sum of squares for the CV; the exact probability of F with the CV is .0006, without the CV it is .001.

Power and sample-size calculations are identical to those of ANOVA, with the exception that adjusted means and variances (or standard deviations) are used in the equations (Cohen, 1977). Adjusted $MS_{S/A}$ is used for σ^2 in Equation 4.6 and δ refers to the desired minimal difference between adjusted means.

8.6.5 Adjusted Means

ANCOVA adjusts both the means and the error term. Adjustment of the error term is usually more important, but adjustment of the means is sometimes also required. The means are adjusted to the values predicted if all cases scored about the same on the CV. Random assignment is used in experimental work in the hope that it equalizes groups before administration of treatment, so, ideally, the groups should have the same mean on the CV before treatment. In any given study, however, random assignment may not create equality. It is common to find adjustment of treatment means in nonexperimental work; indeed, this is one of the reasons that ANCOVA is suspect in nonexperimental studies.

To understand the nature of the adjustment, consider the pattern of means in the example of Table 8.29. Rather than equality, the pattern of means for the CV across the three levels of A is low, medium, and high. Suppose that the correlation between the CV and DV is relatively strong and positive. The first DV pattern is low, medium, and high, the same pattern as the CV obtained before treatment. These results imply that treatment has not changed the DV and significance found in ANOVA should not be found in ANCOVA. The second DV pattern is medium, medium, and medium. In this case, ANOVA would be nonsignificant, but ANCOVA should reach significance because the treatment at a_1 actually raises scores, whereas the treatment at a_3 actually lowers scores. Finally, both ANOVA and ANCOVA are likely to find significance for the third DV pattern, but the effect of treatment is even stronger than the ANOVA suggests once the pattern in the CV is taken into account. In ANCOVA, it is the adjusted means that are tested for differences, and the adjusted means that are

TABLE 8.28   Source Table for One-Way ANOVA for the Small-Sample Example of Section 8.4

Source	SS	df	MS	F
A	41.2	2	20.6	12.88
S/A	19.2	12	1.6	
T	60.4	14		

TABLE 8.29   Adjustment of Means Based on the CV–DV Pattern

CV Pattern	ANOVA Raw Score Means			ANCOVA Adjusted Means		
	a_1 Low	a_2 Medium	a_3 High	a_1	a_2	a_3
First DV Pattern	Low	Medium	High	Medium	Medium	Medium
Second DV Pattern	Medium	Medium	Medium	High	Medium	Low
Third DV Pattern	High	Medium	Low	Higher	Medium	Lower

interpreted when considering statistically reliable effects, doing comparisons, and calculating power. It is useful to compare adjusted and unadjusted means to understand the CV adjustment.

Further, in nonexperimental work with preexisting group differences on the DV, ANCOVA can be quite misleading due to regression to the mean. If there are two groups each measured during baseline (CV) and then on a DV, ANCOVA lowers the mean for the group with the higher CV and raises the mean for the group with the lower mean. The results, known as Lord's Paradox (Lord, 1967), can be quite misleading, as clearly described by Jamiesen (1999).

Each mean in a one-way ANCOVA with a single CV is adjusted by the pooled within-cell regression coefficient, $B_{S/A}$, where

$$B_{S/A} = \frac{SP_{S/A}}{SS_{S/A(x)}} \tag{8.26}$$

An adjusted mean is

$$\overline{Y}'_{A_i} = \overline{Y}_{A_i} - B_{S/A}(\overline{X}_{A_i} - \overline{X}_T) \tag{8.27}$$

The adjusted mean for a level of A is the unadjusted mean for that level minus the difference between the CV mean for that level and the overall CV mean, multiplied by the pooled within-cell regression coefficient.

The pooled within-cell regression coefficient for the small sample is

$$B_{S/A} = \frac{12.8}{17.6} = 0.72727$$

from Table 8.2, and the three adjusted means are

$$\overline{Y}'_{A_1} = 2.40 - 0.72727(2.40 - 3.07) = 2.89$$

$$\overline{Y}'_{A_2} = 3.80 - 0.72727(3.40 - 3.07) = 3.56$$

$$\overline{Y}'_{A_3} = 6.40 - 0.72727(3.40 - 3.07) = 6.16$$

**TABLE 8.30 Unadjusted and Adjusted Means
for the Small-Sample Example of Section 8.4**

Variable	a_1	a_2	a_3	T
X	2.40	3.40	3.40	3.07
Y	2.40	3.80	6.40	4.20
Adjusted Y	2.89	3.56	6.16	4.20

Unadjusted means for the CV (X) and DV (Y) for the small-sample example of Section 8.4.3 are in Table 8.30, along with the adjusted DV means.

The means at a_2 and a_3 are pulled down because those two groups scored above the average on the CV to begin with. The a_1 mean is raised because that group scored below the average on the CV to begin with. Because this is an experiment, this suggests that the larger, unadjusted differences among the means are due partially to preexisting differences in rating tendencies between the groups.

Similar to the issue with effect size, there is a dilemma regarding whether to report adjusted or unadjusted means following ANCOVA. The means that are tested are the adjusted ones, so consistency argues in favor of reporting those. In experimental work, the argument is also in favor of the adjusted means because the unadjusted means are based on group differences on the CV that random assignment should eliminate. A replication of the study with different cases and different random assignment is unlikely to duplicate preexisting group differences on the CV. Therefore, the adjusted means, where those mean differences have been eliminated, are probably the more generalizable. However, in a nonexperimental study, it is probably wise to report both adjusted and unadjusted means along with the means on the CV, similar to those reported in Table 8.30, to assist the reader in interpreting the results of ANCOVA.

8.6.6 Specific Comparisons

Types of comparisons and the circumstances under which they are done are the same as in ANOVA (cf. Sections 4.5.5, 5.6.4, and 6.6.6). The difference is that comparisons are done on the adjusted means and the error term is adjusted beyond that required for the omnibus test, with a separate error term for each comparison.[11]

The F ratio for a comparison (recalling that $\text{MS}'_{A\,\text{comp}} = \text{SS}'_{A\,\text{comp}}$ because $\text{df}_{A\,\text{comp}} = 1$) is

$$F_{A\,\text{comp}} = \frac{\text{SS}'_{A\,\text{comp}}}{\text{MS}'_{\text{error}(A\,\text{comp})}} \qquad (8.28)$$

The numerator, the sum of squares for a comparison, is

$$\text{SS}'_{A\,\text{comp}} = \frac{n\left(\sum w_j \overline{Y}'_j\right)^2}{\sum w_j^2} \qquad (8.29)$$

---

[11]A simpler method, which uses a single adjusted error term, may be used when $\text{df}_{\text{error}} \geq 20$ (Keppel, 1991; Winer, 1971).

where $\overline{Y}_j'$ is an adjusted mean for the DV and remaining values are as defined in Equation 4.10.
The adjusted error term for comparisons is

$$MS'_{error(A\,comp)} = MS'_{S/A}\left(1 + \frac{SS_{A\,comp(x)}}{SS_{S/A(x)}}\right) \tag{8.30}$$

Notice that $SS_{A\,comp(x)}$ is different for every comparison, and is

$$SS_{A\,comp(x)} = \frac{n(\sum w_j\overline{X}_j')^2}{\sum w_j^2} \tag{8.31}$$

where $\overline{X}_j'$ is a CV mean, and the remaining terms are as defined in Equation 4.10.

An orthogonal set of comparisons for the small-sample data of Section 8.4 compares the parking lot view to the average of the other two views $(-2, 1, 1)$ and the ocean view to the ski slope view $(0, 1, -1)$.

$SS_{A\,comp1}$ for the first comparison, using the adjusted means of Table 8.30, is

$$SS'_{A\,comp1} = \frac{5[(-2)(2.89) + (1)(3.56) + (1)(6.16)]^2}{(-2)^2 + (1)^2 + (1)^2} = 12.94$$

The error term for the first comparison requires calculation of $SS_{A\,comp(x)}$, from the CV (X) means of Table 8.30. Thus, $SS_{A\,comp1(x)}$ for the first comparison is

$$SS_{A\,comp1(x)} = \frac{5[(-2)(2.4) + (1)(3.4) + (1)(3.4)]^2}{(-2)^2 + (1)^2 + (1)^2} = 3.33$$

and $MS'_{error(A\,comp1)}$ is

$$MS'_{error(A\,comp1)} = 0.90\left(1 + \frac{3.33}{17.60}\right) = 1.07$$

The F ratio for the first comparison, a_1 versus the combination of a_2 and a_3, is

$$F_{A\,comp1} = \frac{12.94}{1.07} = 12.09$$

For the second comparison, a_2 is contrasted with a_3. $SS_{A\,comp2}$ for the second comparison, again using the adjusted means of Table 8.30, is

$$SS'_{A\,comp2} = \frac{5[(0)(2.89) + (1)(3.56) + (-1)(6.16)]^2}{(1)^2 + (-1)^2} = 16.90$$

The error term for the second comparison requires calculation of $SS_{A\,comp2\,(x)}$, from the means of Table 8.30.

$$SS'_{A\,comp2\,(x)} = \frac{5[(0)(2.4) + (1)(3.4) + (-1)(3.4)]^2}{(1)^2 + (-1)^2} = 0$$

because the CV means are equal for the last two levels of A, and $MS'_{error\,(A\,comp2)}$ is

$$MS'_{error\,(A\,comp2)} = 0.90\left(1 + \frac{0}{17.6}\right) = 0.90$$

the same as the adjusted error term for the omnibus effect of A.

The F ratio for the second comparison, a_2 versus a_3, is

$$F_{A\,comp2} = \frac{16.90}{0.90} = 18.78$$

Critical F for a planned comparison with 1 and 11 df at $\alpha = .05$ is 4.84, making both of the comparisons statistically reliable. Critical F for a post hoc comparison is computed using the Scheffé adjustment of Equation 4.13:

$$F_S = (a - 1)F_c = (2)(3.98) = 7.96$$

Both comparisons are statistically reliable by either criterion.

Effect sizes for comparisons in ANCOVA use forms of η^2. As usual, effect sizes for comparisons are done with respect to the entire analysis (using SS'_T in the denominator) or the effect that they are decomposing. For example, η^2 with respect to the entire analysis for A_{comp1} (group 1 versus the other two groups) is

$$\eta^2 = \frac{SS'_{A\,comp1}}{SS'_T} = \frac{12.94}{37.70} = .34$$

Thus, 34% of the variance in rating, adjusted for prerating, is associated with the difference between group 1 and the other two groups. And η^2 for the same comparison with respect to the main effect of A, a less conservative measure, is

$$\eta^2 = \frac{SS'_{A\,comp1}}{SS'_A} = \frac{12.94}{27.80} = .47$$

This indicates that 47% of the variability attributable to the main effect of A is associated with the difference between group 1 and the other two groups.

Syntax and output for comparisons in ANCOVA are the same as for ANOVA, with inclusion of the CV(s). Table 8.31 shows the orthogonal contrasts just described through SPSS GLM (UNIANOVA). The special contrasts matrix has as many rows as columns, with the first row a series of 1s.

TABLE 8.31   Orthogonal Comparisons for the Small-Sample Example of Section 8.4 through SPSS GLM

```
UNIANOVA
  rating BY view WITH pre_rate
  /METHOD = SSTYPE(3)
  /INTERCEPT = INCLUDE
  /CRITERIA = ALPHA(.05)
  /CONTRAST(VIEW) = SPECIAL( 1  1   1
                            -2  1   1
                             0  1  -1)
  /DESIGN = pre_rate view .
```

Univariate Analysis of Variance

Custom Hypothesis Tests

Contrast Results (K Matrix)

View from room Special Contrast			Dependent Variable
			RATING
LI	Contrast Estimate		5.909
	Hypothesized Value		0
	Difference (Estimate – Hypothesized)		5.909
	Std. Error		2.205
	Sig.		.021
	95% Confidence Interval for Difference	Lower Bound	1.055
		Upper Bound	10.763
L2	Contrast Estimate		3.945
	Hypothesized Value		0
	Difference (Estimate – Hypothesized)		3.945
	Std. Error		1.133
	Sig.		.005
	95% Confidence Interval for Difference	Lower Bound	1.452
		Upper Bound	6.439
L3	Contrast Estimate		−2.600
	Hypothesized Value		0
	Difference (Estimate – Hypothesized)		−2.600
	Std. Error		.600
	Sig.		.001
	95% Confidence Interval for Difference	Lower Bound	−3.920
		Upper Bound	−1.280

The first contrast (L1) corresponds to the row of 1s in the special contrast matrix and is not of interest. L2 compares the parking lot view with the combination of the other two views and L3 compares the ski slope and ocean views. The **Contrast Estimate** is the sum of the weights times the adjusted means $[(-2)(2.89) + (1)(3.56) + (1)(6.16) = 3.94$, within rounding error of the L2 value of 3.945 in the table]. A 95% confidence interval is given for the estimate, rather than an F ratio. This default criterion may be altered. A comparison is statistically reliable if the interval does not contain 0. Both comparisons are significant if planned at $\alpha = .05$. A t ratio may be found by dividing the **Contrast Estimate** by its **Std. Error**. For L2, $t = 3.945/1.133 = 3.48$. And, as always, $F = t^2 = 12.13$, within rounding error of the hand-calculated value of 12.09. The result for the second comparison is identical to that of the hand-calculated value.

Other software programs (SPSS MANOVA, SAS GLM, and SYSTAT ANOVA and GLM) provide either F or t ratios with probabilities as for planned comparisons; Scheffé or other adjustments are needed if the comparisons are post hoc.

Note that the separate adjustments for each ANCOVA comparison show up in the numerator SS'_{Acomp} rather than in the error terms in some computer output, but F ratios produced by all programs match those for the approach in which separate error terms are constructed for each comparison.

8.6.7 Alternatives to ANCOVA

Because of violated assumptions and difficulty in interpreting results of ANCOVA, alternative analytical strategies are sometimes sought. The choice among alternatives depends on the scale of measurement of the CV(s) and the DV, the time that elapses between measurement of the CV and assignment to treatment, the shape of the distributions of the CV and the DV, and the difficulty of interpreting results.

Two alternatives are available when the CV(s) and the DV are measured on the same scale: use of change (difference) scores and conversion of the pretest and posttest scores into a repeated-measures IV. In the first alternative, the difference between the previous CV and DV is computed for each case and used as the DV in randomized-groups ANOVA. In the second alternative, the CV becomes the pretest score and the DV becomes the posttest score, which compose a repeated-measures IV in a mixed randomized-groups, repeated-measures ANOVA.

The difference between change scores, mixed ANOVA, and ANCOVA is a matter of which research question you want to ask because, actually, the three alternatives yield the same statistical outcome. For example, suppose patient satisfaction with treatment is measured both before and after patients are randomly assigned to one of two new types of treatment. If the research question is, "Does one type of treatment produce a bigger change in patient satisfaction than the other?" change scores are appropriate. If the research question is, "Do the two treatments produce a different pattern of patient satisfaction in the pre- and posttest scores?" mixed-design ANOVA is the appropriate analysis. On the other hand, if the research question is, "Do the two types of treatment have different mean satisfaction after adjusting for preexisting group differences in tendency to report satisfaction?" ANCOVA is the appropriate analysis.

The mixed ANOVA approach preserves information about the means, unlike ANOVA on change scores where the means are "lost," which may be an advantage. A disadvantage of mixed ANOVA is that the effect of the IV of interest is no longer assessed as a main effect, but rather as an interaction between the IV and the repeated-measures (pretest, posttest) IV, complicating interpretation.

A problem with change scores and mixed ANOVA is ceiling and floor effects (or, more generally, skewness). A change score (or interaction) may be small because the pretest score is very near the end of the scale and no treatment effect can change it very much, or it may be small because the effect of treatment is small—the result is the same in either case and the researcher is hard-pressed to decide between them. Further, when the DV is skewed, a change in a mean also produces a change in the shape of the distribution and a potentially misleading significance test (Jamieson and Howk, 1992). If either ANCOVA or ANOVA with change scores is possible, then ANCOVA is usually the better approach when the data are skewed and transformations are not undertaken (Jamieson, 1999).

When CVs are measured on any continuous scale, other alternatives are available: matched randomized blocks (Section 6.5.3) and using the CV as a blocking IV. In the matched randomized-block design, cases are matched into blocks—equated—on the basis of scores on what would have been the CV(s). Each block has as many cases as the number of levels of the IV in a one-way design or number of cells in a larger design (cf. Chapter 6). Cases within each block are randomly assigned to levels or cells of the IV(s) for treatment. In the analytic phase, cases in the same block are treated as if they were the same case, in a repeated-measures analysis.

Disadvantages to this approach are the assumption of homogeneity of covariance of a repeated-measures analysis and the loss of degrees of freedom for error without commensurate loss of sums of squares for error if the variables used to block are not highly related to the DV. Implementation of the matched randomized-block design requires the added step of equating cases before randomly assigning them to treatment, a step that may be inconvenient, if not impossible, in some applications. It also requires great faith in the matching procedure.

The last alternative is use of the CV as a blocking IV. Cases are measured on potential CV(s) and then grouped according to their scores (e.g., into groups of high, medium, and low consumer satisfaction on the basis of pretest scores). The groups of cases (blocks) become the levels of another full-scale randomized-groups IV that are crossed with the levels of the IV(s) of interest in a factorial design. Interpretation of the main effect of the IV of interest is straightforward, and variation due to the potential CV(s) is removed from the estimate of error variance and assessed as a separate main effect. Furthermore, the assumption of homogeneity of regression shows up as the interaction between the blocking IV and the IV of interest and is available for interpretation.

Blocking has several advantages over ANCOVA and the other alternatives listed here. First, it has none of the special assumptions of ANCOVA or repeated-measures ANOVA. Second, the relationship between the potential CV(s) and the DV need not be linear; curvilinear relationships can be captured in ANOVA when three (or more) levels of a blocking IV are analyzed. Indeed, blocking is more powerful than ANCOVA if the CV–DV relationship is not linear. Blocking, then, is preferable to ANCOVA in many situations, and particularly for experimental, rather than nonexperimental, research.

With some difficulty, blocking can also be expanded to multiple CVs. That is, several new IVs, one per CV, are developed through blocking and crossed in factorial design. However, as the number of IVs increases, the design rapidly becomes very large and cumbersome to implement.

ANCOVA is preferable to blocking for some applications, however. ANCOVA is more powerful than blocking when the relationship between the DV and the CV is strong and linear. And, if the assumptions of ANCOVA are met, conversion of a continuous CV to a discrete IV (e.g., small, medium, large) can result in loss of information. Finally, practical limitations may prevent measurement of potential CV(s) sufficiently in advance of treatment to accomplish random assignment of equal numbers of cases to the cells of the design. When blocking is attempted after treatment, sample sizes within cells are likely to be highly discrepant, leading to the problems of unequal n.

In some applications, a combination of blocking and ANCOVA may turn out to be best. Some potential CVs are used to create new IVs, whereas others are analyzed as CVs.

8.7 Complete Examples of Analysis of Covariance

8.7.1 One-Way Analysis of Covariance with Five Levels and One Covariate

This example of a one-way ANCOVA evaluates the polishing time for Nambeware as a function of five different types of tableware, after adjusting for diameter of the tableware as a CV. The data are available on the Internet, and are provided by Nambe Mills, Santa Fe, New Mexico. The data set is modified so that IV levels, types of tableware, are coded in a single column, and price has been omitted. The data set contains 59 cases. Data files are NAMBE.*. The goal of analysis is to determine whether polishing time varies with the type of tableware after statistically controlling for its diameter, which presumably is a primary determinant of polishing time.

8.7.1.1   Evaluation of Assumptions

8.7.1.1.1   Sample Sizes, Missing Data, and Normality of Sampling Distributions
Table 8.32 shows MINITAB %DESCRIBE descriptive statistics and histograms for **DIAMETER** and **TIME**, grouped **BY TYPE**.

Table 8.32 shows only three of the groups. There are no missing data for either polishing time (the DV) or diameter (the CV). Sample sizes are discrepant, but not terribly so. Standard errors for skewness and kurtosis are found using Equations 2.8 and 2.9. For example, $s_{skewness}$ and $s_{kurtosis}$ for polishing time for trays (group 4) with $N = 10$ are

$$s_{skewness} = \sqrt{\frac{6}{10}} = 0.775 \qquad \text{and} \qquad s_{kurtosis} = \sqrt{\frac{24}{10}} = 1.549$$

Thus, the z value for skewness for polishing **TIME** of **trays** is 1.67 $[1.293/0.775]$, well below a criterion of 2.58 at $\alpha = .01$, appropriate for this small sample. All of the other tests for skewness and kurtosis produce even smaller z values.

8.7.1.1.2   Outliers
Table 8.32 also permits evaluation of univariate outliers. The test for the largest **DIAMETER** score in the first group (**bowls**) shows $z = (15.20 - 9.4391)/2.8705 = 2.01$, not an outlier at $\alpha = .01$. By this criterion, no cases are univariate outliers on DV or CV (**TIME** or **DIAMETER**) in any of the groups.

8.7.1.1.3 Homogeneity of Variance

Homogeneity of variance also may be checked in the full run producing Table 8.32. Sample sizes, though discrepant, do not exceed a ratio of 4:1 for the largest to the smallest group. However, the largest variance for polishing time is 737.7821 in the `tray` group; the smallest is 18.2028 in the `plate` group. $F_{max} = 737.7821/18.2028 = 40.53$, far exceeding the criterion of 10. No such problem occurs with the CV, `diameter`.

Therefore, a variance-stabilizing transformation is considered for `TIME`. Table 8.33 shows descriptive statistics through MINITAB DESCRIBE after square root (`STIME`) and logarithmic (`LTIME`) transforms.

Note that MINITAB shows standard deviations (`StDev`) but not variances, which are found by squaring *s*. Thus, Table 8.33 shows that F_{max} is still too large with the square root transformation, but acceptable using the logarithmic transform, `LTIME`: $z = (0.2223)^2/(0.0793)^2 = 7.86$. Therefore, remaining analyses are based on `LTIME` rather than `TIME`. The exceptionally large variance in polishing times among trays and the exceptionally small variance in polishing times among plates are noted in the results, however.

8.7.1.1.4 Linearity

Scatterplots between the `DIAMETER` and `LTIME` produced by MINITAB PLOT are in Figure 8.5. Separate data sets for each `TYPE` are formed before plots are requested. Note that only the

TABLE 8.32 Descriptive Statistics for Nambe Tableware Types: MINITAB %DESCRIBE Syntax and Selected Output

```
MTB > %DESCRIBE 'DIAMETER' 'TIME';
SUBC> BY 'TYPE'.
```

Descriptive Statistics

95% Confidence Interval for Mu

95% Confidence Interval for Median

Variable: DIAMETER
Group: 1

Anderson-Darling
Normality Test

A-Squared: 0.404
P-Value: 0.328

Mean 9.43913
StDev 2.87050
Variance 8.27050
Skewness 0.487887
Kurtosis −6.7E-01
N 23

Minimum 5.4000
1st Quartile 7.4000
Median 9.0000
3rd Quartile 12.0000
Maximum 15.0000

95% Confidence
Interval for Mu
8.1978   10.6804

95% Confidence
Interval for Sigma
2.2200   4.0628

95% Confidence
Interval for Median
7.7239   10.7313

Descriptive Statistics

95% Confidence Interval for Mu

95% Confidence Interval for Median

Variable: TIME
Group: 1

Anderson-Darling
Normality Test

A-Squared: 0.552
P-Value: 0.137

Mean 27.1222
StDev 11.1686
Variance 124.738
Skewness 0.783846
Kurtosis −1.4E-01
N 23

Minimum 12.0200
1st Quartile 17.8400
Median 23.2100
3rd Quartile 34.8800
Maximum 53.1800

95% Confidence
Interval for Mu
22.2925   31.9519

95% Confidence
Interval for Sigma
8.6378   15.8075

95% Confidence
Interval for Median
20.3802   31.5361

(continued)

TABLE 8.32   Continued

Descriptive Statistics

95% Confidence Interval for Mu

95% Confidence Interval for Median

Variable: DIAMETER
Group: 4

Anderson-Darling
Normality Test

A-Squared:	0.147
P-Value:	0.947
Mean	14.2800
StDev	5.7275
Variance	32.804
Skewness	0.296832
Kurtosis	0.173092
N	10
Minimum	5.0000
1st Quartile	10.5000
Median	13.8500
3rd Quartile	18.2250
Maximum	25.0000

95% Confidence
Interval for Mu

10.1828   18.3772

95% Confidence
Interval for Sigma

3.9396   10.4561

95% Confidence
Interval for Median

10.1306   18.3820

Descriptive Statistics

95% Confidence Interval for Mu

95% Confidence Interval for Median

Variable: TIME
Group: 4

Anderson-Darling
Normality Test

A-Squared:	0.487
P-Value:	0.171
Mean	49.4030
StDev	27.1621
Variance	737.782
Skewness	1.29256
Kurtosis	1.49166
N	10
Minimum	20.830
1st Quartile	30.228
Median	39.150
3rd Quartile	66.845
Maximum	109.380

95% Confidence
Interval for Mu

29.972   68.834

95% Confidence
Interval for Sigma

18.683   49.587

95% Confidence
Interval for Median

29.772   67.785

Descriptive Statistics

95% Confidence Interval for Mu

95% Confidence Interval for Median

Variable: DIAMETER
Group: 5

Anderson-Darling
Normality Test

A-Squared:	0.310
P-Value:	0.486
Mean	10.8556
StDev	3.5623
Variance	12.6903
Skewness	$-4.5E-01$
Kurtosis	$-2.2E-01$
N	9
Minimum	5.0000
1st Quartile	8.0000
Median	11.1000
3rd Quartile	13.4500
Maximum	16.0000

95% Confidence
Interval for Mu

8.1173   13.5938

95% Confidence
Interval for Sigma

2.4062   6.8246

95% Confidence
Interval for Median

6.9116   14.0214

Descriptive Statistics

95% Confidence Interval for Mu

95% Confidence Interval for Median

Variable: TIME
Group: 5

Anderson-Darling
Normality Test

A-Squared:	0.249
P-Value:	0.657
Mean	29.1944
StDev	4.2665
Variance	18.2028
Skewness	$1.49E-03$
Kurtosis	0.998254
N	9
Minimum	16.6600
1st Quartile	21.3600
Median	23.8800
3rd Quartile	26.3850
Maximum	31.8600

95% Confidence
Interval for Mu

20.9149   27.4739

95% Confidence
Interval for Sigma

2.8818   8.1736

95% Confidence
Interval for Median

21.0825   26.4585

**TABLE 8.33   Variances for Transformed Time Variable:
MINITAB DESCRIBE Syntax and Selected Output**

```
MTB > Name C4 = 'LTIME'
MTB > Let 'LTIME' = LOGT(TIME)
MTB > Name C5 = 'STIME'
MTB > Let 'STIME' = SQRT(TIME)
MTB > Describe 'LTIME' 'STIME';
SUBC>    By 'TYPE'.
```

Descriptive Statistics

Variable	TYPE	N	Mean	Median	TrMean	StDev
LTIME	1	23	1.3991	1.3657	1.3988	0.1762
	2	10	1.7083	1.6912	1.7036	0.1320
	3	7	1.5119	1.5278	1.5119	0.1854
	4	10	1.6407	1.5892	1.6312	0.2223
	5	9	1.3775	1.3780	1.3775	0.0793
STIME	1	23	5.107	4.818	5.081	1.044
	2	10	7.222	7.008	7.148	1.105
	3	7	5.811	5.806	5.811	1.204
	4	10	6.815	6.244	6.641	1.814
	5	9	4.901	4.887	4.901	0.439

syntax for the first group is shown, followed by the scatterplots for all five groups. The graphs cause no concern for curvilinearity.

8.7.1.1.5   Reliability of the Covariate
Diameter of a piece of tableware is a straightforward physical measure, presumably standardized. Therefore, there is no reason to question the reliability of the measurement.

8.7.1.1.6   Homogeneity of Regression
Homogeneity of regression in any of the general linear model programs, including MINITAB, is done by including the CV by IV interaction in a model statement, as shown in Table 8.34. Current worksheet syntax shows that we have returned to the full data set.

The **TYPE*DIAMETER** effect is the test for homogeneity of regression. The assumption has not been violated because P = 0.120 (greater than .05).

8.7.1.2   One-Way Analysis of Covariance

8.7.1.2.1   Major Analysis
The major run for the analysis is similar to that of Table 8.34, but with the CV by IV interaction omitted. Table 8.35 shows MINITAB GLM syntax and output. Recall that MINITAB GLM uses

```
MTB  > Split;
SUBC >    NoMatrices;
SUBC >    NoConstants;
SUBC >    By 'Type'.
```

Current worksheet: namble.MTW(TYPE=1)

```
MTB  > Plot 'LTIME'*'DIAMETER';
SUBC >    Symbol;
SUBC >    ScFrame;
SUBC >    ScAnnotation.
```

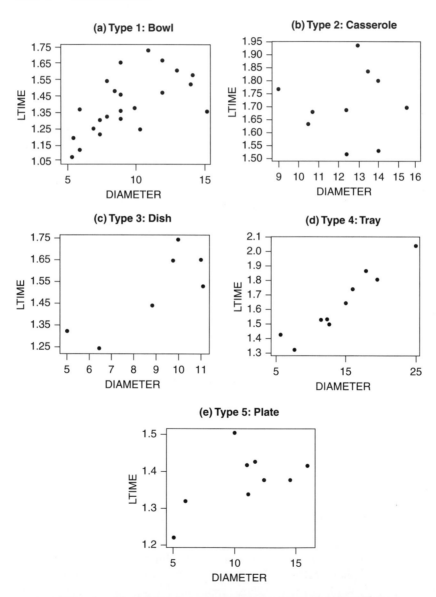

FIGURE 8.5   Scatterplots between LTIME and DIAMETER for Five Tableware Types. Selected MINITAB PLOT Syntax and Output

TABLE 8.34   Test for Homogeneity of Regression: Syntax and Selected Output from MINITAB GLM

```
Current worksheet: nambe.MTW


MTB > GLM 'LTIME' = DIAMETER TYPE DIAMETER*TYPE;
SUBC> Covariates 'DIAMETER';
SUBC> Brief 2.
```

General Linear Model

```
Factor    Type    Levels   Values
TYPE      fixed        5   1 2 3 4 5

Analysis of Variance for LTIME, using Adjusted SS for Tests

Source          DF    Seq SS    Adj SS    Adj MS      F       P
DIAMETER         1   1.23457   0.30332   0.30332   20.52   0.000
TYPE             4   0.46925   0.10075   0.02519    1.70   0.164
TYPE*DIAMETER    4   0.11430   0.11430   0.02857    1.93   0.120
Error           49   0.72439   0.72439   0.01478
Total           58   2.54251
```

Type III sums of squares (unweighted means with all effects adjusted for each other) as the default for analysis of variance and covariance.

The `Analysis of Variance` table shows a significant effect of tableware type on the logarithm of polishing time after adjusting for differences in diameter, $F(4, 53) = 7.41, p < .001$. There also is a significant effect of diameter, after adjusting for differences in tableware types, $F(1, 53) = 44.39, p < .001$.

`Adjusted least squares means` show that casseroles have the longest (logarithm of) polishing time, on average, and plates have the shortest time. However, these observations need to be validated through post hoc analysis. Table 8.36 shows sample sizes, adjusted means, and standard errors (recall that `StdDev` in MINITAB GLM actually is the standard error) for each type of tableware, in a format suitable for publication.

Effect size for tableware type is found by Equation 8.24, where $SS'_T = SS'_{TYPE} + SS'_{Error}$. Therefore:

$$\eta^2 = \frac{0.469}{0.469 + 0.839} = .36$$

The section of output labeled `Coef` shows that the pooled within-groups unstandardized regression coefficient, B, for diameter is 0.033.

8.7.1.2.2   Post Hoc Analyses

Differences among types of tableware are most appropriately evaluated through a Tukey test, available in MINITAB GLM with an additional instruction. Table 8.37 shows the additional syntax and output for the Tukey test of tableware types.

**TABLE 8.35   Analysis of Covariance of LTIME by Type of Tableware
with Diameter as a CV: MINITAB GLM Syntax and Selected Output**

```
MTB > GLM 'LTIME' = DIAMETER TYPE;
SUBC> Covariates 'DIAMETER';
SUBC> Brief 2;
SUBC> Means TYPE.
```

General Linear Model

```
Factor   Type   Levels  Values
TYPE     fixed       5  1 2 3 4 5

Analysis of Variance for LTIME, using Adjusted SS for Tests

Source      DF    Seq SS    Adj SS    Adj MS       F       P
DIAMETER     1   1.23457   0.70247   0.70247   44.39   0.000
TYPE         4   0.46925   0.46925   0.11731    7.41   0.000
Error       53   0.83868   0.83868   0.01582
Total       58   2.54251

Term          Coef      StDev       T       P
Constant   1.15790    0.05824   19.88   0.000
DIAMETER   0.033028   0.004957    6.66   0.000

Means for Covariates

Covariate    Mean    StDev
DIAMETER    10.93    3.853

Least Squares Means for LTIME

TYPE    Mean     StDev
1      1.448   0.02725
2      1.657   0.04053
3      1.579   0.04861
4      1.530   0.04311
5      1.380   0.04193
```

**TABLE 8.36   Logarithm of Polishing Time Adjusted
for Diameter for Five Types of Nambe Tableware**

Type of Tableware	Sample Size	Adjusted Mean	Standard Error
Bowl	23	1.448	0.027
Casserole	10	1.657	0.041
Dish	7	1.579	0.049
Tray	10	1.530	0.043
Plate	9	1.380	0.042

446

TABLE 8.37   Tukey Test of Types of Tableware: MINITAB GLM Syntax and Selected Output

```
MTB > GLM 'LTIME' = TYPE DIAMETER;
SUBC> Covariates 'DIAMETER';
SUBC> Brief 2;
SUBC> Pairwise TYPE;
SUBC> Tukey.
```

General Linear Model

```
Tukey Simultaneous Tests
Response Variable ltime
All Pairwise Comparisons among Levels of TYPE
```

TYPE = 1 subtracted from:

Level TYPE	Difference of Means	SE of Difference	T-Value	Adjusted P-Value
2	0.20834	0.04999	4.167	0.0011
3	0.13099	0.05437	2.409	0.1287
4	0.08167	0.05335	1.531	0.5475
5	-0.06847	0.04996	-1.371	0.6488

TYPE = 2 subtracted from:

Level TYPE	Difference of Means	SE of Difference	T-Value	Adjusted P-Value
3	-0.0773	0.06452	-1.199	0.7520
4	-0.1267	0.05695	-2.224	0.1868
5	-0.2768	0.05836	-4.743	0.0002

TYPE = 3 subtracted from:

Level TYPE	Difference of Means	SE of Difference	T-Value	Adjusted P-Value
4	-0.0493	0.06751	-0.731	0.9484
5	-0.1995	0.06414	-3.110	0.0241

TYPE = 4 subtracted from:

Level TYPE	Difference of Means	SE of Difference	T-Value	Adjusted P-Value
5	-0.1501	0.06024	-2.492	0.1078

Using a criterion $\alpha = .05$, Table 8.37 shows that casseroles (TYPE = 2) take significantly more time to polish than bowls (TYPE = 1) or plates (TYPE = 5), and that dishes (TYPE = 3) take more time than plates. MINITAB Correlation (not shown) indicates a raw bivariate correlation of .7 between logarithm of polishing time and diameter of tableware.

Table 8.38 is a checklist for one-way ANCOVA with a single CV. A Results section in journal format follows.

TABLE 8.38   Checklist for One-Way Randomized-Groups ANCOVA with a Single CV

1. Issues
   a. Sample sizes and missing data
   b. Normality of sampling distributions
   c. Outliers
   d. Independence of errors
   e. Homogeneity of variance
   f. Linearity
   g. Homogeneity of regression
   h. Reliability of CV
2. Major analyses: Main effect or planned comparisons. If significant:
   a. Effect size(s)
   b. Parameter estimates (adjusted marginal means and standard deviations or standard errors or confidence intervals)
3. Additional analyses
   a. Evaluation of CV effect
   b. Evaluation of correlation between CV and DV
   c. Post hoc comparisons
   d. Interpretation of departure from homogeneity of variance, homogeneity of covariance, and/or homogeneity of regression if relevant

---

Results

A one-way randomized-groups ANCOVA was performed on polishing time for five types of Nambe tableware: bowls, casseroles, dishes, trays, and plates, with diameter of item as a covariate. Heterogeneity of variance was reduced by a logarithmic transform of polishing time. Raw polishing times were exceptionally variable for trays and exceptionally stable for plates. Remaining assumptions of ANCOVA were met. Sample sizes for the five types of tableware were, in the order listed above, 23, 10, 7, 10, and 9, with a total $\underline{N}$ = 59. An unweighted means analysis (Type III sums of squares) was used to handle unequal sample sizes and adjust tests of tableware type and diameter for each other.

Type of tableware reliably predicted logarithm of polishing time after adjusting for diameter, $\underline{F}(4, 53) = 7.41$, $\underline{p} < .001$, $\eta^2 = .36$.

Table 8.36 shows logarithm of adjusted means, standard errors, and sample sizes for each type of tableware. A Tukey test revealed that casseroles take significantly more time to polish than bowls or plates, and that dishes take more time than plates, after adjusting for diameter.

Diameter was also significantly related to logarithm of polishing time, after adjusting for type of tableware, $F(1, 53) = 44.39$, $p < .001$, with a pooled within-groups $\underline{B} = 0.033$. The raw bivariate correlation was .70 between logarithm of polishing time and diameter of tableware.

8.7.2 Mixed Randomized-Groups and Repeated-Measures Analysis of Covariance

This example of a factorial ANCOVA with two CVs uses data collected from the National Transportation Safety Board and available with authorization for free use on the Internet. The data set includes 176 stock automobile crashes in which dummies occupied both the driver's and passenger's seats on each crash. The injury variable to be used is chest deceleration. The data file also includes information on type of vehicle and its safety features.

The DV for the analysis is chest deceleration, with vehicle weight and model year as CVs. The randomized-groups IV is type of protection (airbag, manual belt, motorized belt, or passive belt). The repeated-measures IV is location of dummy, in either the driver's or passenger's seat. Data files are CRASH.*.

The goal is to evaluate chest deceleration as a function of type of safety protection (PROTECT), location of dummy (D_P), and their interaction, adjusted for vehicle weight and year. Additionally, the CVs here are of interest in their own right, not just as modifiers of the tests of the randomized-groups IV. That is, CVs are considered continuous IVs, which are themselves assessed after adjusting for vehicle protection and location of dummy.

8.7.2.1 Evaluation of Assumptions

8.7.2.1.1 Sample Sizes and Missing Data

Table 8.39 shows the sample sizes of available data, produced by SPSS DESCRIPTIVES. There were no missing data on the CVs, weight and year; however, several missing values were noted for the DV, **chest deceleration**. Table 8.39 shows three cases missing **passenger** values on the DV in the **airbag** group, one **driver** and two **passenger** values missing the DV in the **manual belt** group, and so on. Because missing data are scattered over the four protection groups (although a bit heavier in the passenger seat), the decision is made to omit cases with values missing in either location for further analysis. The resulting sample sizes are shown in Table 8.40.

TABLE 8.39   Original Sample Sizes for Complete Example of ANCOVA through SPSS DESCRIPTIVES

SORT CASES BY protect.
SPLIT FILE BY protect.
DESCRIPTIVES
VARIABLES=d_chest p_chest weight year
/STATISTICS=MIN MAX .

Descriptives

Descriptive Statistics

Type of protection		N	Minimum	Maximum
Driver airbag	Chest deceleration: driver	32	35.00	64.00
	Chest deceleration: passenger	29	31.00	58.00
	Vehicle weight	32	2190.00	4080.00
	Model year	32	87.00	91.00
	Valid N (listwise)	29		
Manual belt	Chest deceleration: driver	97	35.00	97.00
	Chest deceleration: passenger	96	31.00	71.00
	Vehicle weight	98	1590.00	5619.00
	Model year	98	87.00	91.00
	Valid N (listwise)	95		
Motorize	Chest deceleration: driver	20	41.00	64.00
	Chest deceleration: passenger	21	39.00	77.00
	Vehicle weight	22	2200.00	3630.00
	Model year	22	89.00	91.00
	Valid N (listwise)	19		
Passive belt	Chest deceleration: driver	24	35.00	70.00
	Chest deceleration: passenger	22	32.00	82.00
	Vehicle weight	24	2120.00	3240.00
	Model year	24	87.00	91.00
	Valid N (listwise)	22		

The original sample size of 176 is thus reduced to 165 with a loss of 11 cases due to missing data on the DV. A method 1 adjustment for unequal *n* will be used (cf. Table 5.45).

8.7.2.1.2   Normality of Sampling Distributions

Table 8.41 shows syntax, descriptive statistics, and histograms for each level of **prot_num**.[12] The file first is sorted and then split by **prot_num** so that output is organized by groups. The

---

[12]Prot_num is the same as protect, but in numerical format (1 = driver airbag, and so on). This appears to pose fewer problems for SPSS histograms.

TABLE 8.40 Sample Sizes Used for Complete Example of ANCOVA

Type of Protection (PROTECT) Randomized Groups	Number of Crashes
Driver Airbag	29
Manual Belt	95
Motorized Belt	19
Passive Belt	22

SELECT IF instruction limits the analysis to cases that have valid (nonmissing) data on both passenger and driver chest deceleration.

A glance at the three histograms shown here suggests positive skewness for driver and passenger chest deceleration. Indeed, the skewness for driver chest deceleration in the manual belt group exceeds the $\alpha = .001$ criterion: $z = 0.826/0.247 = 3.34$. Even greater departures from distributional symmetry are noted for passenger chest deceleration in the motorized and passive belt conditions. No reliable departure from normality is evident for the CVs. Therefore, the decision is made to try square root and logarithmic transformations of the DV. Table 8.42 shows the results of the transformation (without histograms).

The square root transform fails to reduce skewness adequately. There is significant skewness in chest deceleration distribution in the motorized group even after the logarithmic transformation. However, the logarithmic transform will be used and the data checked for outliers that may be contributing to remaining skewness.

8.7.2.1.3 Outliers

Table 8.42 shows that the case with the largest value for log of chest deceleration (among passenger dummies) in the motorized belt group indeed is a univariate outlier: $z = (1.89 - 1.6585)/0.0689 = 3.36$. No other univariate outliers are found for logarithm of chest deceleration for either driver or passenger dummies, in any of the protection groups. By referring back to Table 8.41, the only

TABLE 8.41 Descriptive Statistics and Histograms for Protection Categories through SPSS FREQUENCIES: Syntax and Partial Output

```
SORT CASES BY protect.
SPLIT FILE BY protect.
SELECT IF (d_chest < 100 and p_chest < 100).
FREQUENCIES
  VARIABLES=d_chest p_chest weight year /FORMAT=NOTABLE
  /STATISTICS=STDDEV VARIANCE MINIMUM MAXIMUM MEAN SKEWNESS SESKW
    KURTOSIS SEKURT
  /HISTOGRAM NORMAL
  /ORDER ANALYSIS.
```

(continued)

TABLE 8.41   Continued

Frequencies

Statistics

Type of protection			Chest deceleration: driver	Chest deceleration: passenger	Vehicle weight	Model year
Driver airbag	N	Valid	29	29	29	29
		Missing	0	0	0	0
	Mean		46.7586	42.7586	3097.1379	89.9655
	Std. Deviation		7.7167	6.0925	476.8072	1.1175
	Variance		59.5468	37.1182	227345.12	1.2488
	Skewness		.593	.426	.012	−1.083
	Std. Error of Skewness		.434	.434	.434	.434
	Kurtosis		−.675	.823	−.151	.547
	Std. Error of Kurtosis		.845	.845	.845	.845
	Minimum		35.00	31.00	2190.00	87.00
	Maximum		64.00	58.00	4080.00	91.00
Manual belt	N	Valid	95	95	95	95
		Missing	0	0	0	0
	Mean		53.4421	45.8105	2973.7158	88.3789
	Std. Deviation		10.5616	8.4480	726.1261	1.1955
	Variance		111.5471	71.3680	527259.16	1.4293
	Skewness		.826	.728	.768	.560
	Std. Error of Skewness		.247	.247	.247	.247
	Kurtosis		1.853	.337	1.425	−.541
	Std. Error of Kurtosis		.490	.490	.490	.490
	Minimum		35.00	31.00	1650.00	87.00
	Maximum		97.00	71.00	5619.00	91.00
Motorized belt	N	Valid	19	19	19	19
		Missing	0	0	0	0
	Mean		49.4211	46.1579	2750.5263	90.1053
	Std. Deviation		7.5374	8.5976	383.8383	.8753
	Variance		56.8129	73.9181	147331.82	.7661
	Skewness		.543	2.741	.722	−.220
	Std. Error of Skewness		.524	.524	.524	.524
	Kurtosis		−.995	9.501	.323	−1.711
	Std. Error of Kurtosis		1.014	1.014	1.014	1.014
	Minimum		41.00	39.00	2200.00	89.00
	Maximum		64.00	77.00	3630.00	91.00
Passive belt	N	Valid	22	22	22	22
		Missing	0	0	0	0
	Mean		51.0909	44.2273	2728.1818	88.3636
	Std. Deviation		8.1235	10.0330	343.3769	1.5289
	Variance		65.9913	100.6602	117907.68	2.3377
	Skewness		.544	2.559	−.223	.724
	Std. Error of Skewness		.491	.491	.491	.491
	Kurtosis		.330	9.620	−.951	−1.105
	Std. Error of Kurtosis		.953	.953	.953	.953
	Minimum		35.00	32.00	2120.00	87.00
	Maximum		70.00	82.00	3240.00	91.001

TABLE 8.41   Continued

Histogram

Chest deceleration: driver

PROT_NUM: 2.00   Manual belt

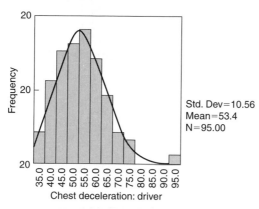

Std. Dev=10.56
Mean=53.4
N=95.00

Chest deceleration: passenger

PROT_NUM: 3.00   Motorized belt

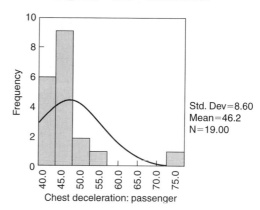

Std. Dev=8.60
Mean=46.2
N=19.00

Chest deceleration: passenger

PROT_NUM: 4.00   Passive belt

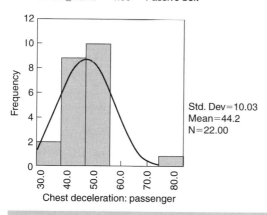

Std. Dev=10.03
Mean=44.2
N=22.00

TABLE 8.42   Descriptive Statistics and Histograms for Protection Categories through SPSS FREQUENCIES

```
SORT CASES BY protect.
SPLIT FILE BY protect.
SELECT IF (d_chest < 100 and p_chest < 100).
COMPUTE sd_chest = sqrt(d_chest).
COMPUTE sp_chest = sqrt(p_chest).
COMPUTE ld_chest = lg10(d_chest).
COMPUTE lp_chest = lg10(p_chest).
FREQUENCIES
VARIABLES=sd_chest sp_chest ld_chest lp_chest /FORMAT=NOTABLE
/STATISTICS=STDDEV VARIANCE MINIMUM MAXIMUM MEAN SKEWNESS SESKW KURTOSIS SEKURT
/ ORDER ANALYSIS.
```

(continued)

TABLE 8.42   Continued

Frequencies

Statistics

Type of protection			SD_CHEST	SP_CHEST	LD_CHEST	LP_CHEST
Driver airbag	N	Valid	29	29	29	29
		Missing	0	0	0	0
	Mean		6.8162	6.5231	1.6643	1.6268
	Std. Deviation		.5556	.4637	6.986E-02	6.179E-02
	Variance		.3086	.2150	4.881E-03	3.818E-03
	Skewness		.479	.175	.364	−.072
	Std. Error of Skewness		.434	.434	.434	.434
	Kurtosis		−.812	.595	−.903	.496
	Std. Error of Kurtosis		.845	.845	.845	.845
	Minimum		5.92	5.57	1.54	1.49
	Maximum		8.00	7.62	1.81	1.76
Manual belt	N	Valid	95	95	95	95
		Missing	0	0	0	0
	Mean		7.2764	6.7409	1.7198	1.6540
	Std. Deviation		.7082	.6118	8.373E-02	7.773E-02
	Variance		.5016	.3743	7.011E-03	6.042E-03
	Skewness		.462	.509	.153	.303
	Std. Error of Skewness		.247	.247	.247	.247
	Kurtosis		.689	−.096	.050	−.391
	Std. Error of Kurtosis		.490	.490	.490	.490
	Minimum		5.92	5.57	1.54	1.49
	Maximum		9.85	8.43	1.99	1.85
Motorized belt	N	Valid	19	19	19	19
		Missing	0	0	0	0
	Mean		7.0111	6.7705	1.6893	1.6585
	Std. Deviation		.5290	.5801	6.476E-02	6.891E-02
	Variance		.2799	.3365	4.194E-03	4.748E-03
	Skewness		.462	2.411	.383	2.069
	Std. Error of Skewness		.524	.524	.524	.524
	Kurtosis		−1.111	7.804	−1.211	6.151
	Std. Error of Kurtosis		1.014	1.014	1.014	1.014
	Minimum		6.40	6.24	1.61	1.59
	Maximum		8.00	8.77	1.81	1.89
Passive belt	N	Valid	22	22	22	22
		Missing	0	0	0	0
	Mean		7.1266	6.6161	1.7032	1.6371
	Std. Deviation		.5628	.6899	6.832E-02	8.444E-02
	Variance		.3167	.4760	4.667E-03	7.131E-03
	Skewness		.316	1.994	.068	1.420
	Std. Error of Skewness		.491	.491	.491	.491
	Kurtosis		.312	7.006	.458	4.701
	Std. Error of Kurtosis		.953	.953	.953	.953
	Minimum		5.92	5.66	1.54	1.51
	Maximum		8.37	9.06	1.85	1.91

univariate outlier noted among the CVs is the largest value of weight in the manual belt condition: $z = (5619 - 2973.716)/726.1261 = 3.64$.

Table 8.43 shows the syntax for the SPSS DISCRIMINANT analyses to assess multivariate outliers in the set of two CVs. The SELECT IF instruction is used from the prior syntax to ensure that the appropriate cases are analyzed. Mahalanobis distance is based on weight and year. Note that

TABLE 8.43   SPSS DISCRIMINANT Analysis to Assess Multivariate Outliers by Protection Groups: Syntax and Selected Output

```
SPLIT FILE OFF.
SELECT IF (d_chest < 100 and p_chest < 100).
DISCRIMINANT
  /GROUPS=prot_num(1 4)
  /VARIABLES=ld_chest weight year
  /ANALYSIS ALL
  /PRIORS EQUAL
  /PLOT=CASES
  /CLASSIFY=NONMISSING POOLED .
```

Discriminant

Casewise Statistics

Case Number	Actual Group	Squared Mahalanobis Distance to Centroid	Case Number	Actual Group	Squared Mahalanobis Distance to Centroid
1	1	.540	23	1	1.444
2	1	2.966	24	1	3.398
3	1	1.787	25	1	1.299
4	1	2.948	26	1	.925
5	1	2.049	27	1	.856
6	1	2.707	28	1	.293
7	1	1.552	29	1	1.692
8	1	2.742	30	2	4.863
9	1	.894	31	2	.355
10	1	.673	32	2	.568
11	1	1.358	33	2	4.425
12	1	1.539	34	2	3.297
13	1	.821	35	2	4.074
14	1	.002	36	2	2.111
15	1	1.005	37	2	.700
16	1	1.444	38	2	2.372
17	1	.827	39	2	12.924
18	1	.485	40	2	14.299
19	1	2.149	41	2	23.312
20	1	.980	42	2	1.395
21	1	4.183	43	2	5.176
22	1	2.654			

the grouping variable is prot_num, a numeric variable created for type of protection. SPSS DIS-CRIMINANT cannot accept groups based on string variables (which may include letters and symbols). The /PLOT=CASES instruction produces the casewise results, which show Mahalanobis distances for each case. Note that the file is not split into protection groups for this analysis, accomplished by SPLIT FILE OFF.

Squared Mahalanobis Distance to centroid is distributed as a χ^2 variable with df equal to the number of predictors (CVs). Critical χ^2 with 2 df at $\alpha = .001$ is 13.816. Squared Mahalanobis Distance for each case from its closest group mean is printed in the last column shown in Table 8.43. A misclassified case will be even farther from its own group centroid. Only the first 43 cases are shown; the only multivariate outlier is case #41 in the manual belt group with $\chi^2 = 23.312$.

Examination of the data for this case revealed that it was the univariate outlier on vehicle weight and was Car #27. The outlier on chest deceleration was Car #136. The decision is made to omit the two outlying cases from further analysis and to describe their characteristics in the results. Thus $N = 163$ for subsequent analyses.

8.7.2.1.4 Independence of Errors
Independence of errors for the repeated-measures portion of the design (location) is handled by use of the appropriate repeated-measures error term for tests of location and the protection by location interaction. Independence of errors is problematic for the randomized-groups IV. It is presumed that cars are not randomly assigned to type of protection. Some stock cars are typically equipped with one (or more) type of protection, whereas other cars are equipped with other types. The hope is that type of belt is not so highly related to other vehicle characteristics as to make generalization beyond the tested vehicles unjustifiable.

8.7.2.1.5 Homogeneity of Variance
Table 8.44 shows SPSS simple descriptive statistics for the cases remaining in the analysis. Car #27 and car #136 are the deleted outliers.

The ratio between the largest variance (.00708) and smallest variance (.00359) for log of driver chest deceleration is far smaller than 10: $F_{max} = 1.97$. Variance ratios for all other variables are similarly acceptable, even though the sample-size ratio is a bit greater than 4:1. Therefore, there is no concern about violation of homogeneity of variance within cells.

8.7.2.1.6 Linearity
SPSS GRAPH is used to produce scatterplots among the continuous variables: logarithm of chest deceleration (driver and passenger), model year, and vehicle weight. Figures 8.6 through 8.10 show syntax and output for the five sets of plots: ld_chest by weight, lp_chest by weight, ld_chest by year, lp_chest by year and weight by year, respectively. Prior filters are left in effect (omitting missing values on the DV and outliers) as well as file splitting by protection.

The most prominent curvilinearity noted is in the relationship between the two CVs, weight and year, for cases in the passive seatbelt group and possibly in the airbag group. Weights are lower for the earlier and later years than in the middle years. Also, the direction of the relationship appears negative in the motorized belt group. However, since the relationships between the DV and each of the CVs are comfortably linear if not particularly strong, no transformation of the CVs is deemed necessary. The scatterplots suggest that the CVs may not be providing strong adjustment to the DV.

TABLE 8.44   Descriptive Statistics for Transformed Variables with Outliers Deleted

SORT CASES BY prot_num.
SPLIT FILE BY prot_num.
SELECT IF (d_chest < 100 and p_chest < 100 and car <> 27 and car <> 136).
DESCRIPTIVES
  VARIABLES=ld_chest lp_chest weight year
  /STATISTICS=MEAN STDDEV VARIANCE MIN MAX .

Descriptive Statistics

Protection: numeric		N	Minimum	Maximum	Mean	Std. Deviation	Variance
driver airbag	LD_CHEST	29	1.54	1.81	1.6643	6.986E-02	4.881E-03
	LP_CHEST	29	1.49	1.76	1.6268	6.179E-02	3.818E-03
	Vehicle weight	29	2190.00	4080.00	3097.1379	476.8072	227345.1
	Model year	29	87.00	91.00	89.9655	1.1175	1.249
	Valid N (listwise)	29					
Manual belt	LD_CHEST	94	1.54	1.99	1.7200	8.415E-02	7.082E-03
	LP_CHEST	94	1.49	1.85	1.6543	7.808E-02	6.096E-03
	Vehicle weight	94	1650.00	5103.00	2945.5745	675.9334	456885.9
	Model year	94	87.00	91.00	88.3936	1.1933	1.424
	Valid N (listwise)	94					
Motorized belt	LD_CHEST	18	1.61	1.79	1.6828	5.993E-02	3.592E-03
	LP_CHEST	18	1.59	1.72	1.6458	4.243E-02	1.800E-03
	Vehicle weight	18	2200.00	3630.00	2736.1111	389.6383	151818.0
	Model year	18	89.00	91.00	90.1667	.8575	.735
	Valid N (listwise)	18					
Passive belt	LD_CHEST	22	1.54	1.85	1.7032	6.832E-02	4.667E-03
	LP_CHEST	22	1.51	1.91	1.6371	8.444E-02	7.131E-03
	Vehicle weight	22	2120.00	3240.00	2728.1818	343.3769	117907.7
	Model year	22	87.00	91.00	88.3636	1.5289	2.338
	Valid N (listwise)	22					

8.7.2.1.7   Reliability of Covariates

Measurement of the two CVs, weight of the vehicle and model year, is straightforward. Therefore, there are no concerns about unreliability of measurement.

8.7.2.1.8   Multicollinearity

Multicollinearity only is a problem if the two CVs, weight and year, are very highly correlated. No such high correlation is suggested by the scatterplots in Figure 8.10. An SPSS bivariate correlation run (not shown) shows $r = .18$, indicating no threat of multicollinearity in the linear relationships among the CVs.

8.7.2.1.9   *Homogeneity of Regression*

The check for parallelism of slopes for the CVs is made by including the interactions between each of the IVs and each of the CVs in an ANCOVA run. Table 8.45 shows syntax and selected out-

```
SORT CASES BY prot_num.
SPLIT FILE BY prot_num.
SELECT IF (d_chest<100 and p_chest<100 and car<>27 and car<>136).
GRAPH
   /SCATTERPLOT(BIVAR)=weight with ld_chest
   /MISSING=LISTWISE.
```

FIGURE 8.6   Scatterplots between Vehicle Weight and Logarithm of Driver Chest Deceleration for the Four Safety Protection Groups: SPSS SCATTERPLOT Syntax and Output

```
GRAPH
    /SCATTERPLOT(BIVAR)=weight WITH lp_chest
    /MISSING=LISTWISE .
```

FIGURE 8.7   Scatterplots between Vehicle Weight and Logarithm of Passenger Chest Deceleration for the Four Safety Protection Groups: SPSS SCATTERPLOT Syntax and Output

put for the homogeneity of regression test through SPSS GLM. The two interactions relevant to the test are in the /DESIGN instruction.

Homogeneity of regression is assessed through the two interactions, protection by weight, and protection by year in this GLM approach to ANCOVA. The first poses no problem, but the PRO-TECT*YEAR is statistically significant at $\alpha = .05$. The decision is made to retain year as a CV despite this, because the violation is marginal and because an example with two CVs makes a more interesting demonstration.

8.7.2.2 Mixed Randomized-Repeated Analysis of Covariance

8.7.2.2.1 Omnibus Analyses

Table 8.46 shows syntax and output for the omnibus ANCOVA of chest deceleration as a function of type of protection and seat location, with vehicle weight and year as CVs. EMMEANS requests adjusted marginal means for both IVs (needed should they turn out to be statistically reliable) and a request for printing parameters provides regression coefficients for the CVs.

Multivariate output has been omitted; it does not differ from univariate output when there are only two levels of the repeated-measures IV, and there is no possibility of violation of sphericity (cf. Section 6.6.2). The Tests of Between-Subjects Effects show that type of protection reliably

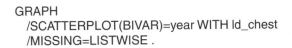

```
GRAPH
   /SCATTERPLOT(BIVAR)=year WITH ld_chest
   /MISSING=LISTWISE .
```

FIGURE 8.8 Scatterplots between Model Year and Logarithm of Driver Chest Deceleration for the Four Safety Protection Groups: SPSS SCATTERPLOT Syntax and Output

GRAPH
/SCATTERPLOT(BIVAR)=year WITH lp_chest
/MISSING=LISTWISE .

FIGURE 8.9 Scatterplots between Model Year and Logarithm of Passenger Chest Deceleration for the Four Safety Protection Groups: SPSS SCATTERPLOT Syntax and Output

affects the logarithm of chest deceleration, $F(3, 157) = 6.293, p = < .0005$, after adjusting for vehicle weight and model year. Type of protection accounts for about 11% of the variance in the logarithm of chest deceleration, partial $\eta^2 = .107$. A look at the marginal means suggests that airbags provide the most protection (leading to the least amount of chest deceleration) and that manual seatbelts provide the least protection. However, this needs to be verified through post hoc comparisons.

There also are significant effects of both CVs. Vehicle weight significantly affects logarithm of chest deceleration, after adjusting for all other effects, $F(1, 157) = 11.279, p = .001$. The output labeled **Parameter Estimates** shows the regression coefficients for the two locations: $B = 0.00004$ and partial $\eta^2 = .071$ for drivers, and $B = 0.00002$ and partial $\eta^2 = .035$ for passengers. Thus, about

GRAPH
/SCATTERPLOT(BIVAR)=year WITH weight.
/MISSING=LISTWISE .

FIGURE 8.10   Scatterplots between Model Year and Vehicle Weight for the Four Safety Protection Groups: SPSS SCATTERPLOT Syntax and Output

3.5% to 7% of the variance over the two locations is accounted for by vehicle weight. The positive coefficients indicate, surprisingly, that the greater the weight of the vehicle, the greater the injury. Model year also significantly affects logarithm of chest deceleration, after adjusting for all other effects, $F(1, 157) = 7.058$, $p = .009$. The output labeled Parameter Estimates shows the regression coefficients for the two locations: $B = 0.00781$ and partial $\eta^2 = .015$ for drivers, and $B = 0.0146$ and partial $\eta^2 = .058$ for passengers. Thus, about 1.5% to 6% of the variance over the two locations is accounted for by model year of the car. The positive coefficients indicate, again surprisingly, that the later the year the vehicle was made, the greater the injury.

The Tests of Within-Subjects Effects show no statistically reliable effects on chest deceleration by location of the dummy or by the location by protection interaction. Nor is there a significant

TABLE 8.45   SPSS GLM Analysis to Assess Homogeneity of Regression: Syntax and Selected Output

```
SPLIT FILE OFF.
GLM
  ld_chest lp_chest BY protect WITH weight year
  /WSFACTOR = location 2 Polynomial
  /MEASURE = chest_de
  /METHOD = SSTYPE(3)
  /INTERCEPT = INCLUDE
  /CRITERIA = ALPHA(.05)
  /WSDESIGN = location
  /DESIGN = protect weight year protect*weight protect*year.
```

General Linear Model

Tests of Between-Subjects Effects

Measure: CHEST_DE
Transformed Variable: Average

Source	Type III Sum of Squares	df	Mean Square	F	Sig.
Intercept	8.775E-03	1	8.775E-03	1.156	.284
PROTECT	2.124E-02	2	1.062E-02	1.399	.250
WEIGHT	8.884E-03	1	8.884E-03	1.171	.281
YEAR	1.929E-02	1	1.929E-02	2.543	.113
PROTECT * WEIGHT	2.548E-02	3	8.493E-03	1.119	.343
PROTECT * YEAR	6.287E-02	3	2.096E-02	2.762	.044
Error	1.146	151	7.588E-03		

interaction between location and either of the CVs, vehicle weight or model year—that is, no violation of homogeneity of regression for the repeated-measures IV. Table 8.47 shows an additional SPSS GLM run in which CVs are omitted and only the repeated-measures portion of the output are examined.

The output shows that power for repeated-measures effects was substantially reduced by using the GLM approach in which interaction between the repeated-measures IV and CVs is included in the analysis model. By using the traditional approach, there is a statistically reliable and substantial effect of location, $F(1, 159) = 58.568$, $p < .0005$, partial $\eta^2 = .269$. The protection by location interaction, however, remains nonsignificant. The location means show that greater average logarithm of chest deceleration is associated with the driver than with the passenger dummy. The lack of a location by protection interaction is especially interesting considering that, with one exception, only the driver's seat was equipped with an airbag.

8.7.2.2.2   Post Hoc Analyses

The omnibus analysis suggests two post hoc analyses: comparisons among marginal means for type of protection and evaluation of the bivariate correlations between injury and the CVs.

TABLE 8.46   Omnibut ANCOVA through SPSS GLM: Syntax and Selected Output

```
GLM
ld_chest lp_chest BY protect WITH weight year
/WSFACTOR = location 2 Polynomial
/MEASURE = chest_de
/METHOD = SSTYPE(3)
/EMMEANS = TABLES(protect) WITH(weight=MEAN year=MEAN)
/EMMEANS = TABLES(location) WITH(weight=MEAN year=MEAN)
/EMMEANS = TABLES(protect*location) WITH(weight=MEAN year=MEAN)
/PRINT = DESCRIPTIVE ETASQ OPOWER
/CRITERIA = ALPHA(.05)
/WSDESIGN = location
/DESIGN = weight year protect.
```

General Linear Model

Within-Subjects Factors

Measure: CHEST_DE

LOCATION	Dependent Variable
1	LD_CHEST
2	LP_CHEST

Between-Subjects Factors

		Value Label	N
Type of protection	d-airbag	Driver airbag	29
	manual	Manual belt	94
	motorized		18
	passive	Passive belt	22

Descriptive Statistics

	Type of Protection	Mean	Std. Deviation	N
LD_CHEST	Driver airbag	1.6643	6.986E-02	29
	Manual belt	1.7200	8.415E-02	94
	Motorize	1.6828	5.993E-02	18
	Passive belt	1.7032	6.832E-02	22
	Total	1.7037	7.982E-02	163
LP_CHEST	Driver airbag	1.6268	6.179E-02	29
	Manual belt	1.6543	7.808E-02	94
	Motorize	1.6458	4.243E-02	18
	Passive belt	1.6371	8.444E-02	22
	Total	1.6462	7.341E-02	163

Tests of Between-Subjects Effects

Measure: CHEST_DE
Transformed Variable: Average

Source	Type III Sum of Squares	df	Mean Square	F	Sig.	Eta Squared	Noncent. Parameter	Observed Power[a]
Intercept	1.907E-02	1	1.907E-02	2.425	.121	.015	2.425	.340
WEIGHT	8.868E-02	1	8.868E-02	11.279	.001	.067	11.279	.916
YEAR	5.549E-02	1	5.549E-02	7.058	.009	.043	7.058	.752
PROTECT	.148	3	4.948E-02	6.293	.000	.107	18.879	.963
Error	1.234	157	7.862E-03					

a. Computed using alpha = .05

TABLE 8.46 Continued

Parameter Estimates

Dependent Variable	Parameter	B	Std. Error	t	Sig.	95% Confidence Interval		Eta Squared	Noncent. Parameter	Observed Power
						Lower Bound	Upper Bound			
LD_CHEST	Intercept	.916	.436	2.099	.037	5.382E-02	1.778	.027	2.099	.550
	WEIGHT	3.56E-05	.000	3.460	.001	1.526E-05	5.588E-05	.071	3.460	.930
	YEAR	7.81E-03	.005	1.566	.119	-2.042E-03	1.767E-02	.015	1.566	.343
	[PROTECT =d-airbag]	-6.4E-02	.022	-2.872	.005	-.109	-2.014E-02	.050	2.872	.814
	[PROTECT =manual]	8.88E-03	.018	.502	.616	-2.602E-02	4.377E-02	.002	.502	.079
	[PROTECT =Motorize]	-3.5E-02	.025	-1.382	.169	-8.452E-02	1.494E-02	.012	1.382	.279
	[PROTECT =passive]	0[b]	.	.	.	.	.	.	.	.
LP_CHEST	Intercept	.281	.411	.683	.496	-.531	1.092	.003	.683	.104
	WEIGHT	2.29E-05	.000	2.370	.019	3.818E-06	4.205E-05	.035	2.370	.654
	YEAR	1.46E-02	.005	3.118	.002	5.368E-03	2.392E-02	.058	3.118	.873
	[PROTECT =d-airbag]	-4.2E-02	.021	-1.999	.047	-8.399E-02	-4.937E-04	.025	1.999	.511
	[PROTECT =manual]	1.18E-02	.017	.707	.481	-2.109E-02	4.461E-02	.003	.707	.108
	[PROTECT =Motorize]	-1.8E-02	.024	-.753	.452	-6.466E-02	2.896E-02	.004	.753	.116
	[PROTECT =passive]	0[b]	.	.	.	.	.	.	.	.

a. Computed using alpha = .05
b. This parameter is set to zero because it is redundant.

TABLE 8.46 Continued

Test of Within-Subject Effects

Measure: CHEST_DE

Source		Type III Sum of Squares	df	Mean Square	F	Sig.	Eta Squared	Noncent. Parameter	Observed Power[a]
LOCATION	Sphericity Assumed	5.516E-03	1	5.516E-03	2.234	.137	.014	2.234	.318
	Greenhouse-Geisser	5.516E-03	1.000	5.516E-03	2.234	.137	.014	2.234	.318
	Huynh-Feldt	5.516E-03	1.000	5.516E-03	2.234	.137	.014	2.234	.318
	Lower-bound	5.516E-03	1.000	5.516E-03	2.234	.137	.014	2.234	.318
LOCATION * WEIGHT	Sphericity Assumed	4.136E-03	1	4.136E-03	1.675	.197	.011	1.675	.251
	Greenhouse-Geisser	4.136E-03	1.000	4.136E-03	1.675	.197	.011	1.675	.251
	Huynh-Feldt	4.136E-03	1.000	4.136E-03	1.675	.197	.011	1.675	.251
	Lower-bound	4.136E-03	1.000	4.136E-03	1.675	.197	.011	1.675	.251
LOCATION * YEAR	Sphericity Assumed	5.137E-03	1	5.137E-03	2.081	.151	.013	2.081	.300
	Greenhouse-Geisser	5.137E-03	1.000	5.137E-03	2.081	.151	.013	2.081	.300
	Huynh-Feldt	5.137E-03	1.000	5.137E-03	2.081	.151	.013	2.081	.300
	Lower-bound	5.137E-03	1.000	5.137E-03	2.081	.151	.013	2.081	.300
LOCATION * PROTECT	Sphericity Assumed	4.081E-03	3	1.360E-03	.551	.648	.010	1.653	.162
	Greenhouse-Geisser	4.081E-03	3.000	1.360E-03	.551	.648	.010	1.653	.162
	Huynh-Feldt	4.081E-03	3.000	1.360E-03	.551	.648	.010	1.653	.162
	Lower-bound	4.081E-03	3.000	1.360E-03	.551	.648	.010	1.653	.162
Error(LOCATION)	Sphericity Assumed	.388	157	2.469E-03					
	Greenhouse-Geisser	.388	157.000	2.469E-03					
	Huynh-Feldt	.388	157.000	2.469E-03					
	Lower-bound	.388	157.000	2.469E-03					

a. Computed using alpha = .05

TABLE 8.46   Continued

Estimated Marginal Means

1. Type of protection

Measure: CHEST_DE

Type of protection	Mean	Std. Error	95% Confidence Interval	
			Lower Bound	Upper Bound
Driver airbag	1.628[a]	.013	1.603	1.653
Manual belt	1.692[a]	.007	1.678	1.705
Motorize	1.655[a]	.016	1.624	1.687
Passive belt	1.681[a]	.014	1.655	1.708

a. Evaluated at covariates appeared in the model: Vehicle weight = 2920.0675, Model year = 88.8650.

2. LOCATION

Measure: CHEST_DE

LOCATION	Mean	Std. Error	95% Confidence Interval	
			Lower Bound	Upper Bound
1	1.691[a]	.007	1.677	1.706
2	1.637[a]	.007	1.623	1.650

a. Evaluated at covariates appeared in the model: Vehicle weight = 2920.0675, Model year = 88.8650.

3. Type of protection * LOCATION

Measure: CHEST_DE

Type of protection	LOCATION	Mean	Std. Error	95% Confidence Interval	
				Lower Bound	Upper Bound
Driver airbag	1	1.649[a]	.015	1.620	1.679
	2	1.607[a]	.014	1.579	1.634
Manual belt	1	1.723[a]	.008	1.707	1.739
	2	1.661[a]	.008	1.646	1.676
Motorize	1	1.679[a]	.019	1.642	1.716
	2	1.631[a]	.018	1.596	1.666
Passive belt	1	1.714[a]	.016	1.682	1.746
	2	1.649[a]	.015	1.619	1.679

a. Evaluated at covariates appeared in the model: Vehicle weight = 2920.0675, Model year = 88.8650.

TABLE 8.47   ANOVA on Injury without CVs: SPSS GLM Syntax and Selected Output

```
GLM
  ld_chest lp_chest BY protect
  /WSFACTOR = location 2 Polynomial
  /MEASURE = chest_de
  /METHOD = SSTYPE(3)
  /EMMEANS = TABLES(location)
  /PRINT = ETASQ OPOWER
  /CRITERIA = ALPHA(.05)
  /WSDESIGN location
  /DESIGN protect.
```

General Linear Model

Tests of Within-Subjects Effects

Measure: CHEST_DE

Source		Type III Sum of Squares	df	Mean Square	F	Sig.	Eta Squared	Noncent. Parameter	Observed Power[a]
LOCATION	Sphericity Assumed	.146	1	.146	58.568	.000	.269	58.568	1.000
	Greenhouse-Geisser	.146	1.000	.146	58.568	.000	.269	58.568	1.000
	Huynh-Feldt	.146	1.000	.146	58.568	.000	.269	58.568	1.000
	Lower-bound	.146	1.000	.146	58.568	.000	.269	58.568	1.000
LOCATION * PROTECT	Sphericity Assumed	1.358E-02	3	4.527E-03	1.820	.146	.033	5.461	.467
	Greenhouse-Geisser	1.358E-02	3.000	4.527E-03	1.820	.146	.033	5.461	.467
	Huynh-Feldt	1.358E-02	3.000	4.527E-03	1.820	.146	.033	5.461	.467
	Lower-bound	1.358E-02	3.000	4.527E-03	1.820	.146	.033	5.461	.467
Error(LOCATION)	Sphericity Assumed	.395	159	2.487E-03					
	Greenhouse-Geisser	.395	159.000	2.487E-03					
	Huynh-Feldt	.395	159.000	2.487E-03					
	Lower-bound	.395	159.000	2.487E-03					

a. Computed using alpha =.05

TABLE 8.47 Continued

Tests of Between-Subjects Effects

Measure: CHEST_DE
Transformed Variable: Average

Source	Type III Sum of Squares	df	Mean Square	F	Sig.	Eta Squared	Noncent. Parameter	Observed Power[a]
Intercept	608.380	1	608.380	68450.951	.000	.998	68450.951	1.000
PROTECT	8.322E-02	3	2.774E-02	3.121	.028	.056	9.363	.718
Error	1.413	159	8.888E-03					

a. Computed using alpha = .05

Estimated Marginal Means

LOCATION

Measure: CHEST_DE

LOCATION	Mean	Std. Error	95% Confidence Interval	
			Lower Bound	Upper Bound
1	1.693	.007	1.678	1.707
2	1.641	.007	1.627	1.655

The SPSS GLM General Factorial procedure has no post hoc tests for ANCOVA. Tukey pairwise comparisons are the logical choice for comparisons among all levels of protection, but are a bit inconvenient when sample sizes are unequal. First, we find the critical F_T according to Equation 4.15, using Table A.3 for q_T with four means and $df_{error} = 120$ (the largest tabled value short of infinity):

$$F_T = \frac{q_T^2}{2} = \frac{3.68^2}{2} = 6.77$$

Marginal pairwise comparisons (without Tukey adjustment) are then run through SPSS GLM as per Section 7.6.1.1, as shown in Table 8.48.

TABLE 8.48   Pairwise Comparisons of Levels of Protection: SPSS GLM Syntax and Selected Output

```
GLM
  ld_chest lp_chest BY protect WITH weight year
  /WSFACTOR = location 2 Polynomial
  /MEASURE = chest_de
  /METHOD = SSTYPE(3)
  /CRITERIA = ALPHA(.05)
  /LMATRIX "air vs. man" protect 1 –1 0 0
  /LMATRIX "air vs. motor" protect 1 0 –1 0
  /LMATRIX "air vs. pass" protect 1 0 0 –1
  /LMATRIX "man vs. motor" protect 0 1 –1 0
  /LMATRIX "man vs. pass" protect 0 1 0 –1
  /LMATRIX "motor vs. pass" protect 0 0 1 –1
  /WSDESIGN = location
  /DESIGN = weight year protect .
```

General Linear Model

Custom Hypothesis Tests #1

Test Results

Measure: CHEST_DE
Transformed Variable: AVERAGE

Source	Sum of Squares	df	Mean Square	F	Sig.
Contrast	.145	1	.145	18.450	.000
Error	1.234	157	7.862E-03		

TABLE 8.48   Continued

Custom Hypothesis Tests #2

Test Results

Measure: CHEST_DE
Transformed Variable: AVERAGE

Source	Sum of Squares	df	Mean Square	F	Sig.
Contrast	1.573E-02	1	1.573E-02	2.000	.159
Error	1.234	157	7.862E-03		

Custom Hypothesis Tests #3

Test Results

Measure: CHEST_DE
Transformed Variable: AVERAGE

Source	Sum of Squares	df	Mean Square	F	Sig.
Contrast	6.188E-02	1	6.188E-02	7.870	.006
Error	1.234	157	7.862E-03		

Custom Hypothesis Tests #4

Test Results

Measure: CHEST_DE
Transformed Variable: AVERAGE

Source	Sum of Squares	df	Mean Square	F	Sig.
Contrast	3.246E-02	1	3.246E-02	4.129	.044
Error	1.234	157	7.862E-03		

Custom Hypothesis Tests #5

Test Results

Measure: CHEST_DE
Transformed Variable: AVERAGE

Source	Sum of Squares	df	Mean Square	F	Sig.
Contrast	3.736E-03	1	3.736E-03	.475	.492
Error	1.234	157	7.862E-03		

Custom Hypothesis Tests #6

Test Results

Measure: CHEST_DE
Transformed Variable: AVERAGE

Source	Sum of Squares	df	Mean Square	F	Sig.
Contrast	1.197E-02	1	1.197E-02	1.523	.219
Error	1.234	157	7.862E-03		

Two of the comparisons reach statistical significance with $\alpha_{FW} = .05$ and the Tukey adjustment: the difference between airbags and manual belts with $F(1, 157) = 18.45$ and the difference between airbags and passive belts with $F(1, 157) = 7.87$. Note that an index table (not shown) identifies the tests using the labels assigned in syntax.

SPSS CORRELATIONS (Table 8.49) provide bivariate correlations among the logarithm of chest deceleration (separately for passenger and driver), vehicle weight, and model year. Cases with missing data and outliers are filtered out as in previous analyses.

Information about statistical significance is inappropriate for these post hoc analyses and is ignored. The output reveals that, indeed, the relationships between injury and the CVs are positive, though small, with correlations ranging from .006 to .262. Thus, weight and year are not particularly impressive CVs in adjusting the DV for testing the effect of protection type. The relationship between the injury to driver and passenger is fairly substantial, $r^2 = (.573)^2 = .33$.

Table 8.50 shows a checklist for a mixed randomized-groups and repeated-measures ANCOVA. A Results section, in journal format, follows.

TABLE 8.49   Bivariate Correlations among Logarithm of Chest Deceleration, Vehicle Weight, and Model Year: SPSS CORRELATIONS Syntax and Output

CORRELATIONS
  /VARIABLES=weight year ld_chest lp_chest
  /PRINT=TWOTAIL NOSIG
  /MISSING=LISTWISE .

Correlations

Correlations[a]

		Vehicle weight	Model year	LD_CHEST	LP-CHEST
Vehicle weight	Pearson Correlation	1.000	.180*	.262**	.216**
	Sig. (2-tailed)	.	.021	.001	.006
Model year	Pearson Correlation	.180*	1.000	.006	.177*
	Sig. (2-tailed)	.021	.	.945	.024
LD_CHEST	Pearson Correlation	.262**	.006	1.000	.573*
	Sig. (2-tailed)	.001	.943	.	.000
LP_CHEST	Pearson Correlation	.216**	.177*	.573**	1.000
	Sig. (2-tailed)	.006	.024	.000	.

*Correlation is significant at the 0.05 level (2-tailed).

**Correlation is significant at the 0.01 level (2-tailed).

a. Listwise N=163

TABLE 8.50   Checklist for Mixed Randomized-Groups and Repeated-Measures ANCOVA

1. Issues
   a. Sample sizes and missing data
   b. Normality of sampling distributions
   c. Outliers
   d. Independence of errors
   e. Multicollinearity
   f. Homogeneity of variance
   g. Linearity
   h. Homogeneity of regression
   i. Reliability of CVs
2. Major analyses
   a. Main effects or planned comparisons. If significant:
      (1) Effect size(s)
      (2) Parameter estimates (adjusted marginal means and standard errors or standard deviations or confidence intervals)
   b. Interactions or planned comparisons. If significant:
      (1) Effect size(s)
      (2) Parameter estimates (adjusted cell means and standard errors in table or plot)
3. Additional analyses
   a. Evaluation of CV effects
   b. Evaluation of intercorrelations
   c. Post hoc comparisons
   d. Interpretation of departure from homogeneity of variance, homogeneity of covariance, and/or homogeneity of regression if relevant

---

Results

A 4 × 2 mixed randomized-groups and repeated-measures ANCOVA was performed on chest deceleration after a vehicle crash. Four types of protection were evaluated: airbags, manual belts, motorized belts, and passive belts. All crashes had dummies in both the driver's and passenger's seats. The repeated-measures independent variable was seat location of the dummy. Covariates were vehicle weight and model year. One hundred seventy-six vehicles were crashed.

There were missing values for either the passenger or dummy chest deceleration for 11 of the crashes. These cases were omitted from analysis along with two outliers: the vehicle with the heaviest weight (5619 lbs) among cars with manual seatbelts and the vehicle producing the greatest passenger chest deceleration among cars with motorized seatbelts (78 units). Other potential outliers were controlled through logarithmic transformation of both driver and passenger chest deceleration, both of which were generally positively skewed. A sample of 163 crashes remained. Homogeneity of variance, homogeneity of regression, linearity among logarithm of chest deceleration, model year, and vehicle weight, and reliability of weight were acceptable. Unequal sample sizes led to a decision to use Type III sums of squares (unweighted means) for the analyses.

There was a statistically significant effect of type of protection on the logarithm of chest deceleration after adjusting for all other effects including the covariates, $F(3, 157) = 6.29$, $p < .0005$, partial $\eta^2 = .11$. A Tukey test at $\alpha = .05$ showed that two of the six differences among adjusted means were statistically reliable. Vehicles with airbags (adjusted mean log of chest deceleration = 1.63, SE = 0.013) produced less injury than vehicles with manual belts (adjusted mean log of chest deceleration = 1.69, SE = 0.007) or vehicles with passive belts (adjusted mean log of chest deceleration = 1.68, SE = 0.014).

Location of dummy also was statistically reliable after adjusting for the main effect of protection and the location by protection interaction, $F(1, 159) = 58.57$, $p < .0005$, partial $\eta^2 = .27$. Dummies located in the driver's seat showed greater (log of) chest deceleration (mean = 1.69, SE = 0.007) than did dummies located in the passenger's seat (mean = 1.64, SE = 0.007). There was no statistically significant interaction between location and type of protection.

Vehicle weight reliably predicted (log of) chest deceleration after adjusting for the main effects, interaction, and the other covariate, model year, $F(1, 157) = 11.28$, $p = .001$. Regression coefficients were 0.00004 for driver dummies and 0.00002 for passenger dummies, with $\eta^2 = .07$ for the driver seat and .035 for the passenger seat. Model year also reliably predicted (log of) chest deceleration after adjusting for all other effects, $F(1, 157) = 7.06$, $p = .009$. Regression coefficients were 0.00781 for driver dummies and 0.0146 for passenger dummies, with $\eta^2 = .015$ for the driver seat and .06 for the passenger seat.

Raw bivariate correlations between (log of) chest deceleration and the covariates were not particularly high. For vehicle weight, $r(161) = .26$ for the driver seat and .22 for the passenger seat. For model year, $r(161) = .01$ for the driver seat and .18 for the passenger seat. The correlation between injuries in the two locations was more substantial, $r = .57$.

8.8 Comparison of Programs

Most programs that do ANOVA also do ANCOVA. About the only exceptions in the four packages subject to major review in this book are SPSS ANOVA (previously ONEWAY) and MINITAB programs other than GLM. Thus, most of the packages have more than one program that handles CVs.

Table 8.51 compares the features of SAS GLM, SYSTAT GLM and ANOVA, SPSS MANOVA and GLM, and MINITAB GLM that are especially relevant to ANCOVA. Other features are reviewed in other chapters.

8.8.1 SPSS Package

The most current program, GLM General Factorial, works well for randomized-groups ANCOVA, providing adjusted marginal and cell means and their standard errors and plotting the adjusted means. Tests of individual CVs are available, but not a combined test.

Marginal means are available for repeated-measures IVs. Syntax also is convenient, with only a single listing of the CV required with repeated-measures IV(s). However, the GLM approach, which adjusts the repeated-measures IV by its interaction with the CV interaction may be undesirable and a separate run is required to obtain the traditional repeated-measures portion of the source table. An alternative data setup is required when there are varying CVs for each level of a repeated-measures IV (cf. Section 8.5.2.2.2).

TABLE 8.51   Comparison of SPSS, SYSTAT, MINITAB, and SAS Programs for Factorial Randomized-Groups ANCOVA

Feature	SPSS MANOVA	SPSS GLM	SAS GLM	SYSTAT ANOVA and GLM	MINITAB GLM
Input					
Factorial designs	Yes	Yes	Yes	Yes	Yes
Repeated-measures IV(s)	Yes	Yes	Yes	Yes	No
List single CV separately for each level of repeated-measures IV	No	No	No	No	No
Type of repeated-measures analysis	Traditional	GLM	GLM	GLM	N.A.
Output					
ANOVA tables include interaction between CV and repeated-measures IV	No	Yes	Yes	Yes	N.A.
Marginal means adjusted for CV(s) for randomized-groups IVs	PMEANS	EMMEANS	LSMEANS	LSMEANS	Yes
Standard errors for adjusted marginal means	No	EMMEANS	STDERR	Yes	Yes
Adjusted marginal means for repeated-measures IV	N.A.	Yes	No	No	N.A.
Cell means adjusted for CV(s) for randomized-groups IVs	PMEANS[b]	EMMEANS	LSMEANS	LSMEANS	Yes
Standard errors for adjusted cell means	No	EMMEANS	Data file	LSMEANS	Yes
Confidence interval for adjusted cell means	No	No	Yes	No	No
Adjusted cell means for repeated-measures IV(s)	N.A.	No	No	Yes	N.A.

TABLE 8.51   Continued

Feature	SPSS MANOVA	SPSS GLM	SAS GLM	SYSTAT ANOVA and GLM	MINITAB GLM
Output (continued)					
Automatic tests of homogeneity of regression	No	No	No	No	No
Estimates of slopes within each group	No	No	No	No	No
Type I as well as Type III sums of squares in a single run by default	No	No	Yes	No	No
Pooled within-cell regression coefficients	Yes	Yes	No	Yes	Yes
Standard error and t for regression coefficients	Yes	Yes	No	No	Yes
Confidence interval for regression coefficients	Yes	Yes	No	No	No
Standardized regression coefficients	Yes	No	No	No	No
Individual tests of multiple CVs	Yes	Yes	Yes	Yes	Yes
Combined test of multiple CVs	Yes	No	No	No	No
Correlations between CVs and predicted DV	Yes	No	No	No	No
Squared correlations between CVs and predicted DV	Yes	No	No	No	No
Plots					
Adjusted means for randomized-groups IVs	No	Yes	No	Yes	No

[a]Requires a repeated-measures IV.

[b]Only for completely randomized factorial design.

SPSS MANOVA addresses the concerns regarding repeated-measures designs, with its traditional analysis. MANOVA also provides a test of all CVs combined (labeled REGRESSION) and is the only program providing correlations, squared correlations, and standardized regression coefficients between CVs and the predicted DV. However, adjusted means are unavailable.

8.8.2   SAS System

SAS GLM also works well for randomized-groups but not repeated-measures ANCOVA and does not provide either regression coefficients for CVs or adjusted marginal means for repeated-measures IVs. The GLM approach requires a separate run to obtain the traditional repeated-measures portion of the source table, and an alternate data setup with varying CVs (cf. Section 8.5.2.2.2). Although a combined test is not given for multiple CVs, the default printing of `Type I SS` (and an appropriate arrangement of model effects) permits a simple calculation to assess the combined effect (cf. Section 8.6.1).

8.8.3   SYSTAT System

SYSTAT likewise works better for randomized-groups than for repeated-measures ANCOVA. An advantage over SPSS and SAS is that adjusted cell means are available for repeated-measures designs, however, adjusted marginal means are not. As for all GLM programs, varying CVs for repeated measures require an alternate data setup. And a separate run without CVs is required if a traditional source table is desired for a mixed design with a constant CV. Regression coefficients are shown for CVs, but without standard errors.

8.8.4   MINITAB Programs

Among the several MINITAB programs available for ANOVA, only GLM handles CVs. The program reports adjusted cell and marginal means and standard deviations, but unadjusted means and SDs must be found using another module within the package. The usual GLM strategy may be used to test homogeneity of regression. Multiple CVs are tested individually, with no test of the set. GLM does not recognize repeated-measures ANOVA, and attempts to adapt the one-score-per-line strategy to ANCOVA result in erroneous df for error.

8.9   Problem Sets

8.1   Use a canned computer program to do an analysis of covariance on the following data set, which is the first problem of Chapter 4 with a CV added. Assume the IV is minutes of presoaking a dirty garment, the DV (Y) is rating of cleanliness, and the CV (X) is the rating of cleanliness before presoaking.

Presoak Time							
a_1 5 min		a_2 10 min		a_3 15 min		a_4 20 min	
X	Y	X	Y	X	Y	X	Y
1	2	1	3	5	8	4	6
5	6	8	9	9	11	5	7
5	6	7	9	5	9	7	9
4	6	4	5	6	9	4	6
3	5	5	7	2	6	7	9
2	3	3	5	9	12	8	9

a. Test for homogeneity of variance.
b. Test for homogeneity of regression.
c. Provide a source table.
d. Check results (and homogeneity of regression) by running the data set through at least one canned computer program.
e. Calculate effect size.
f. Write a results section for the analysis.

8.2 Do a computer analysis of variance on the following data set, which adds two CVs to the first problem of Chapter 5. Assume the IV is minutes of presoaking a dirty garment, the DV (Y) is rating of cleanliness, the first CV (X_1) is the rating of cleanliness before presoaking, and the second CV (X_2) is an index of the fabric thread count.

					Presoak Time							
		b_1: 5 min			b_2: 10 min			b_3: 15 min			b_4: 20 min	
	X_1	X_2	Y	X_1	X_2	Y	X_1	X_2	Y	X_1	X_2	Y
	1	4	2	1	2	3	5	2	8	4	7	6
a_1: Cotton	5	5	6	8	7	9	9	3	11	5	3	7
	5	1	6	7	2	9	5	5	9	7	2	9
	4	6	6	4	4	5	6	5	9	4	1	6
a_2: Poly	3	3	5	5	5	7	2	6	6	7	5	9
	2	4	3	3	8	5	9	1	12	8	4	9

a. Test for homogeneity of variance.
b. Test for homogeneity of regression.
c. Test for absence of univariate and multivariate outliers.
d. Write a results section in journal format. Include evaluation of CVs and the correlation between them, as well as any departure from homogeneity of variance or homogeneity of regression.

8.3 The following mixed randomized-groups–repeated-measures ANCOVA has the same CV for each level of the repeated-measures IV. The randomized-groups IV is keyboard feel on a portable computer: mushy or click. The repeated-measures IV is size of keys: small, medium, or large. The DV is rating of typing speed, with a pretest of typing speed on an IBM desktop computer as a CV.

		Keyboard Size		
	CV:	b_1: Small	b_2: Medium	b_3: Large
	7	1	3	6
	8	2	3	5
a_1: Mushy	8	3	4	4
	11	4	3	7
	13	5	5	8
	15	6	7	9
	14	7	7	8
a_2: Click	13	8	7	7
	15	9	8	7
	14	10	6	8

   a. Do an analysis of covariance using a GLM computer program, evaluating homogeneity of covariance.

   b. Make the adjustment to match results to a traditional analysis.

8.4 Using the results of Problem 8.2, determine the number of cases required to find a significant differ-ence between the two fabrics at $\alpha = .05$ and $\beta = .20$.

8.5 Do an ANOVA (without CV) for the data in Table 8.13, and compare the results with those of Table 8.14.

Extending the Concepts

8.6 The following mixed randomized-groups–repeated-measures ANCOVA has a different CV for each level of the repeated-measures IV. The randomized-groups IV is keyboard feel on a portable computer: mushy or click. The repeated-measures IV is size of keys: small, medium, or large. The DV is rating of typing speed, with a pretest of typing speed on an IBM desktop computer as a CV before each trial. Do an analysis of covariance using a traditional computer program.

| | | **Keyboard Size** | | | | |
| | | b_1: Small | | b_2: Medium | | b_3: Large | |
	CV	DV	CV	DV	CV	DV
	7	1	4	3	3	6
	8	2	5	3	5	5
a_1: Mushy	8	3	4	4	3	4
	11	4	8	3	6	7
	13	5	10	5	9	8
	15	6	11	7	9	9
	14	7	9	7	10	8
a_2: Click	13	8	8	7	9	7
	15	9	12	8	11	7
	14	10	13	6	13	8

9

Latin-Square Designs

9.1 General Purpose and Description

Latin-square designs are used when the researcher has one IV of overriding interest, but other IVs that need to be evaluated in the design because they are expected to have some (often modest) effect on the DV. The other IVs are often considered nuisance variables. The levels of the other IVs could be crossed with the IV of interest in a fully factorial design, but that is likely to make the design prohibitively large and probably gives the other IVs more "stature" than they deserve. Instead, a Latin-square design is used in which the main effect of the IV of interest and the main effects of the other IVs are available for analysis but (most) interactions are not.

Interactions of the IV of interest with the other IVs, and of the other IVs with each other are confounded with tests of main effects and the error term in this design. This means that Latin-square designs are inappropriate when interactions are anticipated. A major consideration, then, in choice of this design is expected absence of interaction.

Latin squares are used both with randomized-groups designs and with repeated-measures designs, although their use with repeated measures is more common in many disciplines. In randomized-groups designs, the other IVs are usually nuisance variables that are unavoidable differences in testing conditions (several different pieces of the same equipment, time of day, different operators or researchers, and the like). Differences associated with these IVs inflate the error term if not accounted for in the analysis, but are otherwise not substantive. A Latin-square design and analysis are likely to increase power by assessing the sums of squares for these IVs and subtracting them from the error term.

In repeated-measures designs, the other IVs are usually cases and position (trial) effects. Position effects are unavoidable in a repeated-measures design in which cases are necessarily measured more than once. Latin-square designs are used to remove potential confounding between position effects and treatment effects by giving cases treatments in different orders. In repeated-measures designs, then, the other IVs may be more substantive (both logically and in terms of sums of squares) than in randomized-groups designs.

The Latin square is an arrangement of treatments. The "square" is a two dimensional layout of three IVs in which rows represent one IV, columns represent another IV, and the third IV, usually the treatment of greatest interest, appears as entries inside the matrix. The test of the effect of interest is,

TABLE 9.1   Basic Latin-Square Design with Four Treatments

	b_1	b_2	b_3	b_4
a_1	c_1	c_2	c_3	c_4
a_2	c_2	c_4	c_1	c_3
a_3	c_3	c_1	c_4	c_2
a_4	c_4	c_3	c_2	c_1

then, carved out of the interaction of the two nuisance variables. All three IVs have the same number of levels. Table 9.1 shows an example, in which C is the IV of interest.[1]

A defining feature of Latin-square arrangements is that each level of the IV of interest—C—appears once in each row and once in each column. Whatever the effects of the different levels of A and B, then, they are spread evenly over the various levels of C. Just as in factorial fixed-effects equal-n designs, the test of C is independent of, averaged over, the main effect of A and the main effect of B. However, as previously mentioned, the main effect of C is not independent of the various parts of potential interactions that may be included in the design.

Different Latin squares contain different segments of the interactions from a complete factorial arrangement. In Table 9.2, X indicates the combinations of A, B, and C generated by the Latin square of Table 9.1. Another Latin square would include other combinations of levels from the full factorial. Interaction, as you recall, is a synergistic effect produced by a particular combination of levels of treatments. The particular Latin square generated for a study may or may not include one or more cells with such synergy. This is why the assumption that there is no interaction—additivity—is so important.

Another difference between the full factorial design and the Latin-square design is the number of degrees of freedom generated: The Latin-square design generates far fewer df than the full factorial. The Latin-square design of Table 9.1, for instance, generates 15 total df, whereas the full factorial design of Table 9.2 generates 63 total df. Degrees of freedom are always a valuable resource to be spent with care, but this is especially true for Latin-square designs.

The same Latin squares are applied to randomized-groups designs and repeated-measures designs, but their purposes are quite different. In a randomized-groups design, a major goal of a Latin-square arrangement is to gain some of the advantages of a full factorial with a substantially reduced number of treatment combinations. A full factorial arrangement of three IVs with four levels each requires 64 treatment combinations, as shown in Table 9.2; the Latin square in Table 9.1 requires only 16 of them. Other advantages include the increased generalizability of results for C over the range of levels of A and B and the increased power that is likely to be achieved by subtracting sums of squares associated with the main effects of A and B from the error term.

---

[1]We have diverged from the usual practice of using A for the IV of greatest interest in order to make the relationship between the mixed design and the Latin-square design as clear as possible.

TABLE 9.2　Segments of Interaction Available in the Latin Square of Table 9.1

c_1:

	b_1	b_2	b_3	b_4
a_1	X			
a_2			X	
a_3		X		
a_4				X

c_2:

	b_1	b_2	b_3	b_4
a_1		X		
a_2	X			
a_3				X
a_4			X	

c_3:

	b_1	b_2	b_3	b_4
a_1			X	
a_2				X
a_3	X			
a_4		X		

c_4:

	b_1	b_2	b_3	b_4
a_1				X
a_2		X		
a_3			X	
a_4	X			

A disadvantage compared with a one-way randomized-group design (with only IV C) is that more groups need to be run. A disadvantage compared with a fully factorial randomized-groups design is lack of information about interactions. And, of course, there is the limitation that all IVs have the same number of levels for the most common applications of Latin-square arrangements; there may be any number of levels, but all IVs have to have the same number of them. The Latin-square design applied to randomized groups is one of a rather large family of incomplete factorial designs. Others are discussed in Chapter 10.

For an example of a randomized-groups Latin-square design, C, the IV of major interest, is four types of assembly procedures potentially affected by two nuisance variables, assembler experience (A) and various temperatures of the room housing the assembly line (B). Sixteen assemblers are blocked into four groups based on experience. The Latin-square arrangement allows the error term to be reduced by variance associated with four levels of assembler experience and four levels of room temperature. However, the design does not permit evaluation of interactions of assembly procedure by experience, assembly procedure by room temperature, experience by room temperature, or of assembly procedure by experience by room temperature.

In a repeated-measures design, the purpose of a Latin-square arrangement is to counterbalance position (trial) effects among cases. In Table 9.1, the B variable is position, and the A variable is the case (or cases) to which levels of C are applied.[2] The first case receives c_1, c_2, c_3, and then c_4 and

---

[2]Note that cases here are labeled A rather than the usual S of repeated-measures ANOVA.

the second case receives c_2, c_4, c_1, then c_3. The goal is to assure that the levels of C are not confounded with the trial in which the treatment is applied, B. This feature permits a repeated-measures IV to be experimental even when all levels of C are applied to the same cases and those cases have memory (for example, experience is carried over from trial to trial). The design also allows evaluation of the effect of position (trial) itself. Sometimes position effects are called practice effects, particularly when applied to animate cases (or perhaps computer programs capable of learning).

For an example of a Latin-square repeated-measures design, C is still different assembly procedures, except that the same four assemblers implement all procedures. The A variable represents the four assemblers and B is the trial in which each of the procedures is implemented. This application controls for such differences as exist among the four assemblers, and for changes in their ability that may occur during the four trials, independent of type of procedure.

9.2   Kinds of Research Questions

The basic question in any Latin-square analysis is whether there are reliable mean differences in the DV as a result of different treatments. If there are more than two treatments, comparisons are possible, in addition to, or in lieu of, the omnibus test.

9.2.1   Effects of the IV(s)

Is there a statistically significant effect of treatment C? Controlling for main effects of A and B, and holding all else constant, are changes in the DV that are associated with different levels of C larger than would be expected by chance? For example, is there a mean difference in production efficiency associated with the assembly procedure used, after controlling for IVs A and B?

In the randomized-groups Latin square, the effects of A and B can also be evaluated. For example, after controlling for assembly procedure and room temperature, is there a difference in production efficiency depending on the experience of the assembler? And, controlling for assembly procedure and assembler experience, is production efficiency affected by room temperature?

The repeated-measures Latin-square design also permits assessment of A and B, should such be desired. Does production efficiency change over trials? Do assemblers get better as they implement more procedures? Worse? Better and then worse? The test of the main effect of differences among assemblers is not often performed because it is usually assumed that such differences exist.

9.2.2   Interactions among IVs

The analysis of a basic randomized-groups Latin-square design permits no evaluation of interactions because main effects are confounded with two-way interactions (e.g., the main effect of C is confounded with the $A \times B$ interaction, and so on). However, there are expansions of the design that do permit evaluation of some interactions. Section 9.5.3.1 discusses one variant of the Latin-square design that permits tests of interactions among types of treatments. In this variant, c_1, c_2, c_3, and c_4 are not four levels of one treatment, but rather two IVs (C and D) with two levels each in factorial arrangement so both main effects and their interaction are available for evaluation. Another expansion involves running the entire Latin-square arrangement at each level of a randomized-groups IV. In this case, the main effect and its interaction with C are available for evaluation. In short, the potential for outfoxing the design is limited only by the ingenuity of the researcher.

9.2.3   Parameter Estimates

What means are expected if a particular treatment is applied to a population? What average production efficiency rating would we expect for a particular assembly procedure? Parameter estimates reported in Latin square, as in any other ANOVA, are means, standard deviations, standard errors, and/or confidence intervals for the mean. The values that are reported are estimated from the sample; however, the sample size is often quite small, which may limit the generalizability of the findings. If parameters are estimated, means and standard deviations or standard errors (and/or confidence intervals) are reported in a narrative format, shown in a table, or presented in a graph, as discussed in Chapters 4 and 5.

9.2.4   Effect Sizes and Power

As for any other ANOVA, effect size is typically reported as proportion of variance in the DV that is predictable from an IV. For instance, how much of the variability in assembly efficiency is associated with differences in production procedures? Section 9.6.3 demonstrates calculation of effect size in Latin-square designs.

Enhanced power often is a driving force behind the choice of a Latin-square analysis, whether repeated measures or randomized groups. Section 9.6.3 also discusses the increase in power associated with these designs.

9.2.5   Specific Comparisons

If there are more than two levels of an IV, which levels are different from each other? For example, is the assembly procedure in which assembly is completed after all parts are available (say, c_1) more effective than the one in which subassemblies are put together as soon as two parts are available (c_2), or the one where top and bottom are assembled separately before they are put together (c_3), or the one that starts in the middle and proceeds to both ends (c_4)? Is that first procedure more effective than the average of all other procedures? These and similar questions may be answered by applying one of a wide variety of comparison procedures, as discussed in previous chapters and in Section 9.6.4.

As usual, comparisons among specific means can be either planned or post hoc. The advantage of planning, as discussed in Section 4.5.5.4 and elsewhere, is greater power.

9.3   Assumptions and Limitations

9.3.1   Theoretical Issues

Theoretical issues in a Latin-square design are identical to those in any other analysis of variance. That is, issues of causal inference and generalizability are of similar concern in Latin-square designs.

9.3.2   Practical Issues

The Latin-square arrangement, as an ANOVA model, assumes normality of sampling distributions, homogeneity of variance, independence of errors, and absence of outliers. Additional requirements for the repeated-measures application of Latin-square analysis are sphericity and additivity.

9.3.2.1   *Normality of Sampling Distributions*

The issue of normality of sampling distributions is associated with sample size and the criterion is the same as for any other ANOVA: Normality of sampling distributions is tenable if degrees of freedom for error exceed 20. However, because there are fewer df in Latin-square designs, this requirement is not often met. Because df are low, inspection of the distributions of DV scores or of residuals is used to assess normality, as demonstrated in Sections 9.7.1.1.1 and 9.7.2.1.1. Solutions for questionable normality (e.g., transformation) are also the same as for any other ANOVA, except that nonparametric tests are unavailable.

9.3.2.2   *Homogeneity of Variance*

In many Latin-square applications, there is only a single score in each cell. Therefore, homogeneity of variance is assessed separately on the margins of the three main effects. That is, variances are compared among levels of A, then separately among levels of B, and then separately among levels of C, using F_{max} and Chapter 3 guidelines for evaluating differences among variances. If there is more than one score per cell, the usual assessment of homogeneity of variance among cells is conducted, as described in Chapter 5.

9.3.2.3   *Independence of Errors*

The ANOVA model assumes that errors (deviations of individual scores around their cell means) are independent of one another, both within each cell and between cells of a design. This assumption is evaluated in randomized-groups designs by examining the details of the research design rather than by statistical criteria. Independence of errors in repeated-measures designs is dealt with as part of the sphericity assumption as discussed in Sections 6.3.2.3 and 6.6.2.

9.3.2.4   *Absence of Outliers*

Univariate outliers can occur in one or more cells (if there are multiple scores in each cell) or in one or more levels of effects in the design. As for homogeneity of variance, outliers are evaluated separately for each level of each IV if there is one score per cell, and within cells if there is a sufficient number of scores in each cell.

9.3.2.5   *Sphericity*

Repeated-measures Latin-square analysis, like other repeated-measures analyses, has the assumption that difference scores between all pairs of levels of the repeated-measures IV have roughly equivalent variances. However, the assumption is unlikely to be violated for the main effect of interest in a Latin-square design, C, because counterbalancing of treatment orders assures that they are not confounded with time. However, sphericity may still be violated if some levels of treatment are more like each other than others because difference scores among pairs of treatments that are similar are probably smaller than difference scores among pairs of treatments that are dissimilar.

The test of position (trials), on the other hand, is likely to be biased by failure of sphericity. This is not a problem unless position is of research interest, and, if it is, the research questions are often better answered by a trend analysis (which does not require sphericity) rather than by the omnibus test. Section 6.6.2 discusses these issues and Section 9.6.1 demonstrates a test of the assumption.

9.3.2.6 Additivity

The assumption of additivity applies to both repeated-measures Latin square and randomized-groups Latin square, but the issues are slightly different. In repeated-measures Latin square, additivity is part of the sphericity assumption discussed in Section 6.6.2.

The additivity assumption in randomized-groups Latin square is that all interactions, $A \times B$, $B \times C$, $A \times C$, and $A \times B \times C$, are negligible or represent only error variance. If treatments do indeed interact, then tests of main effects are misleading. For example, the main effect of C is completely confounded with the $A \times B$ interaction; an apparently large effect of C could actually be due to a large $A \times B$ interaction. Further, since the $A \times B \times C$ interaction serves as (part of) the error term in a randomized-groups Latin-square analysis, a strong three-way interaction reduces the power of the entire analysis. Section 9.7.1.1.3 shows a plot of residuals against predicted values to assess additivity in a randomized-groups Latin-square analysis with one score per cell. Section 9.5.1 shows how to evaluate this assumption in a randomized groups design with more than one case per cell.

9.4   Fundamental Equations

Table 9.3 shows a $3 \times 3 \times 3$ Latin-square arrangement[3] randomly chosen by procedures described in Section 9.5.2. This arrangement could represent either a randomized-groups Latin square (where A and B are two nuisance variables) or a repeated-measures Latin square (where B is position and

TABLE 9.3   Latin-Square Design with Small-Sample Example

	b_1	b_2	b_3
a_1	c_3	c_1	c_2
a_2	c_2	c_3	c_1
a_3	c_1	c_2	c_3

[3]Some texts refer to this as a 3×3 design, because degrees of freedom are equivalent to a 3×3 full factorial ANOVA. We use the three-way notation to emphasize the existence of three IVs.

A is case, analogous to *S* in the designs of Chapters 6 and 7).[4] The IV of primary interest in either design is *C*. The statistical analysis is the same, whether the design is randomized groups or repeated measures.

9.4.1   Allocation of Cases

The Latin square of Table 9.3 provides the arrangement of snow condition (*C*: powder, packed powder, or ice), day of week (*B*: Monday, Wednesday, or Friday), and skiers. The DV is minutes to ski the slope. If this is a randomized-groups study, there are nine different skiers, stratified, say, by skill level (*A*: low, medium, and high). Each skier within each skill level is randomly assigned to a day of the week, and hence a level of snow condition. If this is a repeated-measures study, there are only three skiers (*A*), each one of whom traverses a run on Monday (with one snow condition), a run on Wednesday (with another snow condition), and a run on Friday (with the third snow condition—and a very weary group of snow makers). The three skiers may be assigned sequentially (the first skier is assigned to the first order of snow conditions, and so on) because the orders themselves have been randomized.

Note that in either study, there is only one score per cell. Many applications of Latin-square designs are enhanced by running replicates where more than one score is obtained for each of the nine cells representing combinations of treatment and trials (cf. Section 9.5.1).

9.4.2   Partition of Sources of Variance

The total sum of squared differences is partitioned into four sources:

$$SS_T = SS_A + SS_B + SS_C + SS_{residual} \tag{9.1}$$

or

$$\sum_j \sum_k \sum_l (Y_{jkl} - GM)^2 = n_j \sum_j (\overline{Y}_A - GM)^2 + n_k \sum_k (\overline{Y}_B - GM)^2$$
$$+ n_l \sum_l (\overline{Y}_C - GM)^2 + SS_{residual}$$

The total sum of squared differences between individual scores Y_{jkl} and the grand mean (GM) is partitioned into (1) sum of squared differences between means associated with different levels of *A* ($\overline{Y}_A$) and the grand mean; (2) sum of squared differences between means associated with different levels of *B* ($\overline{Y}_B$) and the grand mean; and (3) sum of squared differences between means associated with different levels of *C* ($\overline{Y}_C$) and the grand mean; and (4) $SS_{residual}$, the remaining sum of squared differences between individual scores and the grand mean. Each *n* is the number of scores that went into the relevant marginal mean.

---

[4]Feel free to modify the notation by changing *A* to *S* when using the following equations for a repeated-measures Latin-square design.

The error term (residual) is found by subtracting the three systematic sources of variance from the total:

$$SS_{residual} = SS_T - SS_A - SS_B - SS_C \tag{9.2}$$

Another way of looking at the partition is that SS_T is first divided into SS_A, SS_B, and SS_{AB}, and then SS_C is "carved out of" SS_{AB} to produce $SS_{residual}$:

$$SS_{residual} = SS_{AB} - SS_C \tag{9.3}$$

This way of conceptualizing the source of variability for C and residual is often more helpful later on.

Total degrees of freedom remain the number of scores minus 1, lost when the grand mean is estimated (cf. Equation 3.6). Note, however, that the total number of scores is not abc, but ab or ac or bc or a^2 because the design is incomplete. Because $a = b = c$, this is most easily expressed as

$$df_T = a^2 - 1 = N - 1 \tag{9.4}$$

Degrees of freedom for A are the number of levels of A minus 1, lost when $\overline{Y}_A$ is estimated.

$$df_A = a - 1 \tag{9.5}$$

Degrees of freedom for B and C are the number of levels of each (a) minus 1, lost when the means are estimated, so that

$$df_B = df_C = a - 1 \tag{9.6}$$

Finally, degrees of freedom for error are the total degrees of freedom minus degrees of freedom for the three effects, which may be expressed in several different ways.

$$df_{residual} = (a^2 - 1) - (a - 1) - (b - 1) - (c - 1) = a^2 - 1 - 3(a - 1)$$
$$= a^2 - 3a + 2 = (a - 1)(a - 2) \tag{9.7}$$

Figure 9.1 diagrams the partition of sums of squares and degrees of freedom for the Latin-square design.

Mean squares are formed by dividing sums of squares by degrees of freedom, as for one-way designs:

$$MS_A = \frac{SS_A}{df_A} \qquad MS_B = \frac{SS_B}{df_B}$$
$$MS_C = \frac{SS_C}{df_C} \qquad MS_{residual} = \frac{SS_{residual}}{df_{residual}} \tag{9.8}$$

F ratios are formed for each of the three sources of variance by dividing the appropriate MS by the single estimate of random variation, $MS_{residual}$. F_A evaluates differences among marginal means

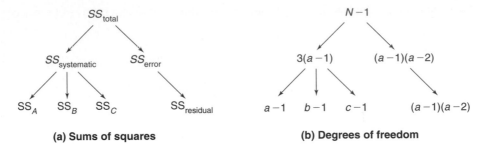

(a) Sums of squares   (b) Degrees of freedom

FIGURE 9.1   **Partition of (a) Sums of Squares and (b) Degree of Freedom into Systematic Sources of Differences among Marginal Means of *A*, *B*, and *C*, and Remaining (Error) Differences among Cases**

for levels of A, the main effect of A. The null hypothesis for this test is $\mu_{a_1} = \mu_{a_2} = \cdots = \mu_{a_j}$, the same as discussed in Section 3.2.3.1 for a one-way ANOVA.

The obtained F_A is

$$F_A = \frac{MS_A}{MS_{residual}} \qquad df = (a-1), (a-1)(a-2) \qquad (9.9)$$

Obtained F_A is tested against critical F with numerator df $= a - 1$ and denominator df $= (a-1)(a-2)$. The null hypothesis is rejected if obtained F_A is equal to or larger than critical F.

F_B evaluates differences among marginal means for levels of B, the main effect of B. The null hypothesis for this test is that $\mu_{b_1} = \mu_{b_2} = \cdots = \mu_{b_k}$.

$$F_B = \frac{MS_B}{MS_{residual}} \qquad df = (a-1), (a-1)(a-2) \qquad (9.10)$$

This is also tested against critical F with numerator df $= a - 1$ and denominator df $= (a-1)(a-2)$. The null hypothesis is rejected if obtained F_B is equal to or exceeds critical F.

Similarly, F_C evaluates differences among marginal means for levels of C, the main effect of C. The null hypothesis for this test is that $\mu_{c_1} = \mu_{c_2} = \cdots = \mu_{c_l}$.

$$F_C = \frac{MS_C}{MS_{residual}} \qquad df = (a-1), (a-1)(a-2) \qquad (9.11)$$

This is also tested against critical F with numerator df $= (a - 1)$ and denominator df $= (a-1)(a-2)$. The null hypothesis is rejected if obtained F_C is equal to or larger than critical F.

9.4.3   Traditional ANOVA Approach to 3 × 3 × 3 Latin Square

Table 9.4 shows hypothetical data in the Latin-square arrangement of Table 9.3, where rows represent A, columns represent B, and cells represent levels of C, and then are rearranged so that columns

TABLE 9.4 Data for Small-Sample Example in Two Different Latin-Square Arrangements

$A \times B$

	b_1	b_2	b_3	Sum
a_1	$c_3 = 4$	$c_1 = 9$	$c_2 = 1$	$A_1 = 14$
a_2	$c_2 = 1$	$c_3 = 6$	$c_1 = 7$	$A_2 = 14$
a_3	$c_1 = 8$	$c_2 = 2$	$c_3 = 5$	$A_3 = 15$
Sum	$B_1 = 13$	$B_2 = 17$	$B_3 = 13$	$T = 43$

$A \times C$

	c_1	c_2	c_3	Sum
a_1	$b_2 = 9$	$b_3 = 1$	$b_1 = 4$	$A_1 = 14$
a_2	$b_3 = 7$	$b_1 = 1$	$b_2 = 6$	$A_2 = 14$
a_3	$b_1 = 8$	$b_2 = 2$	$b_3 = 5$	$A_3 = 15$
Sum	$C_1 = 24$	$C_2 = 4$	$C_3 = 15$	$T = 43$

represent C and cells represent levels of B. The first arrangement is convenient to illustrate calculation of sums for A and B, and the second arrangement is convenient for calculation of sums for C. C is the snow condition with three levels (powder, packed powder, and ice), A denotes which of either three (repeated measures) or nine (randomized groups: high, medium, and low skill) skiers traversed the slope, and B is the day of the week (Monday, Wednesday, or Friday). Time to ski the slope, the DV, is measured in minutes.

Table 9.5 shows the computational equations derived from degrees of freedom (which are first expanded if they contain parentheses). Note that $a^2 = N$, the total number of scores in the entire Latin square.

Table 9.6 shows computation of sums of squares for the small-sample example. Note that as usual the numbers in the denominators are the number of scores in the sums in the numerators that are squared. In this example, three scores are summed for each level of A, and of B, and of C before squaring, and the sums of squares are divided by 3.

Table 9.7 summarizes the results and shows the mean squares and F values based on Equations 9.1 through 9.10.

Each of the obtained F ratios is evaluated separately. With $\alpha = .05$, the same critical value is used to test the main effects of A, B, and C. Based on numerator df = 2 and denominator df = 2, the critical value from Table A.1 from Appendix A is 19.00. Only the obtained F for C exceeds that value. We conclude that there is a difference in time to ski down the slope due to snow condition, but none due to day of week or skill of skiers.

TABLE 9.5   Computational Equations Derived from Degrees of Freedom for Latin-Square ANOVA

Source	Degrees of Freedom	Expanded df	Sum of Squares Equations
A	$a - 1$		$\dfrac{\sum A^2}{a} - \dfrac{T^2}{a^2}$
B	$a - 1 = b - 1$		$\dfrac{\sum B^2}{a} - \dfrac{T^2}{a^2}$
C	$a - 1 = c - 1$		$\dfrac{\sum C^2}{a} - \dfrac{T^2}{a^2}$
Residual	$a^2 - 1 - (a - 1)$ $- (b - 1) - (c - 1)$	$N - a - b - c + 2$ $= N - 3a + 2$	$\sum Y^2 - \dfrac{\sum A^2}{a} - \dfrac{\sum B^2}{a} - \dfrac{\sum C^2}{a} + \dfrac{2T^2}{a^2}$ (or by subtraction: $SS_T - SS_A - SS_B - SS_C$)
T	$a^2 - 1$	$N - 1$	$\sum Y^2 - \dfrac{T^2}{a^2}$

TABLE 9.6   Calculation of Sums of Squares for Latin-Square ANOVA

SS_A	$= \dfrac{14^2 + 14^2 + 15^2}{3} - \dfrac{43^2}{9}$	$= 205.67 - 205.44$		$= 0.23$
SS_B	$= \dfrac{13^2 + 17^2 + 13^2}{3} - \dfrac{43^2}{9}$	$= 209.00 - 205.44$		$= 3.56$
SS_C	$= \dfrac{24^2 + 4^2 + 15^2}{3} - \dfrac{43^2}{9}$	$= 272.33 - 205.44$		$= 66.89$
$SS_{residual}$	$= SS_T - SS_A - SS_B - SS_C$	$= 71.56 - 0.23 - 3.56 - 66.89$	$= 0.88$
SS_T	$= (4^2 + 9^2 + \cdots + 5^2) - \dfrac{43^2}{9}$	$= 277.00 - 205.44$		$= 71.56$

9.4.4   Regression Approach to $3 \times 3 \times 3$ Latin Square

Vectors (columns of weighting coefficients) are required for each of the 2 df for the main effect of A, the 2 df for the main effect of B, and the 2 df for the main effect of C. Table 9.8 shows the scores on the DV (Y), codes for the six X vectors for the main effects, and cross-products of Y with each of the six X vectors. Arbitrarily, linear and quadratic trend coefficients are used for the first and second vec-

TABLE 9.7   Source Table for 3 × 3 × 3 Latin-Square ANOVA

Source	SS	df	MS	F
A	0.23	2	0.12	0.27
B	3.56	2	1.78	4.05
C	66.89	2	33.45	76.02
Residual	0.88	2	0.44	
T	71.56	8		

tors for A, for B, and for C.[5] Therefore, the first X column compares the first and third snow conditions (powder versus ice). The second X column compares the second level of snow with the first and third, pooled (packed powder versus powder and ice). The X_5 and X_6 columns code the trend analysis of day of week. These two columns are difficult to decode because the order of levels of B are scrambled, as they are in the $A \times C$ matrix of Table 9.4. Note that C is coded before A and B in Table 9.8 for ease in decoding. The final six vectors are found by multiplication.

The basic equations for sums of squares and sums of products for the regression approach are the same as illustrated in Table 5.10 for main effects in factorial ANOVA. Table 9.9 shows the equations for finding the sums of squares for the main effect of C, snow condition. Note that this matches the SS_C of Table 9.6 within rounding error.

Table 9.10 shows the equations for finding the sums of squares for the main effect of A, skier. Finally, the sum of squares for day of week (B) is calculated in Table 9.11.

Residual (error) sum of squares is found by subtracting all of the sums of squares for effects from the total sum of squares. First, you find SS_Y, identified as SS_T in Table 9.6:

$$SS_Y = 277 - \frac{43^2}{9} = 71.56$$

and then you obtain $SS_{residual}$ by subtraction:

$$SS_{residual} = SS_Y - SS_A - SS_B - SS_C$$
$$= 71.56 - 66.88 - 3.56 - 0.23 = 0.89$$

Each X vector represents a single df. The df for each effect is the number of vectors for that effect (2) in Table 9.8. Total degrees of freedom (df_Y) is $N - 1 = 9 - 1 = 8$, as per Table 9.6. Degrees of freedom for the error term may be found by subtraction or by use of the equation $N - v - 1$, where v is the number of X vectors for identified SS. Thus $df_{residual} = 9 - 6 - 1 = 2$.

MS values and F ratios are then calculated as in Table 9.7. Interpretation is identical to that of ANOVA by traditional means.

---

[5]Trend coefficients are sensible when the IVs are quantitative or convenient when the researcher just needs an orthogonal set and is not interested in the comparisons per se.

TABLE 9.8 Vectors for Regression Approach to $3 \times 3 \times 3$ Latin-Square ANOVA

		C		A		B		YX_1	YX_2	YX_3	YX_4	YX_5	YX_6
	Y	X_1	X_2	X_3	X_4	X_5	X_6						
$c_1a_1b_2$	9	−1	1	−1	1	0	−2	−9	9	−9	9	0	−18
$c_1a_2b_3$	7	−1	1	0	−2	1	1	−7	7	0	−14	7	7
$c_1a_3b_1$	8	−1	1	1	1	−1	1	−8	8	8	8	−8	8
$c_2a_1b_3$	1	0	−2	−1	1	1	1	0	−2	−1	1	1	1
$c_2a_2b_1$	1	0	−2	0	−2	−1	1	0	−2	0	−2	−1	1
$c_2a_3b_2$	2	0	−2	1	1	0	−2	0	−4	2	2	0	−4
$c_3a_1b_1$	4	1	1	−1	1	−1	1	4	4	−4	4	−4	4
$c_3a_2b_2$	6	1	1	0	−2	0	−2	6	6	0	−12	0	−12
$c_3a_2b_3$	5	1	1	1	1	1	1	5	5	5	5	5	5
Sum	43	0	0	0	0	0	0	−9	31	1	1	0	−8
Squares Summed	277	6	18	6	18	6	18						
N	9												

494

TABLE 9.9   Equations for the Sum of Squares for the Main Effect of *C*

$$SS(reg.X_1) = \frac{[SP(YX_1)]^2}{SS(X_1)} \qquad = \frac{(-9)^2}{6} \qquad = 13.50$$

$$SS(reg.X_2) = \frac{[SP(YX_2)]^2}{SS(X_2)} \qquad = \frac{31^2}{18} \qquad = 53.38$$

$$SS_C \qquad = SS(reg.X_1) + SS(reg.X_2) = 13.50 + 53.38 = 66.88$$

TABLE 9.10   Equations for the Sum of Squares for the Main Effect of *A*

$$SS(reg.X_3) = \frac{[SP(YX_3)]^2}{SS(X_3)} \qquad = \frac{1^2}{6} \qquad = 0.17$$

$$SS(reg.X_4) = \frac{[SP(YX_4)]^2}{SS(X_4)} \qquad = \frac{1^2}{18} \qquad = 0.06$$

$$SS_A \qquad = SS(reg.X_3) + SS(reg.X_4) = 0.17 + 0.06 = 0.23$$

TABLE 9.11   Equations for the Sum of Squares for the Main Effect of *B*

$$SS(reg.X_5) = \frac{[SP(YX_5)]^2}{SS(X_5)} \qquad = \frac{0^2}{6} \qquad = 0.00$$

$$SS(reg.X_6) = \frac{[SP(YX_6)]^2}{SS(X_6)} \qquad = \frac{(-8)^2}{18} \qquad = 3.56$$

$$SS_B \qquad = SS(reg.X_5) + SS(reg.X_6) = 0.00 + 3.56 = 3.56$$

9.4.5   Computer Analyses of Small-Sample Latin-Square Example

Table 9.12 shows how data are entered for a Latin-square ANOVA. This data format provides the basic source table for either randomized-groups or repeated-measures Latin-square designs. However, this format does not permit evaluation of the assumption of sphericity for the repeated-measures design, nor does it provide appropriate error terms for repeated-measures specific comparisons. The assumption of sphericity is tested when either (1) the omnibus effect of position is of research interest or (2) there is reason to believe that some pairs of treatments are more alike than other pairs of treatments. A data arrangement and analysis that incorporate tests of these assumptions as well as tests of the treatment and position effects are described in Section 9.6.1.

Tables 9.13 through 9.16 show computer analyses of the small-sample example of the Latin-square ANOVA of Section 9.4.3 by SPSS GLM, MINITAB GLM, SYSTAT GLM, and SAS GLM.

The SPSS GLM (UNIANOVA) instruction lists the DV (time), followed by the keyword BY, followed by the list of IVs (snow, day, and case). EMMEANS instructions request marginal means for each IV; ETASQ in the /PRINT instruction requests effect size and power statistics. (Note that the choice is GLM—General Factorial if you use menus.) Latin-square analysis is specified in the /DESIGN instruction, where only main effects are listed. This syntax is generated by the menu system when CUSTOM is selected from the MODEL submenu and the three IVs are clicked over (highlighted and selected). The remaining syntax is provided by default through the SPSS menu system.

Tests of Between-Subjects Effects shows the source table of Table 9.7 with the error term (Residual in Table 9.7) labeled Error. The column labeled Sig shows the probability (to three decimal places) that each outcome is a result of chance variation. Thus, the probability that the result with respect to SNOW occurred by chance is .013. The Corrected Model source of variation is the sum of all three main effects plus error. The Total source of variance includes the intercept in its sum; the Corrected Total does not include the intercept and is more useful for effect-size calculations (cf. Section 5.6.2). The column labeled Eta Squared contains effect-size measures described in Section 5.6.2 as partial η^2. R squared in footnote b is the proportion of total variance that is predictable from the corrected model (the sum of all three effects). Adjusted R Squared adjusts that value for bias due to small sample sizes (cf. Tabachnick and Fidell, 2001, Section 5.6.3). Observed Power is described in Section 5.6.3. The Noncent. Parameter (noncentrality) is used to calculate power.

Marginal means appear at the end of the output, with a common standard error for each level of each IV and the 95% confidence interval for the mean. Only the table for SNOW is shown here. The common standard error is found by dividing the square root of $MS_{residual}$ (labeled Error in the output) by the square root of the number of cases in each marginal mean.

Table 9.14 shows syntax and output for the analysis through MINITAB GLM. This differs from the usual setup only in that interactions among IVs are omitted from the GLM instruction.

Output is straightforward, with residual labeled Error. Marginal means appear at the end of output, with a common standard error (labeled STDev) for each level of each IV.

Table 9.15 illustrates syntax and partial output for SYSTAT GLM. Categorical IVs (in this case all three of them) are named in the CATEGORY instruction. The MODEL instruction sets up a model with main effects only, no interactions, and the constant (intercept) on the right side of the equation, and the DV on the left side.

TABLE 9.12 Data Set for Small-Sample Example of Latin-Square Analysis

Snow Condition	Day of Week	Case (Skier)	Run Time
3	1	1	4
1	2	1	9
2	3	1	1
2	1	2	1
3	2	2	6
1	3	2	7
1	1	3	8
2	2	3	2
3	3	3	5

TABLE 9.13   Latin-Square ANOVA for Small-Sample Example through SPSS GLM (UNIANOVA): Syntax and Partial Output

```
UNIANOVA
 time BY snow day case
 /METHOD = SSTYPE(3)
 /INTERCEPT = INCLUDE
 /EMMEANS = TABLES(snow)
 /EMMEANS = TABLES(day)
 /EMMEANS = TABLES(case)
 /PRINT = ETASQ OPOWER
 /CRITERIA = ALPHA(.05)
 /DESIGN = snow day case .
```

Tests of Between-Subjects Effects

Dependent Variable: TIME

Source	Type III Sum of Squares	df	Mean Square	F	Sig.	Eta Squared	Noncent. Parameter	Observed Power[a]
Corrected Model	70.667[b]	6	11.778	26.500	.037	.988	159.000	.753
Intercept	205.444	1	205.444	462.250	.002	.996	462.250	1.000
SNOW	66.889	2	33.444	75.250	.013	.987	150.500	.978
DAY	3.556	2	1.778	4.000	.200	.800	8.000	.222
CASE	.222	2	.111	.250	.800	.200	.500	.062
Error	.889	2	.444					
Total	277.000	9						
Corrected Total	71.556	8						

a. Computed using alpha = .05
b. R Squared = .988 (Adjusted R Squared = .950)

Estimated Marginal Means

1. SNOW

Dependent Variable: TIME

SNOW	Mean	Std. Error	95% Confidence Interval	
			Lower Bound	Upper Bound
1.00	8.000	.385	6.344	9.656
2.00	1.333	.385	−.323	2.989
3.00	5.000	.385	3.344	6.656

TABLE 9.14   Latin-Square ANOVA for Small-Sample Example through MINITAB GLM: Syntax and Partial Output

```
MTB > GLM 'Time' = Snow Day Case;
SUBC> Brief 2;
SUBC> Means Snow Day Case.

Analysis of Variance for Time, using Adjusted SS for Tests
```

Source	DF	Seq SS	Adj SS	Adj MS	F	P
Snow	2	66.889	66.889	33.444	75.25	0.013
Day	2	3.556	3.556	1.778	4.00	0.200
Case	2	0.222	0.222	0.111	0.25	0.800
Error	2	0.889	0.889	0.444		
Total	8	71.556				

```
Least Squares Means for Time
```

Snow	Mean	StDev
1	8.000	0.3849
2	1.333	0.3849
3	5.000	0.3849

TABLE 9.15   Latin-Square ANOVA of Small-Sample Example through SYSTAT GLM: Syntax and Partial Output

```
GLM
CATEGORY SNOW DAY CASE / EFFECT
MODEL TIME = CONSTANT + SNOW + DAY + CASE
ESTIMATE
```

Analysis of Variance

Source	Sum-of-Squares	df	Mean-Square	F-ratio	P
SNOW	66.889	2	33.444	75.250	0.013
DAY	3.556	2	1.778	4.000	0.200
TIME	0.222	2	0.111	0.250	0.800
Error	0.889	2	0.444		

```
------------------------------------------------------------
```

Least squares means.

		LS Mean	SE	N
SNOW	=1	8.000	0.385	3
SNOW	=2	1.333	0.385	3
SNOW	=3	5.000	0.385	3

Squared multiple R is the proportion of variance predicted by all effects combined, as in SPSS. The probability that a mean difference occurred by chance appears in the column labeled P in the source table. Residual is labeled Error. Means and standard errors for each effect are plotted automatically, and printed if PRINT=MEDIUM is specified. Only the descriptive statistics for levels of SNOW (the sole significant effect) are shown here (plots are omitted).

SAS GLM syntax and output appears in Table 9.16. Discrete IVs are identified in the class instruction; the model instruction shows (in regression format) that the DV is a function of the three IVs. (The intercept is included by default.) Marginal means are requested in the means instruction.

SAS GLM shows two source tables. The first is for evaluating the Model with all effects combined, and includes Error (Residual) as well as the Total (identified as Corrected). This table includes R-Square, indicating the proportion of variance predictable from the whole model. Also shown are the square root of the $\text{MS}_{\text{residual}}$ (Root MSE), the grand mean (TIME Mean), and

TABLE 9.16 Latin-Square ANOVA for Small-Sample Example through SAS GLM: Syntax and Partial Output

```
proc    glm data=SASUSER.SS_LATIN;
        class SNOW DAY CASE;
        model TIME = SNOW DAY CASE;
        means SNOW DAY CASE;
run;
```

Dependent Variable: TIME

Source	DF	Sum of Squares	Mean Square	F Value	Pr > F
Model	6	70.66666667	11.77777778	26.50	0.0368
Error	2	0.88888889	0.44444444		
Corrected Total	8	71.55555556			

R-Square	C.V.	Root MSE	TIME Mean
0.987578	13.95349	0.6666666	4.77777778

Source	DF	Type III SS	Mean Square	F Value	Pr > F
SNOW	2	66.88888889	33.44444444	75.25	0.0131
DAY	2	3.55555556	1.77777778	4.00	0.2000
CASE	2	0.22222222	0.11111111	0.25	0.8000

Level of SNOW	N	----------TIME---------- Mean	SD
1	3	8.00000000	1.00000000
2	3	1.33333333	0.57735027
3	3	5.00000000	1.00000000

the coefficient of variation (C.V., the square root of the error mean square divided by the grand mean, multiplied by 100).

The second source table shows the three effects, with the last column (PR > F) indicating the probability of mean differences of that size or larger resulting from chance variation. Marginal means and standard deviations then are provided.

9.5   Types of Latin-Square Designs

The fundamental design in Section 9.4.1 consists of three IVs, each with the same number of levels, and a single score (replication) in each cell. There are advantages for both randomized-groups and repeated-measures designs when each cell contains more than one replication. Two advantages are that the designs generate more degrees of freedom for error, thus greater power, and that other effects become available for analysis.

9.5.1   Replicated Randomized-Groups Designs

In Section 9.4.1 each *ABC* combination is applied to a single case; however, the design is readily extended to replicates where each *ABC* combination is applied to more than one case. In the small-sample example of Section 9.4.1, for instance, there could be several skiers in each cell, as in Table 9.17 (where there are two skiers in each cell).

When there are replications, the design allows a test of the bits and pieces of interactions that happen to be included in the design. If there is no evidence of interaction, the assumption of additivity is supported and an error term with more degrees of freedom is available that is likely to increase the power for testing main effects. There are five steps to the analysis:

Step 1.   Turn the design into a one-way design with a^2 levels (9 levels, in the example) and perform a one-way randomized-groups ANOVA to get SS_{bg} (between groups) and $SS_{S/ABC}$.

TABLE 9.17   Allocation of Cases in a Randomized-Groups Latin-Square Design with Replications

	b_1	b_2	b_3
a_1	$c_3: s_1$ s_2	$c_1: s_7$ s_8	$c_2: s_{13}$ s_{14}
a_2	$c_2: s_3$ s_4	$c_3: s_9$ s_{10}	$c_1: s_{15}$ s_{16}
a_3	$c_1: s_5$ s_6	$c_2: s_{11}$ s_{12}	$c_3: s_{17}$ s_{18}

Step 2. Analyze the data as a Latin square to get SS_A, SS_B, and SS_C (and $MS_{residual}$).

Step 3. Compute $SS_{interactions}$ and $df_{interactions}$, where

$$SS_{interactions} = SS_{bg} - SS_A - SS_B - SS_C \tag{9.12}$$

$$df_{interactions} = df_{bg} - df_A - df_B - df_C \tag{9.13}$$

Step 4. Test $MS_{interactions}$ against $MS_{S/ABC}$.

$$F_{interactions} = \frac{MS_{interactions}}{MS_{S/ABC}} \qquad df = (a-1)(a-2), (N-a^2) \tag{9.14}$$

Step 5. If the test is not significant, breathe a sign of relief, and then use the tests of MS_A, MS_B, and MS_C against $MS_{residual}$ ($= MS_{S/ABC+interactions}$), as obtained in Step 2. If the test is significant, rethink your study because the data violate the additivity assumption of analysis.

Figure 9.2 diagrams the analysis for the randomized-groups Latin-square design with replicates when there are no interactions. $MS_{residual}$ with replicates is usually smaller than that with no replicates because of increased degrees of freedom in the error term. This increases the power of the analysis.

As an example of the steps required for the test of interaction, consider an expansion of the data in the small-sample example of Table 9.4 to two skiers per cell, as seen in Table 9.18.

The corresponding data set appropriate for computer analysis is in Table 9.19. Notice that a column for group has been added to convert the analysis into a one-way design. Information about group membership can either be inserted into the data set itself (often easier) or added by transformation language.

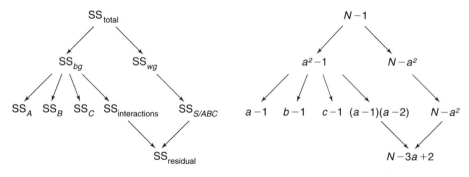

(a) Sums of squares

(b) Degrees of freedom

FIGURE 9.2 Partition of (a) Sums of Squares and (b) Degrees of Freedom into Between- and Within-Groups Sources of Variation, Showing Combination of Sources from Both into a Pooled Estimate of Error for a Randomized-Groups Latin-Square Design with Replicates

TABLE 9.18   Data Set for a Randomized-Groups Latin-Square Design with Replications

	b_1	b_2	b_3
a_1	c_3: 4 6	c_1: 9 10	c_2: 1 4
a_2	c_2: 1 3	c_3: 6 5	c_1: 7 6
a_3	c_1: 8 11	c_2: 2 1	c_3: 5 6

TABLE 9.19   Data Set for Computer Analysis of a Randomized-Groups Latin-Square Design with Replications

A	B	C	DV	Group
1	1	3	4	1
1	1	3	6	1
1	2	1	9	2
1	2	1	10	2
1	3	2	1	3
1	3	2	4	3
2	1	2	1	4
2	1	2	3	4
2	2	3	6	5
2	2	3	5	5
2	3	1	7	6
2	3	1	6	6
3	1	1	8	7
3	1	1	11	7
3	2	2	2	8
3	2	2	1	8
3	3	3	5	9
3	3	3	6	9

The five steps in the analysis are then performed through MINITAB GLM:

Step 1. Turn the design into a one-way design with a^2 levels (9 levels in the example) and perform a one-way randomized-groups ANOVA to get SS_{bg} and $SS_{S/ABC}$ (Table 9.20).

Step 2. Analyze the data as a Latin square to get SS_A, SS_B, and SS_C (and $MS_{residual}$) as shown in Table 9.21.

Step 3. Compute $SS_{interactions}$ and $df_{interactions}$ using Equations 9.12 and 9.13:

$$SS_{interactions} = 140.111 - 3.444 - 1.778 - 126.778 = 8.111$$

$$df_{interactions} = 8 - 2 - 2 - 2 = 2$$

Step 4. Test $MS_{interactions}$ against $MS_{S/ABC}$ using Equation 9.14:

$$F_{interactions} = \frac{SS_{interactions}/df_{interactions}}{MS_{S/ABC}} = \frac{8.111/2}{1.722} = 2.289$$

Step 5. With 2 and 9 df, the interaction is not significant so breathe a sign of relief, and then use the tests of MS_A, MS_B, and MS_C against $MS_{residual}$ shown in Table 9.21, obtained at Step 2.

TABLE 9.20   Analysis to Evaluate Interaction in a Randomized-Groups Latin-Square Design with Replications: MINITAB GLM Syntax and Output

```
MTB > GLM 'DV' = Group;
SUBC> Brief 2.


General Linear Model


Factor   Type    Levels   Values
Group    fixed    9 1 2 3 4 5 6 7 8 9


Analysis of Variance for Time, using Adjusted SS for Tests


Source   DF    Seq SS     Adj SS    Adj MS      F       P
Group     8   140.111    140.111    17.514    10.17   0.001
Error     9    15.500     15.500     1.722
```

TABLE 9.21   Analysis of Main Effects in a Randomized-Groups Latin-Square Design with Replications: MINITAB GLM Syntax and Output

```
MTB > GLM 'DV' = A B C;
SUBC> Brief 2.


General Linear Model


Factor   Type    Levels Values
A        fixed    3 1 2 3
B        fixed    3 1 2 3
C        fixed    3 1 2 3


Analysis of Variance for DV, using Adjusted SS for Tests


Source   DF    Seq SS     Adj SS    Adj MS      F       P
A         2     3.444      3.444     1.722     0.80    0.473
B         2     1.778      1.778     0.889     0.41    0.671
C         2   126.778    126.778    63.389    29.53    0.000
Error    11    23.611     23.611     2.146
Total    17   155.611
```

Note that $SS_{residual}$ (23.611) from Table 9.21 is a sum of $SS_{interactions}$ (8.111) from Equation 9.12 and $SS_{S/ABC}$ (15.500) from Table 9.20.

However, if the test of interaction is significant, the assumption of additivity is violated and the study probably needs to be rerun as a complete factorial. One possible rescue for the study as conducted is to demonstrate that C is not confounded with the $A \times B$ interaction (Winer et al., 1991). An analysis is run in which C is ignored, and the data are analyzed as a two-way full factorial $A \times B$ design (cf. Chapter 5). If the $A \times B$ interaction is nonsignificant, the original test of the main effect of C is then defended as unconfounded.

9.5.2   Replicated Repeated-Measures Designs

Replicates in a repeated-measures Latin-square design also increase the power of the analysis. There are two ways to replicate a repeated-measures Latin-square design: (1) add cases so that each sequence of Cs in the same Latin square has more than one case (the crossover design) or (2) add a randomized-group variable with additional cases in the levels of that variable. In either situation, the study becomes a mixed repeated-measures, randomized-groups design as described in greater detail in Chapter 7.

9.5.2.1   The Crossover Design

In this design, additional cases are measured for each of the orders of the levels of C. The variable A, then, becomes a randomized-groups variable with levels that represent the sequence or order in which the levels of C are administered. The elements that are part of the Latin square are A, B, and C. The number of levels of A is the same as levels of B and C because there has to be a level of A for each sequence of Cs. However, there can be any number of cases assigned to each sequence, as shown in Table 9.22, where there are three levels of A, B, and C, but two cases in each sequence.

Often, in the biomedical arena, there are only two levels of A, B, and C, and C represents a new pharmaceutical agent tested against a placebo or another pharmaceutical agent. The design is called crossover because cases cross over from one level to the other, some going from treatment to control and others from control to treatment. If there are only two or three levels of C, all possible orders of treatment are often included (e.g., c_1, c_2 for some cases and c_2, c_1 for others); if there are numerous levels of C, the order of treatments is most often determined by a Latin square. In drug studies, there is usually a washout period between administrations of the levels of treatment to minimize carryover

TABLE 9.22   Allocation of Cases in a Repeated-Measures Latin-Square Design with Replications: The Crossover Design

			Periods: B		
			b_1	b_2	b_3
	a_1	s_1 s_2	c_2	c_1	c_3
Order or Sequence: A	a_2	s_3 s_4	c_3	c_2	c_1
	a_3	s_5 s_6	c_1	c_3	c_2

effects. The test of order (A) is a test of differences in carryover effects, should they be present. The design is popular enough, especially in biomedical research, and complex enough to have generated at least one book (Jones and Kenward, 1989) with an impressive list of references.

This mixed-design analysis identifies treatment (C) and period (B) as repeated-measures effects with order (A) as a randomized-groups effect. The treatment effect (C) is "carved out of" the $A \times B$ (period by order) interaction just as in the design with no replications (Equation 9.3). As in the replicated randomized-groups design of Section 9.5.1, the "leftover" $A \times B$ interaction ($A \times B_{adj}$) is a test of additivity. There is no interaction of A with C in this design because there are no combinations of A and C. Rather, A is defined across the levels of C.

A data set appropriate for a crossover analysis appears in Table 9.23. There are six skiers randomly assigned to sequence, two receive c_2, c_1, c_3, two receive c_3, c_2, c_1, and two receive c_1, c_3, c_2.

There are two ways to organize the data for computer analysis of this design. One way is to enter the data for A and B in a traditional mixed-design format. Information regarding level of C is then made available through transformation language (e.g., if A is 1 and B is 1, then C is 2, etc.). The other way is to enter the data once for A and B and then for A and C. This organization, which is often easier for a small data set, is shown in Table 9.24.

The easiest way to perform the analysis is to run two mixed-design ANOVAs, one for AB and the other for AC. Most of the sources of variability are obtained directly from the output and one source by subtraction. The three steps for this analysis follow.

Step 1. Run a standard A, B mixed-design ANOVA, as shown in Table 9.25.

Step 2. Run a standard A, C mixed-design ANOVA, as shown in Table 9.26.

Step 3. Combine the results into a source table, as shown in Table 9.27.

There are many things to notice about this source table. First, A and S/A from the Tests of Between-Subjects Effects are the same for either analysis. This is because these elements are

TABLE 9.23 Data Set for a Crossover Design

			Days (Periods): B			Sum
			b_1: Monday	b_2: Wednesday	b_3: Friday	
	a_1	s_1	c_2: 8	c_1: 4	c_3: 5	17
		s_2	9	2	4	15
Order or Sequence: A	a_2	s_3	c_3: 7	c_2: 7	c_1: 2	16
		s_4	5	9	4	18
	a_3	s_5	c_1: 3	c_3: 6	c_2: 9	18
		s_6	3	5	8	16

TABLE 9.24 Data Set for Computer Analysis of a Crossover Design

Case	A	b_1	b_2	b_3	c_1	c_2	c_3
1	1	8	4	5	4	8	5
2	1	9	2	4	2	9	4
3	2	7	7	2	2	7	7
4	2	5	9	4	4	9	5
5	3	3	6	9	3	9	6
6	3	3	5	8	3	8	5

computed from the sums for the cases, as shown in Table 9.23. These sums are the same whether obtained across the levels of B or across the levels of C because the same numbers are involved, just in different order. Second, the error term for the repeated-measures elements of the design, $B \times S/A$ (or $C \times S/A$—called Error(B) or Error(C) in Steps 1 and 2, respectively) are also identical because the numbers involved in the computations are also the same but for order. Finally, sum of squares (and df) for C is taken out of the $A \times B$ interaction from Step 1 to form $A \times B_{adj}$, as in the design with only one case per sequence. $A \times B_{adj}$ is a test of the assumption of additivity as in the randomized-groups design with replications. In this example, there are no sequence (carryover) effects (A), no position effects (B), and no violation of the assumption of additivity ($A \times B_{adj}$). There is, however, a significant difference due to treatment (C, snow condition in the example). Section 9.7.2 shows a full analysis of a crossover design with multiple trials at each level of position, a common complexity added in biostatistical research.

9.5.2.2 The Repeated-Measures Design with a Randomized-Groups IV

The second way to add replications to a repeated-measures Latin square is to add a randomized-groups IV with its associated cases. The randomized-groups IV can represent level of treatment (treatment versus control), a blocking variable (such as gender, skill level, or type of disease), or an additional Latin-square arrangement. In this design, the randomized-groups IV can have any number of levels, but the number of cases at each of those levels is the same as, or some multiple of, the number of levels involved in the Latin square.

The allocation of cases for a design of this type is as shown in Table 9.28, in which the effects that are part of the Latin square ($B, C,$ and S) each have three levels, but the randomized-groups IV (A) has only two. In this design, A is a regular randomized-groups IV that crosses both levels of B and levels of C. That is, all AB and AC combinations are present in the design. The BCS portion of the design at each level of A is identical to that of a repeated-measures Latin square with only one replicate per cell; that entire Latin-square arrangement is duplicated at each level of A.

The small-sample example is readily extended to a design of this type if the randomized-groups variable is defined as, say, gender. As shown in Table 9.29, three male and three female skiers ski on Monday, Wednesday, and Friday under the snow condition prescribed by C.

**TABLE 9.25   Mixed-Design Analysis of *A*, *B* in a Crossover Design:
SPSS UNIANOVA Syntax and Selected Output**

```
GLM
 b1 b2 b3 BY a
 /WSFACTOR = b 3 Polynomial
 /METHOD = SSTYPE(3)
 /CRITERIA = ALPHA(.05)
 /WSDESIGN = b
 /DESIGN = a .
```

Tests of Within-Subjects Effects

Measure: MEASURE_1

Source		Type III Sum of Squares	df	Mean Square	F	Sig.
B	Sphericity Assumed	.778	2	.389	.292	.757
	Greenhouse-Geisser	.778	1.046	.743	.292	.635
	Huynh-Feldt	.778	2.000	.389	.292	.757
	Lower-bound	.778	1.000	.778	.292	.627
B*A	Sphericity Assumed	87.222	4	21.806	16.354	.002
	Greenhouse-Geisser	87.222	2.093	41.680	16.354	.022
	Huynh-Feldt	87.222	4.000	21.806	16.354	.002
	Lower-bound	87.222	2.000	43.611	16.354	.024
Error(B)	Sphericity Assumed	8.000	6	1.333		
	Greenhouse-Geisser	8.000	3.139	2.549		
	Huynh-Feldt	8.000	6.000	1.333		
	Lower-bound	8.000	3.000	2.667		

Tests of Between-Subjects Effects

Measure: MEASURE_1
Transformed Variable: Average

Source	Type III Sum of Squares	df	Mean Square	F	Sig.
Intercept	555.556	1	555.556	833.333	.000
A	.444	2	.222	.333	.740
Error	2.000	3	.667		

TABLE 9.26 Mixed-Design Analysis of *A*, *C* in a Crossover Design: SPSS UNIANOVA Syntax and Selected Output

```
GLM
  b1 b2 b3 BY a
  /WSFACTOR = c 3 Polynomial
  /METHOD = SSTYPE(3)
  /CRITERIA = ALPHA(.05)
  /WSDESIGN = c
  /DESIGN = a .
```

Tests of Within-Subjects Effects

Measure: MEASURE_1

Source		Type III Sum of Squares	df	Mean Square	F	Sig.
C	Sphericity Assumed	85.778	2.000	42.889	32.167	.001
	Greenhouse-Geisser	85.778	1.745	49.144	32.167	.001
	Huynh-Feldt	85.778	2.000	42.889	32.167	.001
	Lower-bound	85.778	1.000	85.778	32.167	.011
C*A	Sphericity Assumed	2.222	4.000	.556	.417	.792
	Greenhouse-Geisser	2.222	3.491	.637	.417	.772
	Huynh-Feldt	2.222	4.000	.556	.417	.792
	Lower-bound	2.222	2.000	1.111	.417	.692
Error(C)	Sphericity Assumed	8.000	6.000	1.333		
	Greenhouse-Geisser	8.000	5.236	1.528		
	Huynh-Feldt	8.000	6.000	1.333		
	Lower-bound	8.000	3.000	2.667		

Tests of Between-Subjects Effects

Measure: MEASURE_1
Transformed Variable: Average

Source	Type III Sum of Squares	df	Mean Square	F	Sig.
Intercept	555.556	1	555.556	833.333	.000
A	.444	2	.222	.333	.740
Error	2.000	3	.667		

TABLE 9.27   Source Table for Analysis of Crossover Design

Source	SS		df	MS	F
A	0.444	From either Step 1 or 2	2	0.222	0.333
S/A	2.000	From either Step 1 or 2	3	0.667	
B	0.778	Step 1	2	0.389	0.292
C	85.778	Step 2	2	42.889	32.167
$A \times B_{adj}$	1.444	$(A \times B - C)$ $87.222 - 85.778 = 1.444$	$(4 - 2)$ $= 2$	0.722	0.542
$B \times S/A$	8.000	From either Step 1 or 2	6	1.333	
Total	98.444	From either Step 1 or 2	17		

TABLE 9.28   Allocation of Cases in a Repeated-Measures Latin Square with a Randomized-Groups IV

		\ **Trials**		
		b_1	b_2	b_3
a_1	s_1	c_2	c_1	c_3
	s_2	c_3	c_2	c_1
	s_3	c_1	c_1	c_2
a_2	s_4	c_2	c_1	c_3
	s_5	c_3	c_2	c_1
	s_6	c_1	c_3	c_2

TABLE 9.29   Data Set for a Repeated-Measures Latin Square with a Randomized-Groups IV

			Days (Periods): B		
			b_1: *Monday*	b_2: *Wednesday*	b_3: *Friday*
Gender: A	a_1: *Men*	s_1	c_2: 8	c_1: 4	c_3: 5
		s_2	c_3: 4	c_2: 9	c_1: 2
		s_3	c_1: 3	c_3: 6	c_2: 9
	a_2: *Women*	s_4	c_2: 7	c_1: 2	c_3: 7
		s_5	c_3: 5	c_2: 9	c_1: 4
		s_6	c_1: 3	c_3: 5	c_2: 8

The data set is organized the same as in Table 9.24 and the same three steps are used to complete this analysis: Run a standard mixed-design ANOVA for AB; then a standard mixed-design ANOVA for AC; and generate a source table with the elements combined for the final analysis.

Step 1. Run a standard A, B mixed-design ANOVA, as shown in Table 9.30, through SYSTAT GLM.

Step 2. Run a standard A, C mixed-design ANOVA, as shown in Table 9.31.

Step 3. Combine the results into a source table, as shown in Table 9.32.

The source table has many of the same features as that of the crossover design (Table 9.27) with two exceptions. First, this design generates an $A \times C$ interaction because A is a true randomized-groups IV and all AC combinations are present in the design. Second, C and $A \times C$ are obtained from $B \times S/A$ rather than from the $A \times B$ interaction, as in Table 9.27. We make a feeble attempt to explain why in the next section.

The randomized-groups IV, A, can be a blocking variable (such as gender or age), a manipulated IV (treatment vs. control), or different Latin squares. When it is different Latin squares, the design looks like that in Table 9.33 and provides a test of potentially different carryover effects if they are of concern in the study. Note that there is a different arrangement of levels of C at a_1 and a_2.

If there is a second randomized-groups IV, D (another blocking variable, another manipulated IV, another Latin square), the randomized-groups part of the design has two IVs, the interaction

TABLE 9.30   Mixed-Design Analysis of A, B in a Repeated-Measures Latin Square with a Randomized-Groups IV: SYSTAT GLM Syntax and Selected Output

```
GLM
CATEGORY A / EFFECT
MODEL B1 B2 B3 = CONSTANT + A/ REPEAT =3, NAMES='B'
ESTIMATE
```

Between Subjects

Source	SS	df	MS	F	P
A	0.000	1	0.000	0.000	1.000
Error	2.444	4	0.611		

Within Subjects

Source	SS	df	MS	F	P	G–G	H–F
B	2.778	2	1.389	0.123	0.886	0.873	0.886
B*A	3.000	2	1.500	0.133	0.877	0.864	0.877
Error	90.222	8	11.278				

TABLE 9.31 Mixed-Design Analysis of *A*, *C* in a Repeated-Measures Latin Square with a Randomized-Groups IV: SYSTAT GLM Syntax and Selected Output

```
GLM
CATEGORY A / EFFECT
MODEL C1 C2 C3 = CONSTANT + A/ REPEAT =3,NAMES='C'
ESTIMATE
```

Between Subjects

Source	SS	df	MS	F	P		
A	0.000	1	0.000	0.000	1.000		
Error	2.444	4	0.611				

Within Subjects

Source	SS	df	MS	F	P	G-G	H-F
C	85.778	2	42.889	38.600	0.000	0.000	0.000
C*A	1.333	2	0.667	0.600	0.572	0.545	0.572
Error	8.889	8	1.111				

TABLE 9.32 Source Table for Repeated-Measures Latin Square with a Randomized-Groups IV

Source	SS		df	MS	F
A	0.000	From either Step 1 or 2	1	0.000	0
S/A	2.444	From either Step 1 or 2	4	0.611	
B	2.778	From Step 1	2	1.389	1.785
C	85.778	From Step 2	2	42.889	55.127
$A \times B$	3.000	From Step 1	2	1.500	1.928
$A \times C$	1.333	From Step 2	2	0.667	0.857
L. S. Residual	3.111	$B \times S/A - C - A \times C =$ 90.222 − 85.778 − 1.333	8 − 2 − 2 = 4	0.778	
Total	98.444		17		

between them and an error term consisting of cases nested within combinations of levels of both IVs. Thus, the upper part of the source table is the same as any two-way randomized-groups ANOVA: *A*, *D*, $A \times D$, and S/AD. The repeated-measures part of the design has the repeated-measures IV of interest, *C*, the position effect, *B*, and all interactions with *A*, *D*, and $A \times D$. Myers and Well (1991, pp. 360–363) show a numerical example for this design.

TABLE 9.33   The Randomized-Groups IV Represents Different Latin Squares

		Trials		
		b_1	b_2	b_3
a_1	s_1	c_2	c_1	c_3
	s_2	c_3	c_2	c_1
	s_3	c_1	c_3	c_2
a_2	s_4	c_1	c_2	c_3
	s_5	c_3	c_1	c_2
	s_6	c_2	c_3	c_1

9.5.2.3   Comparison of the Two Repeated-Measures Designs with Replications

The differences between these two designs (crossover and addition of a randomized-groups IV) are subtle. One difference is the presence of the $A \times C$ interaction. This source is not available in the crossover design, although it is present when A is a genuine randomized-groups IV. In the crossover design, there is no $A \times C$ effect because A does not cross C. There is no a_1, c_1 combination, for instance, because A is defined by the order of *all* the levels of C.[6] On the other hand, when A is a regular randomized-groups IV, such as gender, all combinations of A and C are present, as are all combinations of A and B. That is, both interactions are "real."

The second difference is what part of the AB analysis the Latin-square segment is derived from. Remember that C (and $A \times C$ if present) are "carved out of" the interaction of the other two elements of the Latin square. But the crossover design and the repeated-measures Latin square with a randomized-groups IV have different elements associated with their Latin squares. In the crossover design, those elements are A, B, and C. In the repeated-measures Latin square with a randomized-groups IV, those elements are B, C, and S. Thus, in the crossover design, C is carved out of the $A \times B$ interaction, whereas in the repeated-measures Latin square, C and $A \times C$ are carved out of $B \times S$ (nested in A).

How can you tell which elements are part of the Latin square? Ask yourself, which other element has to have the same number of levels as C and B? In the crossover design, there have to be as many levels of A as there are levels of C and B; however, there can be any number of cases at each level of A. In the repeated-measures Latin square with a randomized-groups IV, on the other hand, the Latin square is duplicated at each level of A, so the number of cases has to match the levels of B and C,[7] but there can be any number of levels of A. Once this pattern is apparent to you, the rest of the design can become endlessly complicated, whereas the IVs that are involved in the Latin square itself remain clear.

[6]Said another way, the Latin square is not complete until you have all the levels of A.

[7]Or be a multiple of those levels.

9.5.3   Less Commonly Encountered Designs

Latin-square designs can become almost endlessly complex. Additional Latin squares can be super-imposed on the first, additional IVs (either randomized groups or repeated measures), can be added, levels of treatment or position can be randomly selected rather than fixed, and so on. Indeed, Winer and colleagues (1991) demonstrate 12 Latin square plans. A few are discussed here, with references to texts that provide greater detail.

9.5.3.1   *Partition of Main Effects in a Latin-Square Design*

The major treatment variable in a Latin-square design, C, can be partitioned into two (or more) sources of variance if the number of levels is even. For example, four levels of C can be partitioned into two levels of C and two levels of D. In the basic Latin-square design of Table 9.1, for instance, c_1 becomes c_1d_1, c_2 becomes c_1d_2, c_3 becomes c_2d_1, and c_4 becomes c_2d_2. The design permits a test of the $C \times D$ interaction as well as the main effects of C and D, instead of just a single main effect of C. Myers and Well (1991, pp. 356–357) demonstrate this design numerically for a repeated-measures Latin-square design.

Winer and colleagues (1991) suggest factorial partition of the A and B variables as well in a randomized-groups design. For example, the four levels of A are partitioned into a 2×2 arrangement and the four levels of B are partitioned into another 2×2 arrangement.

9.5.3.2   *Greco-Latin Squares*

In another variant, a second Latin square is superimposed on the first to produce a Greco-Latin square, as shown in Table 9.34. There are two separate Latin squares, one for C and one for D. This permits isolation of yet another nuisance or treatment variable, in either the randomized-groups or repeated-measures Latin-square design. Then Latin squares may be superimposed on Greco-Latin squares, creating hyper-Greco-Latin squares. The number of IVs that may be superimposed, however, is limited by the degrees of freedom. In the example of Table 9.34, for example, there are no df available for the error term unless there are replications because both C (2 df) and D (2 df) are sub-tracted from the $A \times B$ interaction (4 df). Montgomery (1984) shows a numerical example of a $4 \times 4 \times 4 \times 4$ Greco-Latin square.

The assumption of additivity extends to Greco-Latin squares, but the assumption may be untenable. As more and more IVs are added, the more numerous the potential interactions and the less reasonable the assumption of no interaction.

TABLE 9.34   Greco-Latin Square

	b_1	b_2	b_3
a_1	c_2, d_1	c_1, d_2	c_3, d_3
a_2	c_3, d_3	c_2, d_1	c_1, d_2
a_3	c_1, d_2	c_3, d_3	c_2, d_1

9.5.3.3   *Youden Square*

Incomplete block designs are used when a complete Latin square is impractical either because there are too many treatments or because it is not possible to expose all cases to all treatments. Several such designs are available; Davies (1963) discusses a wealth of incomplete block designs of all types. The one described here is the Youden square for the balanced incomplete block design. In effect, this is an incomplete Latin square in which one or more of the columns (or rows) is missing, so that it is no longer a square.

In a repeated-measures design, it is sometimes impossible to expose all cases to all treatments due to time or other constraints. Suppose, for example, that there are six treatments but each case is only available for five of them. Or, in a randomized-groups design with a blocking IV, there may not be enough cases to go around; each block may contain enough cases for $c - 1$ treatments instead of all c. For instance, with the same six treatments, there may only be 30 (instead of 36) cases available, so that each of the six blocks has only five cases. This could happen, for example, if there are six treatments to be run, but each batch of material is only large enough to extract five samples. The incomplete blocks design is also applicable to a randomized-groups design when one of the nuisance variables, B, necessarily has fewer levels than the other two variables, A and C.

Assignment of cases to treatment is done through the Youden square, in which there are fewer columns (positions) than rows (cases or blocks of cases) or treatments. Table 9.35 is an example of a Youden square with four treatments (C), four cases (A), but only three levels of B, so this is a $4 \times 3 \times 4$ design. Each treatment occurs once in each column in a Youden square and each treatment is deleted once in each row. In a balanced incomplete block design, there is the additional constraint that each pair of treatments occurs together the same number of times as any other pair of treatments. For example, in Table 9.35, each pair of treatments occurs twice.

Davies (1963) provides a variety of Youden square tables. As with Latin squares, the basic Youden square should be randomized (cf. Section 9.6.2). Total sum of squares and sum of squares for B are calculated in the usual way, but there are adjustments to sums of squares for A and for C. These adjustments are automatically provided by software programs when the syntax of Tables 9.13 through 9.16 is used.

9.5.3.4   *Digram Balanced Latin Squares, Changeover Designs*

When there are more than two levels of the IVs in a repeated-measures Latin square, a changeover analysis permits tests of residual effects of the prior treatment. The desire is to test for the presence of differential carryover when one of the levels of treatment has (relatively) long-lasting impact on the DV and thus contaminates responses to the level (or levels) of treatment that follows it. The trick is to analyze for the level of treatment that precedes the current one.

When there is an even number of levels of treatment, a digram balanced Latin square is used in which each treatment follows each other treatment the same number of times. When there is an odd number of levels of treatment, two Latin squares are required (cf. Table 9.33), where one is the mirror image of the other so that each treatment follows each other treatment the same number of times over both Latin squares. In either situation, replicates are highly desirable to generate sufficient df for error and, therefore, power (Cochran and Cox, 1957). A digram balanced Latin-square arrangement with four levels of A is shown in Table 9.36. Note that each level of C follows each other level of C only once.

TABLE 9.35   Basic Youden Square Design for Four Treatments

	b_1	b_2	b_3
a_1	c_1	c_2	c_3
a_2	c_2	c_4	c_1
a_3	c_3	c_1	c_4
a_4	c_4	c_3	c_2

TABLE 9.36   Digram Balanced Latin Square for a 4 × 4 × 4 Design

	b_1	b_2	b_3	b_4
a_1	c_1	c_2	c_4	c_3
a_2	c_2	c_3	c_1	c_4
a_3	c_3	c_4	c_2	c_1
a_4	c_4	c_1	c_3	c_2

TABLE 9.37   Data Set for Digram Balanced Latin-Square Design

		b_1	b_2	b_3	b_4
a_1	s_1	c_1: 7	c_2: 9	c_4: 7	c_3: 6
	s_2	6	10	5	8
a_2	s_3	c_2: 5	c_3: 7	c_1: 9	c_4: 11
	s_4	7	6	12	12
a_3	s_5	c_3: 3	c_4: 6	c_2: 7	c_1: 10
	s_6	4	5	5	9
a_4	s_7	c_4: 5	c_1: 7	c_3: 8	c_2: 8
	s_8	5	9	10	8

Table 9.37 contains a data set using the digram balanced Latin square of Table 9.36 with two replicates (two cases per sequence). The analysis is most easily accomplished by entering data twice, once in a randomized-groups format with cases as an IV (cf. Table 9.12) and also in mixed-design format for AB and AC (cf. Table 9.24). Table 9.38 is the data of Table 9.37 rearranged into a randomized-groups format. In addition to the usual columns for A, B, C, and the DV is a column that codes for the level of C immediately preceding the current one, prior. For treatments at b_1, there are no prior treatments, so prior is coded 0. For treatments at other levels of B, prior reflects the level of C before it. Thus, for the two scores at a_1b_2, prior is 1; for the two scores at a_1b_3, prior is 2; and so forth to the two scores at a_4b_4 in which prior is 3.

The analysis is accomplished in three steps. The first is to use the data set as organized in Table 9.38 in a randomized-groups analysis for prior. The second step is to compute two mixed design ANOVAs, one for AB and one for AC on the data set arranged as in Table 9.24. The third step is to

TABLE 9.38 Data Set for Computer Analysis of a Changeover Design

Case	A	B	C	prior	score
1	1	1	1	0	7
2	1	1	1	0	6
1	1	2	2	1	9
2	1	2	2	1	10
1	1	3	4	2	7
2	1	3	4	2	5
1	1	4	3	4	6
2	1	4	3	4	8
3	2	1	2	0	5
4	2	1	2	0	7
3	2	2	3	2	7
4	2	2	3	2	6
3	2	3	1	3	9
4	2	3	1	3	12
3	2	4	4	1	11
4	2	4	4	1	12
5	3	1	3	1	3
6	3	1	3	1	4
5	3	2	4	3	6
6	3	2	4	3	5
5	3	3	2	4	7
6	3	3	2	4	5
5	3	4	1	2	10
6	3	4	1	2	9
7	4	1	4	0	5
8	4	1	4	0	5
7	4	2	1	4	7
8	4	2	1	4	9
7	4	3	3	1	8
8	4	3	3	1	10
7	4	4	2	3	8
8	4	4	2	3	8

combine them into a source table that reflects the effects of prior in addition to those of A, B, C, and $A \times B_{\text{adj}}$.

Step 1. Run a randomized-groups ANOVA for prior as shown in Table 9.39 using SAS GLM.

Step 2. Run two mixed-design ANOVAs, for AB and AC, as shown in Table 9.40.

Step 3. Combine the results into an ANOVA source table, as shown in Table 9.41.

TABLE 9.39   Randomized-Groups Analysis of Prior in a Changeover Design: SAS GLM Syntax and Selected Output

```
proc glm data=SASUSER.DIGRAM_R;
  class a b c prior;
  model score = a b c prior / ss3;
run;
```

Dependent Variable: SCORE

Source	DF	Sum of Squares	Mean Square	F Value	Pr > F
Model	13	140.1071429	10.7774725	9.07	<.0001
Error	18	21.3928571	1.1884921		
Corrected Total	31	161.5000000			

R-Square	Coeff Var	Root MSE	SCORE Mean
0.867536	14.78210	1.090180	7.375000

Source	DF	Type I SS	Mean Square	F Value	Pr > F
A	3	25.25000000	8.41666667	7.08	0.0024
B	3	59.25000000	19.75000000	16.62	<.0001
C	3	19.75000000	6.58333333	5.54	0.0071
PRIOR	4	35.85714286	8.96428571	7.54	0.0009

Source	DF	Type III SS	Mean Square	F Value	Pr > F
A	3	9.12229437	3.04076479	2.56	0.0873
B	3	33.94408676	11.31469559	9.52	0.0005
C	3	31.55411255	10.51803752	8.85	0.0008
PRIOR	4	35.85714286	8.96428571	7.54	0.0009

The second step is the routine analysis of a crossover design in which the effects of the variable of major interest, C, is "carved out of" the $A \times B$ interaction. In the changeover design, differences due to the prior treatment are also subtracted from the $A \times B$ interaction. Those sums of squares are computed from a randomized-groups run (at Step 1) where Type I and Type III sums of squares for nonorthogonality are available by default. As you recall from the discussion of unequal n in Chapter 5, when sources of variability in a design are not orthogonal, they have overlapping variability. This variability is removed with Type III because overlapping variability is discarded. (This is why the Type III sums of squares for A, B, and C at Step 1 do not match those of the runs in Step 2.) In the changeover design, `prior` is not orthogonal to A, B, and C, and, further, it contains differences due to the effects of A, B, and C as well as differences due to the prior treatment. Differences due to A, B, and C are removed by the Type III adjustment in Step 1, leaving just variability due to prior treatment. However, they are also removed in Type I SS because `prior` is the last listed effect

TABLE 9.40 Mixed-Design Analyses of *AB* and *AC* for a Changeover Design: SAS GLM Syntax and Selected Output

```
proc glm data=SASUSER.DIGRAM_F;
  class a;
  model b 1 b 2 b 3 b 4 = a;
  repeated b 4;
run;
```

The GLM Procedure

Repeated Measures Analysis of Variance Tests of Hypotheses for Between-Subjects Effects

Source	DF	Type III SS	Mean Square	F Value	Pr > F
A	3	25.25000000	8.41666667	5.39	0.0687
Error	4	6.25000000	1.56250000		

Repeated Measures Analysis of Variance Univariate Tests of Hypotheses for Within Subject Effects

						Adj Pr > F	
Source	DF	Type III SS	Mean Square	F Value	Pr > F	G-G	H-F
b	3	59.25000000	19.75000000	17.24	0.0001	0.0008	0.0001
b*A	9	57.00000000	6.33333333	5.53	0.0039	0.0113	0.0039
Error(b)	12	13.75000000	1.14583333				

```
proc glm data=SASUSER. DIGRAM_F;
  class a;
  model c 1 c 2 c 3 c 4 = a;
  repeated c 4;
run;
```

The GLM Procedure

Repeated Measures Analysis of Variance Tests of Hypotheses for Between-Subjects Effects

Source	DF	Type III SS	Mean Square	F Value	Pr > F
A	3	25.25000000	8.41666667	5.39	0.0687
Error	4	6.25000000	1.56250000		

The GLM Procedure

Repeated Measures Analysis of Variance Univariate Tests of Hypotheses for Within-Subject Effects

						Adj Pr > F	
Source	DF	Type III SS	Mean Square	F Value	Pr > F	G-G	H-F
c	3	19.75000000	6.58333333	5.75	0.0113	0.0267	0.0113
c*A	9	96.50000000	10.72222222	9.36	0.0003	0.0026	0.0003
Error(c)	12	13.75000000	1.14583333				

TABLE 9.41 Source Table for Analysis of a Changeover Design

Source	SS		df	MS	F
A	25.250	From Step 2 or Step 1 Type I SS	3	8.417	5.388
S/A	6.250	From Step 2	4	1.563	
B	59.250	From Step 2	3	19.750	17.234
C	19.750	From Step 2	3	6.583	5.744
Prior	35.857	From Step 1	4	8.964	7.822
$A \times B_{adj}$	1.393	$A \times B - C -$ Prior $57.000 - 19.750 - 35.857$	$9 - 3 - 4$ $= 2$	0.697	0.608
$B \times S/A$	13.750	From Step 2	12	1.146	
Total	161.500	From either Step 1 or 2	31		

in the $\mathtt{model}$. Sums of squares due to prior treatment are themselves analyzed and also subtracted from $A \times B$ to complete the analysis. Sums of squares for A should not be adjusted for other effects, so it is the Type I SS that are used (and that match the output for the other runs).

Another variant of the design permits tests of baseline effects when they are assessed between levels of treatment. Baseline measurements can be taken either before the first treatment and/or between treatments. A baseline measurement taken before the first treatment is best handled as a covariate. Baseline measures taken between treatments are discussed by Jones and Kenward (1989).

9.6 Some Important Issues

Issues surrounding basic Latin-square design and analysis are the usual issues of power, effect size, and specific comparisons. Missing data are also a problem because the balanced nature of the design is lost if some scores are lost. Tests of the assumption of sphericity are required in some repeated-measures applications, but the data set has to be arranged to produce the test. Then there are procedures for randomly generating the Latin squares themselves.

9.6.1 Sphericity in Repeated-Measures Designs

Repeated-measures ANOVA assumes that the variances of difference scores among all pairs of treatments are roughly equivalent (cf. Sections 6.3.2.3 and 6.6.2). The assumption is most often violated when treatments are confounded with time because DV pairs measured close together in time are more likely to have similar difference scores than DV pairs measured far apart in time. Because treatments in repeated-measures Latin-square designs are counterbalanced over time, a major source of violation of sphericity is eliminated. However, another potential source of violation of sphericity for treatment is variability in the similarity of treatments, as discussed in Sections 6.3.2.3 and 6.6.2. This possible source of violation should be considered in any repeated-measures design, including Latin square. Sphericity is tested if it is possible that the assumption is violated.

Omnibus tests of position effects in repeated-measures Latin squares are expected to violate sphericity since they are necessarily confounded with time. Position effects are not of interest in many applications and are included in the analysis only to reduce error variance. If position effects are of interest, the assumption of sphericity can be circumvented by use of a trend analysis (cf. Sections 6.3.2.3 and 6.6.2), an analysis that is often more appropriate than the omnibus test of position effects, in any event.

Should you wish to test sphericity, SAS, SPSS, and SYSTAT GLM do it as part of any repeated-measures design. However, the data arrangement of Table 9.12 and the analyses in Section 9.4.5 do not produce the test. Instead, the data are reorganized into the repeated-measures format of Table 9.24, in which all data for each case are entered on a single line. You can enter the data several ways: in either position or treatment order with the other IV created by transformation instructions, or in two separate data sets, one in each order, or with both orders in the same data set (as in Table 9.24). In any event, two repeated-measures analyses are then run, one for the position effect and one for the treatment effect, each with its own test of sphericity.

Table 9.42 shows the small-sample data of Table 9.4 reorganized into repeated-measures format in position order. A glance at the $A \times B$ matrix of Table 9.3 should help clarify the data file (recall that A is analogous to S in a repeated-measures Latin-square design).

Table 9.43 shows SPSS syntax and output for two repeated-measures analyses (one of position and one of treatment effects) with tests of sphericity for each. The IF statements create the treatment IV by defining level of treatment in terms of level of position. The remaining GLM instructions request two runs—the first for the effect of day (position) and the second for the effect of snow—in repeated-measures syntax (see Table 6.40). Case is part of the error term for both runs: case by day ($A \times B$) is the error term for the effect of position and case by snow ($A \times C$) is the error term for the effect of treatment. The remaining syntax is produced by the SPSS menu system for GLM Repeated Measures.

The tests for sphericity appear as Mauchly's Test of Sphericity. The Sig. value of Mauchly's test of .948 for DAY indicates no violation of sphericity for the position effect (an unusual result if the data were real). By Mauchly's test, there is also no violation of sphericity for SNOW.

If sphericity is violated, adjusted df are required (e.g., Huynh-Feldt) or the effect is interpreted from single degree-of-freedom comparisons, as discussed in Section 6.6.2. At this point, you have probably realized that simple repeated-measures Latin-square analysis can also be run either by the procedures of Section 9.4.5 or as two repeated-measures analyses with computation of the appropriate error term[8] and automatic tests for sphericity. MINITAB does not permit this second type of repeated-measures analysis.

TABLE 9.42   Small-Sample Data in Repeated-Measures Format for Test of Sphericity

CASE	b1 = MONDAY	b2 = WEDNESDAY	b3 = FRIDAY
1	4	9	1
2	1	6	7
3	8	2	5

[8]Both AB and AC analyses are run. $SS_{residual} = SS_{AB} - SS_C = SS_{AC} - SS_B$; similarly for df.

TABLE 9.43   Tests for Sphericity in Repeated-Measures Latin-Square Analysis: SPSS Syntax and Selected Output

```
IF(case eq 1) c1=b2.
IF(case eq 1) c2=b3.
IF(case eq 1) c3=b1.
IF(case eq 2) c1=b3.
IF(case eq 2) c2=b1.
IF(case eq 2) c3=b2.
IF(case eq 3) c1=b1.
IF(case eq 3) c2=b2.
IF(case eq 3) c3=b3.

GLM
 b1 b2 b3
 /WSFACTOR = day 3 Polynomial
 /MEASURE = time
 /METHOD = SSTYPE(3)
 /EMMEANS = TABLES(day)
 /CRITERIA = ALPHA(.05)
 /WSDESIGN
 /DESIGN .

GLM
 c1 c2 c3
 /WSFACTOR = snow 3 Polynomial
 /MEASURE = time
 /METHOD = SSTYPE(3)
 /EMMEANS = TABLES(snow)
 /CRITERIA = ALPHA(.05)
 /WSDESIGN
 /DESIGN .
```

(a) First run

Mauchly's Test of Sphericity[b]

Measure: TIME

Within Subjects Effect	Mauchly's W	Approx. Chi-Square	df	Sig.	Epsilon[a]		
					Greenhouse-Geisser	Huynh-Feldt	Lower-bound
DAY	.948	.053	2	.974	.951	1.000	.500

Tests the null hypothesis that the error covariance matrix of the orthonormalized transformed dependent variables is proportional to an identity matrix.

a. May be used to adjust the degrees of freedom for the averaged tests of significance. Corrected tests are displayed in the layers (by default) of the Tests of Within Subjects Effects table.

b.
   Design: Intercept
   Within Subjects Design: DAY

(continued)

TABLE 9.43   Continued

(b) Second run

Mauchly's Test of Sphericity[b]

Measure: TIME

Within Subjects Effect	Mauchly's W	Approx. Chi-Square	df	Sig.	Epsilon[a]		
					Greenhouse-Geisser	Huynh-Feldt	Lower-bound
SNOW	.360	1.022	2	.600	.610	1.000	.500

Tests the null hypothesis that the error covariance matrix of the orthonormalized transformed dependent variables is proportional to an identity matrix.

a. May be used to adjust the degrees of freedom for the averaged tests of significance.
   Corrected tests are displayed in the layers (by default) of the Tests of Within Subjects Effects table.

b.
   Design: Intercept
   Within Subjects Design: SNOW

9.6.2   Choosing a Latin Square

Statistical procedures for Latin-square analysis assume that the Latin square has been randomly chosen from a population of Latin squares. The number of squares in the population depends on the number of levels of C. The higher the number of levels, the larger the population of Latin squares that can be generated. A $2 \times 2 \times 2$ arrangement has only two possible Latin squares (c_1 first or c_2 first), a $3 \times 3 \times 3$ arrangement has 12 possible squares, a $4 \times 4 \times 4$ arrangement has 576 possible squares,[9] and so on. Therefore, generating all possible squares and randomly choosing among them rapidly becomes unwieldy. Some helpful shortcuts are available that start with a standard square and then permute rows, columns, and (possibly) levels of A.

A standard square is one in which both the first row and the first column contain levels of C in ordinal sequence, for example, c_1, c_2, c_3. The remaining elements can be in a variety of orders, but in the simplest (most standard?) one, levels of C continue in ordinal sequence and "wrap around." For example, the simplest $4 \times 4 \times 4$ Latin square is shown in Table 9.44.

This simplest standard square is highly undesirable because levels of C with higher numbers follow levels with lower numbers far too often. Therefore, rearrangement of rows and columns is needed. Several texts provide (more or less) detailed procedures for generating Latin squares by starting with a standard square, and then randomly permuting the rows, and then randomly permuting the columns, and then sometimes randomly redefining the levels of C. Myers and Well (1991) provide procedures that are easily followed. Winer and colleagues (1991) show how to generate orthogonal Latin squares, balanced sets of Latin squares, composite squares, and Greco-Latin squares as well.

---

[9]There are $c(c!)(c-1)!$ possible Latin squares for a $4 \times 4 \times 4$ design.

But the easiest way by far to generate random Latin squares is through appropriate software. SYSTAT DESIGN, NCSS Design of Experiments, and SAS PLAN have that capability. Table 9.45 shows SYSTAT DESIGN syntax and output for randomly generating a $5 \times 5 \times 5$ Latin square. The `SAVE` instruction requests that 25 runs (cells) be saved to a file named `L_DESIGN.SYD`. The `SQUARES` instruction requests that the Latin square itself be printed as output, and the `RAND` instruction requests that a random Latin square with five levels (`LEVELS = 5`) be generated. (It is also possible to request multiple replicates within each cell.)

In the output, B is called `Factor 2`, A is called `Factor 1`, and levels of C are (most confusingly) designated by capital letters inside the square. For example, the first level of B and the first level of A are associated with c_2, the first level of B and the third level of A are associated with c_4, and so on. If this is a repeated-measures Latin square, where case is represented by A and position by B, the first case receives levels of C in c_2, c_5, c_4, c_3, c_1 order.

Table 9.46 shows the output file saved by the instructions in Table 9.45.

TABLE 9.44   Simplest $4 \times 4 \times 4$ Latin Square

	b_1	b_2	b_3	b_4
a_1	c_1	c_2	c_3	c_4
a_2	c_2	c_3	c_4	c_1
a_3	c_3	c_4	c_1	c_2
a_4	c_4	c_1	c_2	c_3

TABLE 9.45   Generating a $5 \times 5 \times 5$ Latin-Square Design through SYSTAT: Syntax and Output

```
DESIGN
SAVE 'L_DESIGN.SYD'
LATIN / LEVELS=5 REPS=1 SQUARES RAND

  Latin-Square Design: 5 Factors, Each With 5 Levels

                 Factor 2
     Factor 1    1   2   3   4   5

            1    B   E   D   C   A
            2    A   D   B   E   C
            3    D   C   E   A   B
            4    E   A   C   B   D
            5    C   B   A   D   E
The design matrix has been saved.
```

**TABLE 9.46 SYSTAT Output
Produced by Syntax in Table 9.45**

RUN	X1	X2	X3
1	1	1	2
2	2	3	2
3	2	5	3
4	5	1	3
5	5	5	5
6	1	3	4
7	4	1	5
8	3	4	1
9	2	1	1
10	3	3	5
11	1	5	1
12	3	5	2
13	3	1	4
14	4	3	3
15	3	2	3
16	5	2	2
17	4	2	1
18	2	2	4
19	1	4	3
20	5	4	4
21	5	3	1
22	1	2	5
23	4	5	4
24	4	4	2
25	2	4	5

The output file shows the random order of "runs," (cells) where the X1 column is levels of A, the X2 column is levels of B, and the X3 column is levels of C. That is, the first run receives the a_1, b_1, c_2 combination and the last run receives the a_2, b_4, c_5 combination. If a column is added for the DV, the 25 treatment combinations are already appropriately organized as a data file for either a randomized-groups or repeated-measures Latin-square analysis, as shown in Section 9.4.5.

9.6.3 Power, Effect Size, and Relative Efficiency

A basic strategy for increasing power is decreasing the size of the error term in the F ratio. Repeated-measures Latin square analyzes the sum of squares for position effects (B) and subtracts them (and their df) from the error term ($A \times S$) that otherwise would be used for a one-way repeated-measures analysis. Although you can use a Latin-square arrangement to control position effects in a research study without analyzing them, this is likely to be unwise. If position effects are substantial, removing them from the error term enhances power. If position effects are "neutral" (neither larger nor smaller than their corresponding df for the error term as a whole), power is unaffected. Power is lower only when position effects are smaller than random error variability because, in this case, you subtract a very small sum of squares for position for each degree of freedom you lose from the error term. In a randomized-groups Latin square, power is enhanced by the inclusion (and subtraction from error variance) of nuisance variables (A and B).

The procedures described in Section 5.6.3 for calculating power and determining the number of cases apply here. The randomized-groups design is treated as a two-way layout and sample-size estimations typically are calculated only for treatment effects. However, estimates can be calculated for other effects as well, and the result used that calls for the largest sample size. Power for a repeated-measures design is calculated using the procedures of Section 6.6.3. Remember that the number of cases must be some multiple of the number of levels of C for a repeated-measures Latin-square design.

Effect size is reported either as η^2 or partial η^2, as described in Section 5.6.2 for randomized groups and Section 6.6.4 for repeated measures. Partial η^2 (Equation 5.14), as an estimate of effect size for snow condition (C) in the small-sample example, is

$$\text{Partial } \eta_C^2 = \frac{SS_C}{SS_C + SS_{\text{residual}}} = \frac{66.89}{66.89 + 0.88} = .99$$

Relative efficiency may be calculated for an unreplicated Latin-square design relative to either the randomized-groups design or the repeated-measures design (Kirk, 1995). Efficiency relative to the randomized-groups designs takes into account the nuisance variables, A and B, which do not occur in the one-way randomized-groups design. Thus, the error term in the Latin-square design should be reduced relative to a one-way design. However, the Latin-square design also generates fewer degrees of freedom; both differences are taken into account in Equation 9.15:

$$\text{Relative efficiency} = \frac{MS_{S/A}}{MS_{\text{residual}}} \left(\frac{df_{\text{residual}} + 1}{df_{\text{residual}} + 3} \right) \left(\frac{df_{S/A} + 3}{df_{S/A} + 3} \right) \tag{9.15}$$

The error term for the one-way randomized-groups design ($MS_{S/A}$) is found from a Latin-square data set by an analysis of the main effect of C, completely ignoring the existence of A and B, or by the following calculation:

$$MS_{S/A} = \frac{SS_T - SS_C}{N - c} \tag{9.16}$$

with $df_{S/A} = N - c$.

For the small-sample example of Table 9.7,

$$MS_{S/A} = \frac{71.56 - 66.89}{9 - 3} = 0.78$$

with $df_{S/A} = 6$, and

$$\text{Relative efficiency} = \frac{0.78}{0.44} \left(\frac{2 + 1}{2 + 3} \right) \left(\frac{6 + 3}{6 + 1} \right) = 1.37$$

Thus, error variance would be over 30% larger if the analysis had been done on a one-way randomized-groups design, with the nine cases randomly assigned to the three levels of A.

Efficiency with respect to a one-way repeated-measures design takes into account position effects, B. Recall that the repeated-measures design already takes into account A (cases), usually labeled S in a repeated-measures design. Thus, efficiency relative to a repeated-measures analysis is

$$\text{Relative efficiency} = \frac{\text{MS}_{AS}}{\text{MS}_{\text{residual}}} \left(\frac{\text{df}_{\text{residual}} + 1}{\text{df}_{\text{residual}} + 3} \right) \left(\frac{\text{df}_{AS} + 3}{\text{df}_{AS} + 1} \right) \tag{9.17}$$

where MS_{AS} is found by running the analysis as a one-way repeated-measures design (i.e., ignoring B) or Equation 9.18 if the data from a Latin square are used:

$$\text{MS}_{AS} = \frac{\text{SS}_T - \text{SS}_C - \text{SS}_A}{(c-1)^2} \tag{9.18}$$

with $\text{df}_{AS} = (c-1)^2$.

Treating the data from Table 9.7 of Section 9.4.3 as a repeated-measures design, then

$$\text{MS}_{AS} = \frac{71.56 - 66.89 - 0.23}{2(2)} = 1.11$$

with $\text{df}_{AS} = 4$, and

$$\text{Relative efficiency} = \frac{1.11}{0.44} \left(\frac{2+1}{2+3} \right) \left(\frac{4+3}{4+1} \right) = 2.12$$

Error variance is more than twice as large when the effect of position is ignored, indicating the advantage of including position effects in the analysis when the Latin-square design is implemented in the study.

9.6.4 Specific Comparisons

Procedures for comparisons differ for randomized-groups and repeated-measures Latin-square designs, just as they do for the ordinary randomized-groups and repeated-measures designs. The difference, as usual, is in the error terms for comparisons. The various forms of effect size also apply to Latin-square analyses.

9.6.4.1 Randomized-Groups Designs

Tests for specific comparisons are straightforward in randomized-groups Latin-square designs. A single error term is used for all comparisons: residual error if there are no replicates or the error term used in Section 9.5.1 if there are replicates. Procedures of Section 4.5.5 are followed for comparisons on marginal means of A, B, or C. Because these comparisons are usually post hoc, appropriate adjustments are made to control the error rate.

Say, for example, that after performing the small-sample randomized-groups Latin-square analysis, we are interested in the pairwise comparison between packed powder and icy conditions. The weighting coefficients we use for levels of C are 0, -1, 1; the corresponding means are 8.00, 1.33, and 5.00. The sample size for each of these means, n, is 3. Following Equation 4.10:

$$F = \frac{n\left(\sum w_j \overline{Y}_j\right)^2 / \sum w_j^2}{\text{MS}_{\text{residual}}} = \frac{3[(0)(8.00) + (-1)(1.33) + (1)(5.00)]^2 / [0^2 + (-1)^2 + 1^2]}{0.44}$$

$$= \frac{40.41/2}{0.44} = 45.91$$

(There is a lot of rounding error in this computation; computer output gives an F value of 45.38.)

Following Equation 4.15, Tukey-adjusted critical F for this pairwise comparison is

$$F_T = \frac{q_T^2}{2} = \frac{8.3^2}{2} = 34.45$$

where Table A.3 in Appendix A is used to find q_T with three means and 2 df for error. Obtained F is larger than critical F_T, so that this test shows a reliable difference in ski time between packed powder and ice.

Partial η^2 for this effect is formed by dividing the SS for the comparison by the sum of the SS for the comparison and the error term, residual.

$$\text{Partial } \eta^2 = \frac{\text{SS}_{\text{comp}}}{\text{SS}_{\text{comp}} + \text{SS}_{\text{residual}}} = \frac{40.41}{40.41 + 0.88} = .98$$

Such is the power of made-up data.

9.6.4.2 Repeated-Measures Designs

Specific comparisons in a repeated-measures Latin-square analysis are more complicated because each comparison requires a different error term, as in any repeated-measures analysis. This is most easily accomplished in a Latin-square analysis by subtracting position effects from each score, and then treating the adjusted data as a simple one-way repeated-measures design.

The position effect is found by subtracting the grand mean from the mean of B for each level. For the small-sample example, GM $= 4.78$, and the three position (DAY) totals are 13, 17, and 13, with means of 4.33, 5.67, and 4.33, respectively. Position effects are found by subtracting GM from the mean for each position:

b_1: $4.33 - 4.78 = -0.45,$

b_2: $5.67 - 4.78 = 0.89,$ and

b_3: $4.33 - 4.78 = -0.45.$

Thus, the effect of the first position, b_1, and the third position, b_3, is to lower scores by 0.45, whereas the effect of the second position, b_2, is to raise scores by 0.89. The nine scores in the $A \times B$ Latin-square

TABLE 9.47   Subtraction of Position Effects from $3 \times 3 \times 3$ Small-Sample Repeated-Measures Latin-Square Example

	b_1	b_2	b_3
a_1	$c_3 = 4 - (-0.45) = 4.45$	$c_1 = 9 - 0.89 = 8.11$	$c_2 = 1 - (-0.45) = 1.45$
a_2	$c_2 = 1 - (-0.45) = 1.45$	$c_3 = 6 - 0.89 = 5.11$	$c_1 = 7 - (-0.45) = 7.45$
a_3	$c_1 = 8 - (-0.45) = 8.45$	$c_2 = 2 - 0.89 = 1.11$	$c_3 = 5 - (-0.45) = 5.45$

arrangement of Table 9.4 are adjusted for these position effects, as shown in Table 9.47. Adjusted scores then are rearranged into treatment (C) order, as in the $A \times C$ arrangement of Table 9.4, as shown in Table 9.48.

This is now treated as the raw data matrix for a standard one-way repeated-measures analysis, with the exception that the degrees of freedom for error, $(a - 1)(c - 1)$, are reduced by 1, lost when position effects are estimated. Section 6.6.6.1.1 shows how to do specific comparisons for a one-way repeated-measures analysis. Effect size for repeated-measures designs is discussed in Section 6.6.4.

9.6.5   Missing Data

Davies (1963) provides a method for estimated missing data in an unreplicated Latin-square analysis that takes into account levels of all three of the IVs in estimating the missing value. The equation for a missing value, Y^*_{jkl}, is:

$$Y^*_{jkl} = \frac{a(A'_j + B'_k + C'_l) - 2T'}{(c - 1)(c - 2)} \tag{9.19}$$

where
$$\begin{aligned}
c &= \text{number of levels of } C \text{ (or } A \text{ or } B) \\
A'_j &= \text{sum of the known values for that level of } A \\
B'_k &= \text{sum of the known values for that level of } B \\
C'_l &= \text{sum of the known values for that level of } C \\
T' &= \text{sum of all known values}
\end{aligned}$$

Say, for example, that the final value in Table 9.4 is missing; that is, that $a_3b_3c_3$ (actually a 5 in the table) is unknown. The known values for the third level of C, 4 and 6, sum to 10 (see the diagonal in Table 9.4). The known values for the third level of B (the third column, 1 and 7) sum to 8, and the known values for the third level of A (the third row, 8 and 2) sum to 10. The sum of all of the known values is $4 + 9 + 1 + 1 + 6 + 7 + 8 + 2 = 38$. There are three levels of each of the IVs, so that $a = 3$, and

$$Y^*_{333} = \frac{3(10 + 8 + 10) - 2(38)}{(3 - 1)(3 - 2)} = \frac{8}{2} = 4$$

TABLE 9.48   Adjusted Scores in Treatment by Cases Matrix for 3 × 3 × 3 Small-Sample Repeated-Measures Latin-Square Example

	c_1	c_2	c_3
a_1	8.11	1.45	4.45
a_2	7.45	1.45	5.11
a_3	8.45	1.11	5.45

This value is inserted into the data and a normal analysis follows, except that one degree of freedom is subtracted from the error term to compensate for estimating the missing value.

Things get more complicated if there are several missing values. In a procedure described by Kirk (1995), all except one of the missing values is "guesstimated" (a reasonable guess based on other values in the data set). Then the remaining missing value is estimated using Equation 9.19. The estimated value is entered into the data set. Equation 9.19 then is applied to one of the "guesstimated" values, and so on until the values stabilize. One degree of freedom for error is deducted for imputing each missing value.

A more complex procedure has been described by Kempthorne (1952), which circumvents the slight positive bias produced by the procedure just described. Kirk (1995) illustrates this procedure.

9.7   Complete Examples of Latin-Square ANOVA

Section 9.7.1 provides an example of a randomized-groups Latin-square analysis, and Section 9.7.2 provides an example of a repeated-measures Latin-square analysis, each with different data sets.

9.7.1   Complete Example of 4 × 4 × 4 Randomized-Groups Latin-Square Analysis

Davies (1963) provides an industrial example in which there are four rubber-covered fabric samples evaluated in four positions of a wear tester. The third factor is the run number, because all four positions of the wear tester are run at the same time. Data sets are FABRIC.*. The goal is to evaluate differences in loss of weight (greater loss = more wear) in fabric samples (C) after a given number of cycles of abrasion with adjustments for position (B) and run number (A), the nuisance variables.

9.7.1.1   Evaluation of Assumptions

The design is fully experimental in that fabric samples are randomly assigned to positions within runs, and the Latin-square arrangement itself is randomly selected. Table 9.49 shows the Latin-square design and data matrix in $A \times B$ (position by run) format.

TABLE 9.49   Data for Complete Example of 4 × 4 × 4 Randomized-Groups Latin-Square ANOVA

	b_1	b_2	b_3	b_4
a_1	$c_2 = 218$	$c_4 = 236$	$c_1 = 268$	$c_3 = 235$
a_2	$c_4 = 227$	$c_2 = 241$	$c_3 = 229$	$c_1 = 251$
a_3	$c_1 = 274$	$c_3 = 273$	$c_2 = 226$	$c_4 = 234$
a_4	$c_3 = 230$	$c_1 = 270$	$c_4 = 225$	$c_2 = 195$

Some practical issues are difficult to assess because of the small sample sizes. Nevertheless, descriptive statistics are useful to evaluate distributions for each main effect.

9.7.1.1.1   Sample Sizes, Normality, Independence of Errors, and Homogeneity of Variance
Independence of errors is assured by the nature of the Latin-square design. Although all four positions are run together, dependence due to runs is eliminated from the error term by the nature of the analysis: Error is the residual variance after effects of position and run are subtracted. There are no missing data.

There are no replications within the 16 cells, so that $n = 1$ in this design. Normality of sampling distributions is questionable with sample sizes this small for tests of each effect. However, a standard measure such as loss of weight in fabric samples is unlikely to produce peculiar distributions in a population of trials.

Table 9.50 shows the descriptive statistics provided by the major SAS GLM run for the three main effects. Descriptive statistics (means and standard deviations) are requested by the `means` instruction. The `ss3` instruction limits the output to Type III sums of squares, which are identical to Type I sums of squares in this balanced design. The `output` instruction is a request for residuals, which are analyzed in Section 9.7.1.1.3. A Tukey HSD test is requested for later analysis in the second `means` instruction, in the form of a 99% confidence interval.

A glance at the standard deviations, particularly for levels of `FABRIC`, indicates serious violation of homogeneity of variance. With the largest variance $(s^2) = (21.00)^2 = 441.00$ and the smallest variance $= (5.32)^2 = 28.30$,

$$F_{max} = \frac{s^2_{largest}}{s^2_{smallest}} = \frac{441.00}{28.30} = 15.58$$

well in excess of the recommended ratio of 10 or less. Therefore, a variance stabilizing transformation of weight loss is considered.

Analyses with log, square root, and inverse transforms of `LOSS` are evaluated, but none of them produces acceptable homogeneity of variance. Therefore, the decision is made to retain the scores in their original form, but to use a more stringent $\alpha = .025$ for the test of fabric. The reliably smaller standard deviation of fabric 4 is also of substantive research interest and is discussed in the section interpreting the major analysis.

TABLE 9.50   Descriptive Statistics from SAS GLM Latin-Square Analysis: Syntax for Full Analysis and Selected Output

```
proc   glm data = SASUSER.FABRIC;
       class CASE POSITION FABRIC;
       model LOSS = CASE POSITION FABRIC / ss3;
       means CASE POSITION FABRIC;
       means CASE POSITION FABRIC / TUKEY CLDIFF ALPHA=.01;
       output  OUT=RESID P=PREDICT STUDENT=STDRESID;
run;
```

```
                   General Linear Models Procedure

          Level of          ----------LOSS----------
          CASE        N        Mean              SD

           1          4     239.250000      20.8706333
           2          4     237.000000      11.1952371
           3          4     251.750000      25.3294953
           4          4     230.000000      30.8220700

          Level of          ----------LOSS----------
          POSITION    N        Mean              SD

           1          4     237.250000      25.0249875
           2          4     255.000000      19.2006944
           3          4     237.000000      20.7364414
           4          4     228.750000      23.8100119

          Level of          ----------LOSS----------
          FABRIC      N        Mean              SD

           1          4     265.750000      10.1447852
           2          4     220.000000      19.2006944
           3          4     241.750000      20.9980158
           4          4     230.500000       5.3229065
```

9.7.1.1.2   *Outliers*

Outliers cannot be evaluated separately for each cell because there is only one score in each combination of *A, B,* and *C*. Therefore, they are evaluated with respect to marginal means. So, for example, the first score in the data matrix, $a_1 b_1 c_2 = 218$ is evaluated against the first mean of *A*, the first mean of *B*, and the second mean of *C*. By comparing with the second mean of *C*,

$$z = \frac{218 - 220.00}{19.20} = -0.10$$

Clearly, this is not an outlier. A check of the remaining values reveals no outliers in the data set.

9.7.1.1.3 Additivity

Additivity cannot be fully assessed in the absence of replications in each cell (cf. Section 9.5.1). Use of the residual error term in the analysis, therefore, contributes to loss of power if the assumption of additivity is violated. The interaction most destructive to interpretability is between position of abrading plates (*B*) and run (*A*) because this interaction is confounded with FABRIC. CASE (run number) represents unmeasured variations in temperature, humidity, and the like. Thus, there would be difficulty if some positions were more susceptible to environmental variation than others (e.g., if higher temperatures produced more wear in position 1 and lower temperatures produced more wear in position 2). This seems unlikely enough that threats to power are not considered consequential in this research.

As a partial test of additivity, SAS PLOT is used to find standardized residuals and predicted values, and plot them from the data set created in the syntax of Table 9.50. Figure 9.3 shows the syntax and output plot for this analysis.

```
proc plot DATA=RESID;
  plot STDRESID*PREDICT;
run
```

FIGURE 9.3   Standardized Residuals as a Function of Predicted Values: Syntax and Selected Output from SAS PLOT

The scatterplot shows no indication of a systematic relationship between predicted values and residuals, supporting the assumption of additivity. A linear relationship, either positive or negative, would indicate a nonadditivity problem.

9.7.1.2 *Analysis of 4 × 4 × 4 Randomized-Groups Latin-Square Design*

Table 9.51 shows the omnibus tests by SAS GLM for the major analysis (syntax is in Table 9.50).

All three effects are statistically reliable, using $\alpha = .05$ for CASE and POSITION, and $\alpha = .025$ for FABRIC. CASE is probably not of interest, reflecting only random fluctuation in environment conditions. Indeed, a look at the means in Table 9.50 over the four trials reveals no simple pattern. Differences among the four positions are known and presumably not of special interest in this research. Thus, CASE and POSITION are simply nuisance variables that might obscure differences among fabrics if not considered—but their significant variance attests to the importance of taking them out of the error term.

Differences among the four fabrics are highly reliable and considerable. Calculating partial η^2 as per Section 9.6.3,

$$\text{Partial } \eta_A^2 = \frac{\text{SS}_{\text{FABRIC}}}{\text{SS}_{\text{FABRIC}} + \text{SS}_{\text{residual}}} = \frac{4621.5}{4621.5 + 367.50} = .93$$

A Tukey test is applied to pairwise differences among the four fabrics, as described in Section 4.5.5.5.2. Here, the test is requested by the TUKEY CLDIFF ALPHA = .01 instruction in the

TABLE 9.51   Omnibus Tests from SAS GLM Latin-Square Analysis, Selected Output: Syntax Is in Table 9.50

General Linear Models Procedure

Dependent Variable: LOSS

Source	DF	Sum of Squares	Mean Square	F Value	Pr > F
Model	9	7076.50000000	786.27777778	12.84	0.0028
Error	6	367.50000000	61.25000000		
Corrected Total	15	7444.00000000			

R-Square	C.V.	Root MSE	LOSS Mean
0.950631	3.267740	7.8262379	239.50000000

Source	DF	Type III SS	Mean Square	F Value	Pr > F
CASE	3	986.50000000	328.83333333	5.37	0.0390
POSITION	3	1468.50000000	489.50000000	7.99	0.0162
FABRIC	3	4621.50000000	1540.50000000	25.15	0.0008

syntax of Table 9.50. (CLDIFF requests that the results of the Tukey test be presented as confidence intervals; alpha is set to .01 to compensate for heterogeneity of variance, more serious for comparisons than omnibus tests.) Table 9.52 shows the results of the pairwise comparisons only for FABRIC—the results for CASE and POSITION are also printed out but are not of current research interest.

Fabric 1 is reliably different from fabric 2 and fabric 4. There are no reliable differences among the remaining three fabrics: 2, 3, and 4. However, fabric 4 also shows the least variability in wear over the trials and positions (cf. Table 9.50).

Means and standard errors are plotted in Figure 9.4 for the four fabrics, as produced by SYSTAT.

Table 9.53 is a checklist for randomized-groups Latin-square ANOVA. An example of a Results section, in journal format, follows for the study described.

TABLE 9.52   Pairwise Comparison from SAS GLM Latin-Square Analysis, Selected Output: Syntax Is in Table 9.50

```
            Tukey's Studentized Range (HSD) Test for LOSS

    NOTE: This test controls the type I experimentwise error rate.

        Alpha                                     0.01
        Error Degrees of Freedom                     6
        Error Mean Square                        61.25
        Critical Value of Studentized Range    7.03327
        Minimum Significant Difference          27.522


  Comparisons significant at the 0.01 level are indicated by ***.

                      Difference       Simultaneous
            FABRIC     Between         99% Confidence
          Comparison    Means             Interval

        1    -3        24.000        -3.522    51.522
        1    -4        35.250         7.728    62.772    ***
        1    -2        45.750        18.228    73.272    ***
        3    -1       -24.000       -51.522     3.522
        3    -4        11.250       -16.272    38.772
        3    -2        21.750        -5.772    49.272
        4    -1       -35.250       -62.772    -7.728    ***
        4    -3       -11.250       -38.772    16.272
        4    -2        10.500       -17.022    38.022
        2    -1       -45.750       -73.272   -18.228    ***
        2    -3       -21.750       -49.272     5.772
        2    -4       -10.500       -38.022    17.022
```

```
>LINE LOSS*FABRIC / SERROR XLABEL='Fabric' YLABEL='Weight Loss'
```

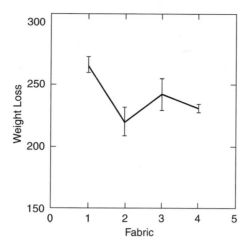

FIGURE 9.4   Mean Weight Loss of Four Abraded Fabrics

TABLE 9.53   Checklist for Randomized-Groups Latin-Square ANOVA

1. Issues
   a. Independence of errors
   b. Missing data
   c. Normality of sampling distributions
   d. Homogeneity of variance
   e. Outliers
   f. Additivity
2. Major analysis, when significant
   a. Effect size
   b. Parameter estimates (means and standard deviations or standard errors or confidence intervals for each group)
3. Additional analyses
   a. Post hoc comparisons
   b. Interpretation of departure from homogeneity of variance, if appropriate

---

Results

A four-level randomized-groups Latin-square analysis was performed on weight loss (in mg) of four fabrics after abrasion by
special-quality emery paper. The test machine consists of plates in
four different positions. There were four trials in which the fabrics were assigned to the different plate positions via a randomly
chosen Latin-square arrangement.

No outliers were observed; however, homogeneity of variance for
the test of differences among fabrics was violated (F_{max} = 15.58).
Transformations failed to produce acceptable homogeneity, so Type I
error rate for the test of fabrics was set to α = .025 and the untransformed values used. There was no evidence that main effects were confounded with interactions among the other two independent variables.

All three tests of effects were statistically reliable. Weight
loss differed by position of plate, F(3, 6) = 7.99, p < .02. Weight
loss also varied over the four trials, F(3, 6) = 5.37, p < .04. Most
important, weight loss differed among the four fabrics, F(3, 6) =
25.15, p < .001, partial η^2 = .93. Figure 9.4 shows means and standard errors for the amount of wear among the four fabrics.

A Tukey test at α = .01 revealed that fabric 1 was significantly worse than fabric 2 and fabric 4, with no reliable differences among fabrics 2, 3, and 4. Fabric 2 showed the least wear on
average; however, fabric 4 had the least variable degree of wear
and was not reliably worse than fabric 2. Therefore, fabric 4 is
the one of choice in terms of consistent resistance to abrasion.

9.7.2 Complete Example of a Repeated-Measures Crossover Design with Multiple Trials

Hirsch and Johnston (1996) tested whether the presence of a floral scent improved performance.
Twenty-one students participated in six trials in which they worked through a set of two paper and

pencil mazes. Participants wore floral scented masks on half the trials, either the first three trials or the last three trials (order randomly determined). The DV was length of time to complete each of the six trials. Data sets are SCENT.*.

Thus, in terms of the layout of the design, there is a single randomized-groups effect, order, and three repeated-measures effects: trial, position, and scent. Therefore, this is a $2 \times 3 \times 2 \times 2$ design overall. All cases in each level of order have the same sequence. The main effect of interest is the effect of scent (mask): Does it take less time to complete a maze in the presence of a floral scent? Position effects are also (mildly) interesting. Is there a carryover effect from the first set of trials to the second—does it take less time to complete the second set of mazes? Also, does order make a difference? Does it matter whether the first set of trials is with the scented or unscented mask?

The experimental nature of the design is assured by randomly assigning participants to orders. Table 9.54 diagrams the layout of the design (but not the analysis), with C = treatment, in which c_1 = unscented mask and c_2 = scented mask; P = first versus second set of trials (position); T = first, second, or third trial within each order; and O = order, where o_1 = unscented trials first and o_2 = scented trials first. Note that the P effect is equivalent to the C by O interaction.

Each case is entered on a separate line in the data set similar to the arrangement used in Table 9.23 (one case per line). One column is needed to code for order. Then, the six performance times for each case are entered in the following order: Unscented trial 1, Unscented trial 2, Unscented trial 3, Scented trial 1, Scented trial 2, and Scented trial 3. Note that the six DVs could also have been entered by their position instead of their scent. If the DVs are coded by scent, scent is tested as a main effect and the position effect is tested by the order $\times$ scent interaction. If the DVs are coded by position, position is tested as a main effect and the scent effect is tested by the order $\times$ position interaction. Because scent is the more important main effect, DVs are coded by scent.

9.7.2.1 Evaluation of Assumptions

Distributional assumptions are to be tested and outliers screened. However, homogeneity of covariance is not an issue for the three levels of trials because they are not of research interest by themselves. The other repeated-measures IVs, scent and position, have only two levels.

9.7.2.1.1 Sample Sizes, Normality, Independence of Errors, and Homogeneity of Variance
Independence of errors is assured by the (presumed) running of each of the participants individually in the randomized-groups part of the design (order effects) and by the use of appropriate error terms in which individual differences are eliminated in the repeated-measures part of the design.

Sample sizes are unequal between the two orders, with $n_1 = 11$ and $n_2 = 10$. This poses no problem with overlapping variance, as all of the sample sizes are equal within each level of order;

TABLE 9.54 Design for Complete Example of Crossover Design

Order	Cases	P_1			P_2		
		t_1	t_2	t_3	t_1	t_2	t_3
o_1	$n = 11$	c_1	c_1	c_1	c_2	c_2	c_2
o_2	$n = 10$	c_2	c_2	c_2	c_1	c_1	c_1

that is, there are no missing data. The inequality in sample sizes makes it slightly more complicated to calculate degrees of freedom for error, however, for evaluating normality of sampling distributions. There are $n_1 + n_2 - 2 = 19$ df for the test of the order effect, just short of assuring normality of sampling distributions for the randomized-groups part of the design. The trials effect is tested with $(n_1 + n_2 - 2)(t - 1) = 38$ df. The scent effect and the order by scent (position) effect are also both a bit deficient in df to assure normality, with df $= (n_1 + n_2 - 2)(o - 1) = 19$. However, none of these insufficiencies is great enough to cause distress as long as there is adequate homogeneity of variance and there are no outliers.

Homogeneity of variance is most directly evaluated by viewing the 12 cell standard deviations (not those labeled Total), as produced by SPSS GLM (Repeated Measures) in Table 9.55. The /WSFACTOR instruction sets up the repeated-measures factors, scents and trials, and requests that the underlying contrasts for the tests of repeated-measures factors be polynomial (default).

Homogeneity of variance is violated by the exceptionally large variance in the Unscented trial 3 data (scented first), with $F_{max} = (29.718)^2/(8.431)^2 = 12.42$. However, as shown in Table 9.56, a square root transformation of the DV (in this case, all six of them) reduces F_{max} to an acceptable level of 7.70. (Note that syntax includes a request for marginal means—/EMMEANS—for the main analysis as well as requests for effect size and power statistics—ETASQ and OPOWER.)

9.7.2.1.2   Outliers

Table 9.56 provides means and standard deviations to permit conversion of raw scores to z scores for testing for outliers in each of the 12 cells. There are no extreme values at $\alpha = .01$ (a reasonable criterion for this sample size) in the transformed data.

9.7.2.2   Analysis of Crossover Design

Table 9.56 shows the syntax for SPSS GLM for the major analysis. Note that it is not necessary to do a separate run for the position effect because it is equivalent to the scent by order interaction. Table 9.57 shows selected output for the omnibus effects marginal means.

The main effect of greatest interest, scent, is not statistically reliable: There is no evidence that performance is affected by the presence of a floral scent. Scent does, however, interact with trials. Thus, the only table of means reproduced here is the one for scents by trials.[10] The means are plotted in Figure 9.5.

The pattern of means suggests that the floral scent enhances performance on the first and third trials, but hinders it on the second trial. Simple effects analysis is required to verify these apparent differences. Table 9.58 shows SPSS GLM syntax and output for a simple effects analysis of scent at each level of trial. Note that scent and trials are defined as a single one-way repeated-measures IV. The comparison is within the SPECIAL matrix. The first row corresponds to the intercept. The next three rows correspond to the three comparisons of interest: scented versus unscented at trial 1, unscented versus scented at trial 2, and unscented versus scented at trial 3, respectively. The last two comparisons are not of current interest (they correspond to a trend analysis on the main effect of trials) but are included because the comparison matrix must be square—that is, the matrix must have the same number of rows as columns.

The contrasts of interest are labeled TRI_SCNT L1, L2, and L3 (for the three trials, respectively) in the output. The obtained F ratio for scents at the first trial is 8.63, $p = .008$; at the second trial, $F = 9.54, p = .006$; and at the third trial, $F = 1.44, p = .246$. (Remaining contrasts are not of interest.)

---

[10]The reliable interaction between order and trials is not of research interest.

**TABLE 9.55 Descriptive Statistics for Crossover Example:
SPSS GLM Syntax and Selected Output**

```
GLM
  unscent1 unscent2 unscent3 scent1 scent2 scent3 BY order
  /WSFACTOR = scents 2 Polynomial trials 3 Polynomial
  /MEASURE = time
  /METHOD = SSTYPE(3)
  /PRINT = DESCRIPTIVE
  /CRITERIA = ALPHA(.05)
  /WSDESIGN = scents trials scents*trials
  /DESIGN = order .
```

Descriptive Statistics

	Order of treatments	Mean	Std. Deviation	N
UNSCENT1	Unscented first	61.2455	19.8943	11
	Scented first	45.8700	8.7142	10
	Total	53.9238	17.1458	21
UNSCENT2	Unscented first	50.5455	15.6079	11
	Scented first	43.4700	10.2875	10
	Total	47.1762	13.5107	21
UNSCENT3	Unscented first	41.1636	10.4219	11
	Scented first	56.1800	29.7176	10
	Total	48.3143	22.6004	21
SCENT1	Unscented first	51.3455	18.8993	11
	Scented first	46.3000	10.4268	10
	Total	48.9429	15.3030	21
SCENT2	Unscented first	54.8818	16.5190	11
	Scented first	56.2500	12.2661	10
	Total	55.5333	14.3051	21
SCENT3	Unscented first	39.5818	8.4312	11
	Scented first	47.4400	11.8875	10
	Total	43.3238	10.7381	21

A Bonferroni adjustment is made for these comparisons, in which the number of comparisons (3) affects the critical probability level. To keep familywise error rate at .05, $\alpha_i = .05/3 = .017$. This adjustment does not affect the results; the floral scent enhances performance on the first trial (partial $\eta^2 = .312$), hinders it on the second trial (partial $\eta^2 = .334$), and does not affect it on the third trial.

There is also no statistically reliable main effect of order; there is no difference in performance between participants who are first exposed to the floral scent and participants who first experience no scent. Nor is the scent by order interaction significant, indicating a lack of position effect. That is, there is no evidence that performance on the second set of three trials is any different from performance on the first set of three trials.

TABLE 9.56 Descriptive Statistics for Crossover Example with Square Root Transformation: SPSS GLM Syntax and Selected Output

```
GLM
 s_u1 s_u2 s_u3 s_s1 s_s2 s_s3 BY order
 /WSFACTOR = scents 2 Polynomial trials 3 Polynomial
 /MEASURE = time
 /METHOD = SSTYPE(3)
 /EMMEANS = TABLES(order)
 /EMMEANS = TABLES(scents)
 /EMMEANS = TABLES(trials)
 /EMMEANS = TABLES(order*scents)
 /EMMEANS = TABLES(order*trials)
 /EMMEANS = TABLES(scents*trials)
 /EMMEANS = TABLES(order*scents*trials)
 /PRINT = DESCRIPTIVE ETASQ OPOWER
 /CRITERIA = ALPHA(.05)
 /WSDESIGN = scents trials scents*trials
 /DESIGN = order.
```

Descriptive Statistics

	Order of treatments	Mean	Std. Deviation	N
S_U1	Unscented first	7.7281	1.2941	11
	Scented first	6.7451	.6440	10
	Total	7.2600	1.1301	21
S_U2	Unscented first	7.0284	1.1231	11
	Scented first	6.5530	.7660	10
	Total	6.8020	.9767	21
S_U3	Unscented first	6.3655	.8414	11
	Scented first	7.3011	1.7871	10
	Total	6.8110	1.4214	21
S_S1	Unscented first	7.0558	1.3103	11
	Scented first	6.7645	.7761	10
	Total	6.9171	1.0732	21
S_S2	Unscented first	7.3260	1.1542	11
	Scented first	7.4588	.8276	10
	Total	7.3893	.9894	21
S_S3	Unscented first	6.2576	.6834	11
	Scented first	6.8336	.9081	10
	Total	6.5319	.8316	21

TABLE 9.57 Selected Output from SPSS GLM Crossover Analysis: SYNTAX Is in Table 9.56

General Linear Model

Tests of Within-Subjects Effects

Measure: TIME

Source		Type III Sum of Squares	df	Mean Square	F	Sig.	Eta Squared	Noncent. Parameter	Observed Power[a]
SCENTS	Sphericity Assumed	5.440E-04	1	5.440E-04	.002	.968	.000	.002	.050
	Greenhouse-Geisser	5.440E-04	1.000	5.440E-04	.002	.968	.000	.002	.050
	Huynh-Feldt	5.440E-04	1.000	5.440E-04	.002	.968	.000	.002	.050
	Lower-bound	5.440E-04	1.000	5.440E-04	.002	.968	.000	.002	.050
SCENTS * ORDER	Sphericity Assumed	.772	1	.772	2.291	.147	.108	2.291	.301
	Greenhouse-Geisser	.772	1.000	.772	2.291	.147	.108	2.291	.301
	Huynh-Feldt	.772	1.000	.772	2.291	.147	.108	2.291	.301
	Lower-bound	.772	1.000	.772	2.291	.147	.108	2.291	.301
Error(SCENTS)	Sphericity Assumed	6.400	19	.337					
	Greenhouse-Geisser	6.400	19.000	.337					
	Huynh-Feldt	6.400	19.000	.337					
	Lower-bound	6.400	19.000	.337					
TRIALS	Sphericity Assumed	4.322	2	2.161	5.269	.010	.217	10.539	.804
	Greenhouse-Geisser	4.322	1.870	2.312	5.269	.011	.217	9.852	.783
	Huynh-Feldt	4.322	2.000	2.161	5.269	.010	.217	10.539	.804
	Lower-bound	4.322	1.000	4.322	5.269	.033	.217	5.269	.587
TRIALS * ORDER	Sphericity Assumed	10.535	2	5.267	12.843	.000	.403	25.686	.995
	Greenhouse-Geisser	10.535	1.870	5.635	12.843	.000	.403	24.012	.993
	Huynh-Feldt	10.535	2.000	5.267	12.843	.000	.403	25.686	.995
	Lower-bound	10.535	1.000	10.535	12.843	.002	.403	12.843	.925
Error(TRIALS)	Sphericity Assumed	15.585	38	.410					
	Greenhouse-Geisser	15.585	35.523	.439					
	Huynh-Feldt	15.585	38.000	.410					
	Lower-bound	15.585	19.000	.820					

(continued)

TABLE 9.57 Continued

Measure: TIME

Tests of Within-Subjects Effects (continued)

Source		Type III Sum of Squares	df	Mean Square	F	Sig.	Eta Squared	Noncent. Parameter	Observed Power[a]
SCENTS * TRIALS	Sphericity Assumed	5.776	2	2.888	7.274	.002	.277	14.549	.917
	Greenhouse-Geisser	5.776	1.720	3.359	7.274	.004	.277	12.509	.883
	Huynh-Feldt	5.776	1.974	2.926	7.274	.002	.277	14.360	.914
	Lower-bound	5.776	1.000	5.776	7.274	.014	.277	7.274	.725
SCENTS * TRIALS * ORDER	Sphericity Assumed	1.788	2	.894	2.252	.119	.106	4.504	.430
	Greenhouse-Geisser	1.788	1.720	1.040	2.252	.128	.106	3.873	.395
	Huynh-Feldt	1.788	1.974	.906	2.252	.120	.106	4.445	.427
	Lower-bound	1.788	1.000	1.788	2.252	.150	.106	2.252	.297
Error(SCENTS * TRIALS)	Sphericity Assumed	15.087	38	.397					
	Greenhouse-Geisser	15.087	32.674	.462					
	Huynh-Feldt	15.087	37.508	.402					
	Lower-bound	15.087	19.000	.794					

a. Computed using alpha = .05

Tests of Between-Subjects Effects

Measure: TIME
Transformed Variable: Average

Source	Type III Sum of Squares	df	Mean Square	F	Sig.	Eta Squared	Noncent. Parameter	Observed Power[a]
Intercept	6074.864	1	6074.864	1264.331	.000	.985	1264.331	1.000
ORDER	9.704E-03	1	9.704E-03	.002	.965	.000	.002	.050
Error	91.291	19	4.805					

a. Computed using alpha = .05

TABLE 9.57   Continued

Estimated Marginal Means

6. SCENTS * TRIALS

Measure: TIME

SCENTS	TRIALS	Mean	Std. Error	95% Confidence Interval	
				Lower Bound	Upper Bound
1	1	7.237	.227	6.762	7.711
	2	6.791	.212	6.347	7.234
	3	6.833	.300	6.205	7.461
2	1	6.910	.238	6.412	7.409
	2	7.392	.221	6.929	7.855
	3	6.546	.174	6.181	6.910

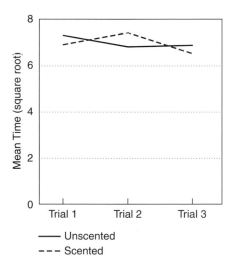

**FIGURE 9.5   Square Root of Mean Time to Solve Mazes over Three
Trials with Scented and Unscented Mask**

Some other statistically reliable effects are noted, but they are not of current research interest: a main effect of trials (which occurs within scent conditions), modified by a trials by order interaction. These findings might be investigated with a strict adjustment for post hoc testing or follow-up research might be designed to verify these effects were they of interest.

Table 9.59 is a checklist for repeated-measures Latin-square ANOVA. An example of a Results section, in journal format, follows for the study described.

TABLE 9.58   SPSS GLM Syntax and Selected Output for Simple-Effects Analysis of Scents at Each Trial

```
GLM
s_u1 s_s1 s_u2 s_s2 s_u3 s_s3 BY order
/WSFACTOR = tri_scnt 6
SPECIAL (1  1  1  1  1  1
         1 −1  0  0  0  0
         0  0  1 −1  0  0
         0  0  0  0  1 −1
        −1  0  1  0  1 −1
         1 −2  1  1 −2  1)

/MEASURE = time
/METHOD = SSTYPE(3)
/PRINT = ETASQ OPOWER
/CRITERIA = ALPHA(.05)
/WSDESIGN = tri_scnt
/DESIGN = order .
```

Tests of Within-Subjects Contrasts

Measure: TIME

Source	TRI_SCNT	Type III Sum of Squares	df	Mean Square	F	Sig.	Eta Squared	Noncent. Parameter	Observed Power[a]
TRI_SCNT	L1	2.233	1	2.233	8.631	.008	.312	8.631	.796
	L2	7.586	1	7.586	9.543	.006	.334	9.543	.834
	L3	1.735	1	1.735	1.436	.246	.070	1.436	.207
	L4	35.014	1	35.014	28.897	.000	.603	28.897	.999
	L5	4.796	1	4.796	.860	.365	.860	.860	.143
TRI_SCNT * ORDER	L1	2.505	1	2.505	9.684	.006	.338	9.684	.839
	L2	1.937	1	1.937	2.437	.135	.114	2.437	.317
	L3	.677	1	.677	.560	.463	.029	.560	.110
	L4	4.735	1	4.735	3.908	.063	.171	3.908	.467
	L5	21.754	1	21.754	3.900	.063	.170	3.900	.466
Error(TRI_SCNT)	L1	4.915	19	.259					
	L2	15.103	19	.795					
	L3	22.956	19	1.208					
	L4	23.021	19	1.212					
	L5	105.971	19	5.577					

a. Computed using alpha = .05

TABLE 9.59   Checklist for Repeated-Measures or Crossover Latin-Square ANOVA

1. Issues
   a. Missing data
   b. Normality of sampling distributions
   c. Homogeneity of variance
   d. Outliers
   e. Independence of errors/additivity/homogeneity of covariance/sphericity
2. Major analyses, when significant
   a. Effect size
   b. Parameter estimates (means and standard errors or standard deviations or confidence intervals for each group)
3. Additional analyses
   a. Post hoc comparisons
   b. Interpretation of departure from homogeneity of variance if appropriate

---

```
                            Results

     A repeated-measures crossover design was used to investigate
the effect of a floral scent on speed of solving mazes. Partici-
pants worked through a set of two paper and pencil mazes six
times, three times while wearing a floral scented mask and three
times while wearing an unscented mask. Participants were randomly
assigned to wear the floral mask on either their first three tri-
als (n = 10) or their second three trials (n = 11). The dependent
variable was time to complete each maze. Independent variables
were the two types of mask, three trials, and two orders of sets
of trials. The interaction between type of mask and order indi-
cates the effect of position (first vs. second set of trials).

     No outliers were observed, however, there was marked hetero-
geneity of variance (Fmax = 12.42). A square root transform of
solution times reduced the heterogeneity to an acceptable level.
```

There was no statistically reliable main effect of type of mask; that is, there was no evidence that the floral scent affected performance. However, there was a significant interaction between type of mask and trials, $F(2, 38) = 7.27$, $p = .002$, as shown in Figure 9.5. Means, standard errors, and 95% confidence intervals for the six combinations of masks and trials are in Table 9.57 [*last table of output*]. A simple effects test with Bonferroni adjustment showed a significant decrease in square root of time to solve mazes while wearing the scented mask (mean = 6.91) as compared with the unscented mask (mean = 7.24) on the first trial, $F(1, 19) = 8.63$, $p = .008$, partial $\eta^2 = .31$. The opposite relation occurred on the second trial. There was a significant increase in square root of time to solve the mazes while wearing the scented mask (mean = 7.39) as compared with the unscented mask (mean = 6.79) on the second trial, $F(1, 19) = 9.54$, $p = .006$, partial $\eta^2 = .33$. There was no reliable difference between types of mask on the third trial, $p > .017$.

There was no reliable effect of position (first vs. second set of trials), as tested by the type of mask by order interaction, $p > .05$.

9.8   Comparison of Programs

SAS, SPSS, SYSTAT, and MINITAB each have one program best suited to Latin-square analysis, whether randomized groups or repeated measures. Table 9.60 reviews features of these programs especially relevant to randomized-groups Latin-square designs. Other features of the programs that may be applied to the design appear in Chapter 5.

Table 9.61 reviews features of the programs especially relevant to repeated-measures Latin-square designs when homogeneity of covariance is of concern. Other features of the programs that may be applied to the design appear in Chapters 6 and 7.

9.8.1   The SPSS Package

In the SPSS Windows menu, general factorial GLM (UNIANOVA) analyzes Latin-square designs in the randomized-groups format, and repeated-measures GLM analyzes Latin-square designs in the repeated-measures format. The programs provide all the basics for Latin-square analysis with the exception of marginal standard deviations for testing homogeneity of variance that must be found

TABLE 9.60   Comparison of SPSS, SYSTAT, MINITAB, and SAS Programs for Randomized-Groups Latin-Square ANOVA

Feature	SPSS GLM	SAS GLM	SYSTAT GLM	MINITAB GLM
Input				
Use model instruction to specify main effects only	No	Yes	Yes	Yes
Other instructions to specify main effects only	DESIGN	No	No	No
Request marginal means and standard deviations for each IV	EMMEANS[a]	MEANS	No	MEANS
Output				
User-specified contrasts	Yes[b]	Yes	Yes	No
Post hoc tests (see Sections 4.7 and 5.7 for details)	Yes	Yes	No	Yes
Predicted values and residuals	Yes	No	No	No
Saved files				
Predicted values and residuals	Yes	Yes	Yes	Yes

[a]Common standard error rather than individual standard deviations.

[b]Confidence intervals, syntax only if other than trend analysis.

through the descriptive statistics program. Predicted values and residuals may be printed as well as saved to a file, which then may be used to plot them.

9.8.2   The SAS System

SAS GLM is used for all sorts of Latin-square analyses, no matter what the format. Predicted values and residuals are saved to file, and may be plotted. The basic Latin-square analysis may be done in repeated-measures format; however, there is no provision for user-specified comparisons or post hoc tests. Performing these tests under the randomized-groups format produces erroneous error terms for a repeated-measures design. SAS PLAN allows you to generate Latin squares and, for a randomized-groups design, a sequence of runs.

9.8.3   The SYSTAT System

SYSTAT GLM also analyzes Latin-square designs in either randomized-groups or repeated-measures format. User-specified comparisons are available for both formats; however, post hoc tests are

TABLE 9.61 Comparison of SPSS, SYSTAT, MINITAB, and SAS Programs for Repeated-Measures Latin-Square ANOVA

Feature	SPSS GLM	SAS GLM	SYSTAT GLM	MINITAB GLM
Input				
Data may be in either randomized-groups or repeated-measures format	Yes	Yes	Yes	No
Request treatment/position means and standard deviations	EMMEANS	MEAN	No	Yes
Output				
Tests and/or adjustments for homogeneity of covariance (see Section 6.7 for details)	Yes	Yes	Yes	No
User-specified contrasts with repeated-measures format[a]	Yes[b]	No	Yes	N.A.

[a]Requires data matrix of adjusted scores, cf. Section 9.5.6.2.

[b]Confidence intervals, syntax only if other than trend analysis.

unavailable. Predicted values and residuals are saved to file for plotting. Programs for descriptive statistics are required for marginal means and standard deviations. SYSTAT DESIGN generates random Latin-square arrangements and provides a random sequence of runs for randomized-groups setups (cf. Section 9.6.2).

9.8.4 MINITAB Programs

MINITAB GLM treats a Latin square as any other ANOVA, with the Latin-square arrangement indicated by the lack of interactions in the listing of terms in the model equation. Lack of a repeated-measures capability means that data for a repeated-measures Latin square, just as any repeated-measures design, must be in the format of one score per line. This also means that no tests or indications of sphericity are available. Marginal means and post hoc tests are available. However, user-specified comparisons in MINITAB require columns of contrast coefficients in the data set, as always. Residuals may be saved to file.

9.9   Problem Sets

9.1 Do a randomized-groups Latin-square analysis on the following data set. Assume that A is assembler experience, B is assembly-room temperature, and C is four types of assembly procedures. The DV is quality of finished computer.

	b_1	b_2	b_3	b_4
a_1	$c_1 = 5$	$c_2 = 7$	$c_3 = 8$	$c_4 = 10$
a_2	$c_2 = 3$	$c_4 = 7$	$c_1 = 2$	$c_3 = 5$
a_3	$c_3 = 11$	$c_1 = 8$	$c_4 = 11$	$c_2 = 10$
a_4	$c_4 = 13$	$c_3 = 10$	$c_2 = 9$	$c_1 = 9$

a. Evaluate assumptions of normality of sampling distributions, independence of errors, and homogeneity of variance.
b. Do the analysis using the traditional approach.
c. Do the analysis using the regression approach.
d. Provide a source table.
e. Calculate effect size(s).
f. Write a Results section for the analysis.
g. List an appropriate follow-up procedure.

9.2 Analyze the following data set as a crossover design. Assume that A is sequence, B is position or trial, and C is treatment (four types of aircraft-speed indicators). The cases are pilots. The DV is accuracy of reading in a short-duration exposure.

Sequence	b_1	b_2	b_3	b_4
a_1	c_1	c_2	c_3	c_4
a_2	c_3	c_1	c_4	c_2
a_3	c_2	c_4	c_1	c_3
a_4	c_4	c_3	c_2	c_1

Sequence		b_1	b_2	b_3	b_4
a_1	s_1	1	9	3	10
	s_2	3	8	3	10
a_2	s_3	2	1	9	10
	s_4	1	2	7	10
a_3	s_5	8	8	1	4
	s_6	6	6	3	5
a_2	s_7	7	4	9	2
	s_8	7	3	10	3

    a. Do the analysis using the mixed-design repeated-measures format.

    b. Check results by running them through at least one canned computer program.

    c. Evaluate all appropriate assumptions using computer programs where necessary.

    d. Provide a source table with appropriate error term.

    e. Calculate effect size(s).

    f. Write a Results section for the analysis.

    g. Use one of the canned computer programs to run a trend analysis on the position effect.

9.3 Use a canned program to analyze the following data for the following incomplete blocks design. Data are shown in the following Youden square, where C is snow condition (powder, packed powder, ice, and artificial snow), and B and A are defined as in the small-sample example of Section 9.4.3. (Note there now are four cases, but each one skis only three runs.)

	b_1	b_2	b_3
a_1	$c_1 = 9$	$c_2 = 1$	$c_3 = 4$
a_2	$c_2 = 1$	$c_4 = 6$	$c_1 = 7$
a_3	$c_3 = 5$	$c_1 = 8$	$c_4 = 5$
a_4	$c_4 = 4$	$c_3 = 5$	$c_2 = 2$

    a. Use the setup of Table 9.12 for entering data for the canned computer program (assume position effects are not of interest).

    b. Provide a source table.

    c. Calculate effect size(s).

    d. Write a Results section for the analysis.

    e. List an appropriate follow-up procedure.

9.4 Find relative efficiency for the following:

    a. The randomized-groups design in Problem 9.1.

    b. The same design assuming it was a repeated-measures Latin square (i.e., A representing cases).

CHAPTER

10 Screening and Other Incomplete Designs

10.1 General Purpose and Description

Screening designs, like Latin-square designs, test numerous main effects that are deliberately confounded with interactions in order to reduce the number of cases required for the study. As "screening" implies, these designs are appropriate for pilot studies in which the researcher has a long list of potentially effective IVs and inadequate information regarding which are important. The results identify important IVs and tell the researcher which ones to omit in future studies. A second application is when a researcher only needs a "quick-and-dirty" answer to a research question. A third application is when there are very few cases available (for reasons of expense, rarity, or whatever) and the researcher wants the most information from the fewest cases. Except for human factors research, these designs have not been used extensively in the social sciences.

For example, a researcher is uncertain about the factors that affect the outcome of a new therapy. Is it the duration of therapy (4 weeks or 8 weeks)? Is it the concentration of sessions (one a week or three a week)? Is it the training level of the therapist (professional or paraprofessional)? Is it the setting in which therapy is delivered (office or clinic)? Is it the privacy of therapy (one-on-one or group)? Five IVs are identified, each with two levels. A complete factorial randomized-groups study of these IVs has $2^5 = 32$ cells, each with a different combination of research conditions. The design requires 64 cases with only two cases per cell—96 cases if there are three per cell, and so on.

However, it is possible to run the study with far fewer cases by giving up analysis of some of the interactions. For example, 32 cases can provide preliminary tests of all five main effects plus all of the two-way interactions. This is accomplished by confounding all of the three-way and higher-order interactions with main effects and the two-way interactions. Screening designs are also available in which some or all two-way interactions are confounded with main effects, as they are in Latin-square designs; for some designs, this reduces the number of cases even more (e.g., from 32 to 8 with the current example). Use of these designs, then, is a good strategy if you have a long list of factors that might affect your outcome and want an efficient way to screen out the unimportant ones. Screening designs let you identify the most important effects to use in future research or focus efforts at improving the quality of your product.

There are numerous types of screening and other incomplete designs, some available for qualitative IVs and others when the IVs are quantitative. Two major designs for qualitative IVs are fractional-factorial designs and a special case of them, the Plackett-Burman designs. In fractional-factorial designs, some or all two-way interactions can be made available for analysis. The number of interactions that can be tested depends on the number of cases; when more cases are run, more unconfounded interactions can be evaluated. Plackett-Burman designs test no interactions, so, of course, they require the fewest number of cases. Taguchi procedures incorporate many of these same designs but emphasize the stability of the DV under different conditions, effect size rather than significance testing for evaluation of IVs, and identification of the best combination of levels of IVs.

The example has both qualitative (e.g., setting for therapy) and quantitative (e.g., duration of therapy) IVs, but each with two levels. If a fractional-factorial design with 32 cases is used, the main effects of all five IVs are tested in addition to all of the two-way interactions. If a Plackett-Burman design is used, only the main effects of the IVs are tested. If a Taguchi approach is taken, the combination of levels of IVs that produces the most stable and best outcome is emphasized.

Other screening designs are used with quantitative IVs or IVs that are blends of two or more factors. Box-Behnken designs, for instance, are used for quantitative IVs with three levels each and permit tests of linear and quadratic trends of main effects and linear trends of two-way interactions. Central-composite designs are similar to Box-Behnken designs but are used for quantitative IVs with five levels each. Mixture designs are used when conditions are blends of two (or more) IVs (e.g., a class that is 100% lecture versus a class that is 50% lecture and 50% discussion, versus a class that is 100% discussion); that is, the levels are proportions. The primary goal with mixture designs is to find the optimal mix (blend) of IVs rather than to see if IVs are statistically significant. Finally, optimal design methods are available that search for the best design when none of the other specific designs is appropriate to your needs.

Major disadvantages of these incomplete designs, like Latin-square designs, are forfeiture of tests of at least some interactions and the implicit assumption that confounded interactions are negligible. With so few cases, the stability of the DV and the representativeness of the cases are also important. Remember that screening designs are usually just that—preliminary studies to help you design the "real" study. They typically do not provide final answers.

10.2   Kinds of Research Questions

The major question to be answered by most screening and other incomplete designs is whether main effects of IVs are associated with mean differences on the DV. Some designs also permit evaluation of some interactions among treatments.

10.2.1   Effects of the IVs

Are there reliable mean differences between levels of any of the IVs? When the effects of one IV are averaged over the levels of all other IVs, and when extraneous variables are held constant by procedures discussed in Sections 1.1, 1.2.1, and elsewhere, are there mean differences in the DV associated with the levels of an IV? For example, does the average therapeutic outcome depend on the duration of therapy? On the concentration of sessions per week? On the training level of the therapist? On the setting in which therapy is delivered? Or on the privacy with which therapy is delivered? These questions are usually answered by applying separate F tests to each IV, as demonstrated in Section 10.4. Taguchi methods (Section 10.5.4), however, use different procedures.

10.2.2   Effects of Interactions among IVs

Some fractional-factorial designs permit questions about some interactions. Holding all else constant, does outcome for one IV depend on the level of another IV? For example, does the effect of concentration of sessions per week depend on the duration of therapy?

Tests of interactions are also F tests, conducted separately for each interaction. However, you will rarely be able to test 3-way, 4-way, or higher-order interactions, no matter how many cases you have. Higher-order interactions are almost always confounded with main effects or lower-order interactions in these designs and are lost to analysis.

10.2.3   Parameter Estimates

Parameter estimates are sample means, standard deviations, and standard errors or confidence intervals for levels of an IV used to estimate values in a population. Because screening designs are rarely the end in themselves, but are used instead to design future studies, population values are rarely estimated from them. Rather, these statistics provide information about the outcome in different levels of an IV and are used to evaluate the wisdom of including the IV in future studies.

Some fractional factorials provide tests of some interactions and parameter estimates for interactions are described in Chapter 5. However, unequal n is often built into the screening designs. As you recall, there are different ways to average over other IVs when sample sizes arc not the same for all cells, as discussed in Section 5.6.5.

Some incomplete designs (e.g., mixture designs) use the regression approach to ANOVA and emphasize prediction equations rather than comparisons among means. Parameter estimates for these designs are typically unstandardized regression coefficients (B weights).

10.2.4   Effect Sizes and Power

Effect size represents the proportion of variance in the DV that is predictable from a main effect or interaction. Effect size for an IV in a screening design is often used primarily to determine the wisdom of including that IV in subsequent research. However, screening designs typically do not generate a great deal of power; few cases are run so power is low and large effects are sought, so a great deal of power is unnecessary.

10.2.5   Specific Comparisons

Because each IV has only two levels in many screening designs, specific comparisons of marginal means are not relevant. The only type of comparison that might be helpful is a simple main effect in a design with a significant interaction, as illustrated in Section 5.6.4.4.1. However, Box-Behnken and central-composite designs, as well as some Taguchi, fractional-factorial, and optimal designs, have more than two levels of at least some IVs (Section 10.5.5), so comparisons may be appropriate. In fact, Box-Behnken and central-composite designs apply to quantitative IVs and have trend analyses and interactions contrasts built into the model. These comparisons are identical to those in Section 5.6.4.

10.3   Assumptions and Limitations

10.3.1   Theoretical Issues

Issues of causal inference and generalizability are identical to those in any other analysis of variance. However, because of the small number of cases tested in screening designs, the stability of the DV and the representativeness and homogeneity of the cases are especially important. If there is a great deal of error in measuring the DV, you are unlikely to demonstrate statistical significance with such a small sample. Further, if cases are heterogeneous, and only a few cases are used to evaluate the IVs, the precise characteristics of the cases assigned to each level may determine the outcome of evaluation of the IV. This is always true, of course, but with larger samples, case differences are expected to cancel each other more effectively than with such small samples. These factors combine to argue against the utility of screening and incomplete designs when the DV is even moderately unreliable or cases are highly heterogeneous.

10.3.2   Practical Issues

As randomized-groups ANOVA models, these designs assume normality of sampling distributions, homogeneity of variance, independence of errors, and absence of outliers. Additivity also is assumed when interactions are confounded with main affects. For designs in which some interactions are analyzed, unequal sample sizes pose added problems, as discussed in Section 5.6.5.

10.3.2.1   *Normality of Sampling Distributions*

In routine research studies, normality of sampling distributions is anticipated if there are 20 or more df for error. Screening designs, with their few cases, rarely generate anywhere near 20 df for error. An alternative method for assessing normality is through visual inspection of the normal probability plot of residuals, as demonstrated in the complete example of Section 10.7.2.1. Residuals are deviations of individual scores around their marginal or cell means. All software packages provide normal probability plots of residuals. Studies that follow results of screening are then planned with sufficient df for error if the underlying sampling distribution cannot be assumed to be normal.

10.3.2.2   *Homogeneity of Variance*

Screening designs often have only one or two cases per cell and many cells are empty. Therefore, homogeneity of variance is assessed separately on the margins for each main effect. That is, variances are compared among levels of A, then separately among levels of B, and so on. If interactions are evaluated, homogeneity of variance is assessed among the scores in the cells for that interaction, collapsed over all other IVs. The guidelines of Section 3.4.3 and elsewhere are used to evaluate differences among variances when they can be estimated. Some designs use so few cases that it is impossible to comply with even these guidelines. In these situations, the follow-up studies are designed to allow evaluation of homogeneity of variance, as usual.

10.3.2.3   *Absence of Outliers*

Outliers are also difficult to test in incomplete designs because many cells are empty or have only a single case. However, outliers can be sought on the margins or show up in the normal probability plot of residuals, illustrated in Section 10.7.2.1, as points that are highly discrepant from all the others.

10.3.2.4   *Independence of Errors*

The ANOVA model assumes that errors (residuals) are independent of one another, both within each cell and between cells of a design. This assumption is evaluated by examining the details of the research design rather than by statistical means (cf. Section 3.4.2).

10.3.2.5   *Additivity*

Analysis of incomplete designs when main effects are confounded with interactions assumes that all confounded interactions are negligible and represent only error variance. Tests of main effects are erroneous if interactions are present. For example, if the test of the main effect of A is completely confounded with the $B \times C$ interaction, a large main effect of A could be due actually to a large $B \times C$ interaction or a combination of the main effect of A and $B \times C$ interaction. Including only the main effect of A in subsequent research is wasteful and failure to test the $B \times C$ interaction results in loss of pertinent information. Additivity in screening designs is evaluated by the logic of the choice of IVs and their potential interactions; it is not readily tested in the absence of a full factorial design.

10.4   Fundamental Equations

The fractional-factorial design is chosen to demonstrate fundamental equations because of its popularity and because the other screening designs with two levels of each IV are easily developed from it.

    A fractional-factorial design has procedures similar to a full factorial design for allocation of cases to conditions, the partition of variance, and calculation of randomized-groups ANOVA. The difference is that not all combinations of conditions are present, and some interactions are confounded—aliased—with main effects or with other interactions. Sections 10.5.1 and 10.5.2.1 show how to determine which interactions are assessable. Section 10.6.1 shows the formation of screening and other incomplete designs to produce the pattern of aliasing (confounding) that is best for your application. A 2^5 fractional-factorial design with 16 combinations of treatments is demonstrated in this section. There are five IVs, each with two levels, hence, 2^5. This is a half factorial because only half of the potential 32 combinations of treatments are present, thus this half-factorial design is called a 2^{5-1} design.

10.4.1   Allocation of Cases

Table 10.1 shows the layout for a 2^5 half factorial with two cases per cell. The 32 cases are randomly assigned into two replications of 16 cases each and then the 16 cases within each replication are randomly assigned to runs (cells). A run is a particular combination of levels of IVs assigned to a particular case. The first case in each cell is in the first replication, the second case in the second replication.

    This is but one of many half-fractional factorials that could be generated, all with a beautiful symmetry. Take a moment to examine the pattern of filled cells in Table 10.1. Half the cells are empty, but each nonempty cell has different cases, making this a randomized-groups design. Because there are two replications—cases—in each cell, there are sufficient degrees of freedom to test all main effects and two-way interactions, but not higher-order interactions. There is stability to the estimates of means on the margins of each IV because they are each composed of 16 scores. Means for the two-way interactions are each composed of 8 scores. Notice that 32 cases are sufficient to assign one case to each cell of a complete factorial but without df for estimating error. The same 32 cases in the half factorial allow assessment of main effects and two-way interactions for 5 IVs.

TABLE 10.1   Assignment of Cases in a 2^5 Half-Factorial Design

				a_1		a_2	
				b_1	b_2	b_1	b_2
c_1	d_1	e_1		s_1 s_2			s_3 s_4
		e_2			s_5 s_6	s_7 s_8	
	d_2	e_1			s_9 s_{10}	s_{11} s_{12}	
		e_2		s_{13} s_{14}			s_{15} s_{16}
c_2	d_1	e_1			s_{17} s_{18}	s_{19} s_{20}	
		e_2		s_{21} s_{22}			s_{23} s_{24}
	d_2	e_1		s_{25} s_{26}			s_{27} s_{28}
		e_2			s_{29} s_{30}	s_{31} s_{32}	

Allocation of cases to a quarter factorial (2^{5-2} design) is shown in Table 10.2. This is, again, only one of many possible quarter factorials for a design with 5 IVs. In this design, only 8 of the 32 cells are filled, and there are no replications. Each main effect is assessable but with means estimated from only four scores. No unconfounded interactions are available for analysis. On the other hand, the main effects of five IVs are tested with only eight cases.

10.4.2   Partition of Sources of Variance

Partition of sums of squares into main effects and interactions, as always, depends on the number of IVs. The difference in fractional-factorial designs is that main effects and interactions are aliased (confounded) with other effects, as discussed in Section 10.5.1. The following partition of SS for the 2^5 half factorial of Table 10.1 permits tests of all main effects (aliased with four-way interactions) and all two-way interactions (aliased with three-way interactions). This design is sensible if you expect three-way and higher-order interactions to represent only random error.

TABLE 10.2   Assignment of Cases in a 2^5 Quarter-Factorial Design

			a_1		a_2	
			b_1	b_2	b_1	b_2
c_1	d_1	e_1	s_8			
		e_2				s_5
	d_2	e_1		s_6		
		e_2			s_7	
c_2	d_1	e_1				s_1
		e_2	s_4			
	d_2	e_1			s_3	
		e_2		s_2		

In this example, the total sum of squares is partitioned into 16 sources:

$$SS_T = SS_A + SS_B + SS_C + SS_D + SS_E + SS_{AB} + SS_{AC} + SS_{AD} + SS_{AE}$$
$$+ SS_{BC} + SS_{BD} + SS_{BE} + SS_{CD} + SS_{CE} + SS_{DE} + SS_{\text{residual}} \tag{10.1}$$

or, using the deviation approach

$$\sum_j \sum_k \sum_l (\bar{Y}_{ABCDE} - GM)^2 = \left(\frac{1}{2}\right) bcden \sum_j (\bar{Y}_A - GM)^2 + \left(\frac{1}{2}\right) acden \sum_k (\bar{Y}_B - GM)^2$$

$$+ \left(\frac{1}{2}\right) abden \sum_l (\bar{Y}_C - GM)^2 + \left(\frac{1}{2}\right) abcen \sum_m (\bar{Y}_D - GM)^2$$

$$+ \left(\frac{1}{2}\right) abcdn \sum_o (\bar{Y}_E - GM)^2$$

$$+ \ldots \text{ interactions calculated as per Equation 5.1 } \ldots + SS_{\text{residual}}$$

The total sum of squared differences between individual scores Y_{ABCDE} and the grand mean (GM) is partitioned into a sum of squared differences associated with A, with B, with C, with D, with E, and the sum of squared differences associated with all two-way combinations of these five factors, and the residual—the remaining sum of squared differences between individual scores and the grand mean. Each n is the number of scores in each cell.

In this example, the error term—residual—is found by subtracting the 15 known systematic sources of variance from the total:

$$SS_{residual} = SS_T - SS_A - SS_B - SS_C - SS_D - SS_E - SS_{AB} - SS_{AC} - SS_{AD}$$
$$- SS_{AE} - SS_{BC} - SS_{BD} - SS_{BE} - SS_{CD} - SS_{CE} - SS_{DE}$$

(10.2)

Total degrees of freedom remain the number of scores minus 1, lost when the grand mean is estimated (cf. Equation 3.6). However, the total number of scores is not *abcden,* but $\frac{1}{2}(abcden)$ because half the cells are empty. In this 2^{5-1} design, with two levels for each of five IVs, the df for each main effect and interaction is 1. Because there are 15 effects, 5 main effects and 10 two-way interactions,

$$df_{residual} = df_T - df_A - df_B - df_C - df_D - df_E - df_{AB} - df_{AC} - df_{AD}$$
$$- df_{AE} - df_{BC} - df_{BD} - df_{BE} - df_{CD} - df_{CE} - df_{DE}$$
$$= \left[\frac{1}{2}(abcden) - 1 \right] - 15$$

(10.3)

Figure 10.1 diagrams the partition of sums of squares and degrees of freedom for a 2^5 half-fractional factorial design.

As in any ANOVA, mean squares for all main effects and interactions are produced by dividing sums of squares by degrees of freedom:

$$MS_A = \frac{SS_A}{df_A} \qquad\qquad MS_B = \frac{SS_B}{df_B}$$
$$MS_C = \frac{SS_C}{df_C} \quad\cdots\quad MS_{residual} = \frac{SS_{residual}}{df_{residual}}$$

(10.4)

F ratios are formed for all main effects and two-way interactions as in Section 5.4.2, with $MS_{residual}$ substituted for the randomized-groups error term. For this example, each *F* ratio is tested against critical *F* from Table A.1 in Appendix A, with numerator df = 1 and denominator df $= \left[\frac{1}{2}(abcden) - 1 \right] - 15$. The null hypothesis for each effect is rejected if the obtained *F* is equal to or exceeds the tabled *F*.

10.4.3   Regression Approach to a 2^5 Half-Factorial ANOVA

The regression approach and the concept of orthogonality "come into their own" with screening and incomplete designs. Basically, the effects that can be tested unambiguously are those that are in orthogonal columns. Orthogonal columns are first set up to test main effects; then, as usual, columns are cross-multiplied to produce interactions. However, because the design is not fully factorial, some of the codes in the columns for interactions are the same as codes in other columns for either main effects or other interactions. The columns with the same codes are aliased. Because the regression approach is clear for these designs (and is the approach taken by most of the software), only data analysis through the regression approach is illustrated.

(a) Sums of squares

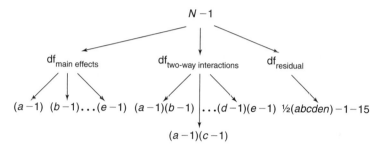

(b) Degrees of freedom

FIGURE 10.1 **Partition of (a) Sums of Squares and (b) Degrees of Freedom into Systematic Sources of Differences among Marginal Means of A, B, C, D, and E; Differences due to Two-Way Interactions $A \times B$, $A \times C$, $A \times D$, $A \times E$, $B \times C$, $B \times D$, $B \times E$, $C \times D$, $C \times E$, and $D \times E$; and Remaining (Error) Differences among Cases**

A sequence of runs is developed either by hand or through software to determine the combinations of levels of IVs presented to cases. Each case is randomly assigned to a run and that run determines the combination of levels of IVs assigned to the case. In Table 10.1, for instance, the first case (s_1) is assigned to the run with the a_1, b_1, c_1, d_1, e_1 combination; the ninth case (s_9) is assigned to the run with the a_1, b_2, c_1, d_2, e_1 combination, and so on.

The half-factorial design for this fictitious example has five IVs (each with two levels) and each combination has two replications (two cases per cell). The goal of the research is to determine which factors contribute to the joy of dancing. The DV is the rating of enjoyment a dancer gives after performing a belly dancing routine.[1] The first IV (A) is whether the dancer views a film of a professional belly dancer before performing his or her own routine. The second IV (B) is whether the dancer is wearing a professional or a practice costume. The third IV (C) is whether the routine is being videotaped. The fourth IV (D) is whether the dancer is performing with live musicians or to taped music. The fifth IV (E) is whether there are other dancers in the audience. Two dancers are assigned to each of the 16 cells in the design, as in Table 10.1.

---

[1]Dancers are extensively trained to produce reliable ratings of enjoyment.

Table 10.3 shows the sequence of runs and the combination of levels of IVs associated with each run. The runs are developed by software in a format appropriate for the regression approach to screening designs that is easily used to analyze the results. There are many things to notice about Table 10.3. The first column gives the numbers for the runs. Because there are two replications, the sequence of runs is repeated twice, one block of 16 runs above the second block of 16 runs. The second column is for the DV score (enjoyment, rated on a 10-point scale). Columns 3 through 7 code levels for IVs A through E, respectively, where 1 or -1 designates the level. Each row of these five columns is a different run because each row represents a different combination of levels of the five IVs. Consider the first row. It is run #2 with a DV score of 8. This case received the a_1, b_2, c_2, d_2, e_2 combination. That is, the dancer randomly assigned to the second run saw a tape of a professional dancer before performing her own routine, but danced in a practice costume, was not videotaped, danced to taped music, and had no other dancers in the audience. Going back to Table 10.1, this dancer was either s_{29} or s_{30}. In Table 10.3, columns 8 through 17 for the two-way interactions are cross-products of columns 3 through 7. The remaining columns cross the DV values in column 2 with the codes of columns 3 through 17 to produce the sums of products. Preliminary sums of squares are at the bottom of columns 3 through 17 and sums of products are at the bottom of columns 18 through 32.

This half factorial is only one of a very large number of sets of runs that accomplish the same purpose. For instance, assignment of IVs to columns is arbitrary. A different assignment results in a different set of runs. The five columns that code for IVs (columns 3 to 7) meet the criteria for orthogonality: Their coefficients sum to zero as do the pairwise cross-products of the columns. Thus, the five main effects and their 10 two-way interactions are mutually orthogonal. Any other set of orthogonal coefficients chosen for the columns coding the main effects has the same properties, but results in a different set of runs.

The pattern of aliasing (confounding) also is available from Table 10.3 with a bit of effort. A three-way interaction in full factorial ANOVA is the product of the three columns that code for the main effects. For example, the ABC interaction is the product of the column for A times the column for B times the column for C. If A, B, and C are multiplied in Table 10.3, the result for the first (and second) block of 16 runs is 1, 1, -1, -1, -1, -1, 1, 1, -1, -1, 1, 1, 1, 1, -1, -1. However, this is exactly the same set of coefficients as for the DE interaction. Thus, in this reduced design, ABC is aliased with DE. With some patience, the other sets of confounded effects in the design are found.

The equations for preliminary sums of squares and sums of products for the regression approach are the same as illustrated in Table 5.10 for main effects in factorial ANOVA. Table 10.4 shows the equations for finding the sums of squares for the main effects, A through E. Table 10.5 shows the equations for the two-way interactions.

You have to find the sum of squares total (SS_Y) in order to compute the sum of squares for residual:

$$SS_Y = 1031 - \frac{(163)^2}{32} = 200.72$$

Residual sum of squares is found by applying Equation 10.2:

$$SS_{residual} = 200.72 - 175.78 - 0.28 - 0.03 - 0.78 - 0.03 - 5.28 - 0.28$$
$$- 0.03 - 2.53 - 0.28 - 0.03 - 0.03 - 0.03 - 5.28 - 2.53$$
$$= 7.52$$

TABLE 10.3   Small-Sample Hypothetical Data Set for 2^5 Half-Fractional-Factorial ANOVA

Run	Y	A X_1	B X_2	C X_3	D X_4	E X_5	AB X_6	AC X_7	AD X_8	AE X_9	BC X_{10}	BD X_{11}	BE X_{12}	CD X_{13}	CE X_{14}	DE X_{15}	YX_1	YX_2	YX_3	YX_4	YX_5	YX_6	YX_7	YX_8	YX_9	YX_{10}	YX_{11}	YX_{12}	YX_{13}	YX_{14}	YX_{15}
2	8	1	-1	-1	-1	-1	-1	-1	-1	-1	1	1	1	1	1	1	8	-8	-8	-8	-8	-8	-8	-8	-8	8	8	8	8	8	8
10	8	1	-1	-1	1	1	-1	-1	1	1	1	-1	-1	-1	-1	1	8	-8	-8	8	8	-8	-8	8	8	8	-8	-8	-8	-8	8
6	7	1	-1	1	-1	1	-1	1	-1	1	-1	1	-1	-1	1	-1	7	-7	7	-7	7	-7	7	-7	7	-7	7	-7	-7	7	-7
14	9	1	-1	1	1	-1	-1	1	1	-1	-1	-1	1	1	-1	-1	9	-9	9	9	-9	-9	9	9	-9	-9	-9	9	9	-9	-9
4	7	1	1	-1	-1	1	1	-1	-1	1	-1	-1	1	1	-1	-1	7	7	-7	-7	7	7	-7	-7	7	-7	-7	7	7	-7	-7
12	7	1	1	-1	1	-1	1	-1	1	-1	-1	1	-1	-1	1	-1	7	7	-7	7	-7	7	-7	7	-7	-7	7	-7	-7	7	-7
8	8	1	1	1	-1	-1	1	1	-1	-1	1	-1	-1	-1	-1	1	8	8	8	-8	-8	8	8	-8	-8	8	-8	-8	-8	-8	8
16	8	1	1	1	1	1	1	1	1	1	1	1	1	1	1	1	8	8	8	8	8	8	8	8	8	8	8	8	8	8	8
1	6	-1	-1	-1	-1	1	1	1	1	-1	1	1	-1	1	-1	-1	-6	-6	-6	-6	6	6	6	6	-6	6	6	-6	6	-6	-6
9	3	-1	-1	-1	1	-1	1	1	-1	1	1	-1	1	-1	1	-1	-3	-3	-3	3	-3	3	3	-3	3	3	-3	3	-3	3	-3
5	1	-1	-1	1	-1	-1	1	-1	1	1	-1	1	1	-1	-1	1	-1	-1	1	-1	-1	1	-1	1	1	-1	1	1	-1	-1	1
13	2	-1	-1	1	1	1	1	-1	-1	-1	-1	-1	-1	1	1	1	-2	-2	2	2	2	2	-2	-2	-2	-2	-2	-2	2	2	2
3	2	-1	1	-1	-1	-1	-1	1	1	1	-1	-1	-1	1	1	1	-2	2	-2	-2	-2	-2	2	2	2	-2	-2	-2	2	2	2
11	2	-1	1	-1	1	1	-1	1	-1	-1	-1	1	1	-1	-1	1	-2	2	-2	2	2	-2	2	-2	-2	-2	2	2	-2	-2	2
7	3	-1	1	1	-1	1	-1	-1	1	-1	1	-1	1	-1	1	-1	-3	3	3	-3	3	-3	-3	3	-3	3	-3	3	-3	3	-3
15	4	-1	1	1	1	-1	-1	-1	-1	1	1	1	-1	1	-1	-1	-4	4	4	4	-4	-4	-4	-4	4	4	4	-4	4	-4	-4
2	3	1	-1	-1	-1	-1	-1	-1	-1	-1	1	1	1	1	1	1	3	-3	-3	-3	-3	-3	-3	-3	-3	3	3	3	3	3	3
10	7	1	-1	-1	1	1	-1	-1	1	1	1	-1	-1	-1	-1	1	7	-7	-7	7	7	-7	-7	7	7	7	-7	-7	-7	-7	7
6	7	1	-1	1	-1	1	-1	1	-1	1	-1	1	-1	-1	1	-1	7	-7	7	-7	7	-7	7	-7	7	-7	7	-7	-7	7	-7
14	8	1	-1	1	1	-1	-1	1	1	-1	-1	-1	1	1	-1	-1	8	-8	8	8	-8	-8	8	8	-8	-8	-8	8	8	-8	-8
4	8	1	1	-1	-1	1	1	-1	-1	1	-1	-1	1	1	-1	-1	8	8	-8	-8	8	8	-8	-8	8	-8	-8	8	8	-8	-8
12	8	1	1	-1	1	-1	1	-1	1	-1	-1	1	-1	-1	1	-1	8	8	-8	8	-8	8	-8	8	-8	-8	8	-8	-8	8	-8
8	7	1	1	1	-1	-1	1	1	-1	-1	1	-1	-1	-1	-1	1	7	7	7	-7	-7	7	7	-7	-7	7	-7	-7	-7	-7	7
16	8	1	1	1	1	1	1	1	1	1	1	1	1	1	1	1	8	8	8	8	8	8	8	8	8	8	8	8	8	8	8
1	6	-1	-1	-1	-1	1	1	1	1	-1	1	1	-1	1	-1	-1	-6	-6	-6	-6	6	6	6	6	-6	6	6	-6	6	-6	-6
9	4	-1	-1	-1	1	-1	1	1	-1	1	1	-1	1	-1	1	-1	-4	-4	-4	4	-4	4	4	-4	4	4	-4	4	-4	4	-4
5	3	-1	-1	1	-1	-1	1	-1	1	1	-1	1	1	-1	-1	1	-3	-3	3	-3	-3	3	-3	3	3	-3	3	3	-3	-3	3
13	2	-1	-1	1	1	1	1	-1	-1	-1	-1	-1	-1	1	1	1	-2	-2	2	2	2	2	-2	-2	-2	-2	-2	-2	2	2	2
3	1	-1	1	-1	-1	-1	-1	1	1	1	-1	-1	-1	1	1	1	-1	1	-1	-1	-1	-1	1	1	1	-1	-1	-1	1	1	1
11	3	-1	1	-1	1	1	-1	1	-1	-1	-1	1	1	-1	-1	1	-3	3	-3	3	3	-3	3	-3	-3	-3	3	3	-3	-3	3
7	3	-1	1	1	-1	1	-1	-1	1	-1	1	-1	1	-1	1	-1	-3	3	3	-3	3	-3	-3	3	-3	3	-3	3	-3	3	-3
15	4	-1	1	1	1	-1	-1	-1	-1	1	1	1	-1	1	-1	-1	-4	4	4	4	-4	-4	-4	-4	4	4	4	-4	4	-4	-4
Sum	163	0	0	0	0	0	0	0	0	0	0	0	0	0	0	0	75	3	-1	-5	-1	-13	3	-1	-9	3	-1	-1	-1	-13	-9
Squares	1031	32	32	32	32	32	32	32	32	32	32	32	32	32	32	32															
Summed		32	32	32	32	32	32	32	32	32	32	32	32	32	32	32															

561

TABLE 10.4   Equations for the Sum of Squares for the Main Effects

$$\text{SS}(\text{reg}.X_1) = \text{SS}_A = \frac{[\text{SP}(YX_1)]^2}{\text{SS}(X_1)} = \frac{75^2}{32} = 175.78$$

$$\text{SS}(\text{reg}.X_2) = \text{SS}_B = \frac{[\text{SP}(YX_2)]^2}{\text{SS}(X_2)} = \frac{3^2}{32} = 0.28$$

$$\text{SS}(\text{reg}.X_3) = \text{SS}_C = \frac{[\text{SP}(YX_3)]^2}{\text{SS}(X_3)} = \frac{(-1)^2}{32} = 0.03$$

$$\text{SS}(\text{reg}.X_4) = \text{SS}_D = \frac{[\text{SP}(YX_4)]^2}{\text{SS}(X_4)} = \frac{(-5)^2}{32} = 0.78$$

$$\text{SS}(\text{reg}.X_5) = \text{SS}_E = \frac{[\text{SP}(YX_5)]^2}{\text{SS}(X_5)} = \frac{(-1)^2}{32} = 0.03$$

and residual df is found by applying Equation 10.3:

$$\text{df}_{\text{residual}} = \frac{1}{2}(2)(2)(2)(2)(2)(2) - 1 - 15 = 16$$

Table 10.6 summarizes the results of the calculations and shows the mean squares and F values. Each F ratio is evaluated separately, as usual. At $\alpha = .05$, the critical value from Table A.1 is 4.49, based on numerator df = 1 and denominator df = 16 for all effects. The main effect of A (viewing a film of a professional dancer prior to the dance) and interactions $A \times B$ (viewing the film or not by wearing a professional costume or not when dancing), $A \times E$ (viewing the film or not by dancing with other dancers in the audience or not), $C \times E$ (being videotaped or not by dancing with other dancers in the audience or not), and $D \times E$ (dancing with live musicians or not by dancing for an audience of other dancers or not) are all significant. Thus, all of the IVs participate in at least one statistically reliable effect—not an entirely happy result for a screening run. (See Section 5.6.1 for interpretation of interactions.)

Note that there are 15 F tests for the small data set: an invitation to inflated familywise Type I error. A prudent researcher would consider a Bonferroni-type adjustment to α_{FW}, $.05/15 = .003$, if this analysis is to be used for final decision making rather than just screening. By this criterion, only the main effect of A is reliable. The remaining "borderline" effects would probably be considered for further research, however.

10.4.4   Computer Analyses of the Small-Sample 2^5 Half-Factorial ANOVA

Data are entered in the format of the first seven columns of Table 10.3: run number (optional), DV, and the codes (1 or -1) for the five IVs. The columns may be in any order. Tables 10.7 through 10.10

**TABLE 10.5   Equations for the Sum of Squares
for the Two-Way Interactions**

$$SS(reg.X_6) = SS_{AB} = \frac{[SP(YX_6)]^2}{SS(X_6)} = \frac{(-13)^2}{32} = 5.28$$

$$SS(reg.X_7) = SS_{AC} = \frac{[SP(YX_7)]^2}{SS(X_7)} = \frac{3^2}{32} = 0.28$$

$$SS(reg.X_8) = SS_{AD} = \frac{[SP(YX_8)]^2}{SS(X_8)} = \frac{(-1)^2}{32} = 0.03$$

$$SS(reg.X_9) = SS_{AE} = \frac{[SP(YX_9)]^2}{SS(X_9)} = \frac{(-9)^2}{32} = 2.53$$

$$SS(reg.X_{10}) = SS_{BC} = \frac{[SP(YX_{10})]^2}{SS(X_{10})} = \frac{3^2}{32} = 0.28$$

$$SS(reg.X_{11}) = SS_{BD} = \frac{[SP(YX_{11})]^2}{SS(X_{11})} = \frac{(-1)^2}{32} = 0.03$$

$$SS(reg.X_{12}) = SS_{BE} = \frac{[SP(YX_{12})]^2}{SS(X_{12})} = \frac{(-1)^2}{32} = 0.03$$

$$SS(reg.X_{13}) = SS_{CD} = \frac{[SP(YX_{13})]^2}{SS(X_{13})} = \frac{(-1)^2}{32} = 0.03$$

$$SS(reg.X_{14}) = SS_{CE} = \frac{[SP(YX_{14})]^2}{SS(X_{14})} = \frac{(-13)^2}{32} = 5.28$$

$$SS(reg.X_{15}) = SS_{DE} = \frac{[SP(YX_{15})]^2}{SS(X_{15})} = \frac{(-9)^2}{32} = 2.53$$

show computer analyses of the small-sample example of the 2^5 half-factorial ANOVA of Section 10.4.3 by four GLM programs: SPSS, MINITAB, SYSTAT, and SAS.

The SPSS GLM syntax in Table 10.7 is the same as for the Latin-square design of Chapter 9, except that two-way interactions are requested in addition to main effects in the TABLES instructions and in the DESIGN instruction. ETASQ and OPOWER request effect sizes and observed power statistics.

The output is the same as for the Latin-square analysis but longer due to inclusion of all two-way interactions. The F ratios in the source table (Tests of Between-Subject Effects) differ slightly from those of Table 10.6, due to rounding error in the hand calculations. At the end of the output are marginal means for main effects and cell means for the two-way interactions. Tables are shown for only one main effect and one interaction. The standard error for each marginal mean is the

TABLE 10.6   Source Table For 2^5 Fractional-Factorial ANOVA

Source	SS	df	MS	F
A	175.78	1	175.78	374.00
B	0.28	1	0.28	0.60
C	0.03	1	0.03	0.06
D	0.78	1	0.78	1.66
E	0.03	1	0.03	0.06
AB	5.28	1	5.28	11.23
AC	0.28	1	0.28	0.60
AD	0.03	1	0.03	0.06
AE	2.53	1	2.53	5.38
BC	0.28	1	0.28	0.60
BD	0.03	1	0.03	0.06
BE	0.03	1	0.03	0.06
CD	0.03	1	0.03	0.06
CE	5.28	1	5.28	11.23
DE	2.53	1	2.53	5.38
Residual	7.52	16	0.47	
T	200.75	31		

TABLE 10.7   Fractional-Factorial ANOVA for Small-Sample Example through SPSS GLM: Syntax and Selected Output

```
UNIANOVA
  rating BY prof_dan costume video music audience
  /METHOD = SSTYPE(3)
  /INTERCEPT = INCLUDE
  /EMMEANS = TABLES(prof_dan) /EMMEANS = TABLES(costume)
  /EMMEANS = TABLES(video) /EMMEANS = TABLES(music)
  /EMMEANS = TABLES(audience) /EMMEANS = TABLES(costume*prof_dan)
  /EMMEANS = TABLES(prof_dan*video) /EMMEANS = TABLES(music*prof_dan)
  /EMMEANS = TABLES(audience*prof_dan) /EMMEANS = TABLES(costume*video)
  /EMMEANS = TABLES(costume*music) /EMMEANS = TABLES(audience*costume)
  /EMMEANS = TABLES(music*video) /EMMEANS = TABLES(audience*video)
  /EMMEANS = TABLES(audience*music)
  /PRINT = ETASQ OPOWER
  /CRITERIA = ALPHA(.05)
  /DESIGN = prof_dan costume video music audience costume*prof_dan prof_dan
  *video music*prof_dan audience*prof_dan costume*video costume*music audience
  *costume music*video audience*video audience*music.
```

TABLE 10.7 Continued

Tests of Between-Subjects Effects

Dependent Variable: RATING

Source	Type III Sum of Squares	df	Mean Square	F	Sig.	Eta Squared	Noncent. Parameter	Observed Power[a]
Corrected Model	193.219[b]	15	12.881	27.480	.000	.963	412.200	1.000
Intercept	830.281	1	830.281	1771.267	.000	.991	1771.267	1.000
PROF_DAN	175.781	1	175.781	375.000	.000	.959	375.000	1.000
COSTUME	.281	1	.281	.600	.450	.036	.600	.113
VIDEO	3.125E-02	1	3.125E-02	.067	.800	.004	.067	.057
MUSIC	.781	1	.781	1.667	.215	.094	1.667	.229
AUDIENCE	3.125E-02	1	3.125E-02	.067	.800	.004	.067	.057
PROF_DAN * COSTUME	5.281	1	5.281	11.267	.004	.413	11.267	.883
PROF_DAN * VIDEO	.281	1	.281	.600	.450	.036	.600	.113
PROF_DAN * MUSIC	3.125E-02	1	3.125E-02	.067	.800	.004	.067	.057
PROF_DAN * AUDIENCE	2.531	1	2.531	5.400	.034	.252	5.400	.588
COSTUME * VIDEO	.281	1	.281	.600	.450	.036	.600	.113
COSTUME * MUSIC	3.125E-02	1	3.125E-02	.067	.800	.004	.067	.057
COSTUME * AUDIENCE	3.125E-02	1	3.125E-02	.067	.800	.004	.067	.057
VIDEO * MUSIC	3.125E-02	1	3.125E-02	.067	.800	.004	.067	.057
VIDEO * AUDIENCE	5.281	1	5.281	11.267	.004	.413	11.267	.883
MUSIC * AUDIENCE	2.531	1	2.531	5.400	.034	.252	5.400	.588
Error	7.500	16	.469					
Total	1031.000	32						
Corrected Total	200.719	31						

a. Computed using alpha = .05
b. R Squared = .963 (Adjusted R Squared = .928)

(continued)

TABLE 10.7   Continued

Estimated Marginal Means

1. Professional dancer film

Dependent Variable: RATING

Professional dancer film	Mean	Std. Error	95% Confidence Interval	
			Lower Bound	Upper Bound
No	2.750	.171	2.387	3.113
Yes	7.438	.171	7.075	7.800

6. Professional costume * Professional dancer film

Dependent Variable: RATING

Professional costume	Professional dancer film	Mean	Std. Error	95% Confidence Interval	
				Lower Bound	Upper Bound
No	No	2.250	.242	1.737	2.763
	Yes	7.750	.242	7.237	8.263
Yes	No	3.250	.242	2.737	3.763
	Yes	7.125	.242	6.612	7.638

same, the square root of $MS_{residual}$ divided by the square root of the 16 cases in each marginal mean. The standard error for each cell mean is the same, the square root of $MS_{residual}$ divided by the square root of the eight cases in each two-way cell. Other output is as described in Section 9.4.5 for the Latin-square design.

MINITAB GLM analyzes a fractional-factorial design like any other, with all of the effects listed in the GLM equation and, if means are desired, in the Means instruction, as shown in Table 10.8. The ANOVA table is followed by marginal and cell means for each of the effects listed in the Means instruction. Results match those of SPSS.

Table 10.9 shows syntax and output for SYSTAT GLM. All desired main effects and two-way interactions are specified in the MODEL instruction. PRINT=MEDIUM provides marginal and cell means and standard errors.

Format for output is the same as for the Latin-square design described in Section 9.4.5. $MS_{residual}$ is labeled Error. Means and standard errors are the same as for SPSS and MINITAB GLM. Plots of all means (and standard deviations) for main effects and interactions are provided (not shown), but interaction plots are difficult to interpret if there is more than one because only the first-listed IV is labeled on the graph.

TABLE 10.8   Fractional-Factorial ANOVA for Small-Sample Example through MINITAB GLM: Syntax and Selected Output

```
MTB > GLM 'RATING' = PROFDAN COSTUME VIDEO MUSIC AUDIENCE PROFDAN*COSTUME &
CONT>       PROFDAN*VIDEO PROFDAN*MUSIC PROFDAN*AUDIENCE COSTUME*VIDEO &
CONT>       COSTUME*MUSIC COSTUME*AUDIENCE VIDEO*MUSIC VIDEO*AUDIENCE MUSIC &
CONT>      *AUDIENCE;
SUBC>    Brief 2 ;
SUBC>    Means PROFDAN COSTUME VIDEO MUSIC AUDIENCE PROFDAN*COSTUME PROFDAN &
CONT>       *VIDEO PROFDAN*MUSIC PROFDAN*AUDIENCE COSTUME*VIDEO COSTUME &
CONT>       *MUSIC COSTUME*AUDIENCE VIDEO*MUSIC VIDEO*AUDIENCE MUSIC &
CONT>       *AUDIENCE.
```

Analysis of Variance for RATING, using Adjusted SS for Tests

Source	DF	Seq SS	Adj SS	Adj MS	F	P
PROFDAN	1	175.781	175.781	175.781	375.00	0.000
COSTUME	1	0.281	0.281	0.281	0.60	0.450
VIDEO	1	0.031	0.031	0.031	0.07	0.800
MUSIC	1	0.781	0.781	0.781	1.67	0.215
AUDIENCE	1	0.031	0.031	0.031	0.07	0.800
PROFDAN*COSTUME	1	5.281	5.281	5.281	11.27	0.004
PROFDAN*VIDEO	1	0.281	0.281	0.281	0.60	0.450
PROFDAN*MUSIC	1	0.031	0.031	0.031	0.07	0.800
PROFDAN*AUDIENCE	1	2.531	2.531	2.531	5.40	0.034
COSTUME*VIDEO	1	0.281	0.281	0.281	0.60	0.450
COSTUME*MUSIC	1	0.031	0.031	0.031	0.07	0.800
COSTUME*AUDIENCE	1	0.031	0.031	0.031	0.07	0.800
VIDEO*MUSIC	1	0.031	0.031	0.031	0.07	0.800
VIDEO*AUDIENCE	1	5.281	5.281	5.281	11.27	0.004
MUSIC*AUDIENCE	1	2.531	2.531	2.531	5.40	0.034
Error	16	7.500	7.500	0.469		
Total	31	200.719				

Least Squares Means for RATING

PROFDAN	Mean	StDev
-1	2.750	0.1712
1	7.437	0.1712

PROFDAN*COSTUME		Mean	StDev
-1	-1	2.250	0.2421
-1	1	3.250	0.2421
1	-1	7.750	0.2421
1	1	7.125	0.2421

SAS GLM also requires a **MODEL** instruction, as seen in Table 10.10, which includes all the effects to be assessed: 5 main effects and 10 interactions. All 15 effects are also in the request for means. Output is limited by requesting only Type III SS (**ss3**), which for this analysis is identical to that of Type I SS. (Section 5.6.5 discusses these types of sums of squares.) Output follows that of the Latin-square example of Section 9.4.5. Cell means and standard deviations follow those for marginal values.

TABLE 10.9 **Fractional-Factorial ANOVA for Small-Sample Example through SYSTAT GLM: Syntax and Selected Output**

```
PRINT=MEDIUM
GLM
CATEGORY PROF_DAN COSTUME VIDEO MUSIC AUDIENCE/EFFECT
MODEL RATING = CONSTANT + PROF_DAN+COSTUME+VIDEO+MUSIC+AUDIENCE+COSTUME*,
   PROF_DAN+VIDEO*PROF_DAN+MUSIC*PROF_DAN+AUDIENCE*PROF_DAN+VIDEO*COSTUME+,
   MUSIC*COSTUME+AUDIENCE*COSTUME+MUSIC*VIDEO+AUDIENCE*VIDEO+AUDIENCE*,
   MUSIC
ESTIMATE
```

```
               Analysis of Variance
```

Source	Sum-of-Squares	df	Mean-Square	F-ratio	P
PROF_DAN	175.781	1	175.781	375.000	0.000
COSTUME	0.281	1	0.281	0.600	0.450
VIDEO	0.031	1	0.031	0.067	0.800
MUSIC	0.781	1	0.781	1.667	0.215
AUDIENCE	0.031	1	0.031	0.067	0.800
COSTUME*PROF_DAN	5.281	1	5.281	11.267	0.004
VIDEO*PROF_DAN	0.281	1	0.281	0.600	0.450
MUSIC*PROF_DAN	0.031	1	0.031	0.067	0.800
AUDIENCE*PROF_DAN	2.531	1	2.531	5.400	0.034
VIDEO*COSTUME	0.281	1	0.281	0.600	0.450
MUSIC*COSTUME	0.031	1	0.031	0.067	0.800
AUDIENCE*COSTUME	0.031	1	0.031	0.067	0.800
MUSIC*VIDEO	0.031	1	0.031	0.067	0.800
AUDIENCE*VIDEO	5.281	1	5.281	11.267	0.004
AUDIENCE*MUSIC	2.531	1	2.531	5.400	0.034
Error	7.500	16	0.469		

```
------------------------------------------------------------------
Least squares means.
                      LS Mean       SE      N
   PROF_DAN   =-1      2.750      0.171     16
   PROF_DAN   =1       7.438      0.171     16
   ---------------------------------------------------------------
COSTUME    =-1
   PROF_DAN   =-1      2.250      0.242      8
COSTUME    =-1
   PROF_DAN   =1       7.750      0.242      8
COSTUME    =1
   PROF_DAN   =-1      3.250      0.242      8
COSTUME    =1
   PROF_DAN   =1       7.125      0.242      8
   ---------------------------------------------------------------
```

TABLE 10.10   Fractional-Factorial ANOVA for Small-Sample Example through SAS GLM: Syntax and Selected Output

```
proc glm data=SASUSER.FRACFA2;
    class PROF_DAN COSTUME VIDEO MUSIC AUDIENCE;
    model RATING = PROF_DAN COSTUME VIDEO MUSIC AUDIENCE
                PROF_DAN*COSTUME PROF_DAN*VIDEO PROF_DAN*MUSIC
                PROF_DAN*AUDIENCE COSTUME*VIDEO COSTUME*MUSIC
                COSTUME*AUDIENCE VIDEO*MUSIC VIDEO*AUDIENCE
                MUSIC*AUDIENCE /ss3;
    means PROF_DAN COSTUME VIDEO MUSIC AUDIENCE
                PROF_DAN*COSTUME PROF_DAN*VIDEO PROF_DAN*MUSIC
                PROF_DAN*AUDIENCE COSTUME*VIDEO COSTUME*MUSIC
                COSTUME*AUDIENCE VIDEO*MUSIC VIDEO*AUDIENCE
                MUSIC*AUDIENCE;
run;
```

```
                    General Linear Models Procedure

Dependent Variable: RATING

Source          DF    Sum of Squares    Mean Square    F Value    Pr > F

Model           15      193.21875000    12.88125000      27.48    0.0001

Error           16        7.50000000     0.46875000

Corrected
  Total         31      200.71875000

        R-Square              C.V.         Root MSE        RATING Mean

        0.962634          13.44104        0.6846532         5.09375000

Source            DF    Type III SS     Mean Square    F Value    Pr > F

PROF_DAN           1    175.78125000    175.78125000     375.00    0.0001
COSTUME            1      0.28125000      0.28125000       0.60    0.4499
VIDEO              1      0.03125000      0.03125000       0.07    0.7995
MUSIC              1      0.78125000      0.78125000       1.67    0.2150
AUDIENCE           1      0.03125000      0.03125000       0.07    0.7995
PROF_DAN*COSTUME   1      5.28125000      5.28125000      11.27    0.0040
PROF_DAN*VIDEO     1      0.28125000      0.28125000       0.60    0.4499
PROF_DAN*MUSIC     1      0.03125000      0.03125000       0.07    0.7995
PROF_DAN*AUDIENCE  1      2.53125000      2.53125000       5.40    0.0336
COSTUME*VIDEO      1      0.28125000      0.28125000       0.60    0.4499
COSTUME*MUSIC      1      0.03125000      0.03125000       0.07    0.7995
COSTUME*AUDIENCE   1      0.03125000      0.03125000       0.07    0.7995
VIDEO*MUSIC        1      0.03125000      0.03125000       0.07    0.7995
VIDEO*AUDIENCE     1      5.28125000      5.28125000      11.27    0.0040
MUSIC*AUDIENCE     1      2.53125000      2.53125000       5.40    0.0336
```

(continued)

TABLE 10.10   Continued

```
                General Linear Models Procedure

            Level of              ---------Rating---------
            PROF_DAN      N          Mean              SD

               1         16       7.43750000        0.81394103
              -1         16       2.75000000        1.00000000

    Level of      Level of             ---------Rating---------
    PROF_DAN      COSTUME      N          Mean              SD
       1             1         8       7.12500000        0.83452296
       1            -1         8       7.75000000        0.70710678
      -1             1         8       3.25000000        0.70710678
      -1            -1         8       2.25000000        1.03509834
```

10.5   Types of Screening and Other Incomplete Designs

There are several types of screening and other incomplete designs for randomized-groups IVs with two or more levels. Before discussing these designs, however, it is useful to define *resolution.*

10.5.1   Resolution of Incomplete Designs

Incomplete designs differ in degree of aliasing and so in the number of interactions that can be tested. The more interactions that can be tested, the higher the resolution. With low-resolution designs, only main effects are tested; with higher resolution, some or all of the two-way interactions can also be tested. Three-way and higher-order interactions are aliased with main effects and two-way interactions in all of these designs and so are unavailable for analysis. Table 10.11 describes designs in terms of their resolution: the kinds of aliasing that occur and the effects that can be tested.

The 2^5 half-factorial design with replications of Table 10.1 (also called 2^{5-1}) is resolution V. The quarter-factorial design of Table 10.2 with no replications is resolution III. Latin-square, Plackett-Burman, and most Taguchi designs are also resolution III. The 2^{4-1} half-fractional factorial of Section 10.5.2.1 is resolution IV. Some resolution III designs are turned into resolution IV designs by a fold-over technique, in which the number of runs is doubled and all the coefficients are reversed ($+$ changed to $-$ and vice versa).

10.5.2   Fractional-Factorial Designs

The fractional-factorial design of Table 10.1 is a half factorial because half of the combinations of a full factorial are used while the other half of the cells are empty. Other fractions of a full factorial are also possible, as shown in Table 10.2. This section discusses other fractions in designs with two levels of each IV and in designs with three levels of each IV.

TABLE 10.11   Resolution in Various Screening Designs

Resolution	Description	When to Use
III	Main effects are independent of each other, but are aliased with interactions.	You are willing to assume that all interactions are negligible and will base future research only on screened main effects.
IV	Main effects are independent of each other and independent of two-way interactions, but some two-way interactions are aliased with others.	You are willing to assume that all third- and higher-order interactions are negligible. You are unable to determine ahead of time which two-way interactions are negligible and which are worth testing.
V	Main effects and two-way interactions are all independent of each other	You are willing to assume that all third- and higher-order interactions are negligible. You want to test all main effects and two-way interactions.

10.5.2.1   Two-Level Fractional-Factorial Designs

The number of runs in a fractional-factorial design in which all IVs have two levels (sometimes called a Box-Hunter design) is always 2 to some power. Recall that a run is the combination of levels of IVs assigned to a case. Two raised to a power is the number of combinations in the study. For example, a full factorial with five IVs has $2^5 = 32$ combinations. A half factorial has one less than the power of 2 in the full factorial. So a half-fractional factorial with five IVs has $2^{5-1} = 2^4 = 16$ runs (as in Table 10.1). A quarter factorial has 2 less than the power of 2 in the full factorial. Therefore, a quarter factorial with five IVs has $2^{5-2} = 2^3 = 8$ runs (as in Table 10.2), and so on.

Generally, the number of runs (not including replicates) in a fractional factorial is

$$r = 2^{k-q} \tag{10.5}$$

The number of runs (r) in a two-level fractional-factorial design is 2 to the power of $(k - q)$, where k is the number of IVs, and q is some number less than k. In a half factorial, $q = 1$; in a quarter factorial $q = 2$; and so on.

The smaller the number of runs relative to the full factorial, the lower the resolution and the fewer the effects that can be analyzed. A 2^5 quarter factorial permits analyses only of main effects (which are aliased with three-way interactions); the two-way interactions are all aliased with each other and with bits and pieces of higher-order interactions. Other parts of higher-order interactions are folded into the residual error term. As shown in Section 10.4, a 2^5 half factorial with two replications permits analysis of main effects (aliased with four-way interactions) and all two-way interactions (aliased with three-way interactions). Typically, fractional-factorial designs are not used to analyze interactions higher than two-way.

The number of replicates affects both the power of the study and the effects that are assessable. With one replicate per run, there is one case for each combination of levels of IVs. With two replicates per run, there are two cases for each combination of levels of IVs, and so on. When there is one replication and sample size is small, analyses of some effects are sacrificed to provide degrees of freedom for error. Obviously, omitted effects should be those that are not of research concern and that are likely to be negligible.

How do you generate a fractional-factorial design by hand[2] and how do you know which effects are aliased? The first step is to determine how many IVs there are (the value of k) and whether tests of only main effects or tests of main effects plus two-way interactions are needed. This determines the resolution of the design, the fraction required, and thus the value of q. The second step is to determine the number of runs required using Equation 10.5. This also determines the minimum number of cases needed if there is only one replication. The third step is to generate a set of orthogonal coefficients for each of the IVs for the required number of runs, as shown, for example, in Table 10.3. The last step is to cross-multiply the coefficients in the IV columns for main effects to produce various interactions. This reveals the pattern of aliasing because columns with the same codes are aliased. Only in fully factorial designs are all of the columns for main effects and interactions different from each other. Once the columns for main effects are coded, the cross-products of columns for various interactions are easily found using a spreadsheet program such as Quattro or Excel or one of the data-entry programs of the statistical packages.

Schmidt and Launsby (1994) present a more formal approach, with jargon, to identifying the pattern of aliasing. Suppose, in a 2^{4-1} design, for example, D (the last main effect) is aliased with ABC (expected to be negligible).[3] The expression $D = ABC$ is called the *half fraction design generator*, and ABC is called the *defining word*. The *defining relation* is $I = ABCD$. The rest of the aliasing pattern is identified by multiplying both sides of the defining relation by the effect in question. To identify the factor aliased with AB,

$$AB(I) = AB(ABCD)$$
$$= A^2B^2CD = IICD = CD$$

where I is the identity column with all entries equal to 1 because any column multiplied by itself $= I$ (e.g., $A^2 = I$). Therefore, the AB interaction is confounded with the CD interaction. Testing one of these interactions lets you know that there is a significant two-way effect of either $A \times B$ or $C \times D$ (or both), but you can not tell which. Similarly, AC is aliased with BD and so on.

Other main effects (besides D) also are aliased. For example,

$$A(I) = A(ABCD)$$
$$= A^2BCD = I(BCD) = BCD$$

This design is of resolution IV because it permits tests of main effects (aliased with three-way interactions) and 3 of the 6 two-way interactions (each aliased with one of the other three). Three-way interactions are aliased with main effects. The four-way interaction is I, a column of ones, and is equivalent to the intercept in a regression model.

Schmidt and Launsby (1994, pp. 483–486) demonstrate aliasing patterns in a 2^{7-3} design. Other tables of aliasing patterns are provided by Davies (1963), Montgomery (1984, pp. 338–339),

---

[2]The easiest way, by far, to generate a fractional-factorial design is through software. This is illustrated later in this section.

[3]You can determine what is aliased with what is in your own study by your assignment of IVs to the letters A, B, C, and D.

and Woodward and colleagues (1990, pp. 246–247). Further discussion of these issues in terms of resolution is in Section 10.6.1.

SAS FACTEX generates a fractional-factorial design when you provide the number of runs, the number of factors, resolution (Section 10.6.1), and, optionally, a blocking variable to represent replications, if any. (SAS FACTEX labels replicates as blocks.) Table 10.12 shows syntax and printed output for the 2^{4-1} design ($2^3 = 8$ runs). A data file is requested: SASUSER.FRACFAC.

TABLE 10.12   Generating a 2^{4-1} Fractional-Factorial Design through SAS FACTEX: Syntax and Output

```
proc factex ;
  factors
    A B C D;
      size design = 8;
      model resolution = 4;
run;
examine aliasing;
quit;
proc factex ;
  factors A B C D;
    size design = 8;
    model resolution = 4;
run;
output out = SASUSER.FRACFAC
  randomize novalran;
quit;
run;
data SASUSER.FRACFAC; set SASUSER.FRACFAC end=adxeof;
  Y =.;
run;
data SASUSER.FRACFAC; set SASUSER.FRACFAC; _adxran = ranuni(0);
proc sort data=SASUSER.FRACFAC
    out=SASUSER.FRACFAC(drop=_adxran);
    by _adxran;
run;
proc print data=SASUSER.FRACFAC;
run;


Aliasing Structure

A
B
C
D
A*B = C*D
A*C = B*D
A*D = B*C
```

The output shows the pattern of aliasing: All main effects are unconfounded with each other and with two-way interactions (although main effects are confounded with three-way interactions), and each two-way interaction is aliased with another. The set of runs for one replicate (block) is output in spreadsheet format in Table 10.13. You may copy the design for as many replicates as you want. Hypothetical values of the DV, Y, have been added by hand in Table 10.13.

Other programs that help you generate two-level fractional-factorial designs are SYSTAT DESIGN, MINITAB DOE, and NCSS Design of Experiments.

The analysis proceeds as in Section 10.4, where only those effects that are interpretable are included in the model. This means that in a resolution III design (cf. Section 10.5.1), you analyze only main effects. In a resolution IV design, you analyze the main effects and the two-way interactions of interest by choosing one from among each set that is aliased. For example, if AB and CD are aliased, you analyze the AB interaction if you believe the CD interaction is negligible. Otherwise, the result may be due to a CD interaction or to both AB and CD interactions. In a resolution V design, all main effects and two-way interactions are available for analysis. In resolution IV and V designs, you can always pool unimportant two-way interactions into the residual term to gain degrees of freedom and power if you expect those interactions to be negligible.

Table 10.14 shows the analysis of main effects only through SAS GLM using the data in Table 10.13. Two-way interactions are pooled into a residual, the error term, because they are expected to be negligible; lsmeans requests marginal means for all main effects.

Only the main effect of A is statistically reliable and only the marginal means for A are shown; remaining marginal means are deleted. Further research is designed to explore A, perhaps through an experiment with more levels of A.

10.5.2.2 *Three-Level Fractional-Factorial Designs*

Fractional-factorial designs in which IVs have three levels are more complicated because interactions as well as main effects have more than one degree of freedom and there is much more opportunity for confounding. In a 1/3 fractional factorial (3^{k-1}), for instance, each effect has three aliases instead of the two in the two-level half-fractional factorial; in a 1/9 fractional factorial (3^{k-2}), each

TABLE 10.13   Output Data Set (SASUSER.FRACFAC) from SAS FACTEX Run: Syntax Is in Table 10.12

OBS	A	B	C	D	Y
1	1	−1	1	−1	12
2	−1	−1	−1	−1	5
3	−1	−1	1	1	6
4	−1	1	−1	1	3
5	−1	1	1	−1	4
6	1	1	−1	−1	11
7	1	−1	−1	1	9
8	1	1	1	1	8

TABLE 10.14   Analysis of 2^{4-1} Fractional-Factorial Design through SAS GLM: Syntax and Selected Output

```
proc glm data=SASUSER.FRACFAC;
  class A B C D;
  model Y = A B C D / ss3;
  lsmeans A B C D/;
run;
```

```
                    General Linear Models Procedure
                       Class Level Information

                    Class    Levels    Values

                      A        2       1   -1
                      B        2       1   -1
                      C        2       1   -1
                      D        2       1   -1

              Number of observations in data set = 8

                    General Linear Models Procedure

Dependent Variable: Y
```

Source	DF	Sum of Squares	Mean Square	F Value	Pr > F
Model	4	70.00000000	17.50000000	9.55	0.0470
Error	3	5.50000000	1.83333333		
Corrected Total	7	75.50000000			

R-Square	C.V.	Root MSE	Y Mean
0.927152	18.67595	1.3540064	7.25000000

Source	DF	Type III SS	Mean Square	F Value	Pr > F
A	1	60.50000000	60.50000000	33.00	0.0105
B	1	4.50000000	4.50000000	2.45	0.2152
C	1	0.50000000	0.50000000	0.27	0.6376
D	1	4.50000000	4.50000000	2.45	0.2152

```
                    General Linear Models Procedure
                       Least Squares Means

                        A              Y
                                    LSMEAN

                        1       10.00000000
                       -1        4.50000000
```

effect has nine aliases, and so on. In addition, more than five IVs are necessary for reasonable tests of two-way interactions, and even then they are often difficult to interpret (Kirk, 1995). For these reasons, the design is not discussed further here; if interested, Montgomery (1984) discusses 3^{k-q} designs and Kirk (1995) provides a general discussion of 3^{k-q} designs and a complete worked-out example of the 3^{4-1} design. When IVs have three levels, the Latin-square design of Chapter 9 and the Box-Behnken and Taguchi designs described in this chapter are probably more practical than the fractional factorial.

10.5.3   Plackett-Burman Designs

Plackett-Burman designs are of resolution III (cf. Section 10.5.1) and maximize the number of main effects that can be analyzed from as few runs as possible. They are used to screen a very large number of IVs and are more flexible than resolution III fractional-factorial designs in the number of runs that can be used.

The most common Plackett-Burman designs have numerous IVs, each with two levels. The number of runs (cases) required is some multiple of 4 instead of the number computed using Equation 10.5 for the two-level fractional-factorial design. The design allows you to study up to k IVs in $k + 1$ runs, as long as $k + 1$ is a multiple of 4. For example, you can study 11 IVs in 12 runs. Schmidt and Launsby (1994) show how to generate Plackett-Burman designs by hand.

Table 10.15 shows SYSTAT DESIGN syntax and generated data set for 11 IVs in 12 runs with two replicates and randomized order of runs. The design matrix also is produced as printed output (not shown).

There are two blocks of runs representing the two replications, 1 to 12 and 13 to 24. The first column (Run) shows the runs in order. Columns for IVs A through K use -1 and 1 to designate the two levels of each IV; there are 12 observations at each of the two levels. The columns are orthogonal, but only if computed over the entire 24 runs. Hypothetical data are added to the last column (Y) of the data set; in practice, data are added after they are collected.

SYSTAT also analyzes the data through GLM. Table 10.16 shows SYSTAT GLM syntax and selected output. Only main effects are analyzed—no interactions. All IVs are declared to be categorical.

The Analysis of Variance table shows that mean differences on H and K are statistically reliable at $\alpha = .05$. Further research examines these two IVs, and perhaps E, with $p = .073$. These two or three variables might be examined in factorial arrangment, with analysis of the interaction(s).

SYSTAT DESIGN extends Plackett-Burman designs to those in which IVs have three or more levels. A request for 9, 27, or 81 runs provides designs with three levels of each of 4, 13, or 40 IVs, respectively.[4] A request for 25 or 125 runs provides designs with five levels each of 6 or 31 IVs, respectively. A request for 49 runs provides a seven-level design for eight factors.

Plackett-Burman designs are generated through NCSS Design of Experiments by specifying the number of runs ($k + 1$) and the number of replicates in the Screening Designs menu. No output is printed, but a data set is generated, which looks similar to Table 10.15. MINITAB DOE generates Plackett-Burman designs by specifying the number of IVs (up to 47) and the number of replicates.

---

[4]Are we serious about 40 factors?

TABLE 10.15 Plackett-Burman Design for 11 Factors in 12 Runs: SYSTAT DESIGN Syntax and Generated Data Set

```
DESIGN
SAVE 'D:\BOOK.ANV\Screen\plackbur.syd'
PLACKET / RUNS=12 REPS=2 LETTERS RAND
```

Run	A	B	C	D	E	F	G	H	I	J	K	Y
1.000	1.000	-1.000	1.000	1.000	1.000	-1.000	-1.000	-1.000	1.000	-1.000	1.000	6.000
2.000	1.000	-1.000	1.000	1.000	-1.000	1.000	1.000	1.000	1.000	-1.000	-1.000	5.000
3.000	-1.000	-1.000	1.000	-1.000	-1.000	1.000	1.000	1.000	1.000	1.000	-1.000	4.000
4.000	1.000	-1.000	1.000	-1.000	1.000	-1.000	1.000	1.000	1.000	1.000	-1.000	2.000
5.000	1.000	-1.000	-1.000	-1.000	1.000	-1.000	1.000	1.000	-1.000	1.000	1.000	8.000
6.000	1.000	-1.000	1.000	1.000	1.000	-1.000	-1.000	-1.000	1.000	1.000	1.000	7.000
7.000	-1.000	1.000	1.000	-1.000	1.000	-1.000	-1.000	1.000	1.000	-1.000	1.000	5.000
8.000	-1.000	-1.000	-1.000	1.000	1.000	1.000	-1.000	-1.000	1.000	-1.000	-1.000	4.000
9.000	-1.000	-1.000	1.000	-1.000	1.000	1.000	-1.000	-1.000	-1.000	1.000	-1.000	3.000
10.000	1.000	1.000	-1.000	1.000	-1.000	1.000	-1.000	1.000	-1.000	1.000	1.000	1.000
11.000	-1.000	1.000	1.000	-1.000	-1.000	-1.000	-1.000	-1.000	-1.000	1.000	1.000	9.000
12.000	-1.000	-1.000	-1.000	-1.000	-1.000	-1.000	-1.000	-1.000	-1.000	-1.000	-1.000	2.000
13.000	-1.000	1.000	1.000	-1.000	-1.000	1.000	1.000	-1.000	-1.000	-1.000	1.000	8.000
14.000	-1.000	1.000	1.000	-1.000	-1.000	1.000	1.000	-1.000	-1.000	-1.000	-1.000	6.000
15.000	-1.000	-1.000	-1.000	1.000	-1.000	1.000	1.000	1.000	1.000	-1.000	-1.000	3.000
16.000	-1.000	1.000	-1.000	1.000	-1.000	1.000	1.000	1.000	1.000	1.000	-1.000	5.000
17.000	-1.000	-1.000	-1.000	1.000	-1.000	1.000	1.000	-1.000	1.000	1.000	1.000	6.000
18.000	-1.000	1.000	1.000	-1.000	-1.000	1.000	-1.000	-1.000	1.000	-1.000	1.000	6.000
19.000	1.000	1.000	-1.000	-1.000	1.000	-1.000	-1.000	1.000	1.000	-1.000	1.000	8.000
20.000	1.000	1.000	-1.000	-1.000	1.000	1.000	1.000	1.000	1.000	-1.000	1.000	8.000
21.000	-1.000	-1.000	-1.000	1.000	1.000	1.000	-1.000	-1.000	-1.000	1.000	1.000	9.000
22.000	1.000	1.000	-1.000	1.000	-1.000	1.000	1.000	-1.000	1.000	1.000	1.000	3.000
23.000	1.000	-1.000	1.000	1.000	-1.000	1.000	1.000	-1.000	-1.000	1.000	-1.000	4.000
24.000	1.000	1.000	1.000	-1.000	-1.000	-1.000	1.000	-1.000	1.000	1.000	-1.000	3.000

TABLE 10.16   Analysis of Plackett-Burman Design through SYSTAT GLM: Syntax and Selected Output

```
PRINT=MEDIUM
GLM
CATEGORY A B C D E F G H I J K / EFFECT
MODEL Y = CONSTANT + A+B+C+D+E+F+G+H+I+J+K
ESTIMATE

Dep Var: Y   N: 24   Multiple R: 0.958   Squared multiple R: 0.918
```

Analysis of Variance

Source	Sum-of-Squares	df	Mean-Square	F-ratio	P
A	1.042	1	1.042	1.190	0.297
B	0.042	1	0.042	0.048	0.831
C	0.375	1	0.375	0.429	0.525
D	1.042	1	1.042	1.190	0.297
E	3.375	1	3.375	3.857	0.073
F	0.042	1	0.042	0.048	0.831
G	1.042	1	1.042	1.190	0.297
H	18.375	1	18.375	21.000	0.001
I	0.042	1	0.042	0.048	0.831
J	0.042	1	0.042	0.048	0.831
K	92.042	1	92.042	105.190	0.000
Error	10.500	12	0.875		

Analysis of Plackett-Burman designs proceeds as in Table 10.16 with only main effects included in the model.

10.5.4   Taguchi Designs

Taguchi designs were developed to facilitate quality control. Like Plackett-Burman designs, they provide tests of the maximum number of IVs with a minimum number of runs. However, the emphasis is not so much on the performance of individual IVs as on effect size and the combination of levels of IVs that produces the optimum (largest or smallest) value of the DV. Taguchi designs can be used to identify the optimal combination of conditions for producing anything from a high-quality paint job to the most favorable therapeutic outcome.

Taguchi's approach differs from the classic ANOVA approach in at least two respects. The first is that two (or more) responses are usually taken for each run, under different environmental (noise) conditions. These two (or more) responses form the levels of the "outer array." The individual responses are the same as responses to any of the other screening designs. However, the two (or more) responses from different environmental conditions are combined into a single DV that reflects both the central tendency and the variability among the responses. The combined DVs are then used to form the "inner array." That is, each combination of levels of IVs (run) has a response in the inner array that is a combination of responses in the outer array.

Taguchi methods emphasize that the optimum combination of levels of IVs is the one where responses are not only at their highest (or lowest) level but also are stable. Thus, the levels of the outer array are combined into a single DV that reflects both central tendency and variability, η (eta; details to follow).

A second difference is in the statistics used for analysis. The DV is a signal-to-noise ratio statistic, η, that takes into account both the central tendency and variability of responses in the outer array. The combination of levels of IVs is sought to produce maximum η. When the importance of individual IVs is evaluated, a "degree-of-contribution" measure, ρ (%), often replaces the F ratio. The statistical approach is discussed in detail by Taguchi (1993) and by Schmidt and Launsby (1994).[5]

The designs are named by the number of runs (treatment combinations) formed by the inner array of IVs, where L_4 is a design with 4 runs, L_{12} a design with 12 runs, and so on. Taguchi designs typically are forms of other resolution III designs, such as the fractional factorial, Plackett-Burman, Latin square, and so on (Schmidt and Launsby, 1994). Although most are resolution III screening designs (cf. Section 10.5.1), some also permit evaluation of some two-way interactions. Table 10.17 summarizes Taguchi designs in terms of the number of IVs and their levels. For example, an L_{18} design has 18 runs with 8 IVs: 1 two-level IV and 7 three-level IVs.

If a traditional ANOVA approach (with F ratios) is used to evaluate individual IVs, and all effects are evaluated, there are often no degrees of freedom left for error. Either more than one replicate is run in order to have some degrees of freedom for error, or a preliminary analysis determines which effects are unimportant and these are pooled in subsequent analyses to provide an estimate of error.

L_8, L_{12}, L_{16}, and L_{32} are Plackett-Burman designs and are coded as described in Section 10.5.3. L_4, L_8, L_{16}, and L_{32} are two-level fractional-factorials that are coded as described in Section 10.5.2.1. L_{27} is a three-level fractional-factorial design. Coding of levels of IVs for most remaining designs is complex and best left to SYSTAT DESIGN, or NCSS.

Taguchi (1993) provides tables for coding many of these designs and also shows patterns of aliasing for them. These tables are useful if you are interested in testing some interactions in lieu of some of the main effects. For example, if the main effect of C, expected to be negligible, is aliased with the interesting $A \times B$ interaction, the statistical result of the column labeled "C" is interpreted as the $A \times B$ interaction. SYSTAT DESIGN also shows aliasing patterns for some Taguchi designs.

Table 10.18 shows a Taguchi L_{12} design generated through SYSTAT DESIGN. Letter labels are requested as well as randomization of runs, with one replicate per cell. Entries in the columns indicate the levels of each of the IVs for that particular run. The pattern of aliasing is also available

---

[5]These sources also discuss a loss function, which translates differences between ideal and actual responses into a financial measure.

TABLE 10.17 Taguchi Designs

Design	Number of Runs	Number of IVs	Number of Levels
L_4	4	3	2 each
L_8	8	7	2 each
L_9	9	4	3 each
L_{12}	12	11	2 each
L_{16}	16	15	2 each
L_{16}	16	5	4 each
L_{18}	18	1	2
		7	3 each
L_{25}	25	6	5 each
L_{27}	27	13	3 each
L_{27}	27	22	3 each
L_{32}	32	31	2 each
L_{32}	32	1	3
		9	4 each
L_{32}	32	1	2
		9	4 each
L_{36}	36	11	2 each
		12	3 each
L_{36}	36	3	2 each
		3	3 each
L_{50}	50	1	2
		11	5 each
L_{54}	54	1	2
		25	3 each
L_{64}	64	63	2

in SYSTAT DESIGN for Taguchi designs if you request `PRINT=LONG`, although only full aliasing (complete confounding) is shown. Effects that are only partially confounded are not identified. That output revealed that none of the interactions is fully aliased in the L_{12} design of Table 10.18.

Table 10.19 shows the output data set with IV entries generated by SYSTAT DESIGN with two hypothetical response values added to the data set; these two responses form the outer array. The two responses, `RESP1` and `RESP2`, represent responses taken by running the experiment under two differing environmental (noise) conditions. Each case provides values for both responses, which then are combined over the outer array into a single S/N (signal-to-noise) ratio (`ETA` in the data set) to serve as the DV.

The final column, `ETA`, is the S/N ratio, converted to a dB (decibel) scale, and is calculated as follows:

$$\eta = -10 \log \left(\frac{1}{p} \sum_1^p Y^2 \right) \tag{10.6}$$

The S/N ratio in dB units (η) for a case is found by squaring each of the p responses for the case, summing them, dividing by the number of responses, taking the log to the base 10, and multiplying the result by -10.

TABLE 10.18   Taguchi L_{12} Design through SYSTAT DESIGN

```
SAVE 'D:\BOOK.ANV\SCREEN\TAGL12.SYD'
DESIGN
  TAGUCHI / REPS=1 TYPE=L12 LETTERS RAND
    Taguchi Design L12: 12 Runs; 11 Factors, Each With 2 Levels
```

	Factor										
Run	A	B	C	D	E	F	G	H	I	J	K
1	1	1	2	2	2	1	1	1	2	2	2
2	2	1	2	1	2	2	2	1	1	1	2
3	2	1	1	2	2	2	1	2	2	1	1
4	1	2	1	2	2	1	2	2	1	1	2
5	2	2	2	1	1	1	1	2	2	1	2
6	1	2	2	2	1	2	2	1	2	1	1
7	2	2	1	1	2	1	2	1	2	2	1
8	2	2	1	2	1	2	1	1	1	2	2
9	2	1	2	2	1	1	2	2	1	2	1
10	1	1	1	1	1	1	1	1	1	1	1
11	1	1	1	1	1	2	2	2	2	2	2
12	1	2	2	1	2	2	1	2	1	2	1

The design matrix has been saved.

TABLE 10.19   SYSTAT Data Set and Hypothetical Response Values for Taguchi L$_{12}$ Design through SYSTAT DESIGN

RUN	A	B	C	D	E	F	G	H	I	J	K	RESP1	RESP2	ETA
1	1	1	2	2	2	1	1	1	2	2	2	5	7	-15.682
2	2	1	2	1	2	2	2	1	1	1	2	4	5	-13.118
3	2	1	1	2	2	2	1	2	2	1	1	3	6	-13.522
4	1	2	1	2	2	1	2	2	1	1	2	2	3	-8.129
5	2	2	2	1	1	1	1	2	2	1	2	1	3	-6.99
6	1	2	2	2	1	2	2	1	2	1	1	6	8	-16.99
7	2	2	1	1	2	1	2	1	2	2	1	4	7	-15.119
8	2	2	1	2	1	2	1	1	1	2	2	5	4	-13.118
9	2	1	2	2	1	1	2	2	1	2	1	2	3	-8.129
10	1	1	1	1	1	1	1	1	1	1	1	7	7	-16.902
11	1	1	1	1	1	2	2	2	2	2	2	3	4	-10.969
12	1	2	2	1	2	2	1	2	1	2	1	1	2	-3.979

For example, the case that received the first run has responses in the outer array of $Y_1 = 5$ and $Y_2 = 7$. The S/N ratio for the responses for that case is

$$\eta = -10 \log\left[\frac{1}{2}(5^2 + 7^2)\right] = -15.682 \text{ dB}$$

The combination of levels of IVs in the inner array with the largest η (closest to zero, in this example, since all of the η values are negative) is the most desirable; in this example, it is the case that received the 12th run where $\eta = -3.979$ dB.

Equation 10.6 is appropriate when the DV is scaled so that smaller values are better. For the example, the case that received the first run has values in the outer array of 5 and 7, whereas the case that received the last run has values of 1 and 2, the best of the outcomes if smaller values are better. If larger DV values in the outer array are better, however, Equation 10.6 is modified by using the reciprocal of Y^2—$(1/Y^2)$—in place of Y^2 in the equation:

$$\eta = -10 \log\left(\frac{1}{p}\sum_1^p \frac{1}{Y^2}\right)$$

For the example, the case that received the 12th run, with scores of 1 and 2, now has the *least* favorable outcome and an η value of 2.04. The case that received the 10th run has both the highest DV values (7 and 7) and the most stable DV values, and produces an η value of 16.90. This value is higher than the value of 16.635 achieved by the case that received the 6th run, with DV scores in the outer array of 6 and 8. With this scaling, the highest value of η is also the most favorable outcome, but now all of the η values are positive (above zero).[6]

---

[6]Other variations of the S/N equation are available when the goal is for Y to achieve a target value or when the response standard deviation is related to its mean (Taguchi, 1993).

Individual IVs may be analyzed with traditional ANOVA using η as the DV. However, without replicates there are no degrees of freedom for error unless some effects are pooled to serve as error. Alternatively, measures of effect size are calculated and interpreted instead of F ratios. In either event, a preliminary ANOVA is used to determine which effects are unimportant.

Table 10.20 shows SYSTAT GLM syntax and selected output for the preliminary analysis to determine which effects to pool for error in this single-replicate design. F ratios are not calculated because there are no df for error. Taguchi provides no clear guidelines for pooling "small" effects into error. One strategy is to begin with a few very small effects, in this case A, F, and G, all of which have mean square values much smaller than the others. SYSTAT GLM syntax is modified to eliminate these as IVs during the next analysis, as shown in Table 10.21.

All effects except E are statistically significant at $\alpha = .05$ by traditional ANOVA methods. However, E is retained in the model because its F ratio exceeds 2, a criterion recommended by Schmidt and Launsby (1994). It should be clear that one's choice of which terms to combine into error after the preliminary analysis has direct impact on the significance of effects in the final analysis.

The Taguchi approach advocates replacing the F ratio with p (%) as a criterion for interpretation, calculated as

$$p_{effect} = \frac{SS_{effect} - df_{effect}(MS_{error})}{SS_{total}}(100) \tag{10.7}$$

TABLE 10.20 Preliminary Analysis of Taguchi L_{12} Design through SYSTAT GLM: Syntax and Selected Output

```
GLM
  CATEGORY A B C D E F G H I J K / EFFECT
  MODEL ETA = CONSTANT + A+B+C+D+E+F+G+H+I+J+K
  ESTIMATE

Effects coding used for categorical variables in model.
```

Analysis of Variance

Source	Sum-of-Squares	df	Mean-Square	F-ratio	P
A	0.587	1	0.587	.	.
B	16.326	1	16.326	.	.
C	13.805	1	13.805	.	.
D	6.011	1	6.011	.	.
E	1.050	1	1.050	.	.
F	0.046	1	0.046	.	.
G	0.426	1	0.426	.	.
H	128.125	1	128.125	.	.
I	21.060	1	21.060	.	.
J	6.242	1	6.242	.	.
K	3.669	1	3.669	.	.
Error	0.0	0		.	

TABLE 10.21   Analysis of Taguchi L$_{12}$ Design through SYSTAT GLM: Syntax and Selected Output

```
GLM
  CATEGORY B C D E H I J K / EFFECT
  MODEL ETA = CONSTANT + B+C+D+E+H+I+J+K

  ESTIMATE
```

Effects coding used for categorical variables in model.

Dep Var: ETA   N: 12   Multiple R: 0.997   Squared multiple R: 0.995

Analysis of Variance

Source	Sum-of-Squares	df	Mean-Square	F-ratio	P
B	16.326	1	16.326	46.221	0.007
C	13.805	1	13.805	39.083	0.008
D	6.011	1	6.011	17.017	0.026
E	1.050	1	1.050	2.972	0.183
H	128.125	1	128.125	362.728	0.000
I	21.060	1	21.060	59.620	0.005
J	6.242	1	6.242	17.673	0.025
K	3.669	1	3.669	10.386	0.048
Error	1.060	3	0.353		

This measure of effect size (converted to a percentage) falls between η^2 and ω^2 (Section 4.5.1) in size. This effect size, because it contains MS$_{error}$, is also sensitive to the choices of IVs to pool into error.[7] For the main effect of *B* in Table 10.21,

$$\rho_B = \frac{16.326 - (1)(0.353)}{197.348}(100) = 8.09$$

Table 10.22 shows the ANOVA table, including both traditional and Taguchi information. *H* is the strongest IV by far, accounting for about twice as much variance as all the other IVs combined. A Taguchi-based strategy also examines the combination of levels of IVs with the largest S/N ratio. As shown in Table 10.19, the best combination of factors occurs in the final run where $\eta = -3.979$. Ignoring the IVs with nonsignificant *F* ratios and/or trivial ρ, the best combination of factors includes lower levels of *D*, *I*, and *K*; and higher levels of *B*, *C*, *E*, *H*, and *J*. Follow-up research could include intermediate, lower, or higher levels of those IVs and possibly some interactions among them. Lev-

---

[7]Note, however, that ρ may be calculated even when there are no df for error, as in the output in Table 10.20. The second term in the numerator of Equation 10.7 is simply 0.

TABLE 10.22   Source Table for Taguchi L$_{12}$ Design

Source	SS	df	MS	F	ρ (%)
(A)	0.587	1	0.587		
B	16.326	1	16.326	46.22	8.1
C	13.805	1	13.805	39.08	6.8
D	6.011	1	6.011	17.02	2.9
E	1.050	1	1.050	2.97	0.4
(F)	0.046	1	0.046		
(G)	0.426	1	0.426		
H	128.125	1	128.125	362.73	64.7
I	21.060	1	21.060	59.62	10.5
J	6.242	1	6.242	17.67	3.0
K	3.669	1	3.669	10.39	1.7
Error	1.060	3	0.353		
T	197.348	12			

Note: Parentheses indicate effects to be pooled into errors.

els of *H*, particularly, could be extended to higher levels, if that is possible. Further experimentation also might be specially designed to assess interactions between *H* and other significant effects.

There is far more to the Taguchi approach than is dealt with here. For example, Taguchi (1993, pp. 75–76) provides the details, including statistics, to estimate the optimum combination of levels and the improvement in quality expected from it.

10.5.5   Response-Surface Methodology

Response-surface methodology is used for designs with quantitative IVs. As in Taguchi designs, the goal is not just to identify statistically significant IVs, but also to reveal the combination of levels of IVs that produces the most desirable response. The three most popular designs are Box-Behnken designs for three-level IVs; central-composite designs for five-level IVs; and mixture designs, used when the combination of IVs forms a constant quantity (e.g., 100%). Taguchi methods may also be applied to response-surface designs, as illustrated by Myers and Montgomery (1995, Chapter 10).

Response-surface methodology is typically applied after the list of potential IVs has been reduced through one or more of the screening designs described earlier. The researcher then tries additional levels of the surviving IVs to determine when the response approaches some optimum level. When the region of optimum response is identified, further analyses are conducted to build a mathematical model to find the combination of levels that produces the optimum response (Myers and Montgomery, 1995). Model adequacy is assessed at each phase of the study by examining residuals, as in any regression model (cf. Tabachnick and Fidell, 2001, Chapter 5).

Many of the designs and techniques in response-surface methodology are beyond the scope of this book. Some, for example, include multiple response measures. Only the more straightforward popular designs and analyses—and those most easily implemented through software—are outlined here. A good resource for a more detailed complete treatment of response-surface methodology is Myers and Montgomery (1995).

Response-surface methodology takes the regression approach to analysis. Early stages in the research focus on IVs with two levels or linear trends of quantitative IVs; later phases often include some (but not all) interactions among IVs and usually explore quadratic trends of IVs, as well. Higher-order interactions and trends are rarely investigated.

10.5.5.1   Box-Behnken Design

Box-Behnken designs are used when there are numerous quantitative IVs, each with three levels. For this reason, the design is infrequently employed in the social sciences. An example, however, might involve therapeutic outcome tested against length of therapy (2, 4, or 6 weeks), concentration of therapy (1, 2, or 3 sessions per week), number of other patients included in sessions (0, 2, or 4), age range of client (20–29, 30–39, 40–49), severity of illness (1 = mild, 2 = moderate, 3 = severe), and so on.

Linear and quadratic trends of main effects and interaction contrasts of linear trends of all two-way interactions are analyzed. For the example, does outcome improve as the duration of therapy increases (linear trend)? Or, is outcome better at 4 weeks than at either 2 or 6 weeks (quadratic trend)? Does the linear trend of duration of therapy depend on the linear trend of, say, age range of clients so that, for instance, older patients require longer therapies (linear by linear interaction contrast)?

Figure 10.2 diagrams the layout for a three-way Box-Behnken design. A Box-Behnken design is especially amenable to a regression approach because each of the effects tested has a single degree of freedom.

Table 10.23 shows a hypothetical data set with four IVs and codes for the 14 effects in this Box-Behnken design. The 14 effects consist of four linear and four quadratic tests of main effects and six linear by linear interaction contrasts. Codes for linear effects are available through software (e.g., SYSTAT DESIGN, which has several Box-Behnken design options, and SPSS Trial Run) or in Schmidt and Launsby (1994), who show codes for three, four, and five IVs. Codes for quadratic trend are generated by squaring codes for linear trend. Note that this is a different type of coding that uses only 0, 1, and −1 as coefficients (cf. Section 3.5.5, effects coding) than the contrast coding used elsewhere in this book. Codes for the linear by linear interaction contrasts are, as usual, the products of the linear codes for the pairs of component IVs.

Table 10.24 shows the syntax and output for generating the linear codes of Table 10.23 through SYSTAT DESIGN. To make the pattern easier to see, randomization of runs is not requested, unlike in an actual set of experimental runs. For analysis, the + and − values in the output file (named BOX-BEN.SYD in Table 10.24) are replaced by 1.000 and −1.000, respectively. The response scores are added to the file by hand after data are collected. (A blocking factor to represent replications, as per SAS FACTEX, may also be requested; the number of blocks depends on the number of IVs, as indicated in the SYSTAT manual: SPSS, Inc., 1999e.)

The data set is evaluated through regression, with columns for quadratic effects and interaction contrasts of linear trend added if the data are analyzed by hand. However, the normal regression

(a) Sums of squares

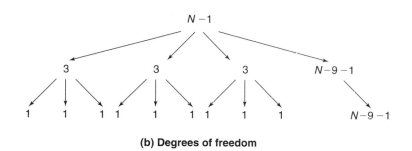

(b) Degrees of freedom

FIGURE 10.2   Partition of (a) Sums of Squares and (b) Degrees of Freedom into Systematic Sources of Linear Trends of A, B, and C; Quadratic Trends of A, B, and C; Linear by Linear Interaction Contrasts among A, B, and C; and Remaining (Error) Differences among Cases

approach described in Section 10.4.3 and elsewhere is inadequate because not all the effects are orthogonal. In particular, the codes for the quadratic effects are correlated with other effects so the cross-products of columns do not sum to zero: They are not orthogonal. Therefore, matrix algebra is required for hand calculation of the regression approach, a grisly procedure with 14 predictors.

However, analysis is available through SYSTAT GLM, SAS GLM, MINITAB GLM, and SPSS GLM, as well as NCSS. Table 10.25 shows syntax and output for the analysis through SYSTAT GLM. Quadratic effects are specified in the MODEL instruction by multiplying a factor by itself (e.g., `A*A`) and interactions are specified by cross-multiplying factors (e.g., `A*B`). Recall that SYSTAT GLM uses only Type III sums of squares for nonorthogonal effects.

The `Analysis of Variance` table shows that there is significant prediction of the response from the 14 effects combined. Individual effects are evaluated at $\alpha = .05$ by using the 95% confidence intervals (`Lower < 95% > Upper`): effects whose intervals do not include zero are statistically reliable. Thus, the significant linear effects for A and B. Only D has a significant quadratic effect. The significant interaction contrast is $A_{\text{linear}} \times B_{\text{linear}}$. C does not appear in any reliable effects. If this screening run does not resolve all questions of interest, follow-up research might involve a full factorial design with A, B, and D to provide tests of all two-way interactions of A, B, and C and the three-way $A \times B \times D$ interaction.

The design can also be analyzed through SAS FACTEX, MINITAB DOE, and NCSS Response Surface Analysis, which include modules that do not require specification of quadratic

TABLE 10.23 Example of Box-Behnken Design with Four IVs

Run	y	A_{LIN}	B_{LIN}	C_{LIN}	D_{LIN}	A_{QUAD}	B_{QUAD}	C_{QUAD}	D_{QUAD}	$A_{LIN}*B_{LIN}$	$A_{LIN}*C_{LIN}$	$A_{LIN}*D_{LIN}$	$B_{LIN}*C_{LIN}$	$B_{LIN}*D_{LIN}$	$C_{LIN}*D_{LIN}$
1	9	-1	-1	0	0	1	1	0	0	1	0	0	0	0	0
2	6	1	-1	0	0	1	1	0	0	-1	0	0	0	0	0
3	1	-1	1	0	0	1	1	0	0	-1	0	0	0	0	0
4	6	1	1	0	0	1	1	0	0	1	0	0	0	0	0
5	3	0	0	-1	-1	0	0	1	1	0	0	0	0	0	1
6	3	0	0	1	-1	0	0	1	1	0	0	0	0	0	-1
7	3	0	0	-1	1	0	0	1	1	0	0	0	0	0	-1
8	2	0	0	1	1	0	0	1	1	0	0	0	0	0	1
9	4	0	0	0	0	0	0	0	0	0	0	0	0	0	0
10	5	-1	0	-1	0	1	0	1	0	0	1	0	0	0	0
11	7	1	0	-1	0	1	0	1	0	0	-1	0	0	0	0
12	5	-1	0	1	0	1	0	1	0	0	-1	0	0	0	0
13	7	1	0	1	0	1	0	1	0	0	1	0	0	0	0
14	8	0	-1	-1	0	0	1	1	0	0	0	0	1	0	0
15	3	0	1	-1	0	0	1	1	0	0	0	0	-1	0	0
16	7	0	-1	1	0	0	1	1	0	0	0	0	-1	0	0
17	2	0	1	1	0	0	1	1	0	0	0	0	1	0	0
18	6	0	0	0	0	0	0	0	0	0	0	0	0	0	0
19	6	-1	0	0	-1	1	0	0	1	0	0	1	0	0	0
20	8	1	0	0	-1	1	0	0	1	0	0	-1	0	0	0
21	5	-1	0	0	1	1	0	0	1	0	0	-1	0	0	0
22	8	1	0	0	1	1	0	0	1	0	0	1	0	0	0
23	6	0	-1	0	-1	0	1	0	1	0	0	0	0	1	0
24	3	0	1	0	-1	0	1	0	1	0	0	0	0	-1	0
25	7	0	-1	0	1	0	1	0	1	0	0	0	0	-1	0
26	3	0	1	0	1	0	1	0	1	0	0	0	0	1	0
27	8	0	0	0	0	0	0	0	0	0	0	0	0	0	0

TABLE 10.24   Box-Behnken Design Generated through SYSTAT DESIGN: Syntax and Printed Output

```
SAVE 'D:\D&A\SCREEN\BOX-BEN.SYD'
BOXBEHNKEN / FACTORS=4 LETTERS

  Box-Behnken Design: 27 Runs; 4 Factors,
                    Each With 3 Levels


               Factor
      Run    A    B    C    D

       1     -    -    0    0
       2     +    -    0    0
       3     -    +    0    0
       4     +    +    0    0
       5     0    0    -    -
       6     0    0    +    -
       7     0    0    -    +
       8     0    0    +    +
       9     0    0    0    0
      10     -    0    0    -
      11     +    0    0    -
      12     -    0    0    +
      13     +    0    0    +
      14     0    -    -    0
      15     0    +    -    0
      16     0    -    +    0
      17     0    +    +    0
      18     0    0    0    0
      19     -    0    -    0
      20     +    0    -    0
      21     -    0    +    0
      22     +    0    +    0
      23     0    -    0    -
      24     0    +    0    -
      25     0    -    0    +
      26     0    +    0    +
      27     0    0    0    0
The design matrix has been saved.
```

components and interaction contrasts. Further, these programs offer plots to help identify regions of optimal response.

Qualitative IVs can be analyzed through Box-Behnken designs, as well, if codes can be applied to levels in a way that makes research sense. For example, if the levels of an IV represent two types of treatment and a control, codes of 1 and −1 are applied to the treatments and 0 to the control. The "linear" trend compares the treatments with each other, whereas the "quadratic" effect evaluates

TABLE 10.25   Box-Behnken Design Analyzed through SYSTAT GLM: Syntax and Selected Output

```
GLM
MODEL RESPONSE = CONSTANT + A + B + C + D + A*A + B*B + C*C + D*D + B*A
                + C*A + D*A + C*B + D*B + D*C
ESTIMATE
```

Dep Var: RESPONSE N: 27 Multiple R: 0.907 Squared multiple R: 0.822

Adjusted squared multiple R: 0.614 Standard error of estimate: 1.392

Effect	Coefficient	Std Error	Std Coef	Tolerance	t	P(2 Tail)
CONSTANT	4.833	0.464	0.0	.	10.417	0.000
A	0.917	0.402	0.278	1.000	2.281	0.042
B	-2.083	0.402	-0.631	1.000	-5.185	0.000
C	-0.333	0.402	-0.101	1.000	-0.830	0.423
D	0.000	0.402	0.000	1.000	0.000	1.000
A*A	0.333	0.201	0.226	0.800	1.659	0.123
B*B	-0.167	0.201	-0.113	0.800	-0.830	0.423
C*C	-0.292	0.201	-0.198	0.800	-1.452	0.172
D*D	-0.458	0.201	-0.311	0.800	-2.281	0.042
B*A	2.000	0.696	0.350	1.000	2.874	0.014
C*A	0.250	0.696	0.044	1.000	0.359	0.726
D*A	0.000	0.696	0.000	1.000	0.000	1.000
C*B	0.000	0.696	0.000	1.000	0.000	1.000
D*B	-0.250	0.696	-0.044	1.000	-0.359	0.726
D*C	-0.250	0.696	-0.044	1.000	-0.359	0.726

Effect	Coefficient	Lower <95%>	Upper
CONSTANT	4.833	3.822	5.844
A	0.917	0.041	1.792
B	-2.083	-2.959	-1.208
C	-0.333	-1.209	0.542
D	0.000	-0.875	0.875
A*A	0.333	-0.104	0.771
B*B	-0.167	-0.604	0.271
C*C	-0.292	-0.729	0.146
D*D	-0.458	-0.896	-0.021
B*A	2.000	0.484	3.516
C*A	0.250	-1.266	1.766
D*A	0.000	-1.516	1.516
C*B	0.000	-1.516	1.516
D*B	-0.250	-1.766	1.266
D*C	-0.250	-1.766	1.266

Analysis of Variance

Source	Sum-of-Squares	df	Mean-Square	F-ratio	P
Regression	107.417	14	7.673	3.960	0.011
Residual	23.250	12	1.937		

the average of the treatments versus the control. The interaction contrasts are between treatments, with the control groups omitted.

10.5.5.2 Central-Composite Designs

Each IV has five levels in this, the prototype of the response-surface design. The IVs are considered continuous, with discrete coding used for convenience during experimentation. Central-composite designs, like Box-Behnken designs, test linear and quadratic effects of each of the IVs and the linear by linear components of the two-way interactions. Thus, the partition of sums of squares and degrees of freedom follows Figure 10.2. Variations among central-composite designs and their properties are discussed in detail by Montgomery (1984).

Standard central-composite analysis is a sequential procedure that begins with a test of the combination of linear effects of all IVs. This first test asks if a model with only linear components is related to the DV. A test of the combination of quadratic effects of IVs and linear interaction contrasts follows. The second test asks if the prediction of the DV is improved by addition of quadratic and interaction contrast components. Follow-up tests determine which individual effects are statistically reliable.

Response surfaces are examined through pairwise plots of IVs, in which contours are shown for values of the DV. A circle inside such a plot indicates that highest (or lowest) values of the DV fall at the levels of the two IVs aligned with the circle. Figure 10.3 shows such a contour plot, in which high values of the DV, Y, are desirable, and the two axes represent levels of A and B. The optimum response occurs in the region of $A = B = 5$ in this plot.

Sometimes the point of optimum response appears to lie outside the range of the levels chosen for some of the IVs. The plots are examined to estimate the direction in which the optimum region lies, to help design follow-up experiments. SAS FACTEX and NCSS Response Surface Analysis

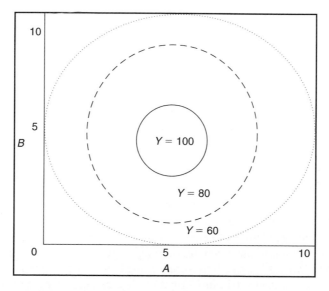

**FIGURE 10.3   Response-Surface Contour Plot of Y
as a Function of A and B**

provide printed estimates of optimum areas for each IV or show directions in which optimum points are likely to be found. A central-composite design generated and analyzed through NCSS is demonstrated in Section 10.8.

There are some alternatives available when analyzing data generated by a central-composite design. For example, if you are uninterested in the interaction contrasts, you can do a full trend analysis (to fourth order) of the main effects.

10.5.5.3 Mixture Models

Mixture designs are used when cases are formed by mixtures or blends of levels of quantitative IVs. These designs require the sum of the levels of the IVs to equal some fixed total for every case or run (e.g., 100%, or "a glassful of beverage"). If, for example, the two IVs are percentage of rum (A) and percentage of Coke (B) in a drink, levels of each might be 0%, 50%, and 100%. Three runs (blends or cases) cover all possible mixtures for two IVs with three levels: all rum and no Coke, all Coke and no rum, and 50% of each. (We leave the DV to the imagination of the reader.) Table 10.26 shows the levels in this mixture design. Two additional runs are required if there are five levels (adding 25% and 75%), as shown in Table 10.27.

Proportions are chosen to cover the response surface of all potential mixtures of these components to facilitate prediction of the optimal blend. Obviously, not all blends can be investigated, particularly since the IVs are considered continuous. Several strategies have been proposed to determine mixtures likely to cover the response surface under different research circumstances (e.g., reduce the number of IVs in each blend). Cornell (1990) provides guidelines for generating many mixture designs, or they can be generated through software such as SYSTAT DESIGN, SAS FACTEX or OPTEX, or MINITAB DOE.

10.5.5.3.1 Lattice Designs

Lattice designs (labeled simplex-lattice by Cornell, 1990) are the most popular of the mixture designs. The number of IVs is flexible, but all IVs have the same number of levels. As shown in Table 10.26, two IVs (A and B) each can have three levels (1.0, .5, and 0), or, as in Table 10.27, each can have five levels (1.0, .75, .50, .25, and 0), or any other number of levels. The number of IVs and their levels determine the minimum number of runs, without replication.

Lattice designs are neither factorial nor orthogonal. For example, the 3×3 design of Table 10.26 would have nine cells in a full-factorial design, one of them representing 0% of both A and B, whereas another represents 100% of both A and B, and so on. Clearly, not all combinations are even feasible. Further, the correlation between A and B is not zero because once the level of A is chosen, the level of B is fixed since A and B sum to 100%. Consequently, there are not enough degrees of freedom to include all IVs in the analysis. On the other hand, the quantitative nature of the IVs makes trend analysis appealing.

The most popular analysis, based on Scheffé and reviewed by Cornell (1990) and Myers and Montgomery (1995), is a multiple-regression approach in which one of the IVs is dropped (and thus acts as the intercept) and interactions are formed for all the IVs, including the dropped one. The original IVs, coded by their proportions in the mixture (as in Tables 10.26 and 10.27), form the linear portion of the model. Two-way interactions form the quadratic portion of the model, and so on.

Table 10.28 shows a data set from Cornell (1990), elaborated by Myers and Montgomery (1995). The three IVs are components of a yarn mixture: A = polyethylene, B = polystyrene, and C

TABLE 10.26   Diagram of a 3 × 3 Mixture Design

Run	A: Rum	B: Coke
1	1.0	0
2	0	1.0
3	0.5	0.5

TABLE 10.27   Diagram of a 5 × 5 Mixture Design

Run	A: Rum	B: Coke
1	1.0	0
2	0	1.0
3	0.5	0.5
4	0.25	0.75
5	0.75	0.25

TABLE 10.28   Lattice Design from Cornell (1990)

A	B	C	ELONG
1	0	0	11.0
1	0	0	12.4
.5	.5	0	15.0
.5	.5	0	14.8
.5	.5	0	16.1
0	1	0	8.8
0	1	0	10.0
0	.5	.5	10.0
0	.5	.5	9.7
0	.5	.5	11.8
0	0	1	16.8
0	0	1	16.0
.5	0	.5	17.7
.5	0	.5	16.4
.5	0	.5	16.6

= polypropylene. The two types of mixtures of interest in this lattice design with three components are pure blends (all one component) and binary blends (.50–.50 mixes of two of the three components). There are no three-component blends. Two replications of each pure blend and three replications of each binary blend are assessed. The DV is elongation of the fabric when a certain force is applied.

Because of the nonorthogonality of A, B, and C in this lattice design, and because trends are interesting with these quantitative IVs, a sequential regression analysis (cf. Section 5.6.5) is run in which the first step includes the linear portions of A, B and C and the second step includes their interactions. Recall that sequential regression provides an analysis for nonorthogonal data because variables entered first take all their own variability plus any overlapping variability shared with variables not yet entered. Variables entered second are assigned only the remaining variability they share with the DV. Thus, each portion of overlapping variability is only analyzed once.

Table 10.29 shows syntax and output from SPSS COMPUTE and REGRESSION for this analysis. The interactions are created through COMPUTE instructions before REGRESSION is run.[8] The first three lines of the REGRESSION syntax are produced by default, except for the request for CHANGE statistics, to ask whether the interactions reliably add to prediction of elongation beyond that afforded by the linear portion. The NOORIGIN instruction makes the CONSTANT equivalent to A, so the main effect of A is left out. The two METHOD instructions list the IVs to be

---

[8]Because linear codes are used for A, B, and C (0, .5, and 1.0), the cross-products of the terms also represent a quadratic trend. In this lattice design, these terms represent the tendency for a .50–.50 mix to be stronger (or weaker) than the pure blends (e.g., to have a quadratic trend).

TABLE 10.29   Analysis of Lattice Design through SPSS REGRESSION: Syntax and Selected Output

```
COMPUTE ab = a*b.
COMPUTE ac = a*c.
COMPUTE bc = b*c.
REGRESSION
  /MISSING LISTWISE
  /STATISTICS COEFF OUTS R ANOVA CHANGE
  /CRITERIA=PIN(.05) POUT(.10)
  /NOORIGIN
  /DEPENDENT elong
  /METHOD=ENTER b c /METHOD=ENTER ab ac bc.
```

Regression

Variables Entered/Removed[b]

Model	Variables Entered	Variables Removed	Method
1	C, B[a]	.	Enter
2	BC, AC, AB[a]	.	Enter

a. All requested variables entered.

b. Dependent Variable: ELONG

Model Summary

Model	R	R Square	Adjusted R Square	Std. Error of the Estimate	Change Statistics				
					R Square Change	F Change	df1	df2	Sig. F Change
1	.654[a]	.427	.332	2.5368	.427	4.477	2	12	.035
2	.975[b]	.951	.924	.8537	.524	32.317	3	9	.000

a. Predictors: (Constant), C, B

b. Predictors: (Constant), C, B, BC, AC, AB

ANOVA[c]

Model		Sum of Squares	df	Mean Square	F	Sig.
1	Regression	57.629	2	28.815	4.477	.035[a]
	Residual	77.227	12	6.436		
	Total	134.856	14			
2	Regression	128.296	5	25.659	35.203	.000[b]
	Residual	6.560	9	.729		
	Total	134.856	14			

a. Predictors: (Constant), C, B

b. Predictors: (Constant), C, B, BC, AC, AB

c. Dependent Variable: ELONG

594

TABLE 10.29 Continued

Coefficients^a

Model		Unstandardized Coefficients		Standardized Coefficients		
		B	Std. Error	Beta	t	Sig.
1	(Constant)	14.995	1.410		10.632	.000
	B	−5.164	2.163	−.602	−2.387	.034
	C	.800	2.163	.093	.370	.718
2	(Constant)	11.700	.604		19.381	.000
	B	−2.300	.854	−.268	−2.694	.025
	C	4.700	.854	.548	5.505	.000
	AB	19.000	2.608	.634	7.285	.000
	AC	11.400	2.608	.380	4.371	.002
	BC	−9.600	2.608	−.320	−3.681	.005

a. Dependent Variable: ELONG

entered on the two regression steps. The first **ENTER** specifies entry of *B* and *C*; *A* is omitted because it serves as the intercept or baseline value. This step analyzes the linear portion of the model because coding for each effect is quantitative: 0, .5, and 1. The second step includes the three interaction terms, *AB*, *AC*, and *BC*. The final line of syntax requests predicted scores, residuals, and standardized residuals.

The **Variables Entered/Removed** table reminds us that variables enter into the regression equation in two steps: first the linear components and then the interactions. In the output, **Model 1** refers to an equation with the intercept (*A*, called **Constant** by SPSS Regression), *B*, and *C*. **Model 2** refers to the complete equation with both linear components and interaction. The **Model Summary** table shows significant prediction of the response with only the linear effects of each component $F(2, 12) = 4.48$, $p = .035$, and enhancement of that prediction when interaction components are added, $F(3, 9) = 32.32$, $p < .0005$. This result indicates that combinations of components have effects on elongation above and beyond the linear effect of each one separately. When all components are included, the model predicts 95% (**R Square** = **.951**) of the variance in elongation with $F(5, 9) = 35.203$, $p < .0005$.

With a bit of maneuvering, the **Coefficients** table gives us the regression equation for predicting elongation. Component *A* is represented in the equation by the intercept (called **Constant** by SPSS Regression). In the full model (**Model 2**), this value is 11.7, the mean of the two data points for a pure mixture of *A*. Thus, *A* is acting as a baseline, supplemented by coefficients for *B* and *C*. The coefficients for *B* and *C* are adjusted by adding the constant to them. The corrected coefficient for *B*, then, is the constant plus the printed value $[11.7 + (−2.3)] = 9.4$, and the corrected coefficient for *C* is $(11.7 + 4.7) = 16.4$. (These coefficients now equal the means of *B* and *C*, respectively.) The prediction equation with corrected coefficients, then, is

$$Y' = 11.7A + 9.4B + 16.4C + 19.0AB + 11.4AC + −9.6BC$$

All components are statistically reliable at $\alpha = .05$, but $\alpha = .01$ provides better control of familywise error. At the more stringent α level, the linear contribution of B is problematic. Component C (polypropylene), with the highest coefficient, makes the largest contribution to yarn elongation, producing the strongest yarn. However, the positive coefficients of the AB and AC interactions suggest that these combinations produce yarn of greater strength than expected from simply adding their linear effects, whereas the negative coefficient of the BC interaction indicates that this combination produces a *weaker* yarn than expected from their linear components.

10.5.5.3.2   Other Mixture Designs

The lattice design is the most flexible mixture design, with the number of IVs and the number of levels independent (although each IV must have the same number of levels). In the three remaining mixture designs mentioned here, centroid, axial, and screening, the number of IVs determines the number of levels.

Centroid designs (called simplex-centroid by Cornell, 1990) are those in which each of the mixtures has equal proportions of each included component. So, for example, a design with five IVs has one mixture composed of 1/3 each of, say, A, B, and C, and no D or E, and then other 1/3 mixtures of all other combination of three IVs from the five. Other mixtures are composed 1/2 each of, say, C and D, with no A, B, or E, and 1/2 mixtures of all other pairwise combinations of two IVs, and so on. Pure mixtures of each component are also included in the design.

Axial designs have some proportion of each component in almost all mixtures. These designs allow an in-depth analysis of the response surface (SYSTAT manual: SPSS, 1999e).

Screening designs are useful when there is a large number of potential components and the goal is to rule out some of them. The design involves running mixtures with proportions of numerous components, but during analysis, some components are effectively reduced to zero by combining terms in statistical tests of the model (Cornell, 1990). The design is similar to the centroid design and differs from the axial design in that most mixtures contain proportions of a few components, rather than emphasizing complete mixtures (SPSS, 1999e).

These designs, and variations on them (including the lattice design), are comprehensively covered by Cornell (1990). A discussion of these and other mixture designs (with several detailed analyses) is offered by Myers and Montgomery (1995).

10.5.6   Optimal Designs

The appropriate design for your experiment may not fit the specifications of any of the designs in the preceding sections. For, example, you may have both qualitative and quantitative IVs; or not all combinations of factor levels are feasible; or you simply cannot manage the number of runs specified in the most appropriate design. Optimal design methods let you specify your model just as you want it, along with any restrictions that you impose.

There may be a number of combinations of IV levels possible, but the optimal design is chosen on the basis of efficiency.[9] You want to choose the most efficient design that meets your needs. SAS OPTEX, SYSTAT DESIGN Wizard, and NCSS search for and identify optimal designs.

---

[9]There are a number of efficiency criteria that, under most circumstances, give similar results. The most popular is D-optimality, available in all three programs.

Finding an optimal design begins with a definition of the IVs of interest and their levels (the candidate set of points). Then, combinations of levels to be excluded, if any, are specified. You also may specify combinations of levels that must be included. The optimal design is chosen from among the remaining combinations of levels.

Consider an example in which there are a total of 8 IVs, 6 IVs with two levels each (A through F), and 2 IVs with five levels each (G and H). These might be alternate items on a questionnaire, with rating of clarity of the whole questionnaire as a DV. There are two possible ways of asking questions A through F. There are five possible ways of asking questions G and H, but some combinations of G and H do not make sense when asked together. Say, six combinations of levels of G and H cannot occur: g_1 and h_5, h_1 and g_5, g_1 and h_4, h_1 and g_4, g_2 and h_5, h_2 and g_5. A second hitch might be that only about 20 potential respondents are available to pilot the questionnaire, so, say, only 18 combinations of all questions can be run.

SAS uses a set of procedures to search for optimal designs. The candidate set is defined through PROC PLAN, which produces a data set. Then the optimization procedure is applied to this data set according to your criteria. Table 10.30 shows the SAS procedures for finding the optimal design for the example. SAS PROC PLAN identifies the eight IVs (**factors**) and the name of the output data file, **CAN**. This is a full eight-way factorial design. Then a DATA step modifies the data set, identifying combinations to exclude (^). PROC OPTEX then is run on the modified data set, in which all eight IVs are identified as **class**ification (quantitative) IVs and a main effects model is specified (without a response variable). The design is limited to 18 runs in the **generate** instruction. Finally, the optimal design is saved as a data set called OPTIMAL and printed out.

TABLE 10.30   Optimal Design for Eight Factors with Restrictions on Combinations and Number of Runs: SAS PLAN and OPTEX Syntax and Selected Output

```
proc plan;
  factors A=2 B=2 C=2 D=2 E=2 F=2 G=5 H=5;
  output out=CAN
    A B C D E F nvals = (1 to 2)
            G H nvals = (1 to 5);
data CAN; set CAN;
  if (^((G=1) & (H=5)));
  if (^((G=5) & (H=1)));
  if (^((G=1) & (H=4)));
  if (^((G=4) & (H=1)));
  if (^((G=2) & (H=5)));
  if (^((G=5) & (H=2)));
proc print data=CAN;
run;
proc optex data=CAN;
    class A B C D E F G H;
    model A B C D E F G H;
    generate n=18;
run;
    output out=OPTIMAL;
proc print  data=OPTIMAL;
run;
```

(continued)

TABLE 10.30   Continued

```
                    The PLAN Procedure
          Factor    Select    Levels    Order
          A            2         2      Random
          B            2         2      Random
          C            2         2      Random
          D            2         2      Random
          E            2         2      Random
          F            2         2      Random
          G            5         5      Random
          H            5         5      Random

                   The OPTEX Procedure
```

				Average Prediction Standard
Design Number	D-Efficiency	A-Efficiency	G-Efficiency	Error
1	46.3151	30.6023	69.0687	1.0061
2	46.0897	28.9577	66.5476	1.0137
3	45.9952	29.3663	70.7333	1.0148
4	45.9293	28.9389	61.9689	1.0187
5	45.7735	28.3197	62.8887	1.0199
6	45.6116	29.1300	64.3602	1.0304
7	45.1925	26.1608	59.7607	1.0481
8	44.9295	25.9535	62.5567	1.0532
9	44.4299	28.0258	62.1805	1.0669
10	44.3151	28.0040	62.1337	1.0518

OBS	A	B	C	D	E	F	G	H
1	2	2	2	2	1	1	2	4
2	2	2	1	2	2	2	4	5
3	2	2	1	1	2	1	5	4
4	2	1	2	2	1	1	3	1
5	2	1	2	1	2	2	1	3
6	2	1	2	1	1	1	5	5
7	2	1	1	1	1	2	3	2
8	2	1	1	1	1	1	2	3
9	1	2	2	2	1	2	2	2
10	1	2	2	1	2	1	4	2
11	1	2	2	1	1	1	3	3
12	1	2	1	1	1	2	1	1
13	1	1	2	2	1	2	5	3
14	1	1	2	1	2	2	2	1
15	1	1	2	1	1	2	3	4
16	1	1	1	2	2	1	3	5
17	1	1	1	2	2	1	1	2
18	1	1	1	2	1	1	4	4

The output first shows the design and then indicates that runs may be done in any order. Then, all 1216 runs[10] are printed (not shown here). SAS randomly selects 10 designs with 18 runs, and orders them in terms of D-efficiency. (Some nonselected designs could have greater efficiency.) Two other efficiency criteria are shown in this table, along with an estimate of prediction error for each. Then, the optimum set among the 10 designs (the one with the highest value of D-efficiency—design 1 in this example) is printed out. In this design, the questionnaire for the first respondent has the second alternative for the first four questions (*A* through *D*), the first alternative for questions *E* and *F*, the second alternative for question *G*, and the fourth alternative for question *H*. The second respondent has a questionnaire composed of the second alternatives for questions *A*, *B*, *D*, *E*, and *F*, the first alternative for question *C*, the fourth alternative for question *G*, and the fifth alternative for question *H*, and so on through the 18 respondents. At least four of the questionnaires should be duplicated and given to additional respondents to provide some estimate of error variance in the analysis phase (NCSS, 1998). Data are then collected and analyzed through any one of the available ANOVA programs.

10.6 Some Important Issues

The two prominent issues in screening and other incomplete designs are using software to generate the designs and choosing the design most appropriate for your needs.

10.6.1 Generating Screening and Other Incomplete Designs

Incomplete designs are tedious and difficult to generate by hand. Section 10.4.3 discussed development of a 2^5 half factorial by hand, but all these designs are much more easily developed through software. Several software packages are available. All of them provide output files in which the levels of the IVs for each run are already coded into columns; DV scores for each run are added as data are collected.

SYSTAT and MINITAB have design generation built into their statistics packages; SAS QC is a module separate from the statistics package. Another package that is particularly easy to use is NCSS (1997, 1998), also reviewed in this chapter. The programs vary widely in the types of designs that are generated and the way they are generated. Table 10.31 compares features of these four programs.

SAS has three programs, FACTEX and OPTEX (in the QC package) and PLAN (in the statistics package). PLAN is best used for designs with repeated measures, such as the Latin-square designs of Chapter 9 and for creating factorial designs. OPTEX searches for the optimal experimental design. FACTEX (accessible either through syntax or the ADX menu in SAS/ASSIST) generates three types of designs reviewed here: two-level, response-surface, and mixture. Tables 10.12 and 10.13 show a fractional-factorial design generated through FACTEX. Other two-level designs accessible through FACTEX are Taguchi and Plackett-Burman designs. The FACTEX response-surface procedure generates Box-Behnken and central-composite designs. Special analytic procedures are available for two-level, response-surface, and mixture designs (cf. Table 10.32). Neither OPTEX nor PLAN is available in the ADX menu system.

---

[10]A full factorial combination ($2 \times 2 \times 2 \times 2 \times 2 \times 2 \times 5 \times 5$) produces 1600 runs; 384 of these are the combinations that are excluded.

TABLE 10.31 Comparison of SYSTAT, MINITAB, SAS, and NCSS for Design of Screening and Other Incomplete Research Designs

Feature	SYSTAT Design	MINITAB DOE	SAS	NCSS
Fractional-Factorial Designs	BoxHunter	Factorial Designs	FACTEX Two-level	Fractional Factorial
Input				
Maximum number of IV levels	11	2	2	2
Specify number of factors	Yes	Yes	Yes	No
Specify number of runs	Yes	No	Yes	Yes
Specify number of replicates	Yes	Yes	No	No
Specify blocking variable	No[a]	Yes	Yes	Yes
Request simulated response variable	No	No	No	Yes
Specify coding of factor levels	No	Yes	Yes	Yes
Specify fraction of a full factorial	No	Yes	Yes	No
Specify resolution	No	No	Yes	No
Specify effects to be estimated	No	No	Yes	No
Specify generator	No	No	No	No
Specify folding	No	Yes	Yes	No
Printed output				
Design matrix	Yes	Yes	Yes	No
Design generator	Yes	Yes	No	Yes
Resolution	Yes	Yes	No	No
Defining relation	Yes	Yes	No	Yes
Pattern of aliasing	No	Yes	Yes	Yes
Special analysis module with plots	No	Yes	No	Yes

TABLE 10.31   Continued

Feature	SYSTAT Design	MINITAB DOE	SAS	NCSS
Plackett-Burman Designs	Plackett	Factorial Designs	FACTEX Two-level	Screening
Input				
Maximum number of levels	7	2	2	2
Specify number of runs	No	Yes	Yes	Yes
Specify number of factors	Yes	Yes	Yes	No
Specify blocking variable	No[a]	No	Yes	No
Specify number of replicates	Yes	Yes	Yes	No
Request simulated response variable	No	No	No	Yes
Specify coding of factor levels	No	Yes	Yes	Yes
Printed output				
Design matrix	Yes	Yes	Yes	No
Special analysis module with plots[d]	No	Yes	No	Yes
Taguchi Designs	Taguchi	Not Available Separately	FAXTEX Two-level	Taguchi
Input				
Specify Taguchi type (see Table 10.17)	Yes	N.A.	No	Yes
Maximum number of levels	5	N.A.	2	5
Specify number of factors	No	N.A.	Yes	Yes
Specify number of runs	No	N.A.	Yes	No
Specify number of replicates	Yes	N.A.	Yes	No
Distinguish between inner and outer arrays	No	N.A.	Yes	No
Specify coding of factor levels	No	N.A.	Yes	Yes

(continued)

TABLE 10.31   Continued

Feature	SYSTAT Design	MINITAB DOE	SAS	NCSS
Taguchi Designs (continued)				
Printed output				
Design matrix	Yes	N.A.	Yes	No
Pattern of aliasing	Yes	N.A.	No	No
Special analysis module with plots[d]	No	Yes	No	No
Box-Behnken Designs	Box-Behnken	RS	FACTEX Response surface	Response surface
Input				
Maximum number of factors	16	7	7	6
Specify blocking variable	Yes	Yes	No	Yes
Specify simulated response variable	No	No	No	Yes
Specify coding of levels	No	Yes	Yes	Yes
Printed output				
Design matrix	Yes	Yes	Yes	No
Special analysis module with plots[d]	No	Yes	Yes	Yes
Central-Composite Designs	Central Composite	RS	FACTEX Response surface	Response surface
Input				
Maximum number of factors	Unlimited	6	8	6
Specify blocking variable	Yes	Yes	No	Yes
Specify simulated response variable	No	No	No	Yes
Specify coding of levels	No	Yes	Yes	Yes
Specify replications	No	Yes	No	No

TABLE 10.31   Continued

Feature	SYSTAT Design	MINITAB DOE	SAS	NCSS
Central-Composite Designs (continued)				
Specify number of center points	Yes	Yes	Yes	No
Specify value of M to construct cube	Yes	No	No	No
Specify value of α for placement of axial points	No	Yes	Yes	No
Specify incomplete blocks	Yes	No	No	No
Printed output				
Design matrix	Yes	Yes	Yes	No
Complete defining relation	Yes	No	No	No
Design generators	Yes	No	No	No
Special analysis module with plots[d]	No	Yes	Yes	Yes
Mixture Models	Mixture	Mixture	FACTEX Mixture	Not available separately[e]
Input				
Maximum number of factors	Unlimited	15	10	N.A.
Specify number of factor levels	Yes	No	No[b]	N.A.
Specify number of runs	No	No	Yes	N.A.
Specify blocking variable	No	No	Yes	N.A.
Specify number of replications	No	No	Yes	N.A.
Lattice design	Yes	Yes	Yes	N.A.
Centroid design	Yes	Yes	No	N.A.
Axial design	Yes	No	Yes	N.A.

(continued)

TABLE 10.31 Continued

Feature	SYSTAT Design	MINITAB DOE	SAS	NCSS
Mixture Models (continued)				
Screening design	Yes	No	Yes	N.A.
Constrained mixture designs	Yes	No	Yes	N.A.
Printed output				
Design matrix	Yes	Yes	No	N.A.
Special analysis module with plots[d]	No	Yes	No	N.A.
Optimal Designs	Optimal	Not available	PLAN and OPTEX	D-optimal
Input				
Maximum number of factors	Unlimited	N.A.	Unlimited	Unlimited
Specify optimality criterion	Yes	N.A.	Yes	No
Specify optimization method	Yes	N.A.	Yes	No
Specify candidate design point (data set)	Yes	N.A.	Yes	Yes
Specify number of solutions	No	N.A.	Yes	No
Specify number of runs	Yes	N.A.	Yes	Yes
Specify number of points to exchange at each iteration	Yes	N.A.	Yes	Yes
Specify maximum number of iterations	Yes	N.A.	Yes	Yes
Specify convergence tolerance	Yes	N.A.	Yes	No
Specify which solutions to be displayed	Yes	N.A.	Yes	No
Specify whether design region is continuous or discrete for each IV	Yes	N.A.	CLASS	Yes

TABLE 10.31 Continued

Feature	SYSTAT Design	MINITAB DOE	SAS	NCSS
Optimal Designs (continued)				
Specify number of duplicates (replicates)	No	N.A.	No	Yes
Specify whether intercept to be included	Yes	N.A.	Yes	Yes
Specify simulated response variable	No	N.A.	No	Yes
Indicate combinations of levels to be forced	No	N.A.	Yes	Yes
Indicate combinations of levels to be excluded	No	N.A.	Yes	Yes[f]
Specify random number seed	Yes	N.A.	Yes	No
Printed output				
Efficiencies of designs	Yes	N.A.	Yes	Yes
Model summary	No	N.A.	Yes	Yes
Statistics regarding individual df effects	No	N.A.	No	Yes
Aliasing structure	No	N.A.	Yes	No

[a]Codes may be added to data set to turn replicates into levels of a blocking factor.

[b]Depends on number of factors and number of runs.

[c]Mixed-level factorial design also are available.

[d]See Table 10.38 for features of analysis modules.

[e]May be generated through D-optimal module.

[f]See NCSS (1998, pp. 2251–2252).

SYSTAT DESIGN has two modes beginning with Version 9: classic and wizard. The classic mode generates and can be accessed through syntax; the wizard does not. Both modes generate full factorial designs as well as fractional-factorial (Box-Hunter) designs, Taguchi designs, Plackett-Burman, Box-Behnken, and mixture designs. Wizard mode generates central-composite and optimal designs as well. The program also generates Latin-square designs (Chapter 9). Patterns of aliasing are available for Box-Hunter and Taguchi designs. Randomization of runs may be specified for all designs. Designs are analyzed through SYSTAT ANOVA, GLM, or REGRESSION. Tables 10.15, 10.18, and 9.45 are examples of experiments planned through SYSTAT DESIGN.

MINITAB DOE generates full factorial as well as fractional-factorial designs with two levels, Box-Behnken, central-composite, and mixture models. Only lattice and centroid are available among mixture models. All generated designs have a custom analysis module with plots, and all designs may be generated with randomized order of runs.

NCSS Design of Experiments generates fractional-factorial, screening, Taguchi, and response-surface designs (Box-Behnken and central composite), and, in the most recent version, D-optimal designs. Fractional-factorial designs are limited to two levels. Screening designs in NCSS include Plackett-Burman designs as well as designs in which the number of runs is a power of 2. Table 10.35 shows a central-composite design produced by NCSS. All of the procedures have the option to simulate responses so you can ensure that the design provides the tests you really want. Generated files are fully modifiable, so that any number of responses may be added and codes for IVs altered. Indeed, the method for excluding combinations of levels of IVs in optimal designs requires deleting unwanted rows from a fully factorial candidate set of runs (NCSS, 1998). Special analysis modules with plots are available for two-level designs without interactions and for response-surface designs (cf. Table 10.32). D-optimal designs may be generated with replicates. The D-optimal module also permits design of mixture experiments, as shown in the manual (NCSS, 1998, pp. 2249–2250). Most of the modules permit generation of a simulated response for each run, useful in planning phases to ensure that the analysis will provide desired information.

10.6.2   Choosing among Screening and Other Incomplete Designs

The first issue is whether one of the incomplete designs in this chapter or Chapter 9 is more appropriate. All of the designs in this chapter apply to randomized-groups IVs; Latin-square designs are the only readily available incomplete designs that apply to either randomized-groups or repeated-measures IVs. Latin square is useful for randomized groups when there are three IVs (two of them usually "nuisance" IVs) and all IVs have the same number of levels. Otherwise, the designs of this chapter are likely to be more useful. Choice of designs in this chapter is made on the basis of the type of IVs (qualitative, quantitative, or a mix of qualitative and quantitative) and the number of levels of each IV. Table 10.32 summarizes these choices.

10.6.2.1   Qualitative IVs

Four types of incomplete designs are available when IVs are qualitative: fractional-factorial, Plackett-Burman, Taguchi, and optimal designs. Fractional-factorial designs are useful when all IVs have two levels or when all IVs have three levels (although use is rare and rather complicated). With replication, you may be able to test at least some two-way interactions. Similarly, some Taguchi designs allow tests of two-way interactions in lieu of tests of main effects.[11] Plackett-Burman designs are useful for

---

[11]Taguchi analyses (S/N ratios, calculation of ρ) may be used with any screening or other incomplete design, even with quantitative IVs (Section 10.5.3).

TABLE 10.32   Choosing a Screening or Other Incomplete Design

Type of Independent Variables	Number of Levels of Independent Variables	Designs
Qualitative	2	2-level fractional factorial or Plackett-Burman or Taguchi
	3	3-level fractional factorial or Taguchi
	More than 3	Taguchi
	Mixed	Taguchi
	Any	Optimal designs
Quantitative	3	Box-Behnken
	5	Central composite
	Mixtures	Mixture models
	Any	Optimal designs
Mixed	Any	Optimal designs

screening a very large number of IVs, each with two levels, in the smallest possible number of runs; however, they are resolution III designs in which no interactions are tested. Optimal design methods are available when none of these designs is appropriate for your purposes.

For two-level IVs, then, choose a Plackett-Burman design if you want the fewest number of runs and can do without testing any interactions; choose a Taguchi design if you find one that meets your particular needs (see Table 10.17), and, otherwise, choose a fractional-factorial design. For IVs with three levels or studies in which IVs have different numbers of levels, your best bet is one of the Taguchi designs. Or when IVs have three levels, you might choose a Box-Behnken design if you can find a coding scheme that makes sense for your research.

10.6.2.2   Quantitative IVs

Box-Behnken (three levels of each IV), central-composite (five levels of each IV), or mixture designs are used with quantitative IVs. In their standard form, both Box-Behnken and central-composite designs test linear and quadratic trends of main effects and linear interaction contrasts. Therefore, the Box-Behnken design probably is adequate for most purposes—the central-composite design requires more runs to accommodate the extra two levels of IVs but does not provide additional information. Optimal design methods are available if your design does not meet these criteria.

Mixture designs are used when the response is to a mixture of levels of IVs and the various blends add up to a fixed total. The degree of trend is limited by the number of levels of the IVs and, therefore, the degrees of freedom available for evaluating each IV. Thus, some designs permit tests of trends higher than quadratic, although such trends are often difficult to interpret. Taguchi analyses are frequently useful with mixture designs to identify the most effective blend(s).

10.6.2.3   *Mixed Qualitative and Quantitative*

None of the specific designs accommodates a mix of qualitative and quantitative IVs, unless the particular characteristics of the qualitative IVs happen to make a trend analysis meaningful. However, any such mixed designs can be handled through optimal design methods.

10.7   Complete Example of a Central-Composite Design

The example illustrated here is an experiment conducted one hot August afternoon by one of us on a Pentium 166-MHz computer running main effects ANOVA on SPSS 7.5 for Windows. The goal was to determine which factors, from among the number of IVs, the number of covariates, or sample size, had an impact on time to complete an analysis.[12] The desire was to determine which factor or factors in the design influenced the processing time of the computer. Each factor had five levels, in keeping with the requirements of a central-composite design. The first factor was the number of IVs (each with two levels) included in the model of the analysis being timed (IVNO: 1 to 5); the second factor was number of covariates included in the model (COVAR: 0 to 4), and the third factor was sample size (SIZE: 50, 150, 250, 350, 450). The DV was processing time for GLM for main effects only; all other settings were left at default for the program. Each of the 20 runs included a different combination of the three IVs.

The data set used was from the sequential logistic regression example of Tabachnick and Fidell (2001, Section 12.7.3). The 5 two-level IVs were created from demographic variables representing marital status, working status, presence of children, race, and age group. The four continuous covariates were attitudes toward marital status, attitudes toward role of women, attitudes toward housework, and socioeconomic level. When the number of IVs (or the number of covariates) was less than 5 (or 4), in a particular run, the variables were randomly selected from among the sets of 5 (or 4). To create the factor of sample size, samples of appropriate size were randomly selected for each run from the 465 available. The criterion for each analysis was educational attainment. The DV for this study was time to complete the analysis.

10.7.1   Generating the Design

NCSS Design of Experiments was used to create the pattern of runs for the three-factor central-composite design. Table 10.33 shows the setup for designing a three-factor central-composite experiment and the resulting runs in which the DV (elapsed time in seconds for SPSS to perform the

---

[12]This experiment was impossible to conduct at a later date on a Pentium II 450-MHz computer running SPSS 9.0. Run time was simply too fast to record without special timing equipment.

TABLE 10.33 Generating a 3-Factor Central-Composite Design through NCSS: Setup and File

1. Open a new (empty) dataset.
2. Open the Response Surface Designs window.
3. Fill in the Design window as follows:
   a. Set Design Type to Central-Composite
   b. Set Sort Order to Random
   c. Set Simulated Response Variable to -blank-
   d. Set Block Variable to -blank-
   e. Set First Factor Value to C1
   f. Set each of the first three Factor Values to −1,1 and remaining three Factor Values to -blank-
4. Fill in the Template window with a name, and save it.
5. Run the procedure.

IVNO	COVAR	SIZE	TIME
4	3	150	0.22
3	0	250	0.22
4	1	350	0.27
1	2	250	0.16
4	1	150	0.17
3	2	250	0.22
3	2	250	0.27
3	2	450	0.27
3	2	250	0.22
2	1	350	0.16
2	1	150	0.17
5	2	250	0.38
3	2	250	0.22
3	2	250	0.22
2	3	150	0.16
3	4	250	0.27
2	3	350	0.21
3	2	50	0.17
4	3	350	0.33
3	2	250	0.17

analysis) from the experimental runs have been added. No printed output is produced by this NCSS run. Variable names were changed from the C1, C2, C3 notation to IVNO, COVAR, and SIZE, respectively, in the data window, and C4, the DV, was changed to TIME. The original codes for the five levels of each IV were −1.73, −1, 0, 1, 1.73. All codes were changed to reflect actual values of the levels of IVs. For example, the lowest level of IVNO was changed from −1.73 to 1, indicating a single IV. The highest level of SIZE was changed from 1.73 to 450, and so on.

The levels of the IVs are specified with unequal frequency. Among the 20 runs, there is a single run with the highest level and a single run with the lowest level of each IV. The middle level of each IV is the most commonly specified. The second and fourth levels of each IV are less frequently specified than the middle level, but more frequent than the extreme levels, as is typical in central-composite designs.

10.7.2   Assumptions and Limitations

10.7.2.1   *Normality, Absence of Outliers, and Independence of Errors*

Degrees of freedom are inadequate to assume normality of sampling distributions. With 20 runs (cases) and nine effects to be tested (linear and quadratic effects of all three IVs, and linear by linear interaction contrasts of the 3 two-way interactions), df for error $= N - k - 1 = 10$. NCSS Response Surface Analysis provides a normal probability plot of residuals by default. This assessment of normality does not take into account sampling distributions for cells but rather considers all data as a single group. Table 10.34 shows the setup for NCSS Analysis of Response Surface Designs and the normal probability plot of residuals.

The data points deviate from the major diagonal (representing normality) at both the lower and upper levels. This suggests that the distribution is not skewed, but rather has heavier than normal tails. This should pose no problem for the current screening analysis.

TABLE 10.34   Analyzing a 3-Factor Central-Composite Design through NCSS: Setup and Residuals Output

1. Open the Analysis of Resp. Surface Designs window.
2. Fill in the Design window as follows:
   a. Set Dependent Variable Y to TIME (4th variable in data set)
   b. Set Factor Variable A to IVNO, Factor Variable B to COVAR, and Factor Variable C to SIZE
   c. Leave remaining boxes -blank- (with 0's for Dec'ls)
3. Leave remaining windows with default values.
4. Fill in the Template window with a name, and save it.
5. Run the procedure.

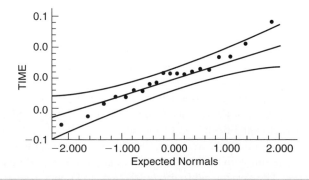

Normal Probability Plot of Residuals

The highest score (the uppermost case on the right) is a borderline outlier. Note that it falls just outside the 95% confidence interval (the curved bands) for the expected normal values. It would be considered an outlier if it were outside a 99% confidence interval with $N = 20$. Independence of errors is assured by the random assignment of levels to runs.

10.7.2.2 *Homogeneity of Variance*

There are insufficient data to evaluate homogeneity of variance for the main effects because there is only one trial of the extreme values for each IV. Also, some combinations of IVs (e.g., IVNO = 1, COVAR = 2, SIZE = 250) occur only once, so that homogeneity of variance cannot be assessed for the interaction terms. Follow-up research with a full factorial design would resolve the issue. The effect of heterogeneity of variance is to raise the Type I error rate beyond the nominal level. This is not fatal if the purpose of the experiment is to screen effects for planning further research. On the other hand, if the results of this experiment are themselves to be interpreted, a prudent course is to set $\alpha = .025$ to compensate for possible violation of homogeneity of variance.

10.7.3 Three-Factor Central-Composite Design

Table 10.35 shows the output of the analysis through NCSS Analysis of Response Surface Designs.

The first part of the output shows descriptive statistics for each of the variables, including the IVs. The next part of the output (omitted here along with the printout of residuals) displays information about the hierarchical model underlying the response-surface analysis.[13]

A sequential ANOVA follows, which evaluates the three linear terms taken together, the three quadratic terms taken together, and the three linear by linear interaction contrasts taken together. The analysis is sequential in that each level is adjusted for prior levels. That is, quadratic effects are adjusted for linear effects, and interaction contrasts are adjusted for main effects (cf. Section 5.6.5 for adjustments for effects in designs with cells of unequal sample sizes).

Lack of fit tests the adequacy of the model and is evaluated in this ANOVA. A significant result suggests that a higher-order model is appropriate (e.g., a model that includes cubic terms or quadratic by quadratic interaction terms). The "pure error" is provided by the replicated observations from at least some of the cells and is what permits a test of lack of fit. A second ANOVA is then presented in which pure error (with lack of fit variance omitted) serves as the error term for tests of effects. The overall regression, including all terms in the model, is statistically reliable, $F(9, 10) = 6.23$, $p = .004$ using total error, with an impressive 84% of the variance in processing time predictable from the combination of nine effects: Incremental R-Squared $= .84$ (note that this is equivalent to multiple R^2 for the whole model). These ANOVAs also suggest that only the linear effects are statistically reliable using either error term.

The next set of ANOVAs, one for each error term, evaluates each IV by including all effects that have that IV as a component. For example, IVNO includes the linear effect of IVNO, the quadratic effect of IVNO, the IVNO(linear) by COVAR(linear) interaction, and the IVNO(linear) by SIZE(linear) interaction. (Interaction terms are reused in evaluation of IVs.) The collective IVNO

---

[13]In hierarchical models, lower-order terms are included in all models in which higher-order terms are included. For example, if an $A \times B$ interaction is in the model, the main effects of A and B also must be there.

TABLE 10.35   Analyzing a 3-Factor Central-Composite Design through NCSS: Selected Output. Setup Is in Table 10.34

Response-Surface Regression Report

Descriptive Statistics Section

Variable	Count	Mean	Minimum	Maximum
IVNO	20	3	1	5
COVAR	20	2	0	4
SIZE	20	250	50	450
TIME	20	0.224	0.16	0.38

Sequential ANOVA Section

Source	df	Sequential Sum-Squares	Mean Square	F-Ratio	Prob Level	Incremental R-Squared
Regression	9	5.794875E-02	6.43875E-03	6.23	0.004240	0.848693
Linear	3	4.986875E-02	1.662292E-02	16.09	0.000373	0.730357
Quadratic	3	0.0032425	1.080833E-03	1.05	0.414101	0.047488
Lin x Lin	3	0.0048375	0.0016125	1.56	0.259424	0.070848
Total Error	10	1.033125E-02	1.033125E-03			0.151307
Lack of Fit	5	5.33125E-03	1.06625E-03	1.07	0.472798	0.078079
Pure Error	5	0.005	0.001			0.073228

Sequential ANOVA Section Using Pure Error

Source	df	Sequential Sum-Squares	Mean Square	F-Ratio	Prob Level	Incremental R-Squared
Regression	9	5.794875E-02	6.43875E-03	6.44	0.027033	0.848693
Linear	3	4.986875E-02	1.662292E-02	16.62	0.004937	0.730357
Quadratic	3	0.0032425	1.080833E-03	1.08	0.436806	0.047488
Lin x Lin	3	0.0048375	0.0016125	1.61	0.298396	0.070848
Total Error	10	1.033125E-02	1.033125E-03			0.151307
Lack of Fit	5	5.33125E-03	1.06625E-03	1.07	0.472798	0.078079
Pure Error	5	0.005	0.001			0.073228

ANOVA Section

Factor	df	Last Sum-Squares	Mean Square	F-Ratio	Prob Level	Term R-Squared
IVNO	4	4.004554E-02	1.001138E-02	9.69	0.001805	0.586490
COVAR	4	5.484821E-03	1.371205E-03	1.33	0.325132	0.080328
SIZE	4	1.703839E-02	4.259598E-03	4.12	0.031517	0.249537
Total Error	10	1.033125E-02	1.033125E-03			0.151307
Lack of Fit	5	5.33125E-03	1.06625E-03	1.07	0.472798	0.078079
Pure Error	5	0.005	0.001			0.073228

TABLE 10.35   Continued

ANOVA Section Using Pure Error

Factor	df	Last Sum-Squares	Mean Square	F-Ratio	Prob Level	Term R-Squared
IVNO	4	4.004554E-02	1.001138E-02	10.01	0.013228	0.586490
COVAR	4	5.484821E-03	1.371205E-03	1.37	0.362427	0.080328
SIZE	4	1.703839E-02	4.259598E-03	4.26	0.071905	0.249537
Total Error	10	1.033125E-02	1.033125E-03			0.151307
Lack of Fit	5	5.33125E-03	1.06625E-03	1.07	0.472798	0.078079
Pure Error	5	0.005	0.001			0.073228

Estimation Section

Parameter	df	Regression Coefficient	Standard Error	T-Ratio	Prob Level	Last R-Squared
Intercept	1	0.3215625				
IVNO	1	−0.085	5.354913E-02	−1.59	0.143522	0.038123
COVAR	1	−0.0475	5.187878E-02	−0.92	0.381428	0.012684
SIZE	1	−4.0625E-04	5.2637E-04	−0.77	0.458086	0.009013
IVNO^2	1	0.01	6.410164E-03	1.56	0.149815	0.036823
COVAR^2	1	0.00375	6.410164E-03	0.59	0.571505	0.005178
SIZE^2	1	−2.5E-07	6.410164E-07	−0.39	0.704710	0.002301
IVNO*COVAR	1	0.00875	1.136401E-02	0.77	0.459117	0.008970
IVNO*SIZE	1	0.0002125	1.136401E-04	1.87	0.091017	0.052907
COVAR*SIZE	1	0.0000875	1.136401E-04	0.77	0.459117	0.008970

Estimation Section Using Pure Error

Parameter	df	Regression Coefficient	Standard Error	T-Ratio	Prob Level	Last R-Squared
Intercept	1	0.3215625				
IVNO	1	−0.085	5.268366E-02	−1.61	0.167576	0.038123
COVAR	1	−0.0475	5.104031E-02	−0.93	0.394757	0.012684
SIZE	1	−4.0625E-04	5.178627E-04	−0.78	0.468281	0.009013
IVNO^2	1	0.01	6.306562E-03	1.59	0.173676	0.036823
COVAR^2	1	0.00375	6.306562E-03	0.59	0.577983	0.005178
SIZE^2	1	−2.5E-07	6.306562E-07	−0.40	0.708153	0.002301
IVNO*COVAR	1	0.00875	1.118034E-02	0.78	0.469274	0.008970
IVNO*SIZE	1	0.0002125	1.118034E-04	1.90	0.115766	0.052907
COVAR*SIZE	1	0.0000875	1.118034E-04	0.78	0.469274	0.008970

Optimum Solution Section

Parameter	Maximum Exponent	Optimum Value
IVNO	2	6
COVAR	2	−57
SIZE	2	4727

Function at optimum	−12.98515
Number of Function Evaluations	504
Maximum Functions Evaluations	500

(continued)

TABLE 10.35 Continued

Residual Section

Row	TIME	Predicted	Residual
1	0.22	0.238125	−0.018125
2	0.22	0.19875	0.02125
3	0.27	0.288125	−0.018125
4	0.16	0.16375	−0.00375
5	0.17	0.206875	−0.036875
6	0.22	0.215	0.005
7	0.27	0.215	0.055
8	0.27	0.26125	0.00875
9	0.22	0.215	0.005
10	0.16	0.171875	−0.011875
11	0.17	0.175625	−0.005625
12	0.38	0.34625	0.03375
13	0.22	0.215	0.005
14	0.22	0.215	0.005
15	0.16	0.171875	−0.011875
16	0.27	0.26125	0.00875
17	0.21	0.203125	0.006875
18	0.17	0.14875	0.02125
19	0.33	0.354375	−0.024375
20	0.17	0.215	−0.045

Plots Section

Grid Plot of TIME

Grid Plot of TIME

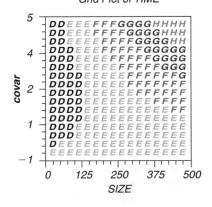

Grid Plot of TIME

factor is reliable using either error. Thus, so far, the output from the four ANOVAs suggests that the linear effect of number of IVs is a statistically reliable determinant of processing time.

The estimation sections evaluate the regression coefficients (cf. Section 4.4.4) of each of the nine effects after adjusting for the eight other effects, a different approach to unequal sample sizes than is used in the sequential ANOVA section. The estimation section of the output calls into question the importance of the linear effect of number of IVs because, with either error term, the linear effect of IVNO is not reliable after adjusting for all other effects, $p = .14$ or $.17$. The last R^2 shows that the effect predicts about 4% of the variance in processing time after adjustment for all other effects. The negative coefficient is misleading because the linear relationship between number of IVs and processing time is positive. This is seen in the plots at the end of the output, in which the highest values of time are produced by the highest levels of IVNO (higher letters indicate higher values). The negative regression coefficient is produced because variance associated with IVNO overlaps with that of other effects; that is, the effects are not independent. This nonindependence among effects is also what diminishes the apparent importance of IVNO, once all other effects are taken into account. Table 10.36 shows regression coefficients, their standard errors, and t-ratios (regression coefficients divided by their standard errors) for all effects in a form suitable for publication.

These results suggest that further research should be designed to explore the effects of a larger number of IVs. This is corroborated in the optimum solution section. Here the optimum number of IVs (to produce the greatest amount of processing time) is estimated to be 6. Therefore, further research should be designed to encompass at least 6 IVs. On the other hand, the lack of quadratic effects implies that intermediate levels of IVNO are not important. Thus, a suggested follow-up experiment would be a one-way design with 2 and 6 IVs as the two levels of IVNO, and perhaps an additional level with 10 IVs, to explore possible nonlinear trends with even more IVs. There is no indication that either the number of covariates or sample size needs to be included in further research of processing time.

Table 10.37 shows a checklist for a central-composite design. A Results section, in journal format, follows.

TABLE 10.36   Parameter Estimates and Standard Errors for All Effects in Central-Composite Analysis

Effect	B Coefficient	Standard Error	t Ratio (df = 10)
IVNO: Number of IVs	−0.0850	0.0535	−1.59
COVAR: Number of covariates	−0.0475	0.0518	−0.92
SIZE: Sample size	−0.0004	0.0005	−0.77
Quadratic IVNO	0.0100	0.0064	1.56
Quadratic COVAR	0.0038	0.0064	0.59
Quadratic SIZE	<0.0001	<0.0001	−0.39
IVNO by COVAR interaction	0.0088	0.0114	0.77
IVNO by SIZE interaction	0.0002	0.0001	1.87
COVAR by SIZE interaction	<0.0001	0.0001	0.77

TABLE 10.37   Checklist for Central-Composite Design

1. Generate the design
2. Issues
   a. Normality of residuals and outliers
   b. Independence of errors
   c. Homogeneity of variance
3. Major analysis
   a. Significance of levels of model (linear, quadratic, interaction). If significant:
      (1) Significance of factors
      (2) Significance of parameter estimates
      (3) Effect size
   b. Design further research:
      (1) Optimum values
      (2) Contour plots

Results

   A central-composite screening design was used to analyze factors that increase processing time for a general factorial main effects ANOVA through SPSS for Windows 7.5, running on a Pentium 166. The three independent variables were number of two-level IVs in the ANOVA (1 to 5), the number of covariates (0 to 4), and the sample size for the run (50, 150, 250, 350, 450). There were 20 runs, with varying combinations of number of factors, number of covariates, and sample size. The design was generated through NCSS Design of Experiments, with random order of runs. Residuals analysis showed acceptable normality and no outliers, but homogeneity of variance could not be assessed because of small cell sizes. Therefore, the criterion for statistical reliability was set to .025 to compensate for possible violation.

The overall sequential multiple regression analysis through NCSS, including linear and quadratic trends of the three main effects and linear by linear interaction contrasts was statistically reliable, $F(9, 10) = 6.23$, $p = .004$, $R^2 = .85$. However, this analysis showed that only the linear trends of main effects were statistically reliable, $F(3, 10) = 16.09$, $p < .001$. Parameter estimates (unstandardized coefficients, B) for all effects with standard errors and t ratios are in Table 10.36. None of these parameter estimates was statistically significant after adjustment for all other effects.

Tests of all three trends (linear, quadratic, and linear-by-linear interaction contrasts) tested collectively for each independent variable showed that only number of factors was statistically reliable, $F(4, 10) = 9.69$, $p = .002$. However, the specific test of the linear trend of number of factors did not reach statistical significance, $p = .14$ after overlapping variance associated with all other effects was removed.

Optimization tests and contour plots suggested that the optimum level of number of factors would be 6 (one more than the maximum number tested in this screening design), and that testing of trends beyond linear probably is unnecessary. Thus, the results suggest a follow-up study with a one-way design with 2 and 6 as the levels of number of factors. A greater number of factors, say, 10, might also be included to explore possible nonlinear trends with more factors.

10.8   Comparisons of Programs

SPSS, SAS, SYSTAT, and MINITAB all have ANOVA programs to analyze incomplete designs. SAS, NCSS, and MINITAB also have modules to analyze some specific designs.

Screening designs are diverse enough that various features of the general ANOVA programs could be applicable to any one of them. Consult the Comparison of Programs sections of Chapters 5 through 9 for features of the SAS, SYSTAT, MINITAB, and SPSS GLM programs. Table 10.38 compares features of analysis modules within programs to generate designs.

10.8.1   SAS FACTEX

Designs generated through the ADX menu system by SAS FACTEX may be analyzed through that same menu system after responses are added for the runs. Data analysis can proceed either with or without prompts, with more options available in the no-prompt form. Any of the two-level designs can be analyzed through the menu system. However, fractional-factorial and Taguchi designs with more than two levels of any IV are analyzed through a standard GLM program. The ADX menu system analyzes IVs with more levels only in response surface (Box-Behnken, central-composite) and mixture designs, which are separate choices.

Options for modifying designs are limited in SAS FACTEX; however, this is the only package that provides output of a standard ANOVA table, a regression table accompanied by parameter estimates, or both. Also, there is output for both Type I and Type III sums of squares. (Type I SS are more appropriate in analyses where unequal n is a feature of the design.) Standard residuals and profile plots are available; however, residuals cannot be added to the data file. This is the only program that plots residuals as a function of observation number, of interest if there is reason to suspect a sequential change in response over runs (cases).

10.8.2   NCSS Design of Experiments

NCSS provides a full range of analyses for two-level and response-surface (Box-Behnken and central-composite) designs. Mixture designs and fractional-factorial and Taguchi designs that have IVs with more than two levels are analyzed through regular regression and ANOVA modules.

There is detailed information about aliasing in two-level designs. Effects cannot be selected specifically during analysis, but they can be pooled and added to the error term if preliminary analysis shows that they are negligible and the design provides no degrees of freedom for error. This is the only program that provides tables of means and mean differences for each two-level effect and combination of two-level effects; one table is sorted by size of effect. For response-surface designs, covariates can be specified and there are many choices for analyzing these designs, including a stepwise (called hierarchical) analysis; ANOVA tables are presented in several formats (cf. Table 10.35). Contour plots are available for response-surface analysis. For all the designs, the only available plot of residuals is a normal probability plot; however, predicted scores for response-surface analysis and residuals for any analysis can be added to the data file for plotting in any format within another NCSS module.

TABLE 10.38   Comparison of SAS FACTEX, NCSS, AND MINITAB Analysis Modules

Feature	SAS FACTEX	NCSS	MINITAB[a]
Fractional-Factorial, Plackett-Burman, and Taguchi Designs	Two-level	Two-level	Factorial
Input			
Specify terms in model	Yes	No	Yes
Specify covariates (continuous factors)	No	No	Yes
Specify pooling of terms	No	Yes	No
Specify significance level for tests of effects	No	Yes	No
Specify size of aliasing to be reported	No	Yes	Yes
Specify number of decimals in means and mean squares.	No	Yes	No
Specify plot characteristics	Yes	Yes	Yes
Save residuals to data set	No	Yes	Yes
Specify sum-of-squares type	Yes[b]	No	No
Select ANOVA or regression-type output or both	Yes	No	No
Specify better or best S/N ratio for Taguchi designs	No	No	Yes
Printed Output			
ANOVA source table	Yes	Yes	Yes[c]
Regression-source table	Yes	No	No
Estimated marginal and cell means	Yes	Yes	Yes
Mean differences for each main effect	No	Yes	No
Sorted means and mean differences	No	Yes	No

(continued)

TABLE 10.38   Continued

Feature	SAS FACTEX	NCSS	MINITAB[a]
Fractional-Factorial, Plackett-Burman, and Taguchi Designs (continued)			
Lack-of-fit tests (residual and pure error)	Yes	No	Yes
Parameter estimates and tests	Yes	No	Yes
Overall R^2 and adjusted R^2	Yes	No	No
Plots			
Normal probability plot of residuals	No	Yes	Yes
Plot of residuals (raw or standardized) vs. predicted (or observed) score	Yes	No	Yes
Store residuals in data file	No	Yes	Yes
Normal probability plot of effects	No	Yes	Yes
Interaction plots of means (profiles)	Yes	No	Yes
Residuals vs. observation number	Yes	No	Yes
Cube plot	Yes	No	Yes
Main effects and interactions for S/N ratio, means, and standard deviations (Taguchi)	No	No	Yes
Box-Behnken and Central-Composite Designs	Response surface	Response surface	RS
Input			
Specify three-level full-factorial design	No	No	Yes
Specify terms in model	Yes	No	No

TABLE 10.38 Continued

Feature	SAS FACTEX	NCSS	MINITAB[a]
Box-Behnken and Central-Composite Designs (continued)			
Specify covariates (continuous factors)	No	Yes	No
Specify minimums, maximums, and number of decimals	No	Yes	Yes
Specify maximum exponents for terms in model	No	Yes	No
Specify whether minimum or maximum is sought	No	Yes	No
Specify characteristics of linear terms	No	Yes	No
Specify characteristics of cubic terms	No	Yes	No
Request search for most parsimonious hierarchical model	No	Yes	No
Specify minimum R^2 to avoid removing term	No	Yes	No
Specify precision accuracy	No	Yes	No
Specify plot characteristics	Yes	Yes	Yes
Specify maximum number of evaluations	No	Yes	No
Save residuals and predicted values to data set	No	Yes	Yes
Specify sum-of-squares type	Yes[b]	No	No
Specify multiple responses to optimize	No	No	Yes
Printed output			
Count, mean, minimum, maximum for each variable	No	Yes	No

(continued)

TABLE 10.38   Continued

Feature	SAS FACTEX	NCSS	MINITAB[a]
Box-Behnken and Central-Composite Designs (continued)			
Estimated marginal means	Yes	Yes	No
Estimated cell means	Yes	No	No
Sequential ANOVA table with trend components	Yes	Yes	Yes
Sequential ANOVA table with trend components using pure error	Yes	Yes	Yes
ANOVA table with IVs (main effect and interactions combined)	No	Yes	No
ANOVA table with IVs using pure error	No	Yes	No
ANOVA table with tests of each effect	Yes	No	No
Regression source table	Yes	No	No
Parameter estimates for all effects	Yes	Yes	Yes
Parameter estimates using pure error	No	Yes	No
Incremental, term, and last R^2s	No	Yes	No
Overall R^2 and adjusted R^2	Yes	No	Yes
Optimum value of each IV (main effect and interaction combined)	No	Yes	No
Function at optimum	No	Yes	No
Scores at minimum and maximum ridges	Yes	No	No
Canonical analysis of response surface	Yes	No	No

TABLE 10.38   **Continued**

Feature	SAS FACTEX	NCSS	MINITAB[a]
Box-Behnken and Central-Composite Designs (continued)			
Predicted value at stationary point	Yes	No	No
Residuals and predicted values	No	Yes	Yes
Effect size	No	Yes	No
Lack-of-fit tests	Yes	Yes	Yes
Plots			
Normal probability plot of residuals	No	Yes	Yes
Plot of residuals (raw or standardized) vs. predicted (or observed) score	Yes	No	Yes
Contour plots	Yes	Yes	Yes
Surface plots	Yes	No	Yes
Interaction plots of means (profiles)	Yes	No	Yes
Residuals vs. observation number	Yes	No	Yes
Cube plot	Yes	No	Yes
Save residuals and predicted values to data file	No	Yes	Yes
Mixture Models	Mixture	Not available separately	Mixture
Input			
Specify terms in model	Yes	N.A.	Yes
Specify mixture components	No	N.A.	Yes
Specify sum-of-squares type	Yes[b]	N.A.	No

(continued)

TABLE 10.38   Continued

Feature	SAS FACTEX	NCSS	MINITAB[a]
Mixture Models (continued)			
Specify blocks	Yes	N.A.	Yes
Printed output			
ANOVA source table	Yes	N.A.	No
Regression source table	Yes	N.A.	Yes
Parameter estimates	Yes	N.A.	Yes
Scores at minimum and maximum of ridges	Yes	N.A.	No
Plots			
Normal probability plot of residuals	Yes	N.A.	Yes
Plot of residuals (raw or standardized) vs. predicted (or observed) score	Yes	N.A.	Yes
Contour plots	Yes	N.A.	No
Surface plots	Yes	N.A.	No
Interaction plots of means (profiles)	Yes	N.A.	No
Residuals vs. observation number	Yes	N.A.	Yes

[a]Taguchi inner- and outer-array designs only.

[b]Prints out results for Type I and Type III sums of squares.

10.8.3   MINITAB DOE

MINITAB DOE has an analysis module for each design it generates, plus an additional module entitled "Analyze Inner/Outer Array," which is a diagnostic rather than an analysis program. Analysis modules are less extensive than available from some of the other programs; however, MINITAB does a good job of generating surface and contour plots for response-surface analyses. This analysis also permits optimization based on multiple responses.

There is no printed output for the analysis of inner and outer Taguchi arrays; however, graphs are provided that plot the main effects of each of the IVs (inner array), as well as all two-way interactions between them. Thus, ineffective IVs are suggested, as well as interactions among IVs that need to be taken into account. By default, the DV in each graph is the mean S/N ratio, computed from the set of responses (outer array) specified. Means and standard deviations of each of the responses may optionally be specified as DVs. The program also lets you specify which S/N ratio is better for your goals: lower, higher, or nominal.

10.9   Problem Sets

10.1   IVs in the following 2^{3-1} half-factorial design are type of cement (Portland or other), reinforcement (yes or no), and additive (yes or no). In each case, the first listed level is coded 1, the second level is coded -1. There are two replicates (blocks). The DV is strength of the dried cement.

Run	Cement Type	Reinforcement	Additive	Strength
1	1	1	1	9
2	1	−1	−1	3
3	1	−1	−1	4
4	−1	−1	1	6
5	−1	−1	1	7
6	1	1	1	8
7	−1	1	−1	7
8	−1	1	−1	8

a. Set up the full coding for the regression approach.
b. Show the aliasing pattern for this design.
c. Do the ANOVA using the regression approach.
d. Calculate effect sizes(s).
e. Write a Results section for this analysis.
f. Use one of the canned computer programs to check your results.

10.2   Generate a Plackett-Burman design with seven factors and eight runs.

10.3   The following L_8 Taguchi design has seven IVs with two levels each, and a response which is replicated.

Run	A	B	C	D	E	F	G	Response 1	Response 2
1	1	1	1	1	1	1	1	3	5
2	1	1	1	2	2	2	2	4	5
3	1	2	2	1	1	2	2	5	7
4	2	1	2	2	1	2	1	9	8
5	2	1	2	1	2	1	2	8	6
6	1	2	2	2	2	1	1	6	4
7	2	2	1	1	2	2	1	8	9
8	2	2	1	2	1	1	2	7	9

a. Find the S/N ratio assuming that small values of Y are desirable.
b. Use a canned program to do a preliminary ANOVA on the main effects to determine ignorable effects.
c. Rerun the ANOVA to find F ratios after removing ignorable effects.
d. Calculate p (%) for all significant effects.
e. Summarize the results in a source table.

10.4 IVs in the following Box-Behnken design are length of ski vacation (2, 4, and 6 days), size of hotel room in square meters (50, 100, 150), and cost of lift tickets ($45, $50, $55). The DV is the rating of the ski trip.

Days	Room Size	Tickets	Rating
−1	0	1	2
0	−1	−1	6
1	0	−1	8
1	0	1	9
0	0	0	5
−1	1	0	3
−1	0	−1	1
1	1	0	10
0	−1	1	4
1	−1	0	7
−1	−1	0	1
0	1	−1	7
0	0	0	6
0	1	1	6
0	0	0	4

a. Code the quadratic trends of the main effects and the linear by linear trends of the interactions.
b. Do the analysis using the regression approach.
c. Write a Results section.
d. Check your work through a canned computer program.

10.5 The data on the following page are from a mixture design to investigate optimum proportions of cinnamon and sugar for cinnamon toast. The DV is a rating of taste on scale of 1 to 10.
a. Calculate the codes for the sugar by cinnamon interaction. (*Hint:* See Table 10.29 syntax.)
b. Run a sequential regression to assess the effects of proportions of sugar and cinnamon on rating of taste, being sure to include the interaction as an effect.
c. Indicate which effects are statistically reliable.
d. Show the prediction equation, using the corrected coefficients.
e. Write a Results section for this analysis.

10.6 Using software, find an optimal design in which there are three qualitative IVs, with $a = 2$, $b = 2$, and $c = 3$. The design should include 12 runs, permit tests of all three main effects, and the A by B interaction.
a. Show the runs that are chosen.
b. What is the D-efficiency of the design.
c. Show a source table with df for each effect (including error and total), assuming there are no replicates.

Run	Sugar	Cinnamon	Rating
1.00	0.33	0.67	4.00
2.00	1.00	0.00	2.00
3.00	0.67	0.33	10.00
4.00	0.50	0.50	7.00
5.00	0.17	0.83	3.00
6.00	0.00	1.00	1.00
7.00	0.83	0.17	6.00
8.00	0.50	0.50	6.00
9.00	0.00	1.00	2.00
10.00	0.67	0.33	9.00
11.00	0.83	0.17	7.00
12.00	0.33	0.67	5.00
13.00	1.00	0.00	2.00
14.00	0.17	0.83	5.00

11 Analysis of Variance with Random Effects

11.1 General Purpose and Description

Random-effects ANOVA is used when levels of an IV are randomly chosen from a population of possible levels. Suppose, for example, a researcher defines the range of reasonable doses of a new drug as 0 to 500 mg, and then randomly chooses five levels of them, say, 15, 89, 236, 251, and 402 mg. Any set of five doses between 0 and 500 mg could be chosen for the levels, including, say, 1, 2, 3, 4, and 5 mg. Because the five doses are randomly selected, dosage is a random-effects IV.

Often, random effects are part of a mixed design that has both fixed and random IVs.[1] For instance, if time of administering the doses is added as a second IV, and its levels are purposefully chosen, say, 8 A.M., 4 P.M., and 12 P.M., time is a fixed IV, and the design has one fixed effect and one random effect. On the other hand, if the times for administering the doses are also randomly chosen, there are two random-effects IVs.

The differences between random and fixed IVs are in how the levels are selected and the generalizability of the findings. Levels of fixed-effects IVs are purposefully chosen to cover the range of levels of interest; the researcher is often unwilling to leave the choice to chance because a randomly selected range could be quite narrow or some levels could be very similar. If the fixed IV is quantitative, levels are usually also chosen with equal spacing between them. The findings generalize only to the range of levels included in the study. Levels of random effects are randomly chosen and, if quantitative, are not equally spaced. The findings, however, generalize to the entire range of values from which the levels are chosen. With the exception of cases, all of the IVs discussed in Chapters 2 through 10 are fixed.

Cases (or subjects) are almost always considered random. When treatments are applied to a set of cases, the researcher is rarely interested in those particular cases, but rather in a larger population of cases. In many experiments, the population of cases is composed of the cases potentially available for the study; for example, all the employees of a firm could be considered a population. If numerous cases are chosen and randomly assigned to various levels of treatment, we generalize the results to all the employees of that firm. If cases are first randomly selected from a larger population (say,

---

[1]This is the second use of the term *mixed* to characterize factorial designs. The other use is to label designs with a combination of randomized-groups and repeated-measures IVs.

the firm is randomly selected from among many), and then employees are randomly selected and randomly assigned to levels of treatment, the generalization has a much wider scope.[2]

The goal, then, of a random-effects IV is to widen the scope of generalization. There is a penalty to pay, however. Random-effects ANOVA is often less powerful than fixed-effects ANOVA because different, and frequently larger, error terms are required. You are permitted a wider scope of generalization only as long as the effect of treatment is large enough to withstand the reduction in power.

Random-effects IVs appear in a multitude of applications, with both randomized-groups and repeated-measures IVs, with one-way, full, and incomplete factorials, and with covariates.

One frequent application of random-effects IVs is in studies that use Generalizability Theory (Chronbach, 1972) for the analysis. The goal of these studies is to determine how reliable (dependable) scores for cases are when used in different situations or at different times. Each score is thought to have both a "true" component (the part that is reliably measuring what you want measured) and error. Generalizability theory uses ANOVA to partition the error component into numerous IVs that represent different features of the testing situation (test items, types of tests, scoring procedures, raters, testing environments, time frames, and so on) to see which are important. The levels of the error IVs are considered randomly selected. The theory has been applied in a wide variety of research areas and summarized by Brennan (1992), Shavelson and Webb (1991), and Marcoulides (1999), among others.

However, the most common use of a random-effects IV is with a nested design, as illustrated in Table 1.3(c), where there is both a fixed- and a random-effects IV. For example, suppose you have three training programs and 15 groups of students, already formed. You randomly assign five groups to each of the three training programs. Training is a fixed-effect IV. Groups are nested within (do not cross) training programs and form a random-effect IV. Cases (students) are nested within groups and form another random-effect IV.

Nested designs can also be useful for increasing the scope of generalization. Consider, for example, a memory experiment in which the researcher is interested in the effects of the emotional content of words, negative or positive, on the number of words recalled. The researcher could put together one list of negative, and one list of positive words, but there is the danger that recall depends on the particular lists used and not on their emotional content. One solution is to generate several lists of negative and several lists of positive words, and nest them within levels of emotional content. If an effect is found for emotional content, but not for list, the researcher has evidence that the emotional content, and not the particular list, affects memory.

Nested designs are like the incomplete factorial designs of Chapter 10 in that not all combinations of levels are present. They are like mixed randomized-group, repeated-measures designs in that cases nest within randomized-groups IVs but cross repeated-measures IVs. There can be additional randomized-groups and repeated-measures IVs, any of which may be fixed or random.

11.2 Kinds of Research Questions

11.2.1 Effect of the IV(s)

Questions about the effect of a random IV are the same as for a fixed IV. Are there reliable mean differences among the levels of treatment, holding all else constant? For example, is there a mean dif-

---

[2]As discussed in Chapter 1, statistical generalization is much more limited than logical generalization, which often extends beyond the population that has been randomly sampled.

ference in productivity among groups of employees who have different types of training? Do different dosages lead to different degrees of symptom alleviation? These questions are answered by applying an F test to each IV, as demonstrated in Section 11.4. However, the F tests differ in their error terms depending on whether IVs are random or fixed, as discussed in Section 11.6.1.

11.2.2   Effects of Interactions among IVs

Questions about interactions are also the same for random and fixed IVs. Holding all else constant, does the pattern of means in the DV over the levels of one IV depend on the level of another IV? For example, does the efficacy of different dosages depend on time of administration of the drug? Interactions are tested by applying F tests, but these tests also use different error terms depending on whether IVs are random or fixed, as discussed in Section 11.6.1.

An important limitation to nested designs is that nested factors do not interact with the IVs in which they are nested. For instance, in the example with type of the training applied to different groups, groups nest within level of training—there is no interaction of groups with type of training to test.

11.2.3   Specific Comparisons

Specific comparisons also follow the same format as fixed-effects ANOVA, but differ in the error terms used to test them. For a quantitative random-effects IV such as dose, for instance, trends are typically the comparisons of interest. Section 11.6.3 demonstrates trend analysis when spacing among levels of the IV is unequal, as happens when levels are randomly chosen.

11.2.4   Parameter Estimates

Parameter estimates for random IVs are the same as for fixed IVs. Sample means, standard deviations, standard errors, and confidence intervals provide estimates of the central tendency and variability in a population at each level of a significant IV. For example, if reliable mean differences in symptom alleviation are found at different dosages, what is the expected amount of symptom alleviation for each dose and what are the standard deviations or standard errors or confidence intervals for each dose? Parameter estimates are calculated as for fixed-effects ANOVA, with the same ambiguity when there are unequal sample sizes in factorial designs (cf. Section 5.6.5).

11.2.5   Effect Sizes

Effect size indicates the proportion of variance in a DV that is associated with a reliable main effect or interaction. How much of the variance in symptom alleviation is associated with dosage? How much of the variance in productivity is associated with differences in training. The η^2 and partial η^2 of Sections 4.5.1 and 5.6.2 apply to random as well as fixed-effects designs. As always, the appropriate error term for the effect is used for partial η^2. The $\hat{\omega}^2$ and partial $\hat{\omega}^2$ of earlier chapters, however, do *not* apply to designs in which there are random effects. Alternative measures are in Section 11.6.5.

11.2.6   Power

What is the probability of finding an IV significant, if indeed, the IV affects the DV? What is the probability of finding an effect of dosage if size of dose does affect symptoms? Power is an important issue in random-effects ANOVA because increased generalizability is often gained at the expense of power. Tests of random IVs are typically less powerful than tests of the same IVs when fixed because of differences in the required error terms. For an IV in a factorial random-effects design, the error term is an interaction (or some other combination of terms) that typically has fewer degrees of freedom than the error term in fixed-effects analysis.

In nested designs, the problem is that the nested IV serves as the error term for the effect of treatment. For example, if five groups of students are assigned to each of three levels of training, the error term for training is based on the variance among means for the groups and on the number of groups within each level, not on scores for the total number of students at each level of training. The reduction in power due to smaller degrees of freedom may be partially offset by lower variability among group means than among individual scores, but, on balance, only partially.

With either design, the problem of reduced power is sometimes dealt with by pooling terms from nonsignificant effects to increase the degrees of freedom. For instance, in the nested design, researchers test the effects of groups first, and then pool error terms, or use the error term based on cases if there is no significant difference among groups. However, it is much safer to plan the study with sufficient numbers of groups to ensure necessary power than to rely on finding no significant differences among groups. Section 11.6.1.2 discusses pooling of error terms. Power and sample-size estimation for random-effects ANOVA are available in the GANOVA program (Woodward et al., 1990).

11.3   Assumptions and Limitations

Assumptions of random-effects ANOVA are the same as fixed-effects ANOVA with the added assumptions that levels of the random IVs are randomly chosen from a population of levels and that the population of levels is normally distributed and independent of error. It is assumed that scores within levels of the random IV have equal variances (homogeneity of variance), and, additionally, that in a factorial design, all pairs of levels of the random IV(s) have homogeneity of covariance, even if they are not repeated measures. Beyond that, assumptions and limitations depend on whether the IV is a repeated-measures IV or a randomized-groups IV.

11.3.1   Theoretical Issues

As with any ANOVA, causal inference depends on the manner in which cases are assigned to the levels of the IV(s), manipulation of the levels of the IV(s), and controls used in the research. Statistical tests may also be used in nonexperimental studies, but causal inference is not attempted.

It is sometimes difficult to decide whether an IV is fixed or random. If an IV is random, the levels of the IV are randomly selected from a larger population of levels to which the researcher wants to generalize. An extension of random selection is that a different set of levels probably would be selected in any replication of the study. Some guidelines for deciding if an effect is random or fixed are as follows:

1. Cases are always considered a random factor. Although they are usually randomly assigned to levels of treatment, they often are not randomly selected from a population. However, they would almost always be a different group in a replication, as is true for other random effects.

2. Groups in nested designs are always considered random factors because, at the very least, they are randomly assigned to levels of treatment.

3. With other IVs, the decision is based on how the particular levels are chosen. Suppose, for example, you have a collection of vacation slides categorized as either landscapes or close-ups and you want to study how well they are remembered. If you just select your favorite five slides in each category, the IV is fixed. However, you probably want to generalize your results to memory for land-scapes and close-ups in general, not to the particular ones used in your experiment. Therefore, you randomly select some number of slides, say, 5, from each category in your collection, or, better yet, from several collections. Type of slide (landscape vs. close-up) is a fixed factor; the five slides in each category are a random factor.

4. A trial factor in a repeated-measures study is typically fixed. However, suppose that there is a very large number of observations—say, a movement response recorded every half-second during a night of sleep. A random trial factor is formed if you randomly select some manageable number of half-second time periods for each case, say, 10 of them, and include only those 10 movement responses in the analysis.

5. A blocking factor can be either fixed or random, depending on how the blocks are formed (Lee, 1975). Blocks form a fixed factor if the ranges defining the levels are chosen in advance and are constant through replications. For example, if you decide to block on operator experience by choosing ranges such as 0–5 years, 6–10 years, 11–15 years, the IV is a fixed factor. On the other hand, if you simply record the years of experience of available operators, and then count off equal numbers of operators into least, middle, and most experienced, the IV is a random factor because replication of the study would typically produce different cutoffs for the three levels of experience.

6. Qualitative IVs are typically fixed. The levels differ in kind, and it is likely that the ones chosen for study are the ones of primary interest (or availability). If, however, the number of "kinds" is very large, and some are randomly selected for study, the levels form a random-effects IV.

7. Quantitative IVs can be easily either fixed or random. The researcher could be interested only in specified levels or in randomly selected levels from a range.

Lee (1975) recommends treating a factor as fixed when in doubt. However, be sure that cases and groups nested within treatments are treated as random, and do not generalize the results of analyses of fixed factors outside the range of levels included in the study.

11.3.2 Practical Issues

Practical issues are the same as for other ANOVA designs, and there are additional assumptions that depend on whether an IV is randomized groups or repeated measures, as discussed in what follows. Violations of assumptions of normality and homogeneity of variance are more consequential in design with random effects.

11.3.2.1 Randomized-Groups Designs

In a completely randomized-groups design, the assumptions and limitations of Section 5.3.2 apply to all IVs, whether random or fixed effects: normality of sampling distributions, homogeneity of variance, independence of errors, and absence of outliers. If a Latin-square or some other incomplete design is used, there is also the assumption of additivity when only one score is in each cell of the design (cf. Sections 9.3.2.6 and 10.3.2.5). If there are covariates, the additional assumptions and limitations of Section 8.3.2 apply: multicollinearity, linearity, homogeneity of regression, and reliability of covariates.

In factorial designs, the additional assumption for random-effects IVs is that covariances between all pairs of levels are equal. For example, if five dosages are levels of one random-effects IV and three times of administration are levels of another random-effects IV, the assumption of homogeneity of covariance is that the relationships between all pairs of levels of dosage are the same (collapsed over levels of time) and that the relationships between all pairs of levels of time are the same (collapsed over levels of dosage). Evaluation of homogeneity of covariance is discussed in Section 11.6.4.

11.3.2.2 Repeated-Measures and Mixed (Randomized-Repeated) Designs

The assumptions and limitations of repeated measures apply to random-effects, repeated-measures IVs whether in a fully repeated-measures design (Section 6.3) or a mixed randomized-repeated design (Section 7.3). The additional assumption, you recall, is of sphericity (Sections 6.3.2.3 and 6.6.2).

11.4 Fundamental Equations

There are two basic types of random-effects ANOVA: nested designs and designs in which one or more factors have levels that are randomly chosen, but factors are not nested within other factors. The simplest of the latter designs is a one-way ANOVA with randomly chosen levels of the single IV. However, analysis of this one-way random-effects design is identical to that of a one-way fixed-effects design, whether randomized groups or repeated measures. It is only when additional IVs are added to the design that the analysis changes, because with additional IVs there is overlap between tests of main effects and interactions.[3] Therefore, the design demonstrated here is the simplest nested design, with a single fixed IV and a random IV nested within the fixed IV.

The fixed IV (A) is length of ski training with two levels: a half-day class or a full-day class. The random-effect IV (B) is group, with two groups of three skiers in each level of training time. B is a random effect IV because the study is intended to draw conclusions about groups of skiers in general, not just the groups of skiers in the study. The DV is time to ski a standard run. Groups form the error term for length of training, and skiers within groups form the error term for groups. Although both length of training and groups can be tested, only length of training is of interest. The traditional ANOVA approach is shown first, followed by the regression approach for nested designs.

11.4.1 Allocation of Cases

Three skiers are randomly assigned to each of four groups, and then two groups are randomly assigned to each of the two treatments. Table 11.1 shows the assignment of the 12 skiers to the two groups of B at each of the two levels of A. Cases are designated S, as usual. The design, of course, is far too small for an actual experiment.

In practice, this design is often used with intact groups (such as classrooms), which are then randomly assigned to levels of treatment. Intact groups are typically formed by convenience or by self-selection, rarely by random selection and assignment. The test of treatment is legitimate because the error term for treatment is based on groups (where random assignment has occurred[4]) rather than

---

[3]There is similar overlap, at least conceptually, in unequal-n factorial designs.

[4]The assumption of independence of errors is also violated if individual cases are used to form the error term when cases within groups are exposed to a level of treatment together.

**TABLE 11.1   Assignment of Cases in a Simple
Nested Design**

Treatment A	a_1		a_2	
Groups B	b_1	b_2	b_3	b_4
Cases S	s_1 s_2 s_3	s_4 s_5 s_6	s_7 s_8 s_9	s_{10} s_{11} s_{12}

on individual cases (where random assignment has not occurred). However, the test of groups uses individual cases for the error term, and is problematic when random assignment to groups has not occurred.

Nesting is also present when cases are first randomly assigned to levels of A, and then randomly split into groups (B) within each level of treatment. This second step is sometimes necessary because treatment is something that must be applied to groups, not to individuals (e.g., when studying social interaction in a group). Otherwise, the more efficient one-way randomized-groups design is used in which each case within a treatment level is run individually or all levels of treatment are run at one time.

Allocation of cases in studies when the levels of one or more IVs are randomly selected but there is no nesting is the same as for fixed-effects designs.

11.4.2   Partition of Sources of Variance

The total sum of squares is divided into three sources: differences due to levels of treatment (A), differences due to groups (B) nested within levels of A (B/A), and differences due to cases nested within levels of B, nested within levels of A ($S/B/A$).

$$SS_T = SS_A + SS_{B/A} + SS_{S/B/A} \qquad (11.1)$$

or

$$\sum_i \sum_j \sum_k (Y_{ijk} - GM)^2 = n_j \sum_j (\overline{Y}_A - GM)^2$$
$$+ \left[n_{jk} \sum_j \sum_k (\overline{Y}_B - GM)^2 - n_j \sum_j (\overline{Y}_A - GM)^2 \right]$$
$$+ \sum_i \sum_j \sum_k (Y_{ijk} - \overline{Y}_B)^2$$

The total sum of squared differences between individual scores Y_{ijk} and the grand mean (GM) is partitioned into (1) sum of squared differences between means associated with different levels of A ($\overline{Y}_A$) and the grand mean; (2) sum of squared differences between means associated with levels B ($\overline{Y}_B$) (which also contain differences due to levels of A) and the grand mean minus the sum of squared differences between means associated with different levels of A ($\overline{Y}_A$) and the grand mean (which results in the sum of squared differences associated with different levels of B); and (3) sum of squared differences between individual scores Y_{ijk} and the means associated with levels of B ($\overline{Y}_B$).

Because A and B do not interact, the "real" sum of squares for B is found by subtraction of sum of squares for A from the regularly computed sum of squares for B that, in this case, contains differences due both to levels of A and levels of B. The notation for groups is B/A (B nested within A) and the notation for cases nested within B is $S/B/A$.

Total degrees of freedom is the number of scores minus 1 (or $abn - 1$), lost when the grand mean is estimated (cf. Equation 3.6). Note that the number of levels of B is now defined as the num-ber at each level of A; for the example, there are two levels of B at each level of A. There are as many levels of B altogether as number of levels of B within cach level of A, times the number of levels of A.

Degrees of freedom for A are the number of levels of A minus 1, lost because the $\overline{Y}_{a_j}$ average to the grand mean, so $a - 1$ of the means can take on any values whatever, but the last mean is fixed.

$$\mathrm{df}_A = a - 1 \tag{11.2}$$

Degrees of freedom for B are derived from the notational scheme in the usual way:

$$\mathrm{df}_{B/A} = a(b - 1) \tag{11.3}$$

Degrees for cases within levels of B and A are also derived from the notation as follows:

$$\mathrm{df}_{S/B/A} = ab(n - 1) \tag{11.4}$$

To verify the equality of degrees of freedom,

$$N - 1 = abn - 1 = a - 1 + ab - a + abn - ab$$

Figure 11.1 shows the partitions of sums of squares and degrees of freedom.

Mean squares are formed by dividing sums of squares by degrees of freedom, as for all ANOVA designs.

$$\mathrm{MS}_A = \frac{\mathrm{SS}_A}{\mathrm{df}_A} \qquad \mathrm{MS}_{B/A} = \frac{\mathrm{SS}_{B/A}}{\mathrm{df}_{B/A}} \qquad \mathrm{MS}_{S/B/A} = \frac{\mathrm{SS}_{S/B/A}}{\mathrm{df}_{S/B/A}} \tag{11.5}$$

F ratios are formed for each of the two sources of variance to be evaluated: A and B/A. F_A eval-uates the main effect of A. The null hypothesis for this test is the same as for a one-way fixed-effects ANOVA, expressed as $\mu_{a_1} = \mu_{a_2} = \cdots = \mu_{a_j}$. However, the appropriate error term is the variation among groups (B) within levels of A. Obtained F_A is computed as

$$F_A = \frac{\mathrm{MS}_A}{\mathrm{MS}_{B/A}} \qquad \mathrm{df} = (a - 1),\, a(b - 1) \tag{11.6}$$

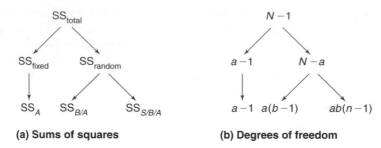

(a) Sums of squares **(b) Degrees of freedom**

FIGURE 11.1   **Partitions of (a) Total Sum of Squares into Sum of Squares due to Differences among Treatments, Differences among Groups within Treatments, and Differences among Cases within Groups; and (b) Total Degrees of Freedom into Degrees of Freedom Associated with Treatments, Degrees of Freedom Associated with Groups within Treatments, and Degrees of Freedom Associated with Cases within the Groups**

Obtained F_A is tested against critical F from Table A.1 in Appendix A with numerator df $= a - 1$ and denominator df $= a(b - 1)$. The null hypothesis is rejected if obtained F_A is equal to or exceeds critical F.

$F_{B/A}$ evaluates differences among marginal means for levels of B (groups), nested within levels of A, called the main effect of B nested within A. The null hypothesis is that group means are the same. This test is not often of research interest,[5] but sometimes is used to decide whether to pool error terms (cf. Section 11.6.1).

$$F_{B/A} = \frac{\mathrm{MS}_{B/A}}{\mathrm{MS}_{S/B/A}} \qquad \mathrm{df} = a(b - 1),\ ab(n - 1) \qquad (11.7)$$

Obtained $F_{B/A}$ is tested against critical F from Table A.1 with numerator df $= a(b - 1)$ and denominator df $= ab(n - 1)$. The null hypothesis of no mean difference among groups is rejected if obtained $F_{B/A}$ is equal to or larger than critical F.

11.4.3   Traditional ANOVA Approach (One Treatment Factor and One Level of Nesting)

Table 11.2 shows an unrealistically small hypothetical data set to evaluate speed of skiing as a function of length of class. Treatment A, length of class, has two levels (a half-day class or a full-day class) and is a fixed-effect IV. B/A is a random-effects IV, in which two different groups of skiers ($b = 2$) are randomly assigned to each length of class; there are four groups altogether. Each group has three skiers, so $n = 3$ for each level of B; there are a total of 12 skiers. The DV is time to ski a common run.

Table 11.3 shows computation equations for sums of squares for A, B/A, $S/B/A$, and T (total). Divisors as well as summations differ in places from those of factorial fixed-effects ANOVA of

---

[5]More complex analyses are useful if differences among groups are of research interest (cf. Section 11.6.2).

TABLE 11.2 Hypothetical Data for Nested ANOVA

Class Length A	a_1: Half Day		a_2: Full Day	
Groups B	b_1	b_2	b_3	b_4
Cases S	7	7	5	4
	6	6	3	2
	10	8	5	5
Sums for B	23	21	13	11
Sums for A	44		24	

$\sum Y^2 = 7^2 + 6^2 + \cdots + 5^2 = 438$

$T = 68$

$a = 2, b = 2, n = 3$

TABLE 11.3 Computational Equations for Sums of Squares for Nested ANOVA

$$SS_A = \frac{\sum A^2}{bn} - \frac{T^2}{abn} = \frac{44^2 + 24^2}{6} - \frac{68^2}{12} \qquad\qquad = 33.33$$

$$SS_{B/A} = \frac{\sum B^2}{n} - \frac{A^2}{bn} = \frac{23^2 + 21^2 + 13^2 + 11^2}{3} - \frac{44^2 + 24^2}{6} \qquad = 1.33$$

$$SS_{S/B/A} = \sum Y^2 - \frac{B^2}{n} = 7^2 + 6^2 + 10^2 + 7^2 + \cdots + 2^2 + 5^2 - \frac{23^2 + 21^2 + 13^2 + 11^2}{3} = 18.00$$

$$SS_T = \sum Y^2 - \frac{T^2}{abn} = 7^2 + 6^2 + 10^2 + 7^2 + \cdots + 2^2 + 5^2 - \frac{68^2}{12} = 52.66$$

Chapter 5. The divisor for B is n rather than an because B does not cross A. That is, there are only n scores in each level of B, not an scores as there would be in a fully crossed $A \times B$ design. Table 11.4 summarizes the results and shows mean squares and F values based on Equations 11.1 through 11.7.

    The error term for treatment A is B/A, and the error term for B/A is S/B/A. Therefore, the degrees of freedom for evaluating F_A are 1 $(a - 1 = 2 - 1)$ and 2 $[a(b - 1) = 2(1)]$, and the degrees of freedom for evaluating $F_{B/A}$ are 2 and 8 $[ab(n - 1) = 12 - 4]$. With $\alpha = .05$, the critical value for F_A is 18.51 and the critical value for $F_{B/A}$ is 4.46. Therefore, there is a statistically significant effect of length of ski class, but no significant differences among groups. Looking at the means, we conclude that skiers trained for a full day take less time to ski a run than do skiers trained for only half a day.

TABLE 11.4   Source Table for Nested ANOVA

Source	SS	df	MS	F
A	33.33	1	33.33	49.75
B/A	1.33	2	0.67	0.30
$S/B/A$	18.00	8	2.25	
T	52.66	11		

11.4.4   Regression Approach (One Treatment Factor and One Level of Nesting)

The regression approach can be taken with nested designs and other varieties of random-effects designs as long as the correct error term is chosen for each effect (cf. Sections 11.5 and 11.6.1) and there is equal n.[6] The only exception is for quantitative IVs in which there is unequal spacing between levels. When levels are unequally spaced, special coefficients for trend analysis must be derived because the coefficients that are readily available are for equally spaced levels. Keppel (1982, Appendix C-3) describes procedures for generating an appropriate set of trend coefficients by hand.

Table 11.5 shows the regression analysis of the nested design of data in Table 11.2. The Y column contains the DV scores. The X_1 column contains coefficients to separate the two levels of A. Columns X_2 and X_3 contain coefficients for separating the four levels of B, two nested in each level of A. Notice that nesting of B is represented the same as nesting of cases in the mixed (randomized-groups, repeated-measures) design of Table 7.7 (columns X_9–X_{32}). Columns X_4 through X_{11} separate cases, nested in levels of B, nested in levels of A. Because there are three cases at each level of B, two columns are required for each AB combination. As in Table 7.7, the coding used to separate cases is completely arbitrary. Columns X_{12} to X_{22} are the cross of Y with columns X_1 to X_{11}, respectively. This table is generated by a spreadsheet program, in which the facilities of the spreadsheet are used to compute SS(reg) for columns X_1 to X_{11}.

Values for ANOVA are readily computed by summing appropriate ss(reg) for columns X_1 to X_{11}, as shown in Table 11.6. Within rounding error, these values agree with the values in Table 11.4.

11.4.5   Computer Analyses of Small-Sample Nested Example

Table 11.7 shows how data are organized for the small-sample nested example. Data may be converted from a spreadsheet program or entered through facilities provided by the statistical program. Columns can be in any order.

Tables 11.8 through 11.11 show computer analyses of the small-sample example of the nested design with one fixed and one random IV by SPSS GLM (UNIANOVA), SAS GLM, MINITAB GLM, and SYSTAT GLM.

SPSS GLM (UNIANOVA) requires two additional lines of syntax to specify the design, as shown in Table 11.8. First, the nested IV, group is declared a RANDOM variable. Second, the

---

[6]As usual, the coefficients are not orthogonal if the design is not balanced, and matrix algebra is required to find sums of squares adjusted for overlap.

TABLE 11.5 Regression Approach to Nested-Design ANOVA

			Y	A X_1	B/a1 X_2	B/a2 X_3	S1/b1/a1 X_4	S2/b1/a1 X_5	S1/b2/a1 X_6	S2/b2/a1 X_7	S1/b3/a2 X_8	S2/b3/a2 X_9
a_1	b_1	s_1	7	1	1	0	2	0	0	0	0	0
		s_2	6	1	1	0	−1	1	0	0	0	0
		s_3	10	1	1	0	−1	−1	0	0	0	0
	b_2	s_4	7	1	−1	0	0	0	2	0	0	0
		s_5	6	1	−1	0	0	0	−1	1	0	0
		s_6	8	1	−1	0	0	0	−1	−1	0	0
a_2	b_3	s_7	5	−1	0	1	0	0	0	0	2	0
		s_8	3	−1	0	1	0	0	0	0	−1	1
		s_9	5	−1	0	1	0	0	0	0	−1	−1
	b_4	s_{10}	4	−1	0	−1	0	0	0	0	0	0
		s_{11}	2	−1	0	−1	0	0	0	0	0	0
		s_{12}	5	−1	0	−1	0	0	0	0	0	0
	sum		68	0	0	0	0	0	0	0	0	0
	sum sq		438	12	6	6	6	2	6	2	6	2
	SS		52.67	12	6	6	6	2	6	2	6	2
	SP			20	2	2	−2	−4	0	−2	2	−2
	ss(reg)			33.33	0.67	0.67	0.67	8	0	2	0.67	2

			S1/b4/a2 X_{10}	S2/b4/a2 X_{11}	YX_1 X_{12}	YX_2 X_{13}	YX_3 X_{14}	YX_4 X_{15}	YX_5 X_{16}	YX_6 X_{17}	YX_7 X_{18}	YX_8 X_{19}	YX_9 X_{20}	YX_{10} X_{21}	YX_{11} X_{22}
a_1	b_1	s_1	0	0	7	7	0	14	0	0	0	0	0	0	0
		s_2	0	0	6	6	0	−6	6	0	0	0	0	0	0
		s_3	0	0	10	10	0	−10	−10	0	0	0	0	0	0
	b_2	s_4	0	0	7	−7	0	0	0	14	0	0	0	0	0
		s_5	0	0	6	−6	0	0	0	−6	6	0	0	0	0
		s_6	0	0	8	−8	0	0	0	−8	−8	0	0	0	0
a_2	b_3	s_7	0	0	−5	0	5	0	0	0	0	10	0	0	0
		s_8	0	0	−3	0	3	0	0	0	0	−3	3	0	0
		s_9	0	0	−5	0	5	0	0	0	0	−5	−5	0	0
	b_4	s_{10}	2	0	−4	0	−4	0	0	0	0	0	0	8	0
		s_{11}	−1	1	−2	0	−2	0	0	0	0	0	0	−2	2
		s_{12}	−1	−1	−5	0	−5	0	0	0	0	0	0	−5	−5
	sum		0	0	20	2	2	−2	−4	0	−2	2	−2	1	−3
	sum sq		6	2											
	SS		6	2											
	SP		1	−3											
	ss(reg)		0.17	4.5											

TABLE 11.6 Sums of Squares for the Regression Approach to Nested-Design ANOVA

Source	Columns		SS	df (number of columns)
A	$SS(reg.X_1)$	33.33	33.33	1
B/A	$SS(reg.X_2) + SS(reg.X_3)$	$0.67 + 0.67$	1.34	2
$S/B/A$	$SS(reg.X_4) + SS(reg.X_5) + \cdots + SS(reg.X_{11})$	$0.67 + 8 + \cdots + 4.5$	18.00	8
Total	SS_Y	52.67	52.67	11

TABLE 11.7 Data Set for Small-Sample Example of Nested Design

Group	Time	Training
1	7	1
1	6	1
1	10	1
2	7	1
2	6	1
2	8	1
3	5	2
3	3	2
3	5	2
4	4	2
4	2	2
4	5	2

DESIGN instruction shows both training and group(training), to indicate that groups are nested within training. Remaining options are produced by default through the Windows menu system.

The segment labeled Tests of Between-Subjects Effects shows the tests of training and group(training), along with the appropriate Error terms for each, identified in footnotes. Note that the label for $S/B/A$ is Error. The segment labeled Expected Mean Squares shows the basis for choice of error terms, as described in Section 11.6.1.

Table 11.9 shows that SAS GLM also requires two special types of syntax for a nested design. The model instruction includes GROUP(TRAINING) to indicate the nesting arrangement, and the random instruction shows that the nested effect is a random IV, and is to be tested using the appropriate error term.

The initial segments of output are the same as results of fixed-effects ANOVA and use inappropriate error terms. The portion of output labeled Type III Expected Mean Square shows formation of error terms, as explained in Section 11.6.1. The final table of output shows tests of TRAINING and GROUP(TRAINING) using appropriate error terms that match results of Section 11.4.3.

Table 11.10 shows syntax and output for an analysis through MINITAB GLM. Nesting is indicated in two ways. First, the nesting arrangement is shown in the model equation as group(training), then group is declared to be a Random IV.

TABLE 11.8   Nested ANOVA for Small-Sample Example through SPSS GLM (UNIANOVA)

```
UNIANOVA
 time BY group training
 /RANDOM = group
 /METHOD = SSTYPE(3)
 /INTERCEPT = INCLUDE
 /CRITERIA = ALPHA(.05)
 /DESIGN = training group(training).
```

Tests of Between-Subjects Effects

Dependent Variable: TIME

Source		Type III Sum of Squares	df	Mean Square	F	Sig.
Intercept	Hypothesis	385.333	1	385.333	578.000	.002
	Error	1.333	2	.667[a]		
TRAINING	Hypothesis	33.333	1	33.333	50.000	.019
	Error	1.333	2	.667[a]		
GROUP(TRAINING)	Hypothesis	1.333	2	.667	.296	.751
	Error	18.000	8	2.250[b]		

a. MS(GROUP(TRAINING))
b. MS(Error)

Expected Mean Squares[a,b]

Source	Variance Component		
	Var(GROUP(TRAINING))	Var(Error)	Quadratic Term
Intercept	3.000	1.000	Intercept TRAINING
TRAINING	3.000	1.000	TRAINING
GROUP(TRAINING)	3.000	1.000	
Error	.000	1.000	

a. For each source, the expected mean square equals the sum of the coefficients in the cells times the variance components, plus a quadratic term involving effects in the Quadratic Term cell.
b. Expected Mean Squares are based on the Type III Sums of Squares.

Table 11.10 shows the number of levels of each of the IVs, and their Type as fixed or random. The source table follows, with values matching those of SPSS and SAS.

Table 11.11 shows syntax and output for the nested design through SYSTAT GLM. The nesting arrangement is shown in the MODEL instruction. SYSTAT has no way of specifying random effects—but that is no problem with only one level of nesting and no other random factors.

The source table shows the same sums of squares and mean squares as the other programs, however, the test of TRAINING uses $S/B/A$ (labeled Error) instead of GROUP(TRAINING) as

TABLE 11.9 Nested ANOVA For Small-Sample Example Through SAS GLM: Syntax and Selected Output

```
proc glm data = SASUSER. SSNESTED;
    class GROUP TRAINING;
    model TIME = TRAINING GROUP(TRAINING);
    random GROUP(TRAINING) / test;
run;
```

General Linear Models Procedure

Dependent Variable: TIME

Source	DF	Sum of Squares	Mean Square	F Value	Pr > F
Model	3	34.66666667	11.55555556	5.14	0.0286
Error	8	18.00000000	2.25000000		
Corrected Total	11	52.66666667			

R-Square	C.V.	Root MSE	TIME Mean
0.658228	26.47059	1.5000000	5.66666667

Source	DF	Type III SS	Mean Square	F Value	Pr > F
TRAINING	1	33.33333333	33.33333333	14.81	0.0049
GROUP(TRAINING)	2	1.33333333	0.66666667	0.30	0.7514

Source	Type III Expected Mean Square
TRAINING	Var(Error) + 3 Var(GROUP(TRAINING)) +
Q(TRAINING)	
GROUP(TRAINING)	Var(Error) + 3 Var(GROUP(TRAINING))

Tests of Hypotheses for Mixed Model Analysis of Variance

Dependent Variable: TIME

Source: TRAINING
Error: MS(GROUP(TRAINING))

DF	Type III MS	Denominator DF	Denominator MS	F Value	Pr > F
1	33.333333333	2	0.6666666667	50.0000	0.0194

Source: GROUP(TRAINING)
Error: MS(Error)

DF	Type III MS	Denominator DF	Denominator MS	F Value	Pr > F
2	0.6666666667	8	2.25	0.2963	0.7514

TABLE 11.10   Nested ANOVA for Small-Sample Example through MINITAB GLM

```
MTB > GLM 'time' = training group(training);
SUBC>    Random 'group';
SUBC>    Brief 2.

    Analysis of Variance for TIME, using Adjusted SS for Tests

Source              DF    Seq SS    Adj SS    Adj MS      F       P
TRAINING             1    33.333    33.333    33.333    50.00    0.019
GROUP(TRAINING)      2     1.333     1.333     0.667     0.30    0.751
Error                8    18.000    18.000     2.250
Total               11    52.667
```

**TABLE 11.11   Nested ANOVA on Small-Sample Example through SYSTAT GLM:
Syntax and Selected Output**

```
GLM
CATEGORY TRAINING GROUP / EFFECT
MODEL TIME = CONSTANT + TRAINING + GROUP(TRAINING)
ESTIMATE

                      Analysis of Variance

Source            Sum-of-Squares    df    Mean-Square    F-ratio       P

TRAINING                  33.333     1          3.333     14.815    0.005
GROUP(TRAINING)            1.333     2          0.667      0.296    0.751

Error                     18.000     8          2.250
```

the error term. Although this is acceptable under some circumstances (cf. Section 11.6.1), the more traditional test of training is obtained by recalculating F:

$$F = \frac{MS_{TRAINING}}{MS_{GROUP(TRAINING)}} = \frac{33.33}{0.67} = 49.75$$

with 1 and 2 df, as per Section 11.4.3.

11.5   Types of Designs with Random Effects

Types of designs with random-effects IVs are numerous: one-way designs (either randomized groups or repeated measures) with a random-effects IV; factorial designs with all random-effects IVs (which are, in turn, any combination of randomized groups and repeated measures); mixed random–fixed-effects designs (with any combination of randomized-groups and repeated-measures IVs), and nested designs (with any degree of nesting) under either randomized-groups or repeated-measures fixed-effects IVs. Nesting under a repeated-measures fixed-effects IV, for instance, might be something like multiple lists of words given to all cases, with Latin-square counterbalancing. The designs may incorporate other complications like incomplete crossing of factors (Chapter 10) and covariates (Chapter 8).[7]

11.5.1   Nested Designs

The simple example of Section 11.4 has one randomized-groups IVs within a fixed-effects IV. Additional levels of nesting also are possible. Figure 11.2 shows two levels of nesting: B/A and $C/B/A$. In this example, groups could be nested within ski resorts, which, in turn, are nested within training. That is, four resorts (Bear Mountain, Snow Summit, Mammoth, and Heavenly) are randomly selected from a list of resorts in California that have both half-day and full-day classes. Two (Bear Mountain and Snow Summit) are randomly assigned to half-day classes and the other two (Mammoth and Heavenly) are randomly assigned to full-day classes. Resorts and groups are random-effects IVs. Length of training is a fixed-effect IV. Table 11.12 shows a hypothetical data set for this design.

   Table 11.13 shows SPSS GLM (UNIANOVA) syntax and selected output for the analysis of this data set. The double nesting is indicated in the **DESIGN** instruction, with **resorts(training)** indicating that resorts are nested within types of training, and with **group(resorts(training))** indicating that groups are nested within resorts, which, in turn, are nested within types of training. Both resorts and groups are identified as **RANDOM**.

   The **Tests of Between-Subjects Effects** table shows that the mean difference between the two levels of training is statistically reliable, even with only 2 df associated with **resort(training)** as its error term. The **Estimated Marginal Means** table shows that groups trained for a full day ski

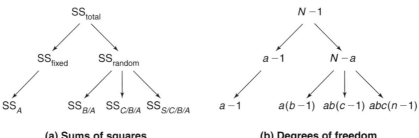

(a) Sums of squares   **(b) Degrees of freedom**

FIGURE 11.2   Partitions of (a) Total Sum of Squares into Sum of Squares due to Differences among Treatments, Differences among Groups within Treatments, Differences among Subgroups within Groups, and Differences among Cases within Subgroups within Groups within Treatments, and (b) Total Degrees of Freedom into Degrees of Freedom Associated with Treatments, Degrees of Freedom Associated with Groups within Treatments, Differences among Subgroups within Groups within Treatments, and Degrees of Freedom Associated with Cases within Subgroups within Groups within Treatments

---

[7]We recommend a simulated data set and trial analyses before embarking on data collection for highly complex designs, to avoid ending up with a data set you do not know how to analyze.

TABLE 11.12   Hypothetical Data for Doubly Nested Design

Class Length A	a_1: Half Day				a_2: Full Day			
Resort B	b_1: Bear Mountain		b_2: Snow Summit		b_3: Mammoth Mountain		b_4: Heavenly Valley	
Groups C	c_1	c_2	c_3	c_4	c_5	c_6	c_7	c_8
Cases S	7	7	8	7	5	4	4	1
	6	6	5	10	3	2	6	2
	10	8	9	7	5	5	4	3

TABLE 11.13   Doubly Nested ANOVA through SPSS GLM (UNIANOVA):
Syntax and Selected Output

```
UNIANOVA
  time BY training group resort
  /RANDOM = group resort
  /METHOD = SSTYPE(3)
  /INTERCEPT = INCLUDE
  /EMMEANS = TABLES(resort)
  /EMMEANS = TABLES(group)
  /EMMEANS = TABLES(training)
  /CRITERIA = ALPHA(.05)
  /DESIGN = training resort(training) group(resort(training)).
```

Univariate Analysis of Variance

Between-Subjects Factors

		Value Label	N
Length of training	1.00	Half day class	12
	2.00	Full day class	12
GROUP	1.00		3
	2.00		3
	3.00		3
	4.00		3
	5.00		3
	6.00		3
	7.00		3
	8.00		3
RESORT	1.00	Bear Mountain	6
	2.00	Snow Summit	6
	3.00	Mammoth Mountain	6
	4.00	Heavenly Valley	6

(continued)

TABLE 11.13   Continued

Tests of Between-Subjects Effects

Dependent Variable: TIME

Source		Type III Sum of Squares	df	Mean Square	F	Sig.
Intercept	Hypothesis	748.167	1	748.167	897.800	.001
	Error	1.667	2	.833[a]		
TRAINING	Hypothesis	88.167	1	88.167	105.800	.009
	Error	1.667	2	.833[a]		
RESORT(TRAINING)	Hypothesis	1.667	2	.833	.263	.781
	Error	12.667	4	3.167[b]		
GROUP(RESORT(TRAINING))	Hypothesis	12.667	4	3.167	1.357	.292
	Error	37.333	16	2.333[c]		

a. MS(RESORT(TRAINING))
b. MS(GROUP(RESORT(TRAINING)))
c. MS(Error)

Estimated Marginal Means

3. Length of training

Dependent Variable: TIME

Length of training	Mean	Std. Error	95% Confidence Interval	
			Lower Bound	Upper Bound
Half day class	7.500[a]	.441	6.565	8.435
Full day class	3.667[a]	.441	2.732	4.601

a. Based on modified population marginal mean.

faster than those trained for half a day. (Remaining tables of means are not reproduced here.) Neither of the random (nested) effects is statistically significant.

Nested designs can have additional IVs that cross treatments, rather than being nested within them. For example, we might add gender to the preceding design, so that there are three women and three men within each of the eight groups, as shown in Table 11.14.

Degrees of freedom for A (training) are $a - 1 = 1$. Degrees of freedom for B (resort) are $a(b - 1) = 2(2 - 1) = 2$. Degrees of freedom for C (groups) are $ab(c - 1) = 2(2)(2 - 1) = 4$, and degrees of freedom for D (gender) are $d - 1 = 1$. Degrees of freedom for the interaction of gender with training are $(d - 1)(a - 1) = 1$. Gender is also crossed with resort and with groups. The degrees of freedom for the gender by resort within training interaction are $(d - 1)a(b - 1) = 1(2)(1) = 2$; and, finally, degrees of freedom for the interaction of gender by groups within resort within training are $(d - 1)ab(c - 1) = 1(2)(2)(1) = 4$.

TABLE 11.14 Hypothetical Data for Doubly Nested Design with Additional Crossed IV

Class Length A		a_1: Half Day				a_2: Full Day			
Resort B		b_1: Bear Mountain		b_2: Snow Summit		b_3: Mammoth Mountain		b_4: Heavenly Valley	
Groups C		c_1	c_2	c_3	c_4	c_5	c_6	c_7	c_8
Gender D	d_1: Women	7	7	8	7	5	4	4	1
		6	6	5	10	3	2	6	2
		10	8	9	7	5	5	4	3
	d_2: Men	6	9	7	9	5	3	4	2
		9	5	7	8	4	6	5	2
		8	7	6	9	4	5	6	1

$a = 2, b = 2, c = 2, d = 2, n = 3.$

Table 11.15 shows the analysis through SAS GLM. Note the difference in specifying double nesting between SPSS and SAS. Double parentheses are not used in SAS; instead, the double nesting is indicated by including all higher-level IVs within a single set of parentheses. (Note that terms within a set of parentheses are separated by an * in the output.)

Only the training and group (within resorts and within training) are statistically reliable. This result is interpreted from the **Least Squares Means** tables. The means for training show that skiers with full-day classes ski faster than those who have only been trained for half a day. Group (within resort and training type) differences are not of particularly substantive interest, however a look at the means shows group 8 (within resort four with full-day training) did especially well. Other **Least Squares Means** tables (for nonsignificant interactions) are not shown here.

11.5.2 One-Way Random-Effects Design

The IV in a one-way random-effects design can be either randomized groups (different cases in each level of the IV) or repeated measures (the same cases in each level of the IV). In either case, the analysis is the same as for a one-way fixed-effects design. This is because it is interaction that creeps into the test of a main effect with a random IV and a one-way design has no interactions.[8]

11.5.3 Factorial Random-Effects Designs

This section discusses factorial designs in which all IVs are random. Such designs can be any combination of randomized groups (Section 11.5.3.1) and repeated measures (Section 11.5.3.2). The difference between random- and fixed-effects ANOVA is in the error terms. Error terms for main effects are

---

[8]Cases are a random factor in any design, including repeated-measures designs. Technically, cases should be declared a random factor in a one-way repeated-measures design (with both cases and the IV declared "between-subjects" factors) and in a Latin-square repeated-measures design (where time is a third "between-subjects" factor; cf. Section 9.4.5). Because no interactions are computed in these designs, however, the software develops the appropriate error term.

**TABLE 11.15   Doubly Nested ANOVA with Additional Crossed IV:
SAS GLM Syntax and Selected Output**

```
proc glm data = SASUSER.DBLNEST;
   class TRAINING GROUP RESORT GENDER;
   model TIME = TRAINING GROUP(RESORT TRAINING) RESORT(TRAINING)
                GENDER TRAINING*GENDER
                GENDER*GROUP(RESORT TRAINING) GENDER*RESORT(TRAINING) ;
   random GROUP(RESORT TRAINING) RESORT(TRAINING)
        GENDER*GROUP(RESORT TRAINING)
        GENDER*RESORT(TRAINING) /TEST;
   lsmeans TRAINING GROUP(RESORT TRAINING) RESORT(TRAINING)
        GENDER*TRAINING GENDER*RESORT(TRAINING)
        GENDER*GROUP(RESORT TRAINING);
run;
```

                  General Linear Models Procedure

Source   Type III Expected Mean Square
TRAINING   Var(Error) + 6 Var(RESOR*GENDER(TRAINI))
                          + 3 Var(GROU*GEND(TRAI*RESO))
                          + 12 Var(RESORT(TRAINING))
                          + 6 Var(GROUP(TRAINI*RESORT))
                          + Q(TRAINING,TRAINING*GENDER)
GROUP(TRAINI*RESORT)   Var(Error) + 3 Var(GROU*GEND(TRAI*RESO))
                          + 6 Var(GROUP(TRAINI*RESORT))
RESORT(TRAINING)   Var(Error) + 6 Var(RESOR*GENDER(TRAINI))
                          + 3 Var(GROU*GEND(TRAI*RESO))
                          + 12 Var(RESORT(TRAINING))
                          + 6 Var(GROUP(TRAINI*RESORT))
GENDER   Var(Error) + 6 Var(RESOR*GENDER(TRAINI))
                          + 3 Var(GROU*GEND(TRAI*RESO))
                          + Q(GENDER,TRAINING*GENDER)
TRAINING*GENDER   Var(Error) + 6 Var(RESOR*GENDER(TRAINI))
                          + 3 Var(GROU*GEND(TRAI*RESO))
                          + Q(TRAINING*GENDER)
GROU*GEND(TRAI*RESO)   Var(Error) + 3 Var(GROU*GEND(TRAI*RESO))
RESOR*GENDER(TRAINI)   Var(Error) + 6 Var(RESOR*GENDER(TRAINI))
                          + 3 Var(GROU*GEND(TRAI*RESO))

      Tests of Hypotheses for Mixed Model Analysis of Variance
Dependent Variable: TIME

      Source   DF   Type III SS   Mean Square   F Value   Pr > F
 *   TRAINING   1   165.020833   165.020833   57.82   0.0169

      Error   2   5.708333   2.854167
Error: MS(RESORT(TRAINING))
* This test assumes one or more other fixed effects are zero.

TABLE 11.15   Continued

Source	DF	Type III SS	Mean Square	F Value	Pr > F
GROUP(TRAINI*RESORT)	4	33.750000	8.437500	13.97	0.0128
RESOR*GENDER(TRAINI)	2	0.375000	0.187500	0.31	0.7494
Error	4	2.416667	0.604167		

Error: MS(GROU*GEND(TRAI*RESO))

Source	DF	Type III SS	Mean Square	F Value	Pr > F
RESORT(TRAINING)	2	5.708333	2.854167	0.36	0.7228
Error	3.5927	28.816638	8.020833		

Error: MS(GROUP(TRAINI*RESORT)) - MS(GROU*GEND(TRAI*RESO))
       + MS(RESOR*GENDER(TRAINI))

Source	DF	Type III SS	Mean Square	F Value	Pr > F
* GENDER	1	0.187500	0.187500	1.00	0.4226
TRAINING*GENDER	1	0.187500	0.187500	1.00	0.4226
Error	2	0.375000	0.187500		

Error: MS(RESOR*GENDER(TRAINI))
* This test assumes one or more other fixed effects are zero.

Source	DF	Type III SS	Mean Square	F Value	Pr > F
GROU*GEND(TRAI*RESO)	4	2.416667	0.604167	0.33	0.8585
Error: MS(Error)	32	59.333333	1.854167		

Least Squares Means

TRAINING	TIME LSMEAN
1	7.50000000
2	3.79166667

GROUP	TRAINING	RESORT	TIME LSMEAN
1	1	1	7.66666667
2	1	1	7.00000000
5	1	3	7.00000000
6	1	3	8.33333333
3	2	2	4.33333333
4	2	2	4.16666667
7	2	4	4.83333333
8	2	4	1.83333333

two-way interactions, and error terms for interactions are higher-order interactions. Only the highest-order interaction uses the error term based on within-cell variability. Calculation of sums of squares, degrees of freedom, and mean squares are otherwise exactly the same as for fixed-effects analysis.

11.5.3.1 Factorial Random-Effects ANOVA with Randomized Groups

The most straightforward factorial random-effects design is one where all IVs are randomized groups (different cases in all combinations of levels). Understanding the rationale for use of interaction as the error term is based on understanding the deviation approach to ANOVA. In an ordinary fixed-effects analysis, the levels of main effects chosen are the only ones of interest and they cover the range of interest. When you look at one main effect, say, A, you collapse over levels of all other effects, say, B. The deviations due to B sum to zero over the levels of B. Some levels of B raise scores and some lower scores, but when all are considered, they sum to zero. Because the test of A is conducted over the levels of B, it is a pure test of the main effect of A; whatever the effects of B are, they cancel each other when examining A. However, with random effects, the levels of B are randomly chosen and there is no guarantee that the deviations produced by these particular levels sum to zero. Instead, the sums of squares for the main effect of A are often contaminated with differences associated with the particular levels of B randomly selected for the study. Because the apparent effects of A depend somewhat on choice of B, it is interaction—of those particular Bs with levels of A—that contaminates the look at A.

Suppose, for example, that the small-sample example of Section 5.4.3 is redefined so that the three professions (administrators, belly dancers, and politicians) are randomly chosen from a compendium of all possible professions and that vacation lengths are randomly chosen from a set of all possible vacation lengths from 1 day to 35 days (where we happened to select 7, 12, and 31 days). For these particular levels of both IVs, there may well be special interaction. Any special interaction of these particular levels of profession with these particular levels of vacation length contaminates both the test of the main effect of profession and the test of the main effect of vacation length. Had we randomly chosen other levels of either variable, their special interactions would similarly confound tests of the two main effects. The contamination is removed by using interaction as the error term, so that F for an IV is a pure test of the main effect. Lindeman (1974) and Maxwell and Delaney (1990) offer more detailed discussions of the issue, along with illustrative examples.

The partitions of sums of squares and degrees of freedom are the same as in Figure 5.1 and all computations of sums of squares, degrees of freedom, and mean squares for this random-effects example are the same as Table 5.7. Only the F ratios for the main-effects change, reflecting the random nature of the choice of IV levels.

$$F_A = \frac{MS_A}{MS_{AB}} \qquad df = (a-1), (a-1)(b-1) \qquad (11.8)$$

$$F_B = \frac{MS_B}{MS_{AB}} \qquad df = (b-1), (a-1)(b-1) \qquad (11.9)$$

Table 11.16 shows the sources of variance, error terms, and F tests for the two-way random-effects ANOVA applied to the data of Table 5.3.

Tests of main effects are evaluated with 2 and 4 df; at $\alpha = .05$, the critical value is 6.94. The test for interaction remains the same as in Section 5.4.3. The consequence of interpreting these IVs as random rather than fixed effects is to greatly reduce power for testing both main effects. In most randomized-groups designs, power is reduced because the degrees of freedom for interaction are markedly smaller than degrees of freedom for S/AB. This example also happens to have a very strong interaction, which further reduces power.

Although partition of sums of squares and degrees of freedom remains the same, error terms are yet more complicated with higher-order factorials. Take, for example, a hypothetical drug study with two randomly chosen levels of reasonable drug dosages, two randomly chosen levels of symptom severity, and four randomly chosen ages (chosen from the population of ages of patients). The DV is amount of symptom relief. Table 11.17 shows the data set and Table 11.18 shows the analysis through MINITAB Balanced ANOVA.

TABLE 11.16 Source Table for Two-Way Randomized-Groups, Random-Effects ANOVA.

Source	SS	df	MS	Error Term	F
A	33.85	2	16.93	AB	0.65
B	32.30	2	16.15	AB	0.62
AB	104.15	4	26.04	S/AB	23.45
S/AB	20.00	18	1.11		
T	190.30	26			

TABLE 11.17 Hypothetical Data Set for Three-Way Randomized-Groups, Random-Effects ANOVA

Age	Dosage	Severity	Relief
1	1	1	3
1	1	1	4
1	1	2	1
1	1	2	2
1	2	1	5
1	2	1	4
1	2	2	2
1	2	2	3
2	1	1	8
2	1	1	9
2	1	2	8
2	1	2	7
2	2	1	9
2	2	1	7
2	2	2	5
2	2	2	6
3	1	1	6
3	1	1	8
3	1	2	5
3	1	2	6
3	2	1	9
3	2	1	8
3	2	2	7
3	2	2	10
4	1	1	10
4	1	1	11
4	1	2	8
4	1	2	7
4	2	1	12
4	2	1	13
4	2	2	10
4	2	2	11

TABLE 11.18   Three-Way Randomized-Groups, Random-Effects ANOVA through MINITAB BALANCED ANOVA: Syntax and Selected Output

```
MTB > ANOVA 'relief' = age|dosage|severity;
SUBC>    Random 'age' 'dosage' 'severity';
SUBC>    EMS.
```

Analysis of Variance (Balanced Designs)

Factor	Type	Levels	Values			
AGE	random	4	1	2	3	4
DOSAGE	random	2	1	2		
SEVERITY	random	2	1	2		

Analysis of Variance for RELIEF

Source	DF	SS	MS	F	P	
AGE	3	214.750	71.583	11.77	0.035	x
DOSAGE	1	10.125	10.125	1.98	0.283	x
SEVERITY	1	24.500	24.500	73.50	0.540	x
AGE*DOSAGE	3	17.625	5.875	6.71	0.076	
AGE*SEVERITY	3	3.250	1.083	1.24	0.432	
DOSAGE*SEVERITY	1	0.125	0.125	0.14	0.731	
AGE*DOSAGE*SEVERITY	3	2.625	0.875	0.93	0.447	
Error	16	15.000	0.937			
Total	31	288.000				

x Not an exact F-test.

Source	Variance component	Error term	Expected Mean Square for Each Term (using unrestricted model)
1 AGE	8.18750	*	(8) + 2(7) + 4(5) + 4(4) + 8(1)
2 DOSAGE	0.31250	*	(8) + 2(7) + 8(6) + 4(4) + 16(2)
3 SEVERITY	1.51042	*	(8) + 2(7) + 8(6) + 4(5) + 16(3)
4 AGE*DOSAGE	1.25000	7	(8) + 2(7) + 4(4)
5 AGE*SEVERITY	0.05208	7	(8) + 2(7) + 4(5)
6 DOSAGE*SEVERITY	-0.09375	7	(8) + 2(7) + 8(6)
7 AGE*DOSAGE*SEVERITY	-0.03125	8	(8) + 2(7)
8 Error	0.93750		(8)

* Synthesized Test.

Error Terms for Synthesized Tests

Source	Error DF	Error MS	Synthesis of Error MS
1 AGE	3.05	6.083	(4) + (5) - (7)
2 DOSAGE	2.23	5.125	(4) + (6) - (7)
3 SEVERITY	0.17	0.333	(5) + (6) - (7)

Significance tests have to be synthesized for the three main effects, as shown in the section labeled `Error Terms for Synthesized Tests`. Further, different software programs use different algorithms for synthesizing tests. Error terms and difficulties associated with them are discussed in Section 11.6.1.

Because the mean squares for interactions are substantial, all tests, except the three-way interaction, are penalized in this analysis. The tests of the two-way interactions are not very powerful with the MS for the three-way interaction serving as error term, with its 3 df. Section 11.6.1.2 shows how to pool error terms to gain power for testing two-way interactions when the three-way interaction is nonsignificant.

There is also no clear error term for the tests of the three main effects, as indicated by the absence of a specified `Error term` accompanying the `Expected Mean Square for Each Term` section of output.

11.5.3.2 Factorial Random-Effects ANOVA with Repeated Measures

Repeated measures in a factorial random-effects ANOVA are most easily handled by considering cases just another random factor, as was demonstrated for repeated-measures ANOVA through MINITAB in Chapter 6. Partition of sums of squares and degrees of freedom does not change from fixed-effects ANOVA with repeated measures.

Consider a design similar to the earlier drug study, with two levels of severity and two of dosage, both with levels randomly selected. Instead of four levels of age, however, there are four patients and only one score for each combination of patient, severity, and dosage. Table 11.19 shows a data set for a "three-way" random-effects ANOVA, where cases form the other "way." Table 11.20 shows the syntax and selected output for the analysis through SPSS GLM (UNIANOVA). The two substantive IVs are SEVERITY and DOSAGE. Table 11.20 shows that neither of these main effects produces a reliable mean difference in RELIEF of symptoms. However, there is a statistically significant interaction

TABLE 11.19 Hypothetical Data Set for Two-Way Repeated-Measures, Random-Effects ANOVA

Patient	Severity	Dosage	Relief
1	1	1	1
1	1	2	6
1	2	1	4
1	2	2	6
2	1	1	7
2	1	2	8
2	2	1	6
2	2	2	3
3	1	1	3
3	1	2	5
3	2	1	5
3	2	2	3
4	1	1	5
4	1	2	8
4	2	1	6
4	2	2	4

TABLE 11.20   Two-Way Repeated-Measures, Random-Effects ANOVA Through SPSS GLM (UNIANOVA)

UNIANOVA
 relief BY patient dosage severity
 /RANDOM = patient dosage severity
 /METHOD = SSTYPE(3)
 /INTERCEPT = INCLUDE
 /CRITERIA = ALPHA(.05)
 /DESIGN = patient dosage severity patient*dosage patient*severity
   dosage*severity patient*dosage*severity.

Tests of Between-Subjects Effects

Dependent Variable: RELIEF

Source		Type III Sum of Squares	df	Mean Square	F	Sig.
Intercept	Hypothesis	400.000	1	.	.	.
	Error	.	.[a]	.		
PATIENT	Hypothesis	12.500	3	4.167	.568	.657
	Error	42.025	5.731	7.333[b]		
DOSAGE	Hypothesis	2.250	1	2.250	.115	.777
	Error	28.809	1.471	19.583[c]		
SEVERITY	Hypothesis	2.250	1	2.250	.115	.777
	Error	28.809	1.471	19.583[d]		
PATIENT* DOSAGE	Hypothesis	11.250	3	3.750	22.500	.015
	Error	.500	3	.167[e]		
PATIENT* SEVERITY	Hypothesis	11.250	3	3.750	22.500	.015
	Error	.500	3	.167[e]		
DOSAGE* SEVERITY	Hypothesis	16.000	1	16.000	96.000	.002
	Error	.500	3	.167[e]		
PATIENT* DOSAGE* SEVERITY	Hypothesis	.500	3	.167	.	.
	Error	.000	0	.[f]		

a. Cannot compute the error degrees of freedom using Satterthwaite's method.

b. MS(PATIENT*DOSAGE) + MS(PATIENT*SEVERITY) – MS(PATIENT*DOSAGE* SEVERITY)

c. MS(PATIENT*DOSAGE) + MS(DOSAGE*SEVERITY) – MS(PATIENT*DOSAGE* SEVERITY)

d. MS(PATIENT*SEVERITY) + MS(DOSAGE*SEVERITY) – MS(PATIENT*DOSAGE* SEVERITY)

e. MS(PATIENT*DOSAGE*SEVERITY)

f. MS(Error)

TABLE 11.21   Comparison of Error Terms in Two-Way Repeated-Measures Fixed-Effects and Random-Effects Designs

Source	Fixed-Effects Error	Random-Effects Error
Dosage	Dosage × Patient	Dosage × Patient + Dosage × Severity − Dosage × Severity × Patient
Severity	Severity × Patient	Severity × Patient + Dosage × Severity − Dosage × Severity × Patient
Dosage × Severity	Dosage × Severity × Patient	Dosage × Severity × Patient

between DOSAGE and SEVERITY. The main effect of PATIENT represents individual differences and is ordinarily not of interest; however, it could be tested in this random-effects model, unlike a corresponding fixed-effects model, because there is an unambiguous error term.

Table 11.21 compares the error terms in a fixed-effects and a two-way random-effects repeated-measures design. The error terms for the main effects of dosage and severity follow the same pattern as in a randomized-groups design, also with complicated adjustments to degrees of freedom. The error term for the dosage by severity interaction is the same as in a repeated-measures fixed-effects design (cf. Section 6.4.5).

Note that sphericity is not tested when the problem is set up this way, as discussed in Section 6.4.1.5 in the context of MINITAB analysis of repeated-measures designs. When repeated-measures IVs have only two levels, there is no opportunity to violate the assumption. However, when there are more than two levels of a repeated-measures IV, the assumption could be violated. To test the assumption, a separate run is required in which data are set up with one line of data per patient, as in the usual repeated-measures analysis. Or a planned trend analysis could be substituted for the omnibus test of the effect.

11.5.4   Mixed Fixed-Random Designs

This section discusses designs in which some effects are fixed and some random. These designs also do not differ from fixed-effects designs in partition of sources of variability, computation of sums of squares, degrees of freedom, and mean squares, and in the error term used to test the highest-order interaction. They do differ in which error terms are used to test some of the main effects and lower-order interactions. Mixed fixed-random designs can include randomized-groups IVs, repeated-measures IVs, and a mix of randomized and repeated-measures IVs, with any number of IVs of any particular type. Recall that there are two uses of the term *mixed:* (1) Fixed and random effects and (2) randomized-groups and repeated-measures IVs.

There are two forms of the randomized-groups mixed fixed-random design: the restricted and unrestricted models. This chapter, like most textbooks, illustrates the restricted model, however, most software programs are based on the unrestricted model. The two models differ in their choice of error term for the random factor: the restricted model uses $MS_{S/AB}$ as the error term, whereas the unrestricted model uses MS_{AB} as the error term. The restricted model is recommended because it is likely to provide a more powerful test of the random factor and because of the rationale described in what follows.

Section 11.5.4.1 discusses a fully randomized-groups design with some fixed and some random-effects IVs. Section 11.5.4.2 discusses a fully repeated-measures design with some fixed and some random-effects IVs. Section 11.5.4.3 discusses a "mixed-mixed" design in which there are both randomized-groups and repeated-measures IVs, some fixed effects and some random effects.

11.5.4.1   Mixed Fixed–Random-Effects ANOVA with Randomized Groups

The simplest of these designs is a two-way randomized-groups factorial, with one IV fixed and the other random. Suppose, in the example of Section 5.4, that levels of profession are randomly selected but vacation lengths are fixed at 1, 2, and 3 weeks. The F ratios, reflecting the error terms for main effects, are

$$F_A = \frac{MS_A}{MS_{S/AB}} \qquad df = (a - 1),\, ab(n - 1) \tag{11.10}$$

$$F_B = \frac{MS_B}{MS_{AB}} \qquad df = (b - 1),\, (a - 1)(b - 1) \tag{11.11}$$

The random-effects factor, A (profession), uses the same error term as in a fixed-effects design. It is the *fixed* factor, B (vacation length), that uses a different error term—the $A \times B$ interaction.[9] Thus, the design can be analyzed through any ANOVA software. If there is no random-effects capability, you simply recalculate using MS_{AB} as the error term, and assess statistical significance using Table A.1 from Appendix A with numerator $df = b - 1$ and denominator $df = (a - 1)(b - 1)$.

The analysis is run through SYSTAT in Table 5.16. The F ratios for profession and the profession by length interaction are interpreted as for the fixed-effects design. To conform to the present example, the F ratio for vacation length is recalculated as

$$F_B = \frac{16.148}{26.037} = 0.62 \qquad df = 2, 4$$

Because of the reduction in degrees of freedom, the factor has suffered a reduction in power. Table 11.22 summarizes the sources of variance, error terms, and F tests for the two-way randomized-groups, fixed-random ANOVA.

TABLE 11.22   Source Table for Two-Way Randomized-Groups, Fixed, Random-Effects ANOVA

Source	SS	df	MS	Error Term	F
A (random)	33.85	2	16.93	S/AB	15.23
B (fixed)	32.30	2	16.15	AB	0.62
AB	104.15	4	26.04	S/AB	23.45
S/AB	20.00	18	1.11		
T	190.30	26			

[9]Although most software programs use the $A \times B$ interaction as the error term for the random as well as the fixed factor, MINITAB Balanced ANOVA permits a restricted model.

A three-way randomized-groups, fixed-random design can have either one or two random IVs. Consider, for example, the levels of age and severity to be fixed in the data of Table 11.17 and dosage levels are randomly selected. Table 11.23 shows the analysis through MINITAB Balanced ANOVA. The restricted model is requested along with expected mean squares (EMS).

Table 11.24 shows the error terms for this three-way mixed design. All effects that include the random IV (DOSAGE) use the within-cell error term. All other effects suffer loss of power by using

TABLE 11.23   Three-Way Randomized-Groups, Fixed–Fixed, Random-Effects ANOVA Through MINITAB Balanced ANOVA

```
MTB > ANOVA 'relief' = age|dosage|severity;
SUBC>    Random 'dosage';
SUBC>    Restrict;
SUBC>    EMS.
```

Analysis of Variance (Balanced Designs)

Factor	Type	Levels	Values	
AGE	fixed	2	1	2
DOSAGE	random	2	1	2
SEVERITY	fixed	2	1	2

Analysis of Variance for RELIEF

Source	DF	SS	MS	F	P
AGE	1	5.062	5.062	0.67	0.563
DOSAGE	1	10.563	10.563	6.26	0.037
SEVERITY	1	10.563	10.563	0.75	0.545
AGE*DOSAGE	1	7.562	7.562	4.48	0.067
AGE*SEVERITY	1	10.563	10.563	2.09	0.386
DOSAGE*SEVERITY	1	14.063	14.063	8.33	0.020
AGE*DOSAGE*SEVERITY	1	5.062	5.062	3.00	0.122
Error	8	13.500	1.688		
Total	15	76.938			

Source	Variance component	Error term	Expected Mean Square for Each Term (using restricted model)
1 AGE		4	(8) + 4(4) + 8Q[1]
2 DOSAGE	1.109	8	(8) + 8(2)
3 SEVERITY		6	(8) + 4(6) + 8Q[3]
4 AGE*DOSAGE	1.469	8	(8) + 4(4)
5 AGE*SEVERITY		7	(8) + 2(7) + 4Q[5]
6 DOSAGE*SEVERITY	3.094	8	(8) + 4(6)
7 AGE*DOSAGE*SEVERITY	1.688	8	(8) + 2(7)
8 Error	1.688		(8)

TABLE 11.24   Error Terms in Restricted Three-Way Randomized-Groups, Fixed–Fixed-Random-Effects Design

Source	Error Term
Age (Fixed)	Age $\times$ Dosage
Severity (Fixed)	Severity $\times$ Dosage
Dosage (Random)	S/ABC
Age $\times$ Severity	Age $\times$ Severity $\times$ Dosage
Severity $\times$ Dosage	S/ABC
Age $\times$ Dosage	S/ABC
Age $\times$ Severity $\times$ Dosage	S/ABC

error terms based on interactions. Note that error terms are different in the unrestricted model produced by most other software.

Compare these results with those of the fully random-effects model of Table 11.18. We now have exact (rather than synthesized) tests of the main effects, however, tests of the fixed effects still severely lack power, with the single df two-way interactions that have more variance (MS) than the main effects. However, the main effect of the random factor now reaches statistical significance, as does one of the mixed interactions, DOSAGE*SEVERITY, because both those effects are tested with the within-cell error term (S/ABC).

11.5.4.2   Mixed Fixed–Random-Effects ANOVA with Repeated Measures

Another variation is the fully repeated-measures design with some IVs fixed and some random. For example, the two-way repeated-measures design of Section 6.4.2.3 could easily have both a fixed effect (month) and a random effect (novel) if the types of novel are randomly chosen from a population of all possible types.

The trick with the analysis is to organize the data as if all IVs, including cases, are randomized-group IVs. Then both cases and the actual random-effects IV(s) are defined as random. The IVs are treated as if they are randomized groups. Table 11.25 shows the data setup for a "three-way" mixed fixed–random-effects ANOVA. Table 11.26 shows the analysis through SPSS GLM (UNIANOVA).

The error terms are summarized and compared with those in a two-way fixed-effects analysis in Table 11.27. Compare these error terms with those of Table 11.21 for a two-way repeated-measures design with both effects random. The error terms are exactly the same as when only one of the effects is random.

The effects of interest in this analysis are MONTH, NOVEL, and their interaction. These effects are reported in the section labeled Tests of Between-Subjects Effects because the data are organized as randomized groups. Power is lost for both tests of main effects, compared to that of the fixed-effects analysis of Section 6.4.2.3, because of the change in error terms. The test of the MONTH*NOVEL interaction is the same as in the fixed-effects analysis. Again, setting up the data and analysis this way provides no test of sphericity.

TABLE 11.25   Hypothetical Two-Way Repeated-Measures Data Set in One-Line-Per-Cell Format

CASE	NOVEL	MONTH	BOOKS
1	1	1	1
1	1	2	3
1	1	3	6
1	2	1	5
1	2	2	4
1	2	3	1
2	1	1	1
2	1	2	4
2	1	3	8
2	2	1	8
2	2	2	8
2	2	3	4
3	1	1	3
3	1	2	3
3	1	3	6
3	2	1	4
3	2	2	5
3	2	3	3
4	1	1	5
4	1	2	5
4	1	3	7
4	2	1	3
4	2	2	2
4	2	3	0
5	1	1	2
5	1	2	4
5	1	3	5
5	2	1	5
5	2	2	6
5	2	3	3

TABLE 11.26   Two-Way Repeated-Measures, Fixed, Random ANOVA: SPSS GLM (UNIANOVA) Syntax and Selected Output

```
UNIANOVA
  books BY month novel case
  /RANDOM = novel case
  /METHOD = SSTYPE(3)
  /INTERCEPT = INCLUDE
  /CRITERIA = ALPHA(.05)
  /DESIGN = month novel case month*novel
  month*case novel*case month*novel*case.
```

Univariate Analysis of Variance

Between-Subjects Factors

		N
MONTH	1.00	10
	2.00	10
	3.00	10
NOVEL	1.00	15
	2.00	15
CASE	1.00	6
	2.00	6
	3.00	6
	4.00	6
	5.00	6

(continued)

TABLE 11.26 Continued

Tests of Between-Subjects Effects

Dependent Variable: BOOKS

Source		Type III Sum of Squares	df	Mean Square	F	Sig.
Intercept	Hypothesis	512.533	1	.	.	.
	Error	.	.[a]	.		
MONTH	Hypothesis	2.867	2	1.433	.045	.957
	Error	60.236	1.911	31.517[b]		
NOVEL	Hypothesis	.133	1	.133	.003	.957
	Error	113.699	2.887	39.383[c]		
CASE	Hypothesis	16.467	4	4.117	.537	.722
	Error	25.325	3.303	7.667[d]		
MONTH * NOVEL	Hypothesis	64.467	2	32.233	26.135	.000
	Error	9.867	8	1.233[e]		
MONTH * CASE	Hypothesis	4.133	8	.517	.419	.880
	Error	9.867	8	1.233[e]		
NOVEL * CASE	Hypothesis	33.533	4	8.383	6.797	.011
	Error	9.867	8	1.233[e]		
MONTH * NOVEL * CASE	Hypothesis	9.867	8	1.233	.	.
	Error	.000	0	.[f]		

a. Cannot compute the error degrees of freedom using Satterthwaite's method.

b. MS(MONTH * NOVEL) + MS(MONTH * CASE) − MS(MONTH * NOVEL * CASE)

c. 1.000 MS(MONTH * NOVEL) + MS(NOVEL * CASE) − 1.000 MS(MONTH * NOVEL * CASE)

d. MS(MONTH * CASE) + 1.000 MS(NOVEL * CASE) − 1.000 MS(MONTH * NOVEL * CASE)

e. MS(MONTH * NOVEL * CASE)

f. MS(Error)

TABLE 11.27 Comparison of Error Terms in Two-Way Repeated-Measures Designs, Both Effects Fixed, both Random and Mixed

Source	Mixed and Completely Random-Effects Error Terms	Fixed-Effects Error Term
Month	Month × Novel + Month × Case − Month × Novel × Case	Month × Case
Novel	Month × Novel + Novel × Case − Month × Novel × Case	Novel × Case
Month × Novel	Month × Novel × Case	Month × Novel × Case

11.5.4.3 Mixed Fixed–Random-Effects ANOVA with Randomized Groups and Repeated Measures

Finally, there are mixed–mixed designs with both random and fixed effects and both randomized groups and repeated measures. Using the example of Section 7.4.3, let us assume that types of novels are randomized groups and randomly chosen and the three months are repeated measures and fixed effects. The first task is to reorganize the data into one-line-per-cell format so that cases are also set up as a random randomized-groups IV, as shown in Table 11.28.

   Table 11.29 shows the analysis through SPSS GLM (UNIANOVA). The syntax uses nesting specification to indicate that cases nest within type of novel (the randomized-groups IV), but cross levels of month (the repeated-measures IV).

   The effects of interest are NOVEL, MONTH, and their interaction. The error terms for NOVEL [tested against CASE(NOVEL) + MONTH – NOVEL MONTH – CASE(NOVEL)] and MONTH (tested against MONTH*NOVEL) are both considerably larger than those in the fixed-effects analysis of Section 7.4.3. However, the test of the MONTH – NOVEL interaction uses the same error term—MONTH – CASE(NOVEL)—as in the fixed-effects analysis and is unaffected by the presence of a random-effects IV. Recall that the test of the highest-order interaction is always the same as for a fixed-effects analysis. Again, no test of sphericity is available with this arrangement of the data.

TABLE 11.28 Hypothetical Data Set for Mixed–Mixed Design

CASE	NOVEL	MONTH	BOOKS
1	1	1	1
1	1	2	3
1	1	3	6
2	1	1	1
2	1	2	4
2	1	3	8
3	1	1	3
3	1	2	3
3	1	3	6
4	1	1	5
4	1	2	5
4	1	3	7
5	1	1	2
5	1	2	4
5	1	3	5
6	2	1	3
6	2	2	1
6	2	3	0
7	2	1	4
7	2	2	4
7	2	3	2
8	2	1	5
8	2	2	3
8	2	3	2
9	2	1	4
9	2	2	2
9	2	3	0
10	2	1	4
10	2	2	5
10	2	3	3
11	3	1	4
11	3	2	2
11	3	3	0
12	3	1	2
12	3	2	6
12	3	3	1
13	3	1	3
13	3	2	3
13	3	3	3
14	3	1	6
14	3	2	2
14	3	3	1
15	3	1	3
15	3	2	3
15	3	3	2

continued at right

TABLE 11.29 Analysis of Mixed–Mixed Design. Novel Is a Randomized-Group, Random-Effects IV; Month Is a Repeated-Measures, Fixed-Effects IV: SPSS GLM Syntax and Selected Output

```
UNIANOVA
 books BY month case novel
 /RANDOM = case novel
 /METHOD = SSTYPE(3)
 /INTERCEPT = INCLUDE
 /CRITERIA = ALPHA(.05)
 /DESIGN = month novel case(novel)
           month*novel, month*case(novel).
```

Univariate Analysis of Variance

Tests of Between-Subjects Effects

Dependent Variable: BOOKS

Source		Type III Sum of Squares	df	Mean Square	F	Sig.
Intercept	Hypothesis	473.689	1	473.689	49.039	.021
	Error	20.578	2	10.289[a]		
MONTH	Hypothesis	.711	2	.356	.020	.980
	Error	71.422	4	17.856[b]		
NOVEL	Hypothesis	20.578	2	10.289	.556	.610
	Error	79.011	4.270	18.506[c]		
CASE(NOVEL)	Hypothesis	26.400	12	2.200	1.419	.224
	Error	37.200	24	1.550[d]		
MONTH * NOVEL	Hypothesis	71.422	4	17.856	11.520	.000
	Error	37.200	24	1.550[d]		
MONTH * CASE(NOVEL)	Hypothesis	37.200	24	1.550	.	.
	Error	.000	0	.[e]		

a. MS(NOVEL)

b. MS(MONTH * NOVEL)

c. 1.000 MS(CASE(NOVEL)) + 1.000 MS(MONTH * NOVEL)
   − 1.000 MS(MONTH * CASE(NOVEL)) − 1.044 − 14 MS(Error)

d. MS(MONTH * CASE(NOVEL))

e. MS(Error)

11.6   Some Important Issues

A major issue in random-effects ANOVA is the choice of error terms. Indeed, this is the only difference between random- and fixed-effects ANOVA. Alternative strategies for analysis of random effects—particularly hierarchical designs—have recently been implemented in software that use iterative algorithms to circumvent the issue of choice of error terms.

Trend analysis, as discussed in Section 11.6.3, of a random IV usually requires adjustment for unequal spacing of levels. Homogeneity of covariance, Section 11.6.4, is an issue in factorial random-effects designs—that is, designs in which random effects cross each other or cross fixed effects.

11.6.1   Error Terms in Random-Effects ANOVA

Error terms are what distinguish between analyses of random- and fixed-effects ANOVA. The reason is that an interaction between a random factor (B) and a fixed factor (A) intrudes on the test of the main effect of the fixed factor. This is because the matrix of cell means from any particular study represents all possible levels of A but not all possible levels of B. This means that you can "trust" the marginal means of B because they are averaged over *all* levels of A, but you cannot trust the marginal means of A, because they are averaged over only some of the possible levels of B. Suppose there are no real (population) main effects of A or B. That is, averaging over all possible levels of B produces about the same means for each level of A, but averaging over only the particular randomly selected levels of B results in different means for each level of A. This happens when the particularly selected levels of B do not happen to have the average response when combined with the levels of A, that is, that these particular levels of B interact with A. Although one fondly hopes that such interaction is absent, the prudent course is to assume the interaction is present and include it in the test of the main effect of A. Little is lost if there really is no interaction, because little is added to the numerator and denominator of the F ratio—only a little more error resulting in a little less power.[10]

Of course, this applies to all main effects in a fully random factorial design. Interaction intrudes on main effects and higher-order interactions intrude on lower-order interactions. Therefore, the expected mean square (EMS—a term we have avoided so far but cannot any longer) in the numerator of an F ratio includes not only treatment plus error but also interactions between treatment and random effects.

Recall from Section 3.2.3.4 that in a fixed-effects ANOVA, the test of treatment is based on the assumption that the components of variance in the F ratio are

$$F = \frac{\text{treatment} + \text{error}}{\text{error}}$$

A second, random, IV in the design changes the numerator to include the potential interaction between treatment and the second IV. Therefore, for the F to be equal to 1 when the null hypothesis

---

[10]Again, this is based on the restricted model. The $A \times B$ interaction intrudes on both fixed and random main effects in the unrestricted model, used by most software.

is true, the interaction must be added to the denominator as well. Thus, the components of variance in the test for treatment become

$$F = \frac{\text{treatment} + \text{interaction} + \text{error}}{\text{interaction} + \text{error}}$$

So let us consider expected mean squares. They are based on population parameters and are represented by Greek letters: σ^2 or θ^2 (theta squared) are used instead of MS to represent expected population variance. The symbol used for population error variance—the real stuff that we can only estimate—is σ_ε^2. This source of variability appears in every expected mean square. In the simplest factorial design, a two-way randomized-groups fixed layout, this is estimated by $\text{MS}_{S/AB}$ and it is all that is needed to serve as the error term for A, B, and the $A \times B$ interaction in that design. However. . . .

11.6.1.1 *Expected Mean Squares*

Population variances for random effects are denoted σ^2; population variances for fixed effects are denoted θ^2. So, for a fixed two-way factorial design, σ^2 (error) is in the denominator and both θ^2 (effect) and σ^2 (error) are in the numerator. There is an additional hitch. The population variance for treatment (θ^2) is multiplied by the number of scores in the marginal mean (i.e., the number of levels of the other factor times the number of scores in each cell) because it affects the calculated mean square. Thus, the expected MS (EMS) for A in a two-way fixed-effects ANOVA is $\sigma_\varepsilon^2 + (b)(n)(\theta_A^2)$. Table 11.30 shows the expected mean squares and error terms for 3 two-way randomized-groups factorial designs: both IVs fixed, A fixed and B random, and both IVs random. The appropriate error term for an effect is the one that has all of the components of the effect *except* the effect itself. Thus, in the design with both IVs fixed, S/AB has the only component that is in A in addition to $(b)(n)(\theta_A^2)$: that is, σ_ε^2.

Table 11.30 shows that the test of the $A \times B$ interaction is the same in all designs, and the error term for the test of the main effects depends only on whether the *other* IV is fixed or random—not whether the IV being tested is fixed or random. Note that the last column of Table 11.30 matches that of the error terms in Table 11.16. Table 11.31 compares error terms in a variety of two-way designs.

Nested designs have their own expected mean squares. Table 11.32 shows EMS and error terms for the simple nested design of Section 11.4, where A is the fixed treatment IV, B is the random IV nested with A, and cases are nested within B.

The EMS for A includes B/A (the random effect) as well as $S/B/A$; therefore, B/A (which also includes $S/B/A$) is used as the error term. These error terms are shown in the SPSS GLM output of Table 11.8, where the error term identified in the first footnote is MS(GROUP TRAINING), which corresponds to $\text{MS}_{B/A}$. In the portion of the table labeled `Expected Mean Squares` the value of 3 corresponds to the three cases in each group (n); the quadratic term includes the number of scores in each level of TRAINING, although not so specified in output. SAS GLM output (cf. Table 11.9) similarly shows expected mean squares for each effect, with Q indicating the quadratic term. Q corresponds to $(b)(n)$ in the EMS for A in Table 11.32. For the small-sample example of Section 4.4.3, the number of levels of B is 2, the number of scores in each level of B/A is 3, so the number of scores in each level of A is $(b)(n) = (2)(3) = 6 = Q$.

TABLE 11.30 Expected Means Squares and Error Terms for Sources of Variance in Three Two-Way Randomized-Groups Factorial Designs

Source	Both IVs Fixed EMS	Both IVs Fixed Error Term	A Fixed, B Random EMS	A Fixed, B Random Error Term	Both IVs Random EMS	Both IVs Random Error Term
A	$\sigma_\varepsilon^2 + (b)(n)(\theta_A^2)$	S/AB	$\sigma_\varepsilon^2 + (n)(\sigma_{AB}^2) + (b)(n)(\theta_A^2)$	$A \times B$	$\sigma_\varepsilon^2 + (n)(\sigma_{AB}^2) + (b)(n)(\sigma_A^2)$	$A \times B$
B	$\sigma_\varepsilon^2 + (a)(n)(\theta_B^2)$	S/AB	$\sigma_\varepsilon^2 + (a)(n)(\sigma_B^2)$	S/AB	$\sigma_\varepsilon^2 + (n)(\sigma_{AB}^2) + (a)(n)(\sigma_B^2)$	$A \times B$
$A \times B$	$\sigma_\varepsilon^2 + (n)(\theta_{AB}^2)$	S/AB	$\sigma_\varepsilon^2 + (n)(\sigma_{AB}^2)$	S/AB	$\sigma_\varepsilon^2 + (n)(\sigma_{AB}^2)$	S/AB
S/AB	σ_ε^2		σ_ε^2		σ_ε^2	

TABLE 11.31 Comparison of Error Terms in Various Combinations of Randomized-Groups, Repeated-Measures, Fixed and Random Two-Way Designs

Source	Randomized Groups Both Fixed	Randomized Groups Both Random	Randomized Groups A Fixed, B Random	Repeated Measures Both Fixed	Repeated Measures Both Random	Repeated Measures A Fixed, B Random	Mixed A RG and Random, B RM and Fixed
A	S/AB	AB	AB	AS	$AS + AB - ABS$	$AS + AB - ABS$	$S/A + AB - B \times S/A$
B	S/AB	AB	S/AB	BS	$BS + AB - ABS$	$BS + AB - ABS$	AB
$A \times B$	S/AB	S/AB	S/AB	ABS	ABS	ABS	$B \times S/A$

RG = randomized groups.

RM = repeated measures.

TABLE 11.32 Expected Means Squares and Error Terms for Sources of Variance in a Simple Nested Design

Source	EMS	Error Term
A	$\sigma_\varepsilon^2 + (n)(\sigma_{B/A}^2) + (b)(n)(\theta_A^2)$	B/A
B/A	$\sigma_\varepsilon^2 + (n)(\sigma_{B/A}^2)$	$S/A/B$
$S/B/A$	σ_ε^2	

So far, EMS and choice of error terms are fairly straightforward. You figure out the interactions that could be included in main effects and add their variances (multiplied by number of scores in the relevant cell) to the EMS that already includes the variance for the effect being tested plus population error, σ_ε^2. Then you look for a term that includes all of the components except the effect to be tested, and use that as the error term. But sometimes that term does not exist. Consider, for example, the three-way randomized-groups designs in which all factors are random. Table 11.33 shows the EMS for that design.

Error terms for the interactions are easily found. Each of the two-way interactions includes population error, its own effect, and the three-way interaction. Because the three-way interaction includes its own effect and population error, it serves as an error term for all the two-way interactions. The three-way interaction needs only population error as its error term, so S/ABC does the job.

Main effects, however, each have 2 two-way interactions in their EMS along with the three-way interaction, population error, and its own effect. There are no terms to serve as error that have the three-way interaction, population error, and 2 two-way interactions. Therefore, the strategy is to combine effects to end up with the correct components. For the error term for A, for example, EMS_{AB} has one of the interaction components needed and EMS_{AC} has the other; both have the three-way component and population error. So adding them together produces an error term with all of the needed components, but an extra three-way interaction component and an extra population error.

TABLE 11.33　Expected Means Squares and Error Terms for Sources of Variance in Two Three-Way Randomized-Groups Factorial Designs

| Source | All IVs Fixed | | All IVs Random | |
	EMS	Error Term	EMS	Error Term
A	$\sigma_\varepsilon^2 + (b)(c)(n)(\theta_A^2)$	S/ABC	$\sigma_\varepsilon^2 + (n)(\sigma_{ABC}^2) + (n)(c)(\sigma_{AB}^2)$ $+ (n)(b)(\sigma_{AC}^2) + (b)(c)(n)(\sigma_A^2)$	$\text{MS}_{AB} + \text{MS}_{AC}$ $- \text{MS}_{ABC}$
B	$\sigma_\varepsilon^2 + (a)(c)(n)(\theta_B^2)$	S/ABC	$\sigma_\varepsilon^2 + (n)(\sigma_{ABC}^2) + (n)(c)(\sigma_{AB}^2)$ $+ (n)(a)(\sigma_{BC}^2) + (a)(c)(n)(\sigma_B^2)$	$\text{MS}_{AB} + \text{MS}_{BC}$ $- \text{MS}_{ABC}$
C	$\sigma_\varepsilon^2 + (a)(b)(n)(\theta_C^2)$	S/ABC	$\sigma_\varepsilon^2 + (n)(\sigma_{ABC}^2) + (n)(b)(\sigma_{AC}^2)$ $+ (n)(a)(\sigma_{BC}^2) + (a)(b)(n)(\sigma_C^2)$	$\text{MS}_{AC} + \text{MS}_{BC}$ $- \text{MS}_{ABC}$
$A \times B$	$\sigma_\varepsilon^2 + (c)(n)(\theta_{AB}^2)$	S/ABC	$\sigma_\varepsilon^2 + (n)(\sigma_{ABC}^2) + (c)(n)(\sigma_{AB}^2)$	$A \times B \times C$
$A \times C$	$\sigma_\varepsilon^2 + (b)(n)(\theta_{AC}^2)$	S/ABC	$\sigma_\varepsilon^2 + (n)(\sigma_{ABC}^2) + (b)(n)(\sigma_{AC}^2)$	$A \times B \times C$
$B \times C$	$\sigma_\varepsilon^2 + (a)(n)(\theta_{BC}^2)$	S/ABC	$\sigma_\varepsilon^2 + (n)(\sigma_{ABC}^2) + (a)(n)(\sigma_{BC}^2)$	$A \times B \times C$
$A \times B \times C$	$\sigma_\varepsilon^2 + (n)(\theta_{ABC}^2)$	S/ABC	$\sigma_\varepsilon^2 + (n)(\sigma_{ABC}^2)$	S/ABC
S/ABC	σ_ε^2		σ_ε^2	

These are dealt with by subtracting out EMS_{ABC}, which only has the extra components, so that $MS_{A\,error}$ can be formed as $MS_{AB} + MS_{AC} - MS_{ABC}$. This error term and the terms for B and C appear in Table 11.33. F ratios based on this term are called quasi-F (also called pseudo-F) ratios, or F'. For example, the main effect of A is tested by

$$F'_A = \frac{MS_A}{MS_{AB} + MS_{AC} - MS_{ABC}} \tag{11.12}$$

Adjusted degrees of freedom for the error term are then calculated using Equation 11.13 so that standard F tables (Appendix A.1) may be used to evaluate F' (Satterthwaite, 1946).

$$df_{A_{adj}} = \frac{(MS_{AB} + MS_{AC} - MS_{ABC})^2}{MS_{AB}^2/df_{AB} + MS_{AC}^2/df_{AC} + MS_{ABC}^2/df_{ABC}} \tag{11.13}$$

SAS GLM output for the three-way random-effects ANOVA (Table 11.18) shows these error terms and their use in evaluating main effects. This strategy can be applied to any design in which there is no straightforward error term for testing an effect, for example, the mixed–mixed design of Table 11.29. One problem with this strategy, however, is that the error MS can be less than zero if the MS that are added are less than the MS that are subtracted. Thus, other strategies for calculating quasi-F ratios are available (Myers, 1979). There also are alternatives to ANOVA in dealing with random-effects designs, as discussed in Section 11.6.2.

11.6.1.2 Pooled Error Terms

Loss of power in random-effects designs stems from loss of degrees of freedom in error terms. Some researchers recommend pooling error terms to overcome this loss of power under some circumstances. For example, Winer (1971) recommends pooling MS_{AB} with $MS_{S/AB}$ if there is no statistically reliable interaction or if prior research indicates that no interaction is to be expected.[11] To consider pooling, preliminary tests are performed on higher-order effects before testing lower-order effects of interest. The procedure is as follows: If an interaction is apparently random variability, it can be pooled with another mean square that has the same expected value except for interaction. Pooling is done by adding the SS for the two effects, adding their df, and then forming a new MS by dividing the new SS by the new df.

Consider, for example, the three-way analysis of Table 11.18. All of the two-way effects use the three-way interaction as the error term, but it is not statistically reliable ($p = .447$). Thus, MS_{ADS} (AGE by DOSAGE by SEVERITY) may be pooled with MS_{error}. The pooled sums of squares and degrees of freedom are

$$SS_{pooled} = 15.000 + 2.625 = 17.625$$

and

$$df_{pooled} = 16 + 3 = 19$$

---

[11]There is a strong interaction in the two-way random-effects example of Table 11.16, so pooling is not feasible.

The new MS to use as error for the tests of two-way interactions is

$$MS_{pooled} = \frac{17.625}{19} = 0.928$$

The test of AGE by DOSAGE now has $F = 5.875/0.928 = 6.33$, now statistically reliable at $\alpha = .05$ with df = 2 and 19. Although the F ratios change little, the increased df_{error} are sufficient to find a reliable $A \times D$ interaction. However, AGE by SEVERITY and DOSAGE by SEVERITY still are not reliable.

Nested models may also use pooled error terms if the designated error terms are not statistically reliable. For example, neither of the random error terms—RESORT(TRAINING) or GROUP(RESORT(TRAINING))—is statistically reliable in the doubly nested ANOVA of Table 11.13. Therefore, the EMS for each term reduces to σ^2, just as it is for $MS_{S/C/B/A}$, labeled **MS(Error)** in Table 11.13). All three effects may be pooled to provide a stronger test of TRAINING, although more power is unnecessary in this case. As a demonstration:

$$SS_{pooled} = 1.667 + 12.667 + 37.333 = 51.667$$

and

$$df_{pooled} = 2 + 4 + 16 = 22$$

The new MS_{error} for the test of TRAINING is

$$MS_{pooled} = \frac{51.67}{22} = 2.35$$

and $F_{training} = 88.167/2.35 = 37.52$, actually less than with the nonpooled error term. However, since df_{error} increases to 22, the p value becomes $< .001$.

One problem with pooling is that Type I error increases once preliminary tests are done—the test of interest can be considered post hoc. This is why some statisticians recommend that pooling never be done. A compromise position to deal with increased Type I error rate is to apply a more conservative α level when using pooled error terms, perhaps .025 instead of .05. However, this may obviate the gain in power from pooling. Another recommendation is to pool terms only when the preliminary test of significance has an $\alpha > .25$ (Myers and Well, 1991, p. 327).

11.6.2 Alternative Strategies to ANOVA

Alternatives to the ANOVA strategy in this chapter are based on maximum likelihood procedures (Eliason, 1993), sometimes referred to as variance-components analysis. Effects in ANOVA are considered variance components in maximum likelihood procedures. These are iterative procedures designed to deal with such problems as unbalanced designs (including unequal sample sizes) and negative variance and df estimates. They also handle repeated measures without some of the restrictive assumptions of the ANOVA models, such as sphericity. Disadvantages of maximum likelihood strategies are that they require large samples and, sometimes, they too produce negative variance estimates. Also, statistical properties of some of the more sophisticated applications (such as random-coefficients models in multilevel modeling (cf. Kreft and DeLeeuw, 1998) are not well known. SAS VARCOMP, SAS MIXED, and SPSS GLM (VARCOMP) all may be used for maximum likelihood analysis of random-effects models.

Tables 11.34 and 11.35 show analysis of the three-way random-effects randomized-groups factorial data of Table 11.17 through SPSS GLM and SAS VARCOMP. Both analyses specify restricted maximum likelihood as the estimation procedure. Table 11.34 shows syntax and selected output for SPSS GLM (VARCOMP). All three IVs are declared RANDOM, and REML is chosen as the METHOD. Remaining instructions are produced through the SPSS menu system.

The variance components of interest are in the Variance Components Estimation table. For example, the variance component for AGE is 8.189, the component for DOSAGE is 0.266, and so on. SPSS provides no direct tests of statistical significance of variance components, but a z value (Wald test) may be calculated by dividing each variance component by its standard error. A variance component (effect) estimate is considered statistically significant if its z value differs sufficiently from zero (the null hypothesis). Standard errors are calculated by taking the square roots of variances in the diagonals of the Asymptotic Covariance Matrix. For example, the variance for AGE in that table is 53.750, for DOSAGE, it is 0.891, and so on, so the standard error for AGE is $(53.750)^{1/2} =$

TABLE 11.34   Three-Way Random-Effects Restricted Maximum Likelihood Analysis: SPSS GLM (VARCOMP) Syntax and Selected Output

```
VARCOMP
 relief BY age dosage severity
 /RANDOM = age dosage severity
 /METHOD = REML
 /CRITERIA = ITERATE (50)
 /CRITERIA = CONVERGE(1.0E8)
 /DESIGN = age dosage severity age*dosage age*severity
          dosage*severity age*dosage*severity
 /INTERCEPT = INCLUDE.
```

Variance Components Estimation

Variance Estimates

Component	Estimate
Var(AGE)	8.189
Var(DOSAGE)	.266
Var(SEVERITY)	1.464
Var(AGE * DOSAGE)	1.247
Var(AGE * SEVERITY)	4.896E-02
Var(DOSAGE * SEVERITY)	.000[a]
Var(AGE * DOSAGE * SEVERITY)	.000[a]
Var(Error)	.887

Dependent Variable: RELIEF
Method: Restricted Maximum Likelihood Estimation

a. This estimate is set to zero because it is redundant.

(continued)

TABLE 11.34   Continued

Asymptotic Covariance Matrix

	Var(AGE)	Var(DOSAGE)	Var(SEVERITY)	Var(AGE * DOSAGE)	Var(AGE * SEVERITY)	Var(DOSAGE * SEVERITY)	Var(AGE * DOSAGE * SEVERITY)	Var(Error)
Var(AGE)	53.750	.180	6.113E-03	-.722	-2.691E-02	.000	.000	9.846E-03
Var(DOSAGE)	.180	.891	-4.85E-18	-.360	2.144E-17	.000	.000	-8.72E-17
Var(SEVERITY)	6.113E-03	-4.854E-18	4.693	-4.442E-17	-1.223E-02	.000	.000	4.788E-17
Var(AGE * DOSAGE)	-.722	-.360	-4.44E-17	1.443	4.923E-03	.000	.000	-1.97E-02
Var(AGE * SEVERITY)	-2.69E-02	2.144E-17	-1.22E-02	4.923E-03	5.382E-02	.000	.000	-1.97E-02
Var(DOSAGE * SEVERITY)	.000	.000	.000	.000	.000	.000	.000	
Var(AGE * DOSAGE * SEVERITY)	.000	.000	.000	.000	.000	.000	.000	.000
Var(Error)	9.846E-03	-8.723E-17	4.788E-17	-1.969E-02	-1.969E-02	.000	.000	7.877E-02

Dependent Variable: RELIEF

Method: Restricted Maximum Likelihood Estimation

7.331 and the standard error for **DOSAGE** is $(0.891)^{1/2} = 0.945$. Thus, $z = 8.189/7.331 = 1.12$ for **AGE** and $0.266/0.891 = 0.30$ for **DOSAGE**. With a critical value of $z = 1.96$ at $\alpha = .05$, there are no statistically reliable predictors of **RELIEF**. This is a more conservative outcome than noted in the traditional analysis of Table 11.18 in which AGE was statistically reliable, but then maximum likelihood analysis is for large samples. SPSS GLM (VARCOMP) does not provide tests of any fixed effects in a mixed fixed–random design.

Table 11.35 shows the same analysis through SAS MIXED. The options chosen are for the `reml` method, `covtest`, which requests Wald z-tests of the parameter estimates using the standard errors derived from the asymptotic covariance matrix, and `asycov`, which requests the asymptotic covariance matrix. Unlike SAS GLM, the program assumes that effects listed in the `model` instruction are fixed; random effects are specified in the `random` instruction.

The `Covariance Parameter Estimates` are the same as SPSS estimates. The `Asymptotic Covariance Matrix of Estimates` shows values similar to those of SPSS, but not exactly the same (note that zero values are shown as blank). This presumably is due to minor differences in the algorithms used by the two programs. The Wald test derives the standard

TABLE 11.35   Three-Way Random-Effects Restricted Maximum Likelihood Analysis: SAS MIXED Syntax and Selected Output

```
proc mixed data = SASUSER.FAC3WAY method=reml covtest asycov;
   class AGE DOSAGE SEVERITY;
   model RELIEF =;
   random AGE|DOSAGE|SEVERITY;
run;
```

```
                 The MIXED Procedure

            Class Level Information

            Class     Levels     Values

            AGE          4       1 2 3 4
            DOSAGE       2       1 2
            SEVERITY     2       1 2
```

Covariance Parameter Estimates

Cov Parm	Estimate	Standard Error	Z Value	Pr Z
AGE	8.1888	7.3309	1.12	0.1320
DOSAGE	0.2656	0.9438	0.28	0.3892
AGE*DOSAGE	1.2469	1.2012	1.04	0.1496
SEVERITY	1.4635	2.1662	0.68	0.2496
AGE*SEVERITY	0.04896	0.2320	0.21	0.4164
DOSAGE*SEVERITY	0	.	.	.
AGE*DOSAGE*SEVERITY	0	.	.	.
Residual	0.8875	0.2807	3.16	0.0008

(continued)

TABLE 11.35 Continued

Asymptotic Covariance Matrix of Estimates

Row	Cov Parm	CovP1	CovP2	CovP3
1	AGE	53.7421	0.1798	-0.7215
2	DOSAGE	0.1798	0.8908	-0.3595
3	AGE*DOSAGE	-0.7215	-0.3595	1.4430
4	SEVERITY	0.006113	1.22E-12	7.589E-8
5	AGE*SEVERITY	-0.02692	7.924E-8	0.004922
6	DOSAGE*SEVERITY			
7	AGE*DOSAGE*SEVERITY			
8	Residual	0.009874	-3.17E-7	-0.01969

Row	Cov Parm	CovP4	CovP5	CovP6	CovP7
1	AGE	0.006113	-0.02692		
2	DOSAGE	1.22E-12	7.924E-8		
3	AGE*DOSAGE	7.589E-8	0.004922		
4	SEVERITY	4.6926	-0.01223		
5	AGE*SEVERITY	-0.01223	0.05382		
6	DOSAGE*SEVERITY				
7	AGE*DOSAGE*SEVERITY				
8	Residual	-3.04E-7	-0.01969		

Asymptotic
Covariance
Matrix of
Estimates

Row	CovP8
1	0.009874
2	-3.17E-7
3	-0.01969
4	-3.04E-7
5	-0.01969
6	
7	
8	0.07877

errors from the covariance matrix, as demonstrated for SPSS. Again, no effects are statistically reliable at $\alpha = .05$.

In addition to restricted maximum likelihood estimation, the two programs provide (unrestricted) maximum likelihood (ML) estimation, a procedure similar to REML that does not take into account degrees of freedom for fixed effects when estimating variance components. SAS and SPSS also implement a noniterative method (minimum norm quadratic unbiased estimation—MIVQUE0 and MINQUE in SAS and SPSS, respectively) that has "considerable flexibility with respect to the form of the models that can be fitted" (SPSS Inc., 1999a). Both programs also have methods that follow the general linear approach.

The reader interested in further information about maximum likelihood methods for models with random effects and nesting is referred to Rao and Kleffe (1988); Bryk and Raudenbush (1992); Searle, Casella, and McColloch (1992); and Kreft and DeLeeuw (1998). The second and fourth sources are devoted to nested (hierarchical) models and introduce random-coefficients models, an elaboration of random-effects models in which the higher levels of nesting (e.g., groups within treatments) may differ not only in level (means), but also in slope.

For example, consider an affirmative action program versus a no-program control as the fixed-treatment IV. Organizations, differing in size, are randomly assigned to treatment or control conditions. The DV is minority salary, measured at the individual employee level—employees, of course, are nested within organizations. Average salaries may differ between organizations as well as between treatments, and this difference is handled in nested ANOVA, because organizations within treatments serve as the error term. In addition, however, the relationship between salary and treatment may differ among organizations of different sizes. That is, the relationship between salary and treatment may depend on organization size. This is similar to the classic ANCOVA problem of heterogeneity of regression (cf. Section 8.3.2.6), but here organization size (the covariate) and salary (the DV) are measured at different levels of the hierarchical design (at the organization level vs. the employee level). All employees within a single organization have the same size "score," leading to nonindependence of errors if classic ANCOVA is used and nesting is ignored. A nested ANCOVA, then, is plagued with heterogeneity of regression because of the different slopes between treatments. Random-coefficients models, however, are designed to take both hierarchical levels of analysis and differing slopes associated with heterogencity of regression into account.[12] Among the programs described in this section, only SAS MIXED handles the random-coefficients models.

11.6.3 Trend Analysis with Unequal Spacing

Trend analysis usually is interesting whenever there is a quantitative IV with more than two levels. Trend analysis is especially interesting when the levels of the quantitative IV are randomly selected from the range of levels of interest because the results generalize to the entire range. Random choice of levels, however, rarely provides levels that are equally spaced, making the trend analysis a bit more demanding, as discussed in Section 4.5.3.6.

Suppose, for example, we are interested in a trend analysis on AGE in the data of Table 11.17. Suppose, in addition, that the levels of age randomly selected from a range of interest, say, 15 to 75, turned out to be 16, 29, 33, and 56. Table 11.36 shows the trend analysis through SPSS GLM (UNIANOVA). Unequal spacing for the trend analysis of age is specified in the /CONTRAST instruction by the spacing of ages within parentheses. Least squares means are requested for age to help interpret the trend analysis.

Custom Hypothesis Tests shows the results of the trend analysis. The 95% confidence intervals for the linear and quadratic effects do not include zero, indicating that both those effects are statistically significant at $\alpha = .05$. The cubic trend is not statistically significant. Figure 11.3 plots the means, showing the direction of the trends.

The rate of growth is steeper between 16 and about 30 than between 30 and 56. The last portion of the line is speculative, drawn by eye, to continue the decrease in rate of growth with increasing age.

---

[12]Within the context of random-coefficients models, slopes are evaluated as intraclass correlations (see, e.g., Bryk and Raudenbush, 1992).

TABLE 11.36 Trend Analysis with Unequal Spacing of Levels in a Three-Way Random-Effects Design: SPSS GLM Syntax and Selected Output

```
UNIANOVA
 relief BY age dosage severity
 /RANDOM = age dosage severity
 /CONTRAST (age) = Polynomial (16 29 33 56)
 /METHOD = SSTYPE(3)
 /INTERCEPT = INCLUDE
 /CRITERIA = ALPHA(.05)
 /EMMEANS = TABLES(age)
 /DESIGN = age dosage severity age*dosage age*severity
             dosage*severity age*dosage*severity.
```

Univariate Analysis of Variance

Custom Hypothesis Tests

Contrast Results (K Matrix)

AGE Polynomial Contrast[a]		Dependent Variable
		RELIEF
Linear	Contrast Estimate	4.894
	Hypothesized Value	0
	Difference (Estimate—Hypothesized)	4.894
	Std. Error	.342
	Sig.	.000
	95% Confidence Interval Lower Bound	4.168
	for Difference Upper Bound	5.620
Quadratic	Contrast Estimate	−1.578
	Hypothesized Value	0
	Difference (Estimate—Hypothesized)	−1.578
	Std. Error	.342
	Sig.	.000
	95% Confidence Interval Lower Bound	−2.304
	for Difference Upper Bound	−.853
Cubic	Contrast Estimate	.633
	Hypothesized Value	0
	Difference (Estimate—Hypothesized)	.633
	Std. Error	.342
	Sig.	.083
	95% Confidence Interval Lower Bound	−9.27E-02
	for Difference Upper Bound	1.359

a. Metric = 16.000, 29.000, 33.000, 56.000.

TABLE 11.36   Continued

Estimated Marginal Means

AGE

Dependent Variable: RELIEF

			95% Confidence Interval	
AGE	Mean	Std. Error	Lower Bound	Upper Bound
1	3.000	.342	2.274	3.726
2	7.375	.342	6.649	8.101
3	7.375	.342	6.649	8.101
4	10.250	.342	9.524	10.976

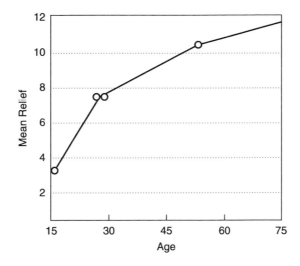

FIGURE 11.3   Mean Relief as a Function of Age

11.6.4   Homogeneity of Covariance

All repeated-measures ANOVA assume homogeneity of covariance/sphericity (cf. Sections 6.3.2.3 and 6.6.2). The assumption also is required for a random-effects IV in a factorial ANOVA. That is, it is assumed that the relationships between all pairs of levels of any IV are the same at all levels of a random IV.

There is no formal test for homogeneity of covariance in random-effects designs akin to Mauchley's sphericity test for repeated measures. However, some idea of the violation of the assumption may be gleaned through viewing the variance-covariance matrices formed around cell means (Lindeman, 1974). For the data of Table 5.3, with the random-effects ANOVA in Table 11.14, cell means are shown in Table 11.37.

TABLE 11.37   Cell Means for Data in Two-Way Random-Effects ANOVA

	b_1: 7 Days	b_2: 12 Days	b_3: 31 Days
a_1: Administrators	0.33	0.67	6.33
a_2: Belly Dancers	6.00	6.00	8.33
a_3: Politicians	6.33	9.00	2.67

TABLE 11.38   Variance-Covariance Matrices for Means in Table 11.37

(a) Variance-covariance matrix for A

	a_1	a_2	a_3
a_1	10.83	2.59	-1.98
a_2	2.59	1.81	-3.88
a_3	-1.98	-3.88	10.10

(b) Variance-covariance matrix for B

	b_1	b_2	b_3
b_1	11.38	3.81	-2.08
b_2	3.81	3.37	-4.75
b_3	-2.08	-4.75	8.24

Because both A and B are random, two variance-covariance matrices are formed. The diagonal elements in the first matrix (A) are formed by finding the variance of each level of A over the three levels of B. The off-diagonal elements are formed by finding the covariances of all pairs of levels of A over the three levels of B.[13] The reverse is done for the variance-covariance matrix for B; means are averaged over levels of A. Table 11.38 shows the variance-covariance matrices for A and B.

Both variances and covariances are far from homogeneous in these two matrices. However, the estimates are highly tentative because of the small samples used to generate them (three samples for each parameter estimate). This possible violation of assumptions of homogeneity of variance and homogeneity of covariance puts the ANOVA results in doubt. A variance-stabilizing transformation might be considered or a more conservative α level for testing effects—perhaps .025 or even .01. Another option is to use SAS MIXED to specify an appropriate variance-covariance matrix.

11.6.5   Effect Size

The $\hat{\omega}^2$ and partial $\hat{\omega}^2$ of Chapter 5 do not apply to ANOVA designs with random effects. An alternative measure, $\hat{\rho}^2$ (rho squared), has been developed as an estimate of population effect size (Vaughan and Corballis, 1969). For a one-way random effects ANOVA,

$$\hat{\rho}^2 = \frac{\text{MS}_A - \text{MS}_{S/A}}{\text{MS}_A + (n - 1) - \text{MS}_{S/A}} \tag{11.14}$$

---

[13]Chapter 2 showed how to calculate variances and covariances.

Note that although the test for significance is the same for one-way fixed- and one-way random-effects designs, the effect size estimate is not.

Partial $\hat{\rho}^2$ is available for statistically reliable effects in a two-way design with both IVs random (Kirk, 1995):

$$\text{Partial } \hat{\rho}^2_A = \frac{(\text{MS}_A - \text{MS}_{AB})/bn}{\text{MS}_{S/AB} + (\text{MS}_A - \text{MS}_{AB})/bn} \qquad (11.15)$$

$$\text{Partial } \hat{\rho}^2_B = \frac{(\text{MS}_B - \text{MS}_{AB})/an}{\text{MS}_{S/AB} + (\text{MS}_B - \text{MS}_{AB})/an} \qquad (11.16)$$

and

$$\text{Partial } \hat{\rho}^2_{AB} = \frac{(\text{MS}_{AB} - \text{MS}_{S/AB})/n}{\text{MS}_{AB} + (\text{MS}_{AB} - \text{MS}_{S/AB})/n} \qquad (11.17)$$

Any values that turn out to be negative are changed to zero. Applying this to the interaction (the only reliable effect) in the two-way random-effects design of Section 11.5.3.1 (cf. Table 11.16):

$$\text{Partial } \hat{\rho}^2_{AB} = \frac{(26.04 - 1.11)/3}{1.11 + (26.04 - 1.11)/3} = .88$$

For a mixed design with A fixed and B random, partial $\hat{\omega}^2$ for A is as defined in Equation 5.15. Partial $\hat{\rho}^2_B$ is as defined in Equation 11.15 and partial $\hat{\rho}^2_{AB}$ is as defined in Equation 11.16. Nested models and those with repeated measures are most easily handled by relying on η^2 and partial η^2 of Section 5.6.2, using the applicable error term for partial η^2.

11.7   Complete Example of Random-Effects ANOVA

The example involves testing the fat content of dried eggs. Data are published in Bliss (1967) and are available on the Internet. The original article describing the experiment (Mitchell, 1950) was not available to us.

Four samples each drawn from a well-mixed can of dried eggs were sent to six testing laboratories, deliberately chosen. Samples were arbitrarily labeled either G or H. Two technicians in each laboratory used the same chemical technique to provide two tests of samples labeled G and two tests of samples labeled H. Therefore, laboratory is a fixed IV with six levels; technicians within laboratories is a second, nested, random IV with two levels; and label of sample (G or H) within technician within laboratory is another two-level, nested, random IV. Therefore, this is a doubly nested $6 \times 2 \times 2$ fixed-random-random design with two replicates (i.e., two testings of each sample by each technician). The DV is fat content determined by acid hydrolysis. The metric is percent fat -41.70% (the latter value presumably is the nominal fat content). The layout of the design is similar to that of Table 11.12, with six levels of A, two levels of B, and two levels of C.

The major effect of interest is differences among laboratories, although differences between technicians within laboratories would likely be of interest to the laboratories. Differences among samples are also potentially interesting because they were randomly selected and arbitrarily labeled from the well-mixed can and, therefore, should differ only by random error. The analysis produces tests of all three main effects (but no interactions because they are precluded by the nesting arrangement).

11.7.1   Evaluation of Assumptions

The usual distributional assumptions for fixed-effects randomized groups apply to this doubly nested design. Because there are no interactions, cells are not defined for this nested design. Therefore, assumptions are evaluated separately on the margin of each of the three main effects: laboratory, technician, and sample.

The design does include repeated measures for the technicians. Each technician provides two tests of the sample labeled G and two tests of the sample labeled H. Individual differences due to cases are dealt with by including technicians as an IV (nested within laboratories). Despite the use of repeated measures, sphericity in not an issue because each of the repeated-measures factors (label of sample and replicates) has only two levels.

11.7.1.1   Sample Sizes, Normality, and Independence of Errors

Independence of errors for the test of laboratories is assured by sending random samples to the six laboratories. Nonindependence of errors within the four tests produced by each technician is accounted for by treating technician as an IV, so that individual differences among technicians do not bias any of the other tests.

Table 11.39 shows syntax and descriptive statistics from SAS MEANS analyses. Data must be sorted by a variable before separate statistics are given for each level of that variable. The 24 levels of sample (with only two scores each) are not shown in the table. Output is shown for only two laboratories and one technician.

This is an equal-n design, with eight scores in each level of laboratory, four scores for each technician, and 24 scores for each label of sample. Normality of sampling distributions is safely assumed for the test of the main effect of samples because $df_{error} = N -$ (number of samples) $= 48 - 24 = 24$ (see Section 11.5.1). However, error df for tests of laboratory and technician are insufficient to assume normality of sampling distributions. Therefore, skewness and kurtosis are examined within each level of laboratory and technician. SAS provides values for these, but not standard errors to use to form tests of them. Standard errors and z-tests for skewness and kurtosis are easy to compute, however, using Equations 2.8 through 2.11.

The standard error for skewness for each of the six levels of laboratory is

$$S_{skewness} = \sqrt{\frac{6}{8}} = 0.866$$

and the standard error for kurtosis is

$$S_{kurtosis} = \sqrt{\frac{24}{8}} = 1.732$$

For the first level of laboratory, then, $z = -0.880/0.866 = -1.02$ for skewness and $z = -0.293/1.732 = -0.169$. At $\alpha = .01$—an appropriate level for evaluating small samples—critical $z = \pm 2.58$. Therefore, neither skewness nor kurtosis exceed acceptable limits for normality. The only level of laboratory that approaches the limits is laboratory 5, with $z = -2.09$ for skewness and $z = 2.31$ for kurtosis.

Standard errors for the 12 technicians are 1.225 for skewness and 2.449 for kurtosis, using Equations 2.8 and 2.9. By using these to form z-tests (Equations 2.10 and 2.11), there is no concern about departure from normality of sampling distributions for any of the technicians' distributions.

**TABLE 11.39 Descriptive Statistics for Egg Testing Data through SAS MEANS:
Syntax and Selected Output**

```
proc sort data = SASUSER.EGGS;
  by LAB;
run;
proc means vardef = DF
  N MIN MAX MEAN STD VAR SKEWNESS KURTOSIS;
  var FATCONT;
  by LAB;
run;
proc sort;
  by TECH;
run;
proc means vardef = DF
  N MIN MAX MEAN STD VAR SKEWNESS KURTOSIS;
  var FATCONT;
  by TECH;
run;
```

```
-------------------------- LAB = 1 --------------------------
                    The MEANS Procedure
                 Analysis Variable: FATCONT

N    Minimum     Maximum        Mean     Std Dev     Variance      Skewness
----------------------------------------------------------------------------
8  0.2400000   0.8000000   0.5800000   0.1969046   0.0387714   -0.8799415
----------------------------------------------------------------------------

                 Analysis Variable: FATCONT

                        Kurtosis
                        ----------
                        -0.2925716
                        ----------

-------------------------- LAB = 5 --------------------------
                 Analysis Variable: FATCONT

N    Minimum     Maximum        Mean     Std Dev     Variance      Skewness
----------------------------------------------------------------------------
8  0.2000000   0.4200000   0.3537500   0.0690626   0.0047696   -1.8081903
----------------------------------------------------------------------------

                 Analysis Variable: FATCONT

                        Kurtosis
                        ----------
                        3.9948441
                        ----------

-------------------------- TECH = 1 --------------------------
                    The MEANS Procedure
                 Analysis Variable: FATCONT

N    Minimum     Maximum        Mean     Std Dev     Variance      Skewness
----------------------------------------------------------------------------
4  0.2400000   0.6200000   0.4375000   0.1774589   0.0314917   -0.1346073
----------------------------------------------------------------------------

                 Analysis Variable: FATCONT

                        Kurtosis
                        ----------
                        -3.8153829
                        ----------
```

11.7.1.2   *Homogeneity of Variance and Outliers*

Homogeneity of variance for the test of laboratories is evaluated by calculating the ratio of highest to lowest variance among the six levels: $F_{\max} = 0.0388/.0048 = 8.08$. With $F_{\max} < 10$ and equal sample sizes in each level, there is no concern about violation of homogeneity of variance.

The largest variance among technicians is 0.0315 and the smallest is 0.0007. This yields $F_{\max} = 45$, seemingly violating the assumption of homogeneity of variance. However, a test of $F_{\max}$ does not reach statistical significance, due to the large number of variances and small number of df for each variance; the critical value for $F_{\max}$ with 3 df (four cases in each variances) and 12 variances is 124 at $\alpha = .05$ (Pearson and Hartley, 1958).

A look at maximum and minimum scores for technician 1 reveals that neither is an outlier: $z = (0.24 - 0.4375)/0.1775 = -1.11$ for the minimum score and $z = (0.62 - 0.4375)/0.1775 = 1.03$ for the maximum score. Therefore, there are no outlying scores for the first technician. Evaluation of minimum and scores for the other technicians reveals that there are no outliers to cloud the test of technicians within laboratories.

Tests for outliers also are applied to each of the six laboratories. For example, in the first laboratory $z = (0.24 - 0.58)/0.1969 = -1.73$ for the minimum score and $z = (0.80 - 0.58)/0.1969 = 1.12$, indicating no outliers at $\alpha = .01$. Tests for the remaining laboratories produce similar results.

Therefore, the only problem identified is the impossibility of testing homogeneity of variance and of evaluating outliers among label of samples within technicians because there are only two replicates. Therefore, the decision is made to set the α level to .01 for the test of label of sample.

11.7.2   ANOVA for Doubly Nested Design

Table 11.40 shows SAS GLM syntax and output for a traditional analysis of the fat content of eggs in this doubly nested design.

Only the test of technicians within laboratories is statistically reliable at $\alpha = .05$: $F(6, 12) = 3.0954, p = .0453$. Neither laboratory nor label of samples within technicians within laboratories displays statistical significance. Effect size for technicians within laboratories is

$$\eta^2 = \frac{SS_{TECH(LAB)}}{SS_{total}} = \frac{MS_{TECH(LAB)}(df_{TECH(LAB)})}{SS_{total}} = \frac{(0.0412458)(6)}{1.0231} = .24$$

Means and standard deviations for the 12 technicians are in the runs producing Table 11.39. With four samples per technician, standard error is calculated as $\texttt{Std Dev}/\sqrt{4}$. Means and standard errors are in Table 11.41 in a form appropriate for a journal report.

Tukey tests are used to compare all pairs of technicians. SAS GLM does not generate Tukey tests for this design. Therefore, the tests are done by hand using $MS_{SAMPLE(LAB*TECH)} = 0.013325$, from the final source table of Table 11.40. The easiest way to do this uses Equation 4.16, modified to incorporate the current error term.

$$\bar{d}_T = q_T \sqrt{\frac{MS_{SAMPLE(LAB*TECH)}}{n}} = 5.62\sqrt{\frac{0.013325}{4}} = 0.324$$

TABLE 11.40   Traditional ANOVA on Fat Content of Eggs in Doubly Nested Design: SAS GLM Syntax and Selected Output

```
proc glm data = SASUSER.EGGS;
  class LAB TECH SAMPLE;
  model FATCONT = LAB TECH(LAB) SAMPLE(TECH LAB);
  random TECH(LAB) SAMPLE(TECH LAB) /TEST;
run;
```

General Linear Models Procedure
Class Level Information

Class	Levels	Values
LAB	6	1 2 3 4 5 6
TECH	12	1 2 3 4 5 6 7 8 9 10 11 12
SAMPLE	24	1 2 3 4 5 6 7 8 9 10 11 12 13 14 15 16 17 18 19 20 21 22 23 24

Number of observations in data set = 48

General Linear Models Procedure

Dependent Variable: FATCONT

Source	DF	Sum of Squares	Mean Square	F Value	Pr > F
Model	23	0.85040000	0.03697391	5.14	0.0001
Error	24	0.17270000	0.00719583		
Corrected Total	47	1.02310000			

R-Square	C.V.	Root MSE	FATCONT Mean
0.831199	21.89116	0.0848282	0.38750000

Source	Type III Expected Mean Square
LAB	Var(Error) + 2 Var(SAMPLE(LAB*TECH)) + 4 Var(TECH(LAB)) + Q(LAB)
TECH(LAB)	Var(Error) + 2 Var(SAMPLE(LAB*TECH)) + 4 Var(TECH(LAB))
SAMPLE(LAB*TECH)	Var(Error) + 2 Var(SAMPLE(LAB*TECH))

Tests of Hypotheses for Mixed Model Analysis of Variance

Dependent Variable: FATCONT

Source: LAB
Error: MS(TECH(LAB))

DF	Type III MS	Denominator DF	Denominator MS	F Value	Pr > F
5	0.088605	6	0.0412458333	2.1482	0.1895

(continued)

TABLE 11.40 Continued

```
Source: TECH(LAB)
Error: MS(SAMPLE(LAB*TECH))
```

		Denominator	Denominator		
DF	Type III MS	DF	MS	F Value	Pr > F
6	0.0412458333	12	0.013325	3.0954	0.0453

```
Source: SAMPLE(LAB*TECH)
Error: MS(Error)
```

		Denominator	Denominator		
DF	Type III MS	DF	MS	F Value	Pr > F
12	0.013325	24	0.0071958333	1.8518	0.0962

TABLE 11.41 Means and Standard Errors for Twelve Technicians in Six Laboratories

Lab	Technician	Mean	Standard Error
1	1	0.4375	0.0887
	2	0.7225	0.0347
2	3	0.3650	0.0301
	4	0.3150	0.0514
3	5	0.3700	0.0389
	6	0.4450	0.0357
4	7	0.3750	0.0786
	8	0.3775	0.0256
5	9	0.3600	0.0129
	10	0.3475	0.0509
6	11	0.3600	0.0308
	12	0.1750	0.0419

with number of means $= 12$, $df_{\text{SAMPLE(LAB*TECH)}} = 12$ and $\alpha = .05$. Technician 2 reports higher fat content than all other technicians except 1 and 6. None of the other differences among technicians is statistically reliable.

Table 11.42 is a checklist of items to consider for doubly nested ANOVA. An example of a Results section in journal format follows.

TABLE 11.42   Checklist for Doubly Nested Analysis of Variance

1. Issues
   a. Independence of errors
   b. Unequal sample sizes
   c. Normality of sampling distributions
   d. Outliers
   e. Homogeneity of variance
2. Major analyses (planned comparisons or omnibus Fs); if significant
   a. Effect size
   b. Parameter estimates (means and standard deviations or standard errors or confidence intervals for each group)
3. Additional analyses
   a. Post hoc comparisons
   b. Interpretation of departure from homogeneity of variance, if appropriate

---

```
                           Results
      A 6 × 2 × 2 doubly nested fixed—random—random ANOVA was per-
formed on fat content (percent fat minus 41.70%) of samples from a
single well-mixed can of dried eggs. Six laboratories, deliber-
ately chosen, were provided with four samples each, two arbitrar-
ily labeled G and two arbitrarily labeled H. Within each
laboratory, two technicians were given two of each sample (G and
H) to test. Thus, technicians were nested within laboratories, and
samples (G and H) were nested within technicians within laborato-
ries. There were two replicates for each sample.
      All assumptions evaluated were met. However, assumptions
about normality and homogeneity of variance could not be evaluated
for the test of sample labels because of the small sample size
(n = 2). Therefore, α was set to .01 for that test, with α = .05
for the tests of laboratory and technicians within laboratories.
There were no outlying cases within levels of laboratory or within
```

measurements of technicians. Outliers could not be evaluated among samples.

No statistically reliable differences were found among laboratories, nor among samples within technicians within laboratories. However, technicians within laboratories were found to differ reliably, $\underline{F}(6, 12) = 3.10$, $\underline{p} = .0453$, $\eta^2 = .24$.

A post hoc Tukey test showed that differences among technicians were largely due to one technician whose reports of fat content (mean = 0.72) were higher than those of all except two of the other technicians; means for the other 11 technicians ranged from 0.18 to 0.45, as shown in Table 11.40. The remaining technicians did not differ reliably from one another.

11.8   Comparison of Programs

SPSS and SAS have a variety of procedures for handling random-effects designs. SYSTAT is not designed for random-effects analysis but may be used to analyze some designs with some hand calculation. MINITAB handles random factors in its GLM and Balanced ANOVA programs.

Table 11.43 shows features of programs that use the traditional ANOVA approach. Only those features relevant to random effects are noted in the table. Other features appear in the Comparison of Programs sections of other chapters. Table 11.44 shows features of programs that use variance components or maximum likelihood approaches.

11.8.1   SAS System

SAS has the most comprehensive set of programs for analyzing random-effects designs. PROC GLM makes available all of its many features to traditional random and mixed fixed–random-effects ANOVA as well as nested designs. About the only shortcoming is the lack of ability to specify trend analysis with unequal spacing to randomized-groups effects.

Maximum likelihood methods are available through VARCOMP and MIXED. The latter is the more recent program and subsumes the former, except that VARCOMP has one method (and not a very popular one) that is unavailable to MIXED.

The newer program is extensive and meant to be at least as comprehensive as SAS GLM—with highly developed facilities for both repeated-measures and random-effects designs. One unique feature is the flexibility to specify an alternative covariance structure when the assumption of homogeneity of covariance is not met in either repeated-measures or random-effects analysis. The program provides many GLM-type features unavailable in other variance components programs, such

TABLE 11.43 Comparison of SPSS, SYSTAT, MINITAB, and SAS Programs for Random-Effects ANOVA

Feature	SPSS GLM (UNIANOVA)	SAS GLM	SYSTAT GLM	MINITAB GLM	MINITAB Balanced ANOVA
Input					
Requires equal sample sizes	No	No	No	No	Yes
Requires special data format	No	No	No	No	No
Special specification for trend (polynomial) analysis with unequal spacing	Polynomial	No	Yes	No	No
Indicate random and/or fixed effects	Yes	Yes	Fixed only	Yes	Yes
Indicate nesting arrangements	Yes	Yes	Yes	Yes	No
Random interactions automatically identified	Yes	No	N.A.	No	Yes
Permits restricted model for two-way mixed fixed–random design	No	No	N.A.	No	Yes
Output					
ANOVA table	Yes	Yes	Yes	Yes	Yes
Expected mean squares	Yes	Yes	No	Yes	Yes
Error terms shown for tests of effects	Yes	Yes	No	No	No

as least-squares means, contrasts, and post hoc tests of differences among means. This is the only program in the group that has capability for random coefficients, multilevel modeling (cf. Section 11.6.2). Anything that can be printed out also can be saved to a data file through the MAKE procedure. Indeed, Table 11.43 only highlights some of the more prominent features of PROC MIXED; many others are documented in the manual (SAS, Institute, Inc., 1997).

11.8.2 SPSS Package

SPSS GLM can analyze all types of random effects. Traditional ANOVA is done through the UNIANOVA module and maximum likelihood procedures are implemented in the VARCOMP module. UNIANOVA implements all the features of fixed-effects analysis for random effects—covariates,

TABLE 11.44 Comparison of SPSS, SYSTAT, and SAS Programs for Alternative Approaches to Random-Effects Designs

Feature	SPSS GLM (VARCOMP)	SAS VARCOMP	SAS MIXED
Input			
Requires equal sample sizes	No	No	No
Requires special data format	No	No	No
Indicate random and/or fixed effects	Yes	Yes	Yes
Random interactions automatically identified	Yes	Yes	Yes
Indicate nesting arrangements	Yes	Yes	Yes
Estimation methods			
Maximum likelihood	ML	ML	ML
Restricted maximum likelihood	REML	REML	REML
Minimum norm unbiased with 0 weight for random effects	MINQUE(0)	MIVQUE0	MIVQUE0
Minimum norm unbiased with unit weight for random effects	MINQUE(1)	No	No
ANOVA with Type I SS	SSTYPE(1)	TYPE1	HTYPE = 1[b]
ANOVA with Type III SS	SSTYPE(3)	No	HTYPE = 3[b]
Option to exclude intercept	EXCLUDE	No	NOINT
Specify covariates	No	Yes[a]	Yes[c]
Specify hypothesis tests and/or model	No	No	COVTEST
Specify linear combination of parameters to be tested			
Specify contrasts	No	No	CONTRAST, ESTIMATE
Specify convergence criterion	CONVERGE	No	Various
Specify maximum number of iterations	ITERATE	MAXITER	MAXITER
Specify maximum number of likelihood evaluations	No	No	MAXFUNC
Specify epsilon value for tolerance	EPS	EPSILON	SINGULAR
Request iteration information	HISTORY	Default	ITDETAILS
Specify α level for tests or confidence limits	No	No	ALPHA
Specify initial estimates of parameters	No	No	PARMS
Sampling-based Bayesian analysis	No	No	PRIOR

686

TABLE 11.44 Continued

Feature	SPSS GLM (VARCOMP)	SAS VARCOMP	SAS MIXED
Input *(continued)*			
Optional covariance structure for repeated measures and random factors	TYPE	No	No
Specify denominator df for fixed effects	DDF	No	No
Specify method for computing denominator df for fixed effects	DDFM	No	No
Specify random-coefficients model for multilevel modeling	Yes	No	No
Output			
Estimates of variance components	Yes	Yes	Yes
Asymptotic variance-covariance matrix	ASYCOV	Yes	Yes
Confidence limits for parameter estimates	CL	No	No
Standard errors and Wald tests for parameter estimates	COVTEST	No	No
Means for fixed effects	LSMEANS	No	No
Multiple comparisons for fixed effects	Several	No	No
Correlation matrix of fixed-effect parameter estimates	CORRB	No	No
Covariance matrix of fixed-effect parameter estimates	COVB	No	No
Multivariate tests for repeated-measures effects	Yes	No	No
Residuals analysis	Yes	No	No
Imputes missing values with repeated measures	Yes	No	No
Save to data file			
Variance components estimates	MAKE	No[d]	VAREST
Asymptotic variance-covariance matrix	MAKE	No[d]	COVB
Asymptotic correlation matrix	MAKE	No[d]	CORB

[a]Only repeated-measures effects may be designated random.

[b]For fixed effects.

[c]Variables not included in the CLASS instruction are treated as continuous covariates.

[d]Any printed output may be saved to data sets through PROC OUTPUT.

comparisons among means, and the like. VARCOMP provides only the basics for a random-effects design, with no information about fixed effects in a mixed random–fixed design. Thus, SPSS is a good choice for traditional analysis, but not for maximum likelihood analysis.

11.8.3   SYSTAT System

SYSTAT GLM analyzes nested effects but does not currently have facilities for random-effects ANOVA. Those designs may be analyzed using the traditional approach and then recalculating F ratios using the appropriate error term (e.g., the calculation following Table 11.11). Other random-effects designs may be similarly analyzed if you are willing to compute expected mean squares and degrees of freedom and apply them to F ratios by hand. Maximum likelihood estimation is available in the nonlinear regression module, but its use requires skills beyond the scope of this book.

11.8.4   MINITAB Programs

MINITAB analyzes random-effects designs within its GLM program, so that all of the GLM features are available for random and mixed fixed–random designs. All IVs, interactions, and nesting arrangements are identified in the model equation, then some or all of the IVs are identified as random. Expected mean squares are available on request.

MINITAB Balanced ANOVA is the program of choice for a two-way randomized-groups mixed fixed–random-effects design. This is the only program that uses the restricted model, most popular in textbooks but missing from most software programs. The program requires equal n but handles any combination of fixed and random IVs in its model equation. As for GLM, expected mean squares are available on request.

11.9   Problem Sets

11.1 For the data in Problem 5.1, assume that presoak time is a random IV with levels = 7, 16, 39, and 45 minutes.
   a. Test all of the assumptions for a mixed fixed–random ANOVA and do the analysis.
   b. Provide a source table.
   c. Calculate effect size(s).
   d. Do a trend analysis and apply an appropriate post hoc adjustment.
   e. Write a Results section for the analyses.
   f. Use one of the canned computer programs to do a variance-components (maximum likelihood) analysis of this data set.

11.2 Do an analysis of variance on the following data set in which organization is nested within treatments and the DV is minority employee salary.

```
Affirmation action treatment

Org1    Org2     Org3
34437   31734    23605
37641   28947    30621
30046   25695    20736
```

```
32755    21747    23596
No treatment control
Org4     Org5     Org6
22189    31073    16241
15874    21550    16962
18630    25390    21673
20891    25517    22972
```

a. Test all relevant assumptions.
b. Provide a source table with pooled error if appropriate.
c. Calculate effect size(s).
d. Write a Results section for the analysis.

Extending the Concepts:

11.3   Show the table of expected mean squares for a doubly nested design.

A Statistical Tables

TABLE A.1   Critical Values of F Distribution

df₂		df₁ 1	2	3	4	5	6	8	12	24	∞
1	0.1%	405284	500000	540379	562500	576405	585937	598144	610667	623497	636619
	0.5%	16211	20000	21615	22500	23056	23437	23925	24426	24940	25465
	1%	4052	4999	5403	5625	5764	5859	5981	6106	6234	6366
	2.5%	647.79	799.50	864.16	899.58	921.85	937.11	956.66	976.71	997.25	1018.30
	5%	161.45	199.50	215.71	224.58	230.16	233.99	238.88	243.91	249.05	254.32
	10%	39.86	49.50	53.59	55.83	57.24	58.20	59.44	60.70	62.00	63.33
	20%	9.47	12.00	13.06	13.73	14.01	14.26	14.59	14.90	15.24	15.58
	25%	5.83	7.50	8.20	8.58	8.82	8.98	9.19	9.41	9.63	9.85
2	0.1	998.5	999.0	999.2	999.2	999.3	999.3	999.4	999.4	999.5	999.5
	0.5	198.50	199.00	199.17	199.25	199.30	199.33	199.37	199.42	199.46	199.51
	1	98.49	99.00	99.17	99.25	99.30	99.33	99.36	99.42	99.46	99.50
	2.5	38.51	39.00	39.17	39.25	39.30	39.33	39.37	39.42	39.46	39.50
	5	18.51	19.00	19.16	19.25	19.30	19.33	19.37	19.41	19.45	19.50
	10	8.53	9.00	9.16	9.24	9.29	9.33	9.37	9.41	9.45	9.49
	20	3.56	4.00	4.16	4.24	4.28	4.32	4.36	4.40	4.44	4.48
	25	2.56	3.00	3.15	3.23	3.28	3.31	3.35	3.39	3.44	3.48
3	0.1	167.5	148.5	141.1	137.1	134.6	132.8	130.6	128.3	125.9	123.5
	0.5	55.55	49.80	47.47	46.20	45.39	44.84	44.13	43.39	42.62	41.83
	1	34.12	30.81	29.46	28.71	28.24	27.91	27.49	27.05	26.60	26.12
	2.5	17.44	16.04	15.44	15.10	14.89	14.74	14.54	14.34	14.12	13.90
	5	10.13	9.55	9.28	9.12	9.01	8.94	8.84	8.74	8.64	8.53
	10	5.54	5.46	5.39	5.34	5.31	5.28	5.25	5.22	5.18	5.13
	20	2.68	2.89	2.94	2.96	2.97	2.97	2.98	2.98	2.98	2.98
	25	2.02	2.28	2.36	2.39	2.41	2.42	2.44	2.45	2.46	2.47
4	0.1	74.14	61.25	56.18	53.44	51.71	50.53	49.00	47.41	45.77	44.05
	0.5	31.33	26.28	24.26	23.16	22.46	21.98	21.35	20.71	20.03	19.33
	1	21.20	18.00	16.69	15.98	15.52	15.21	14.80	14.37	13.93	13.46
	2.5	12.22	10.65	9.98	9.60	9.36	9.20	8.98	8.75	8.51	8.26
	5	7.71	6.94	6.59	6.39	6.26	6.16	6.04	5.91	5.77	5.63
	10	4.54	4.32	4.19	4.11	4.05	4.01	3.95	3.90	3.83	3.76
	20	2.35	2.47	2.48	2.48	2.48	2.47	2.47	2.46	2.44	2.43
	25	1.81	2.00	2.05	2.05	2.07	2.08	2.08	2.08	2.08	2.08
5	0.1	47.04	36.61	33.20	31.09	29.75	28.84	27.64	26.42	25.14	23.78
	0.5	22.79	18.31	16.53	15.56	14.94	14.51	13.96	13.38	12.78	12.14
	1	16.26	13.27	12.06	11.39	10.97	10.67	10.29	9.89	9.47	9.02
	2.5	10.01	8.43	7.76	7.39	7.15	6.98	6.76	6.52	6.28	6.02
	5	6.61	5.79	5.41	5.19	5.05	4.95	4.82	4.68	4.53	4.36
	10	4.06	3.78	3.62	3.52	3.45	3.40	3.34	3.27	3.19	3.10
	20	2.18	2.26	2.25	2.24	2.23	2.22	2.20	2.18	2.16	2.13
	25	1.70	1.85	1.89	1.89	1.89	1.89	1.89	1.89	1.88	1.87

(continued)

TABLE A.1   Continued

df₂	df₁	1	2	3	4	5	6	8	12	24	∞
6	0.1%	35.51	27.00	23.70	21.90	20.81	20.03	19.03	17.99	16.89	15.75
	0.5%	18.64	14.54	12.92	12.03	11.46	11.07	10.57	10.03	9.47	8.88
	1%	13.74	10.92	9.78	9.15	8.75	8.47	8.10	7.72	7.31	6.88
	2.5%	8.81	7.26	6.60	6.23	5.99	5.82	5.60	5.37	5.12	4.85
	5%	5.99	5.14	4.76	4.53	4.39	4.28	4.15	4.00	3.84	3.67
	10%	3.78	3.46	3.29	3.18	3.11	3.05	2.98	2.90	2.82	2.72
	20%	2.07	2.13	2.11	2.09	2.08	2.06	2.04	2.02	1.99	1.95
	25%	1.62	1.76	1.78	1.79	1.79	1.78	1.78	1.77	1.75	1.74
7	0.1	29.22	21.69	18.77	17.19	16.21	15.52	14.63	13.71	12.73	11.69
	0.5	16.24	12.40	10.88	10.05	9.52	9.16	8.68	8.18	7.65	7.08
	1	12.25	9.55	8.45	7.85	7.46	7.19	6.84	6.47	6.07	5.65
	2.5	8.07	6.54	5.89	5.52	5.29	5.12	4.90	4.67	4.42	4.14
	5	5.59	4.74	4.35	4.12	3.97	3.87	3.73	3.57	3.41	3.23
	10	3.59	3.26	3.07	2.96	2.88	2.83	2.75	2.67	2.58	2.47
	20	2.00	2.04	2.02	1.99	1.97	1.96	1.93	1.91	1.87	1.83
	25	1.57	1.70	1.72	1.72	1.71	1.71	1.70	1.68	1.67	1.65
8	0.1	25.42	18.49	15.83	14.39	13.49	12.86	12.04	11.19	10.30	9.34
	0.5	14.69	11.04	9.60	8.81	8.30	7.95	7.50	7.01	6.50	5.95
	1	11.26	8.65	7.59	7.01	6.63	6.37	6.03	5.67	5.28	4.86
	2.5	7.57	6.06	5.42	5.05	4.82	4.65	4.43	4.20	3.95	3.67
	5	5.32	4.46	4.07	3.84	3.69	3.58	3.44	3.28	3.12	2.93
	10	3.46	3.11	2.92	2.81	2.73	2.67	2.59	2.50	2.40	2.29
	20	1.95	1.98	1.95	1.92	1.90	1.88	1.86	1.83	1.79	1.74
	25	1.53	1.66	1.67	1.55	1.66	1.65	1.64	1.62	1.60	1.58
9	0.1	22.86	16.39	13.90	12.56	11.71	11.13	10.37	9.57	8.72	7.81
	0.5	13.61	10.11	8.72	7.96	7.47	7.13	6.69	6.23	5.73	5.19
	1	10.56	8.02	6.99	6.42	6.06	5.80	5.47	5.11	4.73	4.31
	2.5	7.21	5.71	5.08	4.72	4.48	4.32	4.10	3.87	3.61	3.33
	5	5.12	4.26	3.86	3.63	3.48	3.37	3.23	3.07	2.90	2.71
	10	3.36	3.01	2.81	2.69	2.61	2.55	2.47	2.38	2.28	2.16
	20	1.91	1.94	1.90	1.87	1.85	1.83	1.80	1.76	1.72	1.67
	25	1.51	1.62	1.63	1.63	1.62	1.61	1.60	1.58	1.56	1.53
10	0.1	21.04	14.91	12.55	11.28	10.48	9.92	9.20	8.45	7.64	6.76
	0.5	12.83	9.43	8.08	7.34	6.87	6.54	6.12	5.66	5.17	4.64
	1	10.04	7.56	6.55	5.99	5.64	5.39	5.06	4.71	4.33	3.91
	2.5	6.94	5.46	4.83	4.47	4.24	4.07	3.85	3.62	3.37	3.08
	5	4.96	4.10	3.71	3.48	3.33	3.22	3.07	2.91	2.74	2.54
	10	3.28	2.92	2.73	2.61	2.52	2.46	2.38	2.28	2.18	2.06
	20	1.88	1.90	1.86	1.83	1.80	1.78	1.75	1.72	1.66	1.62
	25	1.49	1.60	1.60	1.60	1.59	1.58	1.56	1.54	1.52	1.48

TABLE A.1   Continued

df₂ \ df₁		1	2	3	4	5	6	8	12	24	∞
11	0.1%	19.69	13.81	11.56	10.35	9.58	9.05	8.35	7.63	6.85	6.00
	0.5%	12.23	8.91	7.60	6.88	6.42	6.10	5.68	5.24	4.76	4.23
	1%	9.65	7.20	6.22	5.67	5.32	5.07	4.74	4.40	4.02	3.60
	2.5%	6.72	5.26	4.63	4.28	4.04	3.88	3.66	3.43	3.17	2.88
	5%	4.84	3.98	3.59	3.36	3.20	3.09	2.95	2.79	2.61	2.40
	10%	3.23	2.86	2.66	2.54	2.45	2.39	2.30	2.21	2.10	1.97
	20%	1.86	1.87	1.83	1.80	1.77	1.75	1.72	1.68	1.63	1.57
	25%	1.46	1.58	1.58	1.58	1.56	1.55	1.54	1.51	1.49	1.45
12	0.1	18.64	12.97	10.80	9.63	8.89	8.38	7.71	7.00	6.25	5.42
	0.5	11.75	8.51	7.23	6.52	6.07	5.76	5.35	4.91	4.43	3.90
	1	9.33	6.93	5.95	5.41	5.06	4.82	4.50	4.16	3.78	3.36
	2.5	6.55	5.10	4.47	4.12	3.89	3.73	3.51	3.28	3.02	2.72
	5	4.75	3.88	3.49	3.26	3.11	3.00	2.85	2.69	2.50	2.30
	10	3.18	2.81	2.61	2.48	2.39	2.33	2.24	2.15	2.04	1.90
	20	1.84	1.85	1.80	1.77	1.74	1.72	1.69	1.63	1.60	1.54
	25	1.46	1.56	1.56	1.55	1.54	1.53	1.51	1.49	1.46	1.42
13	0.1	17.81	12.31	10.21	9.07	8.35	7.86	7.21	6.52	5.78	4.97
	0.5	11.37	8.19	6.93	6.23	5.79	5.48	5.08	4.64	4.17	3.65
	1	9.07	6.70	5.74	5.20	4.86	4.62	4.30	3.96	3.59	3.16
	2.5	6.41	4.97	4.35	4.00	3.77	3.60	3.39	3.15	2.89	2.60
	5	4.67	3.80	3.41	3.18	3.02	2.92	2.77	2.60	2.42	2.21
	10	3.14	2.76	2.56	2.43	2.35	2.28	2.20	2.10	1.98	1.85
	20	1.82	1.83	1.78	1.75	1.72	1.69	1.66	1.62	1.57	1.51
	25	1.45	1.55	1.55	1.53	1.52	1.51	1.49	1.47	1.44	1.40
14	0.1	17.14	11.78	9.73	8.62	7.92	7.43	6.80	6.13	5.41	4.60
	0.5	11.06	7.92	6.68	6.00	5.56	5.26	4.86	4.43	3.96	3.44
	1	8.86	6.51	5.56	5.03	4.69	4.46	4.14	3.80	3.43	3.00
	2.5	6.30	4.86	4.24	3.89	3.66	3.50	3.29	3.05	2.79	2.49
	5	4.60	3.74	3.34	3.11	2.96	2.85	2.70	2.53	2.35	2.13
	10	3.10	2.73	2.52	2.39	2.31	2.24	2.15	2.05	1.94	1.80
	20	1.81	1.81	1.76	1.73	1.70	1.67	1.64	1.60	1.55	1.48
	25	1.44	1.53	1.53	1.52	1.51	1.50	1.48	1.45	1.42	1.38
15	0.1	16.59	11.34	9.34	8.25	7.57	7.09	6.47	5.81	5.10	4.31
	0.5	10.80	7.70	6.48	5.80	5.37	5.07	4.67	4.25	3.79	3.26
	1	8.68	6.36	5.42	4.89	4.56	4.32	4.00	3.67	3.29	2.87
	2.5	6.20	4.77	4.15	3.80	3.58	3.41	3.20	2.96	2.70	2.40
	5	4.54	3.68	3.29	3.06	2.90	2.79	2.64	2.48	2.29	2.07
	10	3.07	2.70	2.49	2.36	2.27	2.21	2.12	2.02	1.90	1.76
	20	1.80	1.79	1.75	1.71	1.68	1.66	1.62	1.58	1.53	1.46
	25	1.43	1.52	1.52	1.51	1.49	1.48	1.46	1.44	1.41	1.36

(continued)

TABLE A.1   Continued

df₂	df₁	1	2	3	4	5	6	8	12	24	∞
16	0.1%	16.12	10.97	9.00	7.94	7.27	6.81	6.19	5.55	4.85	4.06
	0.5%	10.58	7.51	6.30	5.64	5.21	4.91	4.52	4.10	3.64	3.11
	1%	8.53	6.23	5.29	4.77	4.44	4.20	3.89	3.55	3.18	2.75
	2.5%	6.12	4.69	4.08	3.73	3.50	3.34	3.12	2.89	2.63	2.32
	5%	4.49	3.63	3.24	3.01	2.85	2.74	2.59	2.42	2.24	2.01
	10%	3.05	2.67	2.46	2.33	2.24	2.18	2.09	1.99	1.87	1.72
	20%	1.79	1.78	1.74	1.70	1.67	1.64	1.61	1.56	1.51	1.43
	25%	1.42	1.51	1.51	1.50	1.48	1.47	1.45	1.43	1.39	1.34
17	0.1	15.72	10.66	8.73	7.68	7.02	6.56	5.96	5.32	4.63	3.85
	0.5	10.38	7.35	6.16	5.50	5.07	4.78	4.39	3.97	3.51	2.98
	1	8.40	6.11	5.18	4.67	4.34	4.10	3.79	3.45	3.08	2.65
	2.5	6.04	4.62	4.01	3.66	3.44	3.28	3.06	2.82	2.56	2.25
	5	4.45	3.59	3.20	2.96	2.81	2.70	2.55	2.38	2.19	1.96
	10	3.03	2.64	2.44	2.31	2.22	2.15	2.06	1.96	1.84	1.69
	20	1.78	1.77	1.72	1.68	1.65	1.63	1.59	1.55	1.49	1.42
	25	1.42	1.51	1.51	1.49	1.47	1.46	1.44	1.41	1.38	1.33
18	0.1	15.38	10.39	8.49	7.46	6.81	6.35	5.76	5.13	4.45	3.67
	0.5	10.22	7.21	6.03	5.37	4.96	4.66	4.28	3.86	3.40	2.87
	1	8.28	6.01	5.09	4.58	4.25	4.01	3.71	3.37	3.00	2.57
	2.5	5.98	4.56	3.95	3.61	3.38	3.22	3.01	2.77	2.50	2.19
	5	4.41	3.55	3.16	2.93	2.77	2.66	2.51	2.34	2.15	1.92
	10	3.01	2.62	2.42	2.29	2.20	2.13	2.04	1.93	1.81	1.66
	20	1.77	1.76	1.71	1.67	1.64	1.62	1.58	1.53	1.48	1.40
	25	1.41	1.50	1.49	1.48	1.46	1.45	1.43	1.40	1.37	1.32
19	0.1	15.08	10.16	8.28	7.26	6.61	6.18	5.59	4.97	4.29	3.52
	0.5	10.07	7.09	5.92	5.27	4.85	4.56	4.18	3.76	3.31	2.78
	1	8.18	5.93	5.01	4.50	4.17	3.94	3.63	3.30	2.92	2.49
	2.5	5.92	4.51	3.90	3.56	3.33	3.17	2.96	2.72	2.45	2.13
	5	4.38	3.52	3.13	2.90	2.74	2.63	2.48	2.31	2.11	1.88
	10	2.99	2.61	2.40	2.27	2.18	2.11	2.02	1.91	1.79	1.63
	20	1.76	1.75	1.70	1.66	1.63	1.61	1.57	1.52	1.46	1.39
	25	1.41	1.50	1.49	1.48	1.46	1.44	1.42	1.40	1.36	1.31
20	0.1	14.82	9.95	8.10	7.10	6.46	6.02	5.44	4.82	4.15	3.38
	0.5	9.94	6.99	5.82	5.17	4.76	4.47	4.09	3.68	3.22	2.69
	1	8.10	5.85	4.94	4.43	4.10	3.87	3.56	3.23	2.86	2.42
	2.5	5.87	4.46	3.86	3.51	3.29	3.13	2.91	2.68	2.41	2.09
	5	4.35	3.49	3.10	2.87	2.71	2.60	2.45	2.28	2.08	1.84
	10	2.97	2.59	2.38	2.25	2.16	2.09	2.00	1.89	1.77	1.61
	20	1.76	1.75	1.70	1.65	1.62	1.60	1.56	1.51	1.45	1.37
	25	1.40	1.49	1.48	1.47	1.45	1.44	1.42	1.39	1.35	1.29

TABLE A.1   Continued

df$_2$ \ df$_1$		1	2	3	4	5	6	8	12	24	∞
21	0.1%	14.59	9.77	7.94	6.95	6.32	5.88	5.31	4.70	4.03	3.26
	0.5%	9.83	6.89	5.73	5.09	4.68	4.39	4.01	3.60	3.15	2.61
	1%	8.02	5.78	4.87	4.37	4.04	3.81	3.51	3.17	2.80	2.36
	2.5%	5.83	4.42	3.82	3.48	3.25	3.09	2.87	2.64	2.37	2.04
	5%	4.32	3.47	3.07	2.84	2.68	2.57	2.42	2.25	2.05	1.81
	10%	2.96	2.57	2.36	2.23	2.14	2.08	1.98	1.88	1.75	1.59
	20%	1.75	1.74	1.69	1.65	1.61	1.59	1.55	1.50	1.44	1.36
	25%	1.40	1.49	1.48	1.46	1.44	1.43	1.41	1.38	1.34	1.29
22	0.1	14.38	9.61	7.80	6.81	6.19	5.76	5.19	4.58	3.92	3.15
	0.5	9.73	6.81	5.65	5.02	4.61	4.32	3.94	3.54	3.08	2.55
	1	7.94	5.72	4.82	4.31	3.99	3.76	3.45	3.12	2.75	2.31
	2.5	5.79	4.38	3.78	3.44	3.22	3.05	2.84	2.60	2.33	2.00
	5	4.30	3.44	3.05	2.82	2.66	2.55	2.40	2.23	2.03	1.78
	10	2.95	2.56	2.35	2.22	2.13	2.06	1.97	1.86	1.73	1.57
	20	1.75	1.73	1.68	1.64	1.61	1.58	1.54	1.49	1.43	1.35
	25	1.40	1.48	1.47	1.46	1.44	1.42	1.40	1.37	1.33	1.28
23	0.1	14.19	9.47	7.67	6.69	6.08	5.65	5.09	4.48	3.82	3.05
	0.5	9.63	6.73	5.58	4.95	4.54	4.26	3.88	3.47	3.02	2.48
	1	7.88	5.66	4.76	4.26	3.94	3.71	3.41	3.07	2.70	2.26
	2.5	5.75	4.35	3.75	3.41	3.18	3.02	2.81	2.57	2.30	1.97
	5	4.28	3.42	3.03	2.80	2.64	2.53	2.38	2.20	2.00	1.76
	10	2.94	2.55	2.34	2.21	2.11	2.05	1.95	1.84	1.72	1.55
	20	1.74	1.73	1.68	1.63	1.60	1.57	1.53	1.49	1.42	1.34
	25	1.39	1.47	1.47	1.45	1.43	1.41	1.40	1.37	1.33	1.27
24	0.1	14.03	9.34	7.55	6.59	5.98	5.55	4.99	4.39	3.74	2.97
	0.5	9.55	6.66	5.52	4.89	4.49	4.20	3.83	3.42	2.97	2.43
	1	7.82	5.61	4.72	4.22	3.90	3.67	3.36	3.03	2.66	2.21
	2.5	5.72	4.32	3.72	3.38	3.15	2.99	2.78	2.54	2.27	1.94
	5	4.26	3.40	3.01	2.78	2.62	2.51	2.36	2.18	1.98	1.73
	10	2.93	2.54	2.33	2.19	2.10	2.04	1.94	1.83	1.70	1.53
	20	1.74	1.72	1.67	1.63	1.59	1.57	1.53	1.48	1.42	1.33
	25	1.39	1.47	1.46	1.44	1.43	1.41	1.39	1.36	1.32	1.26
25	0.1	13.88	9.22	7.45	6.49	5.88	5.46	4.91	4.31	3.66	2.89
	0.5	9.48	6.60	5.46	4.84	4.43	4.15	3.78	3.37	2.92	2.38
	1	7.77	5.57	4.68	4.18	3.86	3.63	3.32	2.99	2.62	2.17
	2.5	5.69	4.29	3.69	3.35	3.13	2.97	2.75	2.51	2.24	1.91
	5	4.24	3.38	2.99	2.76	2.60	2.49	2.34	2.16	1.96	1.71
	10	2.92	2.53	2.32	2.18	2.09	2.02	1.93	1.82	1.69	1.52
	20	1.73	1.72	1.66	1.62	1.59	1.56	1.52	1.47	1.41	1.32
	25	1.39	1.47	1.46	1.44	1.42	1.41	1.39	1.36	1.32	1.25

(continued)

TABLE A.1   Continued

df₂	df₁	1	2	3	4	5	6	8	12	24	∞
26	0.1%	13.74	9.12	7.36	6.41	5.80	5.38	4.83	4.24	3.59	2.82
	0.5%	9.41	6.54	5.41	4.79	4.38	4.10	3.73	3.33	2.87	2.33
	1%	7.72	5.53	4.64	4.14	3.82	3.59	3.29	2.96	2.58	2.13
	2.5%	5.66	4.27	3.67	3.33	3.10	2.94	2.73	2.49	2.22	1.88
	5%	4.22	3.37	2.98	2.74	2.59	2.47	2.32	2.15	1.95	1.69
	10%	2.91	2.52	2.31	2.17	2.08	2.01	1.92	1.81	1.68	1.50
	20%	1.73	1.71	1.66	1.62	1.58	1.56	1.52	1.47	1.40	1.31
	25%	1.38	1.46	1.45	1.44	1.42	1.41	1.38	1.35	1.31	1.25
27	0.1	13.61	9.02	7.27	6.33	5.73	5.31	4.76	4.17	3.52	2.75
	0.5	9.34	6.49	5.36	4.74	4.34	4.06	3.69	3.28	2.83	2.29
	1	7.68	5.49	4.60	4.11	3.78	3.56	3.26	2.93	2.55	2.10
	2.5	5.63	4.24	3.65	3.31	3.08	2.92	2.71	2.47	2.19	1.85
	5	4.21	3.35	2.96	2.73	2.57	2.46	2.30	2.13	1.93	1.67
	10	2.90	2.51	2.30	2.17	2.07	2.00	1.91	1.80	1.67	1.49
	20	1.73	1.71	1.66	1.61	1.58	1.55	1.51	1.46	1.40	1.30
	25	1.38	1.46	1.45	1.43	1.42	1.40	1.38	1.35	1.31	1.24
28	0.1	13.50	8.93	7.19	6.25	5.66	5.24	4.69	4.11	3.46	2.70
	0.5	9.28	6.44	5.32	4.70	4.30	4.02	3.65	3.25	2.79	2.25
	1	7.64	5.45	4.57	4.07	3.75	3.53	3.23	2.90	2.52	2.06
	2.5	5.61	4.22	3.63	3.29	2.06	2.90	2.69	2.45	2.17	1.83
	5	4.20	3.34	2.95	2.71	2.56	2.44	2.29	2.12	1.91	1.65
	10	2.89	2.50	2.29	2.16	2.06	2.00	1.90	1.79	1.66	1.48
	20	1.72	1.71	1.65	1.61	1.57	1.55	1.51	1.46	1.39	1.30
	25	1.38	1.46	1.45	1.43	1.41	1.40	1.38	1.34	1.30	1.24
29	0.1	13.39	8.85	7.12	6.19	5.59	5.18	4.64	4.05	3.41	2.64
	0.5	9.23	6.40	5.28	4.66	4.26	3.98	3.61	3.21	2.76	2.21
	1	7.60	5.42	4.54	4.04	3.73	3.50	3.20	2.87	2.49	2.03
	2.5	5.59	4.20	3.61	3.27	3.04	2.88	2.67	2.43	2.15	1.81
	5	4.18	3.33	2.93	2.70	2.54	2.43	2.28	2.10	1.90	1.64
	10	2.89	2.50	2.28	2.15	2.06	1.99	1.89	1.78	1.65	1.47
	20	1.72	1.70	1.65	1.60	1.57	1.54	1.50	1.45	1.39	1.29
	25	1.38	1.45	1.45	1.43	1.41	1.40	1.37	1.34	1.30	1.23
30	0.1	13.29	8.77	7.05	6.12	5.63	5.12	4.58	4.00	3.36	2.59
	0.5	9.18	6.35	5.24	4.62	4.23	3.95	3.58	3.18	2.73	2.18
	1	7.56	5.39	4.51	4.02	3.70	3.47	3.17	2.84	2.47	2.01
	2.5	5.57	4.18	3.59	3.25	3.03	2.87	2.65	2.41	2.14	1.79
	5	4.17	3.32	2.92	2.69	2.53	2.42	2.27	2.09	1.89	1.62
	10	2.88	2.49	2.28	2.14	2.05	1.98	1.88	1.77	1.64	1.46
	20	1.72	1.70	1.64	1.60	1.57	1.54	1.50	1.45	1.38	1.28
	25	1.38	1.45	1.44	1.42	1.41	1.39	1.37	1.34	1.29	1.23

TABLE A.1   Continued

df₂ \ df₁		1	2	3	4	5	6	8	12	24	∞
40	0.1%	12.61	8.25	6.60	5.70	5.13	4.73	4.21	3.64	3.01	2.23
	0.5%	8.83	6.07	4.98	4.37	3.99	3.71	3.35	2.95	2.50	1.93
	1%	7.31	5.18	4.31	3.83	3.51	3.29	2.99	2.66	2.29	1.80
	2.5%	5.42	4.05	3.46	3.13	2.90	2.74	2.53	2.29	2.01	1.64
	5%	4.08	3.23	2.84	2.61	2.45	2.34	2.18	2.00	1.79	1.51
	10%	2.84	2.44	2.23	2.09	2.00	1.93	1.83	1.71	1.57	1.38
	20%	1.70	1.68	1.62	1.57	1.54	1.51	1.47	1.41	1.34	1.24
	25%	1.36	1.44	1.42	1.41	1.39	1.37	1.35	1.31	1.27	1.19
60	0.1	11.97	7.76	6.17	5.31	4.76	4.37	3.87	3.31	2.69	1.90
	0.5	8.49	5.80	4.73	4.14	3.76	3.49	3.13	2.74	2.29	1.69
	1	7.08	4.98	4.13	3.65	3.34	3.12	2.82	2.50	2.12	1.60
	2.5	5.29	3.93	3.34	3.01	2.79	2.63	2.41	2.17	1.88	1.48
	5	4.00	3.15	2.76	2.52	2.37	2.25	2.10	1.92	1.70	1.39
	10	2.79	2.39	2.18	2.04	1.95	1.87	1.77	1.66	1.51	1.29
	20	1.68	1.65	1.59	1.55	1.51	1.48	1.44	1.38	1.31	1.18
	25	1.35	1.42	1.41	1.39	1.37	1.35	1.32	1.29	1.24	1.15
120	0.1	11.38	7.31	5.79	4.95	4.42	4.04	3.55	3.02	2.40	1.56
	0.5	8.18	5.54	4.50	3.92	3.55	3.28	2.93	2.54	2.09	1.43
	1	6.85	4.79	3.95	3.48	3.17	2.96	2.66	2.34	1.95	1.38
	2.5	5.15	3.80	3.23	2.89	2.67	2.52	2.30	2.05	1.76	1.31
	5	3.92	3.07	2.68	2.45	2.29	2.17	2.02	1.83	1.61	1.25
	10	2.75	2.35	2.13	1.99	1.90	1.82	1.72	1.60	1.45	1.19
	20	1.66	1.63	1.57	1.52	1.48	1.45	1.41	1.35	1.27	1.12
	25	1.34	1.40	1.39	1.37	1.35	1.33	1.30	1.26	1.21	1.10
∞	0.1	10.83	6.91	5.42	4.62	4.10	3.74	3.27	2.74	2.13	1.00
	0.5	7.88	5.30	4.28	3.72	3.35	3.09	2.74	2.36	1.90	1.00
	1	6.64	4.60	3.78	3.32	3.02	2.80	2.51	2.18	1.79	1.00
	2.5	5.02	3.69	3.12	2.79	2.57	2.41	2.19	1.94	1.64	1.00
	5	3.84	2.99	2.60	2.37	2.21	2.09	1.94	1.75	1.52	1.00
	10	2.71	2.30	2.08	1.94	1.85	1.77	1.67	1.55	1.35	1.00
	20	1.64	1.61	1.55	1.50	1.46	1.43	1.38	1.32	1.23	1.00
	25	1.32	1.39	1.37	1.35	1.33	1.37	1.28	1.24	1.18	1.00

Adapted from Table 18 in *Biometrika Tables for Statisticians,* vol. 1, 3rd ed., edited by E. S. Pearson and H. O. Hartley (New York: Cambridge University Press, 1958). Reproduced with the permission of the Biometrika trustees.

TABLE A.2   Critical Values of χ^2 Distribution

df	0.250	0.100	0.050	0.025	0.010	0.005	0.001
1	1.32330	2.70554	3.84146	5.02389	6.63490	7.87944	10.828
2	2.77259	4.60517	5.99147	7.37776	9.21034	10.5966	13.816
3	4.10835	6.25139	7.81473	9.34840	11.3449	12.8381	16.266
4	5.38527	7.77944	9.48773	1.1433	13.2767	14.8602	18.467
5	6.62568	9.23635	11.0705	12.8325	15.0863	16.7496	20.515
6	7.84080	10.6446	12.5916	14.4494	16.8119	18.5476	22.456
7	9.03715	12.0170	14.0671	16.0128	18.4753	20.2777	24.322
8	10.2188	13.3616	15.5073	17.5346	20.0902	21.9550	26.125
9	11.3887	14.6837	16.9190	19.0228	21.6660	23.5893	27.877
10	12.5489	15.9871	18.3070	20.4831	23.2093	25.1882	29.586
11	13.7007	17.2750	19.6751	21.9200	24.7250	26.7569	31.264
12	14.8454	18.5494	21.0261	23.3367	26.2170	28.2995	32.909
13	15.9839	19.8119	22.3621	24.7356	27.6883	29.8194	34.528
14	17.1770	21.0642	23.6848	26.1190	29.1413	31.3193	36.123
15	18.2451	22.3072	24.9958	27.4884	30.5779	32.8013	37.697
16	19.3688	23.5418	26.2962	28.8454	31.9999	34.2672	39.252
17	20.4887	24.7690	27.5871	30.1910	33.4087	35.7185	40.790
18	21.6049	25.9894	28.8693	31.5264	34.8053	37.1564	42.312
19	22.7178	27.2036	30.1436	32.8523	36.1908	38.5822	43.820
20	23.8277	28.4120	31.4104	34.1696	37.5662	39.9968	45.315
21	24.9348	29.6151	32.6705	35.4789	38.9321	41.4010	46.797
22	26.0393	30.8133	33.9244	36.7807	40.2894	42.7956	48.268
23	27.1413	32.0069	35.1725	38.0757	41.6384	44.1813	49.728
24	28.2412	33.1963	36.4151	39.3641	42.9798	45.5585	51.179
25	29.3389	34.3816	37.6525	40.6465	44.3141	46.9278	52.620
26	30.4345	35.5631	38.8852	41.9232	45.6417	48.2899	54.052
27	31.5284	36.7412	40.1133	43.1944	46.9630	49.6449	55.476
28	32.6205	37.9159	41.3372	44.4607	48.2782	50.9933	56.892
29	33.7109	39.0875	42.5569	45.7222	49.5879	52.3356	58.302
30	34.7998	40.2560	43.7729	46.9792	50.8922	53.6720	59.703
40	45.6160	51.8050	65.7585	59.3417	63.6907	66.7659	73.402
50	56.3336	63.1671	67.5048	71.4202	76.1539	79.4900	86.661
60	66.9814	74.3970	79.0819	83.2976	88.3794	91.9517	99.607
70	77.5766	85.5271	90.5312	95.0231	100.425	104.215	112.317
80	88.1303	96.5782	101.879	106.629	112.329	116.321	124.839
90	98.6499	107.565	113.145	118.136	124.116	128.299	137.208
100	109.141	118.498	124.342	129.561	135.807	140.169	149.449

Adapted from Table 8 in *Biometrika Tables for Statisticians,* vol. 1, 3rd ed. (New York: Cambridge University Press, 1958), edited by E. S. Pearson and H. O. Hartley, by permission of the Biometrika trustees.

TABLE A.3 Critical Values of Studentized Range Statistic Distribution

df for $s_{\bar{X}}$	$1-\alpha$	Number of Ordered Means													
		2	3	4	5	6	7	8	9	10	11	12	13	14	15
1	.95	18.0	27.0	32.8	37.1	40.4	43.1	45.4	47.4	49.1	50.6	52.0	53.2	54.3	55.4
	.99	90.0	135	164	186	202	216	227	237	246	253	260	266	272	277
2	.95	6.09	8.3	9.8	10.9	11.7	12.4	13.0	13.5	14.0	14.4	14.7	15.1	15.4	15.7
	.99	14.0	19.0	22.3	24.7	26.6	28.2	29.5	30.7	31.7	32.6	33.4	34.1	34.8	35.4
3	.95	4.50	5.91	6.82	7.50	8.04	8.48	8.85	9.18	9.46	9.72	9.95	10.2	10.4	10.5
	.99	8.26	10.6	12.2	13.3	14.2	15.0	15.6	16.2	16.7	17.1	17.5	17.9	18.2	18.5
4	.95	3.93	5.04	5.76	6.29	6.71	7.05	7.35	7.60	7.83	8.03	8.21	8.37	8.52	8.66
	.99	6.51	8.12	9.17	9.96	10.6	11.1	11.5	11.9	12.3	12.6	12.8	13.1	13.3	13.5
5	.95	3.64	4.60	5.22	5.67	6.03	6.33	6.58	6.80	6.99	7.17	7.32	7.47	7.60	7.72
	.99	5.70	6.97	7.80	8.42	8.91	9.32	9.67	9.97	10.2	10.5	10.7	10.9	11.1	11.2
6	.95	3.46	4.34	4.90	5.31	5.63	5.89	6.12	6.32	6.49	6.65	6.79	6.92	7.03	7.14
	.99	5.24	6.33	7.03	7.56	7.97	8.32	8.61	8.87	9.10	9.30	9.49	9.65	9.81	9.95
7	.95	3.34	4.16	4.69	5.06	5.36	5.61	5.82	6.00	6.16	6.30	6.43	6.55	6.66	6.76
	.99	4.95	5.92	6.54	7.01	7.37	7.68	7.94	8.17	8.37	8.55	8.71	8.86	9.00	9.12
8	.95	3.26	4.04	4.53	4.89	5.17	5.40	5.60	5.77	5.92	6.05	6.18	6.29	6.39	6.48
	.99	4.74	5.63	6.20	6.63	6.96	7.24	7.47	7.68	7.87	8.03	8.18	8.31	8.44	8.55
9	.95	3.20	3.95	4.42	4.76	5.02	5.24	5.43	5.60	5.74	5.87	5.98	6.09	6.19	6.28
	.99	4.60	5.43	5.96	6.35	6.66	6.91	7.13	7.32	7.49	7.65	7.78	7.91	8.03	8.13
10	.95	3.15	3.88	4.33	4.65	4.91	5.12	5.30	5.46	5.60	5.72	5.83	5.93	6.03	6.11
	.99	4.48	5.27	5.77	6.14	6.43	6.67	6.87	7.05	7.21	7.36	7.48	7.60	7.71	7.81
11	.95	3.11	3.82	4.26	4.57	4.82	5.03	5.20	5.35	5.49	5.61	5.71	5.81	5.90	5.99
	.99	4.39	5.14	5.62	5.97	6.25	6.48	6.67	6.84	6.99	7.13	7.26	7.36	7.46	7.56

(continued)

TABLE A.3 Continued

df for $s_{\bar{X}}$	$1-a$	Number of Ordered Means													
		2	3	4	5	6	7	8	9	10	11	12	13	14	15
12	.95	3.08	3.77	4.20	4.51	4.75	4.95	5.12	5.27	5.40	5.51	5.62	5.71	5.80	5.88
	.99	4.32	5.04	5.50	5.84	6.10	6.32	6.51	6.67	6.81	6.94	7.06	7.17	7.26	7.36
13	.95	3.06	3.73	4.15	4.45	4.69	4.88	5.05	5.19	5.32	5.43	5.53	5.63	5.71	5.79
	.99	4.26	4.96	5.40	5.73	5.98	6.19	6.37	6.53	6.67	6.79	6.90	7.01	7.10	7.19
14	.95	3.03	3.70	4.11	4.41	4.64	4.83	4.99	5.13	5.25	5.36	5.46	5.55	5.64	5.72
	.99	4.21	4.89	5.32	5.63	5.88	6.08	6.26	6.41	6.54	6.66	6.77	6.87	6.96	7.05
16	.95	3.00	3.65	4.05	4.33	4.56	4.74	4.90	5.03	5.15	5.26	5.35	5.44	5.52	5.59
	.99	4.13	4.78	5.19	5.49	5.72	5.92	6.08	6.22	6.35	6.46	6.56	6.66	6.74	6.82
18	.95	2.97	3.61	4.00	4.28	4.49	4.67	4.82	4.96	5.07	5.17	5.27	5.35	5.43	5.50
	.99	4.07	4.70	5.09	5.38	5.60	5.79	5.94	6.08	6.20	6.31	6.41	6.50	6.58	6.65
20	.95	2.95	3.58	3.96	4.23	4.45	4.62	4.77	4.90	5.01	5.11	5.20	5.28	5.36	5.43
	.99	4.02	4.64	5.02	5.29	5.51	5.69	5.84	5.97	6.09	6.19	6.29	6.37	6.45	6.52
24	.95	2.92	3.53	3.90	4.17	4.37	4.54	4.68	4.81	4.92	5.01	5.10	5.18	5.25	5.32
	.99	3.96	4.54	4.91	5.17	5.37	5.54	5.69	5.81	5.92	6.02	6.11	6.19	6.26	6.33
30	.95	2.89	3.49	3.84	4.10	4.30	4.46	4.60	4.72	4.83	4.92	5.00	5.08	5.15	5.21
	.99	3.89	4.45	4.80	5.05	5.24	5.40	5.54	5.56	5.76	5.85	5.93	6.01	6.08	6.14
40	.95	2.86	3.44	3.79	4.04	4.23	4.39	4.52	4.63	4.74	4.82	4.91	4.98	5.05	5.11
	.99	3.82	4.37	4.70	4.93	5.11	5.27	5.39	5.50	5.60	5.69	5.77	5.84	5.90	5.96
60	.95	2.83	3.40	3.74	3.98	4.16	4.31	4.44	4.55	4.65	4.73	4.81	4.88	4.94	5.00
	.99	3.76	4.28	4.60	4.82	4.99	5.13	5.25	5.36	5.45	5.53	5.60	5.67	5.73	5.79
120	.95	2.80	3.36	3.69	3.92	4.10	4.24	4.36	4.48	4.56	4.64	4.72	4.78	4.84	4.90
	.99	3.70	4.20	4.50	4.71	4.87	5.01	5.12	5.21	5.30	5.38	5.44	5.51	5.56	5.61
∞	.95	2.77	3.31	3.63	3.86	4.03	4.17	4.29	4.39	4.47	4.55	4.62	4.68	4.74	4.80
	.99	3.64	4.12	4.40	4.60	4.76	4.88	4.99	5.08	5.16	5.23	5.29	5.35	5.40	5.45

TABLE A.4 **Critical Values of Dunnett's *d*-Statistic in Comparing Treatment Means with a Control (1-sided test)**

df for MS$_{error}$	$1 - \alpha$	Number of Means (Including Control)								
		2	3	4	5	6	7	8	9	10
6	.95	1.94	2.34	2.56	2.71	2.83	2.92	3.00	3.07	3.12
	.975	2.45	2.86	3.18	3.41	3.60	3.75	3.88	4.00	4.11
	.99	3.14	3.61	3.88	4.07	4.21	4.33	4.43	4.51	4.59
	.995	3.71	4.22	4.60	4.88	5.11	5.30	5.47	5.61	5.74
7	.95	1.89	2.27	2.48	2.62	2.73	2.82	2.89	2.95	3.01
	.975	2.36	2.75	3.04	3.24	3.41	3.54	3.66	3.76	3.86
	.99	3.00	3.42	3.66	3.83	3.96	4.07	4.15	4.23	4.30
	.995	3.50	3.95	4.28	4.52	4.17	4.87	5.01	5.13	5.24
8	.95	1.86	2.22	2.42	2.55	2.66	2.74	2.81	2.87	2.92
	.975	2.31	2.67	2.94	3.13	3.28	3.40	3.51	3.60	3.68
	.99	2.90	3.29	3.51	3.67	3.79	3.88	3.96	4.03	4.09
	.995	3.36	3.77	4.06	4.27	4.44	4.58	4.70	4.81	4.90
9	.95	1.83	2.18	2.37	2.50	2.60	2.68	2.75	2.81	2.86
	.975	2.26	2.61	2.86	3.04	3.18	3.29	3.39	3.48	3.55
	.99	2.82	3.19	3.40	3.55	3.66	3.75	3.82	3.89	3.94
	.995	3.25	3.63	3.90	4.09	4.24	4.37	4.48	4.57	4.65
10	.95	1.81	2.15	2.34	2.47	2.56	2.64	2.70	2.76	2.81
	.975	2.23	2.57	2.81	2.97	3.11	3.21	3.31	3.39	3.46
	.99	2.76	3.11	3.31	3.45	3.56	3.64	3.71	3.78	3.83
	.995	3.17	3.53	3.78	3.95	4.10	4.21	4.31	4.40	4.47
11	.95	1.80	2.13	2.31	2.44	2.53	2.60	2.67	2.72	2.77
	.975	2.20	2.53	2.76	2.92	3.05	3.15	3.24	3.31	3.38
	.99	2.72	3.06	3.25	3.38	3.48	3.56	3.63	3.69	3.74
	.995	3.11	3.45	3.68	3.85	3.98	4.09	4.18	4.26	4.33
12	.95	1.78	2.11	2.29	2.41	2.50	2.58	2.64	2.69	2.74
	.975	2.18	2.50	2.72	2.88	3.00	3.10	3.18	3.25	3.32
	.99	2.68	3.01	3.19	3.32	3.42	3.50	3.56	3.62	3.67
	.995	3.05	3.39	3.61	3.76	3.89	3.99	4.08	4.15	4.22
13	.95	1.77	2.09	2.27	2.39	2.48	2.55	2.61	2.66	2.71
	.975	2.16	2.48	2.69	2.84	2.96	3.06	3.14	3.21	3.27
	.99	2.65	2.97	3.15	3.27	3.37	3.44	3.51	3.56	3.61
	.995	3.01	3.33	3.54	3.69	3.81	3.91	3.99	4.06	4.13
14	.95	1.76	2.08	2.25	2.37	2.46	2.53	2.59	2.64	2.69
	.975	2.14	2.46	2.67	2.81	2.93	3.02	3.10	3.17	3.23
	.99	2.62	2.94	3.11	3.23	3.32	3.40	3.46	3.51	3.45
	.995	2.98	3.29	3.49	3.64	3.75	3.84	3.92	3.99	4.05

(continued)

TABLE A.4 Continued

df for MS$_{error}$	1 − α	\multicolumn{9}{c}{Number of Means (Including Control)}
		2	3	4	5	6	7	8	9	10
16	.95	1.75	2.06	2.23	2.34	2.43	2.50	2.56	2.61	2.65
	.975	2.12	2.42	2.63	2.77	2.88	2.96	3.04	3.10	3.16
	.99	2.58	2.88	3.05	3.17	3.26	3.33	3.39	3.44	3.48
	.995	2.92	3.22	3.41	3.55	3.65	3.74	3.82	3.88	3.93
18	.95	1.73	2.04	2.21	2.32	2.41	2.48	2.53	2.58	2.62
	.975	2.10	2.40	2.59	2.73	2.84	2.92	2.99	3.05	3.11
	.99	2.55	2.84	3.01	3.12	3.21	3.27	3.33	3.38	3.42
	.995	2.88	3.17	3.35	3.48	3.58	3.67	3.74	3.80	3.85
20	.95	1.72	2.03	2.19	2.30	2.39	2.46	2.51	2.56	2.60
	.975	2.09	2.38	2.57	2.70	2.81	2.89	2.96	3.02	3.07
	.99	2.53	2.81	2.97	3.08	3.17	3.23	3.29	3.34	3.38
	.995	2.85	3.13	3.31	3.43	3.53	3.61	3.67	3.73	3.78
24	.95	1.71	2.01	2.17	2.28	2.36	2.43	2.48	2.53	2.57
	.975	2.06	2.35	2.53	2.66	2.76	2.84	2.91	2.96	3.01
	.99	2.49	2.77	2.92	3.03	3.11	3.17	3.22	3.27	3.31
	.995	2.80	3.07	3.24	3.36	3.45	3.52	3.58	3.64	3.69
30	.95	1.70	1.99	2.15	2.25	2.33	2.40	2.45	2.50	2.54
	.975	2.04	2.32	2.50	2.62	2.72	2.79	2.86	2.91	2.96
	.99	2.46	2.72	2.87	2.97	3.05	3.11	3.16	3.21	3.24
	.995	2.75	3.01	3.17	3.28	3.37	3.44	3.50	3.55	3.59
40	.95	1.68	1.97	2.13	2.23	2.31	2.37	2.42	2.47	2.51
	.975	2.02	2.29	2.47	2.58	2.67	2.75	2.81	2.86	2.90
	.99	2.42	2.68	2.82	2.92	2.99	3.05	3.10	3.14	3.18
	.995	2.70	2.95	3.10	3.21	3.29	3.36	3.41	3.46	3.50
60	.95	1.67	1.95	2.10	2.21	2.28	2.23	2.39	2.44	2.48
	.975	2.00	2.27	2.43	2.55	2.63	2.70	2.76	2.81	2.85
	.99	2.39	2.64	2.78	2.87	2.94	3.00	3.04	3.08	3.12
	.995	2.66	2.90	3.04	3.14	3.22	3.28	3.33	3.38	3.42
120	.95	1.66	1.93	2.08	2.18	2.26	2.32	2.37	2.41	2.45
	.975	1.98	2.24	2.40	2.51	2.59	2.66	2.71	2.76	2.80
	.99	2.36	2.60	2.73	2.82	2.89	2.94	2.99	3.03	3.06
	.995	2.62	2.84	2.98	3.08	3.15	3.21	3.25	3.30	3.33
∞	.95	1.64	1.92	2.06	2.16	2.23	2.29	2.34	2.38	2.42
	.975	1.96	2.21	2.37	2.47	2.55	2.62	2.67	2.71	2.75
	.99	2.33	2.56	2.68	2.77	2.84	2.89	2.93	2.97	3.00
	.995	2.58	2.79	2.92	3.01	3.08	3.14	3.18	3.22	3.25

TABLE A.5   Coefficients of Orthogonal Polynomials

a	Polynomial	$X = 1$	2	3	4	5	6	7	8	9	10	$\sum w_i^2$
3	Linear	−1	0	1								2
	Quadratic	1	−2	1								6
	Linear	−3	−1	1	3							20
4	Quadratic	1	−1	−1	1							4
	Cubic	−1	3	−3	1							20
	Linear	−2	−1	0	1	2						10
5	Quadratic	2	−1	−2	−1	2						14
	Cubic	−1	2	0	−2	1						10
	Quartic	1	−4	6	−4	1						70
	Linear	−5	−3	−1	1	3	5					70
6	Quadratic	5	−1	−4	−4	−1	5					84
	Cubic	5	7	4	−4	−7	5					180
	Quartic	1	−3	2	2	−3	1					28
	Linear	−3	−2	−1	0	1	2	3				28
7	Quadratic	5	0	−3	−4	−3	0	5				84
	Cubic	−1	1	1	0	−1	−1	1				6
	Quartic	3	−7	1	6	1	−7	3				154
	Linear	−7	−5	−3	−1	1	3	5	7			168
	Quadratic	7	1	−3	−5	−5	−3	1	7			168
8	Cubic	−7	5	7	3	−3	−7	−5	7			264
	Quartic	7	−13	−3	9	9	−3	−13	7			616
	Quintic	−7	23	−17	−15	15	17	−23	7			2184
	Linear	−4	−3	−2	−1	0	1	2	3	4		60
	Quadratic	28	7	−8	−17	−20	−17	−8	7	28		2772
9	Cubic	−14	7	13	9	0	−9	−13	−7	14		990
	Quartic	14	−21	−11	9	18	9	−11	−21	14		2002
	Quintic	−4	11	−4	−9	0	9	4	−11	4		468
	Linear	−9	−7	−5	−3	−1	1	3	5	7	9	330
	Quadratic	6	2	−1	−3	−4	−4	−3	−1	2	6	132
10	Cubic	−42	14	35	31	12	−12	−31	−35	−14	42	8580
	Quartic	18	−22	−17	3	18	18	3	−17	−22	18	2860
	Quintic	−6	14	−1	−11	−6	6	11	1	−14	6	780

TABLE A.6 Critical Values of F_{max} Distribution

df for s_X^{2j}	$1 - a$	a = Number of Variances								
		2	**3**	**4**	**5**	**6**	**7**	**8**	**9**	**10**
4	.95	9.60	15.5	20.6	25.2	29.5	33.6	37.5	41.4	44.6
	.99	23.2	37.	49.	59.	69.	79.	89.	97.	106.
5	.95	7.15	10.8	13.7	16.3	18.7	20.8	22.9	24.7	26.5
	.99	14.9	22.	28.	33.	38.	42.	46.	50.	54.
6	.95	5.82	8.38	10.4	12.1	13.7	15.0	16.3	17.5	18.6
	.99	11.1	15.5	19.1	22.	25.	27.	30.	32.	34.
7	.95	4.99	6.94	8.44	9.70	10.8	11.8	12.7	13.5	14.3
	.99	8.89	12.1	14.5	16.5	18.4	20.	22.	23.	24.
8	.95	4.43	6.00	7.18	8.12	9.03	9.78	10.5	11.1	11.7
	.99	7.50	9.9	11.7	13.2	14.5	15.8	16.9	17.9	18.9
9	.95	4.03	5.34	6.31	7.11	7.80	8.41	8.95	9.45	9.91
	.99	6.54	8.5	9.9	11.1	12.1	13.1	13.9	14.7	15.3
10	.95	3.72	4.85	5.67	6.34	6.92	7.42	7.87	8.28	8.66
	.99	5.85	7.4	8.6	9.6	10.4	11.1	11.8	12.4	12.9
12	.95	3.28	4.16	4.79	5.30	5.72	6.09	6.42	6.72	7.00
	.99	4.91	6.1	6.9	7.6	8.2	8.7	9.1	9.5	9.9
15	.95	2.86	3.54	4.01	4.37	4.68	4.95	5.19	5.40	5.59
	.99	4.07	4.9	5.5	6.0	6.4	6.7	7.1	7.3	7.5
20	.95	2.46	2.95	3.29	3.54	3.76	3.94	4.10	4.24	4.37
	.99	3.32	3.8	4.3	4.6	4.9	5.1	5.3	5.5	5.6
30	.95	2.07	2.40	2.61	2.78	2.91	3.02	3.12	3.21	3.29
	.99	2.63	3.0	3.3	3.4	3.6	3.7	3.8	3.9	4.0
60	.95	1.67	1.85	1.96	2.04	2.11	2.17	2.22	2.26	2.30
	.99	1.96	2.2	2.3	2.4	2.4	2.5	2.5	2.6	2.6
∞	.95	1.00	1.00	1.00	1.00	1.00	1.00	1.00	1.00	1.00
	.99	1.00	1.00	1.00	1.00	1.00	1.00	1.00	1.00	1.00

Adapted from Table 31 in *Biometrika Tables for Statisticians,* vol. 1, 3rd ed. (New York: Cambridge University Press, 1966), edited by E. S. Pearson and H. O. Hartley, by permission of the Biometrika trustees.

B Research Designs for Complete Examples

B.1 Facets in Fly's Eyes

The data on which the complete example of a one-way randomized-groups ANOVA are based were collected by Hersh (1924). The purpose of the experiment was to determine the influences of temperature on flies heterozygous for genes of the bar series. Ten probable virgins of one stock (stocks are described in detail by Hersh) were mated with 10 males of another stock in an 8-dram vial containing banana agar inoculated with yeast, and then the bottle was placed at the experimental temperatures. The hatched-out females were counted for facet number and then preserved. The crosses were made in either direction.

The method of counting is described by Hersh as follows:

> The flies were counted upon blackened paraffin in a Syracuse glass. The best slope for placing the flies was easily secured by chipping away at the paraffin. The flies were placed upon the inclined slope of the paraffin and counted under a compound microscope with a Leitz 4 ocular and a Leitz 3 objective. In flies of high facet count the dorsal and ventral areas of the eye were counted separately, and the results added to give the total facet count of the individual. (p. 56)

Temperatures were chosen between 15 and 31°C with an interval of 2°C. Cool and warm rooms in the vivarium building provided the 15 and 25°C temperatures. Incubators in those rooms were converted to produce the 17 and 27°C temperatures. The laboratory incubator provided the 29°C condition. The remaining conditions were maintained in aquaria fitted with temperature control. Because previous research has shown that facet number is "not a good measure of the values of the temperatures," facet counts were tabulated on a "factorial system" described elsewhere (Zeleny, 1920).

B.2 Bonding Strength of Periodontal Dressings

The data on which the complete example of a randomized-groups factorial ANOVA are based were collected by the periodontal department at the USC Dental School in 1983 (Farnoush, Joseph, and Tabachnick, 1985; Sachs et al., 1985).

The purpose of the study was to measure the tensile shear bond strengths of five commercially available noneugenol periodontal dressings, three of which had not been previously investigated. The five periodontal dressing materials were Coe Pak (Coe Laboratories, Chicago), PerioCare (Pulpdent Corp., Brookline, Massachusetts), Peripac (De Trey Freres, S. A., Zurich, Switzerland), and Perio Putty and Zone (both from Cadco Inc., Los Angeles). Perio Putty is a rigid material that hardens with a snap set. The other materials all set with a lesser degree of hardness and rigidity.

A clean, dry, smoothly polished glass slab 15 cm × 7.8 cm × 1.9 cm was used in all trials for adherence of materials. Standardized machined brass cylinders with an outside diameter of 9 mm were filled with periodontal dressing that was mixed according to manufacturers' directions and standardized weight ratios to ensure uniformity of mix. Peripac was supplied ready to use with no mixing required. The materials were pressed into contact with the glass surface for 15 s, released, and allowed to set for either 3 or 24 h, during which time they were stored in a humidor at 37.8°C. Each trial was repeated at least 10 times.

For the tensile test, the glass slab with the cylinders adhered to it was placed in a jig on an Instron Universal Testing Machine (Instron Corp, Canton, Massachusetts), with the cylinder attached to a wire loop engaged by a torque-free tension chain to allow application of tensile force. For the shear test, the glass slab was placed in a jig with the specimens at right angles to a piston in the same machine that generated a compressive force. Thus, a tensile or shear force was applied to the specimens, with the machine set at a crosshead speed of 1 mm per m. Bond failure was characterized by visual inspection as either cohesive or adhesive.

B.3   Reaction Time to Identify Figures

Data for this study were collected by Damos (1989). Twenty right-handed males were required to respond "same" or "different" on a keypad as quickly as possible to a stimulus (the letter F or G) and its mirror image. Each trial consisted of 30 presentations of the stimulus and 30 presentations of its mirror image, 5 presentations in each of 6 orientations: upright (0), 60, 120, 180, 240, and 300 degrees of rotation. In all, the experiment required 10 sessions over two consecutive weeks. Each session had four blocks of nine trials distributed over morning and afternoon periods. Thus, each subject made 21,600 responses during the study. Half the subjects were given stimulus F in the first week and G in the second week; the others were given the letter stimuli in the reverse order. Order of presentation of all stimuli was random on all trials.

The two DVs were average correct reaction time and error rate. Responses to 60° of absolute rotation were averaged with those of 300°, and responses to 120° were averaged with those of 240°. Averages were calculated separately for standard and mirror-image trials.

Data selected for analysis in Section 6.7 were averages from the final (afternoon) period of the last session (10th day), so that all subjects were well practiced with both F and G stimuli. Previous research had shown no reliable differences in response due to letter, so no distinction between F and G stimuli was made in the current analysis. Correct reaction time was the DV selected for analysis. Thus, each of the 20 subjects provided eight reaction-time averages: standard image at four orientations and mirror image at four orientations.

B.4   Auto Pollution Filter Noise

Data for the mixed-randomized–repeated-measures design were available on the DASL page of the World Wide Web, with free-use authorization given. The reference given is Lewin and Shakun (1976, p. 313). Description is as follows:

> The data are from a statement by Texaco, Inc. to the Air and Water Pollution Subcommittee of the Senate Public Works Committee on June 26, 1973. Mr. John McKinley, President of Texaco, cited an automobile filter developed by Associated Octel Company as effective in reducing pollution. However, questions had been raised about the effects of filters on vehicle performance, fuel consumption, exhaust gas back pressure, and silencing. On the last question, he referred to the data included here as evidence that the silencing properties of the Octel filter were at least equal to those of standard silencers.

B.5   Wear Testing of Fabric Samples

The data for the randomized-group Latin-square analysis are from Davies (1963), who describes an experiment:

> . . . relating to the testing of rubber-covered fabric in the Martindale wear tester carried out as a 4×4 Latin Square. The machine consists of four rectangular brass plates on each of which is fastened an abrading surface consisting of special-quality emery paper. Four weighted bushes, into which test samples of fabric are fixed, rest on the emery surfaces, and a mechanical device moves the bushes over the surface of the emery, thus abrading the test specimens. The loss in weight after a given number of cycles is used as a criterion of resistance to abrasion. There are slight differences between the four positions on the machine, and it is known from past experience that if a run is repeated under apparently identical conditions and using apparently identical samples, slightly different results are obtained, ascribable partly to variations in the emery paper and partly to variations in temperature, humidity, etc. (pp. 163–164)

B.6   Odors and Performance

The data for the crossover Latin-square analysis are provided by Hirsch and Johnston (1996) of the Smell and Taste Treatment and Research Foundation. The goal of the research was to assess the effects of odors on performance of cognitive tasks. They recruited "22 volunteers, 12 men and 10 women ranging in age from 15 to 65 years (mean 36, median 34) from the shopping mall at Water Tower Place in Chicago," who were paid a nominal sum for their participation. Participants rated themselves as normally achieving and were given Amoore's pyridine odor threshold test "to establish they were normosmic."

The instruments used were two trail-making (maze) tests, modified from the trail-making sub-test of the Halsted-Reitan Neuropsychological Test Battery which is used to detect neurological problems." Hirsch and Johnston describe the following procedure:

> Prior to testing, subjects accustomed themselves to the masks by wearing unscented masks for one minute. They then underwent testing in randomized, single-blinded fashion. Each subject performed the trials twice: once wearing an unscented mask and once wearing a floral-scented mask. The scented masks had one drop of a mixed floral odorant applied, resulting in a suprathreshold level of scent.
>
> The order of presentation of scented versus unscented masks was random, but the order of maze presentation was constant. Each subject completed the set of two mazes a total of three times sequentially with each mask. The time required to carry out each of the trials was measured. (pp. 119–120)

B.7 Processing Time for ANOVA

Data were collected for the screening experiment on a hot August afternoon in the San Fernando Valley, by the first author enjoying her then-new Pentium 166 in an air-conditioned office. The purpose was to determine which factors affect the computation speed of the SPSS 7.5 GLM procedure: number of two-level IVs, number of covariates, and sample size using a data set described in Tabachnick and Fidell (2001, Section 12.7.3). Five levels of each factor were chosen to demonstrate a central-composite design.

Five dichotomous variables were chosen (or created) from the data set to serve as IVs. In runs with fewer than five IVs, the particular variables were chosen in a haphazard fashion. Four continuous variables also were chosen from the data set to serve as covariates. Again, for runs with fewer than four covariates, the variables were chosen haphazardly, except for runs with no covariates at all. Samples were chosen randomly through SPSS 7.5 for each of the 20 runs. Each run then was executed through SPSS 7.5 and the "elapsed time" in seconds recorded from the "Notes" portion of the output.

B.8 Nambeware Polishing Times

Data for the randomized-groups ANCOVA example were available from the DASL page of the World Wide Web, with free-use authorization. The reference given is Nambe Mills, Santa Fe, New Mexico. The following descriptions are from that Web page:

> Nambe Mills manufactures a line of tableware made from sand casting a special alloy of several metals. After casting, the pieces go through a series of shaping, grinding, buffing, and polishing steps. In 1989 the company began a program to rationalize its production schedule of some 100 items in its tableware line.
>
> The average polishing times for 59 products are related in general to the sizes of the products as indicated by product diameter (or equivalent). However, different types of products have special problems in polishing. For example, casseroles are deeper than ordinary plates and on that account would require more polishing time than a plate of equal diameter. Also it is possible that the increase in polishing time per additional inch of diameter could be different for casseroles than for ordinary plates.

B.9   Chest Deceleration Injuries
in Automobile Crashes

Data for the factorial randomized–repeated ANCOVA example were available from the DASL page
of the World Wide Web, with free-use authorization. Reference is the National Transportation Safety
Board. The following description is provided:

> Stock automobiles containing dummies in the driver and front passenger seats crashed into a wall at
> 35 miles per hour. National Transportation Safety Board officials collected information on how the
> crash affected the dummies. The injury variables describe the extent of head injuries, chest decelera-
> tion, and left and right femur load. The data file also contains information on the type and safety fea-
> tures of each crashed car.

B.10   Fat Content of Eggs

The following description is from the abstract provided on the Internet page accompanying the data
set. Data were taken from Bliss (1967), based on an experiment by Mitchell (1950).

> A single can of dried eggs was stirred well. Samples were drawn and a pair of samples (claimed to be
> of two "types"), was sent to each of six commercial laboratories to be analyzed for fat content. Each
> laboratory assigned two technicians, who each analyzed both "types." Since the data were all drawn
> from a single well-mixed can, the null hypothesis for ANOVA that the mean fat content of each sam-
> ple is equal is true. The experiment is thus really a study of the laboratories.

APPENDIX

C Answers to Selected Problems

Chapter 1

1.1   a. Speaker diameter; 3 levels: 8", 10", 12"

     b. Randomized groups

     c. Quantitative—in inches

     d. Quantitative—in dB

     e. One-way randomized-groups design

     f. Type II error

     g. Make the differences in diameter larger.

1.2   a. Type of drug; 2 levels: "smarts pill" and placebo
       Time; 3 levels: 1 month, 6 months, 12 months

     b. Type of drug is randomized groups
       Time is repeated measures

     c. Type of drug is qualitative
       Time is quantitative

     d. IQ score at each level of time; quantitative

     e. Two-way mixed (randomized-groups, repeated-measures) design

     f. Type I error

1.3   a. Gender
       Content of fabric; 2 levels: polyester and no polyester

     b. Both IVs are randomized groups

     c. Both are qualitative

     d. Gender is not manipulated; content of fabric is manipulated.

     e. Length of time to wear out; quantitative

     f. Two-way factorial randomized-groups design

1.5   There are three IVs, disinfectant, temperature, and ward. Disinfectant and temperature are completely crossed. Two wards nest at each combination of disinfectant and temperature; pieces of equipment (the cases) nest in each ward.

1.6   When the design is a four-way factorial:

Treatment D	Treatment C	Treatment B	Treatment A	
			a_1	a_2
d_1	c_1	b_1	$a_1b_1c_1d_1$	$a_2b_1c_1d_1$
		b_2	$a_1b_2c_1d_1$	$a_2b_2c_1d_1$
	c_2	b_1	$a_1b_1c_2d_1$	$a_2b_1c_2d_1$
		b_2	$a_1b_2c_2d_1$	$a_2b_2c_2d_1$
d_2	c_1	b_1	$a_1b_1c_1d_2$	$a_2b_1c_1d_2$
		b_2	$a_1b_2c_1d_2$	$a_2b_2c_1d_2$
	c_2	b_1	$a_1b_1c_2d_2$	$a_2b_1c_2d_2$
		b_2	$a_1b_2c_2d_2$	$a_2b_2c_2d_2$

When the design is a three-way factorial with D nested:

Treatment C	Treatment B	Treatment A	
		a_1	a_2
c_1	b_1	$a_1b_1c_1d_1$	$a_2b_1c_1d_9$
	b_2	$a_1b_2c_1d_2$	$a_2b_2c_1d_{10}$
c_2	b_1	$a_1b_1c_2d_3$	$a_2b_1c_2d_{11}$
	b_2	$a_1b_2c_2d_4$	$a_2b_2c_2d_{12}$
c_1	b_1	$a_1b_1c_2d_5$	$a_2b_1c_2d_{13}$
	b_2	$a_1b_2c_1d_6$	$a_2b_2c_1d_{14}$
c_2	b_1	$a_1b_1c_2d_7$	$a_2b_1c_2d_{15}$
	b_2	$a_1b_2c_2d_8$	$a_2b_2c_2d_{16}$

Chapter 2

2.1   Sample standard deviation = 10.16 (Equation 2.1)

Estimated population standard deviation = 10.32 (Equation 2.2 or 2.4)

Standard error = 1.83 (Equation 2.6)

95% confidence interval for mean (Equation 2.5)

$$32 - 1.96(1.83) \leq \mu \leq 32 + 1.96(1.83)$$
$$28.41 \leq \mu \leq 35.59$$

2.2   Skewness $= -0.294$; standard error of skewness $= 0.414$; z skewness $= -0.071$ (Equation 2.10)

Kurtosis $= -0.0758$; standard error of kurtosis $= 0.809$; z kurtosis $= -0.94$ (Equation 2.11)

Distribution appears relatively normal.

PROB2.3

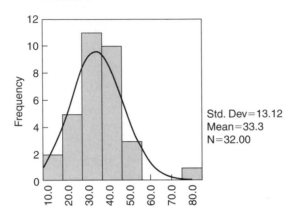

Std. Dev=13.12
Mean=33.3
N=32.00

2.3   The largest score is 78; its z score $= ((78 - 33.25)/13.1173) = 3.41$ (Equation 2.7).

In addition, the score appears disconnected.

2.4   Chi square (χ^2) $= 2.46$ (Equation 2.12); critical value (1 df) $= 3.84$. There is no relationship between the two variables.

2.5   Correlation $= .28$ (Equation 2.14 or 2.15)

$$Y' = 29.784 + 1.278X \text{ (Equations 2.16, 2.17, and 2.18)}$$

The scatterplot is roughly circular.

Overlapping area between height and number of seeds is $r^2 = (.28)^2 = .08$. This represents a small to modest relationship and produces a Venn diagram picture similar to that for the $A \times B$ interaction of Figure 1.2.

Chapter 3

3.1   *Normality of sampling distribution of means:* With 12 cases in each group, the degrees of freedom for error are $a(n - 1) = 22$; therefore, normality is expected.

The assumption of *homogeneity of variance* is violated. The variance of the control group is 32.08 and the variance of the treatment group is 2.63; the ratio is 12.20 (larger than 10). When a square root transformation is applied to the pain scores, the assumption of homogeneity of variance is met $(0.408/0.05 = 8.16)$. [It is also met with a log transform $(0.016/0.003 = 5.33)$.]

There are *no outliers*. Case 6 in the control group has a score of 30 and a z score of $((30 - 15.92)/5.66) = 2.48$. With 22 df for error, and a score of 25 for case 11, this case does not appear to be an outlier, but rather the largest score in a skewed distribution.

Independence of errors is assessed by consideration of details of the experimental design.

It is decided to analyze the data after a square root transformation.

3.2 $SS_A = 1.087$, $SS_{S/A} = 5.080$, $F = 4.708$, $p < .05$.   (Without the transformation, $SS_A = 73.50$, $SS_{S/A} = 381.83$, $F = 4.235$, $p < .05$.)

3.3   The regression approach requires one column for Y (square root of pain), one column to code level of X, and a third column for YX (as shown in Table 3.10). $SS(Y)$, $SS(X)$, and $SP(XY)$ are found as in Table 3.11; $SS(reg.)$ as in Table 3.13.

	Y	X	XY
	3.74	1	3.74
	3.61	1	3.61
	3.87	1	3.87
	3.74	1	3.74
	3.46	1	3.46
	5.48	1	5.48
	4.00	1	4.00
	3.32	1	3.32
	3.61	1	3.61
	3.74	1	3.74
	5.00	1	5.00
	3.74	1	3.74
	3.87	−1	−3.87
	3.46	−1	−3.46
	3.32	−1	−3.32
	3.46	−1	−3.46
	3.46	−1	−3.46
	3.74	−1	−3.74
	3.74	−1	−3.74
	3.16	−1	−3.16
	3.74	−1	−3.74
	3.61	−1	−3.61
	3.16	−1	−3.16
	3.46	−1	−3.46
sum	89.49	0	5.13
sumsq	339.87	24	
ss	6.18	24	
sp			5.13
ss(reg.)			1.09

Chapter 4

4.1   a. Homogeneity of variance: $F_{max} = 5.867/2.267 = 2.59$ (Equation 4.14); assumption is satisfied. (There are sufficient df for error to meet the normality assumption.)

b. Source table:

Source	SS	df	MS	F
Presoak time	66.12	3	22.04	5.59
Error	78.83	20	3.94	
Total	144.96	23		

d. $\eta^2 = 66.13/144.96 = .456$ (Equation 4.3)

$\hat{\omega}^2 = [66.13 - 3(3.94)]/[144.96 + 3.94] = 0.365$ (Equation 4.4)

f. Trend analysis (Equation 4.8):

Source	SS and MS	F
A linear	42.01	10.66
A quadratic	15.04	3.82
A cubic	9.075	2.30
Error	3.94 (MS only)	

$F_S = (4 - 1)(3.10) = 9.30$ (Equation 4.13); only the linear trend is significant.

4.2   a. Source table:

Source	SS	df	MS	F
Group	5.82	4	1.46	1.54
Error	16.00	17	0.94	
Total	21.82	21		

c. $n = [2(.94)/(5.33 - 6.5)^2][1.96 + 0.84]^2 = 1.37[7.84] = 10.74$ (Equation 4.6); approximately 11 cases are needed per group.

4.3   a. Source table:

Source	SS	df	MS	F
A	$16680 - 16333.33 = 346.67$ (equation for SS$_A$ in Table 4.3)	2	173.34	3.97
S/A	$27(43.67) = 1179.09$	27	43.67	
Total	1525.76	29		

b. η^2 is $346.67/1525.76 = .23$ (Equation 4.3)

c. The critical mean difference at the .05 level is (Equation 4.16)

$$d_T = 3.53\sqrt{\frac{43.67}{10}} = 7.38$$

The only mean difference that exceeds this critical value is the difference between the mean at a_1 and the mean at a_3.

d. By using Equation 4.10,

$$F = \frac{10[1(20) + 1(22) - 2(28)]^2 \big/ 1^2 + 1 + (-2)^2}{43.67} = 7.48$$

$$F_s = (3 - 1)(3.35) = 6.70 \qquad \text{(Equation 4.13)}$$

Because 7.48 is larger than 6.70, the mean for the third group is reliably different from the pooled means for the other two groups.

4.4 Problem

	a_1: 2 hours	a_2: 4 hours	a_3: 6 hours	a_4: 8 hours
a.	-3	-1	1	3
b.	1	1	1	-3
c.	1	-1	0	0
d.	1	1	-1	-1

4.5 Problem

	a_1: wl control	a_2: placebo	a_3: old analg	a_4: new analg 1	a_5: new analg 2
a.	1	-1	0	0	0
b.	3	3	-2	-2	-2
c.	0	0	2	-1	-1
d.	0	0	0	1	-1
e.	0	1	0	-1	0
f.	0	1	0	0	-1

Chapter 5

5.1 a. The data set is divided into eight cells. The largest variance is 12.00 (cotton, 10 min) and the smallest variance is 1.33 (polyester, 10 min.). F_{max} is 9.02, less than 10; therefore, the assumption of homogeneity of variance is met.

b. Source table:

Source	SS	df	MS	F	η^2
Material	0.375	1	0.375	0.080	
Soak Time	66.125	3	22.042	4.681	.456
Material × Soak Time	3.125	3	1.042	0.221	
Error	75.333	16	4.708		
Total	144.958	23			

d. See the last column of the source table.

f. Trend analysis source table:

Source	SS	df	MS	F
(Soak Time)	(66.12)	(3)		
Linear Trend	42.01	1	42.01	8.92
Quadratic Trend	15.04	1	15.04	3.19
Cubic Trend	9.08	1	9.08	1.93
Error	75.33	16	4.71	
Total	144.96	23		

$F_S = (b-1)F(3,16) = 3(3.24) = 9.72$; if tested post hoc, none of the trends is significant.

5.3   a. Source table with Type III SS:

Source	SS	df	MS	F
A	4.09	1	4.09	3.80
B	2.14	4	0.54	0.50
$A \times B$	1.85	4	0.46	0.43
Error	15.08	14	1.08	
Total	25.33	23		

b. The unweighted means (i.e., the mean of the cell means on each margin) for A are 5.67 and 6.52 for levels 1 and 2, respectively. The unweighted means for B are 6.00, 5.92, 5.67, 6.38, and 6.50 for levels 1 through 5, respectively. These are the appropriate means because the experiment is intended to be equal to n.

c. With $MS_{error} = 1.08$, alpha $= .05$, and power $= .80$, it would take approximately 27 cases on the margin for each level of A to find a reliable difference between the two levels of A (total $N = 54$).

5.4   Consider the design as follows:

b_1: 4 hours b_2: 6 hours b_3: 8 hours

a_1: coffee

a_2: fruit juice

a_3: beer

a. Marginal comparison of b_3 vs. $b_1 + b_2$.

b. Marginal comparison of a_1 vs. a_2.

c. Simple main effect of A at b_2.

d. Simple comparison of B_{linear} at a_2.

e. Simple comparison of b_1 vs. b_3 at a_1.

f. Simple main effect of B at a_3.

g. Simple comparison of a_1 vs. a_2 at b_1.

h. Interaction contrast of $B_{linear} \times A_{comp}$.

5.5   a. Among the eight cells, the largest variance is 4.3 (deprivation 2, familiar 1, decor 1) and the smallest is .2 (deprivation 2, familiar 1, decor 2); $F_{max} = 21.50$, so the assumption of homogeneity of variance is violated.

b. With untransformed data, the source table is

Source	SS	df	MS	F	Partial η^2
Deprivation	115.60	1	115.60	58.90	.65
Familiarity	40.00	1	40.00	20.38	.39
Decor	44.10	1	44.10	22.47	.41
Deprivation × Familiarity	14.40	1	14.40	7.34	.19
Deprivation × Decor	2.50	1	2.50	1.27	.04
Familiarity × Decor	2.50	1	2.50	1.27	.04
Deprivation × Familiarity × Decor	22.50	1	22.50	11.46	.26
Error	62.80	32	1.96		
Total	304.40	39			

d. See the last column of the source table.

f. The first step is to recode the $2 \times 2 \times 2$ design into a one-way design with eight levels.

Through SPSS ONEWAY, the syntax is

```
IF (deprivat eq 1 and familiar eq 1 and decor eq 1) group = 1.
IF (deprivat eq 1 and familiar eq 1 and decor eq 2) group = 2.
IF (deprivat eq 1 and familiar eq 2 and decor eq 1) group = 3.
IF (deprivat eq 1 and familiar eq 2 and decor eq 2) group = 4.
IF (deprivat eq 2 and familiar eq 1 and decor eq 1) group = 5.
IF (deprivat eq 2 and familiar eq 1 and decor eq 2) group = 6.
IF (deprivat eq 2 and familiar eq 2 and decor eq 1) group = 7.
IF (deprivat eq 2 and familiar eq 2 and decor eq 2) group = 8.
ONEWAY
  eagernes BY group
  /CONTRAST= 1 1 0 0 -1 -1 0 0 /CONTRAST 0 0 1 1 0 0 -1 -1
  /MISSING ANALYSIS.
```

F for contrasting the first level of deprivation against the second level of deprivation at the first level of familiarity is $(-3.512)^2 = 12.33$. F for contrasting the first level of deprivation against the second level of deprivation at the second level of familiarity is $(-7.342)^2 = 53.90$. It is assumed that the critical values were determined ahead of time as part of developing the plan for the sequential analysis. If the decision was, for instance, to set $\alpha = .005$ for the follow-up tests, critical F is about 9.18 and both comparisons are significant.

5.6   If the factors in the $2 \times 3 \times 3$ design are labeled A, B, and C, it takes one column to code A, two columns to code B (call them B_{linear} and B_{quad}), and two columns to code C (call them C_{comp1} and C_{comp2}). Columns for the main effects are A, B_{linear}, B_{quad}, C_{comp1}, and C_{comp2}. There are two columns for the $A \times B$ interaction, $A \times B_{linear}$, $A \times B_{quad}$; there are two columns for the $A \times C$ interaction, $A \times C_{comp1}$, $A \times C_{comp2}$; and there are four columns for the $B \times C$ interaction, $B_{linear} \times C_{comp1}$, $B_{linear} \times C_{comp2}$, $B_{quad} \times C_{comp1}$, and $B_{quad} \times C_{comp2}$. The four columns for the three-way interaction are $A \times B_{linear} \times C_{comp1}$, $A \times B_{linear} \times C_{comp2}$, $A \times B_{quad} \times C_{comp1}$, and $A \times B_{quad} \times C_{comp2}$.

Chapter 6

6.1 To test normality for the marginal effect of type of book:

	Science fiction	Mystery
s_1	$1 + 3 + 6 = 10$	$5 + 4 + 1 = 10$
s_2	$1 + 4 + 8 = 13$	$8 + 8 + 4 = 20$
s_3	$3 + 3 + 6 = 12$	$4 + 5 + 3 = 12$
s_4	$5 + 5 + 7 = 17$	$3 + 2 + 0 = 5$
s_5	$2 + 4 + 5 = 11$	$5 + 6 + 3 = 14$

To test normality for the marginal effect of month:

	Month 1	Month 2	Month 3
s_1	$1 + 5 = 6$	$3 + 4 = 7$	$6 + 1 = 7$
s_2	$1 + 8 = 9$	$4 + 8 = 12$	$8 + 4 = 12$
s_3	$3 + 4 = 7$	$3 + 5 = 8$	$6 + 3 = 9$
s_4	$5 + 3 = 8$	$5 + 2 = 7$	$7 + 0 = 7$
s_5	$2 + 5 = 7$	$4 + 6 = 10$	$5 + 3 = 8$

6.2 Source table:

Source	SS	df	MS	F
Trial	207.275	3	69.092	65.513
Cases	158.225	9	17.581	
Trial × Cases	28.475	27	1.055	

a. There are sufficient df in the Trial × Cases interaction to meet the assumption of normality. In addition, the largest z score in any of the four cells for skewness is 1.02 (negative) and the largest z score for kurtosis is -1.08. The normal probability plots of values at each level of trial lie substantially along the diagonal.

The largest variance is 6.69, the smallest is 3.73; F_{max} is 1.79, so the assumption of homogeneity of variance is met.

The significance value for Mauchley's test of sphericity is .30; there is no violation of sphericity.

b. The only two scores that appear disconnected from the others in their cell are 4 (trial 1) and 9 (trial 3). Box plots identify neither of these as outliers. The z score associated with the value of 4 is $[(4 - 9.3)/2.58] = -2.05$. The z score associated with the value of 9 is $[(9 - 4.7)/2.26] = 1.90$. Neither is an outlier.

c. Partial η^2 (with SS for cases omitted) for the effect of trial is .879.

6.3 The source table for the randomized-groups analysis of the data in Table 6.20 is

Source	SS	df	MS	F
Type of Book	0.133	1	0.133	0.050
Month	2.867	2	1.433	0.538
Type of Book by Month	64.465	2	32.233	12.087
Error	64.000	24	2.667	
Total	131.467	29		

The SS for the main effects and interactions are identical, within rounding error, to those calculated by hand in Table 6.25. SS and df for error, however, in this table have been partitioned into SS_S, SS_{AS}, SS_{BS}, and SS_{ABS} in Table 6.25.

6.4   Source table for the two-way repeated-measures ANOVA:

Source	SS	df	MS	F
Altimeter	1368.90	1	1368.900	13.065
Altimeter × Cases	419.10	4	104.775	
Position	8574.90	3	2858.300	30.940
Position × Cases	1108.60	12	92.383	
Altimeter × Position	3680.90	3	1226.967	7.085
Altimeter × Position × Cases	2078.10	12	173.175	
Cases	2752.60	4	688.150	
Total	19,983.10	39		

a. Because df for the error terms are small, the normality assumption is addressed by inspecting normal probability plots for each of the eight cells, and skewness and kurtosis for those cells. Some of the normal probability plots are not objects of great beauty, but none seems especially worrisome. The z score for the highest skewness (analog-high) is $[1.635/0.913]$ 1.79; the z score for the highest kurtosis (analog-low) is $[-3.028/2]$ 1.51. Both values are acceptable.

   The highest variance among the eight cells is 380.300, the lowest 111.700. F_{max} is 3.40, less than 10.

   Sphericity is not relevant to Altimeter because there are only two levels. Mauchly's test has an acceptable probability value of .35 for the Altimeter × Position interaction. However, for the test of Position, Mauchley's test has a probability of .054, right on the border. Because of the nature of the levels of Position, trend analysis is not appropriate. However, either multivariate results or the results of testing after Huynh-Feldt adjustment are probably appropriate. In this case, the effect of Position meets criteria for significance with any of the tests. The three cases that appeared potential outliers were the 80 in analog-high, the 18 in analog-left, and the 73 in analog-right. z scores for those values were $[(47.4-80)/19.5]$ 1.67, $[(18-39.8)/13.9]$ −1.57, and $[(73-49.2)/14.2] = 1/68$. With the exception of sphericity for Position, assumptions are met.

b. Partial η^2 for Altimeter is .77; for Position it is between .69 (Equation 6.26) and .89. For the Altimeter × Position interaction, it is .64. Partial η^2 is SS_{effect} divided by $(SS_{effect} + SS_{error})$ for that effect; η_L^2 is SS_{effect} divided by $(SS_{effect} + SS_{error} + SS_S)$.

c. Reasonable post hoc comparisons might involve high–low versus left–right followed by high versus low and then left versus right, with Scheffé adjustment. Other reasonable comparisons might be the simple comparisons of position for digital and then for analog altimeters.

6.5   A total of 39 columns are required to set up the problem (plus an additional 39 for the cross of DV score with the other 39 columns). Altimeter requires a single column, Position requires 3, and the Altimeter × Position interaction requires 3. The five cases require 4 columns. Remaining columns are 4 crosses of cases with the single column for Altimeter (for the $A \times S$ interaction), 12 crosses of cases with the 3 columns for Position (for the $B \times S$ interaction), and then 12 crosses of the cases with the 3 columns for the Altimeter × Position interaction (for the $A \times B \times S$ interaction).

6.6   By using Equation 6.20, the relative efficiency of the repeated-measures study over the randomized-groups study is

$$\text{Relative efficiency} = \frac{5.186(27+1)(36+3)}{1.055(27+3)(36+1)} = 4.84$$

6.7   The effects in a three-way repeated-measures design are

Source	df	Error Term	df Error
A	$a-1$	$A \times S$	$(a-1)(s-1)$
B	$b-1$	$B \times S$	$(b-1)(s-1)$
C	$c-1$	$C \times S$	$(c-1)(s-1)$
S	$s-1$		
$A \times B$	$(a-1)(b-1)$	$A \times B \times S$	$(a-1)(b-1)(s-1)$
$A \times C$	$(a-1)(c-1)$	$A \times C \times S$	$(a-1)(c-1)(s-1)$
$B \times C$	$(b-1)(c-1)$	$B \times C \times S$	$(b-1)(c-1)(s-1)$
$A \times B \times C$	$(a-1)(b-1)(c-1)$	$A \times B \times C \times S$	$(a-1)(b-1)(c-1)(s-1)$

Chapter 7

7.1   When the case totals from Table 7.2 are run as a randomized-groups design, the F value (4.68) is the same as that for the test of type of novel (the randomized-groups IV) in the mixed design. That is because the ratio of MS_A to $MS_{S/A}$ is the same in the two analyses. The numbers are not the same, however, because the randomized-groups analysis does not "know" that the totals are formed by combining three scores. If the SS for the mixed design ($SS_A = 20.58$, $SS_{S/A} = 26.40$) are multiplied by 3, they match those of the randomized-groups analysis. Also, after the SS for A and S/A in the mixed design are multiplied by 3, their total is the same as SS_T in the randomized-groups design (140.93), revealing that this portion of the mixed design is a complete partition of case totals in the randomized-groups design.

7.2   a.   Both error terms have fewer than 20 df, insufficient to guarantee normality. The highest z score for skewness in any of the eight cells of the design (classical music at 3 P.M.) is -1.97. The highest z score for kurtosis in two cells (rock at 1 P.M. and classical at 11 A.M.) is 2.29. These scores, on their own, are not high enough to be worrisome with so small a sample size.

     There is no evidence of outliers in the boxplots for the cells. The only score that appears somewhat disconnected from the others is the 6 in the classical–9 A.M. cell; the z score connected with the 6 $[(6 - 3.25)/1.89]$ is 1.45.

     However, the check for homogeneity of variance is not reassuring. The highest variance is 3.58 (classical–9 A.M.) and the lowest is .25 (classical–3 P.M.). F_{max} is 14.32. This data set, then, is a good candidate for transformation.

   b.   For untransformed data, the source table is

Source	SS	df	MS	F
Music	10.125	1	10.125	4.084
Error	14.875	6	2.479	
Time	1.250	3	0.417	0.480
Music × Time	179.625	3	59.875	68.976
Error	15.625	18	0.868	
Total	221.500	31		

   c.   Partial η^2 for Music is .405. For Time, it is .074, and for the Music × Time interaction, it is .92.

   d.   Because the p-value for Mauchly's test of sphericity for Time is .395, the assumption of sphericity is met.

7.3   Answers are in Table 7.19.

7.4   This is a simple main-effects analysis of the randomized-groups IV (Novel) at each level of the repeated-measures IV (Month): A at b_j with S/A at b_j as the error term. This is accomplished by running three, one-way, randomized-groups ANOVAs, one at the first month, the second at the second month, and the third at the third month. F for the difference between types of novels at the first month is 1.857; F for the difference at the second month is 0.441; F for the difference at the third month is 28.409.

7.5   Source table:

Source	Problem a: Error with D Repeated	Problem b: Error with BCD Repeated
A	S/ABC	S/A
B	S/ABC	$B \times S/A$
C	S/ABC	$C \times S/A$
D	$D \times S/ABC$	$D \times S/A$
AB	S/ABC	$B \times S/A$
AC	S/ABC	$C \times S/A$
AD	$D \times S/ABC$	$D \times S/A$
BC	S/ABC	$B \times C \times S/A$
BD	$D \times S/ABC$	$B \times D \times S/A$
CD	$D \times S/ABC$	$C \times D \times S/A$
ABC	S/ABC	$B \times C \times S/A$
ABD	$D \times S/ABC$	$B \times D \times S/A$
ACD	$D \times S/ABC$	$C \times D \times S/A$
BCD	$D \times S/ABC$	$B \times C \times D \times S/A$
$ABCD$	$D \times S/ABC$	$B \times C \times D \times S/A$

7.6   a. The highest z score for skewness is -1.83 (nonpregnant, postglucose, hour 3), and the highest z score for kurtosis is -1.65 (pregnant, fasting, hour 1). In such a small sample, neither of these is worrisome.

The highest variance is 631.583 (pregnant, postglucose, hour 2), and the lowest variance is 63.333 (pregnant, fasting, hour 4). F_{max} is 9.97, slightly less than 10.

There is no evidence in any of the boxplots of the presence of outliers.

The probability level for Mauchley's test of sphericity for Hour is .889, and that for the State (postglucose vs. fasting) $\times$ Hour interaction is .375. The assumption of sphericity is met.

Source	SS	df	MS	F	Partial η^2
Pregnancy	297.563	1	297.563	0.197	.032
Cases/Pregnancy	9061.625	6	1510.271		
State (postglucose vs. fasting)	13,689.000	1	13,689.000	38.692*	.866
State $\times$ Pregnancy	2809.000	1	2809.000	7.940	.570
Cases $\times$ State/Pregnancy	2122.750	6	353.792		
Hour	1465.188	3	488.396	6.953*	.537
Hour $\times$ Pregnancy	1156.188	3	385.396	5.487*	.478
Cases $\times$ Hour/Pregnancy	1264.375	18	70.243		
State $\times$ Hour	506.250	3	168.750	2.588	.301
State $\times$ Hour $\times$ Pregnancy	359.250	3	119.750	1.836	.234
Cases $\times$ State $\times$ Hour/Pregnancy	1173.750	18	65.208		
Total	33,904.939	63			

Note that with seven significance tests, the experimentwise error rate is near .35 if all are tested at the .05 level. If all tests are desired, Bonferroni adjustment to critical values for some or all of them is wise.

b. See the last column of the source table for partial η^2.

c. If .02 alpha level is chosen for all seven tests, the critical value when F has 1 and 6 df is 8.80 and when 3 and 18 df 3.95. By these criteria, only the effects with an asterisk are significant. State, with only two levels, requires no follow-up. Effects of hour are well known. The effect of most interest is the Hour $\times$ Pregnancy interaction. Interaction contrasts are desirable to determine if the trends of hour are different for different pregnancy states. SPSS syntax for the interaction contrast from Table 7.29 is

```
COMPUTE hour_1 = fast_1 + post_1.
COMPUTE hour_2 = fast_2 + post_2.
COMPUTE hour_3 = fast_3 + post_3.
COMPUTE hour_4 = fast_4 + post_4.
EXECUTE.
GLM
hour_1 hour_2 hour_3 hour_4 by preg
/MMATRIX = "linear" hour_1–3 hour_2–1 hour_3 1 hour_4 3
/WSFACTOR = hour 4
/WSDESIGN = hour
/DESIGN = preg.
```

Neither the linear nor quadratic trends differ for different pregnancy states, but the cubic trend does, with an F value of 21.463.

Chapter 8

8.1 a. F_{max} for the DV is $5.867/2.267 = 2.59$ and F_{max} for the CV is $7.200/2.667 = 2.70$; therefore, homogeneity of variance is established for both the DV and the CV.

b. The interaction of the CV (precleanliness) with the IV (Time), with the DV (Cleanliness), is not statistically reliable ($p = .441$); therefore, homogeneity of regression is established.

c. The source table for the analysis is

Source	SS	df	MS	F	Partial η^2
Precleanliness (CV)	74.103	1	74.103	297.615	.940
Time	13.261	3	4.420	17.754	.737
Cases/Time	4.731	19	0.249		

e. See the last column of the source table.

8.2 a. A group variable was created that subdivided the eight cells of the 2×4 design. F_{max} for the cells for the DV (Cleanliness) is $12.000/1.333 = 9.00$. F_{max} for the first CV (Precleanliness, X_1) is $14.333/1.000 = 14.333$. F_{max} for the second CV (Thread count, X_2) is $8.333/2.333 = 3.57$. Homogeneity of variance is not established for the first CV. There are several options: (1) delete the CV, (2) transform the CV, or (3) establish a more stringent alpha level for the tests of the two IVs. Both square root and log transformations of the CV failed to produce homogeneity of variance. For didactic purposes, then, the decision is made to retain the CV (it *was* important in the preceding problem) and establish more stringent alpha levels for the IVs.

b. There were too few df to test homogeneity of regression for the pooled covariates through SPSS MANOVA. Therefore, separate homogeneity tests were made for each CV. For the test of the first CV, the Fabric × Time Precleanliness interaction, $F(3, 8) = 0.03, p = .993$. For the test of the second CV, the Fabric × Time × Thread interaction, $F(3, 8) = 0.76, p = .547$. Thus, the assumption of homogeneity appears to be met.

[For problems with sufficient df, however, the syntax for the test of homogeneity of variance is

```
manova
Y by FABTYPE (1,2) PRESTIME (1,4) with x1, x2
/print = signif(brief)
/analysis = Y
/method = sequential
/design FABTYPE PRESTIME x1 x2
        pool (x1 x2) by FABTYPE
        pool (x1 x2) by PRESTIME
        pool (x1 x2) by FABTYPE by PRESTIME.
```

c. With only three cases in each cell, identification of outliers using z scores and disconnectedness is problematic. Boxplots were examined for the DV and each of the CVs separately in each of the eight cells; no outliers were found. By using the procedure of Table 8.43, outliers were sought among the pair of CVs. None of the cases had a Mahalanobis distance anywhere near the critical value of 13.815; the highest value is 2.884 for case 5.

d. The source table for the analysis is

Source	SS	df	MS	F	Partial η^2
Precleanliness	68.356	1	68.356	146.620	.913
Thread Count	0.119	1	0.119	0.254	.018
Fabric Type	0.000	1	0.000	0.000	.000
Time	10.601	3	3.534	7.580	.619
Fabric Type × Time	0.208	3	0.069	0.149	.031
Error	6.527	14	0.466		

8.3 a. The source table for the analysis using the GLM approach is

Source	SS	df	MS	F
Pretest (CV)	14.583	1	14.583	37.121
Keyboard Feel	4.808	1	4.808	12.240
Cases/Keyboard Feel	2.750	7	0.393	
Key Size	0.793	2	0.397	0.286
Key Size × Pretest	1.270	2	0.635	0.458
Key Size × Keyboard Feel	5.131	2	2.565	1.852
Cases × Key Size/Keyboard Feel	19.397	14	1.386	

b. The source table for the analysis using the traditional approach is

Source	SS	df	MS	F
Pretest (CV)	14.58	1	14.58	37.12
Keyboard Feel	4.81	1	4.81	12.24
Cases/Keyboard	2.75	7	0.39	
Key Size	15.20	2	7.60	5.88
Key Size × Keyboard Feel	12.80	2	6.40	4.95
Cases × Key Size/Keyboard Feel	20.67	16	1.29	

8.4   The adjusted mean for cotton is 6.959 and the adjusted mean for polyester is 6.957; the standard deviation is $(0.466)^{1/2} = 0.683$. With $\alpha = .05$ and power $= .80$, between 1,750,000 and 1,826,720 subjects are required to demonstrate a difference between the two fabrics (estimates differ somewhat with method used).

8.5 F for Time is .480 for in both analyses and F for the Music × Time interaction is 68.98 for both analyses. F for music is 4.084 for the ANOVA and 9.07 for the traditional ANCOVA. Therefore, the traditional approach adjusts the randomized-groups IV, but not the repeated-measures IVs.

8.6   The source table is

Source	SS	df	MS	F
Covariate (RG)	15.22	1	15.22	50.53
Feel (RG)	6.16	1	6.16	20.44
S/A	2.11	7	0.30	
Covariate (RM)	5.01	1	5.01	4.81
Size	13.08	2	6.54	6.27
Feel × Size	10.98	2	5.49	5.26
$B \times S/A$	15.65	15	1.04	

RG = randomized groups
RM = repeated measures

The SPSS MANOVA syntax that produced this output is:

```
manova
DV_S DV_M DV_L by FEEL(1,2) with CV_S CV_M CV_L
   /wsfactor = SIZE (3)
   /wsdesign = SIZE
   /print = signif(brief)
   /design = FEEL.
```

Chapter 9

9.1   a. Because there is a single case in each cell, assumptions are tested separately on the margins of each of the three IVs. For the four levels of Procedure, the IV of primary interest, the boxplots reveal no likely outliers. The z scores for skewness and kurtosis are all acceptable as is F_{max} $(11.583/6.250 = 1.85)$. Because each case experiences only a single combination of levels, independence of errors is likely for all three IVs. For the four levels of Temperature, boxplots and skewness and kurtosis values are all acceptable.

However, $F_{max} = (22.667/2.250) = 10.07$. If a test of Temperature is of interest, a more conservative choice of alpha is in order. For the four levels of Experience, all of the tests are acceptable, including $F_{max} = (4.917/0.917) = 5.36$.

c. In addition to the column for DV scores, three columns for each IV are needed, 9 in all. Orthogonal comparisons of interest can be used to form the columns, or an arbitrary set, such as trend coefficients, can be used. The error term is found by subtraction.

d. Source table:

Source	SS	df	MS	F	Partial η^2
Procedure	35.688	3	11.896	21.148	.914
Experience	97.688	3	32.563	57.889	.967
Temperature	2.188	3	0.729	1.296	.393
Error	3.375	6	0.563		
Total	138.938	15			

e. See the last column of the source table.

g. Assuming Procedure is the only IV of interest, post hoc tests or follow-up experiments focus on that variable. The mean at the fourth level of Procedure (10.250) appears different from the means at the other levels of Procedure (6.250, 7.250, and 8.50, respectively), which may be statistically the same as each other. Tukey tests of differences between all pairs of means or a test with Scheffé adjustment with three means pooled against the fourth might be undertaken.

9.2 b. Data are organized as in Table 9.24. At a minimum, there is a column for Sequence (A) and an additional four columns for DV scores at each level of Position (B). Four additional columns may be added, with the DV scores reorganized into columns for Indicator (C), or the levels of C can be identified through series of IF statements (e.g., IF Sequence = 1 and Position = 1, THEN Indicator = 1, etc.). Two mixed-design runs are required, one to get $SS_{position}$ and the other to get $SS_{indicator}$.

c. Assumptions are evaluated on the margins of Position and Indicator, where a total of eight scores is gathered at each level. However, there are only two scores at the margin for Sequence, totals for the two cases at each level of Sequence; therefore, assessment of assumptions is not possible. A look at residuals of analysis might reveal problems, if they exist.

For the four levels of Position, there are insufficient df for error to guarantee normality; therefore, boxplots and skewness and kurtosis values at each level are inspected. They indicate acceptable normality and no outliers. F_{max} is also acceptable $(12.786/8.554 = 1.49)$, so the assumption of homogeneity of variance is met.

There are also insufficient df for error for Indicator to guarantee normality. However, data at each of the four levels generate reasonable skewness and kurtosis values, and the boxplots reveal no outliers. F_{max} is also acceptable $(2.286/0.857 = 2.67)$.

Mauchley's tests of sphericity revealed no problem for the test of Position ($p = .533$) and no problem for the test of Indicator ($p = .631$).

d. Source table:

Source	SS	df	MS	F	Partial η^2
Sequence	2.844	3	0.948	4.33	.765
Cases/Sequence	0.875	4	0.219		
Position	23.844	3	7.948	7.948/1.052 = 7.555	23.844/(23.844 + 12.625) = .654
Indicator	277.594	3	92.531	92.531/1.052 = 87.957	277.594/(277.594 + 12.625) = .956
Sequence $\times$ Position, Adjusted	283.781 − 277.594 = 6.187	9 − 3 = 6	1.031	1.031/1.052 = 0.980	
Cases $\times$ Position/Sequence	12.625	12	1.052		
Total	323.969	31			

e. See partial η^2 column in the preceding source table.

g. $SS_{position, linear} = 23.256$; $SS_{cases \times position, linear/sequence} = 5.475$. $SS_{position, quad} = 0.281$; $SS_{cases \times position, quad/sequence} = 0.375$; $SS_{position, cubic} = 0.306$; $SS_{cases \times position, cubic/sequence} = 5.775$.

9.3 a. The data set has four columns, one for Case, one for Position, one for Snow, and the last for Time. Each Case has three rows of data, one for each combination of Position and Snow.

b. Source table:

Source	SS	df	MS	F	Partial η^2
Case	0.083	3	0.027	0.018	.017
Position	0.500	2	0.250	0.158	.095
Snow	58.750	3	19.583	12.368	.925
Error	4.750	3	1.583	0.034	
Total	72.250	11			

c. See the last column of the source table.

e. A Tukey test of differences between all pairs of levels of snow is probably appropriate.

9.4 a. $MS_{S/A}$ (through Equation 9.16) is

$$MS_{S/A} = \frac{138.938 - 35.688}{16 - 4} = 8.604$$

The relative efficiency is found using Equation 9.15:

$$\text{Relative efficiency} = \frac{8.604\,(7)\,(15)}{0.563\,(9)\,(13)} = 13.71$$

The Latin-square design is roughly 14 times more efficient than a corresponding randomized-groups design. In this case, there are substantial effects of Experience that would be missed in the randomized-groups design.

b. If the design were repeated measures, Equation 9.18 is first used:

$$MS_{AS} = \frac{138.938 - 35.688 - 97.688}{9} = 6.18$$

Then relative efficiency is found using Equation 9.17:

$$\text{Relative efficiency} = \frac{0.618(7)(12)}{0.563(9)(10)} = 1.02$$

Chapter 10

10.1 a. Four columns are required, one for strength (the DV), one for cement type (A), one for reinforcement (B), and the last for additive (C). Cross-products of the DV with the columns for A, B, and C are required to complete the problem.

b. Each of the main effects is confounded with a two-way interaction, A with BC, B with AC, and C with AB.

c. Source table:

Source	SS	df	MS	F	η^2
Cement Type	2	1	2.0	4.0	.07
Reinforcement	18	1	18.0	36.0	.60
Additive	8	1	8.0	16.0	.27
Residual	2	4	0.5		
Total	30	7			

d. See the last column of the source table.

f. If done through SPSS, the syntax is

```
UNIANOVA
strength BY cement reinforc additive
/METHOD = SSTYPE(3)
/INTERCEPT = INCLUDE
/CRITERIA = ALPHA(.05)
/DESIGN = cement reinforc additive.
```

Through the SPSS menu system, this syntax is produced by choosing Analysis, General Linear Model, Univariate. Once the Dependent Variable and Fixed Factors are clicked over, Model is selected, followed by Specify Model, Custom. Then the three IVs are clicked over, with no interactions specified, followed by Continue and OK.

10.2 Through SYSTAT DESIGN:

Plackett-Burman Design: 8 Runs; 7 Factors, Each With 2 Levels

```
        Factor
Run    A   B   C   D   E   F   G
  1    +   +   +   -   +   -   -
  2    +   +   -   +   -   -   +
  3    +   -   +   -   -   +   +
  4    -   +   -   -   +   +   +
  5    +   -   -   +   +   +   -
  6    -   -   +   +   +   -   +
  7    -   +   +   +   -   +   -
  8    -   -   -   -   -   -   -
```

10.3 a. The S/N ratio for each run is found using Equation 10.6. If a low S/N ratio is desirable, the first run, with the first level of each IV, produces the most desirable outcome.

Run	S/N Ratio
1	−12.30
2	−13.12
3	−15.68
4	−18.60
5	−16.99
6	−14.15
7	−18.60
8	−18.13

b. When all effects are included, there are no df for error. SS for the seven IVs are

Source	SS
A	36.423
B	3.860
C	1.337
D	0.023
E	0.428
F	2.453
G	0.009

c. The decision is made to delete the three effects where SS are less than 1: *D, E,* and *G.* The ANOVA is rerun with these effects deleted to produce the following source table.

Source	SS	df	MS	F	$P_{effect} = \dfrac{SS_{effect} - df_{effect}(MS_{error})}{SS_{total}}(100)$
A	36.423	1	36.423	237.523	81.5%
B	3.850	1	3.850	25.109	8.3%
C	1.337	1	1.337	8.716	
F	2.453	1	2.453	15.997	5.2%
Residual	0.460	3	0.153		
Total	44.523	7			

d. See the last column of the source table.

10.4 a. Variables for testing quadratic trends are produced by multiplying each of the variables by themselves: Days × Days, Tickets × Tickets, and Room-Size × Room-Size. Variables for testing linear interaction contrasts are produced by cross-multiplying the three variables: Days × Tickets, Days × Room-Size, and Tickets × Room-Size.

b. All nine variables are entered at one time into a multiple-regression program with rating as the DV. The source table for the overall relationship is as follows:

Source	SS	df	MS	F
Regression	101.183	9	11.243	9.776
Residual	5.750	5	1.150	
Total	106.933	14		

Inspection of the coefficients and their significance levels reveals that only Days and Room-Size are (linearly) related to rating with F values of $(8.902)^2 = 79.25$ and $(2.638)^2 = 6.96$. Ticket price is not related, nor are quadratic effects of the three variables, nor are the linear interaction contrasts of the three variables.

10.5 a. The sugar by cinnamon interaction is found by cross-multiplying the sugar variable and the cinnamon variable.

b. With sugar identified as the intercept, the source table for the two models (Model 1: cinnamon alone, and Model 2: cinnamon plus sugar × cinnamon) is

Source	SS	df	MS	F
Model 1:				
Regression	10.474	1	10.474	1.303
Residual	88.449	11	8.041	
Model 2:				
Regression	71.171	2	35.586	12.823
Residual	27.752	10	2.775	

c. The first model is not statistically reliable, indicating that increasing the amount of sugar alone or the amount of cinnamon alone is not related to increases in rating. The second model, which includes the interaction of sugar and cinnamon, is statistically reliable. In the second model, the constant (intercept), which represents the linear trend of sugar, is statistically reliable at $p = .012$, and the coefficient is positive, indicating that more sugar is better. The linear trend of cinnamon is not reliable ($p = .082$) and the coefficient is negative, indicating that less cinnamon is better, if anything. The sugar by cinnamon interaction is reliable ($p = .001$), indicating a preference for the mixture.

d. The prediction equation for rating from Model 2 is

$$\text{Rating}' = 3.183\text{Sugar} + [3.183 + (-2.692)]\text{Cinnamon} + 21.700\text{Sugar} \times \text{Cinnamon}$$
$$= 3.183\text{Sugar} + .491\text{Cinnamon} + 21.700\text{Sugar} \times \text{Cinnamon}$$

10.6 a. Only one of many possible sets of runs, equally efficient, is shown here.

Obs	A	B	C
1	2	2	2
2	2	2	1
3	2	2	3
4	2	1	2
5	2	1	3
6	2	1	1
7	1	1	2
8	1	1	3
9	1	1	1
10	1	2	3
11	1	2	2
12	1	2	1

b. D-efficiency is 80.2742.

c. Source table:

Source	df
A	1
B	1
C	2
AB	1
Error	6
Total	11

Chapter 11

11.1 a. The data set is divided into eight cells. The largest variance is 12.00 (cotton, 10 min), and the smallest variance is 1.33 (polyester, 10 min). F_{max} is 9.02, less than 10; therefore, the assumption of homogeneity of variance is met. The error term for Soak Time has 16 df and the interaction (the error term for Material) has 3 df, neither sufficient to guarantee normality of sampling distributions. Therefore, skewness and normal probability plots are examined for each of the eight cells, although with only three scores per cell the assessment is problematic. The highest z score for skewness in any cell was 1.41; the data points line up somewhere along the diagonal of the normal probability plot, and none appears to be an outlier. Boxplots also revealed no outliers in any of the eight cells.

Homogeneity of covariance between pairs of levels for the random IV (Soak) was examined by creating a homogeneity of variance, covariance matrix as in Table 11.38. The values are computed from six scores at each level, combined over the two levels of material. (Note that a covariance is the numerator of a correlation, e.g., numerator of Equation 2.16.) Results are as follows:

	7 min	16 min	39 min	45 min
7 min	3.07	3.33	−0.13	0.27
16 min		5.87	0.53	1.73
39 min			4.57	0.07
45 min				2.27

b. The source table for the analysis is

Source	SS	df	MS	F	Partial η^2
Material	0.375	1	0.375	$0.375/1.042 = 0.360$	.107
Soak	66.125	3	22.042	$22.042/4.708 = 4.68$	.467
Material $\times$ Soak	3.125	3	1.042	$1.042/4.708 = 0.221$	.040
Cases/Material, Soak	75.333	16	4.708		

c. See the last column of the source table.

d. With unequal spacing specified, the significance level for the linear trend of Presoak Time is 0.019, for quadratic trend 0.591, and for cubic trend 0.466. The only potentially significant trend is linear. The problem was done using SPSS GLM, which produced a Difference(Estimate − Hypothesized) value of 3.281, and a corresponding Std. Error of 1.253. When divided, $t = 3.281/1.253 = 2.618$; and $F = (2.618)^2 = 6.86$. This is evaluated post hoc against $F_S = (b − 1)F(1, 16) = (3)(4.49) = 13.47$, and by this criterion, the linear trend is not statistically reliable.

f. When SPSS VARCOMP (through GLM) is run, the Variance Estimate for the Component SOAK is 2.101, and its standard error is $(3.838)^{1/2} = 1.959$. The Wald statistic, then, is $z = 2.101/1.959 = 1.07$, less than critical $z = 1.96$.

11.2 a. Neither of the error terms, Organization/Treatment or Cases/Organization/Treatment, has sufficient df to guarantee normality of sampling distributions. Therefore, skewness and kurtosis and normal probability plots were inspected separately for both levels of Treatment, and separately for the six levels of Organization. All of the values were satisfactory. F_{max} for Treatment is $28,745,730/19,456,156 = 1.478$, and F_{max} for Organization is $18,498,272/7,675,704 = 2.41$. Homogeneity of variance is established for both effects.

No outliers were evident in either the six levels of Organization or the two levels of Treatment.

b. The source table for the analysis is

Source	SS	df	MS	F	Partial η^2
Treatment	284,267,900	1	284,267,900	3.944	.496
Organization/Treatment	288,284,795	4	72,071,198.7	5.362	.544
Cases/Org/Treat	241,935,954	18	13,440,886.3		

c. See the last column of the source table.

11.3 Expected mean squares for a doubly nested design:

Source	EMS	Error Term
A	$\sigma_\varepsilon^2 + (n)\sigma_{C/B/A}^2 + (c)(n)\sigma_{B/A}^2 + (b)(c)(n)\theta_A^2$	B/A
B/A	$\sigma_\varepsilon^2 + (n)\sigma_{C/B/A}^2 + (c)(n)\sigma_{B/A}^2$	$C/B/A$
$C/B/A$	$\sigma_\varepsilon^2 + (n)\sigma_{C/B/A}^2$	$S/C/B/A$
$S/C/B/A$	σ_ε^2	

REFERENCES

Bliss, C.I. (1967). *Statistics in Biology: Statistical Methods for Research in the Natural Sciences.* New York: McGraw-Hill.

Box, G.E.P., & Cox, D.R. (1964). An analysis of transformations. *Journal of the Royal Statistical Society, 26* (Series B), 211–243.

Bradley, D.R. (1988). *Datasim.* Lewiston, ME: Desktop Press. (Available by writing to Drake Bradley, 90 Bardwell St., Lewiston, ME 04240.)

Bradley, J.V. (1982). The insidious L-shaped distribution. *Bulletin of the Psychonomic Society, 20*(2), 85–88.

Brennan, R.L. (1992). NCME instructional module: Generalizability theory. *Educational Measurement: Issues and Practice, 11*(4), 27–34.

Bryk, A.S., & Raudenbush, S.W. (1992). *Hierarchical Linear Models: Applications and Data Analysis Methods.* Newbury Park, CA: Sage.

Cleveland, W.S. (1994). *The Elements of Graphing Data,* 2nd ed. Murray Hill, NJ: AT&T Bell Laboratories.

Cochran, W.G., & Cox, G.M. (1957). *Experimental Designs,* 2nd ed. New York: McGraw-Hill.

Cohen, J. (1977). *Statistical Power Analysis for the Behavioral Sciences,* rev. ed. New York: Academic Press.

Conover, W.J. (1980). *Practical Nonparametric Statistics,* 2nd ed. New York: John Wiley.

Cook, T.D., & Campbell, D.T. (1979). *Quasi-Experimentation: Design and Analysis Issues for Field Settings.* Chicago: Rand-McNally.

Cornell, J.A. (1990). *Experiments with Mixtures: Designs, Models, and the Analysis of Mixture Data,* 2nd ed. New York: John Wiley.

Cronbach, L.J. (1972). *The Dependability of Behavioral Measurements: Theory of Generalizability for Scores and Profiles.* New York: John Wiley.

Dallal, G.E. (1986). PC-SIZE: A program for sample size determinations. *American Statistician, 40,* 52. (Available by writing to Gerard E. Dallal, 53 Beltran St., Malden, MA 02148.)

Damos, D.L. (1989). *Transfer of Mental Rotation Skill.* Technical Report. Los Angeles: University of Southern California, Department of Human Factors.

Davies, O.L., Ed. (1963). *Design and Analysis of Industrial Experiments,* 2nd ed. New York: Hafner.

Dixon, W.J., Ed. (1992). *BMDP Statistical Software Manual.* Berkeley, CA: University of California Press.

Dunnett, C.W. (1980). Pairwise multiple comparisons in the unequal variance case. *Journal of the American Statistical Association, 70,* 796–800.

Egan, W.J., & Morgan, S.L. (1998). Outlier detection in multivariate analytical chemical data. *Analytical Chemistry, 70,* 2372–2379.

Eliason, S.R. (1993). *Maximum Likelihood Estimation: Logic and Practice.* Newbury Park, CA: Sage.

Emerson, J.D. (1991). Introduction to transformation. In D.C. Hoaglin, F. Mosteller, & J.W. Tukey, Eds., *Fundamentals of Exploratory Analysis of Variance.* New York: John Wiley.

Farnoush, A., Joseph, C.E., & Tabachnick, B. (1985, March). Clinical Evaluation of Ceramic Bone Implants in Treatment of Advanced Periodontal Defects. Paper presented at the International Association of Dental Research, Las Vegas.

Fisher, R.A. (1935) *The Design of Experiments.* Edinburgh and London: Oliver & Boyd.

Greenhouse, S.W., & Geisser, W. (1959). On methods in the analysis of profile data. *Psychometrika, 24,* 95–112.

Hadi, A.S., & Simonoff, J.W. (1993). Procedures for the identification of multiple outliers in linear models. *Journal of the American Statistical Association, 88,* 1264–1272.

Harlow, L.L., Mulaik, S.A., & Steiger, J.H., Eds. (1997). *What If There Were No Significance Tests?* Mahwah, NJ: Erlbaum.

Hersh, A. (1924). The effect of temperature upon the heterozygotes in the bar series of drosophila. *Journal of Experimental Zoology, 39,* 55–71.

Himmelfarb, S. (1975). What do you do when the control group doesn't fit the factorial design? *Psychological Bulletin, 82,* 363–368.

Hirsch, A.R., & Johnston, L.H. (1996). Odors and learning. *Journal of Neurological and Orthopaedic Medicine and Surgery, 17,* 119–126.

Hoaglin, D.C., Mosteller, F., & Tukey, J.W. (1991). *Fundamentals of Exploratory Analysis of Variance.* New York: John Wiley.

Huynh, H., & Feldt, L.S. (1976). Estimation of the Box correction for degrees of freedom from sample data in randomized block & split-plot designs. *Journal of the American Statistical Association, 65,* 1582–1589.

Jamieson, J. (1999). Dealing with baseline differences: Two principles and two dilemmas. *International Journal of Psychophysiology, 31,* 155–161.

Jamieson, J., & Howk, S. (1992). The law of initial values: A four factor theory. *International Journal of Psychophysiology, 12,* 53–61.

Jones, B., & Kenward, M.G. (1989). *Design and Analysis of Cross-Over Trials.* London: Chapman & Hall.

Kempthorne, O. (1952). *The Design and Analysis of Experiments.* New York: John Wiley.

Keppel, G. (1982). *Design and Analysis: A Researcher's Handbook,* 2nd ed. Englewood Cliffs, NJ: Prentice Hall.

Keppel, G. (1991). *Design and Analysis: A Researcher's Handbook,* 3rd ed. Englewood Cliffs, NJ: Prentice Hall.

Keppel, G., Saufley, W.H., Jr., & Tokunaga, H. *Introduction to Design & Analysis: A Student's Handbook,* 2nd ed. New York: W.H. Freeman.

Keren, G., & Lewis, C. (1979). Partial omega squared for ANOVA. *Educational and Psychological Measurement, 39,* 119–128.

Kirk, R.E. (1995). *Experimental Design,* 3rd ed. Pacific Grove, CA: Brooks/Cole.

Kreft, I.G.G., & DeLeeuw, J. (1998). *Introducing Multilevel Modeling.* Thousand Oaks, CA: Sage.

Lee, W. (1975). *Experimental Design and Analysis.* San Francisco: W.H. Freeman.

Levene, H. (1960). Robust tests for equality of variance. In I. Olkin, Ed., *Contributions to Probability and Statistics.* Palo Alto: Stanford University Press.

Lewin, A.Y., & Shakun, M.F. (1976). *Policy Sciences: Methodology and Cases.* New York: Pergamon Press.

Lindeman, H.R. (1974). *Analysis of Variance in Complex Experimental Designs.* San Francisco: W.H. Freeman.

Lord, F.E. (1967). A paradox in the interpretation of group comparisons. *Psychological Bulletin, 68,* 304–305.

Marcoulides, G.A. (1999). Generalizability theory: Picking up where the Rasch IRT model leaves off? In S.E. Embretson & S.L. Hershberger, Eds., *The New Rules of Measurement: What Every Psychologist and Educator Should Know,* pp. 129–152. Mahwah, NJ: Erlbaum.

Mauchley, J.W. (1940). Significance test for sphericity of a normal *n*-variate distribution. *Annals of Mathematical Statistics, 11,* 204–209.

Maxwell, S.E., & Delaney, H.D. (1990). *Designing Experiments and Analyzing Data: A Model Comparison Perspective.* Belmont, CA: Wadsworth.

Minitab, Inc. (1997). *MINITAB Release 12.* (Available from Minitab, Inc., 3081 Enterprise Dr., State College, PA 16801 USA, ph. 814.238.3280, fax. 814.238.4383, e-mail: Info@minitab.com, URL: http://www.minitab.com.)

Mitchell, L.C. (1950). Report on fat by acid hydrolysis in eggs. *Journal of the Association Office of Agricultural Chemists, 33,* 699–703.

Montgomery, D.C. (1984). *Design and Analysis of Experiments,* 2nd ed. New York: John Wiley.

Mulaik, S.A., Raju, N.S., & Harshman, R.A. (1997). There is a time & a place for significance testing. In L.L. Harlow, S.A. Mulaik, & J.H. Steiger, Eds., *What If There Were No Significance Tests?* Mahwah, NJ: Erlbaum.

Myers, J.L. (1979). *Fundamentals of Experimental Design,* 3rd ed. Boston: Allyn & Bacon.

Myers, J.L., & Well, A.D. (1991). *Research Design & Statistical Analysis.* New York: HarperCollins.

Myers, R.H., & Montgomery, D.C. (1995). *Response Surface Methodology: Process and Product Optimization Using Designed Experiments.* New York: John Wiley.

NCSS. (1996). *PASS 6.0 User's Guide.* Kaysville, UT: Author.

NCSS. (1997). *NCSS 97 User's Guide* (Vols. I and II). Kaysville, UT: Author.

NCSS. (1998). *NCSS 2000* (Vol. III). Kaysville, UT: Author.

Overall, J.E., & Spiegel, D.K. (1969). Concerning least squares analysis of experimental data. *Psychological Bulletin, 72(5),* 311–322.

Pearson, E.S., & Hartley, H.O. (1958). *Biometrika Tables for Statisticians.* New York: Cambridge University Press.

Rao, C.R., & Kleff, J. (1988). *Estimation of Variance Components and Applications.* Amsterdam: North-Holland.

Rea, L.M., & Parker, R.A. (1997). *Designing and Conducting Survey Research: A Comprehensive Guide.* San Francisco: Jossey-Bass.

Rousseeuw, P.J., & van Zomeren, B.C. (1990). Unmasking multivariate outliers and leverage points. *Journal of the American Statistical Association, 85,* 633–639.

Sachs, H., Joseph, C.E., Farnoush, A., & Tabachnick, B. (1985, March). Evaluation of periodontal dressings in vitro. Paper presented at the International Association of Dental Research, Las Vegas.

SAS Institute, Inc. (1990). *SAS/STAT User's Guide.* Cary, NC: Author.

SAS Institute, Inc. (1997). *SAS/STAT Software: Changes and Enhancements through Release 6.12.* Cary, NC: Author.

SAS Institute, Inc. (1998). *SAS/STAT User's Guide, Version 7–1.* Cary, NC: Author.

Satterthwaite, F.E. (1946). An approximate distribution of estimates of variance components. *Biometrics Bulletin, 2,* 110–114.

Scheffé, H.A. (1953). A method of judging all contrasts in the analysis of variance. *Biometrika, 40,* 87–104.

Schmidt, S.R., & Launsby, R.G. (1994). *Understanding Industrial Designed Experiments,* 4th ed. Colorado Springs: Air Academy Press.

Searle, S.R., Casella, G., & McColloch, C.E. (1992). *Variance Components.* New York: John Wiley.

Shavelson, R.J., & Webb, N.M. (1991). *Generalizability Theory: A Primer.* Newbury Park, CA: Sage.

Siegel, S., & Castellan, N.J., Jr. (1988). *Nonparametric Statistics for the Behavioral Sciences,* 2nd ed. New York: McGraw-Hill.

Spatz, C. (1997). *Basic Statistics: Tales of Distribution,* 6th ed. Pacific Grove, CA: Brooks/Cole.

SPSS, Inc. (1999a). *SPSS Advanced Models 10.0.* Chicago: Author.

SPSS, Inc. (1999b). *SPSS Base 10.0 for Windows: Applications Guide.* Chicago: Author.

SPSS, Inc. (1999c). *SPSS Base 10.0 for Windows: User's Guide.* Chicago: Author.

SPSS, Inc. (1999d). *SPSS Base System Syntax Reference Guide 10.0.* Chicago: Author.

SPSS, Inc. (1999e). *SYSTAT 9.0 Statistics.* Chicago: Author.

Statistical Solutions, Inc. (1997). *SOLAS for Missing Data Analysis 1.0.* Cork, Ireland: Author.

Steiger, J.H., & Fouladi, R.T. (1997). When confidence intervals should be used instead of statistical significance tests, and vice versa. In L.L. Harlow, S.A.

Mulaik, & J.H. Steiger, Eds., *What If There Were No Significance Tests?* Mahwah, NJ: Erlbaum.

Tabachnick, B.G., & Fidell, L.S. (1996). *Using Multivariate Statistics,* 3rd ed. New York: Longman.

Tabachnick, B.G., & Fidell, L.S. (2001). *Using Multivariate Statistics,* 4th ed. Boston: Allyn & Bacon.

Taguchi, G. (1993). *Taguchi Methods: Design of Experiments.* Dearborn, MI: ASI Press.

Tufte, E.R. (1983). *The Visual Display of Quantitative Information.* Cheshire, CT: Graphics Press.

Tukey, J.W. (1977). *Exploratory Data Analysis.* Reading, MA: Addison-Wesley.

Vaughan, G.M., & Corballis, M.C. (1969). Beyond tests of significance: Estimating strength of effects in selected ANOVA designs.

Welch, B.L. (1949). The generalization of student's problem when several different population variances are involved. *Biometrika, 34,* 28–35.

Winer, B.J. (1971). *Statistical Principles in Experimental Design,* 2nd ed. New York: McGraw-Hill.

Winer, B.J., Brown, D.R., & Michels, K.M. (1991). *Statistical Principles in Experimental Design,* 3rd ed. New York: McGraw-Hill.

Woodward, J.A., Bonett, D.G., & Brecht, M.-L.(1990). *Introduction to Linear Models and Experimental Design.* San Diego: Harcourt Brace Jovanovich.

Zeleny, C. (1920). The tabulation of factorial values. *American Nature, 54,* 358–362.

INDEX